WORKING WITH CLASS

Working with Class

SOCIAL WORKERS

AND THE POLITICS

OF MIDDLE-CLASS

IDENTITY

DANIEL J. WALKOWITZ

The

University

of North

Carolina

Press

Chapel Hill

and London

Manufactured in the United States of America

Set in Minion by Keystone Typesetting, Inc.

Designed by April Leidig-Higgins

The paper in this book meets the guidelines for
permanence and durability of the Committee on
Production Guidelines for Book Longevity of the
Council on Library Resources.

Library of Congress Cataloging-in-Publication Data
Walkowitz, Daniel J. Working with class : social
workers and the politics of middle-class identity / by
Daniel J. Walkowitz.
p. cm.   Includes bibliographical references and index.
ISBN 0-8078-2454-2 (alk. paper)
ISBN 0-8078-4758-5 (pbk. : alk. paper)
1. Middle class—United States. 2. Social workers—New
York (State)— New York. 3. Group identity—New York
(State)—New York. I. Title.
HT690.U6W35   1999   98-19359
305.5′5′0973—dc21   CIP

03 02 01 00 99   5 4 3 2 1

Daniel J. Walkowitz, "The Making of a Feminine
Professional Identity: Social Workers in the 1920s,"
American Historical Review 95, no. 4 (October 1990):
1051–75, reprinted in revised form with permission
of American Historical Association.

Daniel J. Walkowitz and Peter R. Eisenstadt, "The
Psychology of Work: Work and Mental Health in
Historical Perspective," *Radical History Review* 34
(January 1986): 7–31, excerpts reprinted with
permission of MARHO: The Radical Historians'
Organization and Cambridge University Press.

Calvin Trillin, "Nobody Here but Us Middle Class,"
The Nation, January 9/16, 1995, 41, reprinted with
permission of Calvin Trillin.

FOR JUDY AND REBECCA

contents

Appendix

figures

preface

When I began this project over a decade ago, two questions provided its subtext: How does one write the history of the working class when everyone thinks he or she belongs to the middle class? And why do my colleagues consider trade unions inappropriate forms of organization for professionals? Finding the answer to these questions, I came to believe, meant confronting the confusion surrounding middle-class identity in the twentieth-century work force, a confusion that extends to professional workers such as college teachers and social workers. Rather than studying teachers, however, I was led by a quite incidental circumstance to study social workers.

Invited in 1982 to write an essay on the historical relationship between work and mental health for a conference sponsored by the National Institute for Mental Health (NIMH) on work as a source of mental illness or as therapy for it, I soon realized that the work of the people trained to provide this therapy offered a special opportunity for pursuing my concerns. The history of social workers involves salient features of modern identity formation in America. First, since social workers were a predominantly, but not exclusively, female labor force that by mid-century serviced a predominantly African American and Hispanic client population, gender and race were always central to how they thought of themselves and their work. Second, professionalization and unionization have also been competing strains of social worker identity since the 1920s. Third, in their appeal to a "forgotten" middle class in late-twentieth-century America, politicians have scripted welfare as a counternarrative of idleness and "privilege." Most important, though, as paid workers occupying a liminal social space between wealthy volunteers and board members who claim agency authority on the one hand and the poor who are dependent on them for aid on the other, social workers play a central role in twentieth-century class formation in America. Indeed, in their daily work of determining eligibility for private philanthropy or public relief, social workers patrol the borders of class. Consequently, social workers, one of the supposed agents in my NIMH study, became instead the subject of my study and the subsequent basis for this project.[1]

The literature on social work, although exceptionally rich, has tended to remain oblivious to the conflicting pressures within this work identity. Instead, with a few important exceptions, historians have chronicled the emergence of social work as a profession, following traditions in the sociology of professions. These later studies have focused on institution building, accepting the language workers adopted within these organizations to define their own reality. However, as Martin Oppenheimer has observed, "[M]ost sociological discussions define professionals by criteria that are narrowly determined, in part by the professionals themselves." For professionals in general, he has noted, the ideology is a reification of the work. "The label [professional] is not a neutral, objective description of a particular reality, but a function of a specific social context that in turn promotes definitions that become part of and help define social reality."[2]

Professionals, Christopher Lasch has reminded us, had to create a "market" for their own "service"; they "invented many of the needs they claim to satisfy" and then rushed to offer their "professional services."[3] Even when there were demonstrable economic crises, professionals offered their own "solutions." In such ways, male-dominated occupations such as law and medicine demonstrated that professionalism served practitioners' interests well: using the claim of an established specialized knowledge base, they effectively controlled entrance into their fields. For women, however, professionalism as an ideology and an identity obscured shifting working conditions in the late nineteenth and early twentieth centuries, changes that failed to fulfill social workers' expectations concerning job autonomy and middle-class living standards.

Professionalism shaped how women organized and defined themselves, and in professions such as social work, they found achievements illusory and problematic. They did have a somewhat higher salary than factory workers and some autonomy in their work. All worked in settings controlled by others who most often were male, however. Visiting teachers, for example, went to schools run by principals and superintendents; probation officers worked under judges and lawyers; medical social workers reported to hospital doctors; psychiatric social workers worked in clinics supervised by psychiatrists. Even family caseworkers in agencies reported to supervisors and managers and found work regimes and budgets controlled by laypersons on boards of directors that represented elite financial groups and policies. Still, increasingly higher educational standards providing some job security may have marked them as professionals, albeit "bureaucratic" or semiprofessionals; both peers and employers acknowledged that they had "careers," with expectations of security, development, and promotion.[4]

This book, although it reworks much of the terrain, is not intended to be another history of social work. Rather, I use the particulars of major debates and struggles in the history of men and women who labor in social work to reflect on the languages of class and identity in twentieth-century America. My focus is on what it means to be middle class, but because people have multiple identities by gender, race, religion, and so forth, all of which are entangled with and feed into their class identity the discussion will often dwell on these competing and interconnected identities. At the same time, this book contributes to an emerging paradigm for writing about subjectivity in identity, one that integrates traditional emphases of social history with some of the lessons of poststructuralism and cultural studies. Identity, in particular, is historical and contingent, located in the subjective interlocution between changing material conditions and the problem of representation—how material needs and ambitions shape the construction of one's self-representation and then how one negotiates one's self-representation with representations offered or imposed by others.

Class identity is forged in the context of the "other," and as attendants to the poor, social workers provide an unusually good perspective on the racial and class components of identity. They not only serve the poor, but as noted above, in public welfare agencies, they attend a client population that is increasingly African American and Hispanic. In the racialization of welfare as black in the second half of the twentieth century, racial and class identities tend to merge in the public imagination, and the confusion between the two becomes a central issue in the politics of class identity. As cultural critics Peter Stallybrass and Allon White have noted, the cultural formation of the bourgeois Imaginary (or the middle-class subject) occurs in liminal and contested public spaces. The repudiation of the "low other" heightens the importance of the "other" to the dominant culture, the top symbolically casting the bottom as an eroticized constituent of its own fantasy life. In this way, social policy and class identity mirror each other: complaints about the poor "breeding like rabbits," hypersexual girls, and juvenile delinquency or street anarchy parallel policy calls to penalize welfare mothers or diagnose political radicalism as irrational mob rule.[5]

In the construction of the "low other," historians are correct to emphasize the specific historical anxieties and ambitions that inform imaginings of the self by the top. Nineteenth-century historians, for example, have seen the middle class constructing itself as a "respectable middle" against a profligate elite and an "unworthy" working class. But in the twentieth century, as women and then African Americans and Hispanics are increasingly entering white-collar occupations, "otherness" has taken on new ethnic, racial, and gender characteristics. In the shifting bourgeois Imaginary of twentieth-century America, lower-class clients in the welfare office become objectified as the grotesque "other," ridiculed and despised as "welfare queens." The issue is not simply whether or not some clients conform to aspects of this stereotype; rather, it is who asserts this (mis)-representation and how it gains authority, for what purposes, and with what implications for all concerned. Identities are malleable and always contested as individuals seek to draw on usable senses of themselves to assert or sustain a secure place—a social and cultural space—within a society in which the material and imaginary conditions that shape how they exist and are understood can never be completely under their control. The struggle to invent and reinvent oneself, then, is always political and historical. This is the politics of identity in the twentieth-century United States, and social workers must confront its contradictions in work on behalf of "other" clients every day.

My strategy for unraveling (and reconstructing) the meanings of middle-class identity in the twentieth-century United States builds on recent trends in the humanities that have provoked labor historians to explore the complex interactions between meaning and experience in various historical periods and to raise political and linguistic questions about the elusive ground on which class and gender identity rests. Joan Scott and others urge attention to how language as a "system of meaning" constructs social identity and, in particular, unlocks its gendered character, "how ideas such as class become, through language, social realities."[6] Social structures and material conditions still matter in history; after all, they provide both the context that shapes subjectivity and the context in which it must be understood. But class definition remains particularly vulnerable to the internal tensions and fluctuating cultural dimensions of identity.

This study addresses directly the instability of class identity. Thus far, this issue has mainly engaged labor historians of the Industrial Revolution. But the need to reconceptualize the language of class in the twentieth-century United States, where labor has shifted from production and extraction to "middle-class" service work and where women have become the core of much white-collar labor, is at least equally compelling. This complex problem requires a complex strategy that can explore several diverse areas of experience in which identity is revealed. This book moves between histories of consumption, politics, the workplace, and trade unions and organizations, keeping at its center the categories of class, gender, and race. Each could be the subject of a separate volume. But rather than being presented as a reductionist mantra of essentialized identities, they must be examined together as malleable, at times almost phantasmal, social constructions that illuminate the relationship between the language and the experiences of class in mid-twentieth-century America.

Two sociological studies have confirmed some of the confusion and ambiguity about the language of class in America in the late twentieth century. In the first, an extraordinarily suggestive participant observation of solidly blue-collar, white, male chemical workers at a northern New Jersey plant, sociologist David Halle finds two operative notions of class: at work, these men describe themselves as working men; at home, they refer to themselves as middle class. Equally important, Halle's portrait notes significant differences by gender and race. Clerical women in the plant, whom the men disparage, form cross-class bonds, broadly extending the idea of working women to include housewives, professionals, and managers. Halle, however, acknowledges the absence of blacks in the plant, correctly. I believe, suggesting that there may be a racial cast(e) to the idea of the middle class.[7]

A second sociological study based on interviews with engineers corroborates the complex language of class in late-twentieth-century America. In this work, Robert Zussman summarizes the ambiguity he finds in the double class identity taken on by engineers who see themselves as part of a "working middle class." Although Zussman's respondents all generally adopt a three-class model, they place virtually everyone within a vast and amorphous "middle" located "between the extremes of wealth and dependent poverty."[8] The oxymoron of a working middle class nicely captures the ambiguity about social workers' class position that has clouded contemporary analyses. As professional white-collar workers in one of the "semiprofessions" or "soft" professions, they are structurally a fraction of the late-capitalist (or "postindustrial") working class. They are dependent on a salary, have incomplete job autonomy, and, on occasion, even unionize. At the same time, however, they generally speak and think of themselves as part of the middle class and share the aspirations, values, and material preferences traditionally associated with that "culture" such as education, privatized family life, and "exotic" travel.

The idea of the expansion of a vast amorphous middle class as a cultural, and as we shall see, political formation exists in tension with countervailing tendencies toward what social analysts and the Census Bureau have heralded as the decline or shrinkage of the middle class from the 1970s to the 1990s. For instance, the Census Bureau reported a decline in the percentage of middle-income families from 71.2 percent in 1969 to 63.3 percent in 1985 as a result of "clusters towards both ends of the income scale." But in contrast to this growing material polarization, interviewed Americans placed themselves within a social world without disparities of wealth during this period. A 1984 New York Times/CBS News poll asking a cross section of Americans to describe their social class position reported that only 8 percent placed themselves within either the "lower" or the "upper" class. The average citizen was no less expansive than politicians who floated proposals for "middle-class" tax breaks with maximums from $80,000 to $200,000 at a time when the median income for a family of four ($35,353 in 1990) was easily less than half the lowest figure. Typical of the confusion were the responses given to a *Baltimore Sun* reporter by the lunch crowds at a South Baltimore tavern and an Inner Harbor galleria in January 1992 to his question about who should benefit from a middle-class tax break. To be sure, no one wanted to be excluded from the benefit, and all people, across various income and occupational levels, saw themselves as middle class. Service workers and even professionals did not see their class position as markedly different from laborers and skilled workers in manufacturing jobs. A tavern waitress saw middle-class income as starting at $20,000 and rising to $28,000 for a single earner; her boss put the top for a family at $50,000. But for a downtown lawyer, this ceiling was much too low; he thought the figure should be closer to the nearly $200,000 a year he and his wife earned.[9]

The widespread availability of consumer goods to a broad middle-income range in the last third of the century has facilitated this ambiguous class meaning. The notion of a ubiquitous and comfortable middle class reflects the fundamental shift in the language and meaning of class during the mid-twentieth century from a primarily socioeconomic category to an increasingly political label. As Peter Sepp, spokesman for the National Taxpayers Union, observed in 1992, the idea of the middle class has become "much more of a political definition than an economic one." These meanings are never completely separate, of course, but if class was a way of speaking of otherness in the nineteenth century, by the late twentieth century, it has become a way of denying a class "other" completely. Social analysts have popularized the notion that a privileged few—speculators, corrupt financiers or politicians, and wily entrepreneurs—exist above and an "underclass" (the term itself suggests efforts to treat the group as a problem outside the realm of class) hopelessly mired in a "culture of poverty" lies below. Everyone else, 80–90 percent of the country, as Zussman has suggested, shares an identity as citizen-taxpayer.[10]

Ironically, this increasingly politicized sense of what it means to be middle class reflects not simple material comfort but anxiety over its economic fragility. The marker for this shift in meaning can be conveniently placed between 1968 and 1972 in the presidential campaign appeals of Richard Nixon to "Middle America" as the repository of the "forgotten American"—the taxpaying middle class. Nixon's campaigns organized fears of inflation, war fatalities, and urban disorder around the powerful conceit that the Great Society had "privileged" the poor. But although Nixon was merely resurrecting William Graham Sumner's social Darwinist usage from the 1870s (in contrast to Franklin Roosevelt's identification of the "forgotten man" as the Okie, the poor, the downtrodden), the shift initiated a new grammar for political campaigns increasingly embraced by both Democrats and Republicans. Thus, Bill Clinton accepted his nomination for president "in the name of the hardworking Americans who make up our forgotten middle class . . . , people who do the work, pay the taxes, raise kids and play by the rules."[11]

In August 1996, Clinton and the Republican-controlled Congress passed a new welfare law that raised the political stakes of the discourse on middle classness. Turning broad authority for policy over to the individual states, placing limits on the time a recipient could receive aid, and instituting tough work requirements, Clinton promised "to end welfare as we have known it." But preliminary evidence suggests that these new strictures will not do so. By early 1998, despite dramatic early reductions in relief rolls, about half of those who had taken jobs had returned to lives of unemployment, poverty, and quiet desperation.[12] And the full impact of the forced time limits had not yet taken place. Even so, in the interim, while critics of the new laws envision a scary scenario with legions of helpless poor mothers and children, conservative supporters draw a picture of abundant opportunity and social mobility among a rising black middle class.[13]

The continuing debate over welfare policy, then, remains deeply embedded in understandings about the nature, extent, and meaning of middle classness in America. And the rising register of race in this debate is crucial. Both conservative and liberal policymakers employ language about dependency that imagines the poor as black and female, as "welfare queens."[14] At the same time, although confusion about the parameters and meaning of the term "middle class" has been shared by those working for wages and salaries. those in blue- and white-collar jobs, and those at lower-, middle-, and upper-income levels, surveys find that blacks, for whom the historical patterns of discrimination have been profound, are the only major ethnoracial group to continue to identify themselves as predominantly working class. It is precisely this shift to more political and racialized meanings of the middle class, its causes, and its various and contested meanings according to one's gender and racial group that this book intends to trace.

acknowledgments

I am delighted to be able to thank the many people who have helped nurture me and this project since the mid-1980s when Peter R. Eisenstadt coauthored an essay with me on the history of work and mental health. Students at New York University and Johns Hopkins University subsequently provided helpful responses to drafts of various chapters. Not all can be mentioned, but I wish to thank especially Daniel Bender, Andrew Darien, Janet Greene, Richard Greenwald, Molly McGarry, and Renee Newman. Adina Back was an insightful assistant during early stages of the research and helped conduct a series of oral histories. Leigh Benin, Karen Brothers, and Felicia Kornbluh generously shared their own research and experiences in social welfare with me and made helpful comments on postwar chapters. David Serlin copyedited part of the manuscript. And Doug Rossinow provided me with a brief but powerfully suggestive analysis of the relationship between blacks and Jews in postwar America for which I am grateful.

Historians know well that librarians and archivists are the too-often underappreciated heroes of historical research. A grant from New York University's Research Council provided early financial support for this project, and librarians in the United States and England made the research possible and often assisted in uncovering wonderful gems in the recesses of their archives. Special thanks go to a few who piloted me through extensive collections and bureaucratic labyrinths: Debra Bernhardt, head of Archival Collections of the Robert F. Wagner Labor Archive, Tamiment Library, New York University; David Klaassen, director of the Social Welfare History Archive, University of Minnesota; Ronald Grele, director of the Columbia University Oral History Research Office, Butler Library; Nikki Tanner, director of the Federation of Jewish Philanthropies of New York Oral History Project; and Bertram J. Black, scientific director of the Jewish Board of Family and Children's Services, and Jerome Goldsmith, executive director of the Federation of Jewish Philanthropies of New York, who provided access to their respective archives. Similarly, for photographic work, thanks to Erika Gottfried and Andrew Lee of the Tamiment Library and Matt Cook of the Chicago Historical Society. Finally, I offer admiration and thanks to the staffs at the New York University Bobst Library, the Johns Hopkins University Library, the British Library, the Senate House Library of the University of London, the Social Welfare History Archive, the Columbia University School of Social Work Library, the U.S. Department of Labor Library, the YIVO Institute for Jewish Research Archive, the Municipal Archive of the City of New York, the Jewish Board of Family and Children's Services Archive, the Chicago Historical Society, the Federation of Jewish Philanthropies of New York Archive, and the Robert F. Wagner Labor Archive and Tamiment Library at New York University.

Colleagues were no less generous in providing help. One group provided references, offered ideas, or helped with troubling passages. Others read drafts of one or another version of lengthy chapters. A third smaller group of stalwarts plowed through the entire manuscript, all with good cheer (at least as expressed to me!) and intelligence. I was not able, smart enough, or prepared to accept the advice of all, for which I bear responsibility. I thank all of them, though, for their help, fortitude, and generosity.

Among the first group are the respondents and audiences at conferences and universities in Canada, Australia, England, and the United States at which I presented versions of various chapters. In addition, I wish to thank Mimi Abramovitz, Betts Brown, Marvin E. Gettleman, Daniel Horowitz, Gail Katz, Lucretia Phillips, Jeffrey Sammons, Herb Schreier, Lewis Siegelbaum, and Judy Stacey. Thanks, too, to Dorothy Fennell for conducting one of the oral histories with me and sharing her research on the United Office and Professional Workers of America, Local 19. Finally, I wish to specially acknowledge the support and assistance of Ramona Knepp, secretary of the Metropolitan Studies Program at New York University.

A second group of colleagues read individual chapters or parts of the manuscript. Thanks go to Eliot Friedson and Wolf Heydebrand for reading early and often primitive drafts of postwar material; to Tom Bender, Robin D. G. Kelley, Regina G. Kunzel, and Rebecca L. Walkowitz for reviewing later versions of introductory chapters; and to Susan Porter Benson, Martha C. Howell, Alice Kessler-Harris, Barbara Melosh, Mary Nolan, Susan Ware, and Marilyn Young for helping to clarify my thinking in my October 1990 *American Historical Review* article, which became the basis of chapter 3. This chapter also benefited from the considerable insights of *American Historical Review* editors David Ransell and Ellen Dwyer, as well as the comments of several anonymous outside readers for the journal. Individual chapters on the postwar era also profited from close readings by colleagues, notably Liz Cohen, James B. Gilbert, Robin D. G. Kelley, Harry Marks, Sam Rosenberg, Burt Schacter, and Judith Smith.

As anyone who ponders the weight of this book might guess, simple thanks are inadequate appreciation for those colleagues who read, edited, and engaged the entire manuscript in its several incarnations. A special place is reserved for the following in my personal pantheon: Michael Frisch, Ronald Grele, Paul Mattingly, Andor Skotnes, and Judith R. Walkowitz. Jeffrey Escoffier advised on and read a final reorganization of the manuscript with an eye to the architecture of the whole and a calming assurance. Clarke A. Chambers deserves special mention. As the dean of social welfare history, he offered a thorough, generous critical reading, and after the copy of the manuscript with his changes was lost in the mail, he read it again! He remained an enthusiastic respondent who could be relied on for insights and regular constructive criticism. To him—and, indeed, to all of these readers—I am deeply indebted.

My editors at the University of North Carolina Press deserve special thanks. Kate Douglas Torrey, who solicited the manuscript, gave me room both to interrupt my work to complete a film project and to take the project in some new directions and, in the end, helped me shape the book. Paula J. Wald copyedited the manuscript with extraordinary care and intelligence and then took the book through production.

Finally, this book could not have been written without the cooperation of social workers who made the history I have begun to relate. I thank in particular those who agreed to be interviewed by me and others. In archival records and oral accounts, social workers have left a vivid record of their struggles and passions for which I am most grateful. No less important has been the example of two professional working women in my own life who have lived the double day as professional workers and family members: Rebecca L. Walkowitz and Judith R. Walkowitz. During the course of my research and writing, I have with admiration and great pleasure watched my daughter, Rebecca, navigate the tensions between a professional and personal life with a steady moral compass. Judy has always been both a professional model and a special personal partner with a bountiful reservoir of intellectual and emotional sustenance for me. To both, this book is dedicated with love, thanks, and admiration.

abbreviations

The following abbreviations are used throughout the book.
An additional list of abbreviations precedes the notes.

AASW   American Association of Social Workers

ABSW   Association of Black Social Workers

AFDC   Aid to Families with Dependent Children

AFL   American Federation of Labor

AFSCME   American Federation of State, County,
and Municipal Employees

AFW   Association of Federation Workers

AWPRA   Association of Workers in Public Relief Agencies

CIO   Congress of Industrial Organization

CORE   Congress of Racial Equality

COS   Charity Organization Society

CSAE   Community and Social Agency Employees

CSF   Civil Service Forum

CSWE   Council on Social Work Education

DPW   Department of Public Welfare of the City of New York

DSS   Department of Social Services of the City of New York

DW   Department of Welfare of the City of New York

ERB   New York City Emergency Relief Bureau

FJP   Federation of Jewish Philanthropies of New York

FSS   Family Service Society

HRA Human Resources Administration of the City of New York

HRB Home Relief Bureau of New York City

JBG Jewish Board of Guardians of New York

JCCA Jewish Child Care Association of New York

JDL Jewish Defense League

JFS Jewish Family Services of New York

JPAS Jewish Protectory and Aid Society

JSSA Jewish Social Service Association

NAACP National Association for the Advancement of Colored People

NABSW National Association of Black Social Workers

NASW National Association of Social Workers

NCCC National Conference of Charities and Correction

NCJCS National Conference of Jewish Communal Service

NCJSS National Conference of Jewish Social Service

NCJW National Council of Jewish Women

NCSW National Conference of Social Work

NCSWE National Council on Social Work Education

NMU National Maritime Union

NWRO National Welfare Rights Organization

SCMWA State, County, and Municipal Workers of America

SSEU Social Service Employees Union

TERA Temporary Emergency Relief Administration

UHC United Hebrew Charities of the City of New York

UJA United Jewish Appeal

UOPWA United Office and Professional Workers of America

UPW United Public Workers

USS United Seamen's Service

WEIU Women's Educational and Industrial Union

WJCS Westchester Jewish Community Service

YMCA Young Men's Christian Association

YWCA Young Women's Christian Association

In the 1920s, a Jew travels from his small Polish shtetl to Warsaw. When he returns, he tells his friend of the wonders he has seen.

"I met a Jew who had grown up in a yeshiva and knew large sections of the Talmud by heart. I met a Jew who was an atheist. I met a Jew who owned a large clothing store with many employees, and I met a Jew who was an ardent Communist."

"So what's so strange?" the friend asks. "Warsaw is a big city. There must be a million Jews there."

"You don't understand," the man answers. "It was the same Jew."

—Rabbi Joseph Telushkin, *Jewish Humor* (1992)

Locating the Middle Class

It is to th[e] . . . white collar world that one must look for much
that is characteristic of twentieth-century existence.
—C. Wright Mills,
  White Collar: The American Middle Classes (1951)

[D]isplacements hurt. This hurts. So we try to tie it up, like a
cut finger. Put a rag around it. . . .
    People in America have always been shouting about the
things they are *not*. Unless, of course, they are millionaires,
made or in the making.
—D. H. Lawrence,
  Studies in Classic American Literature (1923)

A fundamental transformation of work in the late-twentieth-century United
States coincided with a shift in the discourse of class from a primarily economic
category to a political category. From the 1970s to the 1990s, corporations,
increasingly unwilling to provide benefits and social protection for control of
the work force, brought the epoch of welfare capitalism (i.e., Fordism) to an
end.[1] In the corporate restructuring of work, industry has sought to economize
by displacing both blue- and white-collar workers, including middle managers,
who generally had been immune to such reductions in the past. New technologies have created some new jobs, but these have been disproportionately for
women and others willing to take lower-paid jobs. Although managers have
characterized the global reorganization of work with rhetorical niceties such as
"restructuring" or "planned shrinkage," their actions have intensified worker

anxieties and brought insecurity to new sectors of the "working middle class."[2] And the transformation and its effects have been global, touching all parts of the industrialized world, not just the United States. The London research organization Mintel, for example, repeats a story told by researchers in the United States of gender trouble, of a crisis of male identity in the reorganization of work. Charting a "steady fall in male employment since the 1970s" and "a new era of [male] insecurity," Mintel reports that "recession and 'improving technology' . . . favour female employment." Men, it concludes, "appear unprepared for living alone or for being the partner of a breadwinning woman."[3]

The globalization of work represents a third major transition in work and the social relations of production in America, especially in the way it affects the formation and identity of the middle class. The first transition coincided with the rise of industrial capitalism in the 1830–70 era. Writing over forty years ago, C. Wright Mills in *White Collar: The American Middle Classes* described the explosion of the white-collar sector that rendered the old categories obsolete after the turn of the century; this work has remained the basic text for the second transition. The classical nineteenth-century working class, laboring in extraction and production of goods, had been reduced to less than half the employed American work force by 1940. Their place had been taken by new armies of salaried white-collar workers in service, distribution, and coordination—what Mills referred to as the "new middle class."[4]

Workers who confronted these transformed worlds of production and consumption at the turn of the century had three very different characteristics from their nineteenth-century forebears: they were more often female; they more often wore a white than a blue collar; and large numbers of them worked in the public sector. Some historians have placed this transition in the middle of the nineteenth century, but in fact the total numbers of women in the white-collar work force remained quite small until considerably later, and women only constitute a major presence in the twentieth century.[5] Clerical workers were only 0.6 percent of the work force in 1870, a percentage that rose, but only to 2.5 percent in 1900. By 1900, women already constituted 29.2 percent of workers, but it was not until 1960 that they made up a majority of white-collar workers (while remaining only 15 percent of blue-collar workers). The number of white-collar workers exceeded blue-collar workers for the first time three years earlier, in 1957.[6]

The actual work of new white-collar workers differed too. Unlike nineteenth-century self-employed professionals or male clerks, whose occupation served as a way station to the upper echelons of management or ownership, they worked for a salary. They usually had some education, enjoyed a modicum of delegated authority, earned slightly more than their blue-collar counterparts, and, until quite recently, had expectations of greater job security.[7]

After mid-century, the third fundamental economic shift—the global economic reorganization of work—reshaped middle-class white-collar labor. The first industrial imperatives had led to an expansion of white-collar work, although they had less salutary effects on blue-collar labor. As a result of these processes, until 1950 the growth of white-collar work coincided with a decline in agriculture and extraction; after mid-century, white-collar jobs rose as manufacturing work was lost to automation, new technologies, and managerial "efficiencies." The global restructuring of the late twentieth century, then, which in the case of specific industries such as steel can be traced to before World War II, culminated in contractions in middle-class professional and managerial employment, job losses that have been chronicled as the "fall" of the middle class. And the transformation of middle-class identity to primarily a political and cultural rather than an economic formation in late-twentieth-century America has profound implications for the ability of white-collar workers to comprehend and respond to this third economic shift.[8]

In the reorganization of work and its accompanying worklessness, the state increasingly has become a major player. Public schools, of course, have always employed a sizable labor force, but increased consumption and its capitalist downside, economic inequality and poverty, created a raft of new public sector responsibilities and, with them, jobs. Both secondary and higher education grew quickly between the 1930s and the 1960s (reflecting a higher standard of living and the need to obtain skills to perform the new clerical, managerial, and professional jobs). At the same time, the Great Depression, the machinery of war, and burgeoning public welfare rolls transformed the federal and state governments into major employers. Between 1930 and 1960, the number of public employees rose from 3.2 to 8.5 million and the percentage rose from 10.8 to 16 percent of all nonagricultural workers. These numbers continued to grow at a comparable rate for the rest of the century. In 1990 approximately one in three urban workers got a check from a government employer. Adding those dependent on disability payments, Aid to Families with Dependent Children (AFDC), and unemployment insurance to these totals demonstrates both the massive role of the public sector in work and worklessness and the preeminent place of social service workers in this process. White-collar public employment for people such as social workers also came with its own industrial relations baggage since the state could be either a powerful ally or a fierce opponent in trade union negotiations.[9]

Two major shifts, then, have occurred in twentieth-century white-collar work in the United States, one at the beginning and one at the end of the century, and each has had a very different meaning for these workers' class identity. The welfare state, as employer, police, and personal or corporate benefactor, has played an increasingly important role in mediating or shaping these transformations, a process that an abundance of first-rate historical works have been especially good at detailing. Focusing on institutional developments, social policy, and clients of the state, perhaps quite naturally, these studies privilege the perspectives of both administrators and clients and tend to place blame for failures in state policy at the feet of the social workers or bureaucrats "in the middle." The perspective of agents of the state such as social workers has tended to be underrepresented in this story.[10]

Social workers do not always speak with one voice, of course, and they move between "others" both above and below them. Although they are at the center of these transformations, they often exist economically at the margins as a group in the middle or lower middle class and must negotiate their identity within a changing urban social geography.[11] Moreover, their subjectivity reflects changing material conditions and expectations. The social profile, economic situation, and ambitions of the typical social worker change, but so do those of the class "other"; urban poverty, for instance, always pervasive, takes on different meanings as the city becomes marked by an ethnic and then racial "other." Within these transformations lie the remakings of several ideas of American middle-class identity that white-collar workers embraced and articulated over the course of the century to mediate and encounter this changing world. It is to an exploration of these ideas that we now turn.

The Idea of the Middle Class

The history of the middle class has produced a substantial cottage industry in the 1990s, but one that I have found to have remarkably undertheorized the language of class. This deficiency has been especially apparent in the twentieth century, and as contemporary polls suggest, the resulting vagueness about the term "middle class" has extended into popular (mis)understandings. As Judith Stacey concludes from her ethnography of two extended Silicon Valley families in the mid-1980s, the broad use of the term obscures fundamental differences in meaning and material conditions: "So fluid and complex are the occupational, economic, and social statuses of white working families in postindustrial society that few can be captured by a single social class category."[12]

More distressing than the vague use of the term "middle class" in the popular media is the observation by the British historian Geoffrey Crossick, equally applicable to U.S. history, that "historians have too readily taken the language [of class] at face value, for the words used by Victorians to describe their society were no mere reflection of external reality, but an intervention within it." White-collar workers are simply assumed to "be" middle class, and neither the language of class nor its various meanings are interrogated. But a larger political point in Crossick's analysis needs to be emphasized. "Language," he notes, is "bound up with political opportunities and social identities." The meanings of class, then, are forged in the context of concrete struggles and by perceptions of who is an ally and who is an "other." Thus Crossick eloquently articulates the need to bring both historical specificity and a good ear to the discussion, observing that "[i]t is not just that the past is a foreign country; they speak a foreign language there, too."[13]

Writing nearly two decades ago, Mary P. Ryan called for historians to "retrieve . . . middle Americans from historical limbo," and scholars on both sides of the Atlantic such as Cindy Sondik Aron, Burton J. Bledstein, Stuart M. Blumin, Leonore Davidoff and Catherine Hall, Lori D. Ginzberg, Paul E. Johnson, and Olivier Zunz have begun to do just that. But in these works, the conception of the middle class in the eighteenth and nineteenth centuries in England and the United States has been better served than the conception of the middle class in the twentieth century; it has been more easily located in conventional Marxist categories of production among urban traders, shopkeepers, merchants, and professionals—the propertied class—and in the material accoutrements of that class. Some of the most important studies have come from the pens of feminist historians, who, building on the work of Mills, Harry Braverman, and others, have extended and refocused the discussion from production and the workplace to the home and community as well. Central to this discussion, most perceptively in the work of Davidoff and Hall in England and Ryan in the United States, has been the delineation of a privatized middle-class family marked by lower birth rates, privileged children, and mothers on pedestals overseeing the moral order.[14]

Surprisingly perhaps, relatively little historical work has been done on the middle class in the twentieth-century United States, although some very insightful sociological and anthropological work has focused on the 1950s and the post-1980 era. Studies of suburbanization and the family have tended to ignore the middle class as a constructed category with multiple and changing historical meanings.[15] In turn, contemporary analyses neglect the vast numbers of men and women who toil as the lower middle class in the (feminized) "bureaucratic professions" and clerical worlds. Chronicling the "fall" of the middle class and its complicated class identities, these ethnographies draw on interviews with male engineers or chemical workers or study professional-managerial workers. Although this work is often extraordinarily suggestive, it is not deeply sensitive to historical shifts in identity. In sum, the history of the American middle class from 1920 to the present remains territory worked but relatively uncharted.[16]

Two deficiencies in particular undermine the ability of much of this prior work to explain significant parts of the twentieth-century labor force. With some noteworthy exceptions, earlier studies have undervalued the centrality of women white-collar workers (and, of course, gender) and, especially late in the century, race to the history of middle-class re-formation. They have also ignored both subjectivity and its historical multiplicities.

The legacy of nineteenth-century white-collar work shapes the language and understanding of class in the twentieth century, but the category also obscures some fundamental differences and wide divisions within this ever-broadening group. The language of class is the problem, not the answer. What do people (including historians) mean when they call themselves "middle class"? Does it mean the same thing for men as it does for women; does it mean one thing for white women and quite another for black women? And, of course, how do these meanings both change and butt up against one another?

Labor historians acknowledge E. P. Thompson's now old dictum that class is a historical relationship shaped by both economic relations of production and cultural modes, but in execution there is slippage when most historians discuss the middle class; it is never clear whether class "styles" or occupational strata define identity. It is usually unclear whether the middle class they speak of is part of a two- or a three-class societal model. Indeed, an upper class most often remains invisible or obscured in vague musings about the middle class's relationship to a hegemonic or dominant culture.[17]

I am most comfortable with a two-class model that sees the "middle class" as occupying an ambiguous and shifting middle zone of social and political space. Class is not like a marble with hard, well-formed boundaries; rather, it has fuzzy, permeable, and changing boundaries. According to the social theorist Loïc J. D. Wacquant (who builds on Pierre Bourdieu), "The middle class, like any other social group, does not exist ready-made in reality. It must be constituted through material and symbolic struggles waged simultaneously over class and between classes; it is a historically variable and reversible effect of these struggles."[18] Moreover, the "middle's" location in intermediate " 'in between' spaces" makes fuzziness its essential nature, an ambiguity to be captured rather than denied.[19] Thus what follows in this book focuses on the multiple and contested views of the middle class held by various historical actors—namely, social workers and those interacting with them—and on the symbolic strategies and practices they have historically engaged to occupy this middle ground. Although social workers' language of class is (usually) unequivocally "middle class," the meanings they give to that language in their expectations and contested social situations at work and home suggest this more ambiguous social formation. Ironically, social workers' sense of themselves is "middle," situated between the blue-collar workers with whom they share conditions of dependence and the affluent, propertied bourgeoisie with whom they share attitudes about individualism (privacy) and consumer values. Their identity is not fixed, however; rather, during the course of the twentieth century, two nodal forms have contended—a bourgeois working class and a proletarian white-collar class.

The ambiguity, fragility, and marginality of social workers' class position are seen in the constant struggles over who is and who is not a social worker.

Conflicts with Peter Stallybrass and Allon White's "low other" play a central role in shaping class identity, but so do intensely fought battles with much closer social groups. These contests were especially keen in the opening decades of the century and are an important element in the first two chapters of this book. Within social work, the struggle takes place over practical efforts to define "standards" and demands by those with the most agency experience and education to limit entry into the professional association. Initially the field divides over paid workers' efforts to distinguish themselves from unpaid volunteers; later, the contest moves to divisions between public and private sector workers. Nonetheless, many excluded by one group or another in this constantly changing struggle persist in calling themselves social workers and appear to be categorized as such in multiple public and official representations such as the federal census, journalistic accounts, and the visual media. For our purposes, all who define themselves or are defined by others as social workers will be examined, people historically called charity workers, religious workers, psychiatric nurses, or social service or public assistance workers.[20]

The liminal status of social work is revealed by its characterization as either feminized and proletarianized or professionalized. In fact, both characterizations are true but autonomous and antithetical processes.[21] Nineteenth-century clerical work, for instance, was usually a male middle-class occupation involving independent work conceived of as unroutinized and clean. In addition, the job held out the promise of a high salary and social mobility into management, which was understood as not too distant from ownership. Aron's study of federal clericals suggests the more complicated and less promising career path taken by women white-collar workers in the nineteenth century. By the twentieth century, however, the typical clerical was a woman in a managerial bureaucracy or office.

The transition from benevolent charity worker to paid social worker was no less dramatic. In contrast to factory work, these jobs remained clean and paid better. But, as we shall see, bosses presumed that women always had men to support them and that women's wages were supplemental "pin money" earned during an interval in their lives before marriage and family. Office "routines" left a modicum of autonomy, and a few women such as Grace and Edith Abbott, Florence Kelley, Belle Moskowitz, and Mary Van Kleeck seized opportunities to carve out roads to power. For most women, however, the work was basically supervised and dead-end. In fact, it was classical nineteenth-century dependent wage labor that paid a salary, though inadequate to live on alone. Social worker complaints of high caseloads and low wages would echo throughout the twentieth century.

Continual calls from social workers to professionalize reflect their efforts to shore up this marginal status. As such, professionalism functions substantially as an ideology, but like proletarianization, it reflects something of the (limited) autonomy and security in social workers' "career." Indeed, almost all social workers call themselves professionals, whereas only a few orthodox Marxists have ever described themselves as proletarians. But the two processes mirror each other and shape social workers' responses to their work.

The problem for the new, mostly female white-collar clericals, or for that matter the "bureaucratic" professionals, was that they brought the expectations and ideology of independence and autonomy from the nineteenth-century middle class with them but confronted the material realities of dependence in the twentieth-century workplace and home. Their "career" distinguished them from their factory worker counterparts but did not match the perquisites or opportunities of highly paid executives, attorneys, and medical specialists, usually men, who were also white-collar managers and professionals. This more affluent sector of the middle class had considerable "disposable" income, extra money to invest in "securities." Social workers or clericals might share the same expectations, but they could not rest so secure. Complicating their lives were the messages about consumption as a measure of middle-class (or professional) living standards that barraged them every day in the marketplace.

By the mid-twentieth century, however, the middle class had come to define itself by more than the new white-collar occupations. Warren I. Susman and others have explained that this social class was the carrier of a new ideology, a culture of abundance rooted in consumerism. And such attitudes extended across traditional social divisions, beyond the white-collar bureaucrats and service workers.[22]

The responsibility for organizing consumption has remained the chief province of women as homemakers. Once again, historians such as Ryan have described the central place of women and the family in the emerging nineteenth-century middle class. Indeed, consumption and the bourgeois family have long been coterminous. By the twentieth century, however, women had been called on to take these traditional roles into the workplace—in jobs seen to replicate mothering such as teaching, nursing, and social work and in department stores, where they could supervise consumption. Indeed, by the mid-twentieth century, social work itself, especially counseling and therapy, became a modern consumer good, both a "real need" of the "needy" and a status symbol of affluence.[23]

Both independence and consumerism were present in these new workers' lives. Rather than marking the achievement of these people's middle-class identity, however, they were too often only partially fulfilled. As important, they functioned as veils that obscured dependence and subsistence and ultimately beclouded the divergent meanings according to racial and gender differences of class and professional identity.

But, then, how can we examine the languages, representations, and notions of the middle class? As suggested earlier, an especially useful counterpoint lies in the insightful recent work of two sociologists. Although neither Halle's chemical workers nor Zussman's engineers can speak for the white-collar workers who make up the majority of the twentieth-century labor force, both provide graphic testimony of disjunctures between the workplace and the home. It may be that identity divided between work and home will be less self-evident for this majority. Thus, although white-collar voices begin to be heard in both studies, an analysis of a group such as social workers permits examination of cross-class attitudes, of how social service workers define themselves in relation to the social background of their clients.[24]

In the United States, perhaps because racism is so embedded in the political culture, the discourse of class has overlaid a gender bias with a racial bias. The conservative American social critic Rush Limbaugh, for example, gives exaggerated form to widespread prejudices against putative opportunities for women and African Americans in his complaints of "quota queens." Limbaugh's vitriol, as Nancy Folbre has noted, tells as much in its "explicit appeals to race and gender interests" as it tells about the insecurity and fragility of the "middle America" to which he appeals. Ironically, two-parent incomes, while representing new employment possibilities for women, also reflect the often desperate need for additional family income when the man loses his job or finds replacement work with no benefits and a lower wage. These are the new jobs in the global economy for which companies recruit women and minorities willing to work at a lower wage.[25] Not surprisingly, recent books chart the "fall" or "decline" of the middle class.

Equally important as Halle suggests, different racial and gendered languages and experiences of middle classness are themselves rooted in different historical situations. People have multiple and divided identities, some of which are distinct, some of which overlap. They can be professionals and/or trade unionists; they can be Jews or Catholics; they can identify themselves as African Americans, Hispanics, and/or whites; they can be women or men. Moreover, like a person's genetic structure, in different generations different characteristics predominate and others remain recessive. Our task, then, is to historicize identity in all of its multiplicities, contradictions, and tensions. This book will invert Halle's study to look at the attitudes and work of the white-collar social workers— women and men, whites and people of color—who were considered middle class by the blue-collar workers Halle studied.

Why Social Workers?

Social work provides a particularly good point of entry to the study of class formation, the imaginings of it by contemporaries and historians, and the politics of class identity in twentieth-century America. The various meanings of the term "middle class," both for the social workers and for those interacting with them, that historically have shaped social workers' attitudes and behavior constitute this book's central problematic. As workers who both professionalize and, at times, unionize in their struggle to achieve and define their work identity, social workers represent many of the tensions and contradictions that riddled the lives of people navigating the murky waters of class identity during the opening decades of the twentieth century.

The heart of social workers' job as gatekeepers of public and private relief aid has always been patrolling the boundaries of class. The sine qua non of social work involves "casing" the borderline between independency and dependency, between self-sufficient workers like themselves and those they deem "less fortunate." Those in need come to social workers as prospective "clients," dependent on their judgment concerning eligibility for material or emotional aid. Before the client-worker relationship can proceed, social workers must locate and place clients socially; basically, they must determine their eligibility or, in later private service developments, their place in a fee structure. The casework method, early enshrined as the fundamental professional tool of social work, effectively did just that: by asking a series of probing questions about income, family life, and habits, social workers used the case history to mark clients as "authentically" poor.

At the same time that social workers had to mark themselves off from those socially "below" them who were dependent on their judgment, they had to struggle with elites "above" them to claim the authority to hold such power. As workers, they too were "dependent" on others for a wage (albeit they were socially torn over whether dependence on the beneficence of others was morally different from their own labor struggles). In the nineteenth century, "Ladies Bountiful" had volunteered their time, doling out pieties and money donated by their wealthy husbands and themselves to private charities. In the early twentieth century, many of the more prominent of the first generation of paid social workers also came from well-to-do backgrounds, but to justify their wage, they had to distinguish themselves from volunteers. And increasingly—certainly by the 1920s—social workers were a class apart from the society women who could afford to volunteer; as a substantial paid social worker labor force emerged, these women and men had to claim their own social space as "respectable" workers who were different from both the industrial working class to which they tended and the wealthy men and women who controlled agency purse strings and continued to volunteer as Big Brothers or "visitors" to the poor. Professionalization, as we shall see, would in this sense be a political and social project of this occupational group to claim a "middle" social and political space that would provide status and some measure of autonomy and control over their work.

Social workers, then, were centrally located as both subject and object in the transformations of work in the twentieth century. As subject, the social worker was a white-collar worker in what has been generally called a semi- or bureaucratic profession to distinguish it from the more highly paid and not so incidentally mostly male professions of law and medicine, which had an acknowledged specialized base of learning. But, of course, as object, social workers brought their own notions of survival values and social skills to their ministries to those who suffered from the transition and needed assistance.

The popular identification of much social work with public relief and its substantial historical location since 1930 in both the public and the private sector also place the occupation at the center of contemporary debates about American values and "middle-class" political culture. As feminist historians have documented well, welfare state policy and practice historically have been overloaded with political meanings. They cite, for example, debates over charity versus entitlement and gendered differences between means-tested programs serving mostly women and children and grants given without means tests for programs traditionally serving men, such as old-age insurance under the Social Security Act.[26] Once more, a Rush Limbaugh jeremiad suggests the popular conservative political script of such welfare politics. "The poor and the lower classes of this country," Limbaugh has complained to millions of television and radio listeners, "have gotten a free ride since the Great Depression when it became noble to be poor."[27] Finally, and perhaps most important, racial and gender configurations have become the hallmarks of modern urban America and make social workers a good group in which to study the confusion surrounding class identity and class formation in the twentieth-century workplace.[28]

For the most part there is no question about social workers' class self-identity: they think of themselves as middle class. Equally clear, their employment (although not necessarily their work) requires higher education and state certification and constitutes a service—social production rather than production for use. Finally, Halle's discovery of a middle-class living style that chemical workers shared with a range of professionals, clericals, and managers suggests that consumption had fashioned a broadly based middle-class identity at least by the 1980s.

Two caveats from Halle's work demonstrate the need to historicize his case study: the chronological limits of his data to only a four-year period in the early 1980s and, most important, the exclusion of many African Americans from this pattern of class identity. Indeed, this study locates the origins of Halle's double sense of class among professional white-collar workers such as social workers in the 1930s. The history of social workers engages four major characteristics of this ambiguous form of middle-class identity. First, social workers' work routines have historically shared many characteristics with traditional blue-collar labor.

Second, there is no single "professional" social worker identity or work experience; rather, white women and men and women of color (men of color have had less of a presence in social work) have distinct identities that have varied over time. Third, workers draw on multiple identities as cultural resources under different historical circumstances. And fourth, the twentieth-century ideology of professionalism and the idea of the middle class have both functioned as linchpins of a consensus anticlass system of beliefs against alternative and oppositional trade union and working-class identities.

Gender

The predominance of female social workers as both the backbone of the labor force and attendants to the poor, many of whom historically have themselves been female, focuses attention on gender, a central issue in the figuring of class identity. The feminization of the helping professions also has deep historical roots and a profound contemporary impact on the nature of the work—its status, wage structure, and so forth. For example, in her path-breaking book, Mary P. Ryan has noted how the family, as "the cradle of the middle class," establishes bourgeois values of "sexual constraint, temperate habits, maternal socialization," and so forth. Could women, however, be both middle class and workers, especially considering that increasing numbers of those who worked were also married? Both inherited notions of Victorian female respectability and new pressures to emulate the leisure of the rich complicated the working woman's identity. Ironically, as Thorstein Veblen explained at the turn of the century, women who sought paid labor denied their husbands the social status that came from having wives who did not have to work. Thus, women white-collar workers challenged middle-class notions of respectability, femininity, and family and brought on claims that they would neglect their children, undermine their husbands, put themselves at risk in "male" work spaces, and take on "manly" roles to succeed in business.[29]

Gendered divisions within professional white-collar industries such as social work are a central complication in this story. The social service workplace is a heterosocial one, and that fact creates problems for both men and women concerning the ways their professional identity is tied to either femininity or masculinity. Women have always constituted a majority of social workers in the United States, but their percentage has ranged from close to 60 percent during the depression to nearly 75 percent at other times. Women staked a claim to public space but discovered that men still ruled in it, men whose own masculinity depended on their dominance and higher wage. As important, new assertions by single women "adrift" and "bachelor girls" in apartments, their claims of autonomy from the family, and their assumption of more active sen-

COUNTY OF LOS ANGELES

DEPARTMENT OF CHILDREN AND FAMILY SERVICES

MISCELLANEOUS TRANSMITTAL

WRITE IN TITLE OF DOCUMENT TRANSMITTED

TO: Mike Jackson

FROM DISTRICT: Troy Jacobs

DATE: 9/12/00

CASE NUMBER	CLASS OF AID	CASE SURNAME	REMARKS
		Pager Number 213-990-3869 Old cap Code	
		New Cap Code 1690054	
		Old pager not working	

RECEIVED BY	DATE RECEIVED

76M215T DCFS 6-1 (12/94)

suality and sexuality created a crisis of femininity for women as professionals. How would their relations with men as coworkers, bosses, and husbands be mediated by their new assertiveness and demands for professional objectivity?[30]

The history of social work as a locus of female employment also illustrates the analytic challenges and interpretive dilemmas facing the mid-twentieth-century labor historian trying to assess the "new" working class, an increasingly female work force of public employees and white-collar professionals who identify themselves with middle-class life-styles.[31] Women have always predominated in the occupation, but like most workers in the tertiary labor sector, social workers made the transition from voluntary to paid labor early in the century. Female volunteers nevertheless remained an important part of the industry. To this day, volunteers serve as administrators and board members of philanthropic societies and provide a variety of services as Big Sisters and Big Brothers, Junior League members, and counselors for troubled adolescents.

For men, professional work had always been an acceptable arena, but social work was marked as a nurturing occupation appropriate for women. Working-class men rooted their masculinity in the workplace, in the muscular image of the sturdy mechanic. Feminist labor historians such as Ava Baron and Ileen A. DeVault have shown that trade unionists began to transfer their sense of male pride from the workplace to the home with the deskilling of labor under Taylorism, which created, in DeVault's words, a " 'social definition' of masculinity." As a breadwinner, the "manly" worker would provide for his family. The nineteenth-century middle-class man with his higher salary could, of course, provide even better. But what of the male social worker in the twentieth century? Not only was his salary inadequate, but he had to share his work space with even lower-paid women and do so in work encoded as feminine.[32]

Women had a different set of problems: new social spaces like Coney Island and department stores and new styles of independence on the streets and in places such as cafés and dance halls. They were the independent women Kathy Peiss describes; they were adrift, as Joanne J. Meyerowitz notes. But both of these authors seek to remove confusion about class, behavior, and causation that I think is embedded in the historical categories themselves: the confusion of working-class women creating styles that middle-class women adopt, of class as the white-collar occupations of daughters rather than the blue-collar occupations of fathers, and of class as the occupations of native-born WASP women in the 1900s and the occupations of immigrant daughters a generation later.[33]

As an extension of their traditional familial responsibilities, women, represented as "Ladies Bountiful," had always played a major role in ministering to the poor as volunteer charity workers. At the turn of the century, however, women began to have new expectations about work as a paid career at the same time that new opportunities for their paid labor appeared and traditional attitudes against it eased, especially if it was in "appropriate" employment deemed socially imperative. The convergence of suffrage with the need for wartime labor and the supervision of immigrant families and children fostered the entrance of women into paid social service work, first in settlements, then in the proliferating private casework agencies of the postwar era.

Pamphleteers, social critics, and vocational writers littered the opening decades of the twentieth century with books heralding the new employment possibilities for women. But despite all that was new about both work and its relation to gender, many of the attitudes surrounding women's work remained remarkably rooted in the traditional separate-sphere ideology that celebrated domestic forms of work and "maternal" instincts. One "how-to" volume published in 1926 drew on all of these strains of thought: "Every kind of work that women can do is a possibility. At least one of these kinds you can do well, and the world will be the better for your doing it. Some kinds of women's work lead to the creation of beautiful things, some to the relief of distress and the soothing of pain, some to the training of little minds, while still others go to the making of laughter, or to the comfort and pleasure of all."[34]

Among the occupations singled out for the special attention of young women was social work, an activity that had long engaged well-to-do middle-class women as voluntary philanthropy but was now championed as a new "profession" for the leagues of working women. The Women's Educational and Industrial Union (WEIU) of Boston published a series of pamphlets in 1911–12 urging the particular attraction for women of vocations in home and school visiting, charity, settlements, and social service with children. The work might be new, but the WEIU legitimized it by using traditional nineteenth-century evangelical language. In volumes on women's work published in 1914 and 1921, the WEIU elaborated what the authors thought to be women's special opportunities and "calling" for social work.[35]

WEIU writers noted that the remarkable growth in social services in the first decade of the new century had opened up great work opportunities for women. As volunteers, women had always done such work and the day of the volunteers was "far from over," but volunteers "now need to be supplemented by paid experts, released from other ties and uncertainties of business contacts."[36]

This new profession is one of singular interest to woman, for the conservation of human life has always fallen to her lot. She has always been neighbor nurse and social worker; and now what should be more fitting than that she should become "the trained and specialized good neighbor," as expressed by an eminent social worker? As might be expected, the field was filled with an eager, enthusiastic crowd of women, the majority of whom were untrained, but had leisure. From this first chaotic group has gradually emerged the type of trained women and men, who in time, if we may believe the general trend, will be found in control of all philanthropy.[37]

Finally, the growing dominance by the 1930s of daughters of immigrants in social work brought a new reality of work for female social workers that complicated their self-identity as middle class. In contrast to the earlier generation of usually unmarried women, the vast majority of the post-1930 generation married and took on the responsibilities of the double day as both social workers and homemakers. Many took a hiatus from social work to raise families, but their families' growing dependence on two incomes and the double labor of wives jeopardized these women's sense of themselves as middle class. For example, the previous generation, reared in affluence, had access to domestic help. And the contrast with the previous generation was more than a memory—it was apparent in well-heeled volunteers and wives of board members. Moreover, since the double day was a distinct female work pattern experienced by neither their husbands nor their male colleagues, it accentuated the patriarchal regime at work that limited women's promotions and kept them subordinate to male administrators and directors.

Race and Ethnicity

The new profession and the middle-class identity of its members were marked, however, not just by gender but also by race and ethnicity, especially if we include both the Jew and the WASP as ethnic "others." If, as Henry Louis Gates Jr. has demonstrated, "race" is socially constructed and does not exist simply as "blackness," the same can be said of ethnicity. Some turn-of-the-century Baptists, for example, cast Italian Catholics as racial "others," swarthy Mediterraneans who contrasted with "men of real merit who are not quite white folks altogether."[38] Similarly, for Puerto Ricans (or African Americans trying to "pass" as white), being "white" or "black" could mean one thing to them and something else to others, a point often painfully driven home when they applied for a job or sought housing. So, although few African Americans and Hispanics worked in organized social service until fairly late in the twentieth century (the black church did function historically as a self-help welfare institution, of course), race always shaped identity, even as whiteness.

The plasticity of the line between ethnicity and race further complicated the way the story of any one group was embedded in that of another as "other." For instance, just as the racial differences between nineteenth-century Protestant charity missionaries and the Native Americans and immigrants they addressed led to tensions, the racial complexions of ethnicity made visible the strains between German and eastern European Jews. Similarly, as almost exclusively white workers during the first half of the twentieth century, social workers' own status was both enhanced and compromised by their association with poor clients. To be sure, second-generation southern and eastern European women and men entered social work early in the century—in religious agencies, as court officers, as "visiting teachers," and so forth. But the great majority of social workers, while ministering to the "other" on relief, distanced themselves socially from immigrants, black migrants to the city, and people dependent on casual work. At the same time, their low-status, poorly paid work assisting those on the dole or dependent on others placed them at risk of contagion from the "unrespectable."

It is the exclusion of African Americans from the material gains associated with postwar consumer (i.e., middle-class) culture, however, that makes race rather than class the central social problem of modern American society. The abiding tenet of the dominant culture popularized, with ideological fervor, the notion that the benefits of the postwar economic boom and an end to ideology would make consumers of us all in a universal middle class. Blacks' failure, then, to achieve that "promise" must be explained, and the last half of this book traces how a black failure story became deeply entwined with a Jewish counternarrative of success. Thus racial identity became central to social worker subjectivity after World War II. Not only were eastern European Jews often tinged in WASP culture (and, at times, in German Jewish culture) as a racial "other," but Jews themselves had varied and contradictory experiences with blacks. A disproportionate number of Jews took leading roles in the civil rights and welfare rights movements of the 1960s, but at the same time, when upwardly mobile Jews moved to the "better neighborhoods," they belittled their black maids as "schwarzes." Blacks, who they often encountered only as maids, garbage men, and janitors, were the "other" they sought to "help."

Although the conflict between blacks and Jews in New York City was probably more intense than it was anywhere else in the country at the time, its well-publicized acrimony made the racialized success-failure narratives paradigmatic for the nation as a whole. Indeed, the legacy of this problematic and ambiguous history helps inform the way race has been constituted as a "problem" of modern identity in America. As African Americans began to protest their exclusion from the postwar "economic miracle," Jewish social mobility became inscribed as a signifier of white American meritocratic ideology. Neoconservative Jews like Norman Podhoretz could point to American Jews as a primary example of an ethnic group that pulled itself out of the ghetto by dint of hard work and self-denial. As important, they had left behind "ghetto pathologies." This "success" narrative that some Jews told about themselves and that others began to tell about them invested the Jewish experience more and more in the dominant political culture. To the poor and black (two categories that were converging), the Jewish American narrative, then, became a club used to bludgeon them with suspect government policies. To those left out of the "affluent society," Jews were a walking, talking rebuke and thus a highly charged signifier.[39]

In contrast to Jews, who were a major presence in urban social service work, African Americans and Hispanics experienced social work less as a career than as a necessary service until after World War II. Twenty-five percent of those on relief in depression-era New York City were black or Hispanic, but in 1940 less than 2 percent of social workers were black (the number of Hispanics was not documented). The numbers of blacks and Hispanics employed in social work would increase after the war, especially after 1970. Despite the large number of blacks and Hispanics on relief, until mid-century at the earliest, the popular image of the downtrodden remained the "Okie" or the immigrant poor from Europe.

In point of fact, black social service existed well before World War II. Historically it was tied to the black church and the creation of private black institutions in the second half of the nineteenth century. A cadre of African American "professional" social workers did function, however, within a mostly separate social work system dating from the 1920s.[40] But largely excluded from receiving public and private assistance until the mid-1930s, African Americans remained virtually invisible to whites in the early formal history of social work. When blacks came to dominate the popular image of social service after mid-century, it was almost exclusively as recipients politically constructed as "welfare chiselers." The same is true of their image as social workers: until late in the twentieth century, popular accounts presented social work as a white person's profession, but when people of color entered the field, they did so with contested meanings of middle classness and professionalism.

So, although race as blackness became a central part of the story after mid-century, four salient social facts give a racial cast to this history of class identity and formation. First, to reiterate, until the 1970s, social work was usually a white person's job. It is important to consider the ways in which the meaning of whiteness shaped social work as professional work and social policy, especially since clients, increasingly people of color, are seen as "others." Second, social work has always involved a class tension in the relationship between the served and the server, but by mid-century, a disproportionate number of relief clients were women of color and their dependent children. Beginning in the 1930s, public welfare increasingly called on black social workers to minister to black clients, a story that appears to be as much about class as about race.[41] Whites, meanwhile, mainly made use of private services. Third, middle-class black women in large numbers finally earned a niche in public social service work after 1970, but their achievement was mitigated by a racial division in social work that widened the gap between public assistance administration and private work. Fourth, contemporary politics of welfare roots African American (and later Mexican American and Puerto Rican) poverty in a pathological culture and counters it with a Jewish (and later Asian) success story.

Professionalization and Unionization

Social work is one of the few professions to unionize before it fully professionalized. The use of both strategies to sustain worker prerogatives engaged social workers in the discourse on class identity in the twentieth-century United States. Professionalization served as a fundamental social worker strategy for forging a middle-class identity in the pre-1930 era. Following the example of psychiatric and medical social workers, other social workers developed professional organizations in the 1920s; before the decade was over, school social workers also had their own organization, and family and children's caseworkers made up the core of the umbrella professional association, the American Association of Social Workers (AASW). But social workers created their professional identity in response to conflicting pressures. They had to contend with management's efforts to rationalize work and economize, with their families' expectations of attaining and sustaining a higher standard of living, and with their own desire to participate in the new consumer culture. In sum, they had to fulfill new expectations about what constituted professional conditions, a process complicated by the elusive, constructed nature of professionalism, particularly in feminized professions such as social work.[42] Later, when left-wing social workers, often Jewish and from large cities, organized caseworker unions in the 1930s, competing ideologies concerning professionalism and unionism complicated debates among social workers about their middle-class identity. The result was the emergence of the hybrid form of middle- and working-class identity that Halle discovered much later among chemical workers.

The State and the Public-Private Divide

The history of social workers also highlights the central role of the state in American twentieth-century middle-class formation and identity. Whereas the early history of social work was inextricably tied to the history of private philanthropy, beginning in the 1930s, private organizations became increasingly dependent on state aid, and the public sector employed the majority of paid social workers. Both sectors are important loci for understanding work, industrial relations, and the changing social relations in the twentieth century. Each sector continually shaped the options, roles, and history of the other. As important for my story, the public sector's ministrations to the poor and its growing identification with black and Hispanic clients and social workers clarify significant divisions between social workers in each arena concerning claims to respectability and status and, ultimately, differing notions of what it meant for each to be middle class.

As both public employees and administrators of the public's budgetary largess, social workers find themselves constantly in the middle of complex and ambiguous worker, client, and state interactions. As relief workers, they administer the welfare state, and as public workers, they must negotiate with the state as employees. At the same time, asked to minister to clients but not to "coddle" them, social workers try to sympathize and ally with the poor on some occasions and distance themselves on others. Sometimes they seek to do both simultaneously.

Two aspects of social workers' ambiguous relationship to the state need to be emphasized. First, the state is represented by many different players, and they do not speak with one voice. For example, policymakers, bureaucrats, and politicians on the federal, state, and local levels may agree on many policies but disagree on their implementation. At each level, there are also many competing agents of state policy, from social workers to administrators at various bureaucratic stages. State hegemony therefore contains numerous interstices and possibilities upon which to build alliances or resistance, both for clients and, as workers, for social service staff. Second, private agency staffs also labor in the shadow of the state. As Michael B. Katz has noted, the public-private dichotomy has been exaggerated, and private agencies and their staffs remain heavily dependent on public subsidies.[43]

The confusion and tension over social workers' relationship to the state are compounded by the occupation's location in the middle of a confusing welter of political allegations and countercharges set within a politicized fiscal environment. Social workers often find themselves acting as lightning rods for the political storms that swirl around the welfare state. Indeed, throughout its history, social work has been embroiled in political controversy at the heart of state social policy concerning the sources of poverty and the rights and responsibilities of individuals and of the state. Social workers have been attacked from all sides of the political spectrum: from the left as heartless or patronizing bureaucrats meddling in the lives of the poor; from the right as spendthrifts doling out taxpayer monies to the shiftless and irresponsible; from clients as intrusive bureaucrats who stifle and invade their lives. But clients have sought out, respected, and genuinely appreciated the counsel and aid of social workers, especially when they provided referrals and liaison for badly needed social services. Relief investigators and caseworkers are barraged by these polar responses as they confront their work every day. The following anecdote suggests the political and financial context in which poignant human stories unfold daily.

"Child-Protection System Falls Victim to a Paper Maneuver," announced a

New York Times headline early in 1989.[44] Neglect and abuse of children were hardly unfamiliar to the metropolis, but even hardened New Yorkers had been moved by recent cases of battered children found dead. A month earlier, five-year-old Jessica Cortez had been discovered beaten to death on the floor of her family's apartment, and Joel Steinberg had just been convicted of manslaughter for the brutal battering of his adopted six-year-old daughter, Lisa. Now, the *Times* reported, a "public-relations" "paper maneuver" had possibly contributed to the death of a neglected ten-month-old Bronx boy who had suffocated while his mother, Marsha Foot, was out overnight. An investigator from Special Services for Children, a division of the New York City Human Resources Administration (HRA), was supposed to visit the boy's family monthly and periodically test the mother for drug abuse, but the case had been "lost" in a backlog of cases shifted from one overloaded branch of the HRA to another.

"City officials," explained the *Times*, "were trying to reduce caseloads for those units that get a great deal of attention from the press and are usually used as a measure of the success of the child-protection agency." Following the Cortez case, New York City's mayor Edward Koch had "defended the agency's performance," observing that the number of cases each worker handled at a time had dropped from an average of 35.5 in December 1987 to 18.9 in November 1988 "as a measure of the agency's efficiency." But Koch's lower caseload statistics did not reflect working conditions among family service workers, whose caseloads during 1988 in the Bronx averaged from 31.5 to 54.3 cases. Marsha Foot's case had been one of several hundred Bronx cases transferred from protective diagnostic units to flooded family service units, where, the caseworkers' union reported, hundreds of cases often sat in boxes for months at a time.

Amid the personal tragedy of this bureaucratic horror, the *Times* article made two particularly compelling indictments of New York City's social service administration that suggest something of the political and fiscal imperatives under which social service workers must labor. First, the HRA was undoubtedly understaffed and underfinanced, but city administrators responded to this crisis with a charade intended to manipulate the image of social workers' performance instead of attempting to change the work itself. Second, city leaders such as the mayor championed "measures of productivity and supervision" (both of which were illusory) as "an appropriate part of good management."

So contradictions riddled social work in the welfare state as social workers faced tensions in work load and case responsibility and anxieties in fulfilling conflicting roles as the client's aide and benefactor and as a supervisor and cop. But, as I have suggested, social work also had three more general characteristics central to the study of professional white-collar labor and middle-class identity: the substantial role of women in the labor force, the dual place of private and public sector employment, and the tensions between unionization and professionalism.

A central goal of this study is to historicize the problem of middle-class identity. My not-so-modest hope is to make historians, journalists, social commentators, and anyone else who deigns to use the term "middle class" gun-shy about doing so. When they speak of the "middle class," social analysts need to clarify to whom they refer and what they think the category means to their historical actors. Moreover, because definitions of "middle class" shift and are contested, it is necessary to examine the languages of class with historical specificity. And since specific discursive and material struggles on both the local and the national level provide revealing hints of the various and changing meanings of "middle class," the narrative that follows proceeds on both levels.

In the ensuing chapters, a circumscribed geographical focus shares the stage with the national scope of this study. This is especially the case in parts 2 and 3, when the story turns to the efforts to unionize social workers. In these chapters, the narrative traces the local particularities of the larger story by locating the history of social workers' middle-class identity within two New York City social agencies—the Department of Welfare of the City of New York (DW) and the Federation of Jewish Philanthropies of New York (FJP). This highly focused case study provides certain advantages: it personalizes the story; it brings the story back to the shop floor, where various agents of the state—caseworkers, administrators, board members, state bureaucrats—interact; and it highlights historical differences between male and female and black, brown, and white workers. I also interrupt the broader national narrative periodically with incidents drawn from other places to suggest regional differences. But I repeat that this study's basic purpose is not to present an argument about the history or nature of social work or to provide a case study of New York City social workers, although I often do so. Rather, my concern is with the persisting ambiguities of middle-class identity in the twentieth-century United States. Much of what follows does not deal with New York City at all, and the New York City case is intended only to note local differences. There is one important exception, however, in which the New York City story takes on national significance: the contested relationship between blacks and Jews in welfare and city politics in the post-1960 era becomes a paradigmatic national narrative about Jewish success and black failure that lies at the heart of the transformation of the idea of what it means for the white majority to be middle class.

In New York City, I focus on the DW, which employed approximately one of every six people who labored in public sector social work in the nation during the Great Depression. Many of these staff members were hired straight out of college and without specialized training; others had been on relief themselves. I also examine Jewish social workers employed in the private sector by affiliate agencies of the FJP, in particular family casework agencies such as the Jewish Board of Guardians of New York (JBG), the Jewish Child Care Association of New York (JCCA), and Jewish Family Services of New York (JFS). The distinction between the public and the private sector, although evident in the higher work loads and lower salaries in the DW and the greater emphasis on therapy in the private agencies, must not be allowed to obscure the basic similarities of work in both spheres. Indeed, the state has played a major role in private institutions throughout the century, and volunteers have continually contributed services to state agencies.

It is important to acknowledge that New York City is not a typical place and that Jewish caseworkers have a unique history. It is a truism to note that New York City's size is larger, its problems more immense, and its welfare bureaucracy more extensive than elsewhere. The 73,591 social workers counted by the Census Bureau in the New York metropolitan area in 1990 represented the largest concentration in the nation. An area that contained about 6 percent of the nation's population employed nearly 12 percent of the country's welfare service employees, a broad category of clerical workers and professionals labeled by the public as doing "social work." At the same time, the DW bureaucracy, budget, and client demand were legendary, dwarfing that of other cities. Including aid to the homeless, the city alone employed more than 25,000 people in social service.[45] In the best of circumstances, well-intentioned employees have had to wend their way through a labyrinth of forms with federal, state, and local investigators watching over them to make sure that public funds were not being squandered. In the worst of circumstances, clients who were deemed ineligible complained of bias by zealous relief workers anxious to demonstrate their "efficiency." In contrast, the FJP, and in particular, the JBG, have been in social work's therapeutic vanguard, pioneering psychiatric social work in the United States.

The immense scale of social work in New York City distinguishes the social relations and work environment of social work there. For example, large agencies with substantial staffs could be impersonal yet provide the base for worker organization. Thus, the social and political history of New York City's social workers is more radical and sharply contested than that of social workers almost everywhere else. New York City's social workers were some of the most militant and politically left-wing activists in what has historically been a "union town." Jewish social workers were especially articulate and politically active. Yet a large majority of social workers, particularly outside New York City, never unionized. Moreover, the dominance of communists in the New York City social work trade unions during the 1930s made the impact of McCarthyism there greater and more overt than it was elsewhere.

In the discussion of middle-class identity, the sharpness of the debates concerning the class composition of racial and ethnic solidarities and the extremes of articulated positions among New York City's social workers can be especially clarifying. Although personal and political identities are formed in liminal spaces of resistance, more firmly bounded organized activities place them in sharp relief. For example, the cultural critic Homi K. Bhabha has emphasized how competing and overlapping subject positions (gender, race, class, generation, political stance, institutional affiliation, and so forth), the "'in between' spaces," "provide the terrain for elaborating strategies of selfhood—singular or communal—that initiate new signs of identity." The "interstices"—"the overlapping displacement of domains of difference"—are sites where "the intersubjective and collective experiences of *nationness*, community interest, or . . . cultural value are negotiated."[46] In New York City, however, the especially contested history of social workers provides a series of vivid "innovative sites" for the acts of collaboration and contestation that "defin[e] . . . the idea of society itself" and articulate claims to middle-class identity. Some of the claims in New York City— such as being Jewish, Puerto Rican, or communist (or socialist)—will have site-specific resonance; other claims—such as being a woman, a professional, or a trade unionist—will address more general concerns. Most significant, in the closing decades of the century, the coincidence of large Jewish, Puerto Rican, and African American populations in New York City, although unique to the city, made possible what may be the paradigmatic role of race relations in middle-class identity between Jews and blacks. In sum, although the constituent elements of subjectivity with which middle-class identity is constantly negotiated always vary by time and place, New York City social workers illuminate brightly both the process and the shaping of it in twentieth-century America.

In oral histories, social workers often speak with candor and great feeling about the contested nature of these in-between places. But memories of the McCarthy era, bitter union struggles, and complicated race relations caused a handful of contemporaries, many of whom continue to work in New York City social service, to request that they remain anonymous. These individuals are given pseudonyms; other interviewees are identified by their own names.

This book traces middle-class identity through three major shifts. Part 1, covering the first thirty years of the century, focuses on the private philanthropic agencies in which most social workers labored. By examining the class and religious/racial/ethnic dimensions of social workers' professionalizing project and then the gendering of professionalism this part traces how the emerging paid labor force deployed narratives of professionalization to construct a middle-class identity in a new, low-paid, and feminized field.

Part 2, covering the 1930s and 1940s, locates the story more narrowly in New York City, where radical social workers created the professional worker as a countertype to the professional woman of the 1930s. The centrality of unionization to the story of professionalization in New York City gives this section an institutional focus, as it traces the rise of public welfare through the collapse of left-wing social worker unions by mid-century. The New York City social worker community illustrates how a unionization narrative combines with the professionalizing project to reshape middle-class identity as a hybrid worker-professional story. A double sense of class identity emerges that is figured in the oxymoron of the professional middle-class worker. Social workers see themselves as working class on the job and middle class at home.

Finally, part 3 picks up the story at mid-century, when race begins to supplant class as the major "problem" in American society. Against a backdrop of growing numbers of black and Puerto Rican welfare clients, the white public increasingly imagines the city as a threatening black enclave. At the same time, a McCarthyite purge of the left-wing unions facilitates renewed managerial emphasis on efficiency and eligibility. In this context, social workers reprofessionalize and reconstitute their identity as white and less equivocally middle class.

The paradigmatic conflict between blacks and Jews in the late 1960s brings our story back to a focus on New York City. New Left recruits into social work in the city build a new radical union movement, but the heightened middle-class professionalization of the previous decade shapes their efforts. Although progressive social workers once again ally with clients by joining African American activists in the welfare rights movement, they now establish professional craft unions, insisting that their workplace interests are distinct from those of agency-employed clerical and maintenance workers. By the end of that decade, disorder associated with major DW and public school strikes creates a white backlash against social welfare. Complaining that the poor have been privileged by the Great Society, an efflorescent conservative social thought constructs the social mobility of Jews, who are directly implicated in this conflicted history, as a counternarrative to black failure in order to justify welfare cutbacks. Within this political context, social work is fundamentally reorganized after 1970. Administrators Taylorize service work, while professionally trained social workers grow increasingly infatuated with private therapy. These shifts coincide with the emergence of several middle-class identities, segmented by gender and race. The language of class, however, comes to take on an enhanced political and racial meaning rather than an economic social designation. "Middle class," therefore, comes to refer not to class at all but rather to social respectability.

PART one

The Professionalizing Project

In the opening decade of the twentieth century, a new occupation emerged calling itself "social work." It developed in a range of arenas, including schools, hospitals, courts, and Young Men's and Young Women's Christian Associations (YMCAS and YWCAS). Part 1 focuses on the struggles of this new paid labor force, most of whom worked in private philanthropic agencies, to secure a middle-class identity in a new, low-paid, and feminized field. Professionalization became the core strategy of this social and political project.

Each subfield that developed between 1890 and 1920 claimed to be the legitimate heir to this new job title, but three distinct areas—industrial social work, medical or hospital social work, and group work in settlement houses—illustrate their different agendas. Chapter 1 examines how three sets of competing claims were used by different social workers (and by agency board members) to negotiate what constituted respectability or "good" social work: social perspective, loyalty to one's employer, and objectivity.

Chapters 2 and 3 bring the story up to the 1920s: chapter 2 examines the class and religious/racial/ethnic dimensions of the social workers' professionalizing project; chapter 3 looks at the gendering of professionalism. The FJP, which organized in 1917 as part of the effort to consolidate social services across the nation, serves as a window into the overlapping religious, ethnic, and racial aspects of middle-class identity formation. What it means to be a Jew—as an ethnic, religious, or twin identity—has long been a hotly debated question within the Jewish community. In the 1920s, being Jewish had acquired a class meaning that was embedded in winning professional acceptance. Jewish agency workers sought to professionalize specifically as Jewish social workers in New York City, while at the national level social workers fought efforts by the U.S. Census to link their occupation with that of religious workers. At the same time, German Jewish philanthropists denigrated their eastern European brethren as racial "others," but others apart from the separate but influential black social worker community. Chapter 2 concludes by examining the flip side of the would-be middle-class social workers' problem: how to distinguish themselves from elite volunteers and agency board members.

The professional model also had a gendered message for the new female generation of workers who came of age in the 1920s. Whereas the earlier generation of settlement house workers chose career over family, the new one, increasingly made up of granddaughters of immigrants, often wanted to have both work and family, albeit not necessarily at the same time. Focusing on the gendered meaning of social work identity in the 1920s, chapter 3 looks at the heterosexual workplace and examines how the professional "objectivity" and "passionlessness" traditionally associated with male behavior conflicted with attitudes about the nurturing woman and conventions of femininity. Accordingly, female social workers in the 1920s modified the professional model they inherited from the Progressive Era to create an alternative feminine middle-class type: the professional woman.

CHAPTER one

The Invention of the Social Worker

The term "social work" entered the national vocabulary around the turn of the century. Mary E. Richmond was one of the first to use the term in her address as the general secretary of the Baltimore Charity Organization Society (COS) at the 1897 meeting of the National Conference of Charities and Correction (NCCC). Urging the development of training schools, Richmond referred to both "professional social workers" and "professional charity workers." By the turn of the century the term "philanthropy," seen as the science of giving aid, increasingly replaced the term "charity," although the name of the occupation's national association still retained the words "Charities and Correction." Organized in 1873, it changed its name to the American Association of Social Workers in 1917. In response to Richmond's appeal, the New York COS organized the first school of social work in 1898, and it began to function full-time in 1904 as the New York School of Philanthropy.[1] The names of the next three training programs that opened across the country reflected the confusion over terminology and the initial preference for "philanthropy": the Chicago School of Civics and Philanthropy began in 1904; Simmons College (with Harvard University's support) opened its School of Social Work in 1904; and the St. Louis School of Philanthropy offered its first course in 1907. Even after "social work" began to insinuate itself into discussions of the field in the succeeding decade, it had to compete with "social service" and "welfare work."[2]

Many different constituencies may have contributed to the development of the term, but social workers embraced it as a source of higher status. In choosing the title "social worker," the emerging twentieth-century cadre of full-time paid workers who provided social welfare services sought to distinguish their work from personal and religious charity work and organized philanthropy. Reflecting the prejudice of the day that "real" work was paid labor, they wanted to be thought of as "workers." Moreover, they believed that the heart of their enterprise was not moral beneficence but a "social" problem—poverty—to be resolved through formal "social science" expertise. But although the term was intended to distinguish their labor as professional work, it had contradictory connotations. The designation "worker," for example, confused or possibly even undermined their claims to middle-class status. "Social" could be equally compromising. At the end of the nineteenth century, in contrast to political economy and politics, the "social" was imagined as woman's domain. The *Oxford English Dictionary*'s first reference to social work, from the *Girl's Own Paper* in 1890, was typical: " 'Stump Oratory' may safely be regarded as quite beyond the limit of a woman's social work."[3] Indeed, the use of the term to connote women's work in society reflects the ways in which the realm of the "social" is a doubly feminine space. As the feminist historian Denise Riley, writing about social service work, notes, " 'Women' both come under and direct the public gaze . . . as sociological subjects." Although this gendered connotation was not always explicit in discussions of social work, it was always implicit. As such, it also confounded the efforts of many male social work leaders to claim their professional middle-class status.[4]

The publication of the 1910 federal census seemed to justify social workers' anxiety over their status as middle class. As federal enumerators traveled around the country interviewing people about their occupations, they realized they had difficulty categorizing new kinds of social service work. The occupational classification system used by enumerators had not changed substantially since 1870, and the special agent in charge of occupational statistics from 1910 until World War II, Alba M. Edwards, found it "entirely inadequate . . . either to meet the marked changes that had taken place since 1870 in the occupational activities of the people or to meet the increased demands for more accurate and detailed information about these activities." In the 1910 census, directors tried to rectify these problems by reclassifying occupations and adding new categories. To reflect the shift from production to service, for example, Edwards endeavored to reshape the census of occupations along narrow empirical lines. This resulted in a new classification system based not on the product or the place of work but on the relationship of different kinds of work to production—for instance, whether one was a "maker," manager, or salesperson; provided a service; or performed clerical tasks.[5]

The 1910 census classifications brought social workers both good and bad news. Although the census classified nearly half a million teachers as "professionals," it placed 24,461 other individuals with similar demographic profiles into two new groups of "semiprofessionals": religious, charity, and welfare workers and keepers of charitable and penal institutions. This was the good news—by classifying social workers as semiprofessionals, the census at least acknowledged that they were full-time workers. The bad news was the heterogeneous list of occupations with which they were grouped: notaries, fortune-tellers and healers, keepers of pleasure resorts and racetracks, sportsmen, and theater owners, among others.[6]

The reordering of the census reflected Edwards's desire to rank occupations according to status, to distinguish owners ("keepers" would be the census term) from employees and those who sold services from those who made or sold commodities. The "keepers," for instance did not achieve professional standing even in 1930. They had a distinct social profile and had moved outside the mainstream of the field: although their ranks nationwide nearly doubled between 1910 and 1920 from 7,491 to 12,884, approximately two of every three were male. In contrast, as early as 1910, most individuals in the "workers" category were female, and women would increasingly predominate. The number of "workers" increased from nearly 16,000 to over 41,000 between 1910 and 1920, with the percentage of women increasing from 55.7 to 65.6 percent (see appendix, table A.1).[7]

As if the indignity of being listed as a semiprofession and lumped together with sportsmen and fortune-tellers were not enough, the class and professional ambitions of social workers received a second devastating blow five years later. Abraham Flexner's famous address in 1915 before the NCCC was equally disparaging. Promoting a medical model of the "ideal" profession, Flexner argued that social workers, possessing no special skills, could never become "true" professionals.

Flexner's judgment carried considerable weight. Earlier, under the prestigious auspices of the Rockefeller Foundation, he had helped to upgrade medical education by introducing modern science to medical school curricula. His 1915 speech, which set out comparable criteria for measuring professions, became an obsession in social work debates for a long time to come. Social workers fretted over his devastating judgment for the next twenty-five years, remarking on it at annual meetings of the AASW, whose own identity as a professional association was in question. Flexner had not simply insulted social workers; his indictment of their professional standing had undercut the basis of their claim to middle-class status.[8]

Faced with Flexner's critique and the census's damaging classification, social workers mobilized to offer counterevidence. That same year, a joint committee of the New York School of Philanthropy and the Intercollegiate Bureau of Occupations undertook a formal investigation of the occupation. The New York School of Philanthropy, which had begun as the educational arm of the New York City COS, the major social service organization of the generation, spoke for the professional ambitions of the occupation. The investigators, without rancor, challenged their association in the census with the other semiprofessions. "Evidently," they complained in their report, "census tabulators do not yet regard social work as a profession." The remainder of the report then sought to claim professional status for social work.

The joint committee's 1915 report had two objectives: to demonstrate that the census enumeration of social workers was "incomplete" and to discredit its appraisal of social workers. The investigators secured data to argue that the actual number of social workers in New York City was 100 percent greater than the census count. The 1910 census had enumerated 862 men and 1,394 women in New York City who could be classified as religious or charity workers or keepers of charitable or penal institutions, a category that included orphanages and old-age homes. The report accepted both as appropriate categories of social work, totaling "keepers" and "workers" as an inclusive category. In contrast to the census, the investigators counted more than 4,000 women and men at work in the private sector alone. "If to the social workers in private agencies," the report concluded, "we add those in government service, social work takes rank numerically with the most important of the recognized professions." Second, using wage and educational data, the investigators argued that social work techniques and underlying principles were comparable to those of other professions and "not less important than that of the teacher, the lawyer or the physician."[9]

Despite the protestations of social workers, it was not until 1930 that the census moved social and welfare workers into a new category—"other professional pursuits." They were now listed alongside librarians and "county agents, farm demonstration." A 1935 Russell Sage Foundation classic on the new profession attributed the achievement to "the vigilance of the American Association of Social Workers."[10] This tortuous path to respectability, however, would continue to be strewn with category pitfalls; for another fifty years, debates raged over who was and who was not a social worker and whether being a social worker conferred professional status. But as a public marker, the 1930 census shift demonstrated that some social workers had begun to sort out the ambiguity in emerging hierarchical distinctions and that the census had followed their lead: although social and welfare workers achieved the status of professionals, keepers of charitable and penal institutions and the now-isolated religious workers still remained under "semiprofessional and recreational pursuits."[11]

The emergence of the occupation of social work in the census between 1900 and 1930 illuminates both the transformation of work during this era and the difficulty people encountered in finding a language and set of categories for comprehending it. Settlement house, hospital, and industrial social workers; probation officers; and school visitors vied with charity workers from a range of secular and religious philanthropies and churches for classification as social workers. After 1915, they collectively (and increasingly) expressed dissatisfaction with the 1910 categories, but they did so from the perspectives of their different work experiences. While the various types of social service workers debated among themselves and endeavored to prove that their relationships with those they served were appropriate to the social worker title, they also debated with their "bosses"—those who hired or funded their work—over the nature of their work (the labor process) and what it meant to do "efficient" or "good" social work. At the center of their disagreements, then, were questions about their occupational identity rooted in their efforts to negotiate the in-between space between their clients and their employers. Who were social workers; what kind of work did they do; whose work did it resemble; and what was their status, their place in the ranking of jobs? The occupational identity each group struggled to define and claim as a source of authority and middle-class status was that of the social worker.

The Past as Prelude

The "modern" social worker whom the Census Bureau "invented" as a semi-professional in the early twentieth century brought the ideas and experiences of historical predecessors to this debate. The social profile of these workers and their work setting would continue to change as daughters and granddaughters of immigrants entered the field, but the traditions and historical memory of nineteenth-century charity workers both as elite women of independent means and as meddling snobs would shape the way they did the work and thought of themselves in the new era.

First, neither poverty nor the effort to eradicate it was new to America. Poor relief began almost as soon as the first settlers got off the boats in the seventeenth century. The abiding principles of relief that governed AFDC until 1997 and then Temporary Aid to Needy Families, however, had become established by the mid-nineteenth century: promoting "less eligibility" in order to wean putatively dishonest mendicants from the lists and keeping assistance levels below the prevailing rate of wages for a given community in order to encourage habits of work (and, perhaps not so incidentally, provide cheap labor).[12]

Second, the history of welfare and welfare workers has traditionally divided the field into public and private sectors as if they were discrete areas. Indeed, free market enthusiasts would have us believe that the private realm alone is the repository of all that is virtuous and right in society. The fact is that some of the largest private agencies have long relied on public funds for substantial proportions of their operating budgets. As early as 1870, for example, the Children's Aid Society of New York obtained more than half of its $200,000 income from public sources.[13] Reflecting the self-help ethos that informed relief, social welfare historically was mostly private, but it often relied on public funding. In contrast, public care for the poor remained stigmatized by its association with "lowlife" elements and was hard-pressed to attract caring staff. According to Katz, in the antebellum asylum, which often housed the indigent together with both the insane and the criminal, inmates often had to do much of the work, including the nursing of other patients. It was not until the middle of the twentieth century that the state actively insisted on its right to oversee through the use of legally binding contracts the allocation of monies it provided the private sector.[14]

Third, historians of women have begun to document the substantial role of affluent, educated women in relief. In the voluntary charity work spurred by evangelical Christianity during the Jacksonian era, women played a central role that would have a lasting impact on the gendered future of social work.[15] Female benevolent societies and missionary societies sprang up overnight in cities across the Northeast and Middle Atlantic states as revivals encouraged women to bring God and comfort to the "less fortunate." But, as historian Lori Ginzberg has pointed out, these were not just any women; they were "middle and upper-middle-class women . . . [who] shared a language that described their benevolent work as Christian, their means as fundamentally moral, and their mandate as uniquely female."[16] These women, as the historian of women Christine Stansell has observed, "understood class in religious terms" and sought to bridge the substantial differences between themselves and their subjects, but they represented a small elite. "Extremely prominent New York women" formed the Society for the Relief of Poor Widows with Small Children in 1797; daughters of members of this group were among those who organized the New York Orphan Asylum Society in 1806; and 70 percent of the members of the New York Bible Society came from the top 2 percent of taxpayers.[17] These women were hardly "middling." Nonetheless, claiming a "separate sphere" of benevolent work and family life as woman's own, they defined a middle-class identity by mid-century unique to their social profile and relationship to work at that historical moment.[18]

After 1850, the role and gendered character of charity work shifted. Women took on a larger role in charity work, but their authority in agency administration diminished. Thousands of women were introduced to social service work through their participation in local units of the U.S. Sanitary Commission during the Civil War. After the war, they were found, in extensive numbers and with major influence, in the COS. At the same time, as men reconfigured their social roles in public life as trustees and directors of agencies, they reclaimed the administration of poor relief as their own legitimate province. In doing so, men relegated to women the role of helpmate. Male agency directors increasingly hired men as paid agents, compelling women to increase their presence in social welfare as volunteers with diminished status. At the same time, the nature of the authority of "visitors" to the poor shifted: helping the poor, who were now more often of

Irish than of English stock, became less a mission of moral regeneration than an exercise in social control. Although the unpaid staffs often consisted of daughters of the evangelical women of the 1830s, postwar charity reform lost its "evangelical, feminine tone" and became harsher, more "scientific." Female virtue, which had been the measure of good charity work, now took a backseat to "efficiency" and "professionalism"; a woman volunteer had to be more like a man.[19]

The COS, perhaps the quintessential welfare institution associated with the era of "scientific philanthropy," illustrates these shifts in late-nineteenth-century charity and the philosophy that Eric Foner has argued "helped to crystallize a distinctive and increasingly conservative middle-class consciousness" in post–Civil War America.[20] Class antagonism played a more explicit and harsher role in the "scientific charity" of the COS, muting gender alliances and sharpening the edges of class identity at the end of the century. Earlier evangelical women had forged a middle-class identity in contrast to leisured aristocracy in a mission to fallen women; in organizations such as the COS, their daughters forged a middle-class identity by distinguishing themselves from the fallen as members of a class of men and women. Class mattered in both instances, but in rejecting "sentiment" for "science," COS visitors lost much of the gender solidarity that had eased differences between, for example, female moral reformers and "fallen" women in the Jacksonian era.[21]

U.S. reformers embraced the COS in an effort to repress pauperism and the disorder they believed arose from it. The organization was founded in London in 1869, and by the 1880s, in the wake of the turmoil and consternation created by such events as the Paris Commune and the national railroad strike in the United States in 1877, COS branches had opened in major cities across America. COS principles were simple: to create an "independent" poor with "backbone," no material aid was to be given to them except in emergencies, and then only on a temporary basis; volunteers, usually women, were to counsel the poor as "friendly visitors"; and philanthropy was to be placed on a businesslike footing. The COS would investigate, collate data, and proffer advice, although its coercive, moralistic tone was not lost on the poor.

The reorganization of relief as a business would also shape later social work. In this business environment, women were increasingly subordinate volunteers reporting to male directors and superintendents: these women found their "sphere" greatly reduced and their work demeaned as less important.[22] The COS's efforts to become more businesslike prefigured both mounting pressure on social service workers from corporate benefactors and the increasingly businesslike nature of social welfare in the twentieth century. By the late nineteenth century, an interlocking directorate of elites from the worlds of business, finance, and the professions shared resources, members, and social policies. Even as they insisted on the moral nature of their project, they elaborated a business model and increasingly functioned like one. Although the administration of relief from the countinghouse always subjected the poor to austere taskmasters, it would be twentieth-century social workers as dependent wage laborers, not the lady volunteers, who would also feel its impact.[23] In summary, then, by the turn of the century, social workers—still invisible to the Census Bureau and unnamed as such—stood poised to emerge as an independent field of paid labor in a range of social arenas, their work and identity resting on a history riddled by a complicated and deeply interwoven set of gender and class tensions.

Progressive Era Relief

After 1900, the settlement house movement became the key tradition that was claimed, invented, and preserved by the would-be profession and, until recently, by historians as an alternative to both the "Ladies Bountiful," the elite women often seen in poor neighborhoods as austere, prying snobs, and "scientific charity." Social reform emerged during this era and came to dominate public debate on the nature of social work and subsequent historical memory. Many of the reformers came out of the settlement house movement, which most typified these years, and the houses sponsored much of the social research that lay behind proposals for improved public sanitation, housing, safety, education, and protective legislation for women and children. Social reform advocates infused a new political dimension into the debates over diagnosis and treatment and, consequently, over what constituted "proper" social work. Social reformers' concerns with social change became a guiding light for generations of social workers, even as in professional practice they frequently found themselves deploying personal pathology in their diagnoses. Indeed, the reform tradition fueled a historical infatuation with the settlements and their reformers.

Typical Progressive Era settlement house work deviated considerably, however, from the reform ideal. Social service work followed much more in the tradition of scientific charity than historians have earlier acknowledged. Although some radical voices even advanced socialism as the only viable social work reform, welfare capitalism and not social radicalism generally prevailed.[24] In fact, rather than typifying the tradition of social work, the settlements constituted a unique moment in its history and stand apart from much of its subsequent history, when family and child casework would dominate the field.

Settlement workers may have captured the public imagination at the time, but they were never truly representative of the forms of social work that later dominated the field. In contrast to them, significant minorities of industrial and hospital social workers, public health nurses, visiting teachers, and probationary workers influenced the agenda of the fledgling field to a degree that exceeded their numbers. Both industrial and hospital social work, for example, received substantial material and public support from important political constituencies. In addition, work in industry countered the reform bent of the settlements and encouraged pressures for efficiency and social control, and hospital social workers and the mental hygiene movement that developed during World War I became major ideological actors in shaping social work notions concerning diagnosis and therapy Finally, as we shall see in chapters 2 and 3. in the decade following the war, the new dominant place of social workers in family and child casework agencies reshaped the field for a second time. These casework agencies, although not factories, initiated a process of rationalization of social work that would subsequently be elaborated and intensified by the federal relief bureaucracies (the growth of the public sector represents a third shift) that emerged during the Great Depression.

The competition among various types of social service employees over which kinds of work would define the field and the standards by which quality service was to be measured was in fact triangulated. Within the field. some family workers disputed the assumptions of work done on behalf of corporate interests by industrial social workers; in turn, some industrial social workers questioned the professional "objectivity" of work advocating for families. But competing perspectives of businesspeople/philanthropists complicated these internecine social worker struggles. Indeed, this contest among groups of workers and between workers and their "bosses" took place as social workers found themselves under attack on two fronts: the struggle ensued both in the wake of Flexner's 1915 pessimistic prognosis for social work professionalism and as charity leaders pressed to consolidate social services into new federated superagencies. These leaders, then, not only contested the image of the beneficent settlement reformer; they also had the power to give financial legitimacy to their views. Rejecting what they saw as profligacy, businesspeople were anxious to make sure that their resources be used efficiently. As major contributors to social agencies, they now applied the principle of consolidation to charity with renewed zeal: war chests became community chests. Sitting on the boards of the new federated services, these businesspeople insisted that duplicated services be eliminated and pressed their own notions of what constituted "good" social service. In turn, directors of the member agencies formed Councils of Social Agencies that had their own often competing priorities regarding funding and policy.

Several voices—most notably those of the general public and businesspeople—hindered any single group's ability to dominate this discourse. Charity workers who visited families continued to be most numerous, but settlement house work, in addition to visiting teachers and court, industrial, and hospital social work, expanded steadily during the first two decades of the new century. Three of these groups—settlement, industrial, and medical social workers—epitomized the competing social worker perspectives in the two opening decades of the century and will be the subject of this chapter. In the era before 1920, industrial and medical social workers, although fewer in number, came to have a substantial impact on the character of the social worker's craft. Both reflected powerful political and financial interests. But the important political presence of settlement house workers in reform movements gave them a dominant voice in contemporary debates about the field, and it is the latter whom the pre-1920 history of social work has idealized. Thus we begin with them.

Group Social Work: Settlement Houses

The impact of Progressive Era settlement house workers on succeeding generations of social service workers is both less than and greater than their impact as it is conventionally understood. It is less because the work they did came to have particular bearing on later social work as an image of work rather than as a model for it. It is greater because the Progressive Era enthusiasm for efficiency that these reformers embraced would become intertwined with the pursuit of female professional status in a gendered workplace.

The social profile of settlement house workers is primarily that of a unique generation of women working in a unique institution. Allen F. Davis's classic study provides the standard characterization of these workers as well-meaning "middle-class" reformers. Social welfare historian Clarke A. Chambers adds to that portrait, concluding that the prominent women in the field shared authority and power with men more equally than in any other profession (or "semiprofession").[25] As the first generation of young, college-educated "New Women," they possessed a strong desire to "do something important." Indeed, women assumed the majority of settlement house jobs. For example, a WEIU survey of social service workers in the Northeast between 1911 and 1913 collected information on about 1,700 women with 18 different paid and volunteer job titles (in 49 institutions) and found that nearly half—"about 800"—worked in settlements and 284 supervised playgrounds.[26] As the WEIU publication noted, the remarkable growth in social services in the first decade of the new century had opened up great career opportunities for women. Women volunteers would continue to do such work, but their labor would now be supplemented by that of paid experts.[27] The WEIU author recognized that in the transition from volunteer to wage laborer, a generation of new professional workers would emerge, and it would be a female one at that:

> This new profession is one of singular interest to woman, for the conservation of human life has always fallen to her lot. She has always been neighbor, nurse and social worker; and now what should be more fitting than that she should become "the trained and specialized good neighbor," as expressed by an eminent social worker? As might be expected, the field was filled with an eager,

enthusiastic crowd of women, the majority of whom were untrained, but had leisure. From this first chaotic group has gradually emerged the type of trained women and men, who in time, if we may believe the general trend, will be found in control of all philanthropy.[28]

Women constituted two-thirds to three-quarters of the staffs of the "classic" settlements, and they ran and staffed hundreds of other settlements across the country. Most were young women for whom the job was a kind of internship. They worked for a year or two in exchange for room and board and then moved on, perhaps to marry or enter one of the new graduate school training programs in social work. However, women also worked as permanent paid residents, and as the well-known cases of Jane Addams, Mary Simkhovitch, and Lillian Wald suggest, they came to be the most important part of the staff. Largely Protestant women of privilege whose families were "moderately" well-to-do, they had inherited or developed a strong tradition of service, a reforming zeal, and a social consciousness. Many were daughters of ministers; others had fallen under the influence of Social Gospel ministers. Davis found that 90 percent had attended college and 50 percent had gone on to do some graduate work. Most came from old-stock American families, many with ancestry that could be traced back to colonial New England.[29]

Finally, a large proportion of the women were apparently unmarried. Being unmarried did not necessarily mean being single or alone, of course, and feminist historians have elaborated on the female network of these reformers. Historian Judith Ann Trolander has observed that these settlement houses resembled college dormitories, serving as safe places in which young women straight out of college could reside and work. There they could develop the camaraderie and support of a semiprotected, respectable family life. In fact, several of the more prominent women established long-standing intimate relationships with other women. Still, some like Florence Kelley were divorced, and others like Mary Simkhovitch were married.[30]

Although problematic as a data source on social workers, whom it lumps together with charity and religious workers, the 1910 census broadly indicates that the profile of the typical social worker may not have been nearly as uniform as that of the nineteenth-century charity worker or the settlement house mother (see appendix, table A.2). The average social worker at the time did not resemble historian Roy Lubove's classic portrait of elite, native-born settlement house staff; nearly half (42.6 percent) were immigrants or children of immigrants. In fact, in an immigrant center such as New York City, the proportion rose to more than half: as we shall see in chapter 2, three out of every five workers in this category in New York City had a foreign-born parent.[31] Most of these workers undoubtedly staffed the Catholic and Jewish agencies and the Irish, Polish, and

Italian orphanages and old-age homes. This emerging pattern of recruitment of social workers also had implications for class identity. Women's participation in paid white-collar social work conflicted with expectations of them in the past, when they had worked as volunteers. Although still from a more privileged educated class, the new generation of residents, investigators, and visitors were the beginnings of a "middle" class that was very different from that of their "Lady Bountiful" predecessors.

In the history of social service work, the Progressive Era settlement house was also a particular institution in a particular age. Although knowledge of the daily routine of settlement house workers was once limited to anecdotal biographical accounts and descriptions in novels such as Sinclair Lewis's *Ann Vickers*, the picture that has emerged from a rich group of recent monographs is one of remarkable independence, job autonomy, and responsibility. Mary Simkhovitch, for instance, described the daily life at the settlement house as a swirl of activity from early morning into the evening, all organized and supervised by house residents. "The core of all our work," explained Simkhovitch, was work with groups in supervised activities. The scene changed daily, especially the evening activities, which ranged from theatrical rehearsals and performances, concerts, conferences, dances, receptions, and sports to "cooking demonstrations by the young girls for their young men friends." The house also provided daily service programs—a kindergarten and nursery, a thrift shop, and an office where residents could help others with personal and social problems—and contained facilities for sports, crafts, and musical instruction. These activities were supplemented, of course, by extensive involvement in urban reform programs such as those for improved housing, sanitation, and labor legislation.[32]

Well after the settlement house movement lost its dominant place in social work, settlement house staff testified to the traditional place of autonomy in their work. As late as 1927–28, settlement house workers interviewed in a New York Welfare Council study consistently emphasized the creative freedom and autonomy of their jobs. Asked what they liked best about their work, respondents typically replied: "the independence the position allows"; "the opportunity to carry out ideas—to create"; "the fact that you are allowed to carry out your own ideas . . . that there are no set rules or regulations."[33]

The legacy of social worker identity as middle class was also tied to the settlement worker's historical image as a social reformer, an image that recent feminist scholarship has problematized.[34] Not all of those who worked in social service before the war were settlement house reformers, but these forceful and politically engaged "New Women" came to symbolize the age. Many of these women may have been, as Davis argues, more likely to think of themselves as social reformers than as social workers, but it was a Golden Age for social work and they were—and the image prevailed—its "angels."[35] Indeed, citing women such as Florence Kelley and Lillian Wald, historians have lauded the settlement house as the incubator of "maternalist" reformers who would, in the words of one, "make an indelible imprint on U.S. politics."[36] Many of the most prominent women settlement house workers had established an impressive socialist and feminist agenda that went against the grain of work on behalf of the modern corporation. The experience of Mary Simkhovitch's Greenwich House in New York City is illustrative of work that also went on at the Russell Sage Foundation and the New York City cos. Using knowledge gleaned from daily experiences in the settlement, the house's Education Committee produced a series of extraordinary social investigations of the family economy of the poor that demonstrated a feminist and socialist awareness. Simkhovitch's friend Louise Boland More published *Wage Earners' Budgets* in 1903; it was followed by Elsa Herzfeld's *West Side Rookery* (1906); Mary Ovington's study of black life in New York City, *Half a Man* (1911); Louise Hyman's *Industrial Survey* (1912); Mabel Nassau's *Old Age Poverty in Greenwich Village* (1915); and Emily Dinwiddie's *Tenant's Manual* (reprinted as the *Social Worker's Handbook* [n.d.]).[37]

Some social workers joined leading social reformers such as Kelley in support of mother's aid, but as Linda Gordon's history of single mothers and welfare points out, the average social worker was much more likely to focus on the moral reform of mothers than to focus on social reform at the workplace.[38] Social workers in organizations like the cos complained that early settlement house women were too radical and too unscientific and coddled the poor; charity workers emphasized individual causes of poverty, not social ones. Only by the second decade of the new century did some charity workers come to adopt parts of the reformers' perspective, moving from correction to prevention, from charity to social reform. Symbolically, in 1909 Jane Addams was elected president of the NCCC.[39] The 1912 platform was more than symbolic: advocating social insurance and a minimum wage, it offered a sweeping social policy program that reshaped political debates for the next twenty-five years. Not only did Theodore Roosevelt endorse essential parts of the NCCC statement in his presidential campaign, but some of the women who cut their political teeth writing it would go on to help shape New Deal social policy.[40]

The role of settlement house workers as social reformers or agents of social control is not as clear, however, as the vocal opposition of some of them to traditional charity might suggest. Outside New York City and Chicago and away from the more well-known women reformers such as Addams, Kelley, and Wald, the settlement house experience seems to have been more conventional. The experience of women in Pittsburgh settlements, for example, suggests that the institution was generally not a training ground for political activists. These settlements did not groom women for leadership but prepared them for submission to male administrators. Women led Pittsburgh's Kingsley House (1893) and

Kaufmann Settlement (1895), for example, only for the first few years; by roughly 1910 they had come to hold a minority of administrative posts, a proportion that would continue to decline at a rapid pace.[41]

Moreover, the majority of settlement house workers seem to have expressed policies and values little different from those of the COS. Recent historical work has emphasized that these women must be measured against the nativist standards of the day; indeed, they tended to view immigrants as victims rather than as causes of social decay and expressed a genuine appreciation for their native cultures. They were also, however, prone to romanticize those cultures as better suited to a simpler past. Assimilation to the "modern" urban, industrial world would require improved conditions (i.e., child labor laws, improved housing, protective legislation) and Americanization. At best, then, even the most benign settlement aid was tinged with a paternalistic view of immigrants as children. At worst, some settlements were openly racist and others functioned as crude social control institutions for Americanizing immigrant neighbors. Finally, although only some operated overtly as missionary societies, many pressed a Christian agenda.[42]

Ultimately the elite status of most women settlement house workers brought a native-born white perspective to their work, one in which their middle-class identity contrasted the ethnic, immigrant identities of the neighbors they served. Daily programs at the houses encouraged arts, crafts, and cultural activities that would "improve" personal integration into society and promote upward mobility. Moreover, Greenwich House neighbors remembered the imposing presence of Mary Simkhovitch with a mixture of respect and awe, suggesting the ways in which deference rather than equality marked relations between middle-class settlement house residents and their working-class neighbors.[43]

The philosophical basis of this Progressive Era reform tradition rested on the commitment to scientific method and efficiency. Generally, these principles served progressive social ends, although as we shall see, people such as Henry Ford would harness them for other social control objectives. Scientific reform and the cult of efficiency served more benign goals in the hands of social science women associated with the settlement house movement, but their work translated into a drive for consolidation and professionalization of services that would have less salutary results in succeeding decades. In the two opening decades of the twentieth century, however, women social workers/social scientists in private research institutions like the Russell Sage Foundation collected data to justify new programs that could ameliorate the social bases of poverty. At the same time, these women served as a social base for the self-presentation of the social worker as a paid professional: she was the "New Woman," well-educated, autonomous, and responsible, possessing specialized skills celebrated by the new technocratic society.

Regardless of what analysts like the census directors thought of their status, Progressive Era social workers asserted and defined themselves as professionals. Autonomous, responsible, and independent, these well-educated "New Women" created an amiable dormitorylike sorority and a panoply of formal institutions in a "professional subculture." In addition, as reformers these women moved fluidly between settlements, social science research institutions, and political associations, spreading the aura of professional expertise from one to the other. But these "New Women" had created a professional identity that redefined women's roles as domestic without necessarily being familial. Social work was deemed appropriate for women because it allowed them to fulfill their nurturing role. The settlement was a suitable place to do such work because it was a semiprotected, homey environment. As unmarried women, they had not "neglected" familial responsibilities to advance their career; they had, instead, chosen the latter.

Ironically, the commitment to social science and efficiency that social reformers had shared and advanced came to undermine the delicate balance in which a feminine identity coexisted with a professional identity. The leadership of these affluent women in settlement houses provided some, although limited, help to a subsequent generation of women in the casework agencies that came to typify social work, for the Golden Age of the settlement house was just that—a time that had passed and had little relevance to the new casework. Settlement house reformers often lectured in the new social work schools, but their experiences in research agencies and settlements did little to prepare them for work in the postwar bureaucratized casework agencies.

Industrial Social Work

Two programs in the new field of industrial social work, the Ford Motor Company's Sociological Department and Metropolitan Life Insurance Company's welfare program, shaped the emerging discourse within the field about what constituted appropriate social work and its relationship to middle-class identity. These programs represented the first industrial applications of social work. The "industrial social worker" sought to reconstruct worker attitudes to promote "healthy" production.[44]

By 1913 Henry Ford had successfully introduced the assembly line at his automobile manufacturing plant. But although the assembly line guaranteed the technological progress of the company, productivity remained hampered by 10 percent absenteeism and a staggering annual turnover rate of 370 percent. The Ford Motor Company responded by offering $5 a day, double the prevailing auto manufacturing rate, and by creating a Sociological Department. The department monitored the private lives of workers and sought to instill in the largely ethnic working-class employees idealized middle-class (meaning "respectable") midwestern Protestant values such as spending evenings at home, drinking only in moderation, going to bed early, not taking in boarders, and ornamenting the home with store-bought bric-a-brac.

In recruiting industrial social workers, Ford reconstituted native-born, white production workers and supervisory staff from the shop floor as middle-class workers, much as he hoped they would transform his work force of immigrants and poor whites from Appalachia into "reliable" American workers. College-educated sociologists and people who worked in local detective agencies also applied for positions in the department, suggesting that the program was seen as falling between social investigation and policing. Still, most of the staff—the number averaged about fifty—came from the factory, where they had worked as auditors, foremen, and supervisors. The company looked for particular traits in its recruits involving personality "skills" and proficiency in company politics: " 'originality, personality, tact, diplomacy and clear and correct interpretation of the Ford Profit-Sharing Plan.' " Later it also sought people "gifted" in handling domestic disputes and criminals. Carrying an average caseload of 727 workers at a time, investigators scurried about town in Ford automobiles, making about twenty-five visits a day to the friends and families of workers to check on their home life, religiosity, and thriftiness. In turn, their own work was closely supervised by Ford officials.[45]

The reminiscences of George Brown, a typical member of Ford's clerical staff, document the formation of the industrial social workers' distinct identity as middle class against the immigrant "others." One historian has nicely described Brown as a "newly minted white collar man." After taking bookkeeping classes at a YMCA night school, this former shoe worker and bellhop procured a position as a clerk in the Ford Accounts Department. Although he was not an investigator, Brown's views reflected the investigators' attitudes toward assembly line workers. The families, he recalled, "lived like 'hillbillies. . . . A lot of them didn't know what a bathtub was [and a] . . . lot of them were living together as man and wife, but they weren't married at all.' " " 'The investigators,' " he explained, " 'taught those foreigners an awful lot. They, what you'd call, Americanized them.' "[46]

Until wartime inflation eliminated most of the wage difference, the five-dollar-a-day plan and the Sociological Department succeeded quite dramatically in reducing absenteeism and turnover. With the coming of the war, Ford fell back on exhortations of patriotism and traditional wage differentials and incentives. The efforts of the Sociological Department to Americanize and keep track of workers' families proved useful to those who promoted anti-German campaigns and those who systematically tried to smash the radical Industrial Workers of the World.

The welfare program created by Metropolitan Life Insurance Company in 1909 in New York City presents a dramatic contrast to the Ford Sociological Department. Whereas Ford's blue-collar workers made automobiles on an assembly line, Met Life's white-collar clericals pushed paper. In contrast to the situation at Ford, at Met Life both clerks and investigators were white-collar workers. Sharing a sense of a common middle-class social position, they could imagine themselves in each other's place. As at Ford, Met Life managers believed they acted in the best interests of employees and instituted paternalistic policies, but whereas Ford's program was interventionist, punitive, and controlling, Met Life pioneered in creating health services like visiting nurses and advancing social policy to improve health and safety. Of course, it did not hurt that Met Life's corporate interest in extending life coincided with the growing immigrant Jewish community's interest in securing death benefits, always an immediate concern in immigrant communities. Lee K. Frankel, former director of the United Hebrew Charities of the City of New York (UHC), and another Jew, Louis Israel Dublin, a trained accountant who would be elected president of the American Statistical Association in 1924, jointly developed the welfare program.[47]

Although Met Life's corporate policies differed from Ford's in many ways, they also displayed traditional attitudes about gender and conservative expectations that staff could fulfill the role of labor-management specialists. Thus, at Met Life, offices and public spaces were designed, decorated, and assigned in gendered terms; for instance, sewing rooms were provided for women so they could continue to make their own clothes. The company also divided the labor by gender, hiring men and women managers to tend to male and female employees, respectively. Mrs. Glen Cunningham, for example, "oversaw" the health and safety of women employees. Historian Angel Kwolek-Folland uses the term "corporate motherhood" to describe the function of such women. The company provided large private offices for men and filled larger spaces for corporate "family" functions with homey furnishings such as bearskin rugs and lamps. Kwolek-Folland also notes that it was New York City's COS that actually convinced Met Life to start its welfare program. Both the efficiency the COS lauded as scientific charity and its moral benevolence served corporate paternalism and cost reductions well. Thus, these women were also labor-management specialists, with an ear attuned to potential labor grievances. Employees were expected to consult with them about their relations with coworkers and office superiors, as well as about domestic affairs and personal concerns.[48]

Businesspeople's enthusiasm for industrial social work programs such as those at Ford and Met Life created a formidable obstacle for group and medical social workers seeking to make their own work central to the professionalizing project. Under siege by the War Industries Board to maintain production levels and to hold the line on wage reductions, businesspeople increased their appreciation of the role of social work in labor management as a means of ferreting out the troubled—and more often, by their accounts, trouble-making—worker. At the same time, businesspeople sitting on the boards of charity organizations led a renewed drive to bring business practices to social work. They embraced the new mental hygiene movement that had just begun to flourish, a development that had roots in the history of hospital social work.

Hospital Social Work

Hospital social work and the mental hygiene movement constituted a third major area of social service work that advanced itself as the basis for social workers' occupational identity. This branch arose in response to new perceptions of the problems of urban squalor and social adjustment for immigrants; it also reflected the increasing awareness in some quarters that the mental asylum had failed. In 1908 Clifford W. Beers, a well-to-do former mental patient, published his harrowing autobiography detailing the callous and brutal treatment of inmates by an underpaid and overworked nursing staff.[49] The exposé of his harsh confinement caused a furor. But the desire to eliminate such evils was only the beginning of the mental hygiene movement. Seeking to inoculate people against the possibility of developing pathological behavior, mental hygiene reformers enlisted the hospital social worker as home visitor.

Richard C. Cabot, then an internist at Massachusetts General Hospital with a special interest in mental health care, was among the first, in 1905, to employ a full-time paid social worker to assist him in the treatment and diagnosis of mentally ill patients. In *Social Work: Essays on the Meeting-Ground of Doctor and Social Worker* (1919), he promoted the hospital social worker as the new detail worker of the mental health industry, who would "*conquer by dividing the field,* to help humanity by devoting himself to a single manageable task."[50] The social worker in the medical setting was expected to mediate between the hospital, the patient's family, and other social service institutions.

Cabot's discussion of industrial disease suggests the larger conservative social implications of the hospital social worker's increased emphasis on personal and familial pathology. Cabot acknowledges that two diseases are traceable to the conditions of industry: lead poisoning and the "functional neuroses of cigarmakers or telephone operators." But for most problems, he asserts, industry is only one factor "in the complicated skein of causes." Thus, the ten hours an employee spends at work "is often a small factor in producing ill health, compared to the fourteen or sixteen hours he spends outside the industry."[51] As Ida M. Cannon, chief of the Social Service Department of Massachusetts General Hospital, had noted, the hospital social worker's investigation of industrial disease had to consider "personal habits and home conditions of the patients" at least as much as occupation.[52]

In the last analysis, Cabot located the source of a worker's stress outside the workplace. Reflecting the new environmentalism informed by late-nineteenth-century studies of tuberculosis, he prescribed what a later generation might call preventive or holistic medicine—treatment had to move beyond drug therapy and root itself in the social environment, where the bacteria festered. However, Cabot retained an abiding faith in employers—their mental health was never questioned—and in their use of the hospital social worker to solve some of their problems. Cabot offered a "social diagnosis" that both served the changing industrial system and offered personal therapy. The new corporate structure of bureaucratic, "modern industrial plants" removed the boss from the intimate relation with employees that had formerly ensured, he believed, a satisfactory work environment. But, in Cabot's own words, the hospital social worker would maintain "a well-ordered economic system," reducing costly job turnover by promoting industrial harmony: "[T]he object of the employer in setting a home visitor or welfare worker at work is to create the maximum of satisfaction and good spirit among his employees, whereby each will do his best work and be as little likely as possible to change his employment."[53] Factors like deskilled work, routinized task work, and speedups were never considered causes of turnover. Instead, hospital social work, following Cabot's prescription, offered a concoction of self-help, hygiene, moral reform, and scientific job placement to ensure that the skills and mental outlook (attitudes) required by the job fit the skills and mentality of the worker.

Cabot's writings and those of his colleagues at the Boston Psychopathic Hospital laid the groundwork for the use of psychology in social work, but it was the horrors of bombing and trench warfare in World War I that gave the mental hygiene engine its jump start. After the war, hospitals mobilized war nurses in a new mental hygiene movement. This movement had coalesced earlier in the journal *Mental Hygiene*, first published in 1917, which contained articles with titles such as "The Management of War Neurosis and Allied Disorders in the Army" and "Vocational Rehabilitation of Soldiers Suffering from Nervous Diseases."[54] These articles were soon replaced, however, by discussions of psychiatric training and its application to other areas of human activity. Significantly, the area often staked out for study was industrial social work and, more precisely, the industrial worker.

The conservative implications of such social work diagnoses could hardly have been lost on industrial workers. Managers were never studied. Rather, as an article in the first volume of *Mental Hygiene* argued, psychiatry's contribution to "efficiency" in production was to demonstrate that "true education implies a harmonious adjustment between the material and the machine to which it is fed." Applied psychology, the author explained, must "fit" people mentally to their jobs, not vice versa.[55]

It would be a mistake, however, to see psychiatric social workers as simply crude apologists for social injustice. In an article titled "The Movement for a Mental Hygiene of Industry," one of the leaders of the field, E. E. Southard, insisted, for example, that "collective causes" such as maintaining affordable food prices justified collective actions. Southard's view that the role of the industrial psychiatrist was to find individual sources of unrest was echoed both in *Mental Hygiene* and in subsequent debates throughout the twentieth century about the conservative implications of the medical model. The industrial psychiatrist's charge, Southard continued, was to treat the paranoid worker, "a man with a grudge or chip on his shoulder." Such a man, he explained in another article, could be a revolutionary trade unionist of the sort associated with the Industrial Workers of the World. Diagnosed as having a melancholy personality, such people, he explained, led a "life of felt passivity" based on "delusions" and "unpleasant" emotional tone.[56]

To bring its message to the field, the mental hygiene movement almost immediately started its own training program at Smith College. A graduate of this school's first class, Esther Cook, remembered the first announcement of the opening of the school, which appeared on the bulletin boards of women's colleges and social service agencies: " 'On July 8, 1918, Smith College and the Boston Psychopathic Hospital, under the auspices of the National Committee of Mental Health, will open at Smith College a training school for psychiatric social workers. The purpose of the course will be to prepare social workers to assist in the rehabilitation of soldiers suffering from shell shock and other nervous and mental disorders.' "[57]

Massachusetts was a logical place to begin such a venture; the staff of the Boston Psychopathic Hospital, most notably doctors Richard Cabot, E. E. Southard, and Herman Adler, and the hospital's chief of social services, Mary C. Jarrett, had pioneered in the development of psychiatric nursing and medical treatment and would teach the course. Also, female students, obviously thought to be the most appropriate assistants to male psychiatrists (as nurses were to doctors), would be recruited from women's colleges in the area such as the Boston School of Social Work (now the School of Social Work at Simmons College). This school would not remake the field overnight, but its graduates would quickly become the professional avant-garde. And they would spread a Freudian gospel. Forty-three of the seventy women in the first class came with college degrees to take a course whose "main focus," noted Cook, "was on social psychiatry." All the American specialists in the field were there to teach them, but Cook especially remembered their infatuation with Dr. A. A. Brill, Freud's translator: "[H]ow we looked up to him and often sat at his feet in informal evening conferences."[58]

Graduates from programs in psychiatric social work soon became renowned leaders in the field and the avant-garde of a social worker middle class. The intellectual content of psychiatric social work continued to be thin until the 1930s, and even then it remained limited to a few prominent agencies in large eastern cities. The key point for the history of social worker identity as middle class is that the number of psychiatric social workers remained tiny. It was only after World War II that social workers across the country began to claim that psychiatric training was essential to all casework and social work agencies moved quickly to adopt these services in their clinics.

World War I and the Crisis of Social Worker Identity

The debate over the various definitions of what it meant to do "good" (or "professional") social work that underpinned the work force's middle-class identity came to a head during World War I. In the two decades before the war, social workers had succeeded in elevating the representation of the social worker as settlement house "angel" and social reformer to the point that it contested the older image of the "Lady Bountiful." Building on the social reform tradition, some social workers, led by settlement house workers, insisted that quality social service demanded the perspective of the reformer, radical or socialist. Not surprisingly, industrial social workers rejected such "advocacy" and proffered an alternative "neutral" image that emphasized personal rather than social adjustment. Then, as we have seen, the war encouraged the development of new forms of social work in mental hygiene and hospital social work. The Red Cross, for instance, was a hotbed for young women who went into social work in the 1920s. Hospital social workers, undoubtedly encouraged by their close association with medical practitioners, embraced the "objective" stance of the professional.

Most important, in the wake of the Flexner critique, the voices of business-people/philanthropists joined the rising cacophony of voices already claiming to speak to what constituted "authentic" social work. Wartime economies coincided with their desires for a productive and compliant labor force and cost-effective social service. As patriotic war-fund drives heated up, complaints about the costs of charity increased. Indeed, agency services at times have always replicated one another, competing for the same dollars. One businessman stated what many seemed to feel: he was tired of being "'solicited and badgered by every social agency in town.'"[59] So although the news of war and revolution that swirled about social workers seemed to them to merit increased social commitment, philanthropists demanded greater control over costs and services.

In response, philanthropies responsible for fund-raising that relied on businesspeople for donations sought to adopt "businesslike" procedures. Business, which had already begun to see the logic in scientific management, supported the application of scientific management to social service, much as the Met Life and Ford programs had done. Although "consolidation" and "efficiency" would become the bywords for social service in the 1920s, the trend began during the 1910s.

Against the backdrop of these developments, then, the meaning and achievement of social work were contested and elusive, both among social workers and among their clients and funders. Group, medical, and industrial social workers each sought to authorize their own work responsibilities and perspectives as the basis for professional recognition that conferred middle-class status. In doing so, they disclosed a series of abiding political and social disagreements that would continue to wrack social service for decades to come. Ironically, social worker concerns with professional standing and the rise of medical social work (and the first stirrings of psychiatric social work) began to converge in important ways with businesspeople's interests in efficiency and science, and this convergence would shape the debate, especially in the next decade. Again, the origins of this debate could be seen in the 1910s, when, in opposition to the image of the social worker as radical, reformer, or socialist, some of these women and men began to put forth alternative models of the "scientific" hospital social worker (sometimes now called a psychiatric social worker), the "neutral" industrial social worker, and the "efficient" professional social worker. These debates would remain at the heart of the politics of professionalism and middle-class identity for the rest of the century.

Although they disagreed on the ethos that should govern their work, most social workers rejected Flexner's judgment, albeit anxiously, accepting instead the "professional" standing given them by the 1915 joint report of the New York School of Philanthropy and the Intercollegiate Bureau of Occupations discussed earlier. Workers in the field, however, more openly acknowledged that the social and political identities of the social worker incorporated a host of complicated and contested meanings. Census data could only allude to the differences that workers more explicitly queried concerning what it meant to do "professional" work: Were social workers to police or assist those they served? Was social work "objective," or did it require a particular social perspective; did it require one to be an advocate for the poor?

A series of articles during the war years in *Survey*, Paul U. Kellogg's progressive social service review, which came out of the *Charities Review* of the New York City cos, illustrates the early politics of middle-class identity that emerged in debates about the method and perspective of the social work professional. In these articles, the "social problem" is seen as at the heart of social work.[60] Reflecting the reform spirit identified with group settlement workers, *Survey* regularly demanded that social workers meld social action with social justice. Under the heading "Editorial Grist," for instance, John Haynes Holmes of New York City's Church of the Messiah complained that the "typical social worker is still too much concerned with individual cases, and not enough with the social complications of these cases. He is too much of a worker and too little of a reformer." Social workers, he pleaded, should "constitute the bone and sinew of the international peace movement" and enter city and state politics dedicated to the "social problem," that is, the abolition of poverty. Whereas an earlier letter writer had urged the formation of a Social Workers' Party, Holmes saw another hope: "It is obviously socialism—or better!"[61]

This political perspective troubled many social workers either because of its radicalism or because of its imputation that their own work was less efficacious than political action. Writing at the moment of the Russian Revolution to *Survey*, "M." condemned "[a]ny tendency to encourage class consciousness among social workers." This was, he warned, "an erroneous tendency which has manifested itself in the pages of your publication." Writing from the point of view of a businessperson, "M." insisted that social welfare was not the exclusive province of the social worker; "there is as much social welfare in an honestly conducted business enterprise." "M." endeavored to clarify the identity of social workers and what he believed to be their "proper" work. There is "a clear distinction between the professional social worker and the professional reformer," he insisted. The latter's concerns were those of all citizens; the "proper subjects for professional or class concern" were "[q]uestions affecting methods, practices and ethics—in other words, the technique of a profession."[62]

Social workers could not easily ignore such words, coming as they did from the sort of businessperson they depended on for financial support. Indeed, "M." wrote at precisely the moment when businesspeople were rethinking the nature of their commitment to welfare and its administration in more centralized federations. But some social workers had other reasons for welcoming this perspective: "M." spoke to the growing thirst for professional standing, while acknowledging the problematic and complicated relationship of the welfare enterprise to business.

In a 1916 article in *Survey*, for instance, Edith S. Reider, an industrial social worker, challenged the anticapitalist bias she repeatedly encountered among other types of social workers. Social work in the industrial arena, she complained, was not considered a form of social welfare. Arguing for the acceptance of industrial social work, Reider played on the status anxieties of social workers in two ways. First, she tried to counter images of the social investigator as a "snoop" and the charity worker as a "cold statistical Christ." Based on her experiences in the cos, she dared anyone to find "a more overworked lot of girls than we"; the social workers she knew possessed a "personal, helpful touch."[63]

Reider's second point—concerning the problems inherent in social work's historical association with the down-and-out—went directly to the heart of the question of what constituted "real" social work. The issue would, of course, come up in later years. Social service, she argued, was not just for the dependent and, by implication, the degenerate: "It would be unfortunate, indeed, if social service had to be confined to the sub-normal, for many a self-supporting family is in need of constructive social service, and sometimes even temporary relief." Not surprisingly, Reider pleaded for tolerance from her mates. Acknowledging exploitation in industry, she reminded her readers that neither paternalism nor injustice were limited to the industrial sphere: "[B]oth in business and social service there are individuals who should not be trusted at all with the responsibility of dealing with other human beings."[64]

Reider also took up two familiar troublesome images of social workers—the social worker as meddlesome controller and the social worker as frivolous "Lady Bountiful." Both images had well-established histories and some basis for a continued currency. Coming from elite backgrounds, nineteenth-century charity workers often either imposed their own values on the poor or measured the poor's "deservedness" by their own standards of respectability. And the poor often felt imposed upon and said so. Moreover, even as they insisted that they were not being "heartless" or "policing the poor," social workers had to prove that they were making efficient and "proper" use of other people's money. Finally, hostility toward the poor as "undeserving" in many quarters made others only too willing to turn social workers into police and to elide the difference. Thus, John Mitchel, the newly elected mayor of New York City, announced his intentions in 1914 to employ 10,000 people with an intimate feel for city life as "potential social workers—the members of the police force."[65] Even over a decade later, in 1926, D. W. Griffith's popular epic film of greed, intolerance, and prejudice through the ages, *Intolerance*, used social workers, represented as "the vestal virgins of 'Uplift,' " as the contemporary examples of intolerance.[66]

In contrast to the image of the social worker as cop, social workers were more willing to acknowledge the image of the social worker as "Lady Bountiful." They recognized that there was a basis for this image, but they dismissed it as distasteful and outside the mainstream of the profession. For instance, Frances C. L. Robbins voiced appreciation of the "yeoman service in social work" done by volunteers, but she felt compelled to write of the "thoughtlessness" of one volunteer, presumably in the hope that others would take the lesson to heart. The "unfortunate impression" left by this woman's arrival at the home of a client "swathed in furs, in a motor, with chauffeur and footman," Robbins feared, undermined the hour she had spent with the family. "She was Lady Bountiful, superior and patronizing, the object of envy, and the cause of class antagonism."[67] Although many wealthy volunteers and settlement house workers exhibited genuine concern for the poor in a nonpatronizing way, the image of the "Lady Bountiful"—and something of its reality—cast a shadow on the would-be professional social worker.[68]

Even as women social workers tried to put the image of the "Lady Bountiful" behind them, the war opened up new social work possibilities for women that complicated attitudes about their appropriate role. Decisions to replace male social workers who had left for military duty overseas with women created concerns such as those expressed by Sidney A. Teller, a worker in Pittsburgh's Kaufmann Settlement, in a letter to the editor. Writing in response from Louisville, Kentucky, social worker Janet Hall tried to put Teller at ease: "Women are adequately replacing men in heretofore untried fields. . . . May not the 'male social worker,' so anxiously referred to [by Teller], don the Khaki without too much anxiety for the fate of the institutions he leaves behind?"[69]

A decade later, the crisis over the role and image of the female social worker came to a head in the story told in chapters 2 and 3. The full flowering of professional ideology would confront the woman social worker with the contradictory needs to distinguish herself from the female volunteer and to assert her femininity. Meanwhile, during the 1910s, the tensions remained muted. Even though opportunities in social work were more proscribed for women than for men and even though women held most of the jobs, both men and women tended to use men's work as the measure of the job. A booklet issued by the YMCA and the Intercollegiate Bureau of Occupations in 1914, *Salaried Positions for Men in Social Work*, sought to lure men into the poorly paying field by offering forty-five job possibilities in twenty-one lines of social work. At the same time, Katherine Bement Davis, superintendent of the Bedford Reformatory, sought to ease male anxieties about her appointment as New York City's first woman commissioner of correction by announcing that she would run the department "exactly as a man would."[70]

So the emerging discourse about the proper identity and role of the social worker as middle class was not limited to the views of settlement house residents and hospital and industrial social workers; it was shared by workers with various social identities. Gender was but one of those social differences. A second involved race and ethnicity as they were historically constructed about and by various groups of people, whether they be African Americans, elite native-born Protestant whites, Italians, or German or eastern European Jews.

In the Progressive Era, formal social work was generally a white person's job, done by white people for white people. Immigrants, especially the swarthy Mediterraneans some considered "not quite white," were the "others" to be Americanized. African American migration north to industrial cities in the opening decades of the twentieth century gave increased visibility to black communities. In New York City, for instance, blacks increased their numbers by nearly 100,000, from 60,666 in 1900 to 152,467 in 1920. Although they remained a relatively small group in the city, constituting only 2.7 percent of its population, their identification with neighborhoods such as Harlem that were stigmatized later as ghettos gave them a much larger place in the white imagination. Discriminated against in the northern labor market much as they had been in the South, they lived and worked in a tense, symbiotic relationship with the white, immigrant working class with whom they competed for jobs. In the aftermath of the war, when white soldiers sought to return to their jobs, racial conflict often erupted. In Chicago, for instance, when white bosses attempted to reverse wage gains made under the administration of the War Industries Board, massive strikes, most notably in steel, became implicated in race riots that erupted.[71]

Against this tumultuous social backdrop, it is difficult to know what role the small number of African American social workers played. African Americans constituted 3 percent (1,231) of the 41,000 people listed as religious, charity, and welfare workers in the 1920 census. Almost all of them probably worked in church-related agencies or with the Urban League. In New York City, their number had grown in ten years from 28 to 96, reflecting the relative concentration of blacks in the city. In the interim, some of the city's leading settlement reformers did important work to raise racial awareness and help create a receptive audience for African American social service. Beginning in 1905, Mary White Ovington, a wealthy white settlement worker and social investigator from an abolitionist family, published a dozen articles and books on the plight of the African American in New York City. Social workers helped organize the National Urban League in 1910, and the National Association for the Advancement of Colored People (NAACP) was founded in 1909 at a conference organized by Ovington and fellow settlement residents Lillian Wald, Florence Kelley, and Henry Moskowitz.[72]

The settlement house movement's record on race, however, as Ruth Hutchinson Crocker has nicely summarized it in her study of Gary and Indianapolis, was more equivocal. Most settlements, even as they promoted racial reform, in practice maintained a color line. Of the more than 400 settlements in the country, there were about two dozen "black settlements," many of which operated in small southern communities. Many black churches may have functioned as welfare institutions, acting much like neighborhood centers. But most major cities had one formal settlement house for African Americans, such as Indianapolis's Flanner House and Gary's Stewart House. Both of these settlements were formed by "coalitions of black and white reformers," the former under the auspices of the local COS in 1898 and the latter by the Methodist Episcopal church with funds from U.S. Steel in 1920 (a year after the great steel strike). For the most part, white elites provided the money and made up the boards of these facilities, and black elites ran them. By mixing social control with social reform, Crocker acknowledged, these settlements did good work in health care, recreation, and education. She concludes, however, that by "helping to reinforce policies of segregation and inequality that barred black progress," "racism distorted the reform impulse in the Progressive era."[73]

An anonymous 1918 account in *Survey* of "seven Negro industrial welfare workers" in Pittsburgh illustrates the social and political context in which such workers labored. The article, which clearly intended to highlight the contributions of black social workers, demonstrates the limits of enlightened social workers' views on race. When steelworkers were drafted, about 3,000 African Americans entered the industry. Four of the largest companies then specifically hired "colored social service workers" to work with the black workers. Three other companies, including Westinghouse Electric and Pittsburgh Plate Glass, also hired "Negro labor agents who do a large amount of social service work." At their weekly conferences organized by the Urban League of Pittsburgh, these seven black social workers complained of an ongoing problem on the shop floor. Plant foremen, the article explained, were "usually foreigners" who were paid little more than the workers and had "little real authority." With labor in short supply, black workers, it seems, had too much "attitude." Speaking with the voice of a white investigator, the reporter noted that "[t]he Negro resents rough handling and is quick to flash up when his indignation is sustained by a knowledge that there is plenty of work to be had elsewhere."[74]

The tradition of industrial social work defined what the corporation expected of these black welfare workers: they had been hired "to help in reducing the number of causes of discontent." Although the article noted that the "more radical Negro welfare worker believed that only the appointment of Negro foremen would solve the problem," most of the black social workers' solutions emphasized recruiting better foremen and improving their interpersonal relations by encouraging them to get to know the workers by name.[75]

Although black industrial welfare workers appeared to work in a setting separate from that of white workers, as in the settlements, they found themselves in a similarly compromised class position. Race further complicated their lot. As white social workers inched toward a collective identity defined against the immigrant "other" they served, black social workers, a racial "other" themselves, worked to "uplift" and improve the fate of other African Americans in a world apart. In this regard, they were like black middle-class club women of the era, whose slogan was "Lifting while we climb." At the same time, black social workers, who were regularly reminded by segregation and racism of their difference from white workers, espoused patronizing attitudes toward black clients, from whom they wished to be distinguished. Such attitudes would become the core contradiction within a distinct black middle class, whose story became clearer in the 1920s as their numbers grew.

Lumped by the Bureau of the Census in 1910 among fortune-tellers and sportsmen on the one hand and charity workers and asylum "keepers" on the other, hospital, group, and industrial social workers each insisted that their work regime embodied the core values of an independent, "authentic" professional identity. Each believed that the way they related to the people they served was central to the occupation, and each offered a competing model of that social relationship. Company-backed social welfare programs that flourished during the 1920s like Ford's carrot-and-stick paternalism and Met Life's welfare program certainly provided social inspiration (and employment for social workers). But not all social workers acknowledged the validity of such ministrations on behalf of industry as "proper" social work. Instead, they looked to the settlement houses, the visiting nurse programs, hospital social work, and the rise of family and child services out of the charity and reform movements of the nineteenth century. These, they insisted, provided more compelling social prototypes for social work that proved more responsive to a variety of immigrant and working-class concerns.[76]

By the late 1910s, however, as social workers advanced differing views of professionalism—as reform or even socialist or efficient and objective—they also had to confront the dilemma of maintaining the support of businesspeople/philanthropists. Some found it possible to demonstrate that they worked both in and for industry. Others knew that if they wished their voices to be heard, their point of view to be empowered, and their financial position to be improved, they would have to raise their professional status. Most social workers, of course, disagreed with Flexner's assessment of them as "semiprofessionals." Seeing themselves as "emergent" or "transient" professionals, they moved early in the century to establish a "professional subculture" of schools, journals, and organizations to confirm their identity.[77] Responding to Flexner's critique that they lacked a specialized knowledge base and methodology, social workers increasingly sought to develop a rigorous "technique." They found it in a coincident development: in 1917 the publication of Mary E. Richmond's book *Social Diagnosis* quickly established "casework" as the byword for professional practice in the next decade.

Although social workers made little explicit use of the language of middle-class identity in the prewar and wartime discussions, such an identity informed their practices and propaganda. The class "other" remained the immigrant industrial working class, and social workers asserted their own middle classness through claims to their rightful place (and status) in the new occupation. As often as not, social workers sought to leave behind the world of their parents. An older, more privileged generation of charity workers bore the legacy of the nineteenth century, trying to "uplift" the "unfortunate."

The 1920 decision by the Census Bureau to lump religious workers with welfare and charity workers raised a new set of anxieties for social workers. This seemingly modest category change and the focus on casework professionalization entangled social workers with two new sets of "others": clerics and missionaries with modest "technical" expertise and volunteers, from whom paid workers hoped to distinguish themselves. All of these "others," of course, also inhabited the same middle class in which social workers sought to claim membership. The census change also highlighted contradictions concerning religion among the many social workers who worked in the private casework agencies that dominated social work after 1920. Jewish and Catholic social service, for example, employed staffs with conflicting loyalties and multiple, often overlapping social identities. Other agencies, which billed themselves as "nonsectarian," in fact reflected Protestant moral values. Turning to the history of casework and, in particular, the story of New York City's Jewish agencies, the next two chapters look at the "techniques" on which social workers focused. Behind this move was an effort to mark themselves off and exclude others from their professional category. As such, these chapters illuminate as well the complicated ethnic, racial, religious, and gendered meanings of the 1920 census categories for professional middle-class identity.

CHAPTER two

The Professionalization of the Caseworker

During the 1920s, as the federal census merged religious workers with charity and welfare workers, social workers stepped up efforts to distinguish themselves from disparaged "others" marked by overlapping religious, ethnic, and racial identities. At the same time, to validate their paid labor, they had to insulate themselves from two groups that contested their independence from above: "lady" volunteers who did similar work and elite trustees who controlled agency purse strings. To accomplish this task, social workers endeavored to wrap themselves in the mantle of the professional middle class by embracing the ideology and trappings of professionalism. To do so, they heralded two new practices as unique professional (and therefore nonpolitical) "techniques": casework and psychiatry. "Caseworker" became the occupational title for the new social work professional of the 1920s.

The Caseworker

The origins of casework lay in the 1880s. According to Dr. Richard C. Cabot, casework and ultimately the psychiatric nurse or social worker derived from efforts to control tuberculosis in the 1880s when it became clear to doctors that social investigators could help provide treatment by detailing deleterious environmental factors. By the 1890s, cos chapters in various cities had also begun to deploy social scientists to collect urban data for use in analysis and possibly treatment. In Baltimore, Richard T. Ely sent a young graduate student in economics, John R. Commons, off to do casework for the Baltimore cos and then to report back to a joint seminar of economists and historians. Similarly, New

York City's cos forged a working arrangement with Columbia College political science students. In 1899 Mary E. Richmond used the term "case work," which she had appropriated from the London cos, in a slim book, *Friendly Visiting among the Poor*. In 1917 Richmond, who had now become director of the Charity Organization Department of the Russell Sage Foundation, formalized the principles of casework in her landmark text, *Social Diagnosis*. In nearly 500 pages (drawn from thousands of actual cases), Richmond elaborated the proper social investigation procedures based on social evidence; she insisted that specific settings required specific knowledge and treatment. Due to Richmond's influential position and the comprehensiveness of her empirical book, *Social Diagnosis* became the official bible for the caseworker. It laid out the rules for evaluating evidence, walked readers through a lengthy series of typical interviews, and enumerated detailed categories for questioning and diagnosing the "Inebriate," "Feeble-Minded," "Homeless," "Unmarried Mother," "Neglected Child," and "Blind Person." In sum, *Social Diagnosis* provided material evidence to support the claims of social workers that they had the requisite professional knowledge base. Within a year, the book had gone through five printings.[1]

Casework ratified the social worker's prerogatives as middle class. As social workers evaluated cases, they fixed the class position of others above and below them. *Social Diagnosis* identified caseworkers' special knowledge as the ability to classify people and their daily work as processing clients' social location. Their work was to define class. Every day, in determining eligibility for services, they patrolled the boundaries of the lower class. As important to their job security was the status that the "technique" and knowledge base of these procedures provided, thus offering a defense against efforts by those above them to demean or control their work.

Further arming the social worker with a specialized knowledge base was psychiatry, the first stirrings of which in America in the mental hygiene movement coincided with the emergence of the caseworker. But psychiatric theory and treatment would not penetrate most of the social work rank and file for decades.[2] A more sociological form of casework that gave social workers what Thomas W. Laquer calls a humanitarian narrative—a way of talking about the poor, of translating social workers' compassion from "personal impressions" into a nonsentimental, authoritative "report"—persisted until the 1930s (and later).[3] As Theodora L. Wilson, one of the first women graduates of the Smith College School of Social Work, recalled, "[O]n-the-job training was the accepted form of learning for most of us," and it was "piece-meal." The most important pedagogical tool was Richmond's casework method: "Along with the training on the job, there was the weekly morning course at Central Office, for the new workers. Mary Richmond's *Social Diagnosis* was our Bible, and we studied it chapter by chapter and then practiced it rigidly. . . . [T]his thorough gathering of information about a family as recommended by Richmond had real value in that I came to respect evidence, instead of personal impressions, in my evaluation of a family situation."[4]

Even as family caseworkers heralded their new casework method and psychiatric tools, the workaday realities of dependence and routine undercut other aspects of their professional status. The history of family casework in the 1920s became enmeshed in both professionalization and protoindustrialization. Thus, it is important to emphasize that the work and workplace of the typical social worker of the 1920s differed considerably from the work conditions of the Progressive Era volunteer. The earlier generation had concentrated in settlement houses, where they resided—and the image is at least as important here as the reality—in comfortable familial environments; the majority of social workers in the 1920s worked out of family casework agencies. Women still exerted leadership in settlement houses, but the Golden Age of the settlement house was over, however limited a Golden Age it had been. Settlement house reformers often lectured in the new social work schools, but their experiences in research agencies and settlements were of little help in preparing younger women for work in the bureaucratized casework agencies. Thus, when the AASW's Committee of the Vocational Bureau was asked to advise the Federal Classification Board on the classification of government employees, it chose the "family case work field" for its first job analysis "because of the large number of social workers engaged in the field." To justify its work, the committee argued that its reports would "help in defining the field of social work." Produced under the auspices of the Russell Sage Foundation, the first volume of these reports, Louise Odencrantz's *The Social Worker in Family, Medical, and Psychiatric Social Work*, was published in 1929.[5]

In these new casework agencies, social workers invoked professionalism to authorize their own views on wartime and subsequent reorganizations of welfare services. Women social workers' claim to authority was complicated by managerial efficiency drives that undermined their autonomy and by the dominant presence of male administrators and psychiatrists. But professionalism also promised to give social workers status and autonomy on the job, especially in relation to women who worked as volunteers. Thus, the record on autonomy was mixed. Although their independence was constrained, social workers obtained considerable autonomy in their daily work, autonomy that was central to their professional identity. As they traveled around the city on their own, caseworkers met with a client or consulted with a social service representative every half hour or so. A few references from Odencrantz's detailed study of social work typify the range of interventions of a female visitor in a large city:

9:00 A.M.	At Family Court. Spoke to [parole] worker regarding the C family. Arrangements were made to have Mrs. C call at the office to lodge a complaint against her husband[, an unemployed, alcoholic tailor, for lack of support].
9:40 A.M.	At Main Office. Discuss relief eligibility of Mr. L with Self-Support Department.
10:00 A.M.	Discussed with Home Economics department the possibility of sending child to camp for the summer.
10:45 A.M.	Visited lawyer to get legal aid for injured laundry driver.
12:00	Lunch.
12:45 P.M.	E. 96th St. Convinces reluctant Mrs. C to lodge complaint against her husband.
1:25 P.M.	Visited Mrs. S. Arranges physical exam for her. Arranges camp and vocational testing for the eldest child.
1:55 P.M.	Visited Mrs. A. Fails to "give her insight into her husband's [physical] condition." Promises to get doctor's report on daughter's visit to the clinic.
2:35 P.M.	Public School. Gets reports on two children. Gets teacher cooperation with children's plans.
3:10 P.M.	Visited Y Family. Arranges one daughter's tonsillectomy, another's vocational training, and the boy's summer camp and psychological testing.
3:55–4:10 P.M.	Phoned doctors and clinics.
4:10–5:00 P.M.	Dictated day's activities, filed reports, wrote letters.[6]

Odencrantz's summary shows the "typical" female family caseworker doing little of the detailed casework outlined by Richmond and even less psychiatric work. Rather, her work consisted of traveling about town, making arrangements for people, giving advice, providing referrals, and doing paperwork. She was a mediator in an increasingly organized, institutionalized, and bureaucratic world. Much of her eight-hour day was spent moving between nine different work sites, plus a lunch stop. Before lunch she had already traveled from the family court to the main office and to a lawyer's office; after lunch, she visited four different families and went to a public school before returning to the office. In her travels, she engaged problems associated with a wide range of family difficulties: an alcoholic father, alimony, family maintenance, child support, marital problems, school and psychological problems, and physical disabilities. This social worker apparently did not provide the services herself, however; instead, her work mostly consisted of arranging to have each problem addressed by someone else—legal aid, relief agencies, school counselors, vocational counselors, doctors, or visiting nurses. In the one instance in which she provided a psychological service, she "[f]ails to 'give .. insight.' "

Still, this daily routine provided a degree of freedom, discretion, and privileged status on which social workers could build a self-image as middle class. No bosses accompanied social workers on their rounds. They were in a position of responsibility, probably provoking as much fear as respect from clients often desperately in need of aid. But social workers' advice and services only constituted privileged knowledge from the perspective of clients; caseworkers often dispensed information that was commonplace among the better educated and more affluent (but often crucial for the poor). Unlike doctors, lawyers, and engineers, who spoke a specialized language and possessed technical knowledge, social workers served mostly as informed mediators who could provide information about social services and facilitate their use. So, even as social workers proclaimed their professionalism, they made anxious assertions that reflected their own doubts. Writing in his 1931 text on social work training, James Edward Hagerty let the cat out of the bag: thirty institutions of higher education offered training programs for social workers, but, he concluded, "social work is not a profession but a craft" based on "vague and indefinite ideas."[7] As Mary Palevsky, a Brooklyn caseworker, noted, "[O]ver and over again I have heard experienced, but untrained social workers say that intuition, common sense, and life experience are the only necessary preparation for an effective social worker."[8]

Back at the office, social workers found their professional autonomy limited by austere and routinized working conditions in new bureaucracies, the new authority vested in psychiatry, and conflicts with volunteers. In annual reports, JBG executives, who were themselves usually trained social workers, confirmed what caseworkers experienced every day: high caseloads and low salaries persistently undermined professional achievement.[9] Agency managers and executives lauded the Taylorization of social work as a professional advance. For instance, despite annual complaints about its staff, New York City's JBG claimed by 1923 to have become an efficient machine. The executive director reported that it had developed 'a smooth-running, responsible, economical and efficient organization." Apparently using new forms and reporting procedures, record keeping and casework had become more "efficient" and "scientific." New programs in medical, psychiatric, and neurological social work had been established. The JBG had also hired an elite group of statisticians and medical specialists. In sum, over the course of the decade, work in agencies like the JBG became more rationalized.[10]

Rationalization exposed the contradictory effects of the construction of the caseworker as an objective social scientist. Casework armed social workers with a method, with rules of procedure they could point to as a "scientific" knowledge base. But under the banner of professionalism, administrators and board members also endorsed rationalization measures such as the use of specialized assignments with supervision, casework procedures, and standardized report forms as improvements in work. Whether these "improvements" helped social workers remains to be seen. Historian Sharon Hartman Strom suggests that regularized procedures can work to an employee's advantage, minimizing arbitrariness and defining jobs. Still, at the time, no worker voices sang the praises of rationalization. Rather, social workers complained of being overworked, condemning these conditions as routinized.[11]

In fact, across the nation the centralization of social service organizations into citywide Community Chests and Federations of Jewish Philanthropy created tumultuous working conditions, with tightening bureaucratic control and constant reorganization under ever-evolving hierarchies. In New York City, the JBG, for example, completely reorganized staff responsibilities and lines of authority in 1918, 1922, 1925, 1928, and 1930. In 1928 the reorganized structure replaced all old department lines with new crosscutting procedures in which all supervisors would oversee all types of social workers. The reorganization also required remodeling the office. Moreover, new experimental procedures in the psychiatric clinic confronted workers with changed responsibilities about which they surely felt ambivalent. When the JBG established its psychiatric department in 1924, the agency decided that psychiatrists would screen all patients; now, however, social workers would regain some authority. The caseworker would first do a case history of a client before the psychiatric evaluation and then assume responsibility for following up the treatment.[12] Diagnosis remained the province of the psychiatrist; the social worker's task required additional paperwork and responsibility.

Some caseworkers accepted these changes as part of becoming "modern" and "professional"; others countered, circumvented, or openly resisted them as intrusions on their professional status. Although celebrated as the primary knowledge base for professional standing after the war, casework did not produce a distinct set of practices, but it remained a powerful ideological tool in discursive struggles for social workers' professional class legitimacy. It was not the only ideological force, however: in the private, ethnically identified agencies in which most social workers continued to work, the claims of social workers' ethnic, religious, and political identities conflicted with the secularizing professional mandate.

Middletown Revisited

After official documents like the census failed to distinguish their work from that of religious workers, social workers felt an increasing need to secularize their identity. Robert S. and Helen Merrell Lynd captured this secularizing tendency in their classic ethnography of middle-class life, *Middletown: A Study in Modern American Culture*. In Muncie, Indiana, the Lynds uncovered a complex world of social work in which women and men of a shifting and emerging social "middle" sought to claim social space, define their work, and defend its value as secular. "Secularization of charity," its consolidation as an efficient business enterprise, and the growing conflict among business interests, society women, and "professional workers" were at the core of the changes the Lynds saw sweeping through social service in the American heartland since the 1880s.[13] Placing the origins of the secularization of charity in the years between 1880 and 1920, they noted that the Associated Church Charities dropped "Church" from its title in 1900, and ministers ceased to dominate the organization. By 1925, only one social service dollar in five was donated by religious groups.[14]

The meaning of secularization was not as clear or complete, however, as the Lynds suggested. To Muncie business leaders, relief work was one part patriotic duty, one part religious mission, and one part ad campaign. In addition, even though agencies may not have acted in the name of religion and may have relied on public and unaffiliated private monies, the values they espoused, their ideas of the moral, "respectable" life, may have remained unchanged. Moreover, private church-sponsored charities continued to play a central role in dispensing aid. There were, for instance, nine distinct welfare agencies in Muncie and four social service organizations: one was Jewish Welfare and about a quarter of the others—the Salvation Army, the YMCA, and the YWCA—were explicitly Protestant. Less is known about the other organizations, but they included groups like the Red Cross, Boy Scouts, and War Mothers who were likely to proselytize for Protestantism.[15]

The small-town culture of Muncie is a bit misleading, however. Most social workers labored in large industrial cities where Catholic and Jewish social agencies played a greater role in social service. Given that racist state policies failed to provide aid to urban African Americans, the black church also played a major role in social assistance well into the twentieth century. In effect, then, secularization distracted attention from, if it did not render invisible, the continuing religious character of social work and the involvement of religious institutions.

Middletown also chronicles the political process by which social services were consolidated into administratively federated organizations that began in the preceding decade and was repeated across the country. The Community Chest in Muncie typified the development of corporatist charity on Main Street, a provincial world of national chauvinism, jingoism, and hucksterism brilliantly satirized by Sinclair Lewis in *Main Street* (1920) and *Babbitt* (1922). Muncie's Community Chest was organized in 1924–25, the Lynds tell us, to provide "some degree of centralized planning and control." Business would give its share, but civic duty demanded that others (including employees!) also contribute. As a centralized campaign, there would only have to be "one annual war-dance to whoop up enthusiasm and funds." The 1925 campaign was representative. Teams of fund-raisers were divided into militarylike squads with "captains" and "shock troops." The leader then charged the troops: "[T]his city needs a revival. We've been lying back too much on the things we did during the war, and we've got to snap out of it."[16]

In the Lynds' account, the increasing prominence of (male) business executives in social service led to their conflicts with two other groups: "volunteer business class women" and the new professional female social workers. Business executives began to crowd the volunteer women of the "business class" on the governing boards of the federated agencies. These women, in turn, moved to less prominent forms of "charitable work" and into "civic work," forming organizations such as the American Association for University Women.

Wealthy volunteer women did not completely disappear from the local charity boards. Rather, they remained in subsidiary posts, often finding themselves constrained in a narrowing social space between two powerful blocs. They battled with the men on the federated boards above them for fiscal authority and struggled with the women caseworkers below them, who themselves were organizing to demand professional autonomy and authority. The Lynds also placed women caseworkers in the business class, but they portrayed them as more "ambivalent cases" in this class. Both groups of women were part of what the Lynds called the "middle class," but they pursued competing vocational interests and social positions, each seeking to define itself against the other.[17] In a revealing note, the Lynds described how the uneasy triad of male executives, elite female civic volunteers, and female social workers pitted these two groups of women against each other:

> No little opposition to the consolidation of welfare agencies in Middletown comes directly through the opposition of their [female] boards to relinquishing their work. The extent to which these boards have been social affairs is indicated by the fact that the professional worker of the local Visiting Nurses' Association is not allowed to attend the meetings of the board and was not even asked to be present when a worker from a large neighboring city was called in to describe her methods of work. At a meeting of the local Federated Clubs at which the work of the Visiting Nurses' Association was discussed, it was not the professional worker in charge who made the talk, but a society woman on the board.[18]

Middletown illuminates a complex world of social work in which secularization met the challenges of consolidated social services by seeking to claim a social space independent of volunteers, clerics, and board members. However, the dominance of white Protestants of northern European extraction in Middle American cities such as Muncie contrasted with the preponderance of black migrants and immigrants from central and southern Europe in most large industrial cities. In such polyglot cities, agencies and their staffs often waged a continuing struggle to proselytize for the religious, denominational cultures they represented.[19]

Middletown implicated social workers in a process of secularization that generally characterized American middle-class culture. Nonetheless, religion per se continued to have both an institutional and a doctrinal meaning in the large cities where social workers more typically worked.[20] Immigrant cities like New York, Chicago, and Philadelphia teemed with religiously defined populations, especially after 1880, when Catholics from Italy and eastern European Jews constituted the two major groups of arrivals. In response to this massive immigration, private philanthropy, both Catholic and Jewish, bore the brunt of social service to the needy from these groups. In turn, these social work agencies became sites of public debate and political struggle over religion and the process of secularization.

Religion, Ethnicity, and Race in Class Identity

The construction of an "objective," professional caseworker middle-class identity in the 1920s required that social workers separate religious identity and related forms of racial and ethnic identity from occupational identity. This presented an acute dilemma for religious and ethnic group sponsorship of private charity in most of the nation's large cities.[21] In the 1920s, Catholic, Protestant, and Jewish groups continued to provide a broad panoply of social services in every major American city. In succeeding decades, they would debate the policy implications of sectarian charity, questioning everything from the religious training of children, to the kinds of foods to be served clients, to agency and public positions on birth control. Although virtually all general public and private agencies such as the Social Service Bureau, Anti-Tuberculosis Society, and Red Cross advertised themselves as secular or nondenominational, most actually functioned with a Protestant cultural agenda: that is, hostility to parochial schools and religious dietary practices or rituals and support of strict parental discipline and the work ethic. Sometimes this religious message was implicit, as in the cos and the Children's Aid Society; at other times, it was overt, as in the Salvation Army and its evangelical armies for Christ.

The important social roles of the church within the African American community and the political power of its ministers exemplified the problem of defining social work as a secular enterprise when one moved outside the relative homogeneity of Muncie, Indiana. The divide the Census Bureau sought to bridge was particularly wide in the African American community, as two comments from the era on the contested place of religion in black social work illustrate. E. Franklin Frazier, director of the country's only school for black social workers, the Atlanta University School of Social Work, complained in 1924 that churches "are more interested in getting Negroes into heaven than in getting them out of the hell they live in on earth."[22] But such views did not endear Frazier to many black intellectuals and political leaders. Nor did they jibe with the central role accorded the black church in the African American community as a social institution. Largely excluded from public and private assistance, blacks relied on their churches for aid. As Adam Clayton Powell, minister of the Abyssinian Baptist Church in Harlem, wrote in the first issue of *Opportunity*, the journal of the United Urban League, in 1923, the church had to do social work: it "must go into the highways and hedges during the week caring for the sick, the wounded, the distressed and all that are needy, and then on Sunday they will hear us and believe us when we tell them of 'Jesus, the Mighty to save.'"[23]

Pervasive white racism made the situation of the new generation of trained black caseworkers after 1920 quite different from that of white caseworkers. Observing that racism forced black caseworkers to focus on race work, African American historian Stephanie J. Shaw argues that they bridged the class gap between the poor black masses and themselves. In this regard, black professionals, building on the tradition of church-based community service, took on work in the community in addition to their jobs.[24]

Jewish Social Service in New York City

The conflict between religious, ethnic, and class identities was quite different for Jewish social service workers. To Jews, living in a "modern" world of intersecting political, ethnic, and religious identities, ethnicity complicated the question of religion. Whereas nationalism took on new meaning for many peoples, Jews had at best a problematic relationship with the countries they had left—or often fled. Judaism, consequently, could be both a religious and an ethnic identity but not a national identity. In this "modern" world, one label—Jew—came to cover a range of religious positions, from the Orthodox to the Reform to the secular. But the claims of each to be authentic Jews based on religious (or secular) identity conflicted. Being a Jew, for instance, meant something different to a secular or Orthodox Jew, a Zionist or American-centered Jew, or a German or eastern European Jew. It is in this context that the separation of religion from social work and its meaning to social workers need to be reexamined.

Since alternative religious, ethnic, and racial identities were overloaded with political subtexts, they stimulated public fears that the social worker would not be "objective." Some of these anxieties were long-standing. Caseworkers' identity had long been shaped by countervailing political pressures that were both internal and external to their work. As far back as the last half of the nineteenth century, scientific charity leaders caricatured social workers as wasteful and overly indulgent to the poor and demanded that instead they be efficient, rational, and businesslike. As many of the prewar stories about charity workers on the Lower East Side by the Jewish writer Anzia Yezierska suggest, the poor also pictured the social worker as a cruel miser, who was nosy, hard-hearted, cold, and patronizing. Among conservative social critics and many of the poor, these attitudes toward social workers persisted into the twentieth century, but these views had to share ideological space with the idealized portrait of the settlement house reformer in the popular press.[25]

Political, social, and economic changes set loose by World War I hastened the return of the negative depictions. The Russian Revolution in 1917 compounded business anxieties provoked by the militant language and free speech struggles of the Industrial Workers of the World. Another disturbing sign of social change appeared in the increased number of women social workers. Women's assumption of the social work jobs of men who had left to fight raised questions among men about women's ability to do the work adequately, questions that in fact engaged male (and some female) anxieties about masculinity and femininity.[26] Even more disturbing were new racial conflicts in northern cities. Black migration had brought nearly 400,000 African Americans to the industrial North since 1890, and the conclusion of the war found many of them in jobs formerly held by white soldiers. The War Industries Board had held business in check during the war, and the return of soldiers to their jobs coincided with business interests' efforts to restore their authority over the labor force. In this explosive economic and racial mix, in 1919 race riots erupted in twenty-eight cities and whites lynched seventy-eight blacks. Well-publicized dramatic strikes in the steel industry and by the Boston police force that same year further heightened fears of radical insurrection and social anarchy. By 1923, a red scare—a term that should not be allowed to mask the equally strong bias against immigrants, Jews, Catholics, and blacks—gripped individuals who fell within the category that social analysts Robert and Helen Lynd called the "business" or "middle class." In response to the disorder, a right-wing reaction unfolded: in 1919 Attorney General A. Mitchell Palmer conducted his infamous raids and deportations without trial of syndicalist and socialist labor leaders; Congress passed new restrictive immigration laws in 1921 and 1924; and the Ku Klux Klan reorganized. In all, the red scare of the 1920s bears a strong resemblance to the McCarthy era of the 1950s, a better-known moment of political repression and disregard for fundamental civil rights.[27]

In the repressive political climate of the 1920s, the discourse on social worker professionalism often confused social identity with fears arising from radical political identities: for example, was the Jewish social worker a seditious socialist? In the face of political dislocation, social workers often found themselves the target of charges—from both inside and outside their industry—that their behavior was politically biased and irresponsible, in sum, that it was "unprofessional." To defend themselves, they mobilized their own professional organization, the AASW, and, through it, embraced a depoliticized or "neutral" identity as professional caseworkers, an identity stripped of adjectival modifiers that reflected each worker's multiplicity of identities, such as "Jewish" or "radical." Thus, an important element of the "depoliticized" professional defense entailed distinguishing religious work from social work.

New York City, perhaps because of the size and power of its ethnic financial communities, provides a good example of the limits of secularization in the struggle to define social work during the 1920s. A citywide Welfare Council first organized in 1925 to better coordinate social services and avoid duplication, but the powerful ethnic and religious centers of organized charity retained their financial and operating authority.[28] The bulk of charity in New York City continued to be provided by the large religious federations like Catholic Charities of the Archdiocese of New York, the FJP, and the Federation of Protestant Welfare Agencies.

As the principal port of debarkation for European immigrants, New York City had experienced a mushrooming of population since 1880. Jewish immigration played an important part in that growth. The population of New York City, including figures for Brooklyn, which was annexed in 1898, rose from 1.9 million in 1880 to over 3.4 million in 1900; meanwhile, during this period the U.S. population had increased 50 percent, from 50 million to over 76 million. Jews, who numbered only 85,000 in 1880 in New York City, made up approximately 20 percent (650,000) of the city's population in 1900. By 1914, with an estimated 1,335,000 Jews in the city, more than one out every four city residents was a Jew. Ten percent of this total were German Jews, many of whom were well-established second- and third-generation Americans—like industrialist Daniel Guggenheim; financiers Isaac N. Seligman, Solomon Loeb, and Jacob H. Schiff; and department store moguls from the Straus, Stern, and Bloomingdale families. At the same time, poor eastern European Jews from the shtetls of the Pale of Settlement (eastern Poland, the Baltics, and the extreme western part of Russia) swelled the already crowded immigrant quarters of the Lower East Side. The high crime rates reported among these Jews worried both New York City's police commissioner, Theodore A. Bingham, and the established "respectable" German Jews.[29]

In September 1908, Bingham startled the city's Jewish community by announcing that 50 percent of the criminal classes in New York City were Jews. He further marked Jewish youth as an especially serious problem: "'Among the most expert of all the street thieves are Hebrew boys under sixteen who are brought up on lives of crime.' "[30] Bingham's claim, coming on top of an apparent epidemic of white slavery and prostitution among Jewish daughters, turned the "respectable" Jewish community's anxiety into near panic.[31]

Jewish social service in New York City mobilized in the context of this contested political environment, a world riven by differences between German Jews, eastern European Jews, and the society in which both sought respect and survival. Prior to 1900, affluent Jews had already drawn on their own traditions, both secular and religious, to develop a range of social services. As Arthur A. Goren has observed in his history of the New York City Kehillah (an association of Jewish community groups between 1908 and 1922), Jewish communal life has seventeenth-century roots in "rabbinical Judaism." Religious precepts allocated authority to rabbis over the private and public lives of Jews, especially when it came to interring the dead, providing loans to the poor, and giving aid to the sick. The Dutch West India Company forced Peter Stuyvesant, the governor of New Amsterdam, to accept Jews into the colony in 1654, with the proviso that "the poor among them shall not become a burden to the company or the community, but be supported by their own nation."[32] Jewish philanthropists' consistent commitment to private relief until the Great Depression may be attributed to their desire to keep the so-called "Stuyvesant promise," but it also reflected the more ubiquitous American celebration of self-help and individualism. Philanthropic efforts by the well-to-do continued to be the financial backbone of relief in the Jewish community, but by the late nineteenth century, political persecution and economic distress in eastern Europe had encouraged the formation of new political movements with considerable support from within the working-class community, such as the Jewish Labor Bund and Zionism. Although these two movements had different priorities and sometimes divided into secular and religious camps, their efforts were not necessarily incompatible: both raised money and organized on behalf of the community, the former through strikes and the latter through support for Palestine.[33]

These and other traditions, however, also divided the Jewish community and generated disputes both among and within Jewish charities. These disputes often involved questions of Jewish identity that would further complicate questions of social worker identity: What did it mean to be a Jew, and what constituted Jewish social work? In fact, tensions among Jews from different traditions characterized the development of the Jewish community beginning early in the nineteenth century. For instance, when Ashkenazi Jews arrived from central Europe early in the nineteenth century, the more elite Sephardim turned up their noses; in need of aid, the Ashkenazim founded their own orphanage, the Hebrew Orphan Asylum of New York. By mid-century, as the dispute between the Ashkenazim and Sephardim receded, Jewish charity mushroomed. One historian, for example, counts ninety-three Jewish charitable societies serving the city's tiny Jewish population between 1848 and 1860; in contrast, the Irish and German communities, making up nearly half of the city's residents, established only thirteen each.[34]

By the turn of the century, a range of different traditions—secular or religious, German or eastern European—would occasionally fracture the Jewish community even as they helped to organize it. The differences among groups were not always sharp and many Jews articulated multiple identities, but certain polarities emerged. Jewish Labor Bundists, for example, promoted popular, secular, Yiddish culture. Neither Jews committed to religious Zionism nor German Jews necessarily felt at home in Yiddish culture. In the context of a varied community, social service executives, staff, and contributors asked what role religion or politics should play in a Jewish agency's provision of aid to its clients. Should labor reform on behalf of, say, poorly paid garment workers be a part of Jewish social work? Indeed, were Jewish social workers to express the socialism of Bundists from the Pale, they would find themselves standing up against the German Jewish business leaders, department store executives, and garment manufacturers on whom they depended for funds. In this contested world, Jewish social service mobilized to solve the crisis created by Police Commissioner Bingham's slur on their respectability.[35]

It is impossible to determine how many of the less than 2,000 women and men who engaged in some sort of social work in the opening decade of the century in New York City were Jewish because census enumerators did not distinguish workers by religion or ethnicity. Unlike the nationwide portrait of elite, native-born settlement house staff, however, a majority of New Yorkers employed as religious and charity workers in 1910 (60.5 percent) were immigrants or children of immigrants (see appendix, table A.3). In fact, the largest number of male workers were foreign-born whites; there were only eight male and twenty female workers (the same as the number of black women totaled statewide) listed as black. And, of course, if the people who worked in the settlements are subtracted from the data, the immigrant profile of social workers would likely be substantially sharper in Jewish casework agencies.[36]

Something is known of the work performed by the rank-and-file women and men who labored in early Jewish communal service. To help their own people, Jewish immigrants in cities throughout the country formed hundreds of *landsmanshaftn* (hometown societies), organized variously around religious, Bundist (the Workman's Circle), or geographic principles. Similarly, insurance groups were created to provide start-up funds for Jewish businesses or loans in hard times. Meanwhile, the Kehillah tradition of mutual aid stimulated the formation of national organizations such as the American Jewish Committee to advance Jewish political interests nationally and internationally. Finally, the creation of the FJP in 1917 established an umbrella organization under which the many branches of Jewish philanthropy could be collected and administered and could flourish.[37]

Prior to the creation of the FJP, however, and the expansion of paid staffs, Jewish relief was largely charity work conducted by well-to-do German Jewish women; as such, it remained rooted in nineteenth-century calls for self-help. Volunteers from temple sisterhoods provided relief to indigent Jews through two organizations—the UHC and the Jewish Protectory and Aid Society (JPAS). Whereas the UHC traced its origins in 1875 to a depression-induced increase in Jewish poverty, the history of the JPAS was more recent. It was incorporated in 1902 to provide religious, intellectual, and industrial training for delinquent Jewish children and prisoners. Sisterhoods like the Beth El Sisterhood of Personal Service on the Upper East Side, whose leaders were the wives of UHC directors, gave out funds to needy families. Their activities included the operation of nineteen storefronts that distributed secondhand clothes and the Self-Support and Self-Help Department (funded entirely by Jacob Schiff), which provided loans to needy families—163 in 1916 alone. Most of these loans were repaid, which, boasted the UHC, "confirms the traditional Jewish opinion that the granting of loans instead of doles is not only the most meritorious form of benevolence, but one of the wisest and most effective forms of relief, promoting both self respect and reliance."[38]

The creation of the JPAS may mark the beginning of Jewish casework in New York: it was a pioneer casework agency that evolved into the JBG and became a central player in the story of the FJP and Jewish social work in New York. In fact, the JPAS represented a concrete response to the problem of Jewish juvenile delinquency six years before Bingham issued his infamous warning. The JPAS gained its fame from its establishment of cottage homes for delinquents. In 1907 it opened its major facility in Westchester County, the Hawthorne School for Boys, followed in 1912 by the opening of a smaller facility for girls, Cedar Knolls. The Hawthorne School originally had ten cottages with accommodations for 310 boys, whereas Cedar Knolls housed only 22 girls in 1915. The two schools together employed only about a dozen cottage mothers and fathers, and until the 1920s, much of the work was handled by volunteers and a nonprofessional custodial staff. In 1915 the Hawthorne staff included General Superintendent John Klein, a rabbi, a principal, nine cottage fathers and eleven married cottage mothers, an assistant superintendent, a stenographer, a bookkeeper, a director of social activities, a nurse, a bandmaster, a matron, two engineers, three night watchmen, a farmer, a carpenter, and a gardener. The 522 boys in their care that year each received a plot of land to tend and took classes in telegraphy, woodworking, music, mechanical drawing, and machine work. Large numbers of Jewish Big Sisters and Big Brothers provided further assistance. Eighty-one volunteers from the Big Brother Association, for instance, helped ninety-one boys in 1910.[39]

Little is known of these "parents," but their work was largely custodial discipline. Bylaws stipulated that "all the time of the employees belongs to the institution" (they got one day off every two weeks if it could be arranged). In addition, "[g]entlemen must under no circumstances visit the ladies in their private rooms," and they were instructed to "[m]aintain a dignified appearance, refraining from all immoderate conduct."[40]

Before the war, then, Jewish social work remained in its infancy. The School for Jewish Communal Work opened in 1916, but it closed within two years, a victim of the wartime dissipation of emotional and financial resources. It was more likely to be the "meddlesome" visitor from the cos or the volunteer grande dame from the UHC than an officer of the JBG who haunted the byways of the Lower East Side and the fictional stories of Anzia Yezierska.[41] Indeed, settlement house work, the preserve of Protestant women, remained at the center of Progressive Era social work. The day of the Jewish casework agency was yet to come.[42]

Elite "Others": Directors and Volunteers

That day came in the 1920s, but it arrived along with new centralized FJP constraints that threatened the autonomy and job security on which social workers sought to base their professional middle-class identity. By 1917, Jewish philanthropists like Felix M. Warburg, Jacob Schiff's son-in-law, had come to believe that there was a need to coordinate Jewish social services and to minimize the duplication of effort in fund-raising. At the same time, men like Warburg and Schiff also believed that relief had to extend beyond "mere charitable doles" to "rehabilitation." Additional services required additional training, and both demanded increased funds and coordination of services.[43] The FJP was Warburg's answer: an umbrella organization that would provide more "income for the charities and great convenience for the contributors."[44] The organization heralded a new era of expanded and reshaped social work, one that proponents lauded in the language of efficiency and expertise.

The development of centralized, bureaucratized casework agencies transformed organizations like the JPAS. The JPAS reorganized at the same time that the FJP was created, but a professional staff emerged there only after 1920, and they had considerably less freedom and discretion than settlement house workers. Reflecting the shift away from unbridled paternalism, the Jewish Protectory and Aid Society changed its name in 1921 to the more muted form, the Jewish Board of Guardians. Casework of the Big Brother Association and the Hawthorne School was amalgamated in a Department of Prevention and Aftercare, the new heart of the agency. A male supervisor was hired with a mostly male paid staff to attend the boys, reflecting the traditional feeling that troubled boys needed male authority and that the work would be unseemly and dangerous for women. Preventive work soon sought to locate sources of delinquency in the home and child care, however, and women quickly became major fixtures in the agency. By 1921, the JBG's Male and Female Departments had five and seven district workers, respectively, most of whom were enrolled in mental hygiene courses.[45] Nonetheless, centralized FJP decisions undermined key tenets of professionalization such as responsibility and autonomy with routine, bureaucratic oversight and male authority.

From its inception as a consolidated superagency, the FJP insisted that it would only gather money and would not affect the character of Jewish communal work. At the first meeting of the board, Warburg tried to assure skeptics that the FJP did not seek to "control the administration of funds." Agencies would maintain fiscal autonomy.[46] However, if an agency wished to develop a new program, fund new workers to expand services or reduce caseloads, or give staff members a raise, it had to apply to the FJP, which would determine if the proposal was fiscally prudent or deserving. Indeed, since agency boards were often comprised of the same people as those on the FJP's board, or people with similar views, agency board members rarely allowed that consideration of new programs required budgetary decisions at their level. Social workers, however, repeatedly found their requests for raises stymied by the FJP's requirement that they negotiate with the "autonomous" agencies, who would then complain that they had insufficient funds.

The FJP also resembled Muncie's Community Chest. In contrast to the mostly female Jewish caseworkers, who increasingly came from eastern European backgrounds, the men (and a few of their wives) who made up the Boards of Trustees of the FJP and the various agencies were an imposing elite. Before the regular monthly board meetings moved to the fashionable Harmonie Club on East Sixtieth Street in September 1921, all but three monthly meetings took place at Warburg's home at 109 Fifth Avenue; the others were held at the home of Adolph Lewisohn down the block at number 881 and downtown at banker Arthur Lehman's home on William Street and at the Midday Club.[47] Most of the board members were upper-class German Jews, family patriarchs who headed financial empires. They volunteered their time and contributed their money liberally. But these elites usually expected deference, and agency executives and social workers who depended on their support for new programs, capital expenditures, and ultimately their jobs could not easily challenge them. Jacob Schiff's friend and biographer, Cyrus Adler, recalling the investment banker's earnest discussion with a striking tailor at a Henry Street settlement, claimed that Schiff "never assumed airs of superiority or patronage." And Lillian Wald, a strong presence herself, disagreed with Schiff, one of her major benefactors, on more than one occasion.[48] But although wealthy men such as Schiff and Adler often took comfort in believing that they related well to the poor, Morris D. Waldman's memory of Schiff's interactions with social workers was probably more accurate. Then a young social worker, Waldman remembers the awe that greeted the appearance of Schiff at a meeting of one of the agency boards on which he served: "His appearance . . . invariably caused a quiet stir and a sudden hush in conversation in deference not merely to his great wealth . . . but rather because of an aristocratic quality in his personality that palpably, yet subtly, distinguished him and, in a manner, separated him from them."[49]

Jewish women volunteers were no less elite, and recent historical work suggests that they began to assert a new public role for women. Nevertheless, the conclusions of three feminist historians seem correct: these were not "New Women"; equality for them meant sitting on Sabbath school boards, not political or occupational parity with men.[50] In fact, although they may have come to serve on school boards, elite Jewish women found that they had less opportunity to serve on FJP boards where financial decisions—traditionally seen as a male province—were made. In addition, the shift from volunteers to paid staff in FJP agencies threatened to remove one of the traditional sources of authority and fulfillment for these women. Thus, since volunteers had provided most of the agency services before 1920, after 1920 persistent conflicts with paid staff members moved to the center of debates over social worker identity.[51]

The history of the JPAS and its successor, the JBG, dramatically illustrates how the transformation to paid labor pitted caseworkers and volunteers against each other. In 1918 the agency added a psychiatrist to its staff and opened the Department of Prevention and Aftercare. In order to go beyond "visitation, advice, and moral preaching," the agency now insisted that it was necessary to provide individual treatment based on the casework method and "work with the individual through his environment."[52] At the end of 1923, the JBG's staff numbered sixty-five paid workers, forty-five of whom were trained social workers. The other twenty were administrators and clerical staff.

Women made up the majority of the social work staff, but even as they sought status among outsiders, the glass ceiling on work coded as female and the demands of the double day on women as housekeepers and workers limited their professional advancement. Although their numbers grew over time, their rank in the JBG did not. In 1925 fourteen of the twenty-five caseworkers were women, two of whom were listed as married, but the psychiatrist, physician, and chief psychologist were all men. (In fact, there were fewer female physicians nationally in the early twentieth century than there were in the late nineteenth century.)[53] In contrast, the inability to attract male caseworkers to such poorly paid work traditionally coded as female required the JBG to accept men with no training and allow them to work second jobs. In an effort a few years later to raise standards, men who worked second jobs were let go; the agency now simply complained that conditions continued to compel it "to accept men with no training or experience" as caseworkers.[54]

By the mid-1920s, the JBG had become perhaps the most advanced psychiatric social work center in the country, and as such, its work involved more diagnosis and psychological counseling than that of the larger number of workers who did family casework. As early as 1921, the majority of the professional staff of field-workers who assisted the Big Sisters attended courses in psychiatric social work as well as casework, reflecting, according to the JBG's annual report, the new emphasis on preventive care and changing views about delinquency. A mental hygiene clinic, which sought to detect early signs of nervousness and emotional instability, also opened as an adjunct service.[55] Paid women caseworkers nonetheless found their authority on the shop floor severely tested by the male psychiatrists. By 1924, all patients had to be screened by a JBG psychiatrist; previously, the social worker had decided if the patient needed to see a psychiatrist.[56] The conflict between psychiatric social workers and psychiatrists illustrates the tension over gender that will be the subject of the next chapter.

An equally vexing conflict pitted female caseworkers against other women— the elite volunteers. The unenumerated female volunteer force at the JBG must not be underestimated. When the JBG's Big Sister League formed in 1929, for example, it included thirty women "of leisure and ability" who "had training and experience in philanthropic work"[57] Hard-pressed agencies relied heavily on the free labor of women volunteers, especially since these women and their families represented the social class on whom they depended for money. Thus, the JBG expanded its limited service at the mental health clinic when "Miss C. Guggenheim kindly volunteered her services as stenographer and typist." It was important to the agencies and the paid staff as well as to the volunteers that the quality of service be highly regarded, however, so social workers closely supervised volunteers in work that seemed little different from that of the paid staff. As of 1923, for example, the professional staff interviewed each JBG volunteer six times a year. Paid social workers received regular reading assignments, attended lectures, and pursued planned courses of study, and volunteers met in regular study groups, which the JBG described as "practically a prerequisite for active participation in our work."[58]

For some agency administrators, the volunteer also offered a much-needed corrective for the aloofness they felt accompanied social worker professionalization. In his 1926 presidential address to the National Conference of Jewish Social Service (NCJSS), for example, Louis M. Cahn warned professional workers of the dangers of becoming too technical, of losing the "essential ingredient"—"love of mankind"—that laypersons brought to social service. Fearing, furthermore, that the professional social workers' "monopoly of social service" would "result in indifference on the part of the public to the needs of the community," he insisted that "ideals of service . . . need both lay and professional leadership."[59]

Social workers faced the challenge of working beside volunteers and not alienating them while differentiating their work but not their social respectability. This was indeed a big challenge, for although volunteers did work that differed little from that of the professionals, their circumstances differed. The women who dominated both groups, for instance, had home and work responsibilities, but volunteers were not dependent on a wage, "worked" limited hours, and were more often in a position to afford domestic help.[60] So, using the language of professionalism, with its emphasis on autonomy and therapeutic techniques, social workers tried to distinguish the caseworker from the volunteer and supervisory casework from the volunteer's clerical tasks or work as a Big Sister. Meanwhile, many volunteers persisted in seeing social work as largely commonsense counseling.[61] It was little wonder, then, that in 1928 the JBG continued to report that volunteer-professional staff integration was "one of the most difficult problems."[62]

The Politics of Respectability

Agency administrators and board directors agreed that rehabilitating families required competent staff social workers, but they disagreed over what constituted responsible, effective, and respectable social worker performance. At the heart of this debate was the social worker's identity as a "respectable" middle-class citizen. Although both sides often spoke of professionalism, their dispute centered on whether social workers had rights as workers or whether such notions contradicted their professionalism. Superintendent Klein, for example, pointed out that the JPAS's work would be hampered by the difficulty of finding "competent staff . . . due to the limited compensation offered." With news of the Russian Revolution making headlines, the superintendent wanted to reassure his business-minded board of the agency's commitment to respectability. To Klein, besides being trained, being a good (i.e., "competent") social worker meant not being a revolutionary or, more specifically, a Jewish Bundist: "Particular care has always been taken that persons with radical tendencies should not be employed on the school staff; and constant efforts have been made to inculcate in every boy a spirit of true Americanism."[63]

Part of the problem for Jewish agencies was their sense of having a limited pool of recruits. They mostly enlisted Jewish workers, and to provide a steady supply of trained personnel, the NCJSS established the Graduate School for Jewish Social Work in 1925, which by the end of 1937 had trained over 200 social workers. As in most social service agencies, the school's directors came from the world of business: its first president, Julius Rosenwald of Chicago, the head of Sears, Roebuck and Company, was succeeded by Louis E. Kirstein, vice president of Filene's in Boston.[64] However, one rabbinical leader of the Jewish community found the prominence of such businesspeople disturbing and considered it a challenge to Jewish communal spirit. The source of this prolabor message must have made people take notice; his perspective was not characteristic of the rabbinate. Addressing the 1926 NCJSS, Rabbi Abba Hillel Silver poignantly placed the politics of Jewish identity before his audience. Lamenting the absence of the Jewish working man from the boards of synagogues, social service agencies, and community centers, he asked, "Have we no place for him except as a beneficiary or as a possible recipient? . . . Jewish social service is in danger of becoming as utterly bourgeoisie [sic] as the Jewish religion has become in the United States."[65]

Rabbi Silver's support of the working man was not a typical rabbinical stance, and it did not reflect the underlying antiradicalism of communal leaders who dominated the annual meetings of Jewish social service agencies in the 1920s. To many such leaders and those in the Jewish business community who shared their status concerns Jewish radicalism simply reproduced the threat to respectability that Jewish crime had raised earlier in the century. Thus, an identity of interests between Jewish social work, Jewish social workers, and the Jewish labor movement remained an abiding obsession at these conferences. The general session of the inaugural meeting of the NCJSS in May 1923 addressed the topic of "Organized Labor and Social Work." The red scare poisoned the air outside the convention hall. Inside, after a lengthy analysis of the history of Jews in America, Judge Jacob M. Moses, whom the conference report described as the "former impartial Chairman of the Clothing Industry of Baltimore," finally exposed the concern that seemed to be on everyone's mind: "Coming back again to the connection between the Jewish unions and the socialist movement. I think it is very important to get this thing cleared up once and for all and to get rid of the idea that the Jews came over here as a lot of radicals. It is absolutely untrue."[66] Consigning socialists and other radicals to the margins, Moses placed Jews in the American capitalist mainstream. Americanization could safely proceed. Jews were Americans; radicals were an alien "other" to be cast outside the gates guarding both "respectable" Jews and Americans.

Other Jewish communal leaders shared Moses' perspective and distinguished the conservative "mainstream" labor movement of the American Federation of Labor (AFL) from radicals in organizations such as the Industrial Workers of the World. They honored Jewish labor's struggle for social justice but emphasized its growing moderation. Moses, for instance, pointed out the conservative character of the AFL. Noting that labor unions such as the Amalgamated Clothing Workers had developed educational institutions, banks, and health departments, Henry Moskowitz of the FJP announced that "the constructive stage of the Jewish Labor Movement has arrived."[67]

Other agency administrators who responded to Moses sought to keep the left wing at arm's distance while still claiming a middle ground for Jewish social workers. They agreed with Moses' historical account of the division in the Jewish community between the Russian Jews who dominated the labor movement and the German Jews who dominated Jewish philanthropy. As the labor movement had become more respectable, the business community had become more socially responsible. The "Jewish Philanthropic Movement," according to Moskowitz, had "broadened and deepened in its ideals." The Jewish social worker's role was to serve "as mediator and arbitrator."[68]

This mediating role was not as easy for the agencies and the social workers as the agency administrators at the conference suggested, particularly during strikes. Such a role was fraught with tensions between conflicting loyalties to Jewish working-class clients and Jewish bosses/philanthropists. Unfortunately, in regard to this conflict, we know more about agency policies than about the views of individual social workers, although, at least in the 1920s, workers appear to have been in general accord. In answering the question of whether Jewish social service should provide relief to needy families on strike, social agencies had to decide whether the poverty arose from a "legitimate" cause and determine which Jew they would support, the trade unionist or the industrialist. Were there "good" and "bad" Jews, and if the social worker provided aid, was this an unprofessional form of political activism?

A variety of answers could be given, and different agencies took different positions. For instance, when the chair of the 1923 NCJSS annual meeting's Program Committee asked twenty-one Jewish agencies across the country to explain their policies on relief to strikers and their families, seven agencies "seemed to be totally unaware that there is a labor problem." The other agencies' responses ranged from outright opposition to aiding anyone whose dependency could be traced to a strike in Brooklyn, Cincinnati, Philadelphia, and Pittsburgh to reports of good working relations with local trade unions in Omaha, Buffalo, Boston, Denver, Chicago, Baltimore, and Milwaukee. It is difficult to make generalizations about any city, but Brooklyn had a long history of opposition to relief, and Pittsburgh had been the scene of the violent 1919 steel strike in which radicals played a prominent role. In contrast, Baltimore's clothing industry had established a particularly good working relationship with its unions, and it is possible that Milwaukee's and Chicago's well-established socialist political traditions bred greater tolerance for their trade unions. The committee found that, as a rule, in cities where local unions contributed funds to philanthropy, aid was provided to strikers. It was also the case, however, that many Jewish trade unionists across the country considered the local philanthropy to be unsympathetic to their cause and distributed whatever resources they had directly to their members through labor-sponsored welfare organizations. Thus, Jewish workers in Omaha received aid from the Workman's Circle and the Jewish National Worker's Alliance; in Buffalo, the Arbeiter Ring helped the families of its members.[69]

As this range of policies suggests, conflicts between Jewish labor radicalism and professionalism were not easily settled. Five years later, in 1928, when the National Conference of Jewish Communal Service (NCJCS) held its first annual meeting, the debate over how social workers could help in industrial crises reopened. On this occasion, two speakers were invited to express opposing views. Speaking for the "left" was William M. Leiserson, an economist at Antioch College. Formerly a social investigator on the first major study of the impact of industrialization on a metropolis, the Pittsburgh Survey, Leiserson advocated social work activism to make sure that workers got their "fair share" from industry.[70] The "right" was represented not by an antilabor boss but by the leader of a union described as "a leading exponent of social welfare liberalism."[71] The speaker was none other than Sidney Hillman, president of the Amalgamated Clothing Workers. Hillman's point was simple: he welcomed the support of the social worker in labor's cause, but the ultimate objective of the labor movement, he reminded his listeners, was to make social workers and all social service unnecessary.[72] Hillman's opposition to charity was not unlike that of many socialists who wanted justice for workers, not handouts. But Hillman's presence at the conference was significant for two reasons: it illustrated the NCJCS's desire both to reach out to the organized Jewish working class and to mark it off as distinct from its "left" opposition.

Even as Jewish social service leaders strove to domesticate the "radical" labor movement and mitigate the political reverberations within its religious identity, the place of social activism in social work remained a source of anxiety. At the first NCJCS in 1928, for example, when a delegate reported discontent among caseworkers over their subordinate work (presumably to doctors and psychiatrists), the president of the FJP, Solomon Lowenstein, noted that New York City schoolteachers were paid better than social workers because "for a long time [they] have been agitating." A moderate trade unionist himself, who in the 1930s would oppose social worker strike actions, Lowenstein put his finger on the social worker's dilemma: Where did advocating end and agitating begin, and at what point did the social worker step over the line and cease to be "professional"?[73]

Social workers did not agree on the answer. The "left," imbued with the legacy of the Progressive Era reform tradition or various socialist currents, remained skeptical of the "professional" project itself. For instance, speaking in 1923, Bruno Lasker, a *Survey* editor, looked back fondly—and nostalgically—at the sort of people engaged in work on the Pittsburgh Survey as "much nearer some kind of real harmony in thinking. They more or less knew what they were driving at." In contrast, the social workers of the 1920s had 'no common philosophy." They may have been "a near profession," but "some of us don't quite believe it is a profession yet and some of us hope it may never become one."[74]

Other social workers, including many in the occupational mainstream who would join the AASW campaign for professional status, felt otherwise. To these men and women, professionalism was desirable and identification with partisan politics was a threat to its achievement. William Hodson, the president of the AASW and future director of New York City's public welfare effort, argued for politesse rather than politics. In the article "Social Workers and Politics" in a late 1929 issue of *Survey*, Hodson acknowledged that the onset of the depression would increase the pressure for political action. But, he reminded his readers, "John Brown," his fictional social worker, "is not a free agent but the employe [*sic*] of his organization." For John Brown, the citizen, to advocate pensions was one thing; but for John Brown, the secretary of the Family Welfare Society, to do so was quite another. As a political actor, John Brown did not control his identity; the public "does not usually identify" a social worker "by his name alone but by his title as well." But Hodson's example reveals how claims to "objectivity" were politically motivated: "left-wing" politics, not the politics of neutrality or of business, was at issue. "[T]he community in which John Brown lives is conservative and against 'socialistic notions.' Old age pensions are re-garded as something imported from Bolshevik Russia. Shall Brown espouse pensions and thus jeopardize the support of his society? He may shortly be in need of a pension himself!"[75]

Hodson's warning mirrored efforts by the professional arm of social work, the AASW, to create a respectable image for social workers. Like many Jewish executives, social workers were concerned that the public too often confused Jewish identity with labor radicalism; in this context, a nonsectarian identity as caseworker would strip Jewish social work of its association with antibusiness politics.

AASW leaders did not, however, simply fight defensive battles within social work ranks; they also advocated improved working conditions in the agencies. But in appeals to the public and to their boards for increased funding, agency administrators often found themselves in contradictory positions, possibly re-flecting their liminal place as social workers and executives. Social workers in agencies such as the JBG repeatedly found their requests for raises thwarted by the legal fiction of agency autonomy under the FJP fiscal umbrella. The FJP provided the bulk of the JBG's operating revenue, and the JBG's Board of Direc-tors regularly told its staff that it had inadequate funds to offer substantial raises. From the FJP's inception in 1917, its directors regularly insisted that such matters were out of their hands; workers had to ask their "autonomous" agencies for raises.

When it came to negotiating, however, professionalism was an impediment. The prevailing professional ethos rejected trade unionism. Both bosses and AASW opponents of social worker trade unionism claimed that professional "objectivity" dictated against partisan political organizations. To be sure, some

JBG social workers would begin to organize in Workers' Councils and then trade unions at the end of the decade to resist these developments. Until that time, however, their only organizational spokesperson was the AASW, the caseworkers' professional association. Hodson's warning to his fictitious social worker, John Brown, suggested the dilemma facing the social worker as political activist: if he became an advocate for pensions, Brown might "shortly be in need of a pension himself!"

A formal AASW policy on "professional" behavior had already begun to take shape a few years earlier. It involved a landmark case in which Hodson also figured prominently. A conflict had erupted between the Family Service Society (FSS) and the Community Fund of Columbus, Ohio, over centralization and local agency autonomy, and in 1925 the local social workers pleaded with the AASW to intercede on their behalf. The incident is worth examining as a paradigm of shifting concerns over worker rights on the job. It prefigured what would soon become the terms of debate on social worker identity in New York City and nationally. In a preview of the New Deal, the conflict illustrated some of the strains that would accompany the shift from private to public sector service work during the depression. As important, in this midwestern setting, struggles over religious and ethnic versus secular identity receded, thus placing in relief another challenge to social workers' professional legitimacy: the gendered tension between female family caseworkers and male executives and politicians.

The Case of the Columbus, Ohio, FSS

On October 2, 1923, the twenty-three women on the staff the Columbus, Ohio, FSS informed Frank H. Howe, the president of the society, that "we can not conscientiously continue our services" without assurances that "we may hope soon to accomplish some really constructive family social casework here." "[N]o visitor can look after the problems of fifty families," they explained, and their "deep sense of responsibility towards these families" made them demand a "lighter load so that we might help them more, so that we might understand them better, so that we might make fewer mistakes in counselling them."[76] Nearly five months later, the staff escalated their threat while at the same time clarifying the issue as they saw it. In a February 21, 1924, petition, the women notified the FSS that they would resign if their funding agency, the Community Fund, formalized a plan to regulate their service by dividing responsibility for relief between the city's new public relief agency, City Charities, and themselves. The plan, they alleged, would "render impossible" the kind of service they felt was needed.[77] The controversy would not be resolved until years later, and it would become a landmark case in the establishment of the AASW's professional policy.

The dispute between the FSS and the Community Fund originated with the Columbus Plan, a program through which the city for nearly twenty years had turned over public monies to a private agency to administer for relief. That agency had been the FSS. Beginning in 1919, however, every year the FSS expended more money than the city appropriated. In 1919 the excess was only $2,228 over the budget of $12,000, but in 1921, as unemployment increased, the excess rose dramatically to 100 percent more than the $19,000 allocated. Then, in 1922, with "an extreme unemployment situation," expenditures skyrocketed. The city had funded the agency's budget request for $35,000 at $21,000; year's-end expenses tripled that amount, totaling a whopping $65,707.[78]

The city leaders were not pleased. When the FSS came in with a $67,000 request for its 1923 budget, the council members began to debate whether it would be better to distribute relief through a public agency. Meanwhile, they allocated $30,000 and insisted on receiving quarterly reports. At the end of March, it was clear that they had to act: the FSS had already distributed $2,200 more than had been allocated for the entire year. As important, though, the number of relief cases it had served was 25 percent below the number it had originally projected. Relief cost approximately $17 a month per case, an amount that would barely allow an unemployed family to survive. But the bottom line for city leaders was that the FSS overspent while providing more money to fewer families. So, as of July 1923, the city opened City Charities, a public relief agency, and staffed it with a superintendent and two investigators.

The changes that the FSS confronted constituted a kind of rehearsal for the New Deal. Now two agencies were responsible for relief, one public and one private. A division of labor had to be established, but a third player, the Community Fund, complicated the discussion. No longer able to rely on city coffers, the FSS had become one of the forty-six agencies under the Community Fund fiscal umbrella. As issues of financing became confused with policy, the three organizations found themselves at loggerheads. City Charities and the FSS fought over the division of services to the needy, finally agreeing to a plan that divided the work "according to the nature of the service to be rendered." City Charities would provide "all relief within its legal responsibilities," and the FSS would "furnish service and relief supplementary to what the city would give."[79] This plan could not paper over fundamental differences, however, in each group's view of its responsibility for relief and what amount was appropriate. Continuing efforts to work out an arrangement failed, and the relationship between the two agencies steadily deteriorated.

At the same time, although the FSS depended on the Community Fund for support in its struggle with the city relief agency, it found itself in increasing trouble with the fund for continuing to overspend its budget. The dispute between the two sides revealed their fundamentally different notions of social service. City Charities argued that it served the community, both those who provided funds and those who needed to be served by them. It demanded that the FSS open its doors to all who needed help and stretch its budget. Moreover, it insisted, as only one of forty-six agencies supported by the fund, the FSS had to be fiscally responsible. In response, FSS social workers insisted that they had an obligation to provide "real" aid and not be "spread thin" to the point that relief would not help clients. FSS staff believed that they morally and professionally could not reduce aid.[80]

In March 1925 the fund established a committee of five men—a doctor, a general, and presumably three businessmen—to meet with the FSS women. Male authority underlined the economic disparity between the power of the two agencies, which was readily apparent to the FSS's secretary, Walter M. West: "The comparative weight and wealth of the two boards is all on the side of the Community Fund."[8] But regular meetings made no progress. Finally, fed up with what they saw as the FSS's history of continual overspending and lack of cooperation, fund leaders decided in August 1925 they had had enough. The FSS, they complained, had absorbed more of their time than all of the other forty-five agencies in the fund. The FSS would either change its policies and management and permit a joint committee to monitor its intake and fiscal affairs or cease to function as a fund agency!

When the fund insisted on the right to approve personnel and threatened to cut off funds, it attacked not merely the FSS's professional autonomy but its very existence. Agencies that entered a federation or Community Chest had to place their contributors within the superagency's province. Under the best of circumstances, if a federation withdrew its funding from an agency it would be difficult for the agency to win back its contributors; tainted with controversy, it would be nearly impossible. So, flabbergasted at what it saw as "forty-eight hours' notice" that it would be dropped from the fund, the FSS mobilized the AASW. It was well positioned to do so: West was a member of the national AASW Committee on Functional Relations of the Executive Committee, Council, and Chapters.[82]

Enter the AASW. To FSS social workers, the Community Fund's decision to drop them "on short notice and on general charges" raised "a very serious question for all social workers." The AASW agreed. But as the AASW's executive secretary and president, Philip Klein and William Hodson, laid out the guidelines for an investigation into the dispute, they made clear that the AASW had to steer through turbulent political waters. Social worker professionalism, they explained, carried both rights and responsibilities. Social workers had the right to work free "from unnecessary restraint . . . in accordance with the accepted standards and principles of the field." But "the maintenance of good standards of social work" also carried with it a "peculiar responsibility" to "be mindful of their duty to clients, to the other agencies in the community, and to the public as a whole,—a duty of devotion, of sincere cooperation, and of willing adjustment to the general scheme of which they are a part."[83]

Klein and Hodson's memorandum set the tone for the two final reports: a joint report based on an official investigation by one representative from the American Association for Community Organization and one from the American Association for Organizing Family Social Work and the report of an AASW subcommittee reviewing the official investigation. The joint report found fault with both sides, emphasizing that a "clash of personality" rather than substantive issues had prevented successful compromise.[84]

The AASW subcommittee's report shifted the balance of blame to the Community Fund but struck a neutral posture by retaining a critique of the FSS. In a confidential letter to Klein, the FSS's president had warned that it would be difficult to hold the Columbus chapter together without AASW support for its professional autonomy. Although the AASW came through for the Columbus group, the organization demonstrated both to a wary public and to funding agency executives that as a professional association, it would limit its political activism and regulate and discipline its members. The subcommittee chided the fund for "lacking in courtesy and frankness." The fund was wrong to try to force the resignation of FSS leaders; agencies could brook no interference with personnel decisions. And, finally, the fund's "spread-thin" policy lowered standards of "good social work."

The FSS also came in for quite damning criticism. However justifiable FSS efforts to maintain standards of relief may have been, the report insisted that responsible fiscal behavior was essential to a professional code, and in that regard, the agency had failed. The report concluded that the FSS had a seven-year "continuous record of spending in excess of its initial appropriations." Adequate relief was one thing, but the AASW's final measures of "good professional standards in social work" were "sound methods of finance."[85]

Having chastened both sides, the joint committee mediated a settlement according to which the FSS reassumed its place in the Community Fund. Meanwhile, the AASW took advantage of the occasion to develop a "future policy." The Columbus case gave it a base on which to establish a body of "professional principles." Recognizing that more incidents would undoubtedly occur, it proposed to stand ready to investigate, report, and mediate. But scarce resources meant "limiting itself sharply so far as local controversies are concerned." Ultimately, its answer was, in 1926, to create a Grievance Procedure Committee. The committee insisted that its proper province, unlike that of the trade unions, lay in the construction of "professional standards" to be maintained by both social workers and their employers. Significantly, appropriate professional standards did not include striking, making "demands," or collective bargaining.[86]

The Columbus case served as a precedent for the institutionalization of AASW professionalism. When the AASW intervened in Columbus, it found its loyalties divided between largely female caseworkers and male supervisors and executives. From this experience, the Grievance Procedure Committee learned to eschew political advocacy for social workers and to advance "responsible" professionalism that privileged the concerns of male agency executives, fundraisers, and conservative politicians over those of the relief clients. This was a secular professional identity that male board directors from both Muncie's Chamber of Commerce and New York City's FJP would recognize and support. The AASW's profile of a "good social worker" did not square, however, with the political vision of all caseworkers, the majority of whom were women, nor did it satisfy their desire to claim a place for themselves in the expanding consumer culture that increasingly marked middle-class identity. Countervailing pressures of gender and economy led some women social workers to highlight issues of gender, forge a distinct feminine professional identity, and experiment with alternative politicized roles.

CHAPTER three

The Making of a Feminine Professional Ident ty

"Is social work now a profession?," a didactic 1930 essay in *Survey* anxiously queried. "Yes," replied author Hazel Newton, a social worker who had become general manager of the Cooperative Workrooms in Boston. And, she added through the medium of her fictionalized "Miss Case-Worker" named Jane, professionalism meant that social workers were "going scientific." Social workers like Jane were learning to be wary of "putting too much of one's own prejudices, sentiments, loves and hates, into one's job."[1] Against an old-fashioned, voluntary "Lady Bountiful," Newton celebrated the "scientific" "Miss Case-Worker," an "objective" social investigator. Because objectivity and rationality were conventionally associated with male professional culture, however, the scientific model created its own tensions for female social workers.[2]

"Miss Case-Workers" identity reflected more than changed attitudes and methods. In the aftermath of the Columbus dispute, the AASW's increased focus on standards and the politics of social service involved two other salient aspects of the social worker's professional middle-class identity that were encapsulated in the dichotomy between the "Lady" and the "Miss": gender and age. At the same time that professionalism was mobilized to counter disparaging ethnic and religious identities, social workers developed a new professional variant in response to conflicting pressures, of which "gender trouble" was a crucial element. Of course, life is not as tidy as paradigms imply, but as a rule, an older generation of "Ladies" had been replaced by a new generation of "Misses." The caseworkers divided, however, over strategies and by gender. Some men and women seemed to adopt a professional identity to deal with the limits of social and gender differentiation. Some women sought a feminine version of that identity to negotiate the limits of professionalism; some men celebrated a gender-free professionalism that would counter the conventional identification of the "social" as a feminine sphere. And ultimately, a few years later, caseworkers of both sexes would emphasize a workplace identity that met conditions that concerns about neither gender nor professionalism seemed prepared to confront.

This chapter focuses, however, on gender and class within the narrative of professionalism. More specifically, it elucidates the gendered alternative that gained strategic power for female social workers at the end of the 1920s. By that time, social workers had to contend with management's well-established efforts to rationalize work and economize, constraints against which the AASW mobilized well. But other pressures of a more domestic nature placed particular demands on female and male social workers: their families expected to attain and sustain a higher standard of living, and they had their own personal desires to participate in the new consumer culture. In sum, when Hazel Newton wrote in 1930, social workers had to fulfill new consumer expectations about what constituted professional conditions, a process complicated by a collapsing economy and the elusive constructed and gendered nature of professionalism, particularly in feminized professions such as social work.[3]

At the end of the 1920s, women probably represented a larger percentage of social workers than they did at any time before or after. Whereas nearly equal numbers of men and women had held jobs in the field twenty years earlier, by 1930, four of every five social workers (79 percent) were women (see appendix, table A.1). Since social work was a feminized job, however, gender trouble did not confront just women social workers; it threatened male identity, too. "Manly" work was a traditional source of men's pride, and when vocational manuals described social work as compatible with women's essential nurturing nature, they implicitly raised questions about the appropriateness of such work for males. Men like Arthur Dunham did not remember ever thinking being a male caseworker was strange. But Dunham's memory may have been shaped by the fact that he worked as a social service administrator (and, later, a professor of social work) almost from the day he graduated from the University of Pennsylvania School of Social Work in 1919.[4] Indeed, in the 1920s, three aspects of social work seem to have compensated male egos for the preponderance of women in the field: traditional acceptance of male dominance, the male bias in the constructed meanings of professionalism, and job mobility, which permitted men to reimagine themselves as managers.

Female social workers may not have liked male occupational privileges, but few made public outcries against it. Oral histories suggest that deeply ingrained attitudes about women's "essential" domestic priorities shaped women's work histories as well as their relationships with men at work. Some, like Harriet M. Bartlett, a hospital caseworker, felt only "subtle discrimination" as a woman "because she worked in a female field" but recalled nonetheless that many male doctors and hospital administrators did "not accept nurses and social workers on the same level" as themselves. In her reminiscences of being a Chicago caseworker in Jewish social service, Helen Harris Perlman acknowledged her complicity in discrimination against women, contrasting the expectations of her generation of caseworkers with those of settlement house workers. Perlman never thought of social work "as a 'career.' My career was going to be to be married and to have children." Preferential male mobility seemed quite appropriate: "I have to confess, to many women like myself it seemed right that they [men] should [get the jobs]." Years later, she reflected back with a degree of self-conscious irony on her willingness as a woman to forgo promotions in favor of male agency administrators because, "as a friend of mine used to say, I'm much too pretty to know about money."[5]

Self-deprecating female attitudes undoubtedly boosted male pride, but the construction of professionalism around qualities generally thought to be "male" such as "objectivity" and "rationalism" also helped counter the view of the work as feminine. In her study of Jewish clubwomen, for instance, Beth S. Wenger concludes that "Jewish men placed professional social work outside their construction of women's sphere." Clubwomen defended their communal voluntary work, and men used professionalism to transform social work into a "male" sphere.[6] But female social workers also sought professional status, and the widely accepted subordinate position of women in the workplace complicated their professional achievement. Moreover, in cities like New York, Jewish patriarchal traditions combined to undermine the professional aspirations of female Jewish social service workers such as Perlman.

The history of the organization that spoke for the professional status of the occupation, the AASW, evidenced the gender hierarchy in the field. Not only was gender absent from the organization's agenda, but men like the three who played such major roles in the Columbus case—AASW president William Hodson, Executive Secretary Philip Klein, and Walter West—held the lion's share of key offices in the organization. To be sure, some leading women social work educators and researchers were represented on AASW committees. Also, some members, both male and female, worked with other groups advocating alternative positions. But the AASW probably spoke for many of the women as well as the disproportionately large number of men in the higher echelons of social work, especially in the executive offices of private agencies. Its national committees included a roster of the leading figures in the field, many from the major social work institutions of New York City. From the AASW came men such as Hodson, Klein, and West; prominent social work educators such as Porter R. Lee and John A. Fitch represented the New York School of Social Work; and Mary Van Kleeck, Neva R. Deardorff, and Ralph G. Hurlin all did pioneering research for the Russell Sage Foundation. Notable figures from New York City's Jewish social work community, such as Deardorff and M. J. Karpf, also served on various committees.[7]

The increase in the number of social workers, a majority of whom were women, created as much concern as pride within the ranks of the better trained and more elite. Beginning in 1923, as part of a drive to raise "professional standards," a select group of thirty-nine caseworkers and administrators (more than three-quarters of whom were women) met annually under AASW auspices at the Milford Conference to consider their professional status. The strong female contingent bespoke the many leadership opportunities women found in social work, even as their executive ranks remained thin. The final conference report in 1928 concluded that a generic form of social casework did exist in the various branches of social work but only as a de facto practice rather than as a codified and required body of knowledge. Repeatedly, the report stressed that social work had to be "scientific." To start, it recommended that formal graduate education be coordinated by the Council of Social Work Education. A master of social work (M.S.W.) degree would become the entry-level credential. By 1932, the Association of Professional Schools had standardized curriculum and requirements at the twenty-five member schools offering master's degree programs. In addition, following another conference recommendation, the AASW, whose membership had grown from 750 in 1921 to over 5,000 in 1930, created a committee that instituted tougher, more restrictive membership requirements in 1932. In practical terms, these restrictions meant that a majority of practitioners could never qualify for membership.[8]

Also, such AASW concerns with standards did not always meet the needs of the new generation of female social workers who struggled to develop a work identity that would both give them professional status and preserve their femininity.[9] Many practicing agency workers tried to balance career and family. A career, however, required persistence, some luck, and regular promotions—all of which family responsibilities mitigated against. Arlien Johnson's experiences as a prominent social work administrator are a case in point. Discussing her decision never to marry and the cases of three accomplished women she knew who refused to be considered for a deanship because it would interfere with family responsibilities, Johnson intimated that family commitments complicated work decisions for women; women who expected to sustain a career needed both an extended family and a "tolerant" husband.[10]

Not surprisingly, then, a disproportionate number of female social work leaders followed the pattern of 1890–1920 era social workers and remained unmarried. In some cases, this decision was undoubtedly due in part to the fact that the choice of a career met resistance from potential suitors. Evidence from prominent female leaders in all branches of social work practice and education demonstrates that other women chose instead to forge close personal friendships with fellow professional women, relationships that often seemed to "involve sexual intimacy." Jesse Taft and Virginia Robinson, prominent educators at the University of Pennsylvania School of Social Work, shared a home most of their adult lives and adopted two children. Mary Van Kleeck lived with a Dutch woman who was a political economist. Others like Bertha Reynolds and Vita Scudder led single lives. And the list could go on.[11]

By the late 1920s, the willingness of many leaders to forsake heterosexual family life became increasingly disagreeable to many new rank-and-file practitioners. Part of a transformed white-collar work force, the postwar, postsuffrage generation sought both a career and a family, albeit not necessarily at the same time. In addition, the burgeoning consumer family economy in the 1920s further complicated women's work expectations. A professional standard of living dictated new levels of material acquisition supposedly appropriate to a white-collar "middle-class" occupational strata. This consumer culture and ambiguities about respectable women's public roles compelled women to seek a new work identity. But none of the available ideologies and representations produced by mass media or by union and professional associations could serve to orient female social workers in a world of work shaped by the contradictory imperatives of domesticity, career, and consumption. Out of the failure to achieve an autonomous professional work culture and in response to routine in the work itself, social workers created two new typologies: the professional woman and the professional worker. Social workers did not themselves use these terms until the 1960s, but their complaints and analyses in the 1920s anticipated them. Neither the professional woman, a female social worker who accepted the "male" ideology of the dispassionate professional, nor the professional worker, ostensibly a "neutered" white-collar proletarian but in practice "manly," adequately addressed the gendered character of social work. Nonetheless, they framed (and limited) debates among social workers about appropriate roles and responses to their work from the 1920s onward.

The "New Woman"

The struggle to define a new professional identity for social workers in these years was complicated by the rising consumer expectations of the twentieth-century labor force. Nationally, the percentage of employed women classified as professionals grew from 8.2 to 14.2 percent between 1900 and 1930, and women constituted a larger number within the professions than within the labor force in general. Among the occupations in which women concentrated, such as nursing and librarianship, only teaching school was more feminized than social work. By 1930, four of every five people in or preparing for a career in teaching or social work were female. A decade earlier, fewer than three in five social workers were female.

The women who worked in social work also represented a social group that was distinct from their charity work predecessors. To be sure, they were still women privileged by higher education, and in cities with substantial immigrant populations, they were usually native-born. Birth in the United States, however, should not obscure the ties that many in the ethnic charities had to the ethnic community. A substantial number of these women seem to have been grand-daughters of immigrants whose fathers were skilled workmen or clericals. These women were, in fact, the beginnings of a "lower" and "middling" middle class that relied on a paid salary to live a modest life.

The comments on dress and budgeting of Theodora L. Wilson, a caseworker for the Brooklyn Bureau of Charities in the early 1920s, suggest the less-privi-leged social class of this generation of caseworkers. Wilson and her mates were not "Ladies Bountiful." Having to walk the streets of her district, Wilson remem-bered that it was hard to be "concerned about her appearance" on caseworkers' "frightfully low salaries":

> How chic could one look on fifty dollars a month—my starting salary? Our stenographers, who had a slightly different set of values, probably were much more style conscious than we. I'm sure we presented a rather nondescript appearance, except for our Ground Gripper shoes, which were ugly enough to be noticed, but also comfortable enough to walk the streets of our districts. As our salaries increased, I think we were more wont to choose our clothes for their good taste and quality, than because they showed a flair for style. Who needed "style" in an inner city slum? I remember the wisdom of the saleslady who objected to the dark shade of the dress I wanted to buy, when she learned I was a social worker. "You ought to buy something gay, to cheer up the poor dears."[12]

Wilson's reflections on style suggest how the social worker's identity was marked as female and middle class. But ideas about femininity also raised ques-tions about the woman social worker's "objectivity" and professionalism. This female labor force regarded the redefined jobs in private casework agencies and public welfare as respectable work that permitted and even sustained middle-class heterosocial leisure activities. Dependent on a regular income, the new female social worker of the 1920s was not simply an altruist; she had entered paid labor to begin a career. An earlier generation of native-born Protestant women may have felt they had to choose between family and work, but increasing numbers of the new social workers of the 1920s expected to realize both ambi-tions without necessarily confronting the disadvantages that burdensome household responsibilities placed on their careers.[13] In the pages of *The Nation* and elsewhere, elite professional women openly discussed the need to reconcile the public and private spheres of their lives. But essays by social workers suggest that marriage also remained an ultimate goal and an important strategy for economic survival, especially for the increasing numbers of daughters (or granddaughters) of immigrants who retained a vivid memory of childhood poverty. Through mid-century, most female social workers continued to leave work to raise a family. Still, the generation of "modern women" who entered the field in the 1920s prefigured the trend fully evident by 1950 when more than half the women social workers (and an even greater percentage of the men) were married.[14]

In New York City, the city that employed the largest number of social workers, the immigrant origins of the staff were most visible. One in five New York City social workers was born outside the United States, a ratio that dropped to one in ten nationally. Many more social workers undoubtedly were children and grandchildren of immigrants. Historians have documented the process by which first- and second-generation immigrants born in their new country began to assimilate and distinguish themselves from their forebears while maintaining roots in ethnic communities. Historian Andrew R. Heinze has described the "intense acculturation" that characterized the Jewish immigrants' infatuation with mass consumption during these years.[15] But the simple fact that many Irish and southern and eastern European Americans were Catholic and Jews from working-class backgrounds also kept them a world apart from their charity work predecessors. The 1926 roster of the Manhattan office of the Department of Public Welfare of the City of New York (DPW) reflected the increasingly ethnic character of social work. The department included twenty-six female and four male investigators. The chief was a man, Frederick E. Bauer. Most of the women, like Annie Murphy, Mary O'Connor, Margaret Mulcahy, and Catherine Horan, had Irish surnames. Immigrant daughters such as these women would have expected to resume work after varying intervals of childrearing over the decades.[16]

These female social workers of the 1920s received contradictory messages upon entering the field. For all that was new about social work, many of the attitudes toward women's work continued to celebrate domestic forms of work and "maternal" instincts. Social workers were encouraged to play traditional nurturing roles, but in the 1920s, they also came to believe that they could distinguish their work from that of volunteers and from women's "usual" domestic nurturing in the home by becoming "efficient," dispassionate "professionals." For example, WEIU pamphlets asserted that women had special opportunities and "calling" for social work, but when they offered women advice for succeeding in the field, they urged women to adopt the behavioral characteristics valued by the male social work leadership: dispassion, objectivity, and devotion to order and science. As the president of the NCJSS told the annual meeting in 1926, volunteers, again usually women, had brought "love of mankind" to social work, giving free rein to their emotions and impulses. The female professional, however, needed different qualities. To succeed, the "Good Mother" had to adopt attributes of passionlessness and objectivity generally associated with men, traits that easily allowed others to stereotype her as desexed or androgynous.[17]

No less troubling to these women was the discrepancy between the institutional forms professionalism took and the substance it provided. As we have seen, for social workers, professionalism also meant the development of a specialized casework method with new mental health concerns and psychological lingo.[18] The early beginnings of psychiatric social work in the 1920s further exacerbated the tensions in women's efforts to balance work and family roles. The rise of Freudian therapy and child casework emphasized the mother as the primary parent and the crucial importance of early childhood development. As Winifred D. Wandersee has noted, the new child- and family-centered therapies were partially responsive to the decline in child labor and the increase in women's work. Ironically, however, the resulting "treatment" by social workers increased the burden of traditional domestic responsibilities both on themselves and on their adult female clients.[19]

The previous chapter noted the limited ways in which professionalism fulfilled its promise of status and autonomy on the job to social workers. An African American visiting nurse, Florence Jacobs Edmonds, was one of the better-trained workers, for example, but she spent much of her day walking and riding trolleys. Certified in hospital social service, Edmonds had considerable autonomy traveling around New York City in the early 1920s, but professionalism did not prevent doctors from steadily taking over the more satisfying parts of her job, such as doing urinalysis, taking blood pressure, and aiding in childbirth.[20] Much like the typical family caseworker, in numerous visits each day, Edmonds worked as a referral agent, mediator, and helpmate, dispensing often vital commonsense advice.

The sexual division of labor also emphasized the ambiguous character of professional autonomy and opportunity for women social workers. Although bureaucratic centralization limited autonomy, reorganization did create some new opportunities for educated caseworkers and supervisors. Prejudice against women, however, meant that trustees often gave men preference over qualified women for privileged administrative positions: employers saw men as "breadwinners" and argued that women's "natural" familial responsibilities diluted their occupational "value."[21] For example, a 1922 AASW study found that nationally a substantial majority of the new paid family caseworkers in private agencies had attended college. Most of these women had graduated and even received a little graduate training; in an era when probably less than 10 percent of

American women attended college, these social workers were an educated elite.[22] Some of these women received administrative posts, especially in schools of social work, but men predominated in the agency managerial positions. Men also held the professional medical jobs such as that of doctor and psychiatrist, to which social workers increasingly had to defer. In most social service agencies, male doctors in mental hygiene clinics, in psychiatric services, and on medical staffs had the primary authority in treatment and diagnosis.[23] But women continued to fill the fieldwork positions. Agency executives in the 1920s continually complained of the difficulty of recruiting men and the need to pay them a higher family wage, apparently a male prerogative. They also noted that if young male social workers did not rise into managerial positions, they frequently left the field. Within many agencies, "supervisor" seems to have been the senior female job title, and it usually involved the supervision of other women.[24]

The challenge for female social workers of constructing a usable feminine professional identity was further heightened by the promise that work in the 1920s offered admission into the new consumer economy. National trends toward higher living standards powerfully shaped how women defined their new experience as white-collar professionals. Susan Porter Benson has documented the immersion of middle-class females in the twentieth-century culture of consumption. New consumer standards shaped social workers' ambitions as middle-class women and would-be wives. Like most female professionals, they aspired to achieve status and a family wage from their jobs. Shopping in consumer emporiums extended women's traditional roles as domestic providers, but it also placed them under increased pressure: advertising intensified rising consumer expectations, and new leisure activities often required extra "spending money."[25] By the 1920s, female professionals expected to achieve a standard of living and working conditions appropriate to their education and comparable to those of their male counterparts.[26] For most female social workers of the 1920s, these standards remained unrealized ideals, but, like women entering other female-dominated professions, they identified themselves with this middle class and its aspirations. Many older social workers with college educations had fathers who were independent professionals or businessmen.[27] Those who did not have such backgrounds expected that white-collar work—especially in the emerging "semiprofessions"—would confirm middle-class status and permit them to reach what budget studies, home management manuals, and popular magazines lauded in the 1920s as a distinct "American Standard of Living."

Various illustrations in *Survey* pictured how the female social worker might fantasize herself as middle class in this new consumer world: as the "New Woman" flapper, affluent, sleek, and androgynous, ministering, with decency and patronizing humor, to earthy, lower-class families (see figure 3.1). The "American Standard" translated into roomy accommodations with expensive

FIRST AID TO PHILANTHROPISTS

Young Case Worker (making conversation on her first visit): *"The papers say that a rich man in New York wants to give away $8,000,000."*

Client: *"I wish he'd give it to me so's I could get a new set of teeth and eat good."*

Figure 3.1. This sketch contrasts the image of the lithe social worker as flapper with that of the overweight, somewhat surly client. Frontispiece, *Survey*, November 15, 1929, 194; illustration by Greta Ries. Courtesy of Tamiment Institute Library, New York University.

Figure 3.2. Slender and well-coiffed, this middle-class social worker luxuriates in simple elegance, enjoying a good book. Haven Emerson, "The Happy Twins," *Survey*, June 15, 1928, 356. Courtesy of Tamiment Institute Library, New York University.

furniture, paintings, and books. The "professional standard" included automobiles, domestic help, membership in professional societies, and the accumulation of savings and investments.[28] Single and portrayed as from a different class and ethnic background than those of her clients, the social worker was elegantly dressed and surrounded by symbols of affluence such as books and tennis rackets, which represented attributes of her middle-class identity (see figures 3.2, 3.3, and 3.4).

In practice, few social workers could afford the "American Standard," as Elizabeth Healy, a social worker at the Philadelphia Child Guidance Clinic, ruefully observed in 1930. Her dramatic account in *Survey* of a caseworkers' roundtable on self-development on the job was entitled "Get Your Man." Low salaries, Healy claimed, made it impossible for many female social workers to rent and decorate accommodations that would serve as "lures" for men. As Healy summarized the problem, inadequate pay frustrated ambitions to marry and obtain material goods: "Unless we have some place to entertain men we may be putting too much strain on our personalities as bait. When we ask men in after a date, what is it we ask them into? A barren hall leading to our tiny one room refuge, a dull sitting room in a dull boardinghouse, or our living room which we pray has not already been turned into a bed room by our roommate? What lures do we use for our comfort-loving desirables? Fudge alone does not work!"[29]

As Healy's story suggests, female social workers found it difficult to support themselves as single women, much less as members of the middle class. Men's salaries were low, but women's were lower by about 10 percent.[30] The elite psychiatric and medical caseworkers received as much as $150 per month in urban centers, but child and family caseworkers averaged between $90 and $125 per month. Between 1913 and 1926, the real wages of social workers rose only 3 percent. Still, although most social workers' salaries remained slightly below those of skilled industrial workers, for at least white staff, they were appreciably above the average wage of $15–20 per week paid to salespeople at Filene's De-

PROFESSIONAL LAPSES
The dietitian on her holiday—the vitamins left at home

Drawing by Jean Henry

Figure 3.3. In this sketch illustrating the contradictions in social worker leisure, the food is proletarian, but the attire is that of the bourgeois "New Woman." *Survey*, August 15, 1930, 418; illustration by Jean Henry. Courtesy of Tamiment Institute Library, New York University.

A WEARY CASE WORKER IS INVITED FOR A RESTFUL WEEK-END

SUBURBAN HOSTESS: "And then there's my laundress. Her husband walks out on her regularly and turns up again long enough to drink up every cent of her savings (Jackie, it isn't nice to interrupt Mother), and they have another baby. What do you think I ought to do about her?"

Figure 3.4. This sketch suggests that in her leisure time the last thing this single social worker wants to hear are her married friend's complaints about the sort of woman with whom social workers deal on a daily basis. *Survey*, June 15, 1930, 258; illustration by Jean Henry. Courtesy of Tamiment Institute Library, New York University.

partment Store.[31] African American professional women were always paid less than their white sisters, but in the black community, they were an elite. According to historian Stephanie J. Shaw, black professional women "still earned much more than less skilled black workers," and the black community conferred "high status" on them.[32]

Data on the "subsistence" income of those claiming middle-class status during this period is sparse, but 90 percent of ninety-six University of California faculty members' families studied in 1922 earned between $2,000 and $5,000 per year, and three-quarters of the professors' wives complained that the income did not meet their "needs." A reviewer of a comparable study of Yale professors' inability to reach a middle-class living standard ended with an ironic warning to social workers. The reviewer advised that they be more understanding of the failed efforts of others even less fortunate: "People [i.e., social workers] who irritate the poor by scolding because they do not save will possibly leave off such unfair admonishing if they can grasp the fact these studies of comfort standards tell [i.e., that even professionals cannot save money]."[33]

But if professors were having a hard time, the burden undoubtedly fell on their wives. The emphasis on consumption placed a particularly heavy structural and psychological load on women to keep the hearth well supplied and to provide a fulfilling domestic life through consumer goods. But here again many contradictions (and ironies) presented themselves. Work in teaching, nursing, and social service remained poorly remunerated even after it professionalized. Thus, a Baltimore AASW committee determined that a beginning social worker salary of $1,500–$1,800 a year would permit only a " 'bare existence.' " These social workers were able to eke out a living only because most were "local [single] women who live in their own family homes and obtain the maximum of return for the minimum of cost." As one contemporary analyst of social work lamented, low salaries made it impossible to maintain "the standard of living which one would expect [of] a professional person," a standard that contemporary budget studies celebrated. Social workers' income was insufficient to fulfill professional aspirations; it was inadequate to support the travel, study, and book purchases necessary for "professional growth and efficiency."[34]

In sum, as a strategy for female social workers' empowerment, professionalism had contradictory effects. Social workers' wages distinguished their work from that of volunteers, but their incomes were insufficient to maintain a "professional standard of living." The language of professional autonomy justified the wage and the higher status that accompanied it. But changes in procedures that accompanied professionalization undermined autonomy, replacing it with routine, bureaucracy, and male authority. The version of professionalism that social workers inherited from the Progressive Era did little to protect them from charges of incompetence or behavior unnatural to their sex.

Negative depictions of social workers in the emerging mass media of the 1920s further exacerbated the social worker's struggle to develop a positive professional identity. Working out of increasingly rationalized and impersonal bureaucracies, social workers were vulnerable to being stereotyped as heartless investigators.[35]

Literary representations provide especially useful windows into the worlds of gender and consumption central to the social worker's experience and identity. A complicated cultural exchange in the production and consumption of meanings took place in commercial representations of social workers in novels, stories, films, and plays. The representations repackaged what authors observed about sexual identity in the workplace and in the street. The culture industry eroticized these images into light and shadow for popular consumption, revealing what was assimilated, what was ignored, and what the "rules" of exchange might have been.[36]

A few representative popular characterizations of social workers at the end of the 1920s illustrate the stereotypes of social workers that offended and troubled members of the helping profession. The legacy of patronizing charity workers had given social workers a mixed reputation in the larger community and a troubling image in fiction. Progressive Era literary portrayals of social workers, although sparse compared to those of teachers and nurses, tended to be positive, depicting social workers as kindly settlement house and mission workers concerned with saving children.[37] But by the mid-1920s, a noticeable deterioration in the popular image of social workers had occurred, especially as presented in such instruments of the emerging mass culture as advertising, radio, and movies. These media formalized new, unflattering, stock exaggerations of social workers, emblazoning them on screens across the land and popularizing them in dime novels.[38] The coincidence of negative public images and new professional membership standards is significant. Nineteenth-century stereotypes of "friendly visitors" as officious meddlers were given new life by the mass media's dependence on established melodramatic conventions and the increasingly bureaucratic nature of social work and the shuttling of clients between medical specialists and caseworkers armed with forms.[39]

Thus, even as social workers claimed a new professional status, their popular image shifted from that of benevolent altruist—symbolized by "angels" such as Lillian Wald—to that of meddling investigator. A 1923 short story by Anzia Yezierska entitled "The Lord Giveth" presented this revived, unflattering characterization in vivid detail. At the time, Yezierska was a celebrated novelist. The film of her first book, *Hungry Hearts*, had just opened at the Capitol Theatre in New York City, and her Hollywood publicist lauded her as "the sweatshop

Cinderella." In the story, she draws on her own memories of cold, condescending social workers, who, according to Yezierska's daughter, "had humiliated her family and her neighbors," to create Miss Naughton, an "unconscious inquisitor."[40] Insensitive to the traditions of a Jewish rebbe on New York City's Lower East Side who sees full-time study of the Torah as a vocation, the social worker considers the impoverished Jewish family's request for aid an improper use of charity. To his wife, the rebbe's "head is in the next world"; to the prying charity "investigator," the problem is the rebbe's laziness and her agency's limited resources: "You see, we have only a small amount of money, . . . and it is only fair it should go to the most deserving cases."[41]

A decade later, in 1933, the year after the new professional standards for full membership in the AASW took effect, Sinclair Lewis published *Ann Vickers*. Heralded by one reviewer as a "story of a modern American woman, a feminist, a social worker and a prison reformer, but always a rebel against the conventions," the novel melodramatically expresses the ambivalence felt by Lewis (and his audience) toward the "New Woman." Writing during the heart of the depression, Lewis constructed a moral tale of philanthropy, professionalism, and gender roles gone awry. Beneath the story of an idealized heroine confronting a heartless bureaucracy lay what one critic has identified as an unmistakable nostalgia for the "Good Mother."[42] Ann Vickers, always noble, well intentioned, and dedicated, is the light in a tale of shadows and darkness. Everywhere she goes, she encounters a social service system mired in the attitudes of nineteenth-century charity, choosing to do little more than confine, moralize to, or harass the poor.[43] Relief, she admits, provides badly needed aid. But the cold logic of the countinghouse dominates philanthropy; rather than giving the nurturing that is expected of "Good Mothers," she finds, twentieth-century charity is obsessed with record keeping and puritanical notions of need. It has "too much red tape," and "charity workers did tend to become hard, from familiarity with misfortune."[44]

However difficult and frustrating Vickers finds the settlements, their imperfections pale in comparison with the unsanitary conditions, sadistic violence, and staff corruption at Copperhead Gap Penitentiary, an appallingly run southern rural prison at which she takes a position. Vickers encounters a modern Babylon of graft, riots, suicide, political repression, and cruelty. Stymied in her efforts to befriend inmates and reform the institution, she is forced to resign after the staff entrap her in compromising photographs with an alcoholic doctor.[45] Vickers's lot improves somewhat at the Stuyvesant Industrial Home for Women in New York City, where she becomes superintendent. Even there, she remains an embattled voice in the wilderness, convinced that jailers are often worse scoundrels than inmates. Although a caring and at times successful social worker, Vickers remains a beleaguered outsider within her chosen profession.

Ann Vickers left readers with an overwhelmingly negative image of a corrupt social service dominated by unfeeling social workers. Although Lewis and Yezierska were leftist critics of philanthropy, their views were shared across a range of political and cultural productions. For example, the AASW complained that a 1927 movie, *It* which had opened in forty-two theaters across the country, portrayed two social workers as "'hard-boiled,' ignorant looking women—who seize a woman's baby and tell the mother they must put the child in a home until she is well enough to take care of it."[46] The AASW, whose members were disturbed by such negative images, mobilized a national letter-writing campaign directed at the producers of *It*. Within a month, the Famous Players–Lasky Corporation had agreed to replace placards accompanying the film in all forty-two theaters. The term "social workers" on the placards was changed to "meddling neighbors," although the film remained the same. Three years later, in 1930, a production of Elmer Rice's play *Street Scene* was similarly criticized by the Twin City AASW chapter; during the run in Minneapolis, the character of a nosy social worker was changed to that of an "interfering relative."[47]

The Professional Woman

In the last years of the 1920s, two new work identities for social workers began to emerge: the professional woman and the professional worker. Reflecting the world of dissonance created for female social workers by their negative image in the mass media and the contradictory circumstances associated with their professional work, they emerged from the multiple cultural exchanges between workers, clients, and their public audience.[48]

The more dominant of these identities, the professional woman, was a complex construct. In various texts produced in the late 1920s, the professional woman assumed some male attributes, but she was careful not to appear to compete with or threaten men. As Nancy Cott has observed, in a world in which sexual neutrality was considered an essential component of professional identity, acknowledgment of power inequities based on gender was impossible: "The claim to judge practitioners on individual merit as persons (not as men or women) in the dispassionate search for truth and usefulness was essential to the professions' self-definition."[49] Instead, as a way of maintaining her status, the professional woman tried to keep less-qualified women out of the field. During the 1920s, modest agency budgets and low wages combined to encourage the entrance of low-paid, poorly trained workers into social work, recruits who would weaken the professionals' public image and bargaining power. The Milford Conference report, which bemoaned the fact that social work professional development lagged behind that of law, medicine, and even teaching, recommended the promotion of research and coordinated entry-level advanced-degree programs. The bitter interagency dispute involving the Community

Fund in Columbus, Ohio, further stimulated action. Family caseworkers demanded protection from public agency intervention, and AASW executive secretary Walter West, who had been general secretary of the FSS, helped supervise the implementation of new rules. In 1930 the AASW limited membership to those with several years of advanced training or education.[50] These new regulations also restricted the role of volunteers. Still, when a 1932 report on salaries in the social agencies noted that they paid low wages to women because of the presumption that female staff had men to support them, the AASW felt it could and should do little more than issue reports.[51] The AASW's abiding belief was that professionals—administrators and staffs—could work together collegially to achieve solutions.

More aggressive action was directed at those seen as outside the "professional" club; for example, the AASW led the fight to change the "hard-boiled" image of the social worker as depicted in the movie *It* and in Rice's play *Street Scene*. Unfortunately, the AASW proposed professionalism as the solution for problems caused by professionalism: it celebrated the "male" values of objectivity and detachment that contributed to the woman professional's "hard" image. In any case, patching up a troubling image and championing new "standards" did little to change the more complex problems associated with social work conditions.

Female social workers' self-representations expose the complications inherent in the construction of a professional identity around the notion of a woman professional. Three representative contributions by women social workers in 1930 to a regular column in *Survey* entitled "Work Shop" portray women social workers of the period in a variety of ways: as "scatterbrained" or "hard-hearted," as women who need men to organize them, and as women without men. Their unstable, contested ideas of gender and professionalism suggest the confusion and pain some caseworkers experienced when confronted with the image of the female social worker as an aggressive, ambitious "New Woman." The contributions make clear that female social workers felt torn between their roles as women and their roles as professionals, each of which embodied in different ways the qualities of a "good" social worker. The conflict was also over heterosexual domesticity and their ability to participate in the new culture of consumption by being able to afford the accoutrements of middle-class status.[52] By the mid-1920s, in most agencies, "Lady Bountiful," the well-heeled volunteer, had been replaced by "Miss Case-Worker," but she was not a Protestant "Sally"; she was the daughter or granddaughter of immigrants with a name like Mary O'Connor or Margaret Mulcahy.[53] College-educated and upwardly mobile, these women wanted to have careers as well as families. They also expected entry into the culture of consumption befitting a professional standard of living. Low wages blocked their way.

The first contribution to *Survey* is a piece of didactic fiction by Esther Dunham, the wife of prominent social work administrator and professor Arthur Dunham, who, as mentioned earlier, never considered it inappropriate to be a male caseworker.[54] Esther Dunham's "Scatter-Brained Sally" is similarly unperplexed by maleness: she champions the new professional who can learn (from a man) to be efficient (like a man). Dunham's voice is that of an agency executive, but her depiction of female stereotypes would probably ring true among most men and not a few women. Sally, "who had not outgrown her dependence on Mother, is given the task of 'mothering' fifty families" by a welfare agency. But Sally, in what is portrayed as a stereotypically female fashion, responds to the torrent of "slips, forms, face sheets, [and] records" that she encounters every day by behaving frenetically: "I have the brains of a chicken and the disposition of a cat. They told me at school that I had the makings of a good case worker in me. I wish they could see me now! I've worked like a dog for two weeks and all I can say is that I am three hours behind in dictation, that I have a new family to visit tonight, that to-morrow I have ten allowances to deliver in all the corners of this old district besides hosts of relatives and employers and goodness knows what not!"

Fortunately, a man arrives to save the day! Sally's relationship with her boyfriend, who works in the central office, flounders because of her ineptitude; work forces her to cancel dates for four evenings in a row. On the fifth day, the boyfriend arrives, "grim and inexorable," to straighten her out. With his help, she manages to "plan" her dictation, traveling, and scheduling in detail. Within two weeks, Sally and her love life are transformed, and she comes to believe in the new "system." In this fantasy, efficiency does not unsex the social worker; rather, planning allows her the free time to get her man.[55]

But not every "Sally" had a man around to save the day, as Philadelphia social worker Elizabeth Healy noted in a *Survey* essay mentioned above that had appeared two months earlier. According to Healy, a group of women at a caseworkers' roundtable had "offered up a Maiden's Prayer—though it may have sounded like a Lament. A prayer is hopeful, and we were seeking delivery from exile." These "Sallys" did not have problems with their daily routines, although their problem was indeed work related: they could not meet men.

Healy's perspective is more authentically that of a caseworker, not an executive. And she gives voice to a contrasting view of the female worker: women social workers are not scatterbrained; they are too smart, too intimidating for potential male suitors. Whereas in Dunham's fantasy a man solves the social worker's dilemma, Healy's essay places the responsibility for solving these problems on the woman. Although the female social worker's profession may keep her from finding a man, Healy envisions her as a professional woman with a distinct, if limited, place in the gendered public workplace, one secured in part through skillful use of feminine wiles.

When all is said and done, Healy concludes, women have two fundamental problems: the low wages that frustrate their ability to outfit accommodations to "lure" their "comfort-loving desirables" and being female in a male world. The second obstacle is partially of their own making: professional specialization makes female social workers into narrow, self-absorbed individuals. Male professionals can tout their expertise; women cannot. After going out with social workers, several men allegedly commented, "Oh they are brainy girls, nice girls, too, but they leave you pulverized—or at least perforated." In response, Healy concedes that "our promiscuous use of lingo, our conviction of the importance of what we do, and our lack of conspicuous social success, all may be related to our inadequate preparation for being interesting to 'outsiders.'" Besides broadening her horizons, the professional woman social worker has to repress two of her salient professional characteristics: ambition and specialized knowledge. "If we need to, we might remain convinced that the adjustment of human difficulties is a fundamental aim in life. But let's not say so at the dinner table of a former college friend who has invited us in to meet her husband's best friend! Not if we are canny. However, that same dinner table situation may suggest the need of a little personal adjustment if we discover we have no contribution to make in the talk about theaters, comic-strips or sport champions."[56]

Four months later, another social worker, Dorothea de Schweinitz, the assistant executive secretary of the AASW, contested Healy's characterization of social workers. In fact, she intimates, Healy dissembled: "rumor" had it, she begins, that Healy ("and others of the same ilk at the [caseworkers'] round table") "leads a relatively normal existence and has been seen here and there accompanied by a gentleman." Writing in response to Healy's essay, de Schweinitz rejects the idea of the female social worker's responsibility for the domestic crisis, proposing instead a vision of the accomplished single professional woman who does not lack for male companionship. Married to a prominent social work administrator herself, de Schweinitz writes as a woman who has established an independent career and sustained a marriage.[57] Informally surveying female social workers who never married—probably representative of the generation born in the 1870s and 1880s—de Schweinitz finds them advocating an older tradition of career and friendship without marriage. Here the new professional social worker wrote in the genre of social investigation—she was a social worker doing social work on social workers—expressing the less-troubled convictions of the previous generation to a new one.

To de Schweinitz, female careerists are not failed women; the problem is finding secure, self-confident men. After embarking on a career, she argues, women find themselves at odds with the expectations of young men solely interested in domesticated women: "The young ladies, when they were encouraged [by these men] towards anything beyond homemaking, had been charged with the responsibility not of struggle but of making the world more beautiful, good, and generous. Statues of justice, charity, liberty were in the form of woman. Such must be her ideal." She acknowledges that women social workers lack facilities in which to entertain men and become "too absorbed in the work." But to her, the fundamental problem is not the behavior of the woman social worker but the "paucity of males likely to interest the 'bright young woman.'" Social workers' lives, she argues, can include men, albeit not necessarily husbands. Good men are in short supply, but later in life, there is "a variegated procession—widowers, divorcés, restless husbands, and single men with complexes from Oedipus to inertia. The wary social worker recognizes that they seek a kitchen to stir in and a fireplace to poke. . . . A mate? Well, hardly ever, but more comfortable relationships than some previous ones."[58]

The public, however, and, indeed, many social workers had not made such peace with the circumstances of the female professional worker, and these ambivalent accounts can be read as symptomatic texts, reflecting the tensions and contradictions surrounding the work and image of the professional woman. As early as the 1890s, for instance, articles in *American Jewess* asserted that if she were truly middle class (or wished to be considered so), a woman with an able-bodied husband would not work outside the home. And if she tried, she would not get very far in the " 'man's world' of business and the professions."[59] Similarly, Inabel Burns Lindsay, a black caseworker, testified to gender discrimination against her at home and in the workplace in the 1920s and 1930s. She did not work during the first year of her marriage, she explained, because her husband "had some old-fashioned ideas about women working." On the job, since she worked for a "predominantly Negro institution," the Provident Association in St. Louis, she found racial discrimination less a problem than gender bias a woman, she noted, did not "get promoted as readily, nor to as high a rank, as a man."[60]

As the AASW led professional women down the narrow path of professionalism, a few social workers scattered around the country were working out an alternative vision, another way of imagining work in the profession and addressing the needs of the woman worker. Their creation, the professional worker, would gain ideological power in the succeeding decades, but it had its early beginnings in the relatively small but influential group of Jewish social service agencies in the 1920s that were concentrated in a few northern cities.[61] The movement was strongest in New York City, Boston, Philadelphia, and Chicago, but it had representatives across the country.

The Professional Worker

Speaking at the 1923 NCJSS, a Miss Levy from Milwaukee turned the language of standardized scientific management and professionalized social work on its head, making it stand for worker rights rather than routine: "[W]hy don't the social workers of the United States and Canada organize themselves so that they will have a standard salary, a standard vacation and standard rights? They can demand they have a standard pension to retire and get a vacation." Warming to the call to organize, the conference chair encouraged the audience to join the AASW, but social workers concerned with wages and workload saw the AASW as inadequate.[62] Professional executives dominated the AASW, permitting little rank-and-file participation in decision making, although a 1932 survey noted that only 7.5 percent of AASW members were executives. The majority were "practitioners" (80.9 percent) and supervisors, but the "leadership in national and local chapters is by social work executives."[63] To AASW critics, the problematic participation of executives exemplified a more serious inadequacy in the organization's social philosophy, a weakness that became apparent as autonomy in the agencies was increasingly replaced by bureaucratic control later in the decade, even before the onset of the depression. For these critics, Miss Levy's call to arms was answered by an alternative institution that sprang up among some Jewish agency workers in Boston and New York City in 1923–24: the Workers' Council.[64]

Workers' Councils began as an integral part of the emerging professional ethos, the feeling that "professionals" should be consulted and should participate collaboratively in decision making. Whereas the AASW focused on "ethical and technical standards of professional performance," the JBG Workers' Council was organized in 1926 "'by the workers for the interests of the workers rather than by the executive director for the interests of the agency.'" In fact, until late in the decade, the councils acted little differently from the AASW locals, except that executives and supervisors, when permitted to attend meetings, were not allowed to vote. Moreover, the majority of social workers never rushed to join the Workers' Councils, and in succeeding decades, when they did join trade unions, they often remained equally wedded to their professional identity.[65]

The Workers' Councils may have begun in a "professional" conciliatory mode, but they ended the 1920s discussing proletarian issues. The limits of their professional equality and autonomy, of being consulted but lacking authority in fundamental ways, became more apparent to JBG workers by 1928 and 1929. Within the councils and their trade union descendant, the Association of Federation Workers (AFW), which also organized in 1926,[66] social workers created an alternative to the professional woman: the professional worker, a trade unionist. This formulation emphasized exactly what the AASW could not: as much as social workers claimed to be professionals, they were still workers, and poorly paid ones at that.

The Workers' Councils functioned as proto-unions, and in them, the professional worker emerged as a proto–trade unionist, part of a continuous tradition in Jewish social service that emerged full-blown in the 1930s as a left-wing labor movement in both public and private agencies. When some Jewish social workers unionized in 1931, for example, they acknowledged that their new organizations "would remain of little avail unless built upon employee organizations within each agency—the Workers' Councils."[67] "The most important, and really vitalizing force of workers organization within social agencies," argued the chair of the AFW, "is this basic unit of organizational structure.'[68] When FJP agencies imposed a 10 percent wage reduction in 1931, the Workers' Councils and the AFW stood ready for political action. The AFW rewrote its constitution on a "frank economic basis," beginning a long, complicated history of trade union militancy in social work. But it should be recognized that the story began in the 1920s in response to some of the contradictions inherent in the idea of the professional woman.[69]

Although the professional worker's ascendance is more properly part of the history of the 1930s, it is important to note that this formulation had internal problems with earlier roots. Both professional types maintained the sexual division of labor in which women remained subordinate to men and were paid less. Although professionalism's emphasis on individual merit forbade discussion of a social inequity of this sort, effectively making "professional woman" an oxymoron, "professional worker" was a masculine construction. By privileging class divisions over gender, trade unions, which were seen as the preserve of "manly" action, would make the professional worker also the proletarian man.[70]

Still, Jewish social workers from New York City, such as Martha K. Selig, Elizabeth K. Radinsky, Francis Beatman, and Sanford Solender, have testified to the socialist tradition or immigrant experience that informed their early participation in social worker trade unions.[71] The union movement, however, also included prominent non-Jews, such as Mary Van Kleeck. By 1931, it would extend to public welfare agencies. Although it is important to appreciate the cultural and religious backgrounds of these people, the focus should remain on their challenge to the image of the professional woman. Jews and non-Jews alike were drawn to the new image of the professional worker, although this worker always remained a minority in the field. Most female social workers, both the older generation and the daughters of immigrants (and some young native-born women, of course), quietly stood on the sidelines and struggled as individuals with the problems associated with being independent middle-class professionals who were poorly paid, subordinate, "rational" women.

Gender is, then, an essential ingredient in the story of twentieth-century social workers' search for a professional and middle-class identity. To be sure, the politics of reorganization, standardization, and the meaning of what critics variously referred to as "religion," social activism, or lack of "objectivity" played a major part in this struggle; but the development of social work as a profession was also shaped by cultural conventions and limited by the material realities of the home and the workplace. Over these cultural and material forces, female social workers had only limited control. Still, these women thought of themselves as middle class and struggled to construct self-representations compatible with their collective professional or trade union institutional identities, their individual ambitions, and the emerging culture of consumption.

The "New Woman" of the 1920s worked for a living wage in a heterosexual environment and confronted two gendered alternatives to professionalism: the woman professional and the professional worker. Professionalism, an ideology that obscured much of the actual work these women did, could not solve material problems facing women in the profession, nor could it provide an interpretive framework that recognized the way conditions of work were structured by gender. The language of dispassionate, objective efficiency had earlier functioned in the female world of the settlement. Now this language was harnessed to professionalism in a contested heterosexual sphere where its absorption of the principles of scientific management gave it more definite "male" characteristics, encumbering the woman worker's identity with tensions over appropriate behavior. In response, social workers became increasingly anxious, fighting in the late 1920s to win formal professional acceptance from the Census Bureau, medical professionals, and male colleagues. They also struggled to gain acceptance from a skeptical public. As an alternative, female social workers created a variant of the male professional: the professional woman, a practitioner who adopted the "male" work ethos of the dispassionate expert, even while continuing, with evident discomfort, to defer to her male colleagues and bosses.[72]

Through its promotion of professionalism, the AASW helped the concept of the professional woman gain wide currency in the 1920s. During a decade that had seen a retreat from feminism and labor radicalism, by implementing restrictive criteria for membership, the AASW offered the status of an exclusive association as compensation for limited autonomy, low wages, and highly routinized work. More stringent membership criteria also functioned like nineteenth-century apprentice regulations to restrict the supply of "professionally" trained workers and strengthen the power of those in the association. Clients and the larger community now saw social workers less as benevolent "angels" and more as the older nineteenth-century calculating meddlesome investigators celebrated in their rationalized workplace. In turn, in the next decade, social workers would find that the new vitality of the old negative image would hinder depression-fostered battles to improve both their own and their clients' social conditions.

Professional ideology impeded the ability of social workers to comprehend worsening economic conditions that jeopardized both their standard of living and their self-representation as middle class. The professional ethos mystified the work itself. Would-be professionals did not recognize a hierarchical world of bosses and dependent workers. To do so would be to undermine their self-definition as autonomous experts. As the depression deepened, a narrative of unionization that joined with the older narrative of professionalization in self-identification as the professional worker increasingly appealed to social workers. But for women workers this alternative contained meanings about gender that obscured as much as they clarified the meanings of their professional middle-class identity. As a professional woman, the female social worker remained deferential to men, her autonomy and career ambitions constrained; as a professional worker, she became a "neutered" proletarian, but one who was in practice imagined as "manly." In the new configuration, issues of class would ascend as discussions of gender declined.

The forging of middle-class identity as part of a professionalizing narrative also casts the professional worker as the middle-class worker. In the 1930s, this oxymoron, driven by narratives of both unionization and professionalization, would encapsulate the double sides of a new cultural meaning of the middle class. Contesting the older economistic version of professionalism, the new typology, to which we turn in part 2, saw social workers as workers on the job and middle class at home and as consumers.

PART two

The Middle-Class Worker

In the 1930s, unionization of social work set in motion a fundamental refiguring of middle-class identity. Unionization combined with the professionalizing narrative to reshape middle-class identity as a hybrid worker/professional identity. Late-twentieth-century sociological studies of industrial workers have documented this sense of a double class identity: social workers saw themselves as "working class" on the job but "middle class" at home. This identity emerged, however, in the history of social workers during the 1930s around the figure of the professional middle-class worker.

Social workers' hard-won status as middle-class professionals took a beating with the onset of the depression as wage reductions and increased caseloads degraded their living and working conditions. In response, some social workers began to unionize. Although the union movement in social work emerged most fully in New York City, this section is also regularly interspersed with national developments, which help take the story from the rise of public welfare to the collapse of left-wing social worker unions in mid-century.

Chapters 4 and 5 deal with social work during the Great Depression in the new public sector and in the older private agencies, respectively. The notion of the professional worker exposes the ambiguities of middle-class identity in the depression era, when everyone knew of social service workers who had been on the dole themselves. In this political contest, social workers unionized and asserted their "identity of interests" with both clients and agency clerical and maintenance staffs as workers. Moreover, for the woman worker at the center of these chapters, gender took on new meaning in the 1930s. As proletarians, social workers privileged class concerns that were often expressed as "manly" labor; as professionals, their ideology celebrated a world of "objective" (read as "male") personal achievement defined by status in the community and the accoutrements of consumer culture.

Chapter 6 places the politics of war at center stage—first, the patriotic fervor that accompanied war mobilization and then internal sectarian conflicts and the state persecution of radical labor that accompanied the Cold War. However, even as war curtailed some social worker options, it opened up others. War work in psychiatric social welfare offered social workers an alternative and less-controversial arena for an enhanced public identity. If the depression had hardened their image as attendants to the poor, helping families and soldiers readjust to the postwar society broadened social workers' claim to serve all, including the affluent and the "respectable." In this context, wartime dependence on psychiatric social work helped reconstruct social work itself as a consumer good useful to anyone from any social group, just as social workers reasserted their identity as middle class in order to redefine their professional identity in consumerist terms.

four

The Professional Worker in the Public Sector

The burgeoning of public sector social service in the early 1930s represented a profound and dramatic change in the social relations of daily social work: two-thirds of all social workers now worked in the public sector, most staffing New Deal relief agencies. Although the government had long provided considerable funding to private agencies and maintained institutional care facilities for the insane and disabled as well as war veterans, child welfare and maternal care staff had constituted a small part of the social service work force prior to the depression. But no more. The 1940 federal census reported that the number of social and welfare workers grew over the decade by nearly 44,000 workers to 75,197. The 46,000 men and women who now worked in the public sector relief agencies and ran government welfare programs accounted for most if not all of the increase.[1] As significant, men now entered social service at an almost equal rate to that of women. Women established themselves in agencies, often with supervisory positions, and still outnumbered men, but their percentage fell over the course of the decade from 78.7 to 64.3 percent of the social work labor force.[2] Moreover, conventional expectations about male breadwinners shaped social policy and career prospects in men's favor. Federal laws enacted in the 1930s privileged the employment of men and forbid the employment of both husbands and wives at the same agency, effectively compelling families to sacrifice the less well paid woman's job for that of her husband.[3]

This shift in the site of much social service work involved an equally profound change in the work routines, expectations, and subjectivity of all social workers. The recruits into emergency relief and welfare programs were not randomly selected; for example, "because of limited funds and the shortage of trained personnel," the DPW had to place "much reliance" on recruits "from among 'white collar' relief recipients."[4] These recruits often possessed an ambivalent perspective about the class implications of their work, as their more politically schooled colleagues were quick to remind them. As one of the leaders of the Rank-and-File Movement in social work, Jacob Fisher, noted, they might be "children of the professional and business classes," but they had to discard leftover attitudes from the era of social work as benevolence and accept the implications of an "employee psychology, regardless of class background."[5]

Few social workers adopted the class rhetoric of radical organizers like Fisher, but as the Great Depression discredited reigning policies and the economic collapse deepened, few could ignore the fact that working and living conditions had deteriorated. Social work recruits would continue to display the white-collar worker's distinct consumer tastes for exotica, books, and travel, but new material constraints increasingly aligned them with other industrial workers. As the case of Edgar B. Shaw, a former relief investigator for the Home Relief Bureau of New York City (HRB), illustrates, the fates of clients and caseworkers became deeply entwined. A narrow and ambiguous line came to separate the social service worker from the client and, by implication, those who considered themselves middle class from those in the working class during the Great Depression. The fragility and impermanence of this distinction could be seen in Shaw's case. In a June 28, 1933, letter to DPW commissioner Frank B. Taylor, Shaw complained that he had been fired without cause: "a native New Yorker . . . of three generations," who had been "taxpayers for over one hundred and fifty years," he had been forced "to accept Home Relief and deprived from earning a livelihood." Queried by the commissioner, the HRB central office reported that Shaw was transferred to another precinct and later dismissed "because a check-up of his caseload disclosed irregularities." Shaw insisted, however, that he was a victim of "superior employers" who were "not willing to substantiate such charges by granting an open hearing whereby . . . [he] could produce possible evidence to the contrary."[6] Whether Shaw's complaint or the HRB charge was valid is not known, but the ironic HRB recommendation to Shaw was: "Mr. Shaw is eligible for Home Relief and we wrote him on June 27, 1933, suggesting that he apply at his local Home Relief Bureau."[7]

Shaw's problem and the advice proffered him by the central office revealed one of the tragic ironies of the decade—the unemployed could one day be dispensing welfare as a form of work relief and the next day receiving it. As dependent wage laborers who were often compensated less than skilled workers, such social service workers were working class; but with the modest autonomy of a white-collar salary and their strong educational background, they distinguished themselves as middle class. Reflecting on this ambiguity and resulting vulnerability, Irwin Rosen, the director of placement for the Ninety-second Street Young Men's Hebrew Association, who drafted the original Rank-and-File program, explained to the 1936 NCJSS that proletarianization had fractured the middle class into two groups with different class positions: "vast sections of the typical middle class occupational groupings" had been "proletarianized." Managers and supervisors represented "a new middle class" in "fundamental opposition" to "the large lower layer of professionals and technicians" represented by social workers.[8]

It was a simple step from Rosen's argument to the material reality that this "lower layer's" interests were identified with those of the working class. These recruits entered a workplace that was remarkably more proletarian than that of their private sector colleagues. To cope with the great demand for relief and to compensate for the lack of prior social service experience of many recruits, public agencies regimented the work and closely supervised relief workers. Hastily assembled emergency offices were sparsely furnished, and staff were squeezed into whatever space could be found. These large bureaucratic operations had little private space. Moreover, at the same time that the needs and demands of the unemployed mounted, state legislatures exerted constant political pressure on public welfare authorities to economize. Deprived of resources, in turn, public service workers complained that they could often provide only short-term help that failed to fulfill both professional standards of service and client needs; they nevertheless remained reluctant to accept private agency assertions that their work was less professional.

The depression placed comparable fiscal constraints on charity, and private agency social workers such as Rosen and Fisher underwent many similar transformations in work and subjectivity. In contrast to the HRB, private agencies remained small, intimate facilities that emphasized face-to-face relationships between caseworkers, supervisors, and board members. More of the staff continued to be formally trained in social work schools and imbued with the professional ethos surrounding casework, and smaller caseloads permitted them more time to practice extended "treatment." Nonetheless, fiscal constraints led to larger caseloads and wage cuts in private agencies, too. As important, the growth of the public sector created a role crisis for the private agencies: when public agencies assumed responsibility for aid to families and dependent children, as well as aid to the disabled, blind, and elderly in work relief programs such as the Works Progress Administration and the Civilian Conservation Corps, less well funded private agencies had to question their own raison d'être and to ask what social work role was left for them to fill. One answer was to reimagine private sector work as a privileged professional site of advanced training that offered a more secure middle-class status than overburdened public "relief" administration offered.

The 1930s, then, provided a new social and political context of obligations, responsibilities, and opportunities in which many social workers created an alternative self-identity as workers. In the previous decade, the work force of mostly women had constructed the model of the professional woman to distinguish their paid work from activities of volunteers at the same time that volunteers/philanthropists controlled agency fiscal matters from their seats on the boards of directors. In this identity, they could be both feminine and middle class, as figures 3.1–3.4 so graphically illustrated. This identity also helped them navigate the murky waters of a heterosexual workplace and the conflicting constructs of nurturance and objectivity traditionally celebrated as female and male attributes, respectively. The professional variant of social worker identity would hardly disappear; in fact, it embraced the rising enthusiasm for psychiatry to enhance its cultural authority as an arbiter of social and psychological health. But as men entered the field in numbers closer to those of women in the 1930s, both would increasingly embrace a remasculinized proletarian work culture in which "manly" labor was depicted as fighting both depression blues and recalcitrant bosses to protect and sustain their families. This proletarian aspect of their identity at work offered male and female social workers an alternative as professional workers that was neutered, if not masculinized, presenting additional challenges to the woman social worker's feminine identity.

Contingent and multiple subject positions in the 1930s complicated the New Deal social workers' sense of themselves, but the proletarian identity implicit in the social worker trade union movement (especially a movement informed by the Third International's "third period" policies of 1934) placed a filter over race and gender concerns. Thus, in the wake of the 1935 Harlem race riot, Lester B. Granger, the most frequent African American contributor to the left-wing newspaper of the Rank-and-File Movement in social work, *Social Work Today*, offered a class analysis of the racial solidarity represented by black employees of the New York City Emergency Relief Bureau (ERB), who had come to the aid of the Harlem community: "Probably no group of Harlem's citizens have set a more definite impression on their community than the Negro employee of the Emergency Relief Bureau. Here are workers of the white collar class, high school and college graduates, who in other years would have been typical middle class folk with delusions of financial security. The impermanence of their jobs, coupled with membership in the union, the Association of Workers in Public Relief Agencies, has given them a distinctly class conscious outlook."[9]

To be sure, Granger's was one of the most radical voices of the era. But the Marxist idiom of class consciousness, the view of "middle class folk" feeling a kinship with the unemployed and other trade unionists, reflected some of the material realities of the relief worker's own life and revealed that the new double sense of class had become the lingua franca of the era. Even workers in the mainstream of Jewish social work at the time remember regularly reading *Survey* and *Social Work Today* and being "sympathetic to the ideas of these journals."[10] Granger's view of HRB workers as "class conscious" remains an untested assertion, but his hybrid "double" or segmented identity of the middle-class worker spoke to a wide audience. It remains for us to examine, however, how the contingent material and political circumstances of the professional worker model in the 1930s helped to subordinate the multiple identities of femininity, race, and ethnicity to that of worker.

Generations and the Professional Worker Identity

The primary new ingredient in the forging of social worker identity in the 1930s was the rise of a rank-and-file trade union movement in social service. Gender remained an issue, and race increasingly became one, especially in New York City, where public relief workers estimated that blacks, who constituted only 6 percent of the population, made up 26 percent of those on relief by mid-decade.[11] But both race and gender issues were filtered through the lens of class analysis, if not subordinated to it. A rival identity to the professional woman had begun to emerge in the Workers' Councils of the late 1920s, but fueled by the class perspective of a Rank-and-File Movement, it now blossomed into a social movement of professional workers.

The men and women who now rushed to join what they called rank-and-file organizations appeared to comprise a third generation of social workers. The first two generations had been the evangelicals (and "Ladies Bountiful") and what one former social worker analyst writing in *Survey*, Frankwood E. Williams, sarcastically described as professional "Miss Case Workers." In the third generation, the axis had shifted from gender to class—from the professional woman to the professional worker. Moreover, the generational difference exposed a fundamental distinction between executives and caseworkers that had come to inform rank-and-file politics. Thus, the Rank-and-File Movement's statement of principles began by differentiating rank-and-file workers and executives; unlike membership in the AASW, which executives dominated, only social workers, not executives, were eligible for membership in the Rank-and-File Movement's association.[12]

Executives who led social work in 1935 represented the generation of the 1920s: either they had played a major role in bringing about the use of casework methods as the basis of professionalism in the last fifteen years, or, in Williams's words, they were "workers of the previous period who have kept pace with developments." This older generation had pioneered what had become the abiding social work technique after Mary E. Richmond published her classic treatise in 1917—the casework method.[13] But casework was a technique based on an individual medical model that was taken for granted or assumed, never closely examined; it was not a social philosophy. Caseworkers trained in the 1920s were the products of a cultural and educational environment that did little to deepen their social understanding, which stood in contrast to the environment of the 1930s. Williams's critique was harsh but probably not far off base: "The culture broadly expressed [in the 1920s] was in the acceptance of the code of the gentleman, good manners, good taste, courtesy, consideration for others (in the sense of others in the room who may be trying to read), self control (in the sense of not losing one's temper or being sentimental or gushing), poise, moderation, reasonableness, broadmindedness to the point of including almost everything, together with a certain appreciation of good books, plays, pictures, music." Indeed, the consumerist representations of social workers in the pages of *Survey* at the end of the 1920s discussed in chapter 3—as flappers posed with books and tennis rackets nearby—reflected social workers' identification with these symbols of middle-class professional culture.

By the mid-1930s, the situation had changed; considerable numbers of social workers were going beyond their school training and, as Williams notes, "had begun to investigate the economic and social forces that lie back of the generalities assumed by their leaders." Rank-and-File social workers had, in sum, developed "not a philosophy of life but a social philosophy." In addition, Rank-and-Filers appeared to inhabit a different culture; their insistent demands suggested that they possessed a different code of behavior: "They have not shown the customary deference and respect [to executives]." To the old-timers, in the behavior of these young Turks, "nothing remains of a code of orderly procedure." Williams, and, indeed, many others during the decade, reduced this conflict to a familiar central issue: Who is a social worker? "Are the[se Rank-and-Filers], indeed, social workers or are they merely clinging to a professional distinction?"[14]

Left-wingers dominated the unions, and their concerns paralleled those of many left-wing parties that struggled for social justice during the decade. The key difference between the Rank-and-Filers (who also called themselves "practitioners") and those who styled themselves as professionals centered on the latter's commitment to casework technique and the former's emphasis on social work as a site of social and political struggle. Older social workers had established their expertise around the elaboration of the casework technique. Rank-and-Filers, however, although they used the method, saw economic and social forces at work that nullified the use of any technique. The answer for the Rank-and-Filer, then, was a new sense of class work as advocacy rather than classification; it was an integrated program of casework, social action, and client advocacy. In turn, casework executives and many politicians supported increased funding for social programs but still led the fight to separate political activism from social work, arguing that it contradicted professional standards of "objectivity." For professional social workers, objectivity might be stretched to include passing resolutions on state social policy at annual professional meetings, but it certainly did not encompass open identification with clients, demonstrations, picketing, strikes, or—horror of horrors—left-wing challenges to the New Deal itself.

Led by left-wing caseworkers in private agencies in New York City, Philadelphia, and Chicago, social workers in major urban centers across the nation organized during the depression into AFL and later Congress of Industrial Organizations (CIO) unions. By the end of the decade, according to social work historian Leslie B. Alexander, there were approximately 3,300 unionized social workers in private agencies (members of the Social Service Employees Union [SSEU] of the United Office and Professional Workers of America [UOPWA, CIO]).[15] In addition, by the summer of 1938, whereas over 1,000 welfare workers still belonged to the older AFL union (the American Federation of State, County, and Municipal Employees [AFSCME]), another 8,500 had joined the CIO union (the State, County, and Municipal Workers of America [SCMWA]). Although these numbers constituted only a small percentage of the more than 75,000 social service employees enumerated by the 1940 census, a majority—and possibly a substantial majority—of social workers in both the DW and the FJP family and child casework agencies seem to have joined one of the trade unions. For social workers, then, unionization and professionalization had to be reconciled, and this was never more apparent than in the 1930s. According to Alexander's estimate, approximately half of the members of the AASW also joined these highly politicized unions.[16]

To be sure, large numbers of social workers moved in and out of social service and never joined a union at all. But the labor movement affected all of them. Ultimately the union movement would win collective-bargaining rights for social workers and permanently alter working conditions and grievance procedures. The social work trade unionists, along with teachers, also pioneered a new kind of unionism among white-collar workers in the professions and in public service, altering the nature of the discourse about the rights, responsibilities, and obligations of social workers and clients and profoundly challenging the ways workers related to clients, thought about their work, and, ultimately, thought about themselves.

The Rank-and-File Movement

Material realities of the depression era city forced social workers to reimagine their identity as both middle class and proletarian. Nowhere was this more apparent than in New York City. Struck by the unprecedented scale of destitution and unemployment the Welfare Council of New York City offered an "impressionistic view" of the city in the winter of 1930–31. Based on interviews with 900 social workers and public health nurses, it reported that "enormous numbers" of people fearfully confronted the specter of poverty. A census of the unemployed in New York City in 1931, for example, counted 609,035 people— approximately one-quarter of the labor force—"able to work, willing to work, and looking for a job." Many were unemployed for the first time and for diverse reasons. Reduced retail orders closed opportunities for "able-bodied men of good standing in well-paid seasonal occupations (the needle trades and the building trades, notably)." The depression forced other manufacturers to economize in ways that also meant reduced employment for many New Yorkers. Among the unemployed were "clothing workers affected by the removal of factories to places outside New York, where labor costs would be cheaper; middle-aged men who in normal times could have counted on five more years or so in their positions; pocketbook makers who had been displaced by women; Wall Street clerks who had been displaced by improved calculating machines; and many other victims of changes in demand and in methods of production." The result, the social workers interviewed concluded, was "that a wholesale pauperizing process" had gone on that winter.[17]

The harsh depression conditions of the 1930s strengthened the social workers' traditional mission to help the poor, but the dramatic increase in caseloads undermined their efforts to improve standards of service and frustrated their ability to give each case the time it needed. Reiterating the complaint of Columbus's family service staff nearly a decade earlier, New York City caseworkers declared, " 'We spread ourselves thin.' " As the report noted, "They bewail their inability to 'give adequate attention' to the families under their care, to 'complete investigations,' to 'establish relations' . . . in short, to do 'good constructive casework,' 'the kind of work I would wish to do.' "[18]

The poverty around them spurred social workers to action on behalf of others, but fiscal constraints within agencies that placed new restrictions on their behavior, expectations, and professional ambitions charged them to act on their own behalf. Both ambitions came together in a set of new attitudes and organizations that came to be known as the Rank-and-File Movement in social work.

The Rank-and-File Movement grew from a small dissident group within the FJP in the mid-1920s into, by the 1930s, what historian Rick Spano has described as a "social movement."[19] We have seen its origins in the Workers' Councils of agencies such as the JBG. Between 1931 and 1934, the movement had grown to thirteen organizations in eight cities and had blossomed on three fronts. First, protective organizations such as the AFW advanced the trade union cause of private workers in New York City, Philadelphia, Detroit, and Brooklyn; public social service unions had similarly established themselves in Chicago and New York City. Second, following the establishment of a social worker discussion club in New York City to provide an open forum in which union and nonunion social workers could discuss the relationship between social problems and professional practice, other discussion clubs opened in Boston, Chicago, St. Louis, Cleveland, and Philadelphia. Third, Chicago caseworkers established a practitioner group. Functioning as a kind of radical caucus within the AASW and national conferences, this group and others that soon emerged in St. Louis and New York City enabled radical caseworkers to engage a social context for diagnosis and treatment.[20]

By 1937, the Rank-and-File Movement had become a political presence with which politicians and social service administrators had to reckon, and it had changed both the political landscape of social work and the discourse about what constituted "good" social service and "worker" rights—both those of social workers and those of their clients. Starting in 1934, the movement had its own widely read journal, *Social Work Today*. By 1937, the number of Rank-and-File organizations had mushroomed, growing from thirteen in 1934 to fifty-one; in addition, the movement could claim a membership of several thousand and the active allegiance of many thousands more who participated in rallies and strikes.[21]

Most important, the Rank-and-File Movement was not simply a reprise of the social reform impulse that had marked the Progressive Era social worker; rather, it was radical and communist-inspired, and it supported industrial unionism. Unlike many of the social reformers who had cut their reform teeth on social research and the settlements and then went on to help initiate New Deal programs, the Rank-and-Filers criticized the New Deal programs as vastly underfunded palliatives. Filtering their views through Marxist class analysis, these social workers understood the depression and the problem of unemployment as structural. This class perspective also had broad implications for their own identity as workers, their relationship to their clients, the unemployed, and their sense that good casework involved a social diagnosis.

The radicals wanted economic and social surgery of root and branch and organized accordingly. Contrast the Chicago social workers' discussion club's call to organize a union with the decision by the AASW at roughly the same time to tighten its membership qualifications by accepting only those with considerable formal training. The call from Chicago's discussion club to an "open meeting" went out to all who worked in the social service industry regardless of employment status—"'senior caseworkers, caseworkers, case aides, clerical workers, all office workers, all employees of social agencies and institutions in Chicago, ALL EMPLOYED AND UNEMPLOYED.'"[22] Indeed, industrial unionism characterized the social worker unions in both the public and the private sector throughout this era and explains why they switched their affiliation from the craft union–dominated AFL to the CIO in 1937, soon after the CIO split off from the AFL.

In point of fact, many of the Rank-and-File political positions differed little from those of the AASW. In the 1934–36 era, the radicals criticized the New Deal as inadequate, whereas the more mainstream AASW tended to laud its advances. But ultimately, both led the public fight to expand relief programs and improve social worker working conditions. Both were outspoken in their opposition to racial discrimination. Over how to accomplish these goals, however, they parted company. The Rank-and-Filers not only advocated collective bargaining through trade union organization but also advanced industrial unionism in social service; the AASW promoted the autonomy and independence of the professional association, which would establish guidelines for personnel procedures and grievance machinery. The Rank-and-Filers also tended to adopt a two-class social model, at least on the job. Previously, social workers had identified themselves as a "middle" between elite volunteer "ladies" above and immigrant clients below. Rank-and-Filers, however, saw clients as not unlike themselves and, in time, pressed for the development of a welfare rights movement. Whereas in practice, distinctions between professionals and Rank-and-Filers were not absolute—indeed, many Rank-and-Filers also joined the AASW—AASW professionals tended to view the client as an "other" best served by dispassionate, objective advice. The Rank-and-File program differed most, then, in its class perspective: it pressed for solidarity among all workers, rights to collective recognition, "steeply graded income and inheritance taxes," and "elimination of discrimination because of color, nationality, political or religious persuasion, or participation in strikes."[23]

The radical political position of the Rank-and-Filers reflected the strong presence of communists in the movement, although to argue, as did their opponents, that they were merely puppets of the Communist Party probably overstates the formal role of party functionaries in the movement and underestimates the broader day-to-day social concerns that drove them. When the FJP, for instance, decided after five years to recognize the AFW, Benjamin J. Buttenwieser, well known among his more conservative colleagues as the "radical" FJP trustee, insisted that the claim that the union's leadership was largely communist was exaggerated. Trustee George Z. Medalie and FJP president Solomon Lowenstein, both representing more mainstream trustee opinions, acknowledged what in fact seemed to be the case—most FJP social workers were communists (although they were not necessarily party members), and the FJP had to move beyond that fact to deal with policy issues. Medalie, the president of the JBG, claimed that 90 percent of the JBG unionists were communists and that the agency and unionists had always "got along just as well in their discussions." Lowenstein, who nine months earlier had criticized the AFW's role in a strike at Lebanon Hospital as "a failure," now reminded the trustees that the Communist Party was legal in the United States: "he had nothing but praise for the . . . high-minded people of splendid background and training" whom he had met in his work at the FJP.[24]

Indeed, in interviews, FJP leaders from the 1930s without reservation acknowledged joining this radical union. One woman simply noted that she met a disparate group of Trotskyites, Lovestonites, and Leninists in the AFW. Another, Sophie Grossman, when asked if she felt the union was communist-led, placed the role of the party in a utilitarian perspective that many probably shared: "I was not identified with the communist group, but I believed in the things that we as a group, as an agency, as a member of the union were fighting for . . . the benefits that any decent human would require."[25]

There is no mistaking the presence of the Communist Party in the movement, but as Grossman's reflection suggests, members seemed to distinguish its pronouncements, especially on foreign affairs, from the daily activities of agency work.[26] For instance, in his history of the movement, Jacob Fisher, the editor of *Social Work Today*, minimized the role of communists in the movement. But in fact, his magazine mirrored the twists and turns of party dogma through the "ultra-left" "third period" to the United Front moderations of 1936 and the reversal required by the 1939 Hitler-Stalin Pact.[27] Spano correctly notes that many Jewish Rank-and-Filers resisted this final turn, arguing that the movement was thoroughly antifascist. But the fundamental issue remains the authenticity of the Rank-and-Filers' day-to-day concerns, not merely their association with communists. In this regard, as Spano has also observed, the left-wing perspective of the Rank-and-File Movement promoted social diagnosis as an alternative to the focus on personal pathology that framed the way "neutral" professionals approached problems.[28] As important, although the movement occasionally voiced sectarian views, a list of its adherents included many of the most respected and widely read social workers, educators, writers, and caseworkers, such as Mary Van Kleeck from the Russell Sage Foundation; Bertha Reynolds, the associate director of the Smith College School of Social Work; Harry L. Lurie and Eduard Lindeman of the New York School of Social Work; the American Civil Liberties Union's Roger Baldwin; and Fisher, as well as labor leaders such as Chicago's Joseph H. Levy and SCMWA organizer Abe Flaxer.[29]

The Rank-and-File Movement, then, provided a cadre of articulate and passionate spokespersons for the ascendance of a professional worker identity. In the public sector, the most significant organizations were in Chicago and New York City. In the private sector, Jewish agency workers predominated, again in New York City and Chicago but also in Los Angeles, St. Louis, Baltimore, Newark, Detroit, Philadelphia, and Boston. Nowhere were Rank-and-File organizations stronger, however, than among social workers in New York City, where the movement was born. As we turn to New York City to see how and to what extent the movement established its purview in both the public and the private sector, it is important to keep two of its salient features in mind: its considerable influence among 1930s social workers and its radical class analysis and social diagnosis. To be sure, most social workers in the 1930s did not join the Rank-and-File Movement, but in New York City and in the FJP and the DPW in particular, the movement seemed to win majority support. Moreover, the movement was influential beyond its numbers, profoundly altering discourses about "good" social work and social worker identity.

In addition, a class perspective provided the dominant lens through which Rank-and-Filers viewed the social relations of social work and the material conditions in which they and their clients existed. This class perspective changed social workers' relationship to their work, altering their view of their clients and their own sense of self. The movement, for instance, articulated and advanced social diagnosis as an alternative to the personal, medical model that had come to dominate social work by the end of the 1920s. Finally, left-wing concern with proletarian solidarity probably enhanced the movement's consciousness of race, whereas its celebration of "manly" labor may have obscured any similar consideration of discrimination against women workers. It is important to note, however, that social workers' new sense of themselves on the job did not require that they change their sense of themselves at home or in the community. Depressed wages meant that to some extent they did change their private view of themselves, but they continued to place a high value on things associated with middle-class standards—books, education, travel, and distinctive dress.

New York City and Public Welfare: "Professional Workers with a 'Worker' Slant"

The history of welfare in 1930s New York City provides a concrete example of how the social workers' construction of a usable double class identity for hard times emerged in historically specific circumstances. In 1931, as the full impact of the depression began to take its toll, the bottom dropped out of the fragile and provisional New York City welfare net. New York City's unique political culture —including an active reform tradition, a strong labor movement, vibrant socialist and communist communities, an organized Jewish communal tradition, powerful ethnic associations, and a Tammany Hall political machine—mobilized to contest the challenge of the New Deal order. Dependent on the seasonal labor of finishing goods industries, New York City's immigrant working class was particularly vulnerable to economic downturns, and the coming of the Great Depression brought unemployment to the metropolis on a scale that far exceeded the level of unemployment anywhere else in the country. The New Deal would put in place a panoply of services and agencies to meet the crises of unemployment and poverty, but they were built on important precedents in state welfare for which an earlier generation of social workers could justifiably take considerable credit.[30]

However significant they may have been as precedents, early measures were partial, poorly financed, and incompletely implemented.[31] Benefits were shockingly meager, kept to less than half the level that contemporary budget studies agreed was needed to sustain a decent and healthy standard of living; eligibility was also severely restricted. For instance, probably only 20 percent of mothers in need ever became eligible for mothers' allowances and pervasive racism deemed blacks generally "unsuitable."[32] Thus, New Deal policymakers fundamentally had to revise, if not reinvent, the notion of public responsibility for social justice. Brooklyn, for instance, remained adamantly opposed to outdoor relief such as financial assistance; New York City, which had operated a poorhouse since the eighteenth century, opened its first shelter for transients only in 1896. Only in 1907 did city leaders by opening the seven-story Municipal Lodging House at 438 East Twenty-fifth Street, acknowledge their responsibility for the homeless.[33]

By 1931, two years into the financial collapse, it was apparent to many that these institutions and modest efforts by the Hoover administration such as the Reconstruction Finance Corporation were inadequate. As the largest manufacturing state in the nation, New York faced colossal problems. Unemployment in Buffalo, for instance, rose from 6.2 percent of those able and willing to work in 1929 to 32.6 percent in 1932. New York City, which had to open a second and third Municipal Lodging House in 1930–31 on the East Twenty-fifth Street and South Ferry Street piers to house 3,380 people, reported providing 408,100 lodgings and 1,042,247 meals in 1930, numbers that more than doubled the next year. Amid reports of unprecedented levels of poverty and misery, state and local officials entered the breach.[34]

New York governor Franklin D. Roosevelt had initiated action in 1930, noting that "'the situation is serious and the time has come for us to face this unpleasant fact dispassionately and constructively.'"[35] Even with this executive leadership, legislative wheels rolled slowly and it was eighteen months before legislation implementing a Temporary Emergency Relief Administration (TERA), the Wickes Act, was passed. Twenty million dollars in state aid would be funneled to municipalities, which would distribute home and work relief from November 1, 1931, to June 1, 1932, during this "temporary" crisis. "Temporary," of course, came to mean six years.[36]

Nowhere was the task facing the TERA more overwhelming than in New York City. Trained caseworkers were borrowed from private agencies to teach the more-educated relief recipients to become relief workers themselves. Two thousand such people were taken from the relief rolls and hired as investigators and clerks to staff the new agencies. By December 1931, a "makeshift organization" had been installed in seventy-nine unused schools, rentable lofts, and other free spaces.[37]

The dramatic growth of public sector relief work during the New Deal constituted the most striking shift in social work during the 1930s, and that change was most evident in the nation's largest city. The 11,081 men and women who worked for New York City's new Department of Welfare as of January 1, 1938, dwarfed the city's estimated 3,500 private agency social workers. Approximately one of every four social and welfare workers in the country worked in New York City. At their peak in August 1935, the combined staffs of the department's predecessors, the ERB and the DPW, had employed 18,171 people. Even though this total was inflated by the inclusion of a small clerical and maintenance staff (estimated by Commissioner of Investigations William B. Herlands, who Mayor Fiorello H. La Guardia had formally directed to investigate the history of public welfare in the city, to be only 3.5 percent of the total), it represented a staggering transformation of social service labor. With a total operating budget of more than $143 million in 1938, the staff dispensed over $74 million in home relief alone to more than 250,000 applicants, while rejecting a nearly equal number of appeals. Another $51 million went to aid the elderly, blind, and homeless and to support the Works Progress Administration; only $18 million (11.9 percent) was used to pay administrative salaries.[38]

The déclassé social profile of these recruits and the work they did was congenial to a more proletarian outlook at work. Immediate labor demands meant that many new relief workers came to the field without formal training and the professional expectations inculcated by schools of social work. Educational data exists only for the supervisory staff, but even among them, only about half had some college education, and less than one in four had done some postgraduate work.[39] In addition, through the mid-1930s, most TERA employees continued to be paid out of work relief monies. Although formal data is elusive, the broader social base of the labor force suggests that more of these public welfare employees had ties to the immigrant communities often served by the relief agencies than did those who had earlier worked in social work. Recent historical studies have emphasized the potential role of such "new [second-generation] immigrants": when the Great Depression discredited reigning policies, this group drew on its ethnic ties to make class-based demands for full economic and political enfranchisement.[40] TERA publicity could continue to claim that "[a]s time has gone on, personnel and terminology have changed," with "caseworkers" succeeding "investigators," but the reality seems to been more rhetorical than material; any change in role was limited to the supervisory staff and had little effect on the large numbers of people who did most of the work with relief recipients.[41]

The relatively modest social backgrounds of recruits coincided with the distinctly proletarian and bureaucratic work environment they encountered. Historically, complaints of inadequate funds and understaffed offices were familiar in social work, but they took on new meaning in these makeshift facilities beset by lines of desperate people, many of whom had never faced such needs. Relief offices were poorly equipped, frequently lacking necessary furniture and supplies. Rooms were open and overcrowded, making it impossible to provide private counseling.[42] Abe Flaxer, the man who would organize and lead the public welfare trade union, remembered his work as an "investigator" in the ERB around 1934 as decidedly proletarian:

> [The office] . . . had none of the usual accoutrements associated with white collar and professional work. No desks, no chairs, no paper, no paper clips, no files, no secretaries, and was supervised by a rudimentary chain of command. Workers performed their duties twenty to a table, ten on each side. If a worker had the foresight to scrounge a wooden box from his neighborhood grocer or fruit vendor, he or she would sit at the table; otherwise, the worker would do the job standing up. One phone to each table—you had to fight for it. Workers brought their own paper, pens, pencils, paper clips, notebooks. Tempers flared at the loss of a paper clip. To add to the general confusion was the bedlam generated by clients who crowded the premises, shouting for attention.[43]

On the heels of his election, President Franklin Roosevelt modeled his Federal Employment Relief Administration on his New York State program, but the infusion of federal funds did not herald a dramatic improvement in the conditions facing public welfare workers. Pressures on legislators from clients for expanded services met equal pressures from business interests to contain costs. First under the auspices of the Civil Works Administration and later under the Works Progress Administration, federal monies made work relief the cornerstone of public welfare.[44] The singular and contradictory priority given to both relief and cost containment quickly reduced public welfare casework to the policing of eligibility—to patrolling the boundaries of class—and stripped it of higher pretensions. To be sure, to give status to the relief effort, the city's new "reform" mayor, Fiorello H. La Guardia, enlisted veteran social workers with administrative experience and professional prestige. William Hodson was appointed commissioner of public welfare, and Charlotte Carr was induced to take a leave of absence from Hull House to assume the executive directorship of New York City's ERB. But in practice, heavy work loads curtailed "treatment." Social work leaders generally agreed that in order to provide adequate service, social workers should have less than thirty-five cases in the private agencies and sixty in public welfare, but a 1938 study by the American Public Welfare Association found that caseloads for 50 percent of public welfare caseworkers ranged from 100 to 130 cases. Moreover, a breakdown of their daily routine found that paperwork and travel consumed most of caseworkers' time; only about one-third of their day was spent actually meeting with clients.[45]

The Federal Employment Relief Administration shifted the financial burden to the federal government, but for social workers functioning as relief investigators, that only meant they had to deal with an additional layer of regulations on top of the already complicated patchwork of state and city regulations. Unclear lines of authority between old and new agencies further confused the administration of relief. For instance, before the development of the TERA, private agencies had struggled to provide financial assistance. But public welfare also antedated the New Deal, so municipal departments often found themselves providing the same services as those offered by the ERBs. In New York City, for example, the DPW and the ERB coexisted, often uneasily, until they were combined in June 1938 into the DW. When the TERA gave the DPW responsibility and funds for the homeless in 1934, jobs were at stake. ERB employees were paid from work relief; DPW employees were on the city payroll.[46] Not surprisingly, a New York State report evaluating New Deal era relief found "that lack of cooperation between public and private agencies seriously impaired the effective distribution of relief in a number of cities."[47]

Complicating the problem of dispensing relief out of austere and chaotic offices with unclear lines of responsibility was the constant political pressure on relief workers to limit allocations. Providing relief was the emergency need; many political opponents of welfare believed that "treatment" was a luxury and, in any case, not the sort of work the recruits had the experience to perform. Instead, the DPW expected public assistance investigators to certify the needs of each applicant and the applicant's eligibility as a resident of New York State and bona fide unemployed or homeless person.[48] For supervisors reared in the tradition of "objective" social work and administrators wary of taxpayer rebellion, the tendency of relief investigators, themselves employed on work relief, to identify with clients was worrisome. An internal DPW survey of caseloads laid out the "principles" of social work within public welfare: "The policy of the Bureau in respect to eligibility must be reemphasized" and "[c]asework is properly applied to enlist the understanding and cooperation of the client." Moreover, such casework was not to "distract the investigator's attention from factors of eligibility"; it was "not . . . to deal with personal and family problems" "nor absorb a substantial amount of time."[49]

Although politicians and agency administrators often charged both the private and the public sector with politicizing relief and its proper administration, the problem was most acute in the latter. The question of who spoke for the "public" and the rules of worker responsibility to the public had yet to be resolved, and any efforts by social workers and legislators to do so would take place under the intense political glare of taxpayers and relief clients, constituencies that overlapped but often had different needs.

The near obsession with eligibility reflected the contested political economy in which welfare workers had to function; indeed, a hostile political environment would riddle the entire history of welfare. As important, to the extent that the elevated political register compromised social workers' sympathies for the poor, it generated a kind of schizophrenia in their class identity. As "workers," they recognized their kinship with those on relief; as "professionals," they claimed a middle-class standing akin to that of their bosses.

An exchange between domestic relations court judge Herbert A. O'Brien and Commissioner Hodson in 1939 over "proper" social service work in the public sector illuminates the impossible tension within welfare over service and efficiency that social workers faced. Noting that the DW made supplicants feel like "chiselers," Judge O'Brien criticized its procedures as "a sort of witch hunt for impostors rather than distributing relief to the unfortunate poor." O'Brien's conclusion returned to the question of social worker identity: "The grace of charity has been perverted into a science practiced by so-called social workers."[50]

Hodson's response, emphasizing the need for jobs, not relief, and fiscal prudence, would become the semiofficial conservative mantra in subsequent years. Careful investigation of each applicant was a necessity, he explained, "because about half our applicants are not eligible when they apply." Whether or not this ratio had become a presumptive quota under which investigators narrowed the pool of applicants is not clear, but Hodson fell back on the unverifiable (and not quite to the point) comparative claim that New York City's public assistance program took "better care of our people . . . than any other community in the country." "Nobody," he ended, "can make relief an acceptable substitute for the independence of a job and wages."[51]

The Hodson-O'Brien critique of social service policy was only the tip of the iceberg; daily, scores of citizens sent letters complaining about the DW to Mayor La Guardia or Commissioner Hodson. No one felt well served: writers complained of either inadequate aid or excessive spending, or they alleged favoritism or prejudice by relief officers, usually toward some ethnic group. In one instance, for example, a group of World War I veterans forwarded a description of thirteen cases of "improper consideration on the part of those responsible for the Welfare of people." Contrast this, however, with the demand from "A Fellow Citizen" that "definite economies . . . can and should be made at once." Speaking "in the Tax Payer's interest," the writer urged that salaries be lowered, that high-priced caseworkers be fired in favor of "seasoned E.R.B. Workers," and that the mayor and the executive director of the agency, Charlotte Carr, "rid the E.R.B. of all active communists."[52]

Discrimination and ethnic politics complicated both stories of relief and the work of investigators. For example, a 1935 complaint from the J. C. Barbosa Republican Club detailed twenty-one cases of discrimination by relief investigators against Puerto Ricans in East Harlem. The itemized list of grievances from the club reported that the DPW's promise to reopen the case of Pauline Mateo of

62 East 105th Street had remained unfulfilled; the case of Antonio Castagnet of 65 East 103rd Street had been "viciously closed"; and that of Angel Zenaido of 123 East 110th Street had been closed even though the family had "no means of support." Investigating each case, the DPW found complicated stories of miscommunication and abuses on the part of both beleaguered relief investigators and hard-pressed poor families. According to the DPW, Mateo's case had been closed because of the family's "refusal" to explain where they had gotten the money to permit the mother to visit Puerto Rico in June 1934 or to provide the name of the employer who supplied them with home work. Without that information, their case would remain closed. In the case of Castagnet, however, relief was resumed. The suspension had occurred, explained the DPW, because Castagnet had missed appointments with the investigator, "who later was threatened by Mr. Castagnet on the street." And, finally, the DPW concluded that Zenaido's case would remain closed until "the suspicion of concealed resources and income" was cleared up. Zenaido had been on relief for two years until "it was discovered [the] client had earned sufficient money playing 'numbers' to purchase two cars, (Ownership verified) . . . new furniture, and [maintain] . . . a standard of living much higher than possible on Home Relief allowance." Summing up, the club's president, Herman Figueroa, alleged that "[t]he clients poor conditions, and the defective knowledge of the language . . . serve to these investigators as the principal incentive to act arbitrarily in the performance of their duties."[53]

It is difficult to assess the legitimacy, meaning, or cause of these complaints. The DPW immediately reinstituted relief in about half of the cases but, in almost every case, explained the problem as one of changing circumstances or lack of information. Racial and ethnic discrimination, however, were neither new to New York City nor unique to the DPW and undoubtedly help explain some of these problems. But generally social workers, it must be remembered, provided many of the most progressive voices against discrimination. Rather, procedural injunctions imposed by legislators and enforced by administrators that focused on eligibility and cost containment constrained the day-to-day work of relief workers. Taxpayers and the DPW justified these constraints as efforts to ensure that limited funds went to those most in need and deserving, but such relief politics also shaped the behavior and perception of the social worker. In fact, with its focus on eligibility, the "taxpayer public" helped create the image of the hardhearted social worker feared and despised by the relief public. Indeed, in the moral lexicon of New Deal social policy, work relief was preferable to a "handout." In accord with the Victorian principle of "less eligibility," investigators were expected to make sure that aid did not undercut private sector employment. The level of support was not to be determined by family need but by private labor market demands. The "wage" was to be more than the dole but less than market wages in order to encourage low-wage alternatives for industry. Accordingly, the HRB expected relief workers to monitor living standards closely and comply with carefully delineated federal and state regulations. Hearkening back to social workers' own professionalizing injunctions, the HRB required that, above all, they were not to let their "personal, subjective" views of a living wage or client demands interfere with their judgment.

Welfare politics, however, alienated relief workers at least as much from carping politicians and administrators as from the poor, as the fragile security of their own wages made them acutely aware of the problems their recipients faced. Not only had many come off the dole themselves to work in the ERB, but across the country, social workers had found their wages reduced from 6 to 33.3 percent in 1933.[54] In addition, they encountered extraordinarily austere working conditions. Their response to these conditions took two forms that shaped their occupational identity as professional workers: they identified with clients, and they unionized.

The history of the unionization of New York City's public sector social workers remains largely untold, although historians and union organizer Abe Flaxer, in his memoir, have begun to tell some of the tale.[55] It is a dramatic story of intrigue, struggle, and conflict whose full telling is both beyond the scope of this study and deserving of a narrative of its own. In brief, a TERA employees' association formed in September 1933 and, after a series of four meetings in December, grew to a thousand-member organization, the Home Relief Bureau Employees Association. The fledgling organization's immediate success in winning pay raises for relief workers in January 1934 also won it a large following, and by midyear, its 2,500 members represented approximately half of all HRB employees. Flaxer, who previously had organized teachers during lunch meetings, found his efforts at organization frustrated by the dispersed work of social workers, who often ate lunch while traveling between clients, and he turned to those he knew to be well prepared to provide discipline and an organizing apparatus: the Communist Party.[56]

Chaotic work conditions provided sufficient incentive for relief workers to unionize, and the union quickly made important gains for its members. As executive director of the HRB, Charlotte Carr had moved to stabilize working conditions and relief services, and to reflect its own more permanent status, the Home Relief Bureau Employees Association changed its name to the Association of Workers in Public Relief Agencies (AWPRA). By the end of 1935, the AWPRA had celebrated two important victories: on October 29, 1935, the HRB signed a collective-bargaining agreement with the AWPRA, and that was followed by the HRB's adoption of civil service reform to provide social service workers with job security. By the end of 1936, the New York City union had become the strongest, most powerful local in a national union of public agency relief workers. Flaxer led the 6,000-member union into an affiliation with the AFL in a new nationwide organization of public employees, the American Federation of State, County, and Municipal Employees (AFSCME). Flaxer describes the tie with the AFL as a shotgun wedding, however, arranged through the intervention of Congressman Vito Marcantonio. Indeed, the AFL had ample reasons to be a reluctant host to this upstart "red" industrywide union that included clerical and maintenance workers. So, when the CIO formed the next year, public service workers moved into a more hospitable home under its industrial roof. By June 1938, Local 1 of the New York City public welfare employees constituted the largest and most powerful of twenty-eight welfare locals, with 8,500 members across the country in the SCMWA.[57]

As agents of the state, however, relief workers labored in a new and intensely politicized world governed by public sector financing. With the rise of collective bargaining in social work, these social service workers would have to negotiate in a public arena in which the rules of arbitration and the boundaries between fiscal and administrative authority lay in some indeterminate space between legislative assemblies and agency executive suites. With whom was a public worker to negotiate, and who had responsibility for any agreements? Private industry won its Magna Carta in New Deal labor legislation, but the law neither gave public service workers the right to organize nor required legislators to recognize or bargain with them. Legislators argued that public workers had a unique obligation to serve the "public"; as the terminology powerfully suggests, they were "civil servants," expected to serve and be servile. Wisconsin was the sole state to provide collective-bargaining rights for public workers before 1960.[58] Moreover, as both trade unionists and service workers, they confronted a personal dilemma that agency executives and public officials were always ready to throw in their face: as trade unionists, the ultimate weapon of defense was the strike, but the professional ethos of service workers labeled such action as irresponsible. A New York City administrator, for example, criticized a 1935 work stoppage in the HRB by equating relief workers' "duty" with that of firemen: "Our New York City firemen are not built that way [to leave a fire in order to attend a rally], nor trained that way. Nor could any similar situation be remotely imagined in any other group of our Civil Service employees."[59] Indeed, New York City politicians had good reason to proffer such an expectation of obedient service workers, since they periodically had to send police to quell protests by clients and relief workers at welfare centers. Thus, just as welfare clients fought to determine their rights and social entitlements, different service workers struggled over their rights as workers versus their responsibilities to the clients they served.

Social workers, then, found themselves positioned ambiguously between many publics. Legislators, taxpayers, and the police, each of which had multiple voices, made up one set of publics. Clients and the "working class," both broadly filtered through a Marxist lens as the solidarity of all employees in the "welfare industry," were other publics with which left-wing industrial trade unionists shared an identity. As the organizer of Chicago's public sector workers, Joseph Levy, explained, trade union principles broke the illusory professional nexus that had seemed to tie social workers to their administrative brethren: "The new approach to the problem begins with a recognition that the social worker is in an employee relationship to the Board of Trustees or to the State Legislature as the case may be."[60] This new sense of themselves as dependent wage laborers in an adversarial relationship with "bosses" was as important as the rank-and-file social workers' new commitment to "organizations of professional workers with a 'worker' slant." This "slant" meant solidarity with not only other industrial workers but all workers, whether employed or unemployed. That is, it meant solidarity with clients and the belief that, in advocating both with and for them, social workers advocated for themselves. Of course, since relief investigators and clients often changed hats, especially in the early years of the depression, this was not such a foreign notion. So, in this scenario, the "rights" of social workers and those of clients overlapped, and it was a small step to move from welfare rights to the most radical demand of the Rank-and-Filers, "client control."[61]

The Politics of New Deal Social Service in the Public Sector: Two Cases

The state, however, was not monolithic. Even as social workers might contest state social policy that hamstrung them and their clients, relief workers were themselves one of several agents of the state with whom the poor had to deal. Thus relief workers might see themselves in alliance with those in need, but if clients did not agree with workers' determination of their cases, social worker assertions of class solidarity meant little: to such dissatisfied claimants, relief workers were a class "other" whose opinion was to be challenged with an appeal to other state representatives, such as the mayor, a council member, or a supervisor.

Two controversies, one in New York City and the other in Denver, Colorado, illustrate the range and complexity of state policy and how political struggles among the state's many and varied players shaped social worker class identity. In New York City, for instance, Roosevelt and then La Guardia had helped create models for welfare, whereas in Denver, efforts to develop the New Deal welfare state met a hostile political reception. Even at these contrasting regional extremes, however, the heated politics of New Deal social service gave a proletarian cast to a new social worker occupational identity in the public sector. Neither the welfare state nor the union was able to gain a firm foothold in conservative states such as Colorado, but the union movement and the proletarian identity it fostered nonetheless shaped the professional discourse about appropriate social service and social worker identity there. As a subject of national interest, the trade union movement, especially in the left-wing perspective, gave new precedence to social workers' identity as workers. The national circulation of magazines such as *Social Work Today* and *Survey*, even to western outposts of social service, shifted the axis of debate in small but significant ways, as executives, supervisors, and board members, previously thought of as professional colleagues with shared social agendas, now were recast as "employers," as a dominant class "other." In this movement, New York City workers led the way, especially those who worked for the DPW and in the Jewish private agencies, but as the following two cases illustrate, new politically charged class, ethnic, and racial concerns reverberated through virtually every major urban center.[62]

New York City: The Sidonia Dawson Case

The social worker grievance case that received the most publicity during this decade was that of Sidonia Dawson, a supervisory aide in Precinct 18 of the HRB office at 519 West Forty-fourth Street. Dawson was discharged on October 4, 1934, for, according to her supervisor, "activities both inside and outside of the Precinct office during the past week."[63] There was surprisingly little disagreement about whether or not she was involved in these activities; rather, the DPW and the AASW Executive Committee that reviewed the case disagreed with the Rank-and-Filers and others who supported Dawson over their appropriateness. Dawson's offending activities, it seems, involved crossing some unstated line between radical activism and reform advocacy. Dawson, who had organized the HRB Employees Association for her precinct, was now chairman of its Grievance Committee. The historian Leslie Alexander has also noted that Dawson was an African American, although her race is never mentioned in the many full accounts of this case. Although this is an extraordinary omission, it may help explain why the case became a cause célèbre for the Rank-and-File Movement, and it demonstrates how class rather than racial issues dominated the movement's agenda.[64]

All agreed to certain "facts" about the case. Conditions at the precinct office were deplorable: the office was "overcrowded, badly ventilated, [and] miserably placed in a corner of a public school." Upon arriving at the center, applicants took a number and filled out their applications while waiting in the schoolyard for their number to be called. One of the "guards" then took them up the fire escape to be interviewed. Delegates from the Workers Unemployment Union, the Single Women's Unemployment League, and the Unemployed Workers Council—organizations often mobilized by militants in the Communist Party— regularly sought meetings with supervisors at the office to advance welfare rights and their own political image, and the precinct had been the scene of a "series of disturbances." But on September 27, when the controversy involving Sidonia Dawson erupted, specific problems exacerbated this highly politicized and chaotic atmosphere.[65]

First, the supervisor had recently resigned and the office had temporarily been placed under the charge of Florence Elsey, an inexperienced assistant. Second, a woman client had struck a staff member and left the office in a "highly hysterical and excited condition." Into this office, according to the report of an AASW special committee appointed to investigate Dawson's complaint, "supercharged with nervousness and excitement," came a delegation from the Unemployed Workers Council to lay unspecified complaints before acting supervisor Elsey. When the doorman detained the delegation members, they rushed past him into the crowded reception room. Elsey, fearing trouble, then called the police.

At this point, accounts differ. Elsey alleged that the delegation's leader punched one of the policemen; Dawson claimed that the "confusion" arose only after the police "violently seized" the leader. In any case, the delegation members were forcibly ejected, their twenty-year-old leader, Barney Oster, suffering a head wound "so that blood was flowing," and several arrests were made. Dawson, visibly upset at the police's behavior, asked them to desist and leave the premises.

The day's altercation had ended but not Dawson's dispute with Elsey's handling of the matter. The next morning, a flyer entitled "Is the Police Department Running Precinct 18?" appeared on the desks of all office employees. The text accused the supervisor of discriminating against the Unemployed Workers Council representative although she had "treated the hysterical woman as a social service case." Dawson admitted being a member of the committee that had produced the flyer. Then, at a rally later that evening to protest the earlier firing of a Precinct 18 bookkeeper, Dawson recounted the previous day's events and denounced the acting supervisor as callous and indifferent, stating that "if she had summoned the police she should be discharged."[66]

The AASW special committee found that the acting supervisor had fired Dawson for behavior "unbecoming . . . a staff member in a supervisory capacity." The supervisor insisted that she did care about Dawson's complaint of police brutality; Dawson's offense, she averred, was "to make statements about her immediate superior at a public meeting."[67] The judgment of the Executive Committee of the New York City chapter of the AASW, however, was more politically pointed, but it reflected the professional association's equivocal posture as more managerially placed social workers. The AASW opposed the use of police in relief work but recognized the need for order; it advanced the importance of welfare reform but warned against the "destruction of the relief machinery."

Most important to Dawson personally, the AASW, as was its custom, claimed to offer "no final conclusion." Dawson's dismissal remained intact. Moreover, the Executive Committee's report took care to highlight the dangerous line the professional worker had to walk. Dawson, the report noted, had adopted "provocative tactics embarrassing to the administration"; she had failed to follow proper channels, meaning the personnel practices and arbitration machinery that were the cornerstones of AASW policy goals. Most important, to the Executive Committee and many of the politicians and executives to whom it appealed, Dawson had crossed class lines by identifying with clients. The agency "bosses" rather than the clients had become the "other" that determined her primary identity. "A fighting strategy" of social workers was fine as long as it did not involve a fundamental challenge to an "orderly" system of relief—in this case, either from a hostile delegation or from a disrespectful public speech. "[G]enuine concern" for clients was admirable, but "over-identification with the client as against the agency and harassing tactics generally . . . seem to us an unfortunate expression of a fine motive."[68]

Denver, Colorado: Public Relief in an Antiwelfare State

"The county situation here is entirely different from that of New York," complained Blanche Ferguson, the director of the Denver chapter of the AASW, to Walter West in June 1933. Fifteen thousand people were in need of relief, but a shortage of trained staff and monies had reduced service to the point where workers averaged 400–500 cases a month.[69] The opposition to Colorado's system of relief from two groups made the western state's situation different. Colorado antiwelfare politicians, in contrast to the New York case, controlled the state legislature, permitting a conservative state relief committee to block the use of federal funds for administrative purposes. As a result, relief work in Colorado had been slowed to a trickle. Second, private social workers, including many of the top officials in the local AASW, opposed the use of untrained workers or volunteers to take up the slack. For social workers seeking to establish social service and the middle-class status that would secure their position in it, this hostile political climate was familiar. The professional social worker's fight against charity workers who were reluctant to concede that the depression had changed the conditions of social work had been largely won in East Coast and midwestern cities years earlier.

The division within the Denver social work community focused on a conflict between the acting administrator of state relief, Jesse Lummis, and the director of City Charities, Eunice Robinson. Profound political differences separating the two women had grown into a personal feud, no doubt intensified by the depth of feeling each had about the social and professional stakes at issue. Ironically, whereas class had been mapped onto race in the case of Sidonia Dawson, Robinson and "her older [charity] workers" mapped race onto class in the Colorado case. Ferguson, who acknowledged sympathy with Lummis (with whom she played golf), recounted the explicit race bias she had heard Robinson voice against Colorado's poor migrant Mexican workers: "Miss Robinson has taken the stand that the Mexicans who are offered beet contracts and don't take them shall be cut off the charity list, and some families involving forty people have been so treated." Robinson ignored the failure of the beet companies to provide money to the farmers and, in turn, the inadequate wages the farmers paid the Mexicans, Ferguson explained. Rather, she and her "older" colleagues complained of people who "mooched" off of relief and asserted that "people would have gotten along without so much relief if federal money had not been available." Never discussed in the New York City case, race and xenophobia were right up front in Denver's antiwelfare discourse.[70]

Lummis's efforts to implement a substantive welfare program in a state that had virtually no administrative welfare apparatus further offended the older charity workers' sense of professionalism. Finding no social work organization in fifty-eight of Colorado's sixty-three counties in mid-1933 and lacking federal funds, Lummis began to use volunteers and proposed to train new recruits, much as had been done elsewhere. The action that became a symbol of opposition to Lummis, however, was her appointment of Celeste M. Post, a Philadelphia social worker, to the Colorado Relief Committee as a field caseworker. The hiring of Post was particularly infuriating to Lummis's opponents on two counts: first, they thought Post's appointment merely represented an effort by Lummis to undermine charges that she was not hiring trained workers, and second, although Post had previously worked under Lummis at the Denver Tuberculosis Society, she was considered merely another foreign interloper, albeit not "Mexican."[71]

Lummis's days as acting administrator were numbered since she had become a lightning rod for powerful conservative opposition to the development of welfare in Denver. Her opponents, however, were not just male politicians; an older generation of professional women, who were increasingly an embattled minority in social service, led the attack against her. In the AASW, the local president described Lummis's enemies as a "small group" to Post, they were a "small group of social work executives who are most active in opposing anything approaching decent professional standards." Although not the main body of the local chapter, Post noted, the "group largely composes the executive committee of the Denver Chapter."[72]

The virulence with which this older generation attacked Lummis exposed the fragility of their identity as professional women in the topsy-turvy days of early relief. Such women merely mapped their xenophobia onto anxieties about the identity of the social worker, about who would control entry into social service work and who was to be considered a bona fide social worker. In Colorado, too, women mobilized to shape the welfare state, but here elite conservative women tried to resurrect the nineteenth-century image of sacred womanhood as an alternative model of relief. Thus, in June 1933 the Colorado Federation of Women's Clubs voiced opposition to Post's appointment and demanded that "local labor" get job preference. Local unemployment would be reason enough to make such a demand, but these women had a more personal agenda. Although they took the rhetorical "high road" in insisting that women had to address problems of war and poverty, in fact, their vision was of an idealized past of sturdy individuals. As a sympathetic newspaper account described them, "They are women who keep the home fires burning, who organize relief without benefit of [the] Reconstruction Finance Corporation when such relief is necessary, who believe in education, in religion, in morality—in America and Colorado."[73]

The majority of Colorado state legislators seemed to share such conservative views, but although they won the battle against Lummis and made several other efforts to derail relief programs, ultimately they lost the war against the welfare state. Legislators, expressing their own xenophobia, passed a law establishing a Civil Service Commission that required state residence. Then the governor tried his best to stifle relief, too, by withholding federal funds from thirty-eight counties that had refused to collect a controversial automobile tax he had imposed.[74] But finally, the federal government, having already flexed its activist muscles in the elaboration of the New Deal, intervened. Benjamin Glasberg, regional director of federal relief for five western states, invited Elizabeth Kletzsch, a Milwaukee social worker, to take over Denver's entire program of direct relief, including that of the local charities. Lummis had resigned, but Kletzsch's appointment must have been another of Robinson's and her "older workers'" worst nightmares. Kletzsch was not just a "foreigner" but a suspect Jewish one at that. Moreover, forty-six private agencies would continue their social work with Community Chest funds, but Kletzsch would have direct relief immediately transferred to the new city welfare program. As of April 1, 1934, Robinson's agency and three other private charities would no longer receive federal relief funds. Robinson was out of business.[75] Symbolically, the professional woman had ceded her place to the new relief army of professional workers.

five

The Professional Worker in the Private Sector

The coming of the semiwelfare state[1] and its assumption of major responsibility for public assistance required private sector social workers to reinvent themselves. To be sure, depression era cutbacks compelled workers in both spheres to reorient their occupational identity, but the situation of private sector caseworkers differed in important ways. To justify both their funding and their role, caseworkers in the private sector increasingly had to distinguish their work from that of public sector workers as less degraded and more "professional" labor that was in the therapeutic avant-garde. From this era forward, policymakers and social workers would make the material advantages of working conditions in the private agencies and the claims of superior social work treatment there an increasingly important component of social workers' professional identity and status. Indeed, the contrast with Spartan relief offices with heavy caseloads was easily visible and could be quantified. Other aspects, like the quality and degree of counseling, were harder to measure. But the salient point was that social workers in private agencies believed their work was of higher quality—more "advanced"—and private agencies felt increasing pressure to justify their work as such. In doing so, private sector social workers played a key role in helping sustain the beleaguered professional side of their double identity through the depression.

Possibly no agency in the United States in the 1930s better exemplifies the dilemma represented by the seeming oxymoron of the professional worker than New York City's JBG. As a birthplace of the Rank-and-File Movement, the JBG not only contained one of the most radical social worker contingents in the nation but by the early 1930s had already begun to establish its reputation as perhaps the leading center of advanced psychiatric social work. As a psychiatric center, the agency became a major site of an important debate within social work about the value of the psychiatric model—the core of its claim to a professional expertise. This debate also raised questions—even if only implicitly—about the relationship of social work practice to feminism and labor. Moreover, as a site inhabited by radical social workers, the JBG re-engaged the place of ethnic, religious, and radical identities in the history of private philanthropy. And, finally, as an agent of both a radical and a psychiatric center, the JBG's female social worker was often prolabor and a very professional example of the professional woman, and as we saw in chapter 4, social workers had to reconcile countervailing tensions between the two. Thus, by exploring the history of the JBG, this chapter examines how the tension between professionalism and trade unionism played out within the identity of the middle-class worker in its most heightened form. It also looks at the extent to which what it meant to be a woman, a Jew, and a radical continued to complicate professional middle-class identity. First, however, we turn to the general picture in New Deal private agencies to see how depression era developments affected working conditions there and impinged on social workers' professional ambitions.

The Private Sector

Working conditions in New Deal private agencies differed from those in public welfare primarily in the degree of deterioration. Charity workers did not encounter the extremes of disorganization, makeshift facilities, or impersonal bureaucracy that beset public welfare, but their formal training in schools of social work and prior experience in the agencies heightened their awareness of how much conditions had deteriorated. Wage cutbacks and increased workloads gave them a yardstick against which to measure their complaints and energized their protest, not surprisingly, often making them leaders of the nascent trade union movement in social work.

Public and private agency work environments were by no means totally removed from each other, however. Social workers from private agencies helped staff early welfare offices and train new investigators. In addition, many charity workers happily moved into the public sector. Some did so because of financial opportunities or the prospect of exciting new challenges, and others took on public welfare work as a political choice, seeing welfare as a state obligation that did not carry the paternalistic baggage of charity. A well-known example of someone who moved between the private and public sector was Charlotte Carr, who as noted previously took a leave from Hull House to lead New York City's HRB. Countless less-famous others, however, joined Carr. Marsha Treitman, for instance, left United Jewish Aid of Brooklyn in 1935 to become a supervisor of field investigators in the HRB. Scornful of the "pretense" and patronizing attitudes of private charity, Treitman found a home in the DW and continued to supervise caseworkers and consult on casework until her retirement in 1972.[2]

As Denver City Charities workers discovered, even the many social workers who remained in the private agencies found themselves affected by the development of massive state and federal relief programs. The coming of the depression and the rise of the New Deal welfare state created both a financial crisis and an identity crisis for private social work agencies. In the years following the crash, many local government agencies tried to provide some relief. By 1932, lower tax revenues and increased demands bankrupted many municipalities.[3] Private agencies increasingly attempted to share the burden of direct relief, but historically they had preferred to provide service rather than direct aid and they did not always find it easy to make the shift. The transfer of responsibility for administering relief to public welfare (and the funds to do the job), however, compelled private agencies to rethink their mission and program. The depression had also reduced support from agency benefactors. So, deprived of both funds and what had become their central functions, everyone associated with the private agencies sought to redefine their sense of purpose and the meaning of the work they could do, and then they set out to convince the "public"—from state agencies with research funds to private donors—of its importance.

The period of excitement surrounding the rise of welfare was not an auspicious time for private agency workers to have to reestablish their claim to relevance. Nonetheless, social workers could turn to a legacy of developments in "professional techniques." Casework and psychiatric social work often amounted to little more than interviewing and counseling in practice and were limited to the major northeastern cities, but these "techniques" offered the basis for agencies to claim that they provided a unique, advanced service.[4] But private agencies' assertions of their advanced position as leaders and innovators in social work also put them in an ambiguous political position. Private agency executives tended to downplay or denigrate outright public assistance. Such attitudes, however, contradicted their desire to encourage increased state funding of social welfare programs, of which they hoped to get a share to subsidize their own work. At the same time, the need to justify their work led private sector agencies to exaggerate differences between their services and those offered by public assistance. Although some charity work shifted to direct relief after 1929, after 1933 private agencies reverted almost completely to casework. The DPW did family and child casework, too, but its larger caseloads and meager facilities made it an easy target of criticism.

The professional ethos in which trained social workers had been steeped made them particularly sensitive to deteriorating working conditions in the private agencies where they were often employed. This heightened awareness also lay at the center of their growing class confusion: Was their class identity that of the worker or that of the professional, and would it be realized through labor (the union) or therapy (the professional "technique")? At the same time that the private sector social work community strove to define itself as a therapeutic avant-garde, part of the community organized itself as a labor vanguard. Thus, private agency social workers experienced most directly the tensions between the aspirations of a professional identity and those of a trade union identity, and few were better positioned to voice their entwined meanings than the JBG's social workers, who led both the Rank-and-File trade union and psychiatric advances in social work.

The JBG and the Therapeutic Debate

Although the JBG had employed a psychiatrist since 1921, its reputation as the leading psychiatric agency in the country probably dates from the summer of 1932, when John Slawson became its executive director. A renowned psychiatrist, Slawson quickly moved to make psychiatric training the hallmark of agency treatment and the JBG the center of advanced psychiatric training. In his 1932 annual report as president of the Board of Directors of the JBG, George Z. Medalie expressed the agency's public line on the development of public sector social work: it was not a problem but an opportunity to place the JBG, as a "private instrument dedicated to the treatment and prevention of delinquency . . . in the vanguard in the field of behavior maladjustment." In contrast to public agencies, declared Medalie, private organizations such as the JBG had "a unique responsibility" and institutional advantages with which to fulfill it: in his view, they could be "more flexible," they could experiment with new methods and treatment, and, operating outside the public arena, they could be an "impartial nonpolitical instrument" for studying institutions such as the courts.[5]

As the new executive director, Slawson mobilized to realize the JBG's "unique responsibility." A new plan for the organization of the agency was put into effect. The "case reader," apparently the job most involved in client treatment, was to be "preferably a worker trained in psychiatric social work."[6] Slawson also promptly hired two psychiatric social workers from the mental hygiene clinic in Newark as the new directors of casework: Elizabeth Dexter and, as her assistant, Helen Taussig.[7]

One of the approximately forty caseworkers at the JBG during those years, Sophie Grossman, remembered the pervasive headiness of the new fascination with psychiatry. Grossman had been lured to New York City in 1929 from Baltimore by psychiatric casework supervisor Mary Palevsky and the promise of "social opportunities" and "advanced training." At the time, Palevsky worked at Brooklyn's Jewish Social Service Bureau, a sister agency to the JBG. By 1932, she had followed Palevsky to the JBG. Grossman quickly found herself immersed in all the vogue psychiatric venues. She took courses part-time at the New York School of Social Work; she attended Otto Rank's seminar at the JFS; she heard Karen Horney speak at the New School for Social Research; and she discussed cases with Nathan Ackerman, one of the leading figures in family and child psychiatry, after he joined the JBG. She remembered her experiences as "thrilling." Grossman found the new "awareness" of the totally new concepts of "countertransference" and "of one's own reactions to clients" enormously stimulating and captivating. She recalled that people used expressions like "'meaningful behavior.' I'd never heard people talk that way. It was beautiful." She knew she "wanted to be able to think that way."[8]

But besides being thrilling, the field of psychiatric social work was contentious, with competing theories about treatment deeply dividing groups of workers. The heat of the exchanges, of course, only reflected the workers' sense of the discipline's importance. In social work, the major disagreement was between the "functionalists" and the "diagnostics," and people like Grossman remembered daily debates at lunch about the efficacy of each method.

The fundamental difference between the diagnostic or Freudian school and the functional or Rankian school centered on their respective attitudes toward the therapist's and the agency's relationship to the client. The diagnostic school was in the psychiatric mainstream. Following the Freudian tradition, diagnostic treatment was open-ended, interventionist, and psychiatric, treating "total personality" and emphasizing socially accepted norms. In contrast, the functional school was based on the work of Otto Rank, a psychoanalyst and former protégé of Freud's. It considered the will "a key to . . . patient psychology." Emphasizing treatment that was closed-ended, collaborative, and practical, functionalists saw therapy as a way to help clients build their will, although they remained attentive to the limits of both willpower and the agency's functions.[9]

The psychiatric debate may have been, as social work historian John H. Ehrenreich has argued, an important struggle that was fundamentally about how social work was going to deal with "the nature of people's problems, the relation of men and women to the society and to the state, [and] the nature of the new social welfare agencies," but for the purposes of this discussion, at least one historian has suggested that the disagreement also had resonance for social workers' competing actions of class identity.[10] According to Rick Spano, the functionalist emphasis on client agency armed the Rank-and-File Movement with a social alternative to the psychiatric medical model.[11] The evidence, however, for the correspondence between either therapeutic model and a political position is not compelling. Rank's views got a hearing in the Jewish agencies and inspired lunchtime debates over the competing positions at the same time that these social workers unionized and pressed for solidarity with clients. Nowhere in the interviews, minutes, speeches, or journals, however, does anyone make the political connection. Rather, the debate over treatment remained underneath the political table rather than on it.

Thus, the essentially egalitarian diagnostic stance in the functionalist therapeutic relationship did not translate into open political positions. Still, it did involve modes of behavior and attitudes that tended to correspond with the Rank-and-File views on professionalism, trade unionism, and class. In regard to professionalism, for instance, diagnostics relied on medicine and psychiatry and positioned themselves as authorities who "treated" patients; in contrast, functionalists saw themselves as aides who "helped" clients strengthen their own will. The functionalist position on authorizing client views did overlap with debates about client identification, but it remained within the psychiatric camp; it was not Freud or Rank but the class analysis of Marx that most directly challenged the personal diagnosis of the medical model.

In the struggle by JBG social workers to define their identity in the 1930s, the class implications of functionalism probably played a greater role than gender. The same factors that opened up functionalists to charges that identifying with clients made them less professional may have contributed to a more feminist diagnosis, although not to a more egalitarian gender identity. Unfortunately, evidence of their views on gender is limited and at times contradictory, but functionalists certainly did not address "manly" proletarianism. The leading spokesperson for the functionalist school, Jesse Taft, suggests, for example, that female social workers succeeded as functionalists because they were professionals who could use their deference to advantage. She argues that women's traditional subordination to male authority makes women social workers well suited to a nonauthoritarian therapeutic relationship: "A role thus limited in the exercise of knowledge, power, and creativity seems to me to be naturally difficult for a man and particularly for a man with medical training. To become an assistant in an organic growth process comes more naturally to a woman."[12]

Although the successful functionalist social worker may have been "feminine," historian Clarke A. Chambers has suggested that their diagnosis of female clients was feminist: they rejected classical Freudian notions such as infant trauma and patriarchal models such as penis envy. Anticipating 1950s existentialism, their treatment focused on strengthening each client's will, empowering men and women to take control of their own lives. Finally, although essentialist notions of femininity and masculinity crept into the work of even social workers such as Taft, the functionalist school opposed "stereotypes of normative male and female behavior, so often denigrating to women."[13]

It is worth reiterating, however, that there is scant evidence that social workers ever made a political connection between functionalism and the Rank-and-File Movement. The democratic "style" of functionalist casework did not lead to discussions of trade unionism (or of feminism or patriarchy). Nonetheless, in its focus on a common diagnostic goal and project functionalism did encourage an identity of interests between caseworkers and clients. As Taft herself concludes, to the functionalist, the client is "not a sick person whose illness must first be classified, but a human being, like the [social] worker, asking for a specific service."[14]

The impact of psychiatric social work in the 1930s and the furor of the budding therapeutic debate must not be measured by the experience or claims of the JBG. JBG debates in the 1930s, however heated, were atypical of the profession as a whole, and this remained an era during which functionalism was still evolving.[15] In the public agencies where workers were besieged by lines of needy relief applicants, there was little time for psychiatric treatment, even if the new staff had much knowledge of it. Most probably did not. For instance, Helen Perlman, who began to teach at the New York School of Social Work in 1933, remembered that the new theories were slow to penetrate social work beyond the cities of the Northeast. As Perlman recalled, "[P]sychoanalytic theory was practically unknown in social casework *except* in the New York–Philadelphia–Boston circuit." In fact, as historians Regina G. Kunzel and Leslie B. Alexander have noted, it is important not to mistake the rhetoric of psychiatry for its operative reality; psychiatry was much less influential than social work historians and many psychiatric social workers have claimed. The commitment to psychiatry among the elite in the AASW was strong and articulate, and agencies like the JBG were at the forefront of the effort to advance it. But the JBG was the exception, not the rule.[16]

When the depression hit, another social worker in the 1930s, Theodora L. Wilson, remembered the psychiatric legacy as an obstacle as much as an advancement. Wilson recalled the words of radical labor educator A. J. Muste at the 1930 national conference: " 'The social workers have gone psychiatric while the world has gone economic.' " To Wilson, in order to engage the massive social problems of the depression, private agency workers had to be weaned away from psychiatry a view with which Rank-and-File leader Jacob Fisher agreed. Even though they were in the vanguard of the labor movement in social work, it was not until 1932 that New York City's and Brooklyn's Jewish social workers fully mobilized as a fighting trade union movement. And they did so with gusto.[17]

FJP Workers Unionize

As the depression deepened, JBG social workers faced both deteriorating working conditions and the need to prove that their work was superior to the heralded advances in public assistance. They confronted a workplace divided over the practice of therapy, the relative merits of trade unionism and professionalism, and the appropriate relationship to clients. In addition, some of the fiscal implications of the decade-long centralization began to reverberate. Basically, the problem that faced JBG workers was not unlike the problem that faced public employees or charity workers across the country who had been placed under the umbrella of consolidated social service organizations such as Catholic Charities, the Community Chest, or the FJP: Who had the power and authority to redress fiscal complaints? But in access to resources, the two sectors differed. After 1933, the relatively deep pockets and regularity of federal tax revenues contrasted with the philanthropies' dependence on the beneficence and positive disposition of private individuals. As important, the JBG and the FJP both insisted to each other and to their staffs that the agencies had fiscal autonomy, even though budgets had to be approved and funded by the FJP. Social workers, not surprisingly, found this distinction wanting, and it only increased their sense of alienation from the agencies. Executives had been colleagues of social workers themselves, often developing personal relationships with them in small offices. As executives disparaged the distinction concerning agency autonomy, social workers recast both the FJP and agency executives as more distant bosses. In this way, the ideology of the union movement and the institutional constraints fostered by consolidation provided contexts in which social workers came to view themselves and their work as akin to that of other workers, both blue-collar workers in maintenance and white-collar workers doing secretarial work, and that of clients. Thus, JBG social workers' struggle with their agency and with the FJP to win union recognition illustrates how unionization combined with professionalization in the construction of the double identity of the professional middle-class worker.

The struggle to unionize at the JBG and other FJP agencies began in 1932 and took place in three phases over the next six years. In the first phase, from 1932 to 1935, agency social workers initiated plans to unionize in order to roll back wage reductions. In doing so, they had to confront long-standing personal relationships with agency executives who had themselves once been caseworkers and ask with whom the professional worker identified.[18]

The impetus to organize at the JBG came from both inside and outside the agency. Inside the agency, social workers found many of their own friends and kinfolk forced by the depression to turn to them for help, and the shock of recognizing themselves in their clients gave many what one caseworker called a "kin kind of feeling." Helen Harris Perlman was a caseworker in Chicago's Jewish social service from 1927 until she moved to New York City to join the JFS in 1935. She recalled that when a social worker saw "middle-class people" coming for help, "you could imagine your own family or friendship group could be in those lives." The shift, she explained, "had a tremendous effect on the democratization of social work, that is, on the recognition that poverty was not always people's fault." Identifying with clients, then, made a diagnosis that blamed social conditions rather than client pathology more palatable and likely. As important, seeing clients both as middle class and in need, and not unlike themselves, blurred social workers' own class identification, further preparing the way for their double class identity. "[T]he person called 'the client' took on a new kind of dignity in our eyes," concluded Perlman.[19] New respect for clients, who were often workers and trade unionists, as people much like themselves, would, of course, make trade unionism appear more appropriate to social work.

Outside the agency, the economic collapse also created conditions that could lead social workers to protest as trade unionists. The depression put enormous pressure on budgets that were traditionally overextended to begin with, and FJP budgets felt the impact. In 1929 the FJP had been able to balance its budget only by keeping the books open two weeks in January. In 1930 it deferred its planned consolidation with the Brooklyn federation. Then, in 1931, after mortgaging its building to raise funds, the FJP imposed its first wage reduction. As we saw in chapter 3, in response, the Workers' Councils and the AFW at the JBG transformed themselves from benevolent organizations and professional discussion groups into a trade union movement. But even after the reduction, the FJP continued to have a hard time balancing its budget. By 1933, FJP leaders felt they had no alternative but to cut wages a second time.[20]

Agency reliance on the FJP for funds and the simultaneous shibboleth of "agency autonomy" constrained the ability of agency caseworkers to contest the FJP or individual agency procedures or wages. Each agency's wage package was ultimately determined by its budget allocation from the FJP, over which it had little control. Nonetheless, when it came to disputes over wages, benefits, or policies, the FJP insisted that workers were employed by the agency, not by the FJP. But at the same time, FJP trustees felt they could not permit the actions of any individual agency to undermine the power of the others. Thus, the principle of "agency autonomy" gave the FJP considerable political leverage over agencies and a convenient way to deflect worker complaints. For example, in 1933 the Jewish Social Service Association (JSSA) asked the FJP to support a raise for its caseworkers to reflect what it saw as their increased responsibilities. The JSSA had the money to fund the increase but "did not wish to do so if there was a feeling on the part of Federation that it should not do so." And, indeed, there was. Executives of the Committee for the Care of Jewish Tuberculosis, whose staff members were in close contact with JSSA caseworkers, believed that such an increase would have a "disastrous impact" on their negotiations with workers. As another agency executive explained it, executives were universally negative about the JSSA's proposal because they did not want agencies to be placed in competitive positions. Borrowing a line from big business—the world from which most trustees came—every agency would be "autonomous," but the FJP would function like a cartel. As "coordinated policy," no agency would be allowed to "undermine" the others by making separate arrangements.[21]

At the same time that social workers began to witness FJP actions that increasingly resembled those of corporate America, changes within the agencies, some directly related to comparable economizing drives in industry, conspired to further alienate social workers and encourage their unionization. New work routines were one such change. For instance, when Elizabeth Dexter reorganized treatment around psychiatric social work at the JBG in 1932, the new procedures she implemented created a high level of anxiety in the workplace that paralleled concerns at home caused by wage cuts. As relief needs mounted and created a material base for skepticism about psychiatric interventions, Dexter's new reporting procedures for supervisors challenged caseworkers' historic control of their cases. In addition to requiring that supervisors hold weekly seminars to review caseworkers' techniques and their specific cases, she asked them to play a greater role in overseeing caseworkers in order to assess their attitudes and "how they can best be dealt with."[22]

Dexter knew that her directives were treading on dangerous ground and instructed supervisors to "function not in the capacity of checking up on the worker, but in the professional capacity of a consultant." But the distinction was lost on caseworkers, who saw the issue as a source of concern about achieving professional autonomy and concern about workers' control. It had been common practice since the mid-1920s at agencies such as the JBG for caseworkers to meet weekly with supervisors as well as each other to discuss clients. But Dexter, perhaps because of the psychiatric turn these discussions had taken, had crossed some invisible line. Supervisors were now "treating" them, caseworkers claimed. Although this view might have made caseworkers more sympathetic to their clients, Dexter rooted caseworkers' complaints in their pathology; the complainers were the "insecure, incompetent" ones. By March 1934, Dexter had resigned, convinced that compromise was impossible. The new procedures were kept in place, however, although caseworkers were to be given written evaluations of their work with the opportunity to respond. The debacle, however, had created a deep split between former professional colleagues within the agency, a division that could reorient workers' sense of their class interests. As a meeting of the supervisors concluded, "[T]here is a feeling of cleavage between workers as a class and supervisors as a class . . . ; the supervisors think differently as a group on certain subjects and don't attend meetings of the Workers' Council."[23]

The proposed mergers of federations and various agencies made social workers fear not just loss of control on the job but loss of the job itself. Plans for the merger of Jewish child care agencies had been in the works since early 1931 and had been widely circulated in journals such as *Survey*. Calling for the merger of the Hebrew Orphan Asylum, the Hebrew Sheltering Guardian Society, and the

Jewish Children's Clearing Bureau in order to eliminate duplicate services, the plan also envisioned saving money by temporarily closing the Pleasantville Cottage School for troubled orphans. Combined with wage cuts, the mergers convinced AFW members of the "necessity for united action of all employees" on issues involving "common interests, our standard of living and the security of our employment."[24]

In May 1933, 475 people, mostly social workers, answered the AFW's call to arms, signing a petition asking the FJP to rescind wage cuts. The FJP also received protests from the Union of Office Workers and the Union of Technical Men at the affiliated agencies.[25] By 1935, in a dramatic assertion of its working-class identity, the AFW had taken the form of an industrial union: it spoke for maintenance, clerical, and social workers. Of the 4,000 FJP employees at the time, 800 had joined the AFW, which was especially strong among caseworkers and the poorly paid religious teachers and in the JBG, the Jewish Children's Clearing Bureau, and the ISSA.[26]

Executives were variously perplexed, concerned, outraged, and supportive of their caseworkers' rush to join the new industrial union. Many executives had been caseworkers themselves and continued to sympathize with caseworkers' plight. Such agency leaders often tried to meet worker demands and restore wage cuts. After all, aside from the justice of their demands, in order to sustain quality service it was important that agencies maintain good relations with their staffs. JBG executives in fact, were apparently among those most sympathetic to workers' demands. They managed to avoid the second wage cut imposed by many other agencies and in December 1933 asked the FJP to restore wages to the 1931 levels.[27]

Still, the pressure on executives as bosses to maintain social services with depleted resources abrogated their identification with their staffs. Even JBG executives had to be prodded by workers to support their demands. In March 1934, for instance, after the FJP provided monies to restore cuts to all workers who made under $2,000 a year, the JBG claimed that it still had a deficit and limited raises to those making under $1,650 a year. Three months later, after receiving a delegation of workers at their monthly meeting, the trustees agreed to restore the cuts as promised by the FJP. Although the trustees stated that "from a human point of view" the raise was just, their internal debate revealed that fear of losing staff members to other agencies and gender prejudice also played a part in their thinking. The JBG employed an unusual proportion of men (who were thought to deal better with delinquent boys) and shared the bias of the day that men had a unique "responsibility of supporting families."[28]

The growing Rank-and-File Movement was not placated by the partial restoration of wages and by pieties, however. Thus FJP trustees turned to one of their more prolabor representatives to put forth their case—JBG president George Z.

Medalie. Making him chair of the new Personnel Committee, the FJP trustees charged the committee to deal with the "organized demands of the workers regarding working conditions, rights to organize, vacation, etc.," and then exposed their rationale—"so that competition may be prevented between agencies."[29]

Rather than settling matters with the AFW, the formation of the Personnel Committee brought into focus what had become a nagging central problem for social workers in pursuing negotiations: Was the agency's Executive Committee or the FJP's Personnel Committee the "ultimate employer"? The FJP's Distribution Committee had refused to meet with the AFW to discuss social workers' salaries, but from the perspective of social worker and AFW president Jennie Berman, the FJP controlled budgets and assumed "an employer-employee relationship to the workers in its constituent agencies." Pressured by trustees to take a strong stand that made it clear that the FJP was not the agency workers' employer, President Solomon Lowenstein offered the standard FJP position: the FJP was an organization of agencies, not individuals, and agencies had "complete autonomy of internal administration." The FJP passed on agencies' budget requests, but, he explained, they could allocate funds as they wished.[30]

Only one trustee, Benjamin J. Buttenwieser, whose family over the years would provide several of the few prolabor voices at the FJP, dissented from this line. The FJP, he pointed out, had mandated the earlier wage cuts, and "in his opinion," that "proves that Federation itself dictated the salaries of the employees." Accusing the FJP of being "entirely too technical and insufficiently humane," he advocated that the FJP initiate direct negotiations with the workers.[31]

With the exception of Medalie, JBG director and New York City councilman Stanley M. Isaacs was the only other prolabor voice that could be counted on to disrupt the generally conservative trustees' meetings; most FJP executives and board members remained intransigent toward the union. The perspective of trustee H. G. Friedman reflected the general view that the FJP should stonewall the workers. Defending FJP budgetary authority, he argued that the association only sought to coordinate agency policies and that its funding decisions did not bind agencies to any wage policy. His advice to the FJP: be "kindly and considerate" toward workers to defuse their anger, but do "not recognize . . . a direct employer-employee relationship."[32]

Instead of defusing workers' concerns, however, the FJP's repeated insistence that it was not their employer and that consequently it would not meet with them had the opposite effect. The frustration of the overlapping memberships of the JBG Workers' Council and the AFW, who were in effect twice rejected, undoubtedly increased. Although the distinctions made by the JBG and FJP trustees may have made perfect sense to them, their constant reiteration of them to block any discussion with either the JBG Workers' Council or the AFW served only to encourage the workers to shift their identity to that of professional workers rather than professionals pure and simple. By 1934, the AFW had concluded that despite FJP protestations, the FJP was the agency workers' "ultimate employer." Moreover, now that workers had taken on the identity of professional workers, their relationship to executives and trustees had changed, becoming increasingly defined by their role as dependent wage laborers. The AFW was not permitted to meet with FJP trustees, but an AFW statement of principles read to the trustees at their January 1934 meeting both articulated the workers' new sense of class divisions and threw down the gauntlet: the AFW and FJP trustees, it explained, did not have "identical interests" and "cannot rely on the good faith of a professional relationship." If its demands were not met, it warned, it was prepared to "consider further action."[33]

Major strikes in 1935 at two FJP-affiliated hospitals, Lebanon and Beth Moses, were the centerpiece of the second phase in the union drive. These strikes, which were a turning point in worker-management relations at the FJP, highlighted the executives' major fear—the withdrawal of service and loss of ultimate control of the shop floor. The debate surrounding the strikes compelled social workers to address the one question that opponents always raised as problematic in their identity as both professionals and workers: Was striking "appropriate" behavior for a professional middle-class person?

"Further action" by workers was exactly what trustees feared, and not surprisingly, they were often the most vociferous in questioning the respectability and professionalism of striking caseworkers. New York City was a labor town, and the national strike wave of 1934 had stimulated intense organization in the city among workers across the industrial landscape. The garment shops and department stores owned by many German Jews who sat on the FJP boards were no exception. Already up to their necks in industrial action at their own businesses, the last thing they wanted was to allow labor to win a victory in the charities (with their donated monies) that they sought to deny labor in their factories.

No FJP agency better represented the promises and specter of industrial unionism than hospitals, where professional workers such as nurses and social workers worked alongside large numbers of clericals, maintenance workers, and aides. To labor, hospitals offered the opportunity to demonstrate the potential of industrial solidarity; to hospital administrators, industrial unionism undermined the professional ethic of service. Indeed, the threat of workers controlling a health facility elevated wage issues to matters of life and death. Administrators and patients and their families saw the withholding of social services from clients as a serious matter; they considered the withholding of medical services, however, a grievous and life-threatening offense. By 1935, the AFW had made inroads into the service agencies, but hospitals had remained particularly resistant to unionization. Thus, when a delegation of workers from the Hospital for Joint Diseases made its appearance at a February 7, 1935, rally of 500 AFW members, it won the largest applause of the day. As reported in the AFW newspaper, the *Bulletin*, "their presence testified that hospital workers, the most intimidated group in Federation, were at last being won."[34]

The Workers' Councils at Lebanon and Beth Moses had, in fact, been organized for months and had sought in vain to meet with hospital administrators since the spring of 1934 to discuss wages, vacation time, and the right to bargain collectively. By April 1935, although the councils had lost patience, their efforts had won them widespread support from hospital staff. By the end of April, 75 of the 110 workers at Lebanon, including social workers, maintenance staff, and nurses, had joined the AFW. Similar complaints about low wages and the lack of paid vacations, overtime, or sick leave made organizing labor easy; at Beth Moses, "[t]hey flocked into the Workers' Council which signed up 120 within the first week" of recruiting. And the swelled union ranks were angry. The "agency autonomy" line, they claimed, had been used to give them the runaround. The FJP argued that it "could not discuss any of these matters" with an AFW committee from Lebanon because it "was merely the fundraising organization for its affiliated agencies—which are autonomous." When the AFW then tried to meet with the hospital boards through the Workers' Councils, it was "told that what they could give us in the way of [wage] rescinds and increases depended on what Federation would give to them."[35]

Frustrated by months of futile attempts to discuss these matters, the hospital AFW members hoped that a two-hour work stoppage starting at three o'clock on the afternoon of Tuesday, May 14, would call public attention to the situation and put pressure on the FJP to recognize the employee-employer relationship. The Lebanon work stoppage was not the first for FJP workers, but it was the first to affect a hospital, a difference that the *World-Telegram* did not want lost on the public. When 500 workers in the city's Jewish agencies stopped work for two hours in support of the Lebanon workers, an eight-column banner headline raised fears of a public health crisis and placed responsibility squarely on labor: "Staffs at 91 Hospitals Called Out on Two-Hour Strike Today; 100,000 Sick to Be Affected by Union Order." In fact, the AFW had publicly announced that it was "leaving a skeleton staff to man the hospital so that no patient or client would suffer or be inconvenienced because of the stoppage."[36]

The two-hour work stoppage was not unfamiliar to FJP agencies, and its almost ritualized form had, in fact, become, if not accepted, tolerated by the agencies. The AFW had conducted two-hour work stoppages on several occasions during the past year in which workers from virtually every FJP agency had participated. On the whole, agency executives generally turned a blind eye to these stoppages: they tended to sympathize with staff demands and appreciated the limited duration of the strike. Moreover, the union always made sure that skeleton staffs maintained essential services. But although the Lebanon stoppage began with the same script, the hospital administrators changed their role. Lebanon's superintendent, George E. Halpern, and the president of its board, Victor Weil, had tolerated worker organization at the hospital, but they drew the line at strikes. The night before the stoppage, Halpern tried to intimidate employees by forcing them to sign a statement saying that leaving work without a supervisor's approval was tantamount to a resignation. The next day, after twenty-six employees left work at three o'clock, he had a cordon of police block their reentry. Halpern and Weil subsequently claimed that the workers had not left behind a skeleton staff, a charge that the union denied. FJP president Lowenstein, himself no supporter of the stoppage, admitted that if the union had not left behind staff members, it would have been the first time he had ever found that it had not done so. But, arguing that the strikers had jeopardized health service, Halpern notified them that they were dismissed, locked out.[37]

Four days later, a second work stoppage erupted at Brooklyn's Beth Moses Hospital over similar issues. Initially, the Beth Moses struggle paralleled that at Lebanon. Shortly after the Association of Brooklyn Federation Workers enlisted Beth Moses's staff members into a Workers' Council early in 1935, the council's Executive Committee had petitioned hospital superintendent Milton L. Dreyfuss. The demands were quite simple: regular payment on the the first of the month, overtime pay, paid vacations, and restoration of the evening meal. Within a week, however, the five committee members had been fired. The first to be fired, a social worker, reported being told by the head of the Ladies' Auxiliary that she had been "dropped for signing her name to a 'Bolshevistic and Communistic document' (the Council's program)." In response, on May 18, the Association of Brooklyn Federation Workers called for its own two-hour stoppage. In this instance, 100 workers walked out, again leaving behind a skeleton staff. By the end of the day, the Beth Moses administration had locked out all 100.[38]

Although both hospitals had locked out their striking workers, the two administrations resolved these disputes very differently, and the contrast signaled a division in the FJP over how to relate to its professional staffs as workers. The difference also taught FJP leaders an important lesson for the future of employer-employee relations. After ten weeks of picketing, the Beth Moses dispute was settled with relatively little lasting rancor and a minimum of publicity. The hospital fully reinstated all of its employees and agreed to recognize the Workers' Council. In return, the hospital won an important measure of industrial peace: the council pledged not to affiliate with any trade union, and both sides agreed to arbitrate any issues still in dispute.[39]

In contrast, the Lebanon conflict remained unresolved and continued to rankle the staff a year later. Shortly after firing the twenty-six men and women who had stopped work, Superintendent Weil hired replacement workers and settled in to outlast the union and its supporters. Subsequently, he agreed he would consider rehiring twenty-four of the dismissed workers, but only on a case-by-case basis. Ironically, not unlike the debates in social work at the time, Weil basically diagnosed the controversy as a psychological and political problem, not a social or economic one: the hospital had to rid itself of the two "agitators" he felt were responsible for the problems. The AFW would have none of this, however, refusing to allow Weil to "pick off" its leaders and break the union.[40]

Continuing their struggle, Lebanon workers found themselves the beneficiaries of considerable public support. Over $6,000 was raised to support the workers from donations and fund-raising activities such as a boat ride, a dance, a theater party, and a raffle. Over thirty organizations gave money to their cause, the largest amounts coming from the JSSA and the JBG. Powerful New York City unions such as the International Ladies Garment Workers' Union and the Amalgamated Clothing Workers also made contributions to the locked-out workers' fund. The League of Women Shoppers investigated the case and sent delegations to meet with both Lowenstein and Weil. And, most significant to FJP leaders, the Social Justice Committee of all the rabbis in New York City actively intervened with the FJP on the locked-out workers' behalf.[41]

In the short run, all of this support was of little avail. After six months on the picket line and with no sign that the Lebanon management would concede, the locked-out workers admitted defeat. They tried, however, to look for a positive side to what was a bitter result. Not only did the visibility of this struggle help integrate social service workers into the mainstream of the New Deal labor movement, but the contest had increased their awareness of themselves "as salaried employees . . . with much in common with workers' elsewhere." This was the heightened identity of the professional worker, for whom the trade union rather than the professional association was the organization of the moment. As the AFW journal, the *Bulletin*, averred with a rhetorical edge, the lockout had confirmed the industrial character of its members' work—" 'The dispensing of charity' has grown to what is 'equivalent to mass industry.' "[42]

If the defeated workers had been able to sit in on meetings of the FJP trustees, however, they would have discovered that their protracted struggle and public support had won them a political opening within the FJP administrative ranks. Negative publicity from the lockout struck fear into FJP trustees. The image of agency intransigence could hurt donations. As Medalie pointed out to FJP trustees at a closed, off-the-record meeting, the views of these "eminent rabbis" could not be ignored: "[T]he Jewish people of New York . . . regardless of whether or not they are observant, greatly respect their intelligent rabbis." The actions of no single agency in the past had so threatened to put everyone in the FJP at risk, but according to its bylaws, the FJP could not interfere with an agency's "autonomous" relations with its employees.[43] Something, Medalie warned, had to be done to bring peace to Jewish philanthropy lest any single conflict undermine its collective mission and give both the FJP and the Jewish community a "black eye."[44]

The aftermath of the bitter lockout at Lebanon Hospital initiated a third phase of worker organization at the FJP. This phase resulted in not simply union recognition but the affirmation of social workers' identity as trade unionists.

Publicity surrounding the Lebanon lockout convinced FJP trustees and affiliated agencies that they had to find some means of settling disputes with their staffs. The FJP's dependence on philanthropy made it important that it not be seen as intransigent; wealthy contributors, often businesspeople saddled with their own labor problems, were increasingly anxious to avoid endangering their public image by having controversial associations. The growth of the union movement among the FJP staff only augured more conflict. Although Lebanon's locked-out workers had conceded defeat in December 1935, during the next two years, the union movement in the FJP grew into a powerful political force. By the end of 1937, union membership had grown from 300 to 1,200 and claimed to represent 85 percent of all employees. The AFW had also joined the international labor movement, becoming in June 1937 Local 19, one of four UOPWA locals of the SSEU.[45] Rank-and-File leader and editor of *Social Work Today*, Jacob Fisher, was elected president of Local 19, and one of the first acts of the new CIO affiliate was to appoint its first full-time paid organizer in social work: William Piehl, a former JBG caseworker.[46]

As a thriving CIO affiliate, the union lent its support to a wide range of popular progressive issues and, in turn, found itself with new allies in its own cause. In August, for example, Local 19 joined the National Job March and another demonstration sponsored by the American League against War and Fascism. Then, in October the SSEU voted unanimously to place its support in the coming election behind the American Labor Party candidates Mayor La Guardia for mayor and Stanley Isaacs, the FJP trustee, for Manhattan Borough Council president.[47]

However, even as they celebrated their shared identity with other workers, these social workers' fund-raising efforts reflected their distinctively middle-class identity at home and as consumers. The all-day outing and moonlight dance that the Social Workers Committee to Aid Spanish Democracy held at a Westchester County estate in August 1937 is an example. In addition to featuring swimming, athletics, and a campfire, the event raised money with the "sale of some lovely and inexpensive Mexican pottery" as a "special feature."[48]

In return for its support, Local 19 found itself with many powerful friends, who now lined up behind the SSEU in its effort to win recognition from the FJP. The hatters' union, the teachers' union, the newspaper guild, and the fur workers' union all voiced their support for the social workers. Julius Hochman, general manager of the Joint Board of the International Ladies Garment Workers' Union, which had contributed $10,000 to the FJP that year alone, arranged to speak with Lowenstein on Local 19's behalf. Support for the SSEU came from prominent social work educators such as Bertha Reynolds and socialists such as Norman Thomas and B. Charney Vladeck. And Isaacs, who had traditionally been a voice for labor on the FJP's board, returned labor's endorsement of him by making a strong public endorsement of labor. At a mass rally of white-collar workers, Isaacs made the FJP's recognition of the union a public matter: " 'I see no difference between social agencies and other employers so far as the problem of organization of employees is concerned. I see no excuse for the FJP's failure to recognize the Union.' "[49]

The FJP had not forgotten its concern about its public image, however. By October, the SSEU had firmly established itself in FJP agencies, and it was no longer possible for the FJP to appear unwilling to talk with the union. The majority of trustees remained committed to "agency autonomy" and even continued to oppose a proposal from the board's own subcommittees that they agree to submit disputes between agencies and staffs for binding arbitration. Still, although insisting that they would not recognize the union as a bargaining agent, FJP trustees dropped their long-standing unwillingness to meet with union representatives.[50]

The subsequent meeting between labor and the FJP on October 11 was a breakthrough for the union representatives, and they seized the initiative. The issue for the union, Jacob Fisher explained to the trustees, was not a contract or a higher wage but the right of social workers to join a union of their own choosing. Collective bargaining without a contract, he pointed out, had been standard practice in "all major Federation agencies" and some nonsectarian ones for a number of years. Organizations such as the American Jewish Congress, Hadassah, the Jewish National Fund, the United Palestine Appeal, and the Hebrew Immigrant Aid and Sheltering Society had even bargained with contracts, although presumably not with recognized unions. While pressing his case for union recognition, Fisher also held out a large olive branch to the trustees. The union, Fisher pointedly noted, did not seek the right to strike: "We believe a union in social work has a solemn obligation to engage in no activity which would in any way jeopardize the quality of the service rendered."[51]

A series of developments both inside and outside the FJP now worked to bring the issue to a conclusion in December 1937. First, the Wagner Act had recently institutionalized collective bargaining across industry in the National Labor Relations Board. Although the act did not apply to charities, it was only the letter of the law and not the principle that exempted the FJP, as union supporters like Buttenwieser would remind the trustees.[52]

Second, this propitious moment in labor history corresponded with a political opening in the FJP. After complaints from leaders of the Amalgamated Clothing Workers and the International Ladies Garment Workers' Union, in November 1937, the National Labor Relations Board found Lawrence Marx, president of the FJP, guilty of violating the Wagner Act and instructed him to "cease and desist from interfering with, restraining, or coercing their employees [from the clothing firm of Cohn, Hall, and Marx] in the exercise of the right of self-organization."[53] He would be replaced as president the next year by none other than Buttenwieser himself, but in the interim the last thing the FJP needed was a scandal marking it as an antiunion lawbreaker.

In November, as the FJP's newly created Labor Committee met to consider the rights of its workers to join a union, the SSEU renewed its no-strike offer. If "Federation granted a written contract . . . [for] a stipulated period of time" and established arbitration machinery, the *Social Service Employees Union Newsletter* reported, the union "would agree to consider withholding strike action." When the Labor Committee submitted its report to the trustees, this promise of orderly labor-management relations was just the carrot that Buttenwieser needed to win over skeptical conservatives.[54]

In fact, Buttenwieser not only had to reverse the recommendation of the committee's majority report that the FJP only "confer" with its workers but also had to overcome the considerable antiunion pressure on the trustees from the city's business community. "Under the pledge of confidence," lawyers from two large non-Jewish institutions in the city had urged that the FJP not plunge the "whole philanthropic and educational program of the city . . . into the turmoil that would result from the interjection of union activity into it." A representative from a council of the city's association of manufacturers had made a similar entreaty.[55] New York Supreme Court judge Jacob Proskauer who had drafted the majority report, spoke for the vast majority of trustees, who were, of course, substantial businesspeople themselves. The fear that animated the antiunion feeling was that the men and women in Local 19 were not just trade unionists but "reds" with an antagonistic class analysis. Urging that they hold the line against the union, Proskauer told the trustees of his "shock" at hearing a few years ago, as FJP president, "a young lady" who chaired the AFW tell him "that this was a class war." This "psychology," warned Proskauer, "animates . . . a substantial part of these workers." Such sentiment had led FJP administrators to refuse their staff permission to march in the 1935 May Day parade.[56]

Seeking to turn the tide toward support of the minority report, Medalie and Lowenstein joined Buttenwieser in tackling the communist issue head-on. Medalie assured trustees that he had always gotten along fine with BG unionists, 90 percent of whom he claimed were communists. Lowenstein asserted that he had "nothing but praise" for the communists he knew in the agencies and reminded trustees that the Communist Party was legal in the United States. But Buttenwieser, who was probably the trustee most sympathetic to the union cause, cut to the chase: the alternative—continuing to stonewall the workers—would be "the best way" to create the FJP's own worst nightmare. "The best way to promote communism," he warned, "is to deny labor its just desserts."[57]

In a historic vote of 49 to 22, Buttenwieser's minority report, which substituted "to bargain collectively" for "to confer," carried the day. Ten of the opposing votes came from representatives from Montefiore and Mt. Sinai Hospitals. FJP social workers, always seeking a professional identity, now had a trade union identity as well. Of course, the right to join a union and bargain collectively neither guaranteed a union contract nor clarified the issue of agency autonomy. These rights, however, did change forever labor-management relations in the FJP and formalized trade unionism as an integral part of the social worker's identity. On January 10, 1938, the FJP formally recognized the right of SSEU workers in the FJP's offices to collective bargaining. And in July 1938, the SSEU signed its first contract with a social agency, the National Council of Jewish Women (NCJW). Significantly, the contract included a path-breaking hint of SSEU and NCJW feminism—a provision for maternity leave of three to six months without pay. Other gains, although substantial, suggested the limits of worker equality in the union vision. Covering both clerical and professional staff, the contract contained provisions for overtime and an annual vacation of three weeks for clericals and four for professionals. They may have all been "workers," but negotiators obviously agreed that they were not equally so.[58]

The FJP agreement would, in time, shape labor settlements for social work in private agencies across the country. Contracts were not won quickly or easily, however. Even in the more radical New York City Jewish social agencies such as the JBG and the JSSA, contracts were not signed until the early 1940s. Meanwhile, however, the staffs worked out relatively amicable personnel policy agreements that covered many of the same provisions as in formal contracts. The gain for trustees, directors, and executives was no less important: they won an organized way of dealing with protest. Discontent would be negotiated or channeled into grievance procedures. Significantly, it would be twenty-five years before another strike occurred in social service.

Beyond Trade Unionism

Across the country throughout the 1930s, social workers read and heard stories of how unionization was transforming the face of public and private sector social service in New York City. A report of the New York Committee of the

Case-Workers' Section of the NCJSS explained the process as the "de-classing" of Jewish middle-class professionals.[59] In agencies, labor contracts—or at least agreements—began to define the work experience. An ambiguous language of class mirrored complicated class positions, but the identity of the professional worker became social workers' central model for making sense of themselves as both employees and professionals.

The response of caseworkers across the country reflected the ambiguity and tensions in the new identity. In many large northern cities—places like Chicago, Philadelphia, Boston, Baltimore, and St. Louis—caseworkers organized. A substantial majority nationally, however, did not. But their reluctance to unionize was not because social work outside the metropolis was untouched by the depression. The size and scope of New York City's welfare program dwarfed efforts elsewhere, but as the controversy in Denver illustrates, taxpayers, politicians, and clients everywhere complained that public welfare had grown into a vast "industry" staffed by untrained bureaucrats dispensing relief. Similarly— and here the Columbus, Ohio, case is illustrative—private agency work had also become more contested and less secure.

Many social workers laboring in the hinterland—and, indeed, many in the metropolis—had reason to worry about how the class-based politics of trade unionism that was privileged in the identity of the professional worker would address specific concerns of racial or sexual discrimination or professionalism. For example, the upper echelons of the agencies still identified strongly with the AASW. Since many were social workers who had become supervisors and administrators, they most acutely felt the tension implicit in the professional worker's double class identity. To such people, the now-old question of who was a social worker only grew more vexing. The dominant new role of radical CIO social work unions only aggravated their anxiety.

Gertrude Springer, the moderate associate editor of *Survey*, helped to establish a comfortable middle ground for the professional woman as professional worker. In 1938 Springer, a journalist by training, wrote a series of folksy advice columns on social work practice in which she reexamined through her fictional persona, "Miss Bailey," the question of social worker identity. Enormously popular, Springer's columns were anthologized, published as pamphlets, and widely used in workshop training sessions for public assistance workers across the country. In addition, in *Survey Midmonthly*, her stories reached a broad mainstream of the profession.[50] Springer's columns were designed to introduce the legions of new public assistance workers to basic standards and procedures of social work practice. At the same time, she tried to teach relief workers to be humane and flexible rather than rigid about rules. In story after story, Miss Bailey sought to explain the internal logic of clients' actions, urging workers not to impose their own attitudes about "decent" family life and housing on people who were often simply struggling to hold their families together under the strain of great privation.[61]

Miss Bailey's observations in a May 1938 column provided one of Springer's clearest statements to social workers about the dilemma of professionalism versus trade unionism. Adopting her usual sprightly tone, Springer quickly drew her readers into Miss Bailey's didactic narrative. In this story, Miss Bailey found herself in the dining car of a train, where she overheard a woman answer her male companion's question, " 'Who is a social worker nowadays, anyhow?,' " with the plaintive reply, " 'I haven't the least idea. Sometimes it's anybody; sometimes it's somebody. Depends on who's talking about it.' " A case in point, continued a second woman, was her cousin Mary Martin, who worked for " 'widow's pensions' ":

> "[Mary] is scandalized if I call her a social worker—says I'll get her in bad with her office. Yet that kid runs around and visits families and trots children to clinics and sits up half the night making budgets and writing records. When I ask her if that isn't social work what is it, she says that it's social work but that she isn't a social worker. She's an aide. To be a social worker you must have gone to a special school or worked for years and years in some special kind of organization they call 'accredited.' "
>
> "But what does a social worker do that's so different? Doesn't a social worker visit families and write records?"
>
> "Oh yes, of course. Mary says the difference is not in what they do but in the way they do it. Like sending for a doctor when the baby swallows a pin, instead of letting the neighbor women shake it by the heels."[62]

The male companion's conclusion is simple: " '[T]he big shots, the [social work] leaders . . . insist on especially educated and trained workers, but their schools can't supply 'em, can't turn 'em out fast enough. . . . The way I see it the social workers have the standards and the Mary Martins have the jobs.' "

Miss Bailey found the conversation distressing. Why all of this public confusion? " 'Who is us?,' " she asked rhetorically, and then she proceeded to provide three answers. First, there were the AASW members who had met the educational or experiential requirements for membership or, like Miss Bailey herself, had joined during an earlier period of lower standards. AASW rolls included perhaps as many as 9,000 members at the time. Second, there were the many thousands of Mary Martins (maybe as many as 50,000) who did not meet the "accredited" standards of the AASW but who said in effect, " 'We're doing the work, and doing it effectively—at least we continue to have the jobs—so if we aren't social workers what are we?' "[63] The important point for Miss Bailey was that those employed were unionized and that the unions had become militant CIO organizations with nearly 13,000 members.

The dominance of the trade union identity came with a downside, however. Miss Bailey's imaginary cautionary tale concluded with two prescient observations about the shift in the identity of the professional worker from concerns with gender and professionalism to class-based politics. As Miss Bailey notes with an ironic touch, these social workers had grown less " 'concerned with their individual effectiveness or professional identity than with their group strength as a union and their identification with the labor movement. Shades of the founding fathers—or better, mothers! What a change from the good old days when "the cause" compensated for working conditions that didn't bear mentioning; when social workers were "noble" and clients "worthy." ' "[64]

The shift entailed a political price for the new CIO trade unions: now in the public arena, they were held accountable to it. " 'As long as social work was practiced under the wing of privately supported agencies the standards of its personnel were their own business,' " announced Miss Bailey. " 'But now . . . it's different. . . . The public pays the piper and calls the tune, and sooner or later, . . . it will have some check on what it gets for its money when t hires us.' "[65]

Ironically, Springer's fictional persona suggested the limited place of concerns with gender in the professional worker identity. Miss Bailey entered the contested public arena where " 'the public . . . calls the tune' " as a female, but her concerns were not with the worker as a woman. For the most part, Springer's intended audience was the relief worker, a trade unionist who was as likely to be a man as a woman. Confronted with more proletarian working conditions in sparsely furnished relief offices, this "neutered" protagonist had to get by with "manly" persistence. As the professional worker gained ascendance as the core of social worker identity, gender did not disappear. Rather, it shifted to emphasize masculinity and receded to the background. Historian Elizabeth Faue has shown that the iconography of 1930s labor struggles "encoded the class struggle in metaphors of gender," as a "manly struggle" in which the proletariat was inscribed as male and the bourgeoisie as female (see figures 5.1 and 5.2).[66] New Deal labor policy also discriminated in favor of employing men because they were "breadwinners." The economics of gender at the JBG, for instance, raised concerns for agency executives. Because the agency believed that men would be more effective in working with young male delinquents, the percentage of male staff at the JBG was an unusually high 40 percent. For executives, depression constraints were bad enough, but the large number of male employees created additional "problems of remuneration because of the men with families who are pursuing the work of careers."[67] In contrast, male executives tended to view women's work as temporary and marginal, conveniently ignoring the many women who had worked in the agency for most of their adult lives.

Although notions of manliness may have reflected the leadership positions of men like Piehl, Fisher, and Flaxer within the labor movement, women achieved

Figure 5.1. This "manly" depiction of a white-collar woman and blue-collar men urged clerical workers at social service agencies to march in solidarity with their industrial brethren in celebration of May Day proletarianism. Cover of *Ledger* 1, no. 4 (April 1935). Courtesy of Tamiment Institute Library, New York University.

Figure 5.2. "Manly" workers organize and assert their rights, while a diminutive, emasculated clerk cowers behind them. Anonymous, "The N.R.A. and the Office Worker," *Ledger* 1, no. 2 (February 1935): 9. Courtesy of Tamiment Institute Library, New York University.

great prominence as spokespersons within the unions, and although such status is not easily measured, they seemingly gained greater prominence than did women in the executive-dominated AASW. For instance, Helen Mangold, a COS caseworker, was appointed the second SSEU organizer in 1939, and Evelyn Adler, assistant supervisor of casework at the JSSA, was elected Local 19 president. Women who had long been prominent trade union activists were elected to half of the other union offices, too. From Jewish social service, they included Miriam Berkman, a JBG caseworker, who was elected third vice president, and Paula Jacobs Goldstein, a bookkeeper in the FJP office, who was named financial secretary. Goldstein's hobbies of riding horses and playing tennis suggest the continuing ambiguity of these women's class identity, however, even within a left-wing union with a proletarian ideology.[68]

A 1938 UOPWA pamphlet, *The White Collar Workers Organize*, cited the need to end discrimination against women as a reason for joining the union. Women, the author notes, were "denied the best jobs and receiv[ed] lower pay for the same work."[69] But this was a voice in the wilderness and a limited one at that. Nowhere does the author acknowledge that women labored under the burden of the double day or faced a glass ceiling on promotions. Tacitly or willingly—the record does not address gender bias—both men and women appeared to accept prevailing attitudes about the male family wage. Still, from the first, union contracts did make demands for maternity leave. For a variety of reasons, however, class and not gender remained the organizing principle of social worker union struggles. For one thing, the union focused on winning recognition and bargaining rights and restoring wage cuts. As important, however, as Spano has argued, the Rank-and-File Movement's Marxist tradition and its effort to build an industrial solidarity and trade union consciousness emphasized the class "other" of employers.[70]

It would be a mistake to ignore the gendered character of daily work in agency and relief offices, however, especially in the era of the "manly" New Deal proletarian. Historians such as Elizabeth Lunbeck and Regina G. Kunzel have illuminated, for example, how casework practice reenforced gender prejudice against female clients.[71] Highly gendered diagnosis and treatment in psychiatric social work continued a trend already well developed by the 1920s that relied on Freudian models and singled out women and girls as bad mothers and oversexed deviants. The Rankians' emphasis on the will gradually encouraged less-gendered alternative models, but these models seldom appeared in JBG records. For instance, before the caseworkers intervened and asked that sessions be less clinical and address more social and economic problems, from the fall of 1934 to the spring of 1935, the JBG's resident psychiatric staff, John Slawson and a Dr. Levy, conducted a monthly supervisor's seminar to analyze current cases. The fact that nine of the ten supervisors were women did not seem to affect the nature of the discussion: time and time again, the problems of delinquent children were attributed to mothers who "infantilized" them or were ' lax and inconsistent" or "over-protective." Fathers might be authoritarian, but based on the Freudian assumption that children make their primary association with the mother, the burden of blame fell on her. Similarly, girls were inevitably diagnosed as exhibiting "sexual delinquency." The aberrant sexual diagnosis for boys, for whom an active heterosexual life was seen as evidence of manliness, was the opposite of manliness—effeminacy. Levy categorized a boy who stole and "often liked to be alone," for instance, as having "unconscious destructive tendencies and possible homosexual trends." An "effeminate" seventeen-year-old Brooklyn boy was institutionalized to escape an alienating home life in which his parents called him a " 'pansy.' "[72]

On the shop floor, too, gendered attitudes shaped the daily experience of social workers. Notions of manliness may explain why male social workers sought (and often received) promotions to managerial positions, which were supervisory roles not coded as feminine "nurturing" positions. Such attitudes may also help account for the greater tendency of men to forsake "careers" as caseworkers; if they did not become administrators, they often left the occupation. As a case supervisor, for instance, Marsha Treitman criticized men for generally not reading case records carefully. They "were no more interested in that than I am in breeding cockroaches," she explained. Men wanted other jobs.[73] The professional worker's identity as "manly" also did little to assuage female social workers' anxieties as middle-class aspirants about their sexuality and desirability as professional women. The imposing, austere "professional" supervisor in the 1934 cartoon in Social Work Today (see figure 5.3) directs the fashionably coiffed young investigator to "always be professional," but neither the material constraints of the investigator's "$20 a week" salary nor the dowdiness of the supervisor would be lost on female readers. Seeking to convince caseworkers and investigators that their "identity of interests" lay with other wage workers, the trade union movement encouraged them to appreciate their differences with such supervisors. But female social workers could not escape their sense of distance from other women who toiled with their hands, as a skit presented at a Seattle meeting of the National Council of Social Work in 1938 entitled "The Clean Up" illustrates (see figure 5.4). Written by the publicity director of the Chicago YWCA, the skit featured two women custodians cleaning up after a convention of social workers:

O'Hara: Land sakes . . . Gladys! Social workers ain't like ordinary people. They
    don't have things like politics or religion or sex.
Gladys: My goodness, Mrs. O'Hara, what do they have?
O'Hara: Oh, they have things like organization and administration and edu-
    cation.[74]

RELIEF SUPERVISOR (to $20 a week Investigator):—*Now, remember, above all, that your attitude must always be professional!*

Figure 5.3. This sketch in *Social Work Today*, the journal of the left-wing Rank-and-File Movement, ridicules social investigators who persisted in clinging to a professional ideology despite their proletarian wages. William Gordon, "Protecting the Social Service Employee," *Social Work Today* 1 (March/April 1934): 10; illustration by Bernadette Bryson. Courtesy of Tamiment Institute Library, New York University.

The Clean Up

GLADYS *(Helen Cody Baker):* What do social workers do?

O'HARA *(Audrey Hayden):* Do? Why they do the same kind of work that you an' me do—they mop up messes.

Figure 5.4. A skit at the 1938 meeting of the National Council of Social Work that depicted two custodians discussing social workers raised ongoing anxieties about social worker sexlessness. In the skit, one custodian explains: "Social workers ain't like ordinary people. They don't have things like politics or religion or sex." Barbara Abel, "The Clean Up," *Survey Midmonthly*, September 15, 1938. 274. Courtesy of Tamiment Institute Library, New York University.

Responding to the skit's assumption about social worker sexlessness, *Survey Midmonthly* lightly reported "insidious indications of femininity . . . sprouting up through the ranks." A recent charm contest held by a popular women's magazine had elicited a letter from a "field worker for a public social agency" who reported "a new self-consciousness dawning" in a group of women workers: having "become aware of the office clerks' use of the term 'social worker' for anyone whose slip shows," these women had decided—and this was the effort to win the contest—"to become as well dressed as the stenographers." "P.S.," the *Survey* editors added, "the field worker's letter did not win the contest."[75]

The *Survey* editors treated these interventions as light entertainment, but the persisting obsession with social workers' self-image and public image indicated that these issues cut close to the bone. Although the ascendance of the professional worker image shifted organized social workers' public concerns away from gender issues, it did not remove the tension within the professional ideology between femininity and objectivity. In fact, the rise of the union movement and its worker identity probably heightened tensions concerning gender roles, intensifying public fears about whether social worker behavior was suitable for "proper" women.

Race, Ethnicity, and Religion

In contrast to its gender blindness, the Rank-and-File Movement repeatedly voiced concerns about racism. The poverty of the African American community made racism a class issue, and in the 1930s, the Rank-and-File Movement made the fight against racism an active (if subordinate) part of its agenda. But social workers were not new to the cause: since the late 1910s, they had been in the forefront of the battle to end discrimination against African Americans, especially black social workers. A statement by the National Coordinating Committee of Social Service Employee Groups after the 1935 meeting of the National Conference of Social Work (NCSW) in Atlantic City illustrates the self-conscious effort of the left wing to fight for racial equality. Unfortunately, it also illustrates the limits of "professional" concern. Conference organizers, as had been their practice for over a decade, had worked to provide "equality of treatment" in all conference housing and restaurant facilities. However, after the committee protested the fact that two African American members had been denied service in the hotel bar, Edith Abbott, the conference president, declared that the incident was "outside the business of the Conference." Suggesting the parameters she set for gender as well as racial discrimination, Abbott concluded, "If a bar admits men and excludes women, this seems to me again a matter about which we have no concern. This applies also to the matter of racial lines that may be drawn in these fields."[76]

In contrast to Abbott's narrow "professional" agenda, the Rank-and-File Movement put forth a formal program to advance the "Negro in social work."[77] The program not only called for active organizing of black social workers in the labor movement but also set concrete goals for the increased employment of African Americans in New York City in administrative, supervisory, and staff posts. New York was a logical city in which to establish such a program. African American and Puerto Rican clients made up nearly a quarter of the relief rolls but remained relatively invisible in daily accounts of social service; if anything seemed to drive public concerns, it was class conflict, budgetary constraints, and fear of radical dissidents. Both to serve the black community and to provide some employment for it, the Rank-and-File program sought work for African Americans as regional directors, office managers, case supervisors, and investigators on a "20 percent basis." As important, after the 1937 civil service law created an employment list based on an examination, the union movement led the fight in 1937–38 to make the DPW create emergency jobs for African Americans who had been let go on the principle of last hired, first fired.[78] Finally, the Rank-and-File program recognized the great needs of the black community, putting forth an integrationist workplace solution: it asked that African American social workers not be ghettoized in black communities. The authors suggested that racial harmony was elusive even among those most publicly committed to its growth and pointed out to their Rank-and-File audience that equality of caseloads and integration of services would also help improve relationships between white and black workers.

The truth is that social workers shared the racial prejudices that were so deeply ingrained in the American experience. Although social workers, especially in the North, were among the most progressive groups on racial issues, as with gender issues, concerns about racial discrimination ultimately took a backseat to concerns about class issues. Although ethnic consciousness was a familiar political card in the immigrant city, grievances to the DPW often emphasized ethnic and racial bias. Persistent grievances from the Puerto Rican community discussed in chapter 4 suggest the ways in which "whiteness" was encoded in American culture and prejudiced investigators' responses to unfamiliar client habits. Sometimes prejudice was overt. For instance, the insistence of a white social worker from Boston at a 1928 COS seminar in New York City that blacks were "different" (i.e., inferior) made a lasting impression on Inabel Burns Lindsay, one of the first trained black social workers in the country, who also attended the seminar. When such statements were made at meetings, black workers like Lindsay occasionally walked out in protest.[79] But since bias pervaded social relations and was often subtle, black social workers devised less overt strategies of protest. Frankie V. Adams, for example, recalled that because of her "Christian upbringing" she refused "to make a white person mad at me under any circumstance." But when she was deeply offended, she "used what some of the folks say's a 'devilment' reaction to bypass some of the key things that would have been a problem."[80] Nonetheless, however much prejudice warped social service in northern cities such as New York, historians like Spano seem right to suggest that it would have been more abusive and open in the South.[81]

The DPW made special efforts to appoint black administrators and staff in poor black communities, but it did so with a compromised racial agenda. In areas such as Brooklyn's Brownsville and Manhattan's Harlem, where white (and often Jewish) social workers administered to black clients, black workers would be able to serve their own community with more sympathy and understanding. But as historian Stephanie J. Shaw notes, welfare agencies hired many black social workers to advance "race relations" as an alternative to black radicalism.[82] Prior to its appointment of Dorothy I. Haight as its first black personnel supervisor following the 1935 Harlem riot, the DPW did not have a single African American in any key post. Blacks at the time made up slightly more than 6 percent of the city's population and represented 42 percent of the welfare rolls. Haight also recalled the ways in which the history of black-white relations in the city complicated welfare work. Her previous job, she noted, was as an intake interviewer in Brownsville, where clients were usually unemployed black domestics, many of whom undoubtedly served Jewish families. Her supervisor, a Mrs. Kaunitz, asked her to deal with "protesting [black] community groups" because she "found it difficult" to deal with them. By way of explanation, Haight simply added that Kaunitz was Jewish, was married to a doctor, and lived on Central Park West.[83]

The complicated and entwined history of relations between African Americans and Jews in New Deal social service had particular resonance for the future. In time, the experiences of the two groups in New York City took on a highly charged and paradigmatic political meaning for national welfare policy. As we shall see, in the last third of the century, a Jewish success story would be held up as a mirror to a black failure narrative. According to the two stories, Jewish culture made possible exceptional Jewish mobility, whereas the troubled African American family and its culture of poverty left blacks in need of lessons on how to be "white": to work, to limit their family size, and to save money for a rainy day.

The Jewish success narrative emerged out of a pattern of social mobility that, ironically, took shape in the midst of the depression. Jews suffered during the depression like everyone else, but as a disproportionately white-collar group, they suffered less than others. In fact, employment in the teaching and social work professions was an important part of the success enjoyed by a core of the community. By the 1930s, many Jews had been in the country for nearly twenty years, and the community had established a range of institutions to help its members settle, find work, and adapt. In that regard, the FJP was one of the most well funded and responsive ethnic philanthropies in the nation. Still, it is important to note that Jews in New York City benefited considerably from state aid—as employees of the emerging relief bureaucracy, as recipients of public assistance, and as workers in New Deal agencies such as the Civil Works Administration and the Works Progress Administration. By the 1930s, reflecting the mobility of some Jews, Jewish migrants from the immigrant Lower East Side had already established the beginnings of a Jewish suburban enclave in places like the Grand Concourse in the Bronx.[84]

With the achievement of Jewish social mobility and assimilation, however, came two potential conflicts that foreshadowed crucial developments in the narrative of middle-class identity in America: a crisis in Jewish identity and a crisis in the relationship between Jews and the black community whose plight they identified with their own. Increased Jewish acculturation and upward mobility corresponded with the growing establishment of a secular Jewish identity. At the same time, unionism and professionalism combined to make social workers focus more on class solidarities and conflicts than on ethnic or religious identities. The New York City and Chicago federations asked social workers to identify the Jewish content of Jewish social work, but Helen Harris Perlman, for one, "never was able to do that." In fact, although she felt "great pride" in the generosity and social responsibility of the Jewish community (and their sources in Jewish culture and tradition), she did not feel more closely identified with Jews simply because she was of Jewish origin herself. Perlman felt that whatever problems clients had reflected individual ethnic identity and the individuality of all people.[85] Historian Beth Wenger's description of the JSSA's 1934 "March of Time" radio program celebrating the agency's sixtieth year typifies the emphasis on Jewish ethnic identity: the program made "little reference to the Jewish content" of the JSSA's work, but all "the fictitious clients were given Jewish names and ethnic dialects."[86]

Occupational mobility into white-collar jobs such as social work also brought the Jewish worker into potential conflict with blacks who would have to rely on them for public assistance. The reaction to this conflict should be understood in the context of a history of Jewish aid and Jewish identification with black oppression. The immigrant and socialist Jewish community equated anti-Semitism with discrimination against blacks. Moreover, Jews were proud of the major role Jewish philanthropy had played in the history of the National Urban League and the organization of black philanthropy. The image of the victimized black dominated the Yiddish press's discussion of "the race question." And Jews took pleasure in seeing themselves as "good to" blacks, sensitive, and caring. They also delighted in viewing such behavior as part of the Jewish tradition of what it meant to be a "good" Jew.[87]

But as historian Hasia R. Diner has observed, "[I]n a subtle and indirect manner, they [Jews] used the themes of black suffering, black achievement, and black cultural life" to "work . . . out questions of their own status."[88] During the New Deal, a large segment of the African American community became dependent for the first time on public assistance dispensed by disproportionate numbers of Jewish relief workers. Dependence did not foster cohesion, however, especially when the two communities found themselves competing for limited resources. Indeed, assimilation and upward mobility could become an incendiary mix when challenged, as would be the case during disputes over community control of schools and welfare rights thirty years later. By the 1960s, Orthodox Jews would complain about the lack of a religious base in the identity of Jewish social service and about the inequity of a public welfare system that they felt disproportionately aided "lazy" blacks; under the banner of community control, the black community would challenge the teacher and social worker unions it saw as dominated by privileged Jews who imposed their own "middle-class" values on blacks. Thus, the structural and cultural preconditions for narratives of Jewish and black success and failure were put in place during the New Deal.

"Is Unionization Compatible with Social Work?"

As the 1930s came to a close, the issue on which the professional worker's subsequent history would turn remained the impact of loyalty to the trade union on the independence and objectivity of the caseworker. Ironically, the case against trade union affiliation was put forth by Virginia P. Robinson, one of the leaders of the functionalist movement, which advocated a therapeutic model of client agency. In her article "Is Unionization Compatible with Social Work?," published in the *Compass*, the official journal of the AASW, in May 1937, Robinson demonstrated that there was no simple convergence between casework theory and social worker politics.[89] Having originally presented the paper to a prolabor assembly in Philadelphia, Robinson began by complimenting her audience for being "[n]o longer" beholden to "the extremes of Fascism or Communism." By 1937, the Rank-and-File Movement had, in fact, entered its more open Popular Front phase, and Robinson hoped that this would help bridge the differences she saw between "social workers, the small professional group," and "the large, untrained and semi-trained group of rank and filers" in relief who she would be sorry to see "define their job on the level of unskilled, unprofessional labor." The goal of effective social service, she continued, was to raise the level of the unskilled in order to do the highest quality of work. She made two assumptions in answering the question posed by the article's title. First, as a service industry equated with medicine and education, social work "produced" clients, not material goods. Service to the client gave social work, she explained, a special human dimension that was "far more important in terms of human and social values than the product the shop has for sale." Second, the development of quality service, according to Robinson, required that the "unskilled" accept authority, hierarchy, and "discipline"; in language she might have borrowed from a therapeutic manual, it required "the functioning of the agency as a whole." The union, she complained, "cuts the administrative and supervisory functions off from other functions in an effort to make them more like managing functions in industry." In sum, through the union, social workers were taught to think of themselves as workers, and their loyalty was to the union, not to the agency and its leaders, who would train them to become "professionals." The salient issue then was loyalty: Robinson, who couched the issue as one of loyalty to clients' welfare, sought staff loyalty to the agencies and to teachers like herself, not to "an outside group" like the union.[90]

The reply came two years later in a conference address by Jacob Fisher, who was lauded by the *Social Service Employees Union Newsletter* as the person most "entitled to carry membership card #1" in Local 19.[91] "Will John L. Lewis tell me to burn Virginia Robinson—the book not the lady—then the answer is, No," quipped Fisher; "the union is a democratic organization" open to all opinions. But it was precisely the question of union democracy that was at issue, and Fisher knew it. Did the union, especially a union quite correctly seen by its skeptics as in step with Communist Party positions, "inhibit or restrict" the professional activities and "objectivity" of its members? Fisher's answer was unequivocal: "[N]ot in any way."[92]

Rather than being a cause of the problem of democracy in private social service, for Fisher, the social work unions were a solution: speaking for the labor movement and bearing witness for the community, "[t]hey bring a breadth of democracy into the private agency." Objectivity, he explained, does "not mean an ivory tower isolation from the rude conflicts of our time." Rather, to safeguard its essential contribution, social work must be related to the "forces in our time making for progress." There was a problem of democracy in social work, but for Fisher, it lay in the "essentially undemocratic character" of private agencies dependent on the "optional benevolence of the few." The wealthy, albeit often decent, men and women who sat on the boards of directors of these agencies, he reminded his listeners, were "representative neither of the clients, the staff, the contributors nor of the general community."

The key question remained whether social workers could be "loyal to both" the professional association and the trade union. For Fisher, the answer lay in the hundreds of SSEU members in Pittsburgh, Philadelphia, Chicago, New York City, and elsewhere who also functioned as active members of the AASW and the thousands of professional workers—musicians, teachers, nurses, and journalists, among others—who had joined trade unions. Sometimes the methods and goals of the professional association and the trade union differed; sometimes they coincided. The trade union had demonstrated during the depression, however, that it played a particularly vital role in developing innovative social work. Taking a line from the agency book of rationales, Fisher claimed that limited monies had in fact prevented agencies from pioneering new programs and that agency "[p]olicies [had] become fixed, programs congealed." Usurping the professional association's language as his own, Fisher described the trade union as the solution; asserting that the "social work unions are not job-minded," he placed their concerns at the center of the professional ethos: "[R]ange and quality of service to the client is the yardstick by which the union measures the agency's program."[93]

In presenting the union as disinterested and selfless, Fisher was being no more disingenuous than the professional association. But agency executives, board members, and many politicians remained suspicious of his assertions that social work unions, especially these "red" unions, would not compromise loyalty to clients or agency programs and that they were democratic unions representing the "free and inquiring mind." Events in Europe in 1939 and soon afterward would, however, further call these claims into question, especially among many who had flocked to the Rank-and-File Movement. But as the decade came to a close, the social workers' trade union movement had established the identity of the professional worker, winning union recognition and the principle of collective bargaining. Both gains would have a profound and lasting impact on the way these social workers related to their work, their employers, and their clients. But if this historical moment marked the apotheosis of the professional worker, it was also the professional worker's last best moment. The professional worker would soon be at war.

CHAPTER SIX

The Evisceration of the Professional Worker Identity

During the 1940s, World War II abroad and, subsequently, the Cold War at home placed labor and the ideal of the professional worker who identified with other workers under increasing assault. Like other left-wing unions in industry during the war, social workers' unions tended to mirror Communist Party foreign policy in support of controversial issues, such as the Hitler-Stalin Pact, which compromised their militant trade unionism. Simultaneously, wartime dependence on psychiatry for evaluating and then counseling the "everyday soldier" renewed social workers' emphasis on professionalism. Moreover, psychiatry's newfound legitimacy made it increasingly possible for psychiatric and clinical social workers to claim that they had something to offer the "neurotic" masses, not just the poor and delinquent. Being servants of the affluent raised social workers' status (and that of psychiatrists) and provided the preconditions for the commodification of therapy. The increased role of psychiatrists, however, further relegated social workers to the position of aides to these male doctors, forcing female workers as both women and professionals to renew their quest for autonomy.

The beginning of the Cold War marked the final hurrah for the radical trade union movement and with it, the professional worker identity. After the war, renewed labor militancy—which had been nourished by New Deal legislation such as the Wagner Act—encountered a much more frightened and hostile political environment. Federal and state authorities, usually more obsessed with Cold War fears than with labor's claims to justice, passed a series of draconian antilabor laws directed against public employees—for example, New York State's Condon-Wadlin Act and the federal Taft-Hartley Act. Union efforts to respond were frustrated by repressive legislation and by the rigidity and controversial nature of their unions' political positions on international matters, and their militancy was further compromised by anticommunist AFL-CIO unions that offered agency officials a more palliative alternative. As social workers fought these battles over the course of the decade, the professional worker identity, although still rhetorically powerful, lost its political muscle.

At the same time that this identity waned, a more "professional" middle-class alternative took root in which race increasingly displaced class. This heightened racialization of social worker identity as white took place in the 1950s, but the process was set in motion by the blackening of cities and welfare after the war. To begin with, a combination of agricultural distress in Puerto Rico and the lure of a postwar boom on the U.S. mainland initiated a large-scale migration of Puerto Ricans to New York City. For many of the same reasons, a renewed black exodus from the South swelled the flow of poor migrants to the city. When the Department of Child Welfare was merged with the DW in 1947, the large number of African Americans receiving AFDC further enlarged the presence of what the census called "nonwhites" on welfare. In time, policymakers and the public would conceive of blacks and Hispanics who were excluded from America's consumer cornucopia as an "underclass."[1] But that is a story for later chapters. In this chapter, the conjunction of the labor and race stories in New York City during the late 1940s makes New York our logical focus.

The War Years

World War II set the identity of the professional worker back on its heels, but not because of lack of growth in the union movement. The first collective-bargaining contract signed by Local 19—the 1938 contract with the NCJW—covered working conditions for twenty-five employees. By 1940, social work agencies had signed about twenty-five written contracts and made nearly twice that number of informal agreements with social service employee unions, mostly with Local 19.[2] During the war, a small decline in the number of public social work unions was more than offset by a steady gain in the private sector; by the mid-1940s, the SCMWA had twenty-five social work locals with 6,518 members, while at its peak, the UOPWA claimed 6,500 social workers in the SSEU. Although the private agency union movement had spread across twenty-eight cities, New York City's Local 19 had more than half of the total membership. Over half (57 percent) of the members of the local worked in Jewish agencies, where they had won contracts.[3]

Ironically, the imminent demise of the professional worker identity corresponded with what may have been its apotheosis in the unique collaboration between a trade union and a private agency. Between 1943 and 1947, the National Maritime Union (NMU) joined Rank-and-File caseworkers employed by the

United Seamen's Service (USS) in a modest but extraordinary cooperative venture. Staffing commercial ships during the war, merchant seamen suffered great losses yet remained ineligible for military or Red Cross services. Often at sea for long periods of time, they also needed support for daily emergencies while claims were being adjudicated. Their union, the NMU, another left-wing CIO affiliate, moved to enter the breach: in 1941 it established a personal service department to deal with their problems. By the spring of 1943, representatives of government, shipping companies, and the maritime unions had come together to create an agency, the USS, which was to provide seamen with personal service and maintain a loan fund to meet emergencies. With government money, the NMU and the USS thus began a path-breaking program in which a private agency staffed by professionally trained caseworkers would provide "public" relief.[4]

To the seven caseworkers on the USS staff, the experience of working with the union demonstrated that it was possible to bridge the gulf in the double class identity of the professional worker. Bertha Capen Reynolds, the radical social worker who supervised the caseworkers, understood that both the seamen and the caseworkers were participating in a distinctly new form of democratic welfare agency. Middle-class social workers, she explained, were used to playing God when determining the eligibility of working-class clients; in this program, the final say on eligibility rested with the seamen's union and its grievance machinery. To Reynolds, then, this was "an extraordinary opportunity" to see how workers would respond to an agency they "could think of as their own," although it was not public. In addition, Reynolds saw the program as dissolving the historic class divide between caseworkers and clients. She observed that when seamen realized that the caseworkers were, like themselves, union members, they felt none of the unease that was a usual part of worker interaction with "middle-class" caseworkers. Reynolds, who had taken a leave as associate director of Smith College's School of Social Work to direct the USS program, had agreed to provide the NMU with "professional, qualified caseworkers who were also acceptable to the Union as members of the Social Service Employees Union."[5]

The majority of social workers, however, were more aware of the signing of the Hitler-Stalin Pact than the NMU-USS arrangement. Oblivious to the extraordinary but isolated experience of the NMU with welfare, most social workers found the moral compass of the identity of the professional worker increasingly skewed by the tendency of the Rank-and-File Movement to mirror the twists and turns of Communist Party policy. The movement had repeatedly stressed its opposition to fascism, supporting the Abraham Lincoln Brigade's intervention in Spain, for instance. Moreover, liberal social work sentiment, expressed in periodicals such as *Survey Midmonthly* and *Survey Graphic*, generally took the same positions. But the abrupt shift to a noninterventionist stance on the occasion of the pact in August 1939, which *Social Work Today* supported, isolated the communists and troubled many Jews in the movement, some of whom began to articulate an independent antifascist line.[6] Historians such as Rick Spano seem correct in concluding that the Rank-and-File Movement was "more than a mouthpiece for the Communist Party," especially in day-to-day domestic union affairs, remaining in the forefront of the fight for welfare rights and job security and against fascism. It fought hard and well, establishing the principle of trade unionism in social work.[7] But to Jewish agency staff, who provided the core of the Rank-and-Filers, the troubling positions of the Communist Party and the tendency of some prominent union leaders to genuflect before them began to drain the political energy and resonance of the "proletarian" ideology from the identity of the professional worker.

The party's about-face to a position of aggressive antifascism after the United States entered the war as an ally of Russia placed the communists back in step with Jewish social workers' international concerns with anti-Semitism. The party's no-strike pledge did little, however, to improve the working conditions social workers faced on the home front. In fact, the shift of resources from social service to the struggle abroad brought new problems to the workplace. High turnover rates plagued public assistance offices, and officials had to focus on "training" new investigators to use the agency manual, work up budgets for relief recipients, and "visit" clients.[8] Private agencies regularly complained of a shortage of male social workers after many men enlisted or were drafted. The Hawthorne School for Boys, for example, even considered what it saw as an extraordinary step—hiring women to teach shop classes.[9]

The war effort also renewed pressure on Community Chests and the FJP to eliminate duplicate services and consolidate programs. Although the agencies were chronically short of money, the war effort directed funding elsewhere, for example, to the problems of European Jewry. To board members, like those at the FJP, the merger of duplicate programs was a timely response to important changes in the Jewish community. Brooklyn, for example, had three times the number of Jews that Manhattan had but much less access to wealthy Jews, who congregated in Manhattan. In addition, upwardly mobile second-generation Jews (whose story paralleled that of other white ethnics) had begun to move out of areas like the Lower East Side to the Grand Concourse in the Bronx, to Forest Hills in Queens, across the river to Brooklyn, and to the "Golden Ghettos" of Westchester County and Long Island. Jewish community leaders from Westchester, for example, expected that an "exodus" of Jews after the war would swell the Jewish population, which was already at 40,000 in 1943, and the FJP agreed to open a referral office there similar to the one it had placed in Queens a few years earlier.[10]

The suburbanization of many charitable services set in motion a fundamental reorganization of social service in regions like the New York City metropolitan area. Typical was the merger of the Brooklyn and New York City federations. They combined funding campaigns in 1940 and completed a full merger as of July 31, 1944. Three years later, the Westchester Jewish Community Service (WJCS) also became an affiliated agency.[11] Consolidation was not limited to the federations; it took place at all levels of social service. Thus, the FJP amalgamated its child care agencies—the Hebrew Sheltering Guardian Society, the Hebrew Orphan Asylum, the Jewish Children's Clearing Bureau, the Fellowship House, and all of their affiliates—into the New York Association for Jewish Children in 1940.[12] Indeed, the consolidation of resources at the three largest FJP casework agencies—the JFS, the JBG, and the JCCA—in the years during and after the war was not untypical.

The experience at the JBG is a case in point. Mergers had punctuated its history; in fact, it was itself an umbrella organization created in 1921 to consolidate the operations of the Big Brother Association, Big Sister League, Hawthorne School for Boys, and Cedar Knolls School for Girls. According to a 1946 FJP report, these services had been only "mechanically combined" for "outside activities." Now, a quarter of a century later, the JBG had been reorganized into three divisions—the Jewish Child Guidance Institute (Madeleine Borg Clinic), the Division of Community Services, and the Division of Institutional Services. The new integration of services, the JBG explained, was a "far cry from the original mergers" and represented "a functional reorganization [that] accentuates the growth from correction to treatment to prevention."[13]

Across the country, caseworkers, clerical staff, and administrators all found the periodic reorganization and consolidation of existing agencies deeply disruptive and a constant source of anxiety. They all had good reason to worry about their new assignments, if they were fortunate enough to continue to have a job. Former executive directors could find themselves redundant or reduced in authority in a new superagency; social workers suddenly could be required to possess new therapeutic skills or travel to a new office.

These mergers and the shifting use of limited resources they entailed also raised critical issues about responsibility to a community. for instance, about what constituted "Jewish" service in an area where Jews were no longer predominant. In the 1940s, at least, such questions remained muted in the record. However, social workers, as we shall see in the case of the WJCS, were not quiet about the implications of these moves for their jobs—after all, the specter of these shifts had existed since the late 1920s—and they turned to their unions and professional associations to defend them.

The union fought the good fight. Although Communist Party associations may have compromised union solidarity somewhat, the party provided the compensatory benefit of a cadre of dedicated, experienced leaders. Even so, gains were hard to come by. New York State legislation exempted charitable institutions from collective-bargaining labor law, but by 1943, the federal War Labor Board had assumed jurisdiction over them, especially hospitals. But the fact that social workers were bound by War Labor Board provisions meant that the no-strike pledge pertained to them, removing what had proved to be an important union bargaining chip.[14] The FJP's central office had agreed to recognize the UOPWA, but it did not grant the rights to collective bargaining and the deduction of union dues from employees' paychecks until 1944.[15]

Agencies affiliated with the FJP often were even less quick to jump on the union bandwagon.[16] Some agency executives were antiunion, some felt unions were incompatible with social service work, and some opposed the UOPWA in particular as too "red." But it is important to reiterate that many agency executives had been union activists themselves in earlier years when they had worked as social workers in many of these same agencies. This background and the relative intimacy of agency work resulted in a paternalistic pattern of labor relations in many of the casework agencies.[17] Thus, rather than sign union contracts, until the late 1940s, agency executives exchanged letters of agreement with their staffs confirming their mutual recognition of the provisions of a negotiated personnel code. A formal contract, which executives saw as demanding "greater responsibility" of the union, was hammered out at the JBG only after the war, and it took another strike threat in 1946 to win it.[18] The FJP even approved a code in 1949 granting the union the right to cancel the no-strike clause with ten days' notice, and by the end of 1950, the FJP finally agreed to a pension plan the union had been fighting for since the depression.[19]

Workers' celebration of material gains had a hollow ring, however, as right-wing postwar political developments set in motion a shift to a more narrow economic view of labor solidarity. Winning contracts and establishing a permanent union presence in social work did have a lasting impact on working conditions and remained an important component of how social workers viewed their relationship to other workers. Cold War reaction to the trade union movement, however, compelled labor to change, and the balance of elements constituting social worker subjectivity had to change with it.

The Cold War on Labor

After the defeat of Germany and Japan by the Allied forces, American workers awaited a bright new economic day. The desires of the consumer society had been deferred during the war, but now that the United States was the unquestioned leader of the "free world," government and business leaders promised that the new "American Century" would bring its citizens a flood of goods and the highest standard of living in the world. For its part, labor, anxious to recoup losses from the wartime wage freeze, initiated the greatest strike wave in American history. Meanwhile, the economy expanded, although unevenly: private industry jobs became more plentiful and offered higher wages than jobs in the public sector. Indeed, social worker salaries did not recover from the depression until after the war, and then they showed relatively little improvement.[20] Frustrated by the disparity between postwar meliorist rhetoric and the achievements of industrial workers and their own stifled ambitions, public employees protested.

The strike wave of 1946, coupled with the rising fears of communism, emboldened business leaders and politicians to try to regain an upper hand in labor relations. As the federal government eased its wartime regulation of labor-management relations, businesspeople rushed to reverse New Deal labor policies that had stimulated unionization and trade union militancy. Opportunist and right-wing ideologues, such as fledgling California congressman Richard Nixon, played into these needs, mobilizing Cold War fears around the Soviet Union and the potential catastrophe that hostile use of the atomic bomb would unleash on Americans. Conservative politicians also used the fact that voters could hold them liable for public sector strikes to win passage of new antilabor legislation. The Wagner Act and the establishment of a welfare "net" allowed business to cast the New Deal state as labor's helpmate, but the passage in 1947 of the Taft-Hartley Act in Congress placed the state firmly on the side of capital. The act permitted managers to obtain federal injunctions to prevent strikes, prohibited secondary boycotts, and banned the union shop. Moreover, other antilabor legislation required officials in "suspect" unions to register as communists, effectively "admitting" that they belonged to a "seditious" or "alien" organization. The same year, New York State legislators passed the Condon-Wadlin Act outlawing strikes by public employees. Within a few years, forty-five states had adopted such prohibitions with severe penalties for strikers.[21]

In this politically charged context, labor unions that were suspected of identifying with the Soviet Union were especially vulnerable. The SSEU and the United Public Workers (UPW) were such unions: aggressive and socially conscious, they were open to charges that they were seditious because of the conformity of their positions on foreign policy with those of the Soviet Union. For their part, the unions averred that the Cold War and the Marshall Plan took money from welfare programs and diverted it to defense. But such views presumed that the Soviet Union was not a threat, a position that an increasingly vocal number of people found untenable and even dangerous. In July 1947, for instance, one such group, American Business Consultants, published an "objective study" of the UOPWA in *Counterattack: The Newsletter of Facts on Communism*. American Business Consultants did not disclose who had hired them, but it seems to have been anticommunists within the CIO and not "business" at all since the report was part of the docket used by the CIO in building its case to expel the union. The report listed four prominent past and present UOPWA leaders as communists—Bernard R. Segal, Norma Aronson, Mary Van Kleeck, and Lewis Merrill. The charge was not necessarily wrong, but its import was that all union policies flowed from Moscow; that people like ex–union president Merrill, who had "served as an obvious Kremlin lieutenant for many years," took orders from the Soviet Union; and that the rank and file did not have minds of their own but were "dupes."[22]

The attack on the radical social worker trade unions was part of the profound conservative shift in the labor movement and labor-management relations at mid-century. Labor historian Nelson Lichtenstein has aptly described the new "labor-capital accord" that developed as "the peculiarly American system of inter class accommodation that jelled in the 1940s—a decentralized system characterized by extremely detailed, firm-centered collective bargaining contracts, a relatively low level of social welfare spending, and a labor market segmented by race, gender, region and industry."[23] On domestic issues, the SSEU and the UOPWA were independent-minded unions with a broad social perspective that craft unionists in groups such as the AFSCME found troubling. Convinced that the AFSCME was too narrowly tied to craft unionism and professional voluntarism, Abe Flaxer had taken much of the membership into the SCMWA in 1936. In the next decade, the SCMWA aggressively continued to oppose the AFSCME. Now, as the Cold War generated attacks on radical labor, many often socialist but unremittingly anticommunist labor leaders who had been struggling to regain a foothold in social service saw an opportunity. If management would recognize them, they would be the "respectable" voice of labor.[24]

Anticommunism in social work was, of course, not new. FJP leaders had expressed concerns since the mid-1920s that identification with the left would jeopardize Jewish respectability and social worker "objectivity." By the mid-1930s, these concerns were echoed in attacks on social worker unions by the Dies Committee, the congressional predecessor to the House Un-American Activities Committee. The Cold War, especially following on the heels of the 1946 strike wave, simply organized these attitudes, helped give them wider credence, and provided them with an aura of legitimacy. Such views served the common interests of a range of politicians, businesspeople, and alternative labor voices looking to gain power. With the more restrictive labor legislation in place by 1947, only one piece was missing before the "labor-capital accord" could be completed: the radical unions had to be replaced with a more "respectable" and, hopefully, "cooperative" labor movement. Not surprisingly, then, in poignant stories collected in "confidential" AASW grievance files for the years between 1946 and 1954, dozens of caseworkers from every section of the country, from public and private agencies, sectarian and nonsectarian, stated that they had been fired or penalized for union activities or "left-wing" politics.[25] Once again, the history of the radical social worker unions in New York City typified the ruthlessness with which conservatives and anticommunist liberals in both government and social work agencies hounded hundreds of "suspect" social worker trade unionists.

Postwar New York City

The election of a strongly prolabor mayor, William O'Dwyer, in New York City in November 1943 gave public sector workers hope of improving their position, and transit workers, tugboat crews, and 7,500 Western Union employees all went out on strike in 1946. Previous mayor Fiorello La Guardia had spoken warmly of labor, but intent on keeping a lid on the city budget, in practice he had offered labor few material gains.[26] Social workers pressed their demands with renewed vigor, too. In the DW, Frank Herbst, president of the left-wing SCMWA, claimed that 2,000 DW employees were ready to stop work in April 1946 if salary inequities, especially among clericals, were not alleviated.[27] Meanwhile, at the FJP, after threatening a work stoppage, the SSEU signed a contract for an 18 percent wage increase for 300 social workers and clerical workers at the "big three" agencies: the JBG, the JFS, and the JCCA.[28] Three years later, private agency social workers not covered by social security also won a pension plan.[29]

Complaints about working conditions and personal budgets suggest mounting frustration with the double ambitions that the professional worker identity tried to satisfy; gains as trade unionists did not necessarily translate into middle-class gains. Wage hikes, although the percentage of increase was high, in actual dollars did little to meet social workers' consumer ambitions. The 1946 settlement won caseworkers a minimum wage of $2,400 year, but a "middle-aged" social worker had claimed a year earlier that he and his wife could not subsist "at a Professional Level" on a gross annual income of $2,688. Their income did not permit them to buy many books or magazines, pursue advanced courses of study, or belong to a professional organization, all of which were expected of professionals. A "middle-class" American reported in *Welfare*, the SSEU newsletter, that he was unable to afford "to go to a movie, a concert and the opera in any one month. . . . And, of course, he has nothing for savings, life insurance, vacations, let alone the normal American middle-class convenience of a car." The final irony of this social worker's plight was that his income did not meet his own agency's "budget standards set for moderate cost living."[30]

Eking out a "middle-class" "professional standard" was even more of a problem for women social workers. In a militant speech at the 1946 UOPWA national convention, Vice President Joseph H. Levy, a former Rank-and-File organizer from Chicago, noted that women were consistently discriminated against in the "'industry,' although most of the professional workers are women." How, he asked, as professionals can they afford to "dress as they must, buy meals, and maintain their health at such rates of pay?"[31]

Women's problems were compounded if they were also African American or Hispanic. A 1945 article in *Welfare* reported that Dorothy Canada, for instance, an African American social worker at the Brooklyn Bureau of Social Service who earned $1,900 a year, lived with her mother in a $38 a month apartment that was "rarely heated in winter and [has] . . . no hot water." Moreover, *Welfare* pointed out, discrimination forced African Americans such as the Canadas to pay more for "everything they get . . . in addition to living on a starvation salary." As in the depression, such deprivations helped social workers "identify" with their clients, but, making a subtle but significant shift, *Welfare*, the voice of the radical UOPWA, now saw such identification with the poor as a detriment to "valid social work practice."[32]

The author's rhetorical conclusion suggests that social workers had begun to emphasize their own comfort as a basis for their productive work: "Isn't it more likely that the Dorothy Canadas could do even a better job than the fine job they are doing, if they could afford winter coats, warm apartments, decent lunches, and the other minima of an American standard of living?"[33] This change from identifying with clients to identifying with middle-class consumer standards reflected the diminution of a proletarian perspective within the professional worker identity. Of course, the shift in the balancing of their class identity back toward its predominant middle-class perspective also diminished social workers' inclination to rely on trade unionism to redress continued complaints of deteriorating working conditions.

In private agencies, social workers looked to the promise of a brighter postwar future, but worsening working conditions made the present seem like the past. Comparatively lighter workloads and less bureaucracy continued to make work in the private sector an attractive avenue for social mobility out of government relief offices. In many postwar agencies, caseloads did not decline but increased and cases became more difficult. Although they gave no earlier figure for comparison, the Hawthorne and Cedar Knolls facilities reported that the proportion of children diagnosed as "most disturbed" had steadily increased to about 23 percent of admissions by 1948–49.[34] The other JBG services reported a larger share of cases involving adults who required longer treatment and greater application of the still relatively new psychological and psychiatric techniques.[35] The "case worker's dilemma," as posed by two family and child caseworkers in 1947, was how to "meet 1947 standards with 1934 caseloads?" Their sarcastic answer was that caseworkers should grow an "extra dozen hands to juggle telephones, reports and budgets," become two-headed so they could talk to twice as many people, and learn to fly so they could "flit from home to home."[36]

Regimented procedures and constrained budgets in day-to-day work routines also severely limited the autonomy associated with professional social work in private agencies. JBG regulations, for example, required that caseworkers maintain daily and monthly tally sheets. Caseworkers were expected to fill out a detailed two-page form that specifically directed their questions for each case, but space was allotted for a narrative evaluation that left considerable room for caseworker initiative, even if diagnosis and treatment increasingly came from psychiatrists and supervisors. But these procedures produced a tremendous amount of paperwork. Agency casework loads, ranging from forty-five to seventy-five cases, were lighter than DW loads but took no less time. Social investigators were expected to visit each case at least once and preferably twice a month; family therapy was more intensive and involved additional meetings with family members.[37]

The informal, open-ended character of the work and agency paternalism also created conditions easily exploited by supervisors. A 37.5-hour six-and-a-half-day work week was not long by nineteenth-century standards, but the hours really applied only to clerical and maintenance staffs; social workers, as "professional staff," received up to a week's extra vacation time in lieu of additional pay for overtime hours. Grievance machinery, when it existed at all, remained inside the agency and ended with the chief administrator. The public prejudice against striking service workers was formalized in the FJP's personnel codes, which forbid strikes, pickets, and lockouts.[38] Unless social workers moved into supervisory positions, their choices were to quit the work force altogether, leave for jobs elsewhere, or change agencies.

Harsher conditions in the DW, however, did not provide much of an alternative: bureaucratic details and paperwork undermined professional autonomy throughout social work agencies, but the problem was very serious in the DW. The DW's 1945 "Manual of Social Service Policies in Public Assistance" left very little room for clinical maneuvering. Statutory eligibility requirements had to be followed rigorously. Detailed guidelines provided instructions for purchases of every type of commodity, from household furnishings and fuel to clothing. Ascetic propriety seemed to be the norm: a table setting for a family of six could cost no more than $7.25; there was to be enough cutlery for everyone in the family to eat at the same time; and "in selecting furniture," cost was to "be considered in relation to the durability and sturdy construction." As little as possible was left to chance—or to the judgment of the investigator. For example, a girl between the ages of ten and fourteen was entitled to a hat costing up to $1.05; a boy the same age was not. Moreover, these lists were periodically updated, and investigators had to be sure to sort out the latest allotments from the scores of new requirements, executive orders, and work procedures that arrived daily on their desks.[39]

The staff found physical conditions and caseloads at the DW equally demoralizing. In a letter to incoming mayor O'Dwyer in January 1946, DW commissioner Edward E. Rhatigan complained that "[t]he buildings in which we are located are undesirable, our equipment is outmoded, and our staff shortages present a serious threat to the services that the Department must give to the community."[40] Moreover, DW caseloads of between 85 and 120 cases were substantially heavier than those at private agencies, and social workers encountered constantly changing bureaucratic structures.[41]

In both public and private sectors, then, routinized paperwork, heavy caseloads, low wages, and limited mobility frustrated social workers and induced many to leave the field; others turned to their trade unions and professional associations to improve their conditions. High turnover, the need for further training, and the constant effort to maintain funding levels compelled executives and governing boards at both government and private agencies to cast a wary eye on these developments even as they regularly continued to review and revise procedures. The history of social worker unions in New York City illustrates how Cold War politics added to this set of administrative, labor, and fiscal problems, poisoning the political history of social workers and agencies and tolling the death knell for the professional worker identity.

Welfare Workers and Welfare Politics, 1945–1950

Two fears—fear of a racialized "other" and fear of communists—converged to restructure social relations among welfare workers, clients, and the public in postwar New York City. In August 1947, a front-page article in the *New York Times* raised the first fear. The article brought to public attention a social development that had "officials worried": monthly, 2,000 Puerto Ricans were moving to the city. Claiming that 600,000 Puerto Ricans already lived in the city, the article reported that the new arrivals were placing an enormous burden on housing, health, and welfare services.[42] Fear seems, in fact, to have wildly inflated the numbers given in the *Times* account. A 1948 report by C. Wright Mills for the Bureau of Applied Social Research projected the actual number of Puerto Ricans in New York City at the time at closer to 160,000.[43] Indeed, rather than simply describing a "worry," the inflated account in the nation's "newspaper of record" gave official credence to an emerging racialized welfare script, a story that would shape the public discourse about welfare rights, abuses, and services for the rest of the century. "Worry" was an understatement; this anxiety was part of a growing public hysteria about a racialized "other" in welfare.

The migration of many Puerto Ricans to New York City in the late 1940s and the DW's absorption of the Department of Child Welfare during this same period, which dramatically increased the percentage of African American AFDC clients, made visible the change in the racial composition of the city's poor.[44] Unfortunately, racial prejudice in America has often been based on imaginings of a visible "other" as omnipresent and on a view of the victims of social injustice as its perpetrators. In truth, little is known about how "whiteness" has been understood in America, either by Puerto Ricans or by others. Although many Puerto Rican clients may have considered themselves "white" (63 percent listed their "color" as white in 1948), this was not necessarily how the general public viewed them.[45] In general, racial coding in the United States inclines people of northern and eastern European stock to ascribe "blackness" to "others" much more than "others" have been inclined to ascribe "blackness" to themselves.[46] The mapping of a heightened racial consciousness onto class in the DW makes the New York City story an important precursor of national developments in the race politics of welfare and poverty. In particular it illuminates how in the last half of the twentieth century the poor are imagined as black and brown and the "middle class" as white.

The end of the war unleashed a second fear that compounded the growing anxiety about public relief: communists, politicians warned, were subverting welfare at great cost to taxpayers. Indeed, the SCMWA had merged in 1946 with another left-wing CIO union, the United Federal Workers of America, to form the UPW. As an industrial union representing clerical and professional workers, New York City's Local 1, UPW, had special appeal to the particularly vulnerable provisional workers and claimed a substantial majority of the nearly 6,000 welfare workers. Local 75, UPW, represented the New York City supervisors.[47]

Antiracist and client-oriented UPW policies that mirrored Communist Party positions were deeply suspect among critics, many of whom were already predisposed against welfare. One historian of the period has noted that in this era "when many of the attacks on the growing relief rolls had a strong anti-Black and Puerto Rican tone" the UPW local elected Eleanor Goding, a black woman, as president. In addition, union contracts that made demands on behalf of people other than workers were unusual, even among unions in manufacturing and heavy industry. Blue-collar trade unions such as the United Automobile Workers did not, for instance, press contract demands on behalf of car owners for automobile safety or better models.[48] In contrast, UPW contract demands in 1948 included provisions to improve client services: a 30 percent increase in client budgets and improved medical and social services at each welfare center. For relief workers themselves, the union demanded increased wages, lower caseloads, and formal recognition. Finally, demanding day-care facilities for both staff and clients, the union demonstrated an awareness that workers' needs were not inseparable from those of the clients they served.[49] In contrast, the conservative Civil Service Forum (CSF), gaining courage and support from the passage of the Taft-Hartley Act, joined newspaper attacks on welfare policies that were supposedly soft on clients.

After the war, the strikes of public employees and the rising cacophony of

McCarthyism brought intense political pressure on DW administrators. The mayor and the welfare commissioner might find themselves one day defending the DW against allegations of inadequate relief and the next day resisting charges of DW corruption and client immorality. For example, the president of the Welfare Council, which consisted of representatives from public and private agencies throughout the city, alleged in February 1947 that New York City was "complacent in facing its social and health needs."[50] Three months later, Commissioner Rhatigan had to defend the placement of thirty-seven families on welfare (120 of the 233,000 people then on relief) in hotels, who ironically were not sent there by the DW but by Catholic Charities. Rhatigan pleaded that people should "not be diverted by stories of luxury relief, Communism, [or] Christian Fronters." The real problem, he reminded citizens, was a citywide housing crisis, in which the DW had scrupulously followed every state regulation concerning housing for the homeless. Finally, the mayor tried to divert public complaints about DW profligacy and bureaucracy by publicizing recommendations by his Executive Committee on Administration that would decrease paperwork and put more relief workers into the field investigating clients.[51] But the welfare hotel issue would not die. Separate city and state investigations of the DW proceeded, and in late October 1947, Rhatigan was forced to resign.

Benjamin Fielding, the commissioner of licensing, temporarily took on the job of DW commissioner, continuing to defend the department against its critics. Fielding had been commissioner for only a week, however, when he was forced to enter Doctor's Hospital because of exhaustion. During that time, he had announced that 7,000 "employable" relief clients (of 80,000 on home relief) would be dropped from the welfare rolls if they did not find jobs and had issued seven executive orders demanding "punctuality and full time on the job" from social investigators. Nothing had prepared him, however, for the hullabaloo caused by disclosures of a New York State investigation of DW corruption. The investigator found that eligibility had been established in only twenty-two of forty-two sample cases and then dramatically announced that a "woman in mink with $60,000 lived on relief in a hotel," for which the city paid $7.50 a night! Such abuses, the investigator concluded, testified that the "underlying principle of the city's relief administration was: 'The client is always right.' "[52]

Fielding's three months as commissioner functioned as a kind of holding action in which the commissioner defended his beleaguered staff, but three developments came together during his interregnum that shaped and armed his successor's administration.[53] First, regardless of the varied racial identity of Puerto Ricans, race as "nonwhite" was increasingly scripted onto class in the DW.[54] Second, state and city politicians kept the DW constantly under the gun in a seemingly endless stream of investigations. Third, anticommunism became an organized and unimpeachable tenet of social policy. The well-publicized testimony of ex-commissioner Rhatigan before state hearings in Albany in early December 1947 highlighted this development.

Forced to resign as "soft" on welfare "profligacy," Rhatigan intended to set the record straight. Even with a "terrific rate of turnover," staff shortages, heavy caseloads, and the "to do" in the press, the ex-commissioner noted, the percentage of clients ineligible for welfare was no higher than at other times. Instead, Rhatigan offered alternative scapegoats for the problems with welfare. First, he shifted the blame from himself to O'Dwyer, claiming that the mayor had met his repeated requests for a full complement of social investigators only after the crisis hit the newspapers. Then, he attacked a "philosophy of liberality" among social workers and communists in the CIO union.

Rhatigan characterized the liberal philosophy as a " 'let's not waste all our time to see that every penny is spent correctly' " approach, which was taught in all the social work schools and learned in the state agencies. The amalgamation of welfare services for dependent children, services for the aged and the blind, and home relief also encouraged this profligate philosophy. The result, he argued, was an openhanded treatment that confused those who could not work with those who could, extending unwarranted generosity to the latter.

According to Rhatigan, the main problem was the central role of communists in the DW. Morale, he declared, was seriously damaged in the department by the constant battle between the UPW and the CSF. Welfare Council 330 of the CSF was, in fact, a small caseworker organization in the DW that at its peak claimed no more than 500 members. Since it had pledged not to strike and rejected the right to bargain collectively or form an open shop, the DW was delighted to recognize it as an alternative to the UPW.[55] The CSF probably had one-tenth of the UPW's membership, but Rhatigan represented it as an equal and identified the UPW as the "problem." Together, Rhatigan estimated, the two groups represented 99 percent of the staff; they fought constantly, "espous[ing] different philosophies and us[ing] different tactics." Choosing not to examine how these philosophies related to client care, Rhatigan emphasized the potential administrative problems that occurred when the DW was confronted with Communist Party discipline. He claimed that he could not answer whether or not the UPW was "dominated" by communists, although it was widely reputed to be, but contended that the union 'has followed the communist party line for some ten years and there are communists in the Department. This creates quite a problem."

Faced with this "problem," Rhatigan complained that his options were limited. A putative list of communists in the DW was being bandied about in Albany—the Herlands list—but even if such a list existed, Rhatigan reminded the committee, employees could not be summarily dismissed simply for being communists. His parting advice: identify the communists, prevent their promotion, and fire them "if their communistic philosophy affected their service in the Department."[56]

Raymond M. Hilliard, the new DW chief, arrived in New York City in mid-March 1948, soon proclaiming that he expected to do more than identify the communists; he intended to " 'set our house in order.' "[57] Hilliard had cut his welfare teeth as an attorney who prosecuted cases of fraud for the Illinois Emergency Relief Commission. He had then sharpened them as executive secretary of its successor organization, the Illinois Public Aid Commission, where he gained a reputation for toughness by returning $10.5 million of the $50 million welfare budget to state coffers by implementing meticulous and frequent reviews of eligibility. He now applied his techniques in New York City.[58]

Hilliard's stormy three-year assault on client ineligibility, social investigator inefficiency, DW budgetary fat, and communist pollution of the department cannot be separated from the heightened racial subtext that had begun to insinuate itself into the ways social investigators, DW administrators, and the general public understood the problems of poverty, unemployment, and single motherhood. Hilliard had promised to announce on July 1, 1948, his plans for the reorganization of the DW, but in the six weeks leading up to his announcement, two incidents placed the growing concern over the presence of African Americans and Puerto Ricans on welfare rolls in bold relief. The first event reflected a new and heightened racialization of welfare politics as "black." When the UPW demonstrated in late May for increased relief benefits, additional housing, and more staff, it chose to do so in the African American communities of Harlem in Manhattan and Bedford-Stuyvesant in Brooklyn. The UPW sponsored the protests despite Hilliard's complaint that demonstrations were "unprofessional," and it knew that poverty especially wracked New York City's black communities and hoped to mobilize them as additional numbers in the calculus of welfare politics.[59]

The second racially coded event reflected how racial "otherness" in welfare had begun to take on the attributes of being "undeserving" and pathological that previously had been associated with the poor. This case involved yet another state investigation of alleged "misuse of relief funds" in the DW, this time conducted by John M. Murtagh, the New York State commissioner of investigation. The front-page headline of an article on the investigation in the *New York Times* called attention to the ethnic background of those accused: "Recipients Send Money out of Country, Fly to Puerto Rico." The article did not discuss the circumstances surrounding such behavior; rather, the "facts" were presented as a self-evident indictment. Investigators had observed a single Manhattan post office for a three-day period during the previous December and noted that within three days of receiving their checks, 118 relief recipients had purchased money orders and sent them overseas. Although the article maintained the anonymity of the "recipients," their ethnic identity was made clear to readers by a "second case": during the week prior to Christmas, twenty-three people on relief had flown from New York City to Puerto Rico.[60]

In addition to the ethnic and racially coded rescripting of the "undeserving" welfare "other," Murtagh presented twenty-five "findings" against the union. The first fourteen focused on investigators' inadequate attention to "the essence of eligibility"; the last eleven, giving lengthy and itemized indictments, placed the blame for welfare's problems entirely at the feet of the UPW. So armed, Hilliard was ready to battle the union.[61]

On July 1, 1948, two years before the CIO expelled the UPW, Hilliard conducted a protracted campaign to break up the UPW local and banish its left-wing leadership. Simultaneously he announced that he would reorganize the DW with singular attention to reviewing eligibility and institute a "reexamination and complete reinvestigation of our public assistance caseload." Hilliard did not feel that social investigators were overworked; rather, he asserted that the department standard of seventy-five cases, as well as the actual load of eighty-five cases, "is one of the lightest caseloads in the country and I fail to see how a person can be overworked under these circumstances."[62] Hilliard believed that relief allowances were more than adequate, declaring with much public fanfare that his family had been living for a month on a relief allowance of $124.50, had eaten well, and still had $28.54 left (see figure 6.1)![63]

Hilliard agreed with his predecessor that the problem in welfare was communism, but he gave his analysis a gendered twist. He was convinced that communists in the department championed popular causes like increased relief and improved working conditions in DW offices for ulterior political motives and that they seduced the impressionable "young women recently out of college" who were recruited into the agency "to evade the rules." Hilliard assumed that if more men could be lured into social work, the profession could better resist communist wiles. In fact, agency executives, both public and private, sought to hire more men but did not have the money to attract them. The work force remained predominantly female, and so people like Hilliard first attempted to purge the leaders (who were often male) and then adopted a gendered strategy to deal with the women. Presuming that the pliability of women would make them more receptive subjects, he planned to "retrain" them in "proper" work attitudes.[64]

A short-term solution required more drastic action, and here Hilliard resorted to familiar McCarthyite abuses of civil liberties. Setting out first to silence the communists' voices, Hilliard forbid political activities such as demonstrating, leafleting, and pamphleteering by city employees.[65] Then, following the formal CIO expulsion of the UPW as, in its words, "an instrument of the Commu-

Figure 6.1. This illustration prefigures neoconservative Jewish criticism of "liberal" welfare in the 1970s. In the photograph, DW commissioner Raymond M. Hilliard is seen "during a meal with his wife, mother and two sons at his home on Riverside Drive" demonstrating "that a family of six can get by on $96 a month." The handwritten note beneath the photo from the editor of an unidentified Yiddish-language publication congratulates Hilliard on his tough welfare policy. Scrapbooks, Raymond M. Hilliard Collection, Chicago Historical Society. Courtesy of Chicago Historical Society.

nist Party," Hilliard issued Executive Order 291 on March 9, 1950, removing Local 1 from its list of recognized staff bodies. When UPW organizing persisted, Hilliard proceeded to discipline, penalize, or dismiss any worker who " 'casts discredit upon the Department,' " much as he had during the past year. Although all were penalized without specific charges for disregarding a blanket order forbidding any union activity during or after office hours, only leaders were dismissed; some fifty-odd others were suspended or lost promotions.[66]

Many social workers understood that these events threatened the proclient values that animated both their work and their identity as professional workers. Some public assistance workers took to the streets, holding rallies and picketing Hilliard. Rain spoiled the largest planned demonstration, however, and suspensions dampened much remaining ardor. Nonetheless, a rally of 3,000 DW employees in February 1950 forced Hilliard to retract the firing of militants who had refused to reinvestigate 40 percent of their cases.[67] A poem in the *Super-Ego Newsletter*, a rank-and-file broadside published in 1950, captured the gist of the social workers' complaint:

Who cares for feelings,
Let casework go hang,
   But get the ineligibles
   Out with a bang!
Look into their relatives
Into their past,
   And if they're not needy
   Get them out fast.
The workers then started
protesting this speed.
   More time, it was stated
   Is also a need.
But this outrage, said Hilliard
Must cease and desist.
   Unprofessional tactics
   When workers resist.
Yet if this continues
When all's said and done,
   Of clients and workers
   There'll be nary a one.
And then Mr. Hilliard
What will you do?
   There won't even be
   A need for you![68]

Eight JBG social workers from Local 19, UOPWA, understood the wider implications of the UPW purge and Hilliard's final coup de grace: the requirement that all employees take a blanket loyalty oath. In a letter to O'Dwyer, the eight warned that Hilliard's order "will suppress free discussion, criticism and legitimate trade union activity." Hilliard's actions, they argued, focused attention uncritically on worker loyalty and client eligibility and would have a chilling effect on social worker rights and initiative.[69] Indeed, parallel developments in the FJP showed just how much the Cold War at home could freeze opposition to the new restrictive and repressive DW administrative mentality and, with it, the spirit of the professional worker in the private sector.

FJP Caseworkers and FJP Politics, 1947–1951

In contrast to anticommunism in the DW, where the politics of the union served as a lightning rod for a highly publicized and politicized anticommunist crusade, anticommunism played a smaller part in private Jewish agencies. Among the many possible reasons for this are fears of an anti-Semitic backlash against the agencies; general sympathy for labor, especially among agency executives who as caseworkers had once been union members; and the FJP's reluctance to jeopardize fund-raising efforts by drawing public attention to the presence of "reds" in Jewish charity. Accordingly, the FJP's Labor Committee rebuffed the JCCA representative who proposed in 1949 that no affiliated agency should sign contracts "with any union officials who had not filed anti-Communist affidavits." Individual agencies were free to do as they pleased, and no general policy was recommended.[70] But the specter of communism had haunted many of the Jewish businesspeople who sat on the FJP agency boards since the 1920s. So, at the same time that Cold War fears began to mobilize political attacks on labor and welfare, anticommunist sentiments began to make a sustained appearance at agency board meetings.

Two cases are symbolic of the new conservative political climate in Jewish (and non-Jewish) social service and typical of the feverish assaults on social worker civil rights during these years. The first was the 1947 case of an unnamed woman union member fired by the NCJW in New York City. It will be remembered that the NCJW had been the first to sign a union contract in 1938. Times had changed, however. Alleging that this woman had used her "connection with the council to promote the Communist party line," the NCJW pleaded with Philip Murray, the anticommunist CIO leader, to help make her ouster permanent to assure the "good reputation and possibly the very survival" of the agency. But there was little Murray could do as the case went to court.[71]

The subsequent arbitration of the case revealed a frightening mix of paranoid politics, vague charges, and abuses of fundamental civil rights in a deeply ideological era. The NCJW called as witness to support its allegations against the woman Sidney Hook, the chairman of the New York University Department of Philosophy. Hook, a former communist, was becoming a fixture on the anticommunist political circuit as an authority on the "Red menace." The purported miscreant, he explained, had "written a child-study manual 'weighted' on the side of communism," had suggested a reading list for NCJW chapters that did not include any anticommunist literature, and had told "off-color" jokes on two occasions before mixed audiences.[72]

Seven months later the woman was reinstated, but neither the woman nor the NCJW could take full pleasure in the ruling. The woman was guilty, the arbitrator explained, of "subverting the policies of the council," but the NCJW was "equally responsible for failure to check her activities and to correct her errors." The woman returned to work, but the NCJW was not required to pay her back pay. Moreover, the next year, the agency's new contract with the SSEU contained a vague clause allowing for the dismissal of an employee who carried out any program other than that of the NCJW.[73]

The second case involved the struggle over reorganized services at the WJCS. With the opening of a new office in Mt. Vernon in the southern part of Westchester County, the WJCS was reorganized in early 1950. Cases were redistributed geographically and caseworkers were assigned according to their specialties, but although all transcriptions would be done in Mt. Vernon, several workers would now split their week between the Mt. Vernon office and the White Plains office in the northern part of the county.[74] The contest over these new assignments provides an intimate look at how services and work shifted with population changes at mid-century, how the conflicts played into the simmering right-wing reaction, and how antiunion administrators and trustees used charges of anticommunism to crush the labor movement.

Shifting work assignments could cause resentment against the director and charges of personal favoritism that could lead to staff turnover—or, as occurred at the WJCS, to unionization. As one board member wrote the chair of the WJCS's board, "Mr. Antman [the director] is demoralizing the staff of the agency by playing one person against the other. This has made the staff distrust him, and fear him. . . . He abuses workers and does not seem to care about anybody's feelings." Moreover, Joseph Antman reserved the agency car for his personal use and had his paper for school typed "by the agency's stenographers while agency work waited." Finally, Antman did not permit "professional staff" to "meet regularly on committees with the board," a normal professional courtesy at other agencies.[75] Lengthy efforts to fashion an acceptable personnel code with Antman failed because he insisted on broad, arbitrary dismissal clauses that included "insubordination, self-provoked discharge . . . [and] inability to fit in with the human relations activities of the agency." In December of that year, the eleven staff members (nine of whom were women) unanimously selected the left-wing Local 19, SSEU, to represent them.[76]

Social relations at the small FJP agencies were personal and paternal, but when administrators' fears about communism translated into active opposition to a union, social relations could be vicious. It was in this spirit that, with the support of the Board of Directors, Antman delivered his response to the union in late February 1951. After locking out the workers when they arrived at the office, he had the White Plains police arrest them for trespassing.[77]

The denouement of the WJCS story was tied to developments in the FJP. Early the next month, the FJP's president publicly announced that the FJP would not renew contracts or deal with Local 19. Strong statements against the board's actions were made by two representatives, Mrs. Alfred Lindau and Stanley M. Isaacs, the ex-borough president, but they proved to be the only dissenters among the approximately eighty people usually attending such meetings. Maurice B. Hexter, the antiunion executive director of the FJP, articulated the general sentiment when he argued to "[p]rolonged applause" that the issue was the legitimacy of Local 19 and that the FJP was "ten years late" in opposing the union.[78]

The FJP board members' autocratic antiunion actions contrasted with the generally more paternalistic behavior of agency executives, a difference that reflected their distinct social backgrounds. Like their staffs, many of the executives were Jews of eastern European ancestry; some would have had some contact with immigrant socialist culture. Thus, Antman's outright hostility to Local 19 was unusual; most agency executives retained ties to their staffs and union sympathies. In contrast, board members were still disproportionately German Jews, businesspeople and financiers with names like Lehman, Straus, Lewisohn, Loeb, Guggenheim, Sulzberger, and so on. For these people, the decision to break with Local 19 was relatively easy, whereas agency executives had to continue to live with their staffs. The JBG's answer was typical: public confidence and financial support required that the agencies not deal with a union "so generally identified in the public mind with policies inimical to the policies and interests of our own government and of the American people." The JBG and the FJP immediately announced that they would welcome and recognize an alternative anticommunist union, the Community and Social Agency Employees (CSAE), Local 1707, CIO, which had been waiting in the wings for the past two years.[79]

Antman took a hard-nosed tack much in keeping with the FJP's board. Armed with the FJP's repudiation of Local 19, Antman fired the local leader, Leon Luchansky. Six members accepted the firing; five backed their ousted leader. They, too, were fired. The five then mobilized support from clients and donors. Pressured, the agency agreed to reinstate them, but with the stipulation "that the workers would abandon their efforts to have a union in WJCS, and that one of their active leaders [Luchansky?] would resign."[8]

Union organizers despaired, but there was little they could do. Agency paternalism, board intransigence, and the purge of radicals had combined to weaken the union movement. Ironically, as board members of agencies like the WJCS, department store owners stonewalled social workers who attempted to organize unions while simultaneously signing contracts with their own clerical workers. Board members, it seems, recognized the union weakness in social service and made no effort to negotiate with unions there. However, the fact that the UOPWA represented both caseworkers and clerical workers was not lost on Local 19's social workers and only brought their weakness home to them. Not surprisingly, when three women resigned from the union following the lockout, it created a disheartening division among the workers. Many social workers had professional aspirations that made them reluctant trade unionists, especially in a "red" union popularly characterized in the mainstream press as towing a rigid "line."[31]

After the dismantling of the left-wing unions, most staff quietly joined the anticommunist alternatives waiting offstage. As early as mid-1948, for example, an anticommunist division of the Marine Warehousemen got permission from the CIO to enroll UOPWA "bolters" into a rival "right-wing union." Among the first to join were employees from the NCJW.[82] By 1951, the FJP had signed new contracts with Local 1707, CSAE; the DW immediately recognized Local 371, AFSCME, which now included many former members of the CSF.[83]

War, Neurosis, and Class

The purge of the left-wing unions and the demise of the professional worker in New York City were stories that resonated with social workers nationwide, facilitating across the land the acquisition of new professional accoutrements—psychiatry, the broadening class base of social work therapy, and the rising standards of living that permitted therapy's commodification. In turn, the resurgent professionalization would inaugurate in the next decade a reconstituted middle-class identity that, stripped of proletarian pretensions, privileged issues of race and consumption over those of class. Central to this revitalized social work professionalism, however, was the growing prestige of psychiatry.

Until the second half of the century, engagement with psychiatry appears to have been the exception in social work, not the rule. Prior to World War I, neurologists and mental disease specialists remained at the bottom of the medical pecking order. Based in asylums, they were seen as custodians of the mentally deficient and the criminal. Progressive Era reform and the World War I experience with "shell shock" led to the popularizing of mental hygiene and the emerging field of neuropsychiatry. Chapter 2 described how agencies such as the JBG introduced Freudian diagnosis and psychiatric services into social work training by the early 1920s. But except for casework at a few private agencies on the East Coast, most casework remained rooted in sociological interviews, placement, and budget advice.[84]

The exodus of refugee psychoanalysts from Europe to the United States in the late 1930s initiated a second psychiatric wave, which had a considerably greater impact on social workers in the postwar era. Many of the elite refugees were doctors and lawyers, but in order to practice in the United States, they had to obtain American certification. Instead, many chose to become social workers and social work educators. Led by these analysts, by the late 1930s, the center of psychoanalysis had shifted to the United States.

This second psychiatric impulse helped put social work in step with postwar consumer culture. Historian John C. Burnham, for example, has suggested that the German Jewish and WASP elite in psychiatry embraced a new ideal of cosmopolitan culture that made therapists both more receptive to immigrant clients and more bourgeois. As cosmopolites, WASPs rejected "100% Americanism" and all it implied, and German Jews rejected the village culture of the ghetto. Still, although Burnham contends that this cosmopolitanism enmeshed the psychiatric community in the values of postwar consumer culture, serious questions about this community's encounter with and psychiatric "evaluation" of eastern European Jewish refugees and working-class clients remain to be explored.[85]

Psychiatric work in World War II caught the public imagination and dramatically enhanced the role and status of the psychiatrist and of psychiatric social work. The study of the psychological profiles of military recruits and the treatment of war trauma enhanced the understanding of mental illness as a cross-class problem—not simply working-class pathology—and, in the postwar years, gave new prestige to the commodification of therapy as a service that "all" could "afford." At the beginning of the war, the analyst Henry Stack Sullivan helped develop procedures to screen military recruits and weed out those deemed "ill-suited for the rigors of military life." As Gerald N. Grob has noted in his summary of wartime psychiatry, although these mass screening procedures proved unreliable, evidence from psychiatric studies of "battle fatigue" and stress in the 1943 Tunisian campaign suggested that " 'the realities of war' " and " 'traumatic stimuli' " could combine " 'to produce a potential war neurosis in every soldier.' "[86] The diagnosis of neurosis and the recognition of its universality were profound developments in the history of psychiatric interventions: here was a respectable alternative to delinquency and the socially devastating diagnosis of pathological behavior. Many "normal" people could suffer a neurosis that psychiatry could claim to prevent or treat.

The extraordinary number of people involved in some sort of psychiatric intervention during the war not only made clear its general applicability but also raised it to an issue of national security. Prevention and treatment, identifying individuals with potential problems and rehabilitating those who were psychological casualties, became a matter of critical importance for the nation and its military. In the screening of recruits, more than 1.75 million people were rejected for neuropsychiatric reasons, including mental deficiency During the war, military hospitals received 1.1 million admissions for some type of neuropsychiatric disorder, although the actual number of soldiers treated was somewhat smaller due to readmissions (Over 61 percent of these admissions were in the United States and were not thought to be from battle stress.) *Psychology for the Fighting Man: What You Should Know about Yourself and Others* even became a paperback best-seller in 1943. Although the military had assigned only thirty-five people to the army medical corps psychiatric sections at the time of the bombing of Pearl Harbor, by the end of the war, it had appointed 2,400 physicians to psychiatric services, many of whom had little previous training. (That number, in fact, exceeded the total 1940 membership of the American Psychiatric Association.) Moreover, psychiatry had become institutionalized in the military, and psychiatrists had been given officer ranks: William C. Menninger, a member of the Topeka Psychoanalytic Society, headed army psychiatry, and John M. Murray, from the Boston Psychoanalytic Society, led the army air force psychiatric services.[87]

The transformation of the image of the psychiatrist from that of a slightly seedy, sinister asylum superintendent as depicted by Sinclair Lewis in *Ann Vickers* (see chapter 3) to that of a kindly, wise older man with a notepad and analytic couch has been nicely summarized by Burnham in his account of psychiatry's influence on American culture. Americans' expectations of a better life after the war coincided with a growing infatuation with psychiatry as a way of securing "happiness." By 1945, Menninger reported no less than six Hollywood films then in production that had a psychiatric angle. As a *Life* magazine article celebrating the psychiatric "boom" noted, "[I]t is rare to find a Hollywood musical these days without some sort of pseudo-Freudian 'dream sequence,' a convention dating from the huge success of Moss Hart's *Lady in the Dark*, which concerned the efforts of a mixed-up editor of a fashion magazine to solve her difficulties through psychoanalysis." Writing in the *New Republic* in 1948, Frederic Wertham summarized the broad new appeal of psychiatry: "popular reading in psycho-pathology" had become "an important social phenomena."[88]

The growth of psychiatric services meshed with the combination of high expectations, anxieties, and tensions associated with postwar American culture. The conversion of war production to the manufacture of consumer goods initiated an era of economic growth that saw real incomes and standards double between 1945 and 1973. Not everyone shared in that growth, of course, and in the war's immediate aftermath, it remained but a promise. Cold War fears threat-

these high expectations. Simultaneously, the return of veterans from the
war was accompanied by efforts to reimpose, at considerable psychic cost, actual
and imagined prewar social roles in the workplace and the home. According to
historian Regina G. Kunzel, popular prescriptive literature of the postwar era
celebrated a "family centered culture and rigidly differentiated and prescriptive
gender roles . . . [in which] a therapeutic approach to social problems gained
immense popularity."[89] Thus, the "insight" of psychiatrists was increasingly seen
as a way to help people "adjust" to the vicissitudes of both "modern" consumer
culture and "traditional" family life.

The postwar emergence of a therapeutic society that was increasingly infatuated with the notion that talking with a psychological "expert" could help people
cope with everyday stress encouraged any number of careers to offer "professional assistance" as advice, counseling, or therapy. Such developments propelled changes at even a vanguard psychiatric agency such as the JBG. The fact
that some influential members of Sigmund Freud's inner circle, including his
daughter, Anna Freud, and the JBG's chief psychiatrist in the late 1930s, J. H. W.
Van Ophuijsen, did not believe it was necessary to have an M.D. to perform
psychotherapy facilitated the introduction of the JBG's professional staff into the
world of psychotherapy. Experience during the war with psychological treatment furthered the agency's commitment to psychotherapeutic techniques. In
October 1945, the newly appointed executive associate, Bertram Black, announced that the agency's task would be to assimilate "newer knowledge on
human behavior that the war has released." And his goal was evident in his new
staff appointments. By 1946, the JBG's psychiatric staff had grown to fifteen
(approximately one-third of the professional employees) and included the nation's most famous "baby" doctor, Benjamin Spock, as consulting pediatric
psychiatrist. The chief psychiatrist was now Nathan W. Ackerman, who would
go on to found one of the leading training institutes for marital and family
counseling. Reflecting tensions in social roles as well as new attitudes, divorce
rates would begin to escalate in the postwar era, and marital and family counseling would be among the increased services offered by social workers to the
general public.[90]

The fact that many social worker therapeutic projects, such as marital counseling, were also performed by countless other folks undermined the accredited
social worker and complicated the task of defining social work. Psychiatrists
with medical degrees, ministers (and rabbis and priests), and clinical psychologists—not to mention journalistic columns giving advice to the distraught, love-
lorn, and hapless as well as best-selling self-help books—all offered to help
people cope with their problems. Social work's overlap or confusion with other
occupations was not new; social workers' need to distinguish their work from
that of religious workers, nurses, volunteers, and psychiatrists had been a con-

stant source of concern since early in the century. In the postwar era, however, the arena of conflict had shifted to psychotherapy, where social workers found themselves trapped in an uneasy middle ground. Above them were the psychiatrists and psychoanalysts, who complained about competition from underqualified social workers who offered therapy without state accreditation as therapists. Below them were the enterprising counselors and advisers who were free to simply hang out a shingle and offer advice. A resurgent professionalism guided the social workers' quest for stable ground on which to begin their long march toward therapeutic accreditation.

The use of psychiatric techniques quickly won some social workers a measure of recognition: two JBG social workers received teaching positions at Smith College, and several others were invited to participate in institutes for family caseworkers. Then, in recognition of its leading role in psychiatric social work, in 1948 the federal government acknowledged the JBG as one of only two agencies in New York City for advanced psychiatric training. Director Herschel Alt proudly noted that the JBG's Jewish Child Guidance Institute had "been working toward a greater degree of professionalization, and we invest a great amount of training in our workers."[91] Thus, at the same time that the identity of the professional worker grew less tenable, psychiatry emerged to help secure social workers' status and to encourage the reascendance of the enhanced professional identity as a modern professional, an identity that would flower in the 1950s.

Alt's celebration of professionalization reflected social workers' different construction of the term in the postwar era based on new measures of expertise and training. Institutes for children such as the one at the JBG had been created in the earlier professionalizing era of the 1920s. To be professional at that time meant participation in emerging institutional structures in which workers exchanged and shared information: conferences, journals, casework seminars, and graduate work at one of the new graduate schools of social work.[92] There was a great infatuation with Freud's work among the New York City intelligentsia, but on the whole, the content of social work remained limited to popular psychology and casework interview techniques. Only in postwar America—and not just in Manhattan—was psychiatric theory and technique celebrated as the sine qua non of professional social work and incorporated into general practice.

An opinion poll conducted by Cleveland's Welfare Council in 1945 on postwar expectations about social work illustrates the ways in which the emergence of neurosis as a diagnosis and the commodification of therapy facilitated the social worker's heightened identity as middle class. Interviews with 700 female family heads found that public attitudes about the work and class identity of social workers and their clients had changed dramatically since 1930, well before postwar consumerism.[93] Reporting on the poll, *Survey Midmonthly* included an illustration showing John Q. Public looking at three stereotyped portraits, one of a plutocratic male board member, one of a spinsterly (but not poor) social worker, and one of a heavyset poor woman client (see figure 6.2). The caption asked whether these distinct class profiles were "true or false." The answer, the poll implied, was "false." Asked whether social work was " 'for poor people only or for all sorts of people, including those who can pay for service,' " 75 percent of the respondents replied, " 'for everybody.' " Since the onset of the depression, the poll suggested, the image of "the social worker as a hireling carrying a basket for Lady Bountiful" had shifted, so that now all three pictures could, in fact, be that of a client. Although only 19 percent of those queried actually had a "well-informed" idea of what social workers did, the pollsters concluded optimistically—and a bit defensively—that social workers could now throw off "inferiority complexes" caused by their earlier image as patronizing, low-status, and sexless old biddies who associated only with the poor and "face the public" with confidence.

Like all good entrepreneurs, private agencies sought to increase their "market share" and find new customers. With the mushrooming of federal relief programs during the depression, these agencies attempted to distinguish themselves from public assistance by claiming expertise in advanced treatments and services that extended beyond providing jobs and financial aid. The Cleveland poll suggested that their efforts to market their therapeutic "skill" as a commodity appropriate to people of all social classes were meeting success: 25 percent of the respondents said they would turn to a social worker for help with family problems.[94] So, like their colleagues in the 1920s, private agency social workers entered the 1940s seeking to meet professional consumer standards; in the postwar era, they began to transform themselves into therapists providing a middle-class consumer good, free of the stigma associated with service to the poor. Although it took place over several decades, this transformation accelerated in the 1940s.

But how much had the client profile and the work actually changed by 1945? The line between clients and social investigators had blurred early in the New Deal when HRB workers might be found administering aid one day and receiving it the next. The HRB recruited depression era social workers who saw themselves as "middle class," with distinct expectations and interests and a background in white-collar trades, but fragile living and working conditions and trade union militancy led them to emphasize their "identity of interests" with the working class.[95] The significance of the Cleveland poll's postwar images, then, lies less in a changed client profile than in a subtle but significant shift in social workers' confidence concerning their identity as middle class and in their conviction that their service was now equally appropriate to the poor and to the affluent.

Recent work on illegitimacy by Kunzel illustrates how social workers also began to elaborate different signifiers of class for different patient populations

Three Portraits—True or False?

Courtesy *Community*

Figure 6.2. In its 1945 report on an opinion poll concerning postwar expectations for social work, the Cleveland Welfare Council suggested that the stereotypes shown in this sketch were false. The social worker was no longer imagined as a sexless biddy, both men and women now served on boards, and, most important, the client now might resemble anyone. With the rise of therapy and counseling, social workers could be of help to all, regardless of their social position. Jack Yeaman Bryan, "Vote of Confidence for Social Work," *Survey Midmonthly*, November 15, 1945, 285. Courtesy of Tamiment Institute Library, New York University.

during this era. Noting the rising number of white middle-class single women applying to homes and agencies for help during this era, she found that social workers increasingly described them in terms of demeanor—as having a "soft voice" or an "educated accent" or as "poised, calm and assured, quiet, unruffled, friendly and smiling."[96] Not surprisingly, during this same period, agencies began to provide aid on a fee-for-service basis, using rate schedules that gradually increased as the income level of the client increased.[97] Although fees obviously served agencies' needs for money, the cost also alleviated middle-class clients' fears of being associated with welfare relief. Such clients, as one social worker from the Florence Crittenton Homes, Rose Bernstein, candidly explained, also needed a different "class" diagnosis: " '[T]he extension of unmarried motherhood into our upper and educated classes in sizable numbers further confounds us by rendering our former stereotypes less tenable. Immigration, low mentality, and hypersexuality can no longer be comfortably applied when the phenomena has [sic] invaded our own social class.' " The diagnosis of unwed mothers as neurotic, as Kunzel points out, was the answer: middle-class white women (and men, although undoubtedly for different reasons) were "neurotic," a condition seen as a "normal" aspect of the modern condition, whereas working-class and African American women remained mired in "pathological" behavior.[98]

The diagnosis of the neurotic may have encouraged the broadening of social service, but as Linda Gordon's work on family violence has suggested, psychiatric diagnosis remained prejudiced against women and girls.[99] Essentialist assumptions about women's appropriate nurturing roles endured as agencies (and most social workers) continued to privilege male caseworkers as breadwinners and never questioned women's double day. Not surprisingly, women were still paid and promoted less than men. If anything, by helping to obscure gender issues further, prevailing economic agendas in the 1930s facilitated the rise of the professional worker as a neutered identity. The postwar era brought the wrath of McCarthyism down on the CIO unions in social work, but McCarthyism was hardly intended to put working women's needs back on the table. Rather, it encouraged the resurgence of a feminine professional identity in the 1950s as the prevailing image for social workers, an image remarkably congenial to the right-wing currents in the air. As soldier-husbands returned from the war expecting to take back their former jobs, popular pressure on Rosie the Riveter to "readjust" to her traditional role as homemaker mounted, lest she emasculate her mate. For female social workers, such pressure would undercut professional aspirations in ways reminiscent of the construction of a gendered professional identity in the 1920s: they would have to be perfect nurturing housewives as well as dispassionate professionals. The reconstruction of professional identity is a story to be picked up in the next chapter; it was in the 1940s, however, that social workers' language of class and sense of middle-class identity began to shift, part of what historian Ira Katznelson describes as labor's "transformation from social democratic insurgency into a mere interest group."[100]

It was the issue of race, however, that would be most central to the reconstruction of middle-class identity in mid-century America, as two appeals to the JBG in 1949 suggested. The JBG reported that it had received a number of requests to place black children at the Hawthorne School; up until that time, it had accepted only Jewish children. At the same time, the Atlanta University School of Social Work, a training program for African Americans, asked the JBG to employ one of its graduates as a psychiatric social worker. The agency almost always had "a mixed staff," Director Alt vaguely explained, but it had no formal policy on the hiring of African Americans. To be sure, from early in its history, the JBG had taken on students from the Atlanta school for advanced training; still, the JBG's permanent professional staff was almost uniformly Jewish and white. Meanwhile, JFS executives raised parallel concerns: as the federal government provided a mounting share of private agency funds for services in increasingly black neighborhoods, how would federal guidelines shape agencies' programs, limits on the number of clients, and decisions about who agencies would serve?[101] In immediate terms, these questions asked what it meant to be a private agency and what it meant to do Jewish social work. More generally, they asked how race and the state would shape social work policy, worker autonomy, and the politics of identity.

As social workers began to think anew about the new social relations of social work, the weakening of the professional worker identity diluted a social perspective at a critical time. In this context, Dorothy I. Haight's recollections of the support African American social workers such as herself received from the left-wing unions emphasize the lost potential for racial and class solidarity. Although she was not a communist, she fondly recalled that she and other black leaders in Harlem had worked with communists in the United Front and had learned from them "about tactics, staying power, [and the] struggle necessary to build a democratic society."[102] Instead, at the same time that social workers' own identity as unequivocally middle class strengthened, the postwar psychiatric "boom" expanded social work's market to middle-class consumers, who could, for a fee, purchase treatment for "neurosis." The fact that psychiatry, the professional method of choice, accommodated traditional gender roles, however, compromised the ambitions of women social workers, placing renewed emphasis on gendered professional identities that had never been far below the surface. Perhaps most important, the postwar consumer expansion did not meet the expectations of all Americans equally and especially excluded African Americans as an "underclass." As several commentators on the late 1940s have observed, the substitution of race for class in both representation and public discourse in a society that continued to have massive economic inequalities is the great "unsolved problem of American life."[103]

As social work reached the mid-century point, then, the "industry" began to segment its labor market. It had long been divided by gender in diagnosis, treatment, and employment mobility; it would now be segmented along racial and class lines. Class, of course, had been the basic divide between clients and social workers since the days of nineteenth-century benevolence. The Cleveland poll and *Survey Midmonthly*'s illustration of social workers' expectations of their "appropriate" clients (see figure 6.2) illustrate how class began to take on new nonclass meanings in the 1940s as social work was transformed into a consumer commodity that treated "middle-[non]class neurosis." In the past, class had been central to social workers' subjectivity, to how they viewed, understood, and located themselves; they had used indigent clients as the "other" against which they constructed an identity for themselves as "middle class." But mid-century consumerism was a watershed for middle-class subjectivity, a point after which the "other" was increasingly not a class but a "below" group, an "underclass" with an imprisoning pathology and a defining racial identity.

The JFS and the JBG's concerns about the identity and site of the community they should serve suggested, however, that the segmentation of social work by race would also be locational: in the next quarter century, social worker subjectivity would be divided between those who labored in the public sector and those who labored in the private sector and between those who tended to an "underclass" of relief supplicants and those who treated paying "neurotics." Already by mid-century, of course, the spatial division of social service was coming to have well-defined racial differences as politicians and the press drew public attention to the substantial presence of Puerto Ricans and African Americans in public relief. Consequently, old questions about what constituted "real" social work and who was "really" a social worker would increasingly evoke a range of new answers on which neither the public nor those in social service work, black or white, could agree. Ultimately, the division would also be between different identities that social workers had long sought to submerge—ethnoreligious and racial—and the expression of this division in New York City between blacks and Jews would become paradigmatic for the nation. With the demise of the radical social worker unions, the gutting of the professional worker identity, and the rise of "professional" nonsocial perspectives, the racial, ethnoreligious, and gender segmentation of what constituted "middle-class" identity for social workers became central to the politics of welfare and what it would mean to be middle class in the last half of the twentieth century.

Race and the Classless Class

Race began to supplant class as the major "problem" in American society by mid-century. The "affluent society" of postwar America made promises to everyone but increasingly left African Americans behind, marking "the poor" as a racial category. These racial messages also had profound gender encodings. This was particularly true for women social workers, who, because they worked with people from "tough" neighborhoods, had been conventionally portrayed as vulnerable representations of white womanhood. Against a backdrop of welfare clients who were increasingly black and Puerto Rican, the white public came to imagine the city as a threatening black enclave.

Part 3 shifts the focus from trade unionism to culture as consumption became central to middle-class identity. The New York City story continues to provide a case study of national developments in social work, although its union record remained more extensive than elsewhere. In the city, the further consolidation of private agencies and the suburbanization of Jewish services heightened the growing racial divide. At the same time, the purge of the left-wing unions in 1950 facilitated a conservative shift in social service, muting opposition as disloyalty. In this context, chapter 7 traces the emergence of the modern professional, a variant of the professional woman identity. This type took center stage in drives to rerationalize services through "efficiency"—"checking on eligibility" by looking for "men under beds" and monitoring caseloads to encourage the rapid turnover of cases. The experience of social workers during this era paralleled the beginning of another fundamental shift in the meaning of middle-class identity: as juvenile delinquency, anticommunism, and rationalization set loose unimaginable fears, social workers' identity, reconstituted as white and affluent, became a way of speaking more about racial and gender anxieties than about class anxieties.

In chapter 8, the New York City narrative becomes central, however, as the city during the 1960s became the site of a paradigmatic racial-ethnic conflict between blacks and Jews that had national resonance. The professional impulses and heightened racial awareness of the 1950s had shaped the entry of the New Left into social work in the 1960s. New Left recruits into social service led an independent trade union initiative in New York City, in which, in contrast to their radical predecessors, they did not permit the clerical staff to join their union. The double identity of the professional worker had lost its hold on these reprofessionalized social workers; as craft-oriented worker-professionals, they were more inclined to see themselves as unremittingly "middle class" and separate from their clerical support staff (perhaps due to the changing racial composition of the increasingly black clerical work force). The decade ended with a major strike in 1967 in the newly renamed Department of Social Services. The strike foundered, however, on the same racial and ethnic shoals of Jewish-black relations that threatened New York City politics at the time (most dramatically seen in the 1968 Ocean Hill–Brownsville school dispute). By the end of the decade, reacting to the disorder and the sense that the poor had been privileged by the Great Society, neoconservative Jewish intellectuals and Republican conservatives began to construct the social mobility of Jews, who were directly implicated in this conflicted history as both teachers and social workers, as a counternarrative to black failure in order to justify withdrawing welfare from African Americans.

The epilogue concentrates on several profound changes in social work that shaped middle-class identity after 1970: the shift in the racial composition of the labor force, especially in the public sector; the segmentation of social work with the creation of a census service occupation, welfare service aides; and the rise of the predominantly white female social work therapist. These shifts coincided with the emergence of several middle-class identities, segmented by gender and race. Moreover, as a group's identity is often different from that ascribed to it by others, the popular culture continued to denigrate social work as welfare work done by interfering busybodies and heartless bureaucrats. Such caricatures evoked different responses, however, from the groups of people doing what historically had been seen as social work—public assistance, child and family casework, and therapy or counseling. Each group saw itself as middle class but differed in how it viewed the other group. Each group also differed in its views on what constituted social work identity. The language of class came to take on an enhanced political and racial rather than socioeconomic meaning. After 1970, "middle class" became an established way of talking not about class but about social respectability coded as the consuming behavior of white people.

Race and the Modern Professional

The era of the 1950s is conventionally associated with two seemingly discrete processes: the Cold War and the "affluent society" of the "organization man" (to borrow from the titles of two influential books of the period). But although historians have identified the "neo-Victorianism" of the suburban family as congenial to Cold War attitudes, the transformation of work and identity during these years must be examined in relation to a fundamental shift in the multiple subject positions that unlock what historian Thomas C. Holt has called the "iron triangle" of gender, race, and class.[1]

The Cold War's politics of containment had its domestic equivalent in what another historian has perceptively called the "culture of containment," in which blacks and women were objects, the externalized and disowned subversives of white men. Suburbanites, who often saw blacks as their nannies, maids, garbage men, and janitors, increasingly perceived the city as "other," as a place of pathological behavior that endangered social order, the nuclear family, and the "American way." At the same time, public and private agencies generally demanded loyalty oaths from their employees. Public buildings provided bomb shelters, and schoolchildren drilled for bomb attacks by hiding under their desks. Newspapers uncritically headlined the crude tactics and civil liberties abuses of Senator Joseph R. McCarthy and the House Un-American Activities Committee and the infamous trials of Alger Hiss and the Rosenbergs as Russian spies. Similarly, sci-fi films of the 1950s featured alien pods and blobs that could transform themselves to look like humans; everyone was suspect. Domestic, urban popular culture revealed the "other" face, and in New York City, it was increasingly Puerto Rican and black.

Although otherness can be conferred on someone, it is also determined by one's own sense of self, and a series of interconnected social readjustments after the war set the context for the era's new subjective positions. First, men returned to the home front after the war and reentered the job market just as federally subsidized incentives encouraged the resettlement of women at the hearth and in motherhood. The G.I. Bill, for example, offered men higher education and occupational mobility, whereas Veterans Administration mortgages made it possible for more families to purchase suburban homes in which the postwar mother was expected to raise her "booming" postwar babies. These state-subsidized benefits did not fully pay the bills, however; domestic ideology aside, many women had to work the double day as mothers and wage earners themselves if the family was to meet mortgage payments. But the revitalization of the bourgeois ideal of the family shaped social workers' attitudes about the well-adjusted family and provided the context in which female social workers had to fashion both themselves and those they assisted. However, echoing earlier themes in the history of social work, the ideal existed in tension with the harsh realities of social workers' working conditions and clients' modest benefits. In the decades following the war, the linkages between this ideal and the ability of social workers to meet it in their own lives or through "successful" work with clients would come under increasing strain, intensifying the pressure on many of them by the end of the 1960s to choose between the two.[2]

The prescriptive literature of the era encouraged women to leave the work force and return home, and employment figures for social work indicate that many women heeded the advice, whereas discriminatory work conditions limited the choice of those who remained. Of the estimated 75,000 social workers employed in the United States in 1950, nearly 70 percent were women. By 1960, however, the percentage of women in social work had declined to a historic low of 57 percent. But this decline was not simply caused by a decrease in the number of women; rather, the field had expanded dramatically to meet the greater demands of urban poverty and the broadened "middle-class" client base of "neurotics," and a larger proportion of men had taken the new jobs.[3] The increased number of men in social work, however, confronted traditional expectations that such nurturing work was for women, which ultimately would create a crisis for the male social workers' identity.[4]

Class and cultural differences between social workers and their clients complicated gendered identities. Before World War II, such complications were mediated by a shared racial or ethnic as well as class identity. This homogeneity was radically altered after the war; within thirty years of the war's close, a steady African American and Hispanic migration from the rural South and the Caribbean made racial "minorities" an easily identifiable core of the urban poor. This powerful reracialization of poverty in the metropolis changed what it meant to be middle class and a denizen of the city. New York City remained predominantly white, but African Americans and Puerto Ricans came to dominate the welfare rolls; not incidentally, the city and the suburbs were transformed into opposing black and white social landscapes, respectively. Although African Americans constituted only 13 percent of the city's population in 1960, they made up 45 percent of the welfare rolls. Hispanics were 8 percent of the population and 30 percent of the relief recipients.[5] For the vast majority of urban social workers, social difference now meant race.

This shift not only shaped social worker identity but also created an identity crisis and a moral dilemma for financially strapped private self-help agencies. Traditionally, for example, the FJP served old Jewish neighborhoods. The shift in the image of the quintessential urbanite from that of an unemployed white ethnic male to that of an indigent African American mother forced agencies to revise their notion of service.

The presence of black and Hispanic social workers in New York City who developed their own professional identity further complicated the racial story of this era. For these approximately 600 African American and Hispanic social workers, professional and middle-class identity was shaped by both class and racial difference. These men and women were part of a distinct black and Hispanic middle class with roots in the post–Civil War black church. The black social worker community itself had formal roots in the training and sponsorship of African Americans in social work by the Atlanta University School of Social Work and the Urban League since the early 1920s. As early as the 1940s, social work was one of the least-segregated professions in the city and one of the best jobs an African American could hope to obtain. Blacks remained underrepresented in New York City social work, but although their total numbers remained small and their percentage stayed the same, the doubling of the number of "nonwhite" social workers between 1940 and 1950 reflects the relatively progressive legacy of social work. At a time when African Americans in cities like New York constituted only about 10 percent of the population and continued to face systematic discrimination, they made up approximately 7 to 8 percent of the social welfare labor force.[6]

Most important, a suburban ideal emerged in the face of the fundamental racial recomposition of America's cities during the postwar decades. The consumerism of the 1950s seriously affected the practices and attitudes of less-established, usually feminized professional workers, who had already taken on the identity of the middle class but who could now come closer to grasping it as a material and desirable reality. Indeed, to distinguish these workers from higher-paid, usually male "professionals," analysts often labeled them "semiprofessionals." Marginality, however, only increased the status value of material adornments that could cloak one in respectability. A cornucopia of consumer goods and opportunities—electrical appliances, automobiles, travel, split-level homes

—enabled millions of middle-income Americans in suburban enclaves such as Levittown to aspire to a visibly higher standard of living. Private homes with grass, trees, and "modern" conveniences became available to a broader income range.

Increasingly, social workers displayed the trappings of middle-class consumer culture. In Milwaukee, for example, a 1950 survey described social workers as living for the most part in middle- or upper-middle-class residential areas. More than half had fathers who were professionals, semiprofessionals, proprietors, or managers. Over 60 percent owned automobiles, albeit modest Chevies or Fords. Indeed, car ownership was often a job requirement; 49 percent of public assistance agencies nationally required caseworkers to own an automobile. The study concluded: "[H]ere are people with many personal endowments who also have many social opportunities." The "adequacy" of their salaries was questionable—although Milwaukee salaries were above the national average—but "certain compensations are usually recognized as accruing from the humanitarian function of social work and from the professional associations which are made possible."[7] Although the profile of New York City social workers differed somewhat—for instance, they were more likely to use public transportation—most of the Milwaukee findings applied to them as well.

Although many social workers probably never fully realized the consumer dream, like many other "middle-class" Americans, they were susceptible to the popular media's idealization of this consumerism as a standard experience. The "riches" portrayed in the new television sit-coms peopled by families such as the Cleavers in *Leave It to Beaver*, the Nelsons in *The Adventures of Ozzie and Harriet*, the Andersons in *Father Knows Best*, the Stones in *The Donna Reed Show*, and the Ricardos in *I Love Lucy*[8] may have been out of reach for the majority of viewers, but they represented a desired "reality." These were racial scripts that treated the middle class as white and increasingly suburban. The example of Riley, who still punched a clock, in *The Life of Riley* suggested that even a blue-collar worker's identity could shift to the middle class in his comfortable suburban home. These sit-com families lived in what critic David Marc has characterized as "Eisenhower Waldens," suburbs with idyllic small-town names like Mayfield, Hilldale, and Springfield. The Ricardos first lived in an apartment on the fashionable Upper East Side in New York City, but they moved to Westport, Connecticut, in 1957. In any case, as entertainers, they tended to interact with the rich and famous. More typical city dwellers were working-class families like the Kramdens and the Nortons in *The Honeymooners*, which featured a boisterous bus driver and a sewer worker. As Marc has pointed out, by 1957, "sit-com America" had become a domain of whites, Anglo-Saxons, and Protestants, "where adolescence and moral ambiguity were trotted out each week and proven to be no match for the paternal instincts of a rational white breadwinner." Ethnic sit-coms like *The Goldbergs, I Remember Mama*, and *Amos 'n Andy* had all but disappeared from television.[9]

In this cultural and social context, the 1950s constituted a watershed in the middle-class identity of feminized professional occupations such as social work. At the same time that politicians and much of the taxpaying public began to mark poor welfare clients as racially different, this new identity of whiteness cemented social workers' sense of themselves as professionally distinct. Although skilled workers, such as those studied by David Halle, continued to give voice to the instability of their class identity thirty years later, for professionals such as social workers, the 1950s represented an era in which the professional worker of the 1930s dramatically receded in favor of a more fixed middle-class subjectivity.[10] The charged postwar political environment provided a context in which these racial, gendered, and class tensions came together to shape the reorganization of work and how people such as New York City's social workers understood and responded to it.

By 1950, social worker trade unionists in New York City, where the left-wing union movement was centered, had witnessed firsthand the ways in which the Cold War conjoined fears of foreign attack with those of the enemy within. Anticommunist purges also split the ranks of other New York City public sector workers. Left-wing teachers in Local 5, who had been expelled from the American Federation of Teachers in 1940, suffered a similar fate in 1950 as part of the UPW Local 555 of the teachers' union. The purge also took its toll on left-wing hospital workers in the UPW, although the tight-knit progressive core of the small, autonomous Local 1199 of the retail drug employees union weathered the red scare to form the nucleus of an enduring hospital workers' union. Finally, the left wing was similarly purged in the transit workers' union, although, in contrast to Abe Flaxer of the UPW, its leader Mike Quill shifted to the right and spared both his organization and his job.[11] But the anticommunist terror of the era cast a long shadow over open public debate on issues of civil rights, civil liberties, and disarmament, as well as any subject for which critics could detect any sign of class sympathy, such as that of the welfare poor. New York's governor Thomas Dewey justified minimizing state aid to welfare, for example, by arguing in 1952 that he opposed the "Communist concept" that children were "the property of the state." Reflecting values celebrated in the conservative culture of the 1950s (and after), Dewey urged reliance on self-help, voluntary associations, and family, church, and school.[12]

The political culture of the Cold War provides one context for understanding how social workers reshaped their identity as middle class, white, and professional in this decade; consumerism and its unequal development provides another. The 1950s bore an unfortunate resemblance to the Gilded Age a century earlier: the dark fears of danger and angry passions of McCarthyism lurked beneath a veneer of consumption and affluence. In aggregate terms, these years heralded the rise of what the economist John Kenneth Galbraith, in his bestseller of the same name, called the "affluent society." As sociologist Wini Breines has observed, "Between 1947 and 1960, the average real income for American workers increased by as much as it had the previous half century." By the end of the decade, a panoply of new consumer goods filled the average household. Sixty percent of Americans owned a home; 75 percent owned an automobile; 87 percent owned a television; and 75 percent owned a washing machine.[13]

But aggregate figures obscure those whom affluence bypassed, for not all Americans shared equally in the new consumer culture. Material gains seemed fragile to many, jeopardized by enemies abroad and subversives at home. James B. Gilbert's history of the obsession with the rise of juvenile delinquency in the 1950s describes the "powerful undercurrent of doubt" that persisted in the popular culture of the period. Unsettling social changes involving gender, race, and disorder troubled those concerned with the stability of the ladder of mobility. Indeed, like so much else in these people's lives, the expansion of credit often made "ownership" of consumer goods ephemeral and fraught with insecurity, placing them only one step ahead of the collection agency: by 1960, consumer indebtedness had skyrocketed since the end of the war from $8.3 billion to $56.1 billion.[14] Three discrete pieces of social data on conditions in social service reflect the fragility and limits of material success. By 1960, three people of every four on New York City welfare rolls were either African American or Hispanic. Child welfare was the fastest-growing area of social work. And although the median age of social workers rose from forty to forty-three, it remained essentially unchanged for men and four years older for women. More women, it appears, were either staying at work longer or returning to work after having children. Thus, aggregate real wages rose, but the pressure to "keep up with the Joneses" made the two-income "middle-class family" less an option than a necessity.[15]

The war helped set these dislocating changes in motion. Rosie the Riveter symbolized for many women the fact that they could do a wide range of jobs previously coded as men's work, and after the war, many women did not want to quit work. The traditionally negative image of the working mother, which by the late twentieth century had become a middle-class commonplace, may have begun to be reinvented by these women in this period as no contradiction in terms. Still, although marriage and birth rates rose during this decade and the divorce rate fell, as millions of American women entered the work force, the dominant postwar culture condemned working mothers as jeopardizing the American family, and the rhetoric of "Momism" castigated women who stepped outside domestic roles.[16]

New challenges to racism also destabilized existing social relations. During

World War II, new opportunities had opened up for blacks in both industry and the military. Then, Jackie Robinson's courageous and symbolic struggle to integrate "the national pastime" in 1947 caught the public imagination. Robinson's battle exposed the depth of racism in basic American institutions and demonstrated that some people—black and white—were prepared to fight for change.[17] By 1954, the U.S. Supreme Court's decision in *Brown v. Board of Education of Topeka*, which held that separate education was not equal provided a legal base on which to build the growing awareness of civil rights. By the last half of the decade, this awareness translated into active resistance to segregation in the Montgomery, Alabama, bus boycotts and the emergence of the civil rights movement.

At the same time, as African Americans began to express a new sense of rights, three federal programs symbolized opportunities that were disproportionately available to whites. Veterans' benefits provided black and white working-class soldiers with opportunities for higher education and occupational mobility into white-collar professions, but whites were more often in a position to take advantage of these openings. Even when family obligations or social expectations did not prevent them from attending college, black veterans were less likely to have the requisite educational background to pursue higher education. At the same time, G.I. loans and Federal Housing Administration mortgage insurance made it relatively easy for people, especially white people, to buy homes in the new suburban housing developments. Bias in the banking and real estate industries and restrictive covenants in housing associations kept most blacks out. In turn, congressional funding of a 37,000-mile national highway system (1947) and the Interstate Highway System Act (1957) offered speedy and easy access to suburbs, placing the American dream of home ownership within the reach of the aspiring and white affluent.[18]

As important as the rise of consumerism and suburbanization was the pattern of discrimination that accompanied them. The inequity of the "affluent society" had a racial cast to it, increasingly leaving African Americans and Hispanics behind and dependent on welfare. In this context, American cities such as New York, which urban elites had always imagined as white (or "nearly" white since many Protestant elites had questioned the "whiteness" of southern and eastern European immigrants), were now blackened. More significant, as several historians of African Americans have noted, "race" now came to function as "'a global sign, a metalanguage' that speaks to myriad aspects of life that otherwise fall outside the reverential domain of race."[19] Instead of class, the dominant white culture now considered race the country's major "problem."

Popular culture reflected and may have even helped generate middle-class fears concerning the race "problem." During the Harlem renaissance of the 1920s, whites had comfortably exoticized blues and jazz, but black culture's penetration of white culture in the 1950s with rock 'n' roll played into many older people's fears of disorder and instability; the raw emotion and sexual exuberance of the music and the dancing seemed to such people to invite uncontrollable behavior. The 1955 film *Blackboard Jungle*, for instance, reflected popular culture's understanding of juvenile delinquency and suggested how the new social relations of gender and race came together in ways some found threatening.[20] The first Hollywood film to paint the inner-city "slum" in racial hues, *The Blackboard Jungle* was both a box-office smash and a public concern. It was also the first film to feature rock music, and teenage audience members reportedly danced in the aisles to its opening song, "Rock around the Clock" by Bill Haley and the Comets. In contrast to this youthful enthusiasm, the American Legion rated it the movie "that hurt America the most in foreign countries in 1955."[21]

The Blackboard Jungle is set in a New York City public high school, and race prejudice is a constant theme. Although the worst delinquent in the movie is a white boy of Irish descent, the leading troubled adolescent is a black student played by Sidney Poitier, and a second central teen gang member is Puerto Rican. An equally important theme of the film is the threat these delinquents pose to the future, which is represented by the pregnant Ann Dadier. Her husband, Richard, the idealistic young teacher at the center of the story, saves a woman colleague from being raped; however, as a working woman, her virtue is suspect among nonworking wives like Ann, who presumes that the female teacher must have dressed provocatively. Ann is depicted as a traditionally high-strung, anxious woman, wholly dependent on her husband. Reduced to hysterical jealousy by crank letters and phone calls from one of the delinquent youths who alleges that her husband is having an affair, she gives birth prematurely, and the resolution of the child's survival parallels that of Richard Dadier as a teacher in the troubled urban school.

In much the same way that *The Blackboard Jungle* depicts the urban public high school in newer racial as well as older ethnic terms, the movie interprets juvenile delinquency and the "urban problem" as tied to disruptive gender roles and the decline of the family. As the police detective explains to Dadier, who is characterized as the "understanding" liberal who refuses to press charges against students who assaulted him, the war effort had taken Mom and Pop out of the home and allowed gang leaders to replace them: "Mr. Dadier, I've handled lots of problem kids in my time, kids from both sides of the tracks. They were five to six years old in the last war; father in the army, mother in defense plant. No home life. No church life. No place to go. They formed street gangs. It's way over my head Mr. Dadier. Maybe the kids today are like the rest of the world: mixed up, suspicious, scared. I don't know. But I do know this: gang leaders are taking the place of parents, and if you don't stop them. . . ."

As another popular feature film, *West Side Story*, which was based on a play, noted sarcastically, it was the "kindly social worker" who was called on to deal with these "problem" youths.[22] The task was not made easier by their critical popular image. In the play, for instance, a gang member ridicules the typical female social worker who "treats" them by portraying her as patronizing and unsympathetic. From its introductory dance routine to its brutal climax, *West Side Story* depicts a Puerto Rican gang, the Sharks, as increasingly threatening the numerical strength and supremacy of the Jets, an older gang described as "an anthology of what is called American." Juvenile delinquency may have been, as described by A-rab (a Jet imitating a psychiatrist), a "social disease," but these young would-be clients represented the middle-class professional's diagnosis of the problem as personal pathology: "It ain't just a question of misunderstood; deep down inside him, he's no good!"

Finally, client hostility to the social worker was one thing, but the public identification of social work as a female profession further complicated social workers' sense of authority, prestige, and self-worth. The public remained skeptical about the role of the working woman, and in the field, women still had to navigate through the murky waters of job discrimination. But the many men in social work also had to find a language and a role that would free them from the wage and status limitations placed on work coded as appropriate to the woman's sphere.

The purge of the radical unions in 1950–51 severely constrained social workers' voices on issues of gender and race, however, as the history of the trade union movements in the FJP and the DW illustrates. Recall in chapter 6, for example, that when the Board of Trustees of the FJP voted on May 14, 1951, to sever ties with Local 19, UOPWA, FJP executive director Maurice B. Hexter received "prolonged applause" for his denunciation of the union and his claim that the FJP was "ten years late" in opposing the union.[23] Similarly, a year earlier, when the DW replaced its "communist-led" union, social service administrators in both the private and the public sector recognized new unions with perspectives on race, gender, and politics that differed radically from those of their predecessors. During the 1940s, Local 19's Executive Committee had addressed issues of race and gender. Women were underrepresented in leadership roles but nonetheless played an equal role in advancing radical causes. As late as 1951, David Livingston, president of District Council 65 of the Distributive Workers Union, which had merged with remnants of the UOPWA after the CIO purge, continued to suggest Local 19's progressive social agenda. Livingston advanced a radical feminist analysis of discrimination in the workplace and the union against women, and especially black women, who bore a double load as mothers and workers.[24] In contrast, the new unions and the FJP's Board of Trustees were run by men with narrower economist perspectives. For example, in the DW, the 1955 AFL-CIO merger united the two company unions that had replaced the militant Local 1, UPW, in Local 371, District Council 37, AFSCME. Rather than give priority to organizing the growing numbers of caseworkers, Local 371 emphasized legislative and political lobbying on behalf of public employees, a strategy that has led historians to characterize it as "a timid union more concerned with its own survival and patronage than that of the welfare employees it represented."[25]

By the end of the decade, women's voices had also become muted in social worker politics. In elections that were uncontested until the end of the decade, Local 371 annually reelected a male union bureaucrat, Francis J. Petrocelli, to head its slate of officers. Not surprisingly, the position of recording secretary was filled by a woman, as were a few lesser posts. More surprising perhaps was that when the former union militants reorganized at the decade's end, they would do no better; although it would be a mistake to exaggerate the old radicals' feminism, something had happened during the decade that had buttressed men's expanding dominance over social work politics at the supervisory and managerial levels and had hardened professional and gender lines. When former UPW leaders put forth a dissident slate in 1960, the entire seven-person slate was male, although a woman would emerge as its leader in the mid-1960s.[26]

The Cold War, then, provided the social and political context for the purge of both of these CIO unions as well as for a significant shift in social service policy and work. In place of social activism, a new disciplinary social policy emerged, one that made productivity and efficiency the measure of service, in terms of both dollars saved and numbers served. With the left-wing social analysis effectively isolated, the shift in policy also privileged the medical or personal therapeutic model it had long contested. Diverse emphases within social work persisted (for example, family systems–oriented social work, group work, medical social work, community organization work), but the domination of the medical model neatly coincided with social work's ascendant postwar commitment to psychiatric treatment.

The conservative social tenor of the age might have been sufficient to produce these changes since comparable shifts seem to have taken place across the country. The fear engendered by the repressive climate of McCarthyism persisted through the 1950s, however, and silenced voices that had previously championed client advocacy and a social diagnosis of poverty rooted in unemployment, discrimination, and exploitation. Moreover, this climate of fear was especially evident in New York City, where Jews and radical unions—often conflated by popular culture—gave a particular ethnic and political cast to social work. To be sure, New York City's social workers were not the only ones to suffer under McCarthyism; National Association of Social Workers (NASW) grievance records document cases of besieged social workers in every part of the country. And these accounts were only the tip of the iceberg. The attack on New York City's left-wing unions had a "chilling effect" that extended even to the large number of social workers who remained unorganized throughout the era.[27]

The Reorganization of Social Service
Work in New York City

After the purge of the left-wing unions, most New York City social workers quietly joined the anticommunist alternatives waiting offstage; the FJP signed new contracts with Local 1707, CSAE, and the DW immediately recognized Local 1193, social investigators' union, AFSCME, AFL, and Local 371, Government and Civic Employees' Organizing Committee, CIO. Following the AFL-CIO merger in 1955, the two DW locals combined to form Welfare Employees Local 371 within District Council 37, AFSCME.[28] The anticommunist credentials of the Trotskyist and socialist leaders of the CSAE replicated the well-known red-baiting positions of the former CSF members who shaped Local 371.[29] Advocating bread-and-butter trade unionism, these new unions muted the radical issues of client advocacy and withdrew from political action involving national and international affairs. Avowed communist leaders of the old unions such as Bernard R. Segal, Norma Aronson, and Abe Flaxer were blacklisted and left the field. Other leaders, like Jacob Fisher, whose membership in the Communist Party remains unknown but who openly identified with left-wing causes, suffered a similar fate. Fisher resigned from his job as a statistician with the Social Security Administration after being suspended in 1954 as "a security risk," and it would be three years before he found comparable work with a private consulting firm.[30] In an infamous *Saturday Evening Post* article, DW chief Raymond M. Hilliard bragged that he had fired 191 DW workers for "inefficiency." "Less important troublemakers" he had isolated in the "far reaches of Brownsville in Brooklyn," "known as 'Siberia' in the Department." "Dupes and dopes," he concluded, "who had trustingly followed the party line were allowed to pull out of the union and make a new start."[31]

The lesson of this purge was not lost on less-prominent radical social workers, especially in the conservative climate of national and New York State politics. Although DW commissioners sometimes felt compelled to be conservative by political constraints more than by temperament or personal ideology, Hilliard was the first of three commissioners to focus on cost-cutting and eligibility. A year after he had purged radicals from the DW, Hilliard resigned to become executive director of the New York City Welfare Council, an association that coordinated the activities of 250 social agencies. But Hilliard's predecessor, Edward E. Rhatigan, had complained that a "philosophy of liberality" prevailed among social workers, a view he characterized as " '[L]et's not waste all our time to see that every penny is spent correctly.' "[32] Following the decision to end recognition of the UPW in the DW, and free of militant opposition, Commissioner Hilliard unleashed a program to rationalize welfare, increase efficiency, and remove the undeserving from relief rolls.

Partnering Hilliard as assistant commissioner was Henry L. McCarthy. Then, in March 1951, after Mayor William O'Dwyer fled the city to avoid testifying about his relationship with organized crime and Hilliard resigned to become executive director of New York City's Welfare Council, Mayor Vincent R. Impellitteri selected McCarthy as the new DW chief. From 1947 until the end of McCarthy's administration in 1959, Hilliard and McCarthy worked together to reshape the DW. Although McCarthy thought that his social philosophy was more progressive than that of Hilliard, in fact, their policies at the DW were of a piece.[33]

Unlike Hilliard, McCarthy was cut from liberal cloth. From 1945 to 1946, McCarthy, who was married to a Jew, had been the first non-Jew to work for the American Jewish Committee. A supporter of Israel and civil rights, during these years he worked alongside Norman Podhoretz and Gertrude Himmelfarb and their staff on *Commentary* magazine. Then, after working with Hilliard in Illinois, he joined the commissioner in New York City. In his oral history, he described himself as a "Norman Thomas socialist" who supported left-wing causes célèbres such as the cases of Sacco and Vanzetti, Hiss, and the Rosenbergs. In his own words, he was "more liberal than the social workers" and "always a pro-union man."[34]

However, to be "pro-union" had multiple meanings in an era when some unions were being purged and replaced by others. McCarthy, for instance, took equal pride in fighting unions. Known as "Mr. Inside" to Hilliard's "Mr. Outside," McCarthy ran the DW's day-to-day operations, and he later claimed that the difference between himself and Hilliard was often lost on social workers in the DW. As a team, Hilliard and McCarthy purged and silenced the DW's radical voices, put in place new controls on work routines, and established an extensive corporate welfare system within the department that taught and rewarded "efficiency" and agency loyalty.

Rural and upstate Republican legislators who controlled New York State's welfare policy were usually even more conservative than New York City politicians, and there was little the DW commissioner could do. As commissioner, in 1952 McCarthy accused state legislators of refusing to pass along the federal welfare "windfall" to the city, and Hilliard, now speaking for the Welfare Council, criticized the "illogicality" of the state's city welfare policy. Their complaints fell on deaf ears, but Hilliard's in particular must have had a hollow ring to social investigators who had been pressed by him to focus on eligibility and to reduce services. Hostile to state aid to the poor as a "communist concept" and viewing the indigent as weakened by dependence on public coffers, Governor Dewey forced the city to raise its sales tax from 2 to 3 percent in 1951 to meet local welfare costs.[35]

The conservative political and ideological opposition to welfare that constrained the city's DW budget resonated with popular middle-class attitudes about indulgent social investigators and lazy, immoral, or corrupt welfare clients. At the end of 1951, a two-year study of staff shortages in social work by the National Council on Social Work Education (NCSWE), which had been financed by the Carnegie Foundation, revealed that there was a problem with the public image of the social worker. Describing perceptions reminiscent of stereotypes early in the century, the council found a "caricature in the public mind of the social worker as a 'do-gooder,' as a 'cold and heartless' dispenser of other people's money, or as a 'starry-eyed individual who has more sympathy than sense.' "[36]

Ironically, even as they complained about the misguided state policy, DW commissioners Hilliard and McCarthy put city policies into effect that built on such caricatures of the social worker. Having disciplined their "liberal" staff with suspensions and firings, Hilliard and McCarthy implemented what might be called a New Paternalism, establishing a Welfare Training Institute; a company magazine, the Welfarer; and programs to reward and encourage departmental loyalty and national patriotism. Charging that the DW's Negro History Week celebration had been run by "left-wingers" in the past—a claim denied by the New York City branch of the NAACP—Hilliard required that his handpicked appointee, Ruth Whitehead Whaley, "screen and approve" all future speakers.[37] In addition, the DW formed tennis and softball teams and a bowling league, ran a Miss New York Hat contest, and sponsored its own orchestra and chorus (see figures 7.1 and 7.2). Bomb shelters were established in welfare centers, and photos of the department's contingent in the May 1, 1951, Loyalty Day parade were highlighted in the Welfarer (see figure 7.3). In one photo, five women in tailored suits lead the parade, carrying the DW banner. These "respectable" women are the frontline troops, positioned to put the department's "best"—or "prettiest"—face forward. Behind them are the male administrators, including then ex-Commissioner Hilliard and Commissioner McCarthy. Unencumbered by banners, the "leaders" are set back from the women to emphasize their position of leadership. The women strut their gender, whiteness, and middle classness; the men, all of whom are identified in the Welfarer by title as well as by name, strut their status, authority, and, of course, their race and gender.

The training at the Welfare Training Institute built on gendered assumptions about work while imposing a new political regime characterized by an emphasis on efficiency and productivity. Focusing on eligibility, the institute measured the quality of work by the number of clients removed from welfare rolls. By April

Figure 7.1. This photograph shows the carefully orchestrated interracialism at the DW's February 1950 Negro History Week celebration at Hunter College. Charging that the celebration previously had been run by "left-wingers," Commissioner Raymond M. Hilliard appointed Ruth Whitehead Whaley to screen all participants. *Left to right*: Reverend W. O. Carrington, First American Episcopal Church; Guichard Parris, National Urban League; Rabbi Allen A. Steinbach, Ahvah Sholem Temple; Monsignor J. Jerome Reddy, Catholic Archdiocese of Brooklyn; and Ruth Whitehead Whaley. Scrapbooks, Raymond M. Hilliard Collection, Chicago Historical Society. Courtesy of Chicago Historical Society.

1951, over 4,000 field investigators had completed the four-and-a-half-week course, which was designed to transform every "liberal" social investigator and inefficient "Nellie the Investigator" into an efficient social worker.[38]

Nellie the Investigator was a unique cartoon series prepared for the Welfare Training Institute in 1952. Regularly reprinted in the *Welfarer*, the series represented the managerial perspective at a time when there were few alternative images available to social workers. In earlier decades, *Survey* had been one place where reform-minded social workers could represent themselves to themselves. In the postwar years, *Survey* regularly ran articles on Third World poverty and the urgent need for social service. Regular columns addressed the concerns of African American social workers. But in 1952, short of funds in an increasingly crowded field of liberal opinion magazines, its aging editor decided to shut *Survey* down. In the words of social work historian Clarke A. Chambers, the magazine's closing "irrevocably weakened" social work's commitment "as a

Figure 7.2. Clubs sponsored by the DW built loyalty and élan as alternatives to the left-wing union. Here DW choristers sing at the central office Christmas party, December 1949. Scrapbooks, Raymond M. Hilliard Collection, Chicago Historical Society. Courtesy of Chicago Historical Society.

whole to broad social action."[39] *Survey's* demise reduced the professional dialogue to a monologue limited to a series of professional journals focused on scholarly research in the field. Reflecting the changing character of professionalization, the language and representation of social workers now appeared increasingly distant.

The September 1952 strip of *Nellie the Investigator* caricatured the female social worker while appealing to her professional ambition. At 1:00 P.M., Nellie says at her desk: "I guess I'll do some dictation." At 1:10 she says in the dictation room: "Darn! I forgot my fieldbook." She then rifles through her desk in search of the fieldbook, wildly scattering papers. Back in the dictation room, Nellie searches through her handbag, asking, "Where the dickens are those notes on my pending?" "Gosh—I can't do that now. I forgot that the medical social worker wants to see me at 1:30." As Nellie races off, papers scatter in her wake: "And I haven't reviewed the case!"[40]

The text accompanying this typical monthly installment of *Nellie* sought to instruct New York City welfare workers in proper work habits and procedures by explicating what was "right" and what was "wrong" with Nellie's work. What was "right" was briefly noted: the *Welfarer* assured investigators that manage-

Figure 7.3. Female social investigators strut their gender while male executives march authoritatively behind them in the 1951 DW Loyalty Day parade. The parade was established as an alternative to the left-wing union's traditional May Day parade. Ex-Commissioner Raymond M. Hilliard, First Deputy Commissioner Joseph P. Piccirillo, and Commissioner Henry L. McCarthy can be seen in the second row. *Welfarer* 3, no. 6 (May 1951): 7, in Vincent R. Impellitteri Papers, DW, Departmental Correspondence, box 11 (1951), Municipal Archive of the City of New York. Courtesy of Scrapbooks, Raymond M. Hilliard Collection, Chicago Historical Society.

ment appreciated that they worked hard and got the job done. Still, much more was wrong: "Nellie did not forget [dictation]—she just remembered too late," for "poor Nellie had a pace that would stop a clock. However, with proper organization, she would have been able to get through the day with a minimum of lost motion and a maximum of accomplishment." "Time," the text told social workers, "is never used to the best advantage when the timing of dictation or other work is left to 'guessing.'"

Although the choice of her name may have been coincidental, "Nellie" conjures up the traditional stereotype of the emotionally wrought woman, the "nervous Nellie." Exploiting the prejudices of the day, the cartoonists concluded that Nellie's handbag would probably never be organized. Complaints about heavy caseloads have punctuated the history of social work, but in the cartoon world, Nellie's job problems were of her own doing and could be solved with better work habits. If she had kept her notes in a fieldbook, Nellie would have been better prepared: "proper organization" was an "investment in efficient, smooth and rapid completion of . . . [a] job."[4]

Cartoons such as *Nellie the Investigator* may have amused real-life Nellies, taught them a few organizational tricks, and reminded them of departmental priorities, but they did not lighten caseloads or increase pay. In fact, a 1952 study of three city welfare offices issued by the New York State Department of Social Welfare reported high turnover, expanding caseloads, and shabby, stressful work conditions. Ironically, Hilliard's and McCarthy's objectives were stymied by working conditions they ignored; almost three years after they took control of the DW, the report found that poor supervision, and not poor workers, had led to inadequate documentation of eligibility in four-fifths of the cases.[42]

Determining the truth of these charges is impossible. For our purposes, however, the point is that eligibility remained the byword at the agency, the measure of the quality of work. As the focus on productivity and cost-cutting set the tone for social work, the greatest burden and responsibility fell on the clients. In the first six months of his administration, Hilliard issued press releases heralding the reduction of citywide caseloads by 4,415 cases and 9,572 people. With increased unemployment, the figure rose again in 1949–50, but by 1953 the caseloads had fallen from over 175,000 cases citywide in the summer of 1950 to a postwar low of 132,398 cases involving 246,334 people. Precise causation is impossible to establish, but Hilliard took full credit, whereas McCarthy, in his oral history, credited the Korean War for the drop.[43]

Although DW administrators may have tried to convince social workers that they were like Nellie, whose problems were sloppiness and inefficiency, social workers themselves regularly complained of heavy caseloads and long hours. Low wages, not messy handbags, undercut their consumer aspirations for a middle-class life-style.[44] Similarly, political attacks on their job integrity consistently challenged their status ambitions.

Nellie may have represented a lighthearted effort on the part of DW managers to inculcate work discipline, but for both administrators and social workers, she was also a disheartening caricature of women's purportedly irrational nature. Encoded in this meaning was a traditional female variant of professional identity that advised women's deference to men, whether they be coworkers, supervisors, psychiatrists, or administrators.

Changes in private sector social work in New York City's Jewish agencies paralleled those in the DW. Not surprisingly, the purge of Local 19 in the FJP did not herald an improvement in working conditions. Casework agencies, which were still dependent on the FJP for most funds not provided by state subsidies, remained hard-pressed financially. Increasingly, whenever possible, fees for service were exacted from clients, but budget gaps remained, which constantly needed to be filled through reduction in services, increased productivity, or lower costs, mostly by containing wage increases.

State and federal patient-care subsidies increasingly accounted for large shares of agency budgets. By the mid-1950s, although the amount of its contribution had almost doubled since the war, the FJP's share had declined to less than half of the JBG's budget, and the agency had become increasingly dependent on private and public funds. By mid-decade, more than one in four dollars of the JBG's budget came from public coffers. (See appendix, table A.4.)

Public funding, combined with the need to reduce services, had profound implications for the admissions policies and race relations of the FJP and its affiliate agencies; these factors also shaped the work experiences of social workers. The Race Discrimination Amendment to the city budget in 1942 required that publicly funded social service agencies accept referrals of children regardless of race, and New York State subsidies for various JBG programs carried similar provisions that raised problems for the agency concerning its mission to the Jewish community. State aid to agency shelters, for instance, required the admission of all children for whom no other arrangements could be made. JBG executive director Herschel Alt explained to his trustees in October 1953 that such an admissions policy "poses a real problem, as this group is composed of Negro, Puerto Rican, Protestant and Catholic children, with no Jewish children at all." Because the JBG's interest lay in treatment and research, not in the care of homeless children, he averred, the agency "must have the freedom to select the children for these projects." Consequently, Alt reported that he had advised the city that the JBG would accept non-Jewish children into its program but that "because JBG was sponsored and chiefly financed by the FJP for persons of the Jewish faith," it "might be necessary to give preference to Jewish children."[45]

Alt had raised a vexing issue with long-term implications for sectarian social service, but one that could be deferred a while longer. The agency's response did not provoke public opposition, and Alt reported that the problem remained speculative. But of course funding problems did not go away, and their solutions risked attracting the attention of public regulators. Asking for more federal and state aid made it difficult for these Jewish agencies to close facilities, especially in neighborhoods where the constituency was now African American and Hispanic rather than Jewish. Moreover, Jewish supervisors and caseworkers only had to look around the neighborhoods they served to be confronted by the problem and a series of long-standing questions about identity and priorities, questions that had regularly been raised at the annual NCJSS since the 1930s. What did it mean to be a Jewish agency? Was there a Jewish form of social work? What balance was to be struck in keeping an agency open and serving one's ethnic community?[46] These were questions that agencies could avoid until the state demanded answers in the 1960s, but they reflected the changing racial composition of the city and its meaning for social workers identity in the 1950s.

Continuing fiscal constraints, however, compelled management to focus on two alternatives to cutting services: lowering wage costs and increasing productivity. Low wages, however, already undermined efforts to reduce turnover, which was reported by some JBG agencies, for instance, to run as high as 25 percent annually. The CSAE negotiated substantial wage increases that were comparable to those the left-wing UPW had won, but social work wages were still below middle-class living standards.[47] Social workers' wages, for instance, which paled in comparison to those of public school teachers, who were usually seen as their peers, made it difficult to attract additional people into the field. Teachers averaged $3,010 a year in 1950—more than even male social workers earned.[48] Thus, the shortage of trained social workers and their already low wages left management with few choices other than to seek increased productivity, and to do this it basically had to break the social worker's control of the shop floor. In the FJP's efforts to do so, the ensuing FJP scenario bore a striking resemblance to the DW drama.

Managers claimed that the new therapeutic treatments at Jewish casework agencies required the Taylorization of social work. As it reviewed projections for 1955, the FJP's Distribution Committee noted that the expense of psychiatric treatment had become "a very substantial part" of costs. It exhorted agencies to review "the cost per interview or . . . the productivity rate of the worker." The measure of productivity—the number of case interviews per month—provoked extended protests from both agencies and social workers who argued that quality treatment took more time. Since the FJP set salaries and guidelines for the organization, the agencies, although they expressed sympathy for their staffs, sought to improve social workers' efficiency by reorganizing interviewing schedules, developing more interview forms, and counting cases.[49]

Of course, psychiatric clinical treatment itself could be routinized. As a University of Pennsylvania sociologist studying the JBG reported in 1951, "a certain degree of routinization in clinical work" resulted in standardized therapy.[50] But the new emphasis on psychiatry undercut social worker professionalism—authority and autonomy—even as it purported to demand it. Agencies increased both the number and the roles of psychiatrists and psychologists on staff. The mostly female social workers who had always been subordinate to male executives now found themselves working with male doctors and psychologists but subordinate to them for diagnosis as well. Finally, the growing place of psychiatric therapy tended to expand the reliance on a medical therapeutic model, a philosophical orientation that took on symbolic meaning with the introduction of drug therapy by psychiatrists into agency treatment in the mid-1950s.[51]

So as social workers assumed professional legal status during the 1950s, their working conditions and social status did not improve; rather, they suffered from weaker unions and more routinized procedures, especially in the DW. Moreover, female social workers became increasingly subordinate to male experts, so much so that one historian has recently characterized them as becoming more like aides.[52] Although overstated, the contradictions of professionalization in a period of deprofessionalizing changes elicited a familiar defense mechanism. In the private casework agencies, in particular, female social workers were subordinated to a growing number of elite men; they also now faced heavy caseloads and low wages in Taylorized settings. In these ways, the work became more industrialized. Against the backdrop of Cold War politics in social service and the reorganization of work and social policy, one worker eloquently challenged demands that social workers be more productive and efficient: Was a social worker "a Social Investigator using casework methods or a Criminal Investigator using the techniques of the D.A.?"[53] This question of occupational identity had important consequences for social workers' identity as professional and middle class, however, and it is to this problem that we now turn.

The Modern Professional

The 1952 demise of popular vehicles such as *Survey* for the articulation of social workers' point of view left only more-distanced professional voices to speak for them. Management's construction of *Nellie the Investigator*, for example, left New York City women social workers with an image that may well have undermined their feelings of competence. Of course, it is difficult to know how much social workers absorbed the ideology embedded in such images. Male colleagues would have been more likely to hold such views about female semiprofessionals, but women had to confront such views in the popular culture as well as the office. *Our Miss Brooks*, a comedic television series in the 1950s that featured Eve Arden as a spinster English teacher, provides an appropriate example. Miss Brooks was competent in the classroom, but she was daffy elsewhere and her veiled overtures toward another schoolteacher, Mr. Boynton, were unrequited. As Marc has observed, late-1950s sit-coms placed families in the suburbs whereas New York City–based sit-coms such as *Private Secretary*, *Meet Millie*, *My Friend Irma*, and *My Sister Eileen* focused on single working women who were desperately seeking to avoid spinsterhood.[54]

In fact, on the job and in their writings, female social workers employed in private agencies projected a more competent image than that of Nellie or sit-com working women. The modern professional woman who emerged in professional journals, in the oral histories of prominent social workers conducted under the auspices of the NASW, in interviews conducted by the FJP Oral History

Project, and elsewhere exuded businesslike efficiency and demeanor.[55] However, in the deference the professional woman showed to male colleagues, she worked in Nellie's shadow. Even the most accomplished women generally chose to leave the problems of administering welfare to men or felt that domestic responsibilities required them to do so. After all, as dutiful wives and daughters, women continued to work the double day at home and at the office. Commenting on greater male mobility in social work, social work educator Helen Harris Perlman confessed that "to many women like myself it seemed right." Until her awakening to feminism in the 1960s, she "several times undermined the position of women—I've not forgiven myself for this—by arguing . . . [with] my dean [at the University of Chicago School of Social Work] to forgo promotions [to women] in favor of men." It might have been a small consolation to Perlman to have learned from another prominent educator, Arlien Johnson, that stereotypical expectations of women's domestic priorities led various accomplished women in the same era to avoid pursuing deanships.[56] In addition, at work, women social workers embraced therapeutic advances that engaged them in what was commonly understood to be a traditional female familial sphere—the emotional and psychological life of families and children. Union work and identification with clients, important parts of the profession's history, increasingly receded.

The contradictions in the construction of a new variant of the professional identity, the modern professional, in the 1950s are illuminated by D. H. Lawrence's wry observation about Americans' penchant for psychic inversions—the compulsion to displace or compensate for countervailing tendencies in their lives. In such a way, the heightened ideological commitment to professionalization was a counternarrative to opposing trends: in contrast and in response to the deprofessionalizing tendencies of the era—loss of autonomy to male experts and increased routine and bureaucratization due to the greater emphasis on efficiency and productivity—social workers constructed a modern professional identity to defend themselves. As work destabilized, they sought to fix this identity and to protect and assert it through a powerfully reorganized professional association, the NASW, that united the seven social work subdisciplines. The language of identity was muted in the formal professional journals but can be derived from memoirs, case records, and grievances as well as from certain social determinants: the Cold War political legacy the reorganization of work and consumption, and the racial recomposition of the city. It is important to remember, however, that identities are multiple and complex, often combining elements of class, race, gender, age, political orientation, ethnicity, and other features. To simplify the narrative, the following discussion separates these realms. Of course, they are not discrete; they overlap, play off one another, and combine in ways that none of these separate categories describes.

Social workers elaborated the identity of the modern professional out of the complexity, overlap, and contradictions of the era, and once again, the New York City case is illustrative. The powerful left-wing union movement among the city's social workers especially charged their political experience, and its purge had a lingering legacy on workers in both Jewish agencies and the DW. What happened in New York City, however, was not without widespread repercussions, as McCarthyism had a chilling effect nationally, intimidating and distorting progressive perspectives on race and gender in social work or silencing them entirely. As radical social worker Verne Weed has observed, "Hundreds of social workers had job problems, were harassed by the FBI, called before HUAC; but few of these reached the public eye and for good reason. It was not to the individual's advantage to publicize them."[57]

The biographies of two prominent Jewish women social workers in New York City, Leah Weiss and Martha K. Selig, illustrate the hostile political environment in which administrators typically reorganized work and social policy and in which social workers fashioned their modern professional identity. Their experience corresponds to the experiences documented in many other FJP oral histories. In these histories, the Cold War, and not just the McCarthyite purge of the left in unions, emerges as a force that shaped the discourse about effective social work.[58]

Little in Weiss's and Selig's backgrounds would have forecast their involvement in and commitment to the radical union movement. Weiss's parents were Orthodox Jews, and her father, a conservative real estate salesman, voted for the conservative Republican Alf Landon for president in 1936. Selig traced her origins to aristocratic Polish grandparents who raised her. She graduated from Hunter College during the depression, became a certified clinical psychologist, and taught at City College. Both women became union organizers in the 1940s at kindred FJP agencies. Their differing accounts, however, reflected political divisions at the time and the centrifugal pressures forcing them toward a unitary mode of behavior.

After serving as a caseworker and supervisor from 1932 to 1944 at the Pleasantville Cottage School, the Jewish residential facility for orphans in Westchester County, Selig became the first female executive director of an FJP agency. In the 1940s, she represented her staff at Pleasantville in negotiations with the new FJP president, Maurice Hexter. Her second meeting with Hexter, she explained, occurred "over a union negotiating table." She remembered not knowing what a union was but asking for better living conditions and a salary increase. "He sat at the end of the table and he said, 'I'm here to break the union before it gets started.' And I said, 'I'm here to see that you don't. Now let's talk.' And that was the beginning of our marvelous friendship." Hexter did, however, succeed in breaking the union a few years later.[59]

Weiss's account of her experience at the JBG's Hawthorne School for Boys is a more bitter chronicle of the left-wing union's fate. Before becoming an administrator in the early 1950s, she was a "very active" union member, serving on the negotiating committee. Unlike many of her colleagues (who presumably were communists), she was not a member of the Communist Party, but she remembered the leaders of the union as the "best people of the staff, professionally." But forty years later, discussing the purge of the old union—which involved FBI investigations—still made her anxious about confidentiality. She remembered the purge as a deeply "emotional issue"; she and her colleagues were only too happy to have the whole matter disappear "as the union disappeared."[60]

After the purge, Weiss adapted to the new order. She recalled that people became less involved in radical politics and more interested in professional advancement; the staff became absorbed in activities that "promoted professional skills." The staff complained about the new demands for productivity and accountability that followed the purge, but the administration, remembered Weiss, did not see this as a union matter. The new union responded nonetheless by spreading petitions and undertaking a study of its own on how the new routines adversely affected their work with clients. But administrators offered little more than heartfelt sympathy and admiration for the staff. The workload remained unchanged, but the generally quiescent industrial relations under the new union may help explain the lack of further recriminations. Weiss, for instance, was relieved that, after the initial purge, her agency never seemed to discriminate against anyone who had been a member of the left-wing union in granting promotions.[61]

However, the experience of a third female social worker, Marsha Treitman, suggests that even if there were no recriminations for left-wing associations, McCarthyism had a chilling effect on a range of social issues as late as 1959. Adopting the nonethnic pseudonym Laura Lewis, Treitman authored a book of children's verse that year entitled *Enter In*. Intended to combat racism, the book was illustrated with multiracial pictures. Treitman decided to publish it under a pseudonym to avoid compromising or jeopardizing her professional career and to increase sales of the book.[62] Integrationist sympathies were a political liability in the afterglow of McCarthyism, especially for Jews. Anti-Semitism and the disproportionate number of Jews active in the civil rights movement made them easy targets for right-wing politicians who were quick to associate civil rights activism with communism. As important, Treitman's volume suggests that both race and the specter of McCarthyism had become major features on the social worker landscape by the decade's end that heightened the growing social distance between social investigators and clients.

McCarthyism silenced people on more than just racial issues; in related ways, it shaped therapeutic debates and professional standards of what constituted personal and therapeutic "success." Once again, Marsha Treitman's history is a case in point. A case supervisor for the DW, Treitman remained active in the union until its 1951 purge. With the left-wing union experience behind her, in the 1950s Treitman participated in what she referred to as social workers' "love fest with Freud." She had taken courses at the New York Psychoanalytic Institute and now enrolled in additional courses in pychoanalysis at the William Allyson White Institute. She recalled the 1950s as a time of escalating emphasis on Freudianism: after evaluating financial need, the caseworker's main function throughout this era, she noted, was to provide personal service, which meant "fostering psychological services in order to practice on their clients."[63]

Social work's psychiatric "love fest" in the 1950s corresponded with the resolution of the therapeutic debate between the Rankian functionalists and the Freudian diagnostics that had raged since the 1930s. The debate had never taken explicitly political form, but the Cold War atmosphere in the agencies rendered the Rankian client-orientation approach suspect. In the postwar era, the more middle-class clientele in the private agencies also gave new authority to a personal rather than a social diagnosis; for these clients, "getting along" on the corporate ladder was the issue, not poverty. But the therapeutic debate subsided by the mid-1950s because the repressive political climate put social issues on a back burner and because psychiatry moved beyond the Rank-Freud division and took on new therapeutic strategies best described as eclectic, such as behavioral modification, existential models, Jungian group therapy, and self-help groups (modeled on Alcoholics Anonymous).[64] A majority of social workers always accepted the diagnostic framework, but in the 1950s, the ground of the debates shifted with the introduction of these different strategies, and general therapeutic practice incorporated several fundamental functional-school techniques.[65]

This resolution of the functionalist-diagnostic conflict had professional implications. The diagnostics encouraged a psychiatrically informed social work that was to be the basis for increased professional status. As previously noted, these techniques intensified social worker dependence on psychiatrists. Perhaps as important, the functionalists' legacy—fees for service, the therapeutic "hour," and rules to provide structure for clients—contributed to the routinization of the work that social workers now defended as purely professional.

There is no definitive evidence as to whether this movement toward therapy and professionalism reflected new recruitment into social work or simply new clothing on old workers. The answer is probably both, especially after the agencies and government quieted the most dynamic, articulate, and passionate voices for the professional worker alternative. In this conservative political environment, many New York City social workers, reading the handwriting on the wall, simply chose to take advantage of the narrower economist and professional agenda of the new unions. After all, professional development had always been a goal of radicals, too—albeit its purpose was to make them more effective social activists. Others, however, as we shall see in chapter 8, took their politics underground to await another day. Still, two examples from the social work staff at the JBG's Hawthorne School, an agency renowned for its radical politics and its psychiatric training, illustrate the new views among both new recruits and old-timers. Leah Weiss, former chairperson of the Local 19 chapter at the Hawthorne School, remembered that social workers became less politically radical as the decade wore on and more self-absorbed and involved in the profession rather than union activities. The career of Sam Liebner, who joined Hawthorne in February 1953 as a psychiatric social worker trained in the diagnostic school, illustrated her point. Liebner considered the staff at the JBG to be like him—politically active but committed to "good clinical practice." Before becoming an administrator in 1955, Liebner was an active member of the new union and served on the strategy committee, and the terms in which he described his role suggest that the new unions had become more compatible with a restrained professional demeanor and a narrower agenda. "A good social worker," he stated in retrospect, "could fight passionately for social justice via a union or professional organization or as a citizen," but this had to be done "without politicizing clinical work." Liebner believed he had "resisted being overly zealous and sectarian"; in contrast to those who waged destructive "Talmudic struggles," he was a "pragmatist."[66]

In sum, the Cold War, consumerism, and the rise of psychiatry, which had simultaneously accommodated a more conservative social policy and regimented work discipline, had undermined the ideal of the professional worker and allowed for the fixing of a new type, the modern professional. Although they worked as aides to psychiatrists, these professionals could still claim a distinct knowledge base, increasingly had advanced educational degrees, and often saw clients who were referred from agencies on their own. Indeed, having the status of a professional may have compensated for meager material gains. Social worker professionalism ran counter to a diminution in worker autonomy and the continuing history of heavy caseloads and low wages. But the modern professional was also integral to the remaking of middle-class identity. McCarthyism made it both dangerous and unprofessional to express an identity of interest with poor or African American or Hispanic clients. This, and the unequal distribution of the consumer cornucopia, provided the political, economic, and cultural context in which the racial recomposition of the city and the welfare client as a black or Hispanic "other" reshaped the social worker's self-identity as middle class.

The Remaking of the Middle Class

The native-born old middle class of the nineteenth century established its identity in opposition to an ethnic "other" seen as a class problem; in contrast, the white and ethnic new middle class of the mid-twentieth century forged its identity against a black or Hispanic "other" seen as a race problem. Class identity, of course, is relational, and the calcification of social workers' middle-class identity in the 1950s owes as much to their growing sense of distance from white-collar clerical workers in their offices as it does to their sense of distance from clients. Thus, although the UPW had been an industrial union, it is significant that, after its dismantling, DW social investigators and clericals split into two separate unions. Even though the unions formally merged in 1955, as one historian of the movement has noted, the new union, Local 371, was dominated by supervisors and clericals, and disaffected caseworkers lost interest in it.[67] In a society in which working-class or interracial sympathy was often suspect, unambiguous professionalism proved a safer identity than one tinged with militant trade unionism or support for integration.

As it became more fixed, social workers' identity as middle class also began to become less a way of talking about the social and cultural relations of production. Rather, "middle class" increasingly became an amorphous category defined by consumerism, whiteness, and, hence, moral and political legitimacy. Several countervailing tendencies of the age worked in tandem as part of the shift. First, although consumerism had been an important component of class identity since the 1920s, class had initially been rooted primarily in the workplace; then, in the 1930s, consumerism increased its hold in the double identity of the professional worker at home and on the shop floor. In the postwar era, however, middle-class identity became rooted in consumerism based in the home and community.

Historians have only recently begun to unravel the history of consumerism, but the experience of Jewish Americans seems quite typical of the experiences of ethnic communities that had been in the United States for several generations. Although second-generation Jews had established "suburban" beachheads in New York City's outer boroughs before 1930, in the postwar era, they and their children began to create paradigmatic Jewish suburban middle-class (and white) communities outside New York City in Scarsdale, Great Neck and other towns on Long Island, Maplewood, New Jersey, and countless other places. This process was repeated across America, both outside older Jewish communities in older cities and in the new "golden" Jewish meccas, Miami and Los Angeles. In these affluent and materialist settlements, even the modern temples, where rabbis complained that too many congregants only participated on High Holy

Days or during their children's bar and bas mitzvahs, seemed secular in contrast to memories of Lower East Side shuls [68]

Second, the collapse of New Deal corporatism and the left-wing CIO agenda paved the way for the reracializing of the city as "black" and dangerous and gave heightened new meaning to whiteness as a marker of middle-class respectability. In what labor historian Nelson Lichtenstein has called the rise of the private welfare state, the postwar federal government's use of subsidies and its legal support of loyalty oaths and use of injunctions against labor strikes to crush radical unions freed corporations to implement further segmentation and de-skilling of labor. In this environment, skilled and professional workers separated themselves from more marginal workers, who were increasingly black and female, and wage relations were dissociated from larger political issues.[69] Rather than providing a base for common class interest, then, occupation would confer distinct professional status for social workers; the meaning of middle class, now rooted in a consumer economy that increasingly excluded African Americans and Hispanics, became racialized as "white."

In the 1950s, social workers perceived a growing social distance between themselves and poor clients, a gulf in which attitudes about a "culture of poverty" among clients and racial difference became a major component of social worker identity. Seeing themselves as middle class, social workers increasingly acknowledged their social and cultural distance from relief clients, although this distance was always evident to outsiders and clients. For instance, a 1951 article in *Survey* highlighted the gap between "the interests, goals and culture of the masses of children" and those of "[t]eachers, [who] like social workers and clinicians, are earnestly trying to *change the culture.*" The article included a photograph of a Miss Brooks look-alike; bespectacled, with her hair tied back, in a dress with a high collar, she was a "most earnest middle class teacher . . . puzzled at the ways of slum children."[70] (See figure 7.4.) A second example suggests both the pervasive ambiguity in the racial attitudes of white social workers who labored in the poor and increasingly black areas of the city and how some of them began to translate Oscar Lewis's culture of poverty theory from a critique of institutionalized racism to a problem of black pathology.[71] Although Marsha Treitman's 1959 integrationist children's book demonstrates her own antiracist commitments, in a 1991 interview, she retrospectively explained the high incidence of poverty and child welfare within the African American community as a problem of "black promiscuity."[72]

Even as the racial recomposition of the city as a place of black and Hispanic "others" defined the new professional middle-class identity as white, explicit discussion of racial difference does not appear in social workers' records. After all, such talk constituted unprofessional behavior. Still, a couple of court and

Black Star: Photo by Shigeta-Wright

Even the most earnest middle class teacher
becomes puzzled at the ways of slum children

Figure 7.4. Exuding respectability, this teacher conformed to the straitlaced image of the teacher or social worker in 1950s popular culture. Her appearance distanced her iconically and socially from her students or clients. Allison Davies, "Ability and Survival," *Survey*, February 1951, 61; photo by Shigeta-Wright. Courtesy of Tamiment Institute Library, New York University.

grievance cases expose the way social welfare policy on eligibility helped to encode a racial "other" and possibly led social workers to experience themselves as "white."

An October 1951 decision of the New York City domestic relations court concerning neglected children demonstrates the Hilliard regime's introduction of classism and racism in the name of efficiency and morality. In the case, a welfare investigator had petitioned to remove three children from the custody of their foster mother, fictitiously named Johanne Carlson. The children had been in the Carlson home for years, but the DW now alleged that the foster mother was "neglectful," "unstable," and "overly strict." The children's mother, whom the case investigator described as incapable of providing "proper parental control and supervision over her children due to alcoholism and syphilis of the central nervous system," remained an unsatisfactory alternative. The court, however, rejected the petition, charging that the supervisory personnel of the DW were "attempting to take punitive action against her because she protested the inadequacy of the relief allowance for the care of the children, and because 'Sarah' [one of the children] had written [two] letters to the Mayor of the city" threatening suicide if the authorities removed her from the Carlson home.

Central to the court's findings was its ' discovery" that the DW in this and five other cases had helped create the conditions of neglect for which it held mothers responsible. In the case of one Puerto Rican mother, for instance, having judged her neglectful, "the Department of Welfare had already withdrawn public assistance, which directly resulted in the family being dispossessed from its quarters." The department, the report concluded, "then filed a complaint charging as one of its elements of neglect, that the mother has no house for the children."[73]

In actuality, such cases were overloaded with moral ambiguity. It is hard to know whom to support—alcoholic mothers, "overly strict" foster mothers, or overzealous social investigators. Accusing families of "neglect," however, was not a new charge. But it combined long-standing judgments about the customs and mores of the poor with new concerns about the increasing numbers of African American and Hispanic clients that had been made even before the efficiency drive of the 1950s. For example, the DW had cut off funds for a woman and three children because she refused to give information on an additional three children living with her. In fact, these children had a different father who did not live with her but who provided for the children. The mother did not wish to disclose employment or any other information about the putative father "for fear he would lose his job if his employer knew about the children."[74]

Two of the "neglectful" mothers in these five cases were identified as Puerto Rican; the others were identified only by their poverty and "unrespectable" lifestyles. Several mothers had illegitimate children; another had a husband in prison. Federal welfare policy, however, had been established on the idea that a family consisted of a woman dependent on a male breadwinner. The consequence of this policy was that women with children who were without the support of men became eligible for relief. The irony was that inadequate wages and growing consumer expectations abetted the very behavior that welfare critics thought to be immoral: they encouraged women not to marry and to obscure other means of support, that is, to "cheat" the DW and "hide" husbands.[75]

"Respectable" social investigators seemed oblivious to the client's logic, as well as to the general conditions of the client's life. In the DW's eligibility drive, the court consistently heard the testimony of social investigators "so convinced . . . that their procedure was a correct, proper, legal and just one" that they "at first refused to grant" the court's request that the clients receive "temporary emergency relief." It was "shocking" to the court to hear "witness after witness" from the DW assert "what is apparently becoming the present day policy of the Department of Welfare."[76]

The ambiguity of cases involving people of different ethnic backgrounds was hardly new to social work, but the possibility of a racist reading of these circumstances was increasingly overdetermined by the coincidence of escalating physical violence in poor welfare neighborhoods and the color of poverty as depicted in popular entertainments such as *Blackboard Jungle* and *West Side Story*. Fear and the threat of violence in what were referred to as "slums" and "ghettos" of the city increasingly became a formative motif of the middle class and challenged all social workers as they entered these dangerous zones to do their job. During the administration of Commissioner McCarthy, one New York City caseworker was killed, two were raped, and there were various incidents of assault.[77] But race as difference would distinguish the professional identity of white social workers from that of their African American and Hispanic colleagues. For example, racially charged client grievances suddenly began to appear in union records during the late 1950s, suggesting that race relations may have begun to deteriorate in social work. In one case, W. Allen, "a Local member," complained that the DW, "worried at excess of Negroes on staff," had fired Minnie Tilley, a black relief investigator, on the pretext that she lived outside the city.[78]

Another case is the first postwar report of a mugging to appear in SSEU records. In February 1959, three youths attacked Harry Schaeffer, a presumably white social investigator for the DW, in the middle of Harlem at Lenox Avenue and 125th Street. Although nothing is officially known of the assailants' race, the incident spoke to the growing climate of danger, fear, and vulnerability that marked the city and the job.[79] Harlem had been a black community for over thirty years, so such social workers' fears hint at the way race increasingly structured a new arena of vulnerability for upwardly mobile and white social workers. Race as difference now heightened the self-identity of the vast majority of social workers as white.

The Black Middle Class

African Americans in social service shared much with their white colleagues and predecessors, but their race and its sameness with that of the clients they served (who whites marked as "other") shaped their identity as middle class in distinct ways. Black social workers had much the same reason to want to separate themselves from disreputable clients as their white colleagues had, but to do so meant emphasizing difference. So whereas race increasingly dominated the formation of white middle-class identity, class continued to play a much stronger role in the construction of black middle-class identity, much as it seems it always had.[80]

To be sure, if the meaning of whiteness appeared only around the edges of social policy and discourse, the meaning of blackness for the substantial minority of African American social workers was even more elusive. Again, the evidence comes mostly from social determinants and only occasionally from social workers' own testimony. As noted earlier, compared to other occupations—especially most skilled trades, professions, and managerial jobs—African Americans fared well in social work. During the early years of the century, even though they constituted only 2–3 percent of the population in cities like New York, their number of jobs in religious, charity, and welfare work was equal to their share of the city population. (See appendix, table A.5.) Many of the men were undoubtedly ministers, but of course, the black church had long functioned as an important social reform institution within the African American community. For example, during the antebellum era, black ministers encouraged abolitionism, while religion among slaves served as a vital source of cultural coherence and resistance to slavery; more recently, black clergy from groups as different as the Southern Christian Leadership Conference and the Black Muslims provided leadership to the civil rights and black power movements of the mid-twentieth century. Outside the church, African American settlement house workers were also an early and integral part of the emerging black bourgeoisie. The Music School Settlement for Colored People of New York, for instance, flourished in Harlem between 1911 and 1917. Apparently administered mostly by African Americans, it was directed by an African American, J. Rosamond Johnson.[81]

By the 1920s, African American social workers had established their own professional apparatus as part of an organized black middle class. From its founding in 1910, the National Urban League advanced social reform causes and welfare work on behalf of African Americans, and in 1923 it began publishing a national journal, *Opportunity: A Journal of Negro Life*. Three years earlier, the Atlanta University School of Social Work, dedicated to the training of African American social workers, opened its doors. By the mid-1920s, the Association of Colored Social Workers had been formed, with an Executive Council based in Harlem. When fifty black social workers attended the 1927 national meeting of the NCSW in Des Moines, they witnessed the reelection of one of their number to a second three-year term on the Executive Committee.[82]

The category of social work, however, remained quite fluid, and the ranks of the black middle class were swelled by allied groups of workers. For instance, a 1927 article in *Opportunity* on social work in New York City counted 350 "colored teachers" in the public school system as well as 21 nurses whom the Urban League Center of the Henry Street Settlement employed in Harlem every month. Each group, the author noted significantly, worked with both black and white children and families.[33] The New York Colored Mission employed a paid staff of six matrons and visitors, a maintenance worker, and thirteen volunteers. In addition to providing material relief and nursing care to the community, the mission operated five houses in Harlem, functioned as a placement bureau (mostly for domestic work), and gave nearly 16,000 "respectable women" a night's lodging in 1926 alone.[84]

The dramatic expansion of public welfare provided new opportunities for African Americans and other minorities in social service, although they were not as uncomplicated and rosy as the numbers and the achievements of individuals might suggest. The total number of African American social workers tripled during the 1930s and doubled again a decade later. As significant, although the percentage of African American social workers in New York City in 1960 (11.1 percent) paled in comparison to the growing dominance of African Americans on welfare rolls (45 percent), it almost matched their share of the city's population (13 percent).[85] Symbolizing the new racialization of welfare as black, James R. Dumpson, an African American, became first deputy commissioner of welfare in 1957, and in 1959 Mayor Robert F. Wagner Jr. appointed him commissioner.[86]

The achievement of African American social workers (and a small number of Asians and Hispanics) did not obliterate or obscure the fact that there were distinct black and white middle classes. As New York City social worker Marsha Treitman remembered, "[I]t took years before the blockade against [equal opportunities for black social workers] was lifted."[87] Indeed, African American social workers were increasingly ghettoized into public assistance and, specifically, into DW districts where they served black and Hispanic clients. They had helped staff the offices in Harlem since the 1930s; now they aided the growing centers of African American and Hispanic poverty in Brooklyn and the Bronx, too, areas that were increasingly associated with violence. In the private sector, they were more often employed by Protestant and Catholic charities than by Jewish agencies.[88]

Social workers living in Harlem knew they paid premium prices for commodities and food, and they found their efforts to move elsewhere stymied by racial discrimination in housing. Dorothy I. Haight, a social worker who became president of the National Council of Negro Women, lived there because it was "her neighborhood," the place where the people she identified with lived.[89] Ann Tanneyhill's reason for living in Harlem, however, reflected the limited "choices" of most black women social workers. The longtime secretary of the Urban League, Tanneyhill explained that when she arrived in New York City around 1930, "there was no place else [for a black person] to live." She commented that living in Harlem was the first time she had ever lived in "a ghetto." Still residing in Harlem nearly fifty years later, she noted, "Maybe I would [leave] if I could afford to . . . , but I can't." In any case, Harlem was her neighborhood, and unlike her white colleagues, she could state, "I don't feel afraid in Harlem."[90]

It is important to acknowledge that African Americans' experiences with job discrimination in social work were a best-case scenario of the employment prospects for African Americans at the time since the profession stood in the vanguard of the civil rights movement. The NCSW actively supported civil liberties and the emerging civil rights movement each year at its annual meeting as "matters of professional self-interest." The NCSW had labored since the 1930s to hold annual meetings in cities and facilities that did not discriminate against persons of color. Paul U. Kellogg, *Survey*, and the Rank-and-File Movement actively operated on that principle, too, and regularly advanced the discussion of racial issues at national conferences. By the late 1950s and especially in the 1960s, the Family Service Association of America and the National Federation of Settlements sponsored forums on cross-racial adoption and interracial harmony. Still, white social workers increasingly problematized race as "blackness" and identified middle-class respectability as "white" and suburban. On civil rights, as one delegate told the 1949 NCSW meeting, "social work did not have clean hands." Another delegate reiterated the point in 1956, noting that social agencies remained segregated in the South and that they discriminated against blacks in the North.[91]

The growing preponderance of single black mothers on welfare and the pervasive ambiguity of racial attitudes among white workers toward the poor and increasingly black areas of the city also informed a racialized welfare policy that disproportionately denied public funds and services to African American single mothers and their children and subjected them to harassment by welfare officials.[92] Distinct attitudes toward black and white illegitimacy, for example, provide an illuminating barometer of the ways racist attitudes toward sexuality permeated social policy. In their compelling studies of illegitimacy, Regina G. Kunzel and Rickie Solinger have documented the racialized script of postwar sexuality. Kunzel argues that "'neurosis' was, in a relative sense, a privileged [middle-class] category." For white women, sexual promiscuity was a personal problem to be overcome through psychological rehabilitation; indeed, by the 1960s, Solinger notes, it would be recast as a characteristic of the "liberated woman" in the sexual revolution. In contrast, sexually active black women continued to be cast as promiscuous. Seen as suffering from a pathology embedded in the black family and black culture, they were beyond the simple assertion of individual will; black sexuality was a population bomb ready to explode on the white middle-class taxpayer. "In short," Kunzel observes, "the (white) girl could change," but the black girl could not.[93]

The division between the black and white middle classes complicated the response of black social workers to the disparagement, if not outright hostility, of whites toward blacks. If black social workers had to negotiate between race and class work, between demands for respectability and demands for justice, they also had to handle two sides of the class coin: while emphasizing their class difference with clients, it was equally important to emphasize their class solidarity as professionals with white social workers. In the racially charged environment of even the most progressive institutions, some African Americans found themselves expressing equality by deferring, whereas some whites did so by patronizing. At the 1926 NCSW in Des Moines, for instance, members were told that they "would be expected to observe the traditions of the South on the Negro question" if they chose to hold the conference in Memphis the next year. Blacks elected not to speak from the floor out of "respect for the wishes of the majority" and a "sense of fairness to the South," whose representatives were "also a minority group" in the urban-dominated field. The members voted to meet in Memphis and to try to hold an integrated conference, a goal they achieved with remarkable and virtually total success.[94]

The career of Rietta May Herbert, an African American social worker employed in New York City welfare work from 1935 to 1965, suggests the complicated character of African American middle-class identity. Herbert spent most of her career as a social investigator and supervisor of child welfare in the Harlem offices of the DW. A magna cum laude graduate of Howard University with some graduate credit in accounting at Columbia University, Herbert was promoted through the ranks after her supervisor noted "her ability to quickly establish the presumptive eligibility for relief." Shortly after her husband's premature death in 1947, she attended Smith College, receiving her M.S.W. in 1951. Fully credentialed, and with eligibility all the rage in the 1950s, she became a supervisor in 1952, responsible for overseeing the work of child welfare caseworkers in one of the Harlem offices.

What may be most remarkable about Herbert's papers, which include her autobiography, case records, and professional papers, is the general absence of any discussion of race. In a few instances, the race of a client is identified, but Herbert presents herself as a professional woman whose voice is indistinguishable from the voices of white social workers that appear elsewhere. Only in the 1959 case of a black client does racial dissonance surface in the record, although this case seems to be equally part of a discourse on class for African American social workers. The three voices in the record expose the complicated subjectivities of the era for black women. A foster mother, Mrs. J., was upset at what she saw as constant interference by the DW, which regularly checked up on her. She expressed the suspicion of many black relief recipients that middle-class agents of the welfare state were racist. But the black middle-class caseworker interpreted Mrs. J's complaint as the pathological response of the embittered poor: "Foster mother then ventilated a great deal of her hostility by exclaiming that was why so many babies, especially Negro children, remained in hospitals—because we did not trust foster parents to make their own decisions and we expected a lot of foster parents but did very little in return." In the margin, Herbert added her own comment, expressing an equivocation about racial difference not otherwise heard in the record: underlining the phrase "especially Negro children" in the text, Herbert wrote, "[W]hat's going on here?"[95]

One answer may lie in the occasional instance of an African American or Hispanic voice that intrudes on the predominant white discourse of social work and suggests that, even as blacks and Hispanics constructed their own identity as middle class, they were singled out as "others," as an identity apart. One such case was that of Anthony Quiñones, a Puerto Rican relief investigator who was the only person in the DW grievance records ever investigated for enforcing eligibility restrictions. Again, a "true" interpretation of the situation remains elusive, but the singularity of the prosecution could not have been lost on Quiñones: African American and Hispanic investigators were often suspected of leniency toward people from their own communities, but in this case, a Puerto Rican investigator was reprimanded for "mishandling" the case of Mary Hernandez, another Puerto Rican. Quiñones had allegedly removed her from welfare unfairly. After being slashed by her husband with a barber's blade, Hernandez had borrowed $200 from her children's godfather to go to Puerto Rico to get a divorce. Quiñones maintained, however, that she had refused to divulge the source of the money and had told him that "she was ill and wanted to go home." Claiming that he had done no wrong, Quiñones petitioned Local 371 to defend him against harassment by the Department of Investigation. Unfortunately, there the record ends.[96]

The evidence is limited and the findings are tentative, but cases like those of Minnie Tilley, the black relief investigator who was fired, and Anthony Quiñones suggest that the DW's sensitive racial policies specially marked African American and Hispanic social workers in the 1950s as professional "others." Indeed, even benign NASW and agency policies to recruit black and Puerto Rican staff marked their presence in social work as "special." Thus, although the profound racial divisions in American society had always kept them distinct, the middle-class identities of black and white social workers sharpened in relation to each other during the racialization of the city in the 1950s and the growing assertiveness of the civil rights movement after 1957. This process would become more visible (and complicated) in the subsequent decades, but its roots lay in the 1950s.

The Gendered Middle Class

There were masculine and feminine variants on the middle-class identity of the modern professional. The public association of welfare with AFDC, for instance, in which families were increasingly headed by single mothers, meant that poverty and its "treatment" inscribed a profoundly gendered script for both clients and social workers.[97] Heightened postwar anxieties about the deleterious impact of women working outside the home increased pressures on working women to meet domestic responsibilities as well. The demands of the double day burdened women unequally in the labor market, and the rapid influx of men into social work further constrained women's occupational mobility into the upper echelons of the profession. Thus, whereas two-thirds of the caseworkers in the country were female in 1960, twice as many men held executive positions.[98] At the executive director level, women such as Martha K. Selig were unusual. Most social workers were single women who left their jobs when they married in order to raise families. Those who wished to stay (or returned to work after their children had grown up) found themselves locked into jobs with limited opportunities for advancement. Such social workers scurried from agency to agency in search of better work. As a result, half of the workers in both public and private agencies in 1950 had worked for their present employer for less than three years.[99]

Lower salaries and dependence on a single rather than a family wage placed the three-quarters of women social workers who were single or widowed in the worst position. Every section of the country mirrored the national statistics. Public assistance workers, who numerically dominated the field, earned the least. Workers in private agencies fared better but still earned about $150 less annually than schoolteachers, who were usually seen as social workers' peers.[100] Not surprisingly, male caseworkers' annual wages of $2,860 were $200 above those of female caseworkers; even black male caseworkers averaged $20 a year more than women as a group. The gender salary gap widened, too, as social workers moved up the ladder, where men predominated. When women achieved mobility into executive offices, as the wage differentials suggest, they remained at the lowest ranks. Nationally, male and female executives received $4,400 and $3,180 a year, respectively.[101] The sexual division of labor and the wage distinctions testify to a pervasive pattern of de facto discrimination against women, even if it did not often become a public issue in this era.

The fundamental sexism that underlay social relations in the office also limited the achievements of even the most successful women, such as Marsha Treitman, Leah Weiss, and Martha Selig. In remembering their careers, these women insisted that their opinions were always respected and that they were never compartmentalized as having special "women's knowledge." But their narrations reveal their specialization in "female" areas. Whereas successful men moved into managerial positions, successful women social workers such as Treitman, Weiss, Selig, and Herbert became the leading practitioners of family and child therapy, the advance guard for protecting what was traditionally seen as women's sphere. Treitman, for instance, became the training supervisor of the DW's Bureau of Special Services; Weiss became a director of a clinic for disturbed children; Selig, who pioneered the opening of suburban services in Nassau and Queens Counties, appeared before the trustees in December 1952 to deliver the "Report on Family and Children's Services"; and Herbert became a senior representative of child welfare for the New York State Department of Social Welfare. These were accomplished women, whom agencies relied on for their state-of-the-art knowledge of family and child services. But being a woman seems, at least implicitly, to have been part of their expertise in such fields. For such women professionals, who remained at the forefront of family and child casework their entire adult lives, social work was no longer a job but a female career path.[102]

At the same time, these women all knew their professional place—and it was behind men. Weiss, for example, remembered questioning Herschel Alt, the JBG executive director, about why he had appointed a man as head psychiatric social worker instead of her. She thought she should have gotten the job. As she recalled, Alt replied candidly, " 'You are more qualified, but he's a man.' "[103] Similarly, Selig, the top executive woman at the FJP in the 1950s, could never forget that she was a woman and subordinate. Reflecting on the FJP's rejection of her recommendation that it buy land in Nassau County, she recognized that her managerial post may have been incompatible with her sex: "Perhaps if I were not a woman they would have paid more attention to my comments on real estate. But that's one of the problems of being a woman and working in my position as Executive Director for Community Services." She consistently found herself the lone woman in meetings with men.

Although we have no record of how men responded to her, Selig found herself re-creating the model of a designing, manipulative female that men denigrated: "I also learned from Hexter, although he was never sexist, that men come into the field of communal service not to be ruled by a woman! . . . [W]hen I wanted something done, I got one of the top men on the committee to introduce the concept." She also gave men credit for her own ideas. Treated as "one of the boys" by her colleagues, she nevertheless "had to be conscious I was a woman and really manipulate the situation." "The important thing," she concluded, "was to get it done. . . . I don't care what the ERA says. If a woman does something, she may be called aggressive. If a man does the same thing, he is said to be taking great initiative."[104]

The instability of gender identity also proved to be a problem for male social workers in this decade. The movement of men into social work during the 1950s in larger numbers than ever before pressed them to find a distinctive male sphere, an alternative to the domesticated associations attached to this professional activity. At the same time, some black social workers may have found themselves with the opposite problem: being channeled by social agencies into "ultramasculine" work with gangs may have fed rather than undermined their male egos as "superstuds."[105] But the same nurturing functions that made social work appropriate for women threatened the white male social worker's notion of masculinity. Of course, male social workers in the 1950s were not the first

white-collar workers to confront the dilemma of establishing a masculine identity in fields characterized as feminine. Industrial workers traditionally rooted
their "manliness" in physicality and the sense of themselves as skilled. Faced
with deskilling, men transferred their sense of pride and status as "real men" to
their roles as providers for the family.[106] As breadwinners, white-collar workers
excelled. But association with jobs that were seen as part of the female preserve
and as requiring what the culture coded as feminine attributes demanded that
male social workers define manliness differently. Professional "objectivity"—
rationality characterized as male—helped, as did the elaboration of a base of
specialized knowledge (and a belief in it) with the growth of psychiatric social
work in the 1950s.

Finding it difficult to reconcile casework with a masculine professional identity, men either moved into management or left the field altogether. According
to Marsha Treitman, men generally did "poor work" because they disparaged
reading case records, presumably as dead-end work more appropriate for
women. The inferior quality of their work was not a matter of genes, however;
men, said Treitman, simply wanted other jobs.[107] Sam Liebner's career path
exemplified the sort of job definition and mobility that helped men assimilate to
the field. After working for a year and a half at the Rockland State Psychiatric
Hospital to pay off his school loans, Liebner began work at the Hawthorne
School in 1953 as a psychiatric social worker. Two years later, he was an administrator, a job he held until leaving Hawthorne in 1962. A social work educator
for the next twenty years, he also maintained a private clinical practice as a
therapist.[108] Thus, men in social service developed an alternative professional
identity as administrators or managers, although they generally could aspire to
be only middle managers. Even as men came to make up nearly half the number
of social workers tabulated in the census, social work retained a female identity.
Nellie the Investigator's flightiness might be dismissed by readers, but the appropriateness of a woman as the typical social worker was not. Miss Brooks, the
teacher as social worker, and other images from the decade attest to that. Male
social workers avoided becoming feminine and, thus, "semiprofessionals" by
becoming white-collar managers whose status and respectability were conferred
by their authority over others. Their underlings may have been only women, but
at least they shared a class and racial background. In contrast, the modern
professional white woman who remained in the industry found her status diminished by the class and racial makeup of clients.

In the 1950s, consumerism, fear, and race came together to define the reprofessionalized social worker's middle-class identity. Social workers' acquisition of
the material accoutrements of what came to be characterized as the suburban

life-style as well as their educational level made them feel a world apart from their poor, urban clients. Although only 16 percent of social workers had earned the professional degree, the M.S.W., two-thirds nationally had completed college, and half had begun graduate work.[109] But union social workers in New York City saw their security and the status exemplified by their union jeopardized by McCarthyism, much as middle-class American popular culture expressed broader Cold War fears of subversion by alien "others," domestic and foreign. These fears worked in conjunction with the racialization of the city to facilitate the development of a hardened and punitive welfare policy. The racial recomposition of the city had in fact only just begun, but the high numbers of Hispanic and African Americans on welfare rolls made them visible. The professional worker identity that emphasized the shared interests of social workers and clients had reached its zenith during the depression, when left-wing ideology and the union bridged the racial gap between workers and clients and accentuated class solidarity. For the modern professional of the 1950s, however, the African American or Puerto Rican welfare client was a racial "other." Race and privileged access to consumer goods rather than class antagonism had begun to define what it meant to be middle class. In this sense, a distinctive modern professional identity was born that was relatively fixed as middle class and white and was unambiguously committed to the medicalization of crime and poverty. At the same time, although race continued to give the smaller number of black social workers a distinct professional identity, class played an equally prominent role in shaping the black middle class as a group apart from black social workers' "other" clients.

In New York City, the silencing of the left-wing social diagnosis gave free rein to ascendant psychiatric circles, a shift that occurred across the country, even where the union movement had little presence. Agencies increasingly measured the quality of work by its attention to eligibility and its productivity, playing a numbers game that focused on alleged client abuse rather than on social problems such as unemployment, homelessness, or poverty. Not all social workers accepted this regime; indeed, complaints of staff "leniency" from politicians and superintendents such as Hilliard undoubtedly had some legitimacy as some investigators considered the focus on eligibility an appalling cutback in social services and used whatever cracks they could find in the bureaucracy to resist its implementation. This informal resistance to welfare restrictions no doubt increased in the 1960s with the rise of the welfare rights movement and social worker militancy and became more familiar and acceptable to social activists in welfare.[110] In the 1950s, however, the modern professional was remarkably well suited to the focus on efficiency and an analysis based on individual "adjustment": the commitment to "objective" client analysis and an individualistic Freudian psychiatric model satisfied the conservative political currents swirling through social welfare. Not surprisingly, the final issue of the *Welfarer* in 1952 heralded the growing interest at the DW in alcoholic dependency, a personal pathology applicable to both the poor and the "affluent society."[111]

Although caseworkers could celebrate their increased professionalization, social work itself continued to be characterized by heavy caseloads and poor pay. Indeed, the new productivity standards meant increasing routinization and additional paperwork. In these ways, during the 1950s, social workers seemed to have tolerated or even accepted meager working conditions in exchange for the status and culture of professionalism.

Distinctly male and female versions of the professional social work identity also existed and continue to the present. In fact, social work remained typed as a female occupation even after men constituted nearly half of all social workers in the 1950s. Reversing the stereotype of women's work as representing only an interval in women's lives, men saw social work as a stepping-stone to a career in management, a position enhanced by its responsibility for the supervision of middle-class women rather than client "others." Men dominated the better-paid administrative posts in the agencies—and in the unions.

Subordinate to men, but professional, women had to find other ways to achieve professional advancement. One way was to create the illusion of advancement for both themselves and the general public, and agencies found themselves forced to promote almost all social workers to senior caseworkers after a few years of employment. The title offered a bit more money but little additional authority and no more mobility than that provided by the caseworker title in previous decades.[112]

Another way was to set up a protective legal wall of licenses and certificates—a white-collar professional concomitant to craft regulations. If New York City's new CSAE and AFSCME social worker locals did not effectively resist efficiency and productivity drives—indeed, former CSF members in the CSAE had already endorsed such activities—social workers would have to look to their professional associations to defend their interests. In social workers' quest to professionalize, these associations took on greater prominence.

As of October 1, 1956, the six specialized social work associations—psychiatric, medical, group, research, community organization, and social work schools—and the general association federated to form the NASW, which had a single standard: two years of graduate study. When it came to defending social workers against discrimination, union busting, or McCarthyism, however, neither the NASW nor its predecessor, the AASW, did more than issue reports and write letters. Sixty-seven grievances from across the country were brought to the national association between 1947 and 1957, each of which was investigated with great care. Repeatedly, agencies were found guilty of disregarding fundamental civil liberties and ignoring personnel procedures, if they even had any. The

NASW could only exert moral suasion with the agencies. It could urge them to adopt personnel procedures and reinstate workers. Some agencies complied, but generally only in work-related procedural cases agencies like the Salvation Army and the Red Cross, which frequently terminated caseworkers for union activity or political philosophy, stonewalled the NASW.[113] The NASW was more effective as a legislative lobby, leading the fight for state certification, licensing, and job requirements tied to higher levels of graduate educational training.[114]

For many social workers, the ultimate means of achieving professional advancement was to leave the "industrial" setting as they understood it and go into business for themselves. Any notion of independence was at best partial, however, since they remained dependent on agencies for referrals and on the state for third-party insurance payments. Still, self-employment did promise greater autonomy and the potential for a higher income. By the end of the decade, the JBG suggested that the only way to hold on to workers might be to allow them to make some extra money in private practice.[115] But during this period, only a few did; in fact, the small number of social workers whom the census enumerated as self-employed in the United States declined from 390 (0.5 percent) in 1950 to 301 (0.3 percent) in 1960.[16] As self-employed clinicians, they could leave Nellie the Investigator, her working-class clients, and any radical social context for diagnosis behind to realize their professional ambitions by tending to the personal neuroses of the "affluent society." To the vast majority of social workers, however, the identity of the therapist remained part of the future. For the present, they had to find some other way to assert their rights in the workplace.

eight

Jews, Blacks, and a Counternarrative for the Middle Class

The experiences of Jewish social service workers in New York City and the communities of the black poor converged during the 1960s to provide ethno-racial material from which Americans constructed a new narrative of middle-class identity. Naturally, not all social workers were Jews, nor were all welfare recipients black; and other white ethnics certainly came into conflict with blacks in the job market and in urban neighborhoods.[1] As fiscal constraints closed in on social workers and their clients, however, the experiences of blacks and Jews in New York City, and the stories told of each group by the other, by themselves, and by outsiders, became paradigmatic narratives to justify an emerging politics of race, welfare, and middle-class identity.

The renewed emphasis on professionalizing in the 1950s also had a funda-mental impact on middle-class identity. Galvanized by the civil rights movement and the reformist zeal of President John F. Kennedy's New Frontier, New York City social workers in the 1960s once again organized a radical trade union that was committed to serving, at least in part, as an advocate for clients. This resurgent radicalism in social work encouraged many who previously had felt discouraged about filing for benefits to enroll for welfare. By mid-decade, social workers, spurred by New Left recruits, had helped organize the National Welfare Rights Organization (NWRO). But the legacy of racialized professionalism from the preceding decade also informed the ways that social workers began to em-phasize their class difference from other workers. In contrast to the double identity of the professional worker, as worker-professionals social workers now emphasized their distinct interests and, accordingly, organized as a craft union without their clerical and maintenance staffs. Like the New Jersey chemical workers David Halle interviewed in the early 1980s, industrial and clerical workers were "working men" on the job and "middle class" at home, but social work professionals now came to see themselves as a group apart, as middle-class professionals in all spheres.

To be sure, state fiscal constraints on welfare also inhibited social workers' solidarity with clients. Straining to provide both guns and butter to meet the demands of a voracious war abroad and an incendiary urban crisis at home, the federal government forced states and municipalities either to find alternative sources of revenue or to contain costs. But retrenchment occurred at a time when the poor claimed benefits in large numbers and when welfare came to constitute the largest share of urban budgets. Not surprisingly, then, mayoral fiscal strategies of the era focused on controlling social service and its unions: mayors sought sweetheart union deals, put pressure on private charities such as the FJP to take on a larger share of nonsectarian clients, and tried to contain welfare costs.

Municipalities could control welfare budgets in two ways: by reducing the costs of labor and by reducing benefits, both of which seemed to pit the fate of social workers against that of clients. Social workers, of whom disproportionate numbers in New York City were Jewish, drew on their identities as professionals and trade unionists to sustain their wage levels and their identity as middle-class consumers. Welfare recipients also defended their rights as consumers: the NWRO demanded "MORE MONEY NOW!" and the right of its members to make their own choices on how to spend it.[2]

As important for our story, the political and fiscal turmoil in social service combined with the growing ethnic/religious/racial conflict in the city to stimulate a fundamental reorganization of social work that had profound implications for the racial division of middle-class identities. Increasingly during the decade, welfare politics intruded on both white and black aspirations at the same time that it involved each group in the fate of the other. Welfare officials directed social workers to dispense aid in ways that clients often found demeaning and delimiting, while at the same time the mayor proposed automating caseworker tasks and replacing caseworkers with service aides, low-paid workers just one step (but a welcome step for the black unemployed) above welfare recipients. White social work professionals considered such changes decidedly unwelcome and responded accordingly: in subsequent decades, they would increasingly seek to move into a separate world of private practice as therapists.

The Crisis of "Jewish" Social Service

At the first meeting of the FJP Board of Trustees in the new decade, a long-awaited report on the dispersion and resettlement of New York City's Jewish population in the boroughs and suburbs laid out two of the preconditions for a black counternarrative to the story of Jewish social mobility: the dramatic racialization of the city and the transformation of Jewish social services that had taken place since World War II.[3] Begun in 1917 as a Manhattan-based association, the FJP now served a clientele spread over five boroughs and nearly a half dozen counties. Many other Jews had moved to nearby New Jersey and southern Connecticut. Although the Jewish agencies that served the latter were not associated with the FJP, their constituents also availed themselves of the FJP's superior services.[4]

The "growing nonsectarian [that is, black] nature of our sectarian institutions," as FJP executive vice president Joseph Willens described the problem in 1957, resurrected earlier anxieties about obligations to the general population that the state might exact from the FJP as the price of its financial aid. For two decades, FJP officers had raised vexing questions about the implicit threat of state aid to the Jewish character of their mission. Noting that agencies were increasingly made up of Jewish boards and Jewish staffs who served black and Hispanic clients, Willens voiced concern that the imbalance between staff and clients was "socially not good. In my opinion, it is morally wrong." Willens emphasized that he was not critical of the shift to non-Jewish patients, but he pointed out that it brought up a series of soul-searching questions: "Is it the responsibility of the Jewish community to conduct such agencies? What makes an agency Jewish?" Is it the board? The staff? The clients?[5]

Although these were old questions, many recognized that they now existed in a changed political and social environment. The suburban settings of television sit-coms, for instance, reflected the popular sense of major urban demographic shifts. Chapter 7 observed that popular culture increasingly imagined cities and welfare rolls as racialized settings dominated by blacks and Puerto Ricans, even though the majority in both remained white. Suburban "sprawl" could be traced along the new federal highway system, a network of four-lane express highways leading out of the urban workplace to the twin symbols of the mid-twentieth century's consumer economy: the shopping mall and the housing development.

In his 1957 remarks Willens neatly summarized the worrisome meaning of these changes for the FJP's Jewish identity, expressing a perspective that most members probably accepted. Willens believed that the FJP had lost its place at the center of Jewish communal life in the city. In the search for monies from the Jewish community, he argued, the FJP now competed with the United Jewish Appeal (UJA), Jewish agency bond drives, Joint Defense Appeals in support of Israel, and fund-raising by Brandeis and Yeshiva Universities and other new Jewish institutions. Missing in his account were references to the rich history of *landsmanshaftn* (associations of people from the same village), Yiddish theater and folk choruses, and the Jewish labor movement that would have undermined the uniqueness of these changes and demonstrated that the FJP had always shared center stage in Jewish communal life.

At the same time that changes worried Jews, the hopeful national mood of President Kennedy's New Frontier buoyed the expectations of ethnic and racial groups that had long experienced discrimination. The election of the handsome, youthful Massachusetts senator as president gave the nation hope that the turmoil of the civil rights and antiwar movements would be replaced by Camelot. The troubling and optimistic views of change, understood empirically and felt emotionally, galvanized FJP executives and social workers to tackle the changed place of the Jewish community in the city with some ambivalence.

The response initiated by the FJP's Jewish Education Committee represented one pole in the debate over Jewish identity, a position that expressed the emerging place of the Jewish success narrative in the FJP as it sought to address the growing secularization of Jewish life. In 1954 the committee initiated a voluntary program of orientation and training seminars for workers in Jewish communal services and Jewish family and child casework agencies. After five years, 300 professional workers from 45 FJP agencies, including the JFS and the JBG, had participated in a program with five courses, each of which had twelve sessions. According to Earl Morse, an FJP trustee on the committee, the program presumed that there was a Jewish component to Jewish casework and that family and child services would benefit by understanding it. The program, Morse contended, "was designed not to make better Jews out of Jewish Social Workers but to . . . make the Social Workers more effective in their work with Jewish clients."[6]

Morse's analysis of the Jewish experience about which the committee attempted to educate social workers, however, was an exposition of a success narrative of the Chosen People that had messianic and eugenicist implications. Forgetting Police Commissioner Theodore A. Bingham's 1908 report that half of the delinquents in New York City were Jews, Morse argued that "numerous studies . . . by social scientists . . . indicat[e] that among Jews there is less infant mortality, less alcoholism, less juvenile delinquency, less adult crime, lower separation and divorce rates, less suicide, to make only a partial list." Morse attributed this superior record to a distinct set of "Jewish *group* values," a cultural legacy that determined social behavior. Noting the "amazing" upward social and economic mobility of Jews, Morse then asked rhetorically whether there was a correlation between Jewish mobility and these mores. He never raised the implicit question of the obverse relationship for the new black constituency in FJP agencies, nor did he suggest that the agencies should train staff to understand these clients too. Morse offered a perspective that contrasted Willens's view that the agencies should add blacks to their governing boards. Believing that the first commitment of the FJP was to the Jewish community, Morse saw "Jewish" social work as work performed by Jews and for Jews. Morse's diagnosis of social problems simply presumed a black culture of poverty in which personal failure was rooted in the cultural history of a people, not in economic or social discrimination.[7]

Willens and Morse did not necessarily disagree, however, about this social diagnosis. Neither offered a full-blown analysis or program. Rather, the contrast between them illustrated tendencies in each position—Willens's tendency to include and "help" others and Morse's to exclude and "help" one's own community. Each position raised critical moral and financial questions that did not necessarily contradict the other position. The tendencies often overlapped: one could "help" and include from the perspective of "cultural superiority." Still, both could agree with Morse's understanding that the problem at hand partially lay outside the FJP's immediate control in the public realm and that its answer would be critical to the future of Jewish identity and the FJP's philanthropic mission: "Whether an agency is to be for non-Jews or Jews, whether it shall be sectarian or nonsectarian presupposes a profound understanding of the social forces both in the general and in the Jewish community."[8]

Tensions between the needs of Jews and blacks both inside and outside the FJP would grow in the next decade and bring these contrasting tendencies of inclusion and exclusion to a head. At the same time, as welfare came to be seen as black poverty, a powerful Jewish success narrative similar to that articulated by Morse would become increasingly important in the construction of both social worker identity and modern welfare policy. Nowhere was this more apparent than in New York City, where Jewish social workers had come to play a major role once again in a radicalized social work trade union movement that sought to unite the interests of white and Jewish social service staff with those of black clients.

Two articles that appeared on consecutive pages of the November 13, 1963, *New York Times* reflected this debate within the FJP and illustrated the growing importance of the public sphere—including both the weight of opinion and state intervention—as an arena and as a force with which the FJP and social workers had to reckon. The two stories reveal that by the mid-1960s the historical relationship between Jews and blacks in the city had begun to fracture and the state had begun to interject itself into the long-smoldering issue of Jewish social service to nonsectarian clients.

The first account joined Jews and blacks in the same narrative as victims of discrimination. A banner headline announced, "185 in Bronxville Join to Fight Exclusion of Jews and Negroes." Bronxville, a wealthy white suburb in southern Westchester County, had come to be regarded by the Anti-Defamation League of the B'nai B'rith and others as "the holy square mile" in which Jews and blacks were conjoined as undesirable "others." A feature story with a four-photo spread reported that, with the exception of some black maids, both Jews and black homeowners had been excluded from the neighborhood.[9] A second story, however, depicted the fates of Jews and blacks as mirrored opposites. An article on the next page entitled "Child Care Policy on Race Irks City; Dumpson Says Shelters Are Segregated Institutions" illustrated that the civil rights movement had helped to bring the struggle against segregation to the North. The "policies of private agencies" that had few black and Puerto Rican children, New York City's African American commissioner of welfare, James R. Dumpson, noted, were forcing the DW to maintain segregated children's centers: "Hillcrest Center had 213 Negro children out of 221 and Children's Center had 372 Negro and 114 Puerto Rican children out of a total of 558." Dumpson chose not to name the agencies responsible for this situation but simply explained that their "selective" policies sought "to maintain racial balance in their own institutions"—"balance" meaning overwhelmingly "white"—by allowing "religious identification of children to supersede need in selection of care."[10]

Since most Puerto Ricans and some blacks were Catholic, Dumpson's target was not hard to guess. Citing his remarks about "selective" racist policy and how "religious identification" was being given preference over social "need," the JBG promptly placed the matter on the Executive Committee's agenda for the next day. The JBG noted that non-Jewish clients made up 11.9 and 9.7 percent of the clients at its two major child care agencies, the Madeleine Borg Clinic in Manhattan and the Hawthorne–Cedar Knolls School in Westchester County (ironically, not far from the exclusive Bronxville community), respectively.[11] These percentages masked the even smaller percentages of black and Puerto Rican clients. The records do not indicate, however, whether or not the JBG saw these figures as a problem. It would not be possible to ignore Dumpson's complaint for long, but for now, the JBG took no action.

The Emergence of a Paradigmatic Counternarrative

The strong presence of Jews, blacks, and Puerto Ricans in New York City gave a unique shape to social worker identity and placed the ethnic/racial dimension of the conflict between them in bold relief. At the same time that the FJP increasingly worried that accepting state money to provide services to the black community jeopardized Jewish identity, Jews and blacks found themselves in a series of intense relationships in welfare. The extraordinary growth of relief rolls across the country in the last half of the decade set events in motion that propelled the conflicts of the era in New York City.

As Frances Fox Piven and Richard A. Cloward documented in 1971, "the nation experienced a 'welfare explosion'" in the 1960s that was highly racialized. They attributed this cataclysmic social event to protest growing out of the civil rights movement and to the development of Great Society programs to address if not counter, the protest. Eight hundred thousand families (a 107 percent increase) were added to the welfare rolls between January 1960 and February 1969, increasing numbers of whom, especially in the large cities, were black and Hispanic; the 1950s had seen the rolls grow by only 100 000 (17 percent). Increases in New York City and other cities reflected this pattern in its most intense form: "[T]he steepest increase (217 percent) occurred in the five most populous [counties] . . . : New York, Philadelphia, Cook County (Chicago), Wayne County (Detroit) and Los Angeles."[12]

The history of welfare politics in New York City highlights equally significant aspects of this "explosion" for black and Jewish relations. To begin with, 71 percent of the increase occurred in the four years after 1964, a development that correlated with the rise of the NWRO. Social workers—many of whom were Jewish—played a vital role in the organization of the NWRO. They collectively agitated for expanded social service to meet the needs of the burdensome welfare rolls, but resulting landmark welfare strikes in 1965 and 1967 that coincided with the rise of black nationalism found the NWRO pushing white allies to the side.[13] Urban riots, assassinations, and violent antiwar protest during these years only added to the growing public sense that the national ship was out of control in a stormy sea of black and white racism.

The scope and drama of these events and the stories told about them, especially since the national news media were centered in New York City, informed the master narratives of post-1968 social policy and accentuated the racial component of contemporary middle-class identity. Although the Jewish and black communities often split among themselves in these conflicts, the reaction of conservatives both inside and outside the Jewish community stimulated their celebration of a success narrative of the Jewish experience in the United States not unlike that voiced by Morse a decade earlier. In this modern formulation of the classic Horatio Alger myth, Jews came to America and achieved great material success by dint of their hard work, strong families, and emphasis on education. In this scenario, radical Jewish protest was either forgotten or domesticated into organized labor and collective bargaining. The Jewish spin on this myth often added a "racial" component, ranging from suggestions that Jews were "chosen" to the anti-Semitic view that begrudgingly characterized their financial achievements as that of clever but greedy and ruthless Shylocks. This Jewish success narrative was held up by some Jews and non-Jews as a counterstory to the black experience. By the end of the decade, this narrative would have increasing political resonance with neoconservative views on black pathology and Jewish (white) meritocracy.

The story of Jewish success requires special attention. In the minds of the majority of social workers in the FJP and many welfare caseworkers, the Jewish success narrative was intimately linked to their emerging sense of what it meant to be middle class. The Jewish success story was in fact one of several contested narratives. For instance, the Jews who had a particularly strong presence in the Old and New Left, in both the antiwar and civil rights movements that helped to stimulate Great Society programs and an upsurge in welfare rolls, saw their history differently. They continued to see their relationship to the poor as one of shared discrimination and commitment to radical change and state entitlement. Reorganized and remobilized social worker unions in New York City reflected this Jewish and left-wing membership in their reprise of a fundamental element of the older professional worker identity: an identity of interests with and on behalf of their clients, most notably in the development of the welfare rights movement. Black and Hispanic leaders were at the heart of the national welfare rights movement, and it received the active support of the Protestant National Council of Churches and various Catholic dioceses.[14] Jews, however, had a disproportionate and visible presence. Many came out of the civil rights movement and became community activists (Saul Alinsky's 1969 book, *Reveille for Radicals*, became the bible for such efforts) and rank-and-file members of Students for a Democratic Society.[15] White radicals in Students for a Democratic Society promoted community-organizing programs in 1965 and 1966 in white working-class communities, and those who became social workers then extended that project to the welfare rights movement. According to Piven and Cloward, "Great Society social workers and VISTA volunteers became the organizers of NWRO groups."[16]

A shared history of discrimination and radical protest traditions brought Jews and blacks together in New York City, but national and international developments—and the media and political accounts of them—conspired to draw these allies apart, estrange them, and make them symbolic opposites. Thus, by the mid-1960s, the Orthodox Jewish and black communities found themselves living cheek by jowl in various neighborhoods in Brooklyn and Manhattan.[17] During this same period, both groups developed outspoken, militant, radical activist cadres to defend the more nationalist and socially conservative elements in their communities. The Arab-Israeli War in 1967 coincided with the growth of black militancy and the Nation of Islam in the United States. The Orthodox Jewish Hasidic community began to assert itself in the FJP in mid-decade, but its religious concerns were soon overshadowed by the strident nationalism of the militant Jewish Defense League (JDL). These developments paralleled the emergence of the Black Panthers and the black power movement. One outcome was mutual suspicion. Many in the Jewish community had become increasingly anxious about anti-Semitic remarks by Elijah Mohammed and the charismatic Malcolm X; during the same period, Jewish American Zionism, which the Arab-Israeli War subsequently reinvigorated, kindled blacks' hostility to an international loyalty they viewed as chauvinist and imper alist. The hostility of some in each community to nationalist or socioeconomic conflicts became, however, the general fear of many and as blacks began to move into Jewish neighborhoods, many Jews did not stay. Murray Polner described the transformation of the Jewish ghetto of Brownsville in Brooklyn: "[S]ynagogues gave way to black Baptist and Pentecostal churches almost overnight, it seems. . . . By the mid- to late-1960s virtually all the Jews had fled, either because of fear of crime, which was genuine, or their own racist sentiments, also genuine." [18]

This out-migration included large numbers of secular and reform-minded Jews, and Polner's commentary calls into question the existence of a single Jewish identity that could embrace both the Orthodox and the secular, the conservative and the radical. In fact, the Orthodox communities in Brooklyn's Williamsburg and Crown Heights neighborhoods blossomed after other Jews moved out to claim their upward social mobility. [19] There were poor Jews, too, but in contrast to the rampant unemployment of black males in the ghetto, the relative financial security of many of the Orthodox could be seen daily as they took their private buses and vans to jobs at their own Manhattan-based gold, jewelry, and electronics shops. The insularity and seemingly alien ways of the Orthodox, with their flowing *peyas* (sideburns), black frock coats, and broad-rimmed hats, made them an easily visible symbol of difference to their poorer black neighbors.

Many Jews had moved their families to homes in white suburbs in New Jersey or Westchester or Nassau County but had kept their shops in the old community. Increasingly they served black customers. If enterprising black vendors set themselves up on the street, shop owners asked the police to remove them, claiming that they were unfair competition because they did not have overhead costs. Such disputes had old origins in the pushcart wars of the Lower East Side, but now they had a racial script that changed their meaning and made them even more volatile. [20] In addition, high prices and limited credit made the shop-keepers, especially when seen as people living outside the community, easy targets for claims of exploitation and bias. Indeed the new department store complexes in shopping malls could offer reduced prices because of high-volume sales to affluent, creditworthy middle-income (white) families. At the same time, white businesspeople in the old communities became targets of crime and violence.

Conflicts between Jews and blacks became increasingly visible at the same time that long-smoldering and acrimonious struggles over community control of schools broke out in the late 1960s. Teaching was a major avenue of Jewish social mobility, and the teachers' union in New York City had fought long and hard to win job security for its members. It was also true, however, that even though southern school desegregation received national attention, public schools in northern cities like New York remained segregated. Black children congregated in overburdened local schools in black ghettos, where they continued to receive inferior educations. With school decentralization under Mayor John Lindsay promising community control of local schools, leaders of the black community of Ocean Hill–Brownsville sought to select their own teachers, who they hoped would also be more sensitive to black culture and history. To the Jewish teacher trade unionists, however, such currents of black nationalism threatened to sweep away their own gains and undermine their professional integrity and control of the workplace.[21]

There is no hard data on opinions, but qualitative evidence suggests that many Jews and blacks began to see themselves as on opposite sides in these struggles. Jeffrey S. Gurok's history of Yeshiva University, for example, highlights the effort by a student editorialist in the college newspaper to reverse "a pernicious trend within their own community." Jews were mistakenly, the editorialist wrote, equating "black equality . . . with riots, black anti-Semitism, and terrorized Jewish merchants and teachers." Too many Jews, the writer warned, had begun to " 'dissociate' themselves from the 'civil rights movement' and to find kinship with the 'Jewish Defense League which . . . fights might with might.' Other Jews . . . had simply become massively apathetic" about the plight of black people.[22] In subsequent years, the ethnic and racial elements of this conflict would surface in debates over the merits of open admissions at the City University of New York. The university retained many Jewish professors who remembered (and sometimes romanticized) the success of generations of immigrant Jews and contrasted it with the need to provide remedial programs to accommodate minorities who were poorly prepared. By the 1980s, earlier liberal Jewish support of affirmative action was swept away by an insurgent neoconservative opposition to quotas, which Protestant-controlled institutions had long used to discriminate against Jews.[23]

The history of New York City social workers illustrates the multiple strands of the complicated Jewish and black narratives of success and failure that informed social policy and the politics of identity in modern America. Richard Nixon's appeals to a "forgotten" "silent majority" in "Middle America" in his successful campaigns for the presidency in 1968 and 1972 built on the new ressentiment toward welfare, read as "black." Constituting Middle Americans as suburbanite taxpayers, this perspective saw the burgeoning welfare rolls not just as a burden but as providing an unfair advantage to those minorities who had not "achieved" what others had worked hard to attain. The titles of books that the new Republican ideologues used as their basic texts reflected their view that the Great Society had discriminated against a majority of the middle class and created a moral crisis rooted in the city: after the 1968 election, the Republican "bible" became Kevin Phillips's *Emerging Republican Majority*; other books followed with titles such as

America vs. America: The Revolution in Middle-Class Values and *Religion and the New Majority: Billy Graham, Middle America, and the Politics of the 70s.*[24] Championing reductions in welfare, this perspective, in effect, threw the Jewish success story in the face of blacks. Middle-class Jewish success remained generally implicit in these accounts but was nonetheless central to Jews' resentment of black and "liberal" elites who were supposedly responsible for jeopardizing their neighborhoods. Phillips, for example, saw the origins of this hostility in New York City's 1966 referendum on the Police Civilian Review Board that announced that "poor and middle-class Jewish districts, plagued by rising crime rates . . . opposed the liberal urban coalition of Harlem and Park Avenue."[25]

Increasingly, Jews who were caught up in the tumultuous racial politics of late 1960s New York City, even while rejecting Nixon, warmed to this analysis. Some, like the Orthodox Jews who lived in the East Flatbush section of Brooklyn adjacent to the black community of Bedford-Stuyvesant, viewed the swelling of black relief rolls and NWRO militancy close up and increasingly found them inequitable and unsettling. Other Jewish observers were no less concerned about the growing animosity. In a 1972 essay, for example, Jewish literary critic Cynthia Ozick complained of "[b]lack distrust of th[e] heritage of Jewish sympathy": "Jews are nowadays reminded that this difference—America felt simultaneously as Jewish Eden and black inferno—has always been exactly the thing that called into question the authenticity of Jewish sympathy; that this disparity from the beginning made the Jews suspect to resentful blacks, that Jewish commitment to black advancement, much less black assertion, *had* to be undermined by the Jews' pleasure in an America open and sweet to them."[26] Representing their earlier common struggle with blacks against institutionalized bias as "their" help "for" blacks, such Jews felt that their efforts on behalf of blacks had been forgotten. Instead, it seemed as if the state privileged blacks at the expense of hardworking Jewish businesspeople, teachers, and taxpayers. In this context, the "success narrative" of Jews in America, advanced by neoconservative Jews such as Norman Podhoretz and Irving Kristol in the influential magazine *Commentary* was Jewish ressentiment toward "ungrateful" blacks. This narrative found broad acceptance both inside the mainstream Jewish community and outside it among government policymakers and became the counterstory to a "failure narrative" of blacks. By the 1970s, the neoconservative turn of some prominent Jewish intellectuals, the Arab-Israeli wars of 1967 and 1973 and the hostility of some leading black nationalist voices made the solidarity between blacks and Jews that had been seen in the 1963 protest against Bronxville bias considerably less common.[27]

In the 1960s, the dominance of this Jewish success/black failure narrative remained incomplete; it found considerable opposition within the Jewish community, especially from within social worker ranks. Jewish caseworkers were among those most prepared to ally with the poor, and their history refuted a simplistic picture of black and Jewish polarization. A resurgent radical social worker trade union movement in the early 1960s declared its shared concerns with clients (increasingly seen as black), even while FJP executives sought to distinguish Jewish social service from social work in nonsectarian communities. Thus, the labor history of the social worker unions in the 1960s and several landmark strikes among FJP workers and in the DW complicated and even challenged the counternarrative that emerged out of the 1960s in New York City.

Two labor struggles in the DW, a four-week-long strike in January 1965 and a six-month dispute in 1967, highlight the symbiotic and changing relationship between blacks in the NWRO and Jewish social workers. These conflicts would figure and be figured at the center of the emerging counternarrative of the middle class.[28] As highly public events, these strikes shaped popular attitudes and mobilized enormous political forces, including a more interventionist state. In addition, the strikes took place around the time of the 1968 conflict between the black community of Ocean Hill–Brownsville and what it saw as the Jewish teachers' union. It is an ironic story of Jews and blacks, of predominantly Jewish social workers who fought, at least in part, in the interest of NWRO clients. Occurring at a time of controversial antiwar protest, public service worker strikes engaged heated issues of professional responsibility and social dissent, forcing the state to take an active role. Finally, the resolution of the strikes during this decade in both the DW and FJP agencies would be watersheds in social service labor relations, muffling (although not quite silencing) social worker union voices that identified with clients. As important, the strike resolutions fit into a new narrative of race and welfare politics. Although there is little evidence of explicit racial motivation, after the 1967 DW defeat and the changes in the work process that followed in its wake, many white women social workers during the next decades sought alternatives to casework. The strike defeat, then, was part of the general defeat of an alternative social and political protest movement that advanced a sense of class difference and inequality. As such, the defeat of the radical social worker trade union movement would inter the last major movement of white resistance to the emergent nonclass expression of modern middle-class identity.

The DW and the SSEU

The legacy of the enhanced professionalism of the 1950s made the middle-class social workers who organized a new radical social worker union in 1961 fundamentally different from their 1930s predecessors. Their commitment to fighting for clients' rights promised to strengthen the bonds between Jews and blacks in New York City's DW, but their allegiance to a professional ideology ultimately fatally undermined their ability to resist divisive managerial attacks. Professional workers had established solidarity with their staffs in an industrial union; in contrast, radical professionals in the 1960s who also fought on their clients' behalf refused to allow maintenance and clerical workers (who were more likely to resemble their clients) into their union.

Dissident social workers in the DW began to mount open opposition to what they saw as corruption and weakness in Welfare Employees Local 371, District Council 37, AFSCME, at the end of the 1950s. Formed after the merger of the AFL and CIO in 1955, Local 371 had failed to win the broad-based support formerly held by the UPW; membership in Local 371 remained at about 1,000, paling in comparison to the 5,000 who had joined the old left-wing union. Critics of the new union attributed its poor support to its officers' political cronyism and self-interest. Union officials prided themselves on their close relationship with Commissioner Dumpson, and as historian Mark H. Maier has noted, "the union relied on favors from department officials as the main service it could offer members. . . . [T]he prime beneficiaries of the close cooperation between the union and the department were Local 371 presidents Raymond Diana, Anthony Russo, and Frank Petrocelli, all of whom stepped from union office to important city government positions."[29]

In 1959 passive displeasure with Local 371 became active opposition. Led by former UPW member Sam Podell of the East New York Welfare Center in Brooklyn, the Committee for a More Militant and Representative Union in Welfare ran a partial slate of four candidates against the union slate renominating Petrocelli.[30] The entire opposition slate lost but by less than 150 votes for each candidate.[31] Buoyed by its showing, the Podell group kept up its attack in consecutive unsuccessful campaigns during the next years. Finally, convinced that entrenched leaders controlled the election process, the dissidents initiated a different strategy in 1961: the creation of a new independent union representing DW caseworkers—the SSEU.[32] Field investigators, the predominantly female caseworkers who generally felt neglected by Local 371, supplied a ready base for the new union.[33]

Anxious to hold down labor costs and minimize dissent, Mayor Robert F. Wagner Jr. readily acceded to the SSEU's request for recognition. As Maier has argued, strikes by militants at other District Council 37 locals made undermining any locals within the council, even as moderate a group as Local 371, more important to him than the suspect past of UPW leaders.[34]

Well-publicized SSEU activism in 1962 soon won the union a large following. Local 371 had repeatedly signed contract agreements with caseload-reduction promises that went unfulfilled. The SSEU's response, although unsuccessful, demonstrated that it was prepared to be an activist union: several SSEU militants at the Brooklyn Borough Hall Welfare Center led a brief strike protesting the city's failure to live up to its agreement. Then, debunking Local 371's paper victories, four SSEU leaders complained to authorities in Washington, D.C., that New York City did not meet federal guidelines mandating a maximum caseload of sixty. When an outraged Commissioner Dumpson tried to withdraw recognition of the SSEU and suspended four of its leaders, he only managed to martyr them. The four were allowed to remain on the job while they appealed their cases (which they won six years later), and the publicity spurred union growth.[35]

Old-time radicals like Podell played an important role in the early history of the SSEU, but newer recruits to social work did as much or more to shape the union's militancy and political agenda. None of these new recruits was more important than Judith Mage, vice president for publicity from 1963 to 1966 and president from 1966 to 1969. Mage typified the generation of politicized young people schooled in the civil rights and antiwar movements that increasingly dominated youth political culture after the late 1950s. Described by Jewel Bellush and Bernard Bellush as "a product of New York City's radical politics, the middle-class Jewish intelligentsia, and an experimental education at Antioch College," Mage was part of the New Left in social work that energized groups such as the Social Workers Committee for Nuclear Disarmament and Peace.[36] To be sure, other leaders, such as Joseph Tepedino, SSEU president from 1963 to 1966, were also pragmatic liberals with a strong social conscience galvanized by the reforming spirit of the era. But Mage was typical of the more radical wing of the SSEU, to which she added a particular sectarian zeal and a commitment to building alliances with the "working class."

Under the leadership of Mage and her supporters, the SSEU resurrected the 1930s Rank-and-Filers' view of social workers' "identity of interests" with clients. As in the 1930s, this class perspective paid scant attention to gender issues, even under the leadership of women such as Mage. The 1960s variant of the professional worker remained at best a neutered type, and until the women's liberation movement began to challenge these notions late in the decade, it was more often masculinist. Male psychiatrists, administrators, and radical leaders expected and usually won the persisting deference of women. Nonetheless, a significant undercurrent of gender discrimination did fuel the struggle between Local 371 and the SSEU. Caseworkers felt that the male leadership of Local 371 privileged concerns of administrative and supervisory ranks where men congregated. Not surprisingly, the SSEU recruited and won the allegiance of social worker ranks where women predominated—caseworkers, children's counselors, home economists, child care workers, cottage parents, and so forth.[37]

However, there were some fundamental differences in perspective and organization between the New Left SSEU and its Old Left predecessors. In particular, New Left radicals bore the mark of the professionalizing impulse of the intervening decades. New Left radicals who were recruited into social work recognized that racism was central to the emerging urban class structure, but they rejected Old Left proletarianism in favor of their own professional concerns. In contrast to C. Wright Mills's idea of professionals as part of a new middle class, by mid-decade many in the New Left began to advance a theory of the "new working class" in which campus radicals cum professionals were seen as proletarianized laborers who had to build alliances with industrial workers.[38] This hybrid radicalism underscored long-standing contradictions in the oxymoron of the professional worker. Support for the welfare rights movement and community organizing among the poor fit nicely with this idea. But this working class was "new," and the SSEU was also the product of 1950s professionalism and the historical circumstances of its creation. Many members of the SSEU were young professionals who had recently come to New York City in search of socially relevant work as an alternative to a career in business. Many were also Jewish, and further complicating their sense of themselves and their interests was the extent to which, as secularists and workers, they may have identified themselves as radicals and social workers rather than Jews.[39] Indeed, they often claimed all three identities, which provoked a crisis for them late in the decade. But in 1964 it was the caseworkers' identity as worker-professionals (rather than professional workers) that Local 371 had offended.

The reemphasis on professionalism in the 1950s had occasioned a significant shift in social workers' sense of what it meant to be a middle-class professional, a shift that was reflected in their decision to form a craft union. The professional worker's double identity, which had been so vital in the 1930s, may have become increasingly important for clerical and industrial workers in the postwar era, but the SSEU experience suggests that for professionals, the workplace and the home were now both distinct middle-class arenas. Thus, caseworkers' feelings that Local 371 had excluded them coincided with their own preference that white-collar professionals alone shape the SSEU. The industrial unionism that had characterized social service unions from their inception was to be no more; the SSEU organized itself as a craft professional union of caseworkers and all others who had felt excluded by Local 371. Clerical workers remained in District Council 37, AFSCME. Not only did the SSEU make no effort to organize them, but its statement of principles presumed that there should be distinct organizations for clerical workers and caseworkers: "Although the SSEU does not include clerical workers, we are strongly in favor of the organization of the clerks, who are also underpaid, into a militant union, which they do not now have. We would cooperate with and aid the clerical staff in every possible way, but we feel that at present a social service union is the most effective way for the social service staff to achieve its goals."[40]

In October 1964, after the SSEU decisively defeated Local 371 in representative elections at twenty-one of twenty-two welfare centers, it had to face the contradictions between the middle-class orientation of its craft union organization and the proletarian orientation of its workerist ideology: it would seek to build alliances with and for clients from an exclusive base.[41] Ironically, SSEU members fought hard on behalf of their clients at the same time that they resisted a formal alliance with their own clerical and maintenance staffs. As Piven and Cloward observed in their landmark history of mid-twentieth-century welfare policy, contrary to social workers' public image as a hard-bitten lot (which some historians desirous of representing clients' voices have unwittingly accepted as the whole story), many social workers were quite uncomfortable with welfare's restrictive and punitive policies and organized to change them. Since the eligibility drives of the 1950s, welfare manuals had elaborated incomprehensible procedures designed to discourage enrollment through a mixture of intimidation, harassment, and shaming and an array of seemingly endless forms. On the Lower East Side, Piven and Cloward estimated that fully one in two eligible families either never applied for welfare or were rejected on procedural grounds.[42] This realization led Piven and Cloward to speak to George A. Wiley, the associate national director of the Congress of Racial Equality (CORE), about organizing poor people for welfare rights.[43] Wiley, of course, did so, and the NWRO resulted. In this context, the "explosion" to follow merely gave those eligible what they deserved.

Change was slow to come, however, and in the interim, many SSEU caseworkers simply worked to undermine what they felt to be restrictive and inhumane provisions. In Piven and Cloward's words, the "political environment" of attacks on welfare "fraud" and "dependence" compelled welfare officials to "design procedures that serve the economic ends of groups outside of the relief system." As various social welfare historians have noted, conservative politicians who were obsessed with containing costs and reducing rolls were responsible for the restrictive policies, not social workers. To be sure, administrators and social investigators had to enforce these provisions, and a few investigators seemed to have taken almost malicious delight in well-publicized "midnight raids" in search of "men under the bed." Moreover, black and Hispanic clients continued to suffer discriminatory treatment by caseworkers, especially in the South. Still, by political design, neither relief investigators nor recipients benefited from the Spartan and harsh welfare regime.[44] Relief investigators' response, according to one of the SSEU's leaders, William Schleicher, was to manipulate categories to provide needed aid, making bimonthly claims for low monthly rent payments so that additional monies would be available to offset inadequate allowances for clothing, food, or shelter.[45]

Schleicher remembered such manipulation as "common knowledge within the union," a view borne out by the experience of Leigh Benin, an investigator in the DW in the late 1960s. Benin remembered the "atmosphere of desperation" that pervaded welfare at the time. After graduating with a bachelor's degree in

philosophy from Queens College in 1965, Benin started working for the DW—
"What else could one do as a liberal arts major?"—on January 3, 1966. The city's
welfare rolls were expanding, and the department needed additional investigators; Benin simply took the "easiest route to full-time employment." After two
weeks of "orientation," Benin was assigned forty cases at a welfare center on
Thirty-second Street in midtown Manhattan that had a particularly challenging
charge to serve newcomers to the city. The caseload soon grew to sixty to seventy
cases; most clients were people from Puerto Rico or the South who had no
resources and "had to be set up from scratch." Few of the caseworkers spoke
Spanish, and unlike caseworkers at neighborhood centers, social workers at this
center had to visit clients in all parts of the city. The workload and immediate
client demands made relief rather than counseling the core of the job. In some
circumstances, Benin made referrals to counselors, and in a few instances, he
provided "unconscious" and "spontaneous" counseling; he recalled that he "just
followed [his] instincts." Mostly, he requested money for people.[46]

Benin found the daily work unlike anything he had ever experienced before.
His sharpest memories were of a constant stream of people discussing their
problems in a noisy, cluttered room filled with desks piled high with cases.
Phones rang constantly. People were always shouting in different languages. He
remembered being sent to neighborhoods he had never seen before like the
South Bronx and Bedford-Stuyvesant; there he walked up tenement steps and
found families with nothing in their apartments to eat but plantains. He could
not have imagined this "incredible poverty" without seeing it. Requests for
special grants for furniture and food added to the reams of paperwork already
required. Sometimes, he recalled, if he could not get authorization for what
someone needed, he would obtain approval for something else and shift the
funds; a grant for a sofa would help pay the electric bill. Combined with "un-
believable overwork," the experience could be very humbling: "[Y]ou knew that
no matter how much you gave a family, it would not help enough." Feeling that
he had to do something to improve the situation, within a year of starting at the
DW, Benin joined the SSEU.[47]

SSEU social workers, then, set an agenda that fundamentally challenged what
they saw as the abiding professional ethics and cronyism of their AFSCME com-
petitor. The SSEU opposed fundamental managerial prerogatives as well as professionalism, insisting not only that issues of caseloads and working conditions
be placed on the table but also—a quite unheard-of assertion—that services on
behalf of clients be discussed.[48] In the latter regard, Local 371 contrasted its
position with that of the SSEU: "LOCAL 371 *does not believe* that the primary
responsibility of *any Union* in the Department of Welfare is owed to client
organizations."[49] Of course, the SSEU disagreed, reminding all welfare client
groups that they shared "a very important goal: TO CHANGE THE DEPARTMENT

OF WELFARE! . . . It is clear that under the present Welfare System the client is robbed of his dignity. But it is also true that the Welfare System has robbed the welfare worker of his dignity, too."[50]

Not surprisingly, Mayor Wagner was not prepared to discuss such seemingly impertinent challenges to his authority. But no one familiar with the union was surprised either when, on January 4, 1965, it led 8,000 DW employees out on strike.[51] Not to be outdone by the SSEU, AFSCME clerical and supervisory workers went out in support of the strike, and the DW was compelled to close down most of its operations almost immediately. The shutdown placed hundreds of thousands of poor families and children in dire straits. AFSCME leader Jerry Wurf rejected a SSEU plea to call out District Council 37 in support of the strike, but otherwise New York City's labor movement rallied behind the strike.

Both the NWRO and the mayor noted the differences between the rival unions. Wiley communicated with SSEU organizers. As important, the civil rights movement gave its support to the radicals: recognizing that caseloads and working conditions affected clients as well as staff, the director of CORE, James Farmer; the president of the Brotherhood of Sleeping Car Porters, A. Philip Randolph; and thirteen local branches of the NAACP voiced support for the SSEU.[52]

Wagner remained intransigent. Early in the walkout, he had terminated the contracts of all strikers. By the middle of the second week, he decided to risk his liberal credentials (in a city where the mayor needed the liberal vote) and imposed the antistrike provisions of the Condon-Wadlin Act. For the last two weeks of the month-long strike, nineteen strike leaders sat in jail. Only after AFL-CIO president George Meany intervened did Wagner agree to mediation. Three months later, a contract had been hammered out, although not before the SSEU conducted a one-day sit-in at City Hall. The contract terms, which largely met all of the union demands, represented a major victory for the SSEU. Although social worker trade unions had signed many "agreements" with the DW in their thirty years of operation, on June 7, 1965, the SSEU signed the "first collective bargaining agreement to cover public welfare employees in the United States."[53]

The larger meaning of the strike settlement for the subsequent history of the union lay, however, in the reactions to the terms of the settlement. First, the union won its demand for a semiannual clothing grant for welfare recipients. To management, this concession usurped one of its sacrosanct domains—the conditions of relief—and, if anything, quickened its desire to see that no such settlement ever happened again. To (Jewish) workers and (black) clients, however, this gain was tangible proof that DW investigators would not leave the politics of welfare and civil rights behind the doors of DW offices.

Second, the settlement brought state government into new threatening relations with social workers, compelling it to challenge their power both in the workplace and at the bargaining table. On a positive note for labor, the settlement marked the death knell of Condon-Wadlin. The court released the jailed leaders on the convenient legalistic interpretation that their illegal actions had not occurred in its "view and presence." A year later, the state legislature passed a special law exempting the striking welfare workers from prosecution. But legislators supplanted Condon-Wadlin with the Taylor Law, which offered recognition to public unions but imposed harsh new financial penalties on striking public sector workers. Condon-Wadlin had imposed a three-year salary freeze on strikers; Taylor docked people two days' pay for every day they were out on strike.[54]

The strike settlement also initiated a new role for city government as a future player in labor-management conflicts. The structure of the panel that mediated the 1965 strike, a three-part group with representatives from the union and the city and a neutral third party, would hereafter become the model for municipal labor relations in New York City. As important as its structure was the way it defined the parameters of worker protest and contained the sense of managers as "others": tripartitism required binding arbitration and limited disputes to matters of compensation and grievance machinery.

The SSEU opposed the concessions that accompanied the tripartite arrangement but to no avail. As his term came to a close in 1966, Mayor Wagner asked Victor Gotbaum to lead the city's tripartite committee to mediate future disputes. Gotbaum, who had recently been promoted to executive director of District Council 37, had helped mediate a settlement of the 1965 strike. In his historical account of the strike, Maier has argued that Gotbaum felt that binding third-party arbitration was a reasonable alternative to what he believed were futile efforts to legalize strikes by public sector workers.[55] To be sure, many professionals were ambivalent about strike actions. The arrangement did more than take the strike weapon out of their hands, however; it conceded to management one of the major, if not most symbolic, gains in the strike—any discussion of working conditions.

Gotbaum's willingness to accept tripartitism might have been seen as "flexibility" by the mayor, as "practical" by the AFSCME, and as a "sellout" by the SSEU. But its consequences would pay dividends to both city officials and the AFSCME and would bode ill for the SSEU's future. In labor conflicts, the AFSCME could promise the city orderly negotiations of a limited agenda. In return, when the AFSCME competed with the independent union for control of social service workers, it gained political favor from the mayor's office in jurisdictional disputes. At the same time, Gotbaum could promise workers that the city could no longer be intransigent about mediation; it would have to sit down with the union and presumably reach settlements that would free staff from strikes in which they lost pay and professional status.[56]

The SSEU did not have to wait long to see its worst fears realized: the tripartite mediation panel approved the terms of the 1965 settlement by three to two, the two SSEU representatives opposing any settlement that did not include a schedule for the implementation of its terms. The SSEU's skepticism proved well founded since the provisions for a clothing allowance and lighter workloads were never implemented. Nor could a protest easily be remounted since the tripartite arrangement now placed these issues outside the union's purview.

In its subsequent efforts to strengthen its hand and make sure that its contract with the city was enforced, the SSEU found itself stymied as much by the legacy of its craft union organization and a divisive factionalism as by Gotbaum's favorable position at City Hall. The election of John Lindsay as mayor and his appointment in 1966 of a liberal social work educator, Mitchell Ginsberg, as commissioner of welfare had raised hopes among the social work rank and file of a less punitive welfare policy. Ginsberg did reverse Dumpson's ban on the dissemination of birth control information and ended the "midnight raids." The applause of social workers turned to hostility, however, after Ginsberg refused to implement the semiannual clothing grants and defended the decision by claiming that it was based on the city's managerial authority.[57] When the 1965 contract expired at the end of 1966, SSEU workloads remained little changed from workloads two years earlier.

As SSEU leader Judith Mage warned of a new strike unless the DW bargained "seriously," municipal officials leaked warnings of their own that had dire implications for caseworkers. The headline of a mid-December 1966 SSEU flier announced the threat to its members: "New Welfare Title May Eliminate Caseworkers." The leaflet noted that the *Civil Service Leader* had just "learned of a City plan to create a new title, that of 'case aide' which may eliminate the caseworker and other investigator titles in the Department of Welfare." Moreover, the proposal pitted the DW's (predominantly black) clients against its (predominantly Jewish) social workers as each struggled to hold or gain an economic base. According to the report, unskilled aides, who would not be required to have college degrees or pass qualifying tests, "would be recruited from among the present welfare clients . . . at a starting salary of $3,800 per year." In this scenario, caseworkers had reason to worry whether their starting salaries of $5,750 would soon be a thing of the past.[58]

City government's tough stance prompted Local 371 to suggest to the caseworkers that they might fare better if they combined forces. But SSEU leaders remained suspicious of the older men and supervisors who still dominated the AFSCME local, and the local's overture received a cold response from the independent union. Meanwhile, increasingly after 1966, the SSEU itself became fractured by the sectarian politics that had come to divide the New Left. Each faction attempted to be more "radical" than the others. Communist Party members operated a Unity Party, and Maoists in the Progressive Labor Party set up a Rank-and-File Committee. Although each group may have had no more than thirty active members, as engaged and zealous proponents, they spoke loudly and often, with an impact that extended beyond their small numbers. Two even smaller Trotskyist groups, the Workers League and the Spartacist League, further complicated internal union politics. Finally, various socialists, social democrats, and anarchists formed the Movement for a Militant and Democratic Unionism and affiliated with the Peace and Freedom Party.

In an environment rent by sectarian politics, compromise, whether with Local 371 or with DW officials, was unlikely. In the 1956 election for union officers, Mage's "left-wing" slate, running on a platform of greater engagement in community affairs, defeated the "right-wing" slate led by older leaders such as Joseph Tepedino. The election did not stop the flow of fratricidal attacks on Mage by groups from all sides, however, each claiming to be the "real" radicals. In this contested climate, on January 16, 1967, Mage led the SSEU out on the first of three strikes within the next six months.[59]

The chronology of these actions is less important than their legacy: in late July 1967, the union emerged from a six-week work-in substantially weakened.[60] During the work-in, the union had asked workers to report to work but to not do any of their required tasks. Before the protest had ended, however, nearly half of the 1,000 workers whom the city had suspended for "intimidating fellow workers and interfering with service to clients" had returned to work. To avoid folding, the SSEU agreed to mediation, a process that removed virtually all of its workplace grievances from the table.[61]

The 1967 strikes also left the SSEU beholden to Gotbaum. Although as many as 30 percent of the AFSCME members seemed to have supported one or more of these actions, Local 371 did not join the strikes. Gotbaum's intervention to help settle the disputes, however, if only in the hope that the SSEU would survive to merge with his union someday, quite likely saved the SSEU from an early death.

As important, the fact that the remarkable growth the SSEU had enjoyed in its early years had been stymied made the union vulnerable to AFSCME domination. There were many possible reasons for the SSEU's failure to grow after 1966. As we shall see, the AFSCME's favorable position at City Hall was an important part of this story, but undoubtedly, the SSEU's internal sectarian squabbles also undermined its efforts to reach new members. The SSEU failed as well, however, in attempts to expand its base by winning additional members with other job classifications. Galvanized by Gotbaum's new leadership, Local 371 resisted an SSEU raid on supervisors. More general reasons for the union's stagnation lay in fundamental shifts in the political orientation and middle-class identity of New York City's social workers. The SSEU, for instance, continued to exclude the DW's clerical workers from the union.[62] Equally significant, the SSEU did not tap two enormous areas of potential union growth created by the war on poverty—community organization programs and antipoverty workers.

To be sure, initial SSEU success organizing among these groups soon turned to naught for reasons that may have more to do with hostile AFSCME intervention than with SSEU ideology. Employees of Job Orientation in Neighborhoods formed an SSEU-affiliate union, Joint United Staff, but after Mayor Lindsay reorganized New York City social service in 1967 into the HRA, the U.S. Department of Labor, which had jurisdiction over federal workers in municipal agencies, placed these employees in an HRA bargaining unit already largely represented by District Council 37. Whether this was happenstance or, as Benin's history of the struggle argues, "collusion between DC 37 and the City" is unknown. To Mage, what had happened was clear: "[T]he Department of Labor gerrymandered this election."[63]

But antipoverty workers and caseworkers were also very different groups of people with distinct class and racial identities, and as Benin has recognized, those differences had come to have new meaning by late 1967. Benin, who had been fired by the civil service and was one of twenty-nine caseworkers suspended by the city during the 1967 work-in, became the coordinator of antipoverty organizing for the SSEU. As he correctly recalled, the two groups had very different social profiles: caseworkers were generally college educated, and about 80 percent were white, whereas approximately 85 percent of antipoverty workers were black and Hispanic. The latter lived in poor communities in which they had a history of political activism; caseworkers lived in middle-income communities, and fewer of them had a background in urban protest movements.[64] More important, however, by 1968, riots in major cities, Martin Luther King Jr.'s assassination, and the rise of the black power movement had increasingly aroused new suspicions among former allies in the struggle for social justice. Only two years before, it will be recalled, civil rights leaders had lent active support to the SSEU's strike, and caseworkers had helped organize the welfare rights movement. Some alliances would continue: for example, thirty-four social workers were arrested in 1968 for protesting the inadequacies of basic AFDC grant allowances.[65] But as black separatist ideology spread and grew more militant, the NWRO became more independent of white radical "sponsors" and led more frequent disruptions at welfare centers. The result, as summarized by Maier, was "increasingly hostile relations between welfare workers and welfare recipients."[66] By 1968, many among antipoverty workers and the poor, who had been the inspirational sources of the New Left's radical identification with the community of the poor, had forsaken the New Left politically as well as institutionally.

By this time, the city had also maneuvered to give the SSEU little choice but to merge with the AFSCME. To lessen the stigma of welfare, the DW was renamed the

Department of Social Services of the City of New York (DSS) in 1967. Reorganization of social service, however, increasingly isolated social workers from anti-poverty workers. Although the full impact of this shift would be felt in ensuing years, the DSS implemented automated relief work that could be handled by clerical aides and stripped welfare of even its modest commitment to counseling. Lindsay may have buried any final SSEU hopes when he signed Executive Order 40 in June 1967, which authorized the recognition of the majority union in any industry. In the future, the city would negotiate citywide terms only with that group. A diminished SSEU could either stay out in the cold or join the AFSCME. Any future mediation, however, would take place within the tripartite structure of the city's new Office of Collective Bargaining.[67] In 1969 the SSEU reaffiliated with Local 371, AFSCME.

Community and Social Agency Employees, Local 1707

A series of dramatic strikes by radical, private agency social workers employed by the FJP took place during the same years as the SSEU strikes. As in the case of the welfare strikes, these FJP conflicts never generated the national concern that accompanied the more famous teachers' strike of 1968. In New York City, however, like the welfare struggles, FJP strikes were highly visible public events in which newspapers increasingly depicted Jewish agency social worker strikes as jeopardizing the well-being of poor and black children. Thus, all of these social service conflicts in New York City fed into and helped construct the emerging Jewish and black counternarratives that would come to underlie the languages of class and race in late twentieth-century America.

In the aftermath of Commissioner Dumpson's 1963 complaint about private agency bias against nonsectarian clients, the FJP became increasingly sensitive to any adverse publicity that might call into question its "objective" professionalism or the equity of its services. Fund-raisers worried that any public activity that smacked of controversy might jeopardize funding. By the end of four consecutive years of bitter strikes at FJP agencies between 1962 and 1965, the tension between racial and Jewish identity that had never been far from the surface became explicit.

In contrast to Local 371, AFSCME, caseworkers dominated the local union representing private agency staff at the FJP, Local 1707, CSAE, and felt no need to create a radical alternative such as the SSEU. In fact, Local 1707 followed a political trajectory not unlike that of its radical public sector equivalent. After the purge of the UOPWA and the departure of well-liked communist leaders such as Bernard R. Segal, the multiple political strands in the union united behind CSAE president Sam Friedman, himself an old socialist. Although the various left-wing groups shared a social vision, they differed in strategies and priorities, and the socialists' anticommunist credentials and less confrontational tactics sat well with FJP executives. The new union did not lose any of its militancy, but it sought to avoid strikes, and broader social and political issues ceased to be union priorities. Instead, union contract demands focused on grievance machinery, wages, and benefits.[68]

As in the SSEU, Local 1707 social workers' commitment to professional ideology continued to influence how they thought of themselves and the behavior they thought appropriate to that image. The political economy of private philanthropy also encouraged this professional emphasis: to win the financial support of private benefactors and justify receiving state monies, agency staff still had to proclaim that their services were qualitatively distinctive and better than public aid. The fact that FJP agencies such as the JBG and the JFS remained at the forefront of social work education and advanced training undoubtedly attracted social workers with a greater predisposition toward professionalism.[69] Thus, when Local 1707 took a more militant turn in the 1960s and pressed social demands that extended beyond narrow professional self-interest, it did so without the flair, enthusiasm, and militant action of prior years. Still, Sam Liebner remembered the union struggles at FJP agencies in the early 1960s as "very heady times." As he recalled, many agency social workers focused on the war on poverty, but the staff divided between those who saw social work as a way to eliminate poverty and effect a "basic change in the economic system" and those who saw community work as the responsibility of private citizens, not professionals.[70]

The radical social agenda of New Left social workers in the FJP fit comfortably within a liberal civil rights tradition in Jewish philanthropy; militant strikes, even if they were conducted on behalf of clients, were quite another matter. The strike weapon, however it was advanced, threatened the professional's self-image, especially in a specialized private agency such as the JBG with a long tradition of advanced psychiatric training. For instance, in early February 1962, a petition by JBG "professional workers" expressed dismay at the prospect of a strike because strikes were counter to their psychiatric mission. Arguing that "we are all dedicated to freeing ourselves and others of the adverse effects of irrational emotions," they urged arbitration as the rational course. It was with great relief, then, that they learned on February 15 that the strike had been averted by yet another last-minute settlement.[71]

News from upstate the next day, however, turned their relief to horror. Although 61 percent of FJP workers had approved the settlement, the residential staff at the Hawthorne–Cedar Knolls School (the two schools had been merged in the previous decade), the cottage parents, were in open rebellion. The CSAE's domination by professional staff and city-based workers left cottage parents feeling unrepresented. Their situation was not unlike that of the social investigators in Local 371, an irony that seemed lost on the CSAE caseworkers. As JBG social worker Sam Liebner recalled, the cottage parents "felt sold out." Indeed, the cottage parents were different from the professional staff; Liebner referred to them as "natural people." Although they were required to have little formal training, they were responsible for delinquent or "problem" children, and their work was extremely stressful. The school usually employed retired people or childless couples and expected them to draw on their life experiences in order to "parent," on average, twelve or thirteen adolescent or preadolescent boys and girls (206 in all) living in each of sixteen cottages at the school. As one of their leaders, Albert Benghiat, explained, the cottage parents had made futile attempts for six years to improve "intolerable conditions" for child care at Hawthorne–Cedar Knolls; there were no aides for cottage parents and too few psychiatric caseworkers. So, complaining that overwork, inadequate pay, and dangerous conditions undermined responsible treatment, eight cottage couples initiated a walkout and demanded that contract negotiations be reopened.[72]

Local 1707, which had striven to avoid strikes that might tarnish the image of the agency or its members' professionalism, could fall in line behind the cottage parents or risk Local 371's fate. The union did more than join the strike; it assumed leadership of it and proceeded in the next two years to initiate new strikes. The union and civil rights activists also made a symbolically important exchange of support, one that would shape expectations in years to come. In February 1962, CORE joined the picket line in support of the walkout, and eighteen months later, the CSAE rented buses to send members and citizens to the civil rights movement's 1963 March on Washington.[73] After ten days on strike, the union and the JBG reached a settlement the cottage parents won no immediate gains, but the JBG agreed to implement procedures to adjudicate the grievances that had precipitated the walkout.[74]

The union came away from the strike stronger than it had been when it entered it, despite the fact that it lost some of its most valuable leaders at Hawthorne.[75] Although many of the union leaders at Hawthorne, including cottage parents Al and Rose Benghiat, who had worked there six and a half years, resigned from the agency rather than accept reprisals, those who remained cast their votes for the new militancy. JEG trustees noted with apprehension that the union officers chosen at the September 1962 annual election were "reflective of the group which led the strike" and that the new leaders were arranging " 'trials' of members who did not walk out, threatening them with loss of union membership and management's consequent mandatory dismissal from the Agency," although they offered no evidence for such a claim.[76]

Local 1707 displayed its new muscle in strikes in each of the next three years. In October 1963, workers at the FJP's central offices struck for three days to win increases in wages and medical and dental benefits. Bitter and substantially more protracted strikes in the next two years, however, resulted in more stable labor-management relations in the FJP. At the same time, as both workers and managers developed new highly publicized tactics, both sides came to appreciate the vulnerable position in which such shutdowns placed the philanthropic enterprise.

The 1964 strike lasted twenty-two days and involved over 1,000 social workers, psychologists, home care assistants, and aides in the six FJP casework agencies: the JBG, the JFS, the JCCA, Louise Wise Services, the Jewish Community Service of Long Island, and the Altro Health and Rehabilitation Service. At face value, the strike focused on bread-and-butter issues of wages, hours, union security, and improved grievance machinery. These agencies had been conducting combined negotiations with the FJP on an increasingly formal basis for the past decade, and the FJP had approved a 1963 committee recommendation to merge the bulk of services provided by the JBG, the JFS, and the JCCA into one organization.[77] The shutdown of all counseling services affected an estimated 13,000 families in the New York City area. Supervisors kept the JBG's Hawthorne–Cedar Knolls facility open, but the JCCA sent home two-thirds of the children at its Pleasantville Cottage School. JCCA management consistently took the most conservative, hard-line positions at this time, and the extent to which its decision reflected the lack of personnel or was a publicity strategy is not clear. Publicity, in fact, became a major new weapon in the dispute.[78]

In retrospect, the results of the strike appear less noteworthy than the new and more militant tactics that characterized it. A strike involving workers who provided a service reopened old ethical questions about social workers as professionals, especially in the context of the widely held view that such workers had a moral obligation not to withhold service from the needy. But the withholding of service also reinforced Dumpson's complaint about the failure of private agencies to serve "the public"—a public that was nonsectarian and racially different.

There were, in fact, many different "publics." Moreover, as CSAE member Sam Liebner recognized, "the public" was an important pressure point in labor struggles: "In fact, the only leverage one has in a social agency is the good will of the public. You don't have a profit motive."[79] But the public could be welfare recipients and legislators or taxpayers and benefactors, depending on circumstances. And these definitions of the public had an uneasy coexistence since both social workers and legislators needed popular support, the former for funding, the latter for reelection. Agencies and their staffs relied on the goodwill of legislators and donors for funds, but workers often disagreed with executives on how clients constituted as the public could best be served: at the same time that radical workers struck partly on clients' behalf, executives emphasized that the ideology of professional "responsibility" to clients opposed social workers' strikes (and many social workers agreed).

In this and a subsequent strike, both sides demonstrated that they had come to recognize the central role that various publics could play in their disputes. Each side employed a range of tactics that were increasingly becoming a staple of social conflict in the country; these tactics reflected the militant strategies of the civil rights and antiwar movements, the increasing awareness that television and print media could shape public opinion and influence support, and the unique situation of having to appeal to "the public" on issues in social service. In regard to labor, for instance, two days into the 1964 strike, Local 1707 cast itself as the protector of children and appealed to the city to withhold aid to struck child care agencies that had been forced to suspend services. Most of the aid went to the large residential treatment center at Hawthorne–Cedar Knolls, which helps explain why managers there made such an effort to keep the facility operating. Five days later, FJP workers held a twenty-five-hour sit-in at FJP headquarters on Fifty-ninth Street. Most worrisome to management, however, were the use of secondary boycotts at Hawthorne and the threat of violence. Strikers tried to stop milk deliveries at Hawthorne and discouraged nonresidential doctors from giving medical examinations there. According to Executive Director Goldsmith, intimidation succeeded in poisoning the atmosphere: the FJP reported that three men driving a car with Los Angeles license plates had "threatened" Hawthorne workers unloading a food-delivery truck.[80]

For its part, the FJP focused on public relations. Public relations had slowly evolved in the FJP over the past two decades, during which time the central office and each major agency had appointed a "professional" in public relations to speak for it. But in the heated environment of the mid-1960s—and shortly before the 1964 strike—at the advice of its counsel, the FJP retained the firm of Victor Weingarten to handle all public relations. The FJP's public relations efforts, however, appear to have become a matter of damage control more than affirmative publicity. The Weingarten firm did secure a strong antiunion editorial in the *New York Post*. Elsewhere, it was less successful. The *New York Times*, for instance, began its coverage of the strike with the personal account of a striking social worker who continued to meet his professional responsibilities: "A striking social worker discharged his duty to his conscience as well as his union yesterday by going directly from a picket line to the bedside of a hospitalized child who is deeply distrustful of adults." FJP publicist Donald J. Merwin noted that this striking worker, Jack Pinsen, was "a personal friend" of the *Times* reporter, Martin Tolchin.[81]

Merwin felt particularly aggrieved because he had accompanied Tolchin to Hawthorne. The next day, after some trustees "expressed dissatisfaction with the story," the *Times* sent a second reporter, Richard Hunt, to Hawthorne. Merwin felt that Hunt was "visibly antagonistic (and understandably so) because he was being asked to cover the same ground as a respected colleague." After spending several hours with him, Goldsmith and Merwin thought Hunt "had softened up a bit," but his story was also basically sympathetic to the union. Indeed, Merwin felt that the FJP was "fortunate to come away . . . as well as we did," especially considering what might have happened if the trustees' interventions had become public knowledge.[82] Adverse publicity, argued Merwin, could weaken public support. Merwin concluded: "With certain special circumstances, I am convinced that the less publicity we get, the better it will be."[83]

Finally, on March 9, the nineteenth day of the strike, after the union accepted but the FJP scorned a proposal by prolabor Manhattan councilman Paul O'Dwyer that the case be submitted to arbitration, the New York State Mediation Board stepped in and negotiated a settlement.[84] The settlement met some of the workers' demands, and the JBG reported net savings of $11,183 as a result of the strike.[85] After management agreed three days later not to make reprisals against anyone in the union or management who supported the strike, the CSAE signed the contract. Despite its promise, four months later, the FJP demanded that four supervisors who had refused to cross the picket line sign a "no strike pledge" or be "retired, dismissed or transferred to lower-pay jobs."[86]

With the strike behind it, the FJP's Personnel Committee knew it was "imperative" to find "some more constructive . . . alternative to the biannual disruption of services."[87] No-strike pledges might intimidate supervisors, but they were obviously not enforceable because of the union. Moreover, the January 1965 strike in the DW had already demonstrated the limitations of a law such as the Condon-Wadlin Act forbidding strikes by public employees. Then, in October–November 1965, an even longer strike erupted in the FJP. This time it was five weeks before state and city mediators could settle the dispute. Before the conflict was over, however, the union had turned the "art" of public relations against the FJP. In the 1965 strike, workers held sit-ins at FJP offices and hit the agency where it was most vulnerable—in the public eye under the gaze of funders. The union began its strike with a picket of the dinner that kicked off the annual fund-raising appeal, and its sit-in gained it a spot on the local television news.[88]

Two aspects of the settlement may have paved the way for a new regime of labor-management cooperation in the FJP. First, although the union dropped its financial demands, it won two long-sought gains: a union shop for all permanent employees and a thirty-five-hour week during six months of the year (during the other six, employees would work a thirty-seven-and-a-half-hour week). Second, the union's agreement to a three-year contract initiated a new era of labor peace in the FJP under collective bargaining.[89] By end of 1965, the constant state of conflict between FJP workers and managers had exhausted both sides, not to mention the patience of their funders.

In the 1965 strike settlement, FJP social workers showed their middle-class colors and those colors were "white": these workers might remain social activists in their private lives, but their union activity seemed to become increasingly "professional" and divorced from ethnoracial "others." FJP workers may have supported the civil rights and welfare rights movements, but as a general rule, identification with clients did not extend to bringing non-Jews into their sectarian services. The small Louise Wise agency, as we shall see, was a noteworthy exception; its progressive leadership made the agency fully nonsectarian by the mid-1960s. In general, the reprofessionalizing of the 1950s made the FJP's variant of the New Left professional worker less proletarian than consumerist. As part of the "new working class," these social workers organized less as a class than as a class fraction—as a professional-managerial group—to improve their own personal lives as working professionals. Discrimination against women workers crept into the union's agenda on only one occasion. In 1962, cottage mothers, whose salaries were 70 percent of those of their husbands, asked for wage parity.[90] But negotiators quickly and quietly dropped the issue, and neither it nor questions of sectarian discrimination appeared in further union deliberations until the rise of the women's movement at the end of the decade. Unfortunately, when NWRO voices rose later in the decade and black and Jewish communities increasingly found themselves figured in contrasting success narratives and competing claims for justice, FJP silences echoed loudly.

Backlash: Race and Ressentiment

The specter of changes in their work hung over social workers, but the defeat of the New Left in social work by the end of the decade was also the result of internal division and contradictions among professional workers. The legacy of the professionalism and anticommunism of the 1950s drove the New Left to distinguish itself from any association with the Old Left. In doing so, however, the SSEU and Local 1707 rejected the lessons of UPW and UOPWA industrial unionism as well. If the trade union social worker of the 1930s had created a professional worker identity based on an "identity of interests" with clerical workers and clients, the New Left variant was a reprofessionalized hybrid in a craft union structure.

By the 1960s, rather than class identity at least partially tied to the workplace, consumerist distinctions between social workers and both clerical workers and clients had also increasingly become the core of middle-class identity. For instance, speaking of themselves as "human beings" with "aspirations," Local 1707 pressed the JBG for higher wages in 1964, reminding it that they were "consumers with economic needs."[91] Caseworkers continued to be mostly female, and the response by mostly male administrators and trustees and by press accounts suggests that patronizing gender and class prejudice always remained an important, albeit lightly veiled, element in social welfare politics. Preferential occupational mobility for male social workers also structured female professional ambitions. Even as therapy was commodified as a middle-class "need," professional ideology and its feminine variant helped shift the social worker's focus from workplace conditions to personal and professional development. Even the language of conflict became psychologized along gendered lines, especially in the private sector, where both managers and social workers debunked demands in a feminized code as "hysterical" and emphasized their special "professional" status in the therapeutic avant-garde.

The headline of Martin Tolchin's March 9, 1964, article on negotiations to settle the Hawthorne strike, "Psyches Conflict in Strike Parley," illustrates the psychologizing of identity. Tolchin continued the therapeutic metaphor in the article's subtitle: "Mediator Is Termed 'Group Therapist' in Walkout at Six Welfare Agencies but 'Neurosis" Remains; Union Asserts Management Is 'Ambivalent' in Giving 'Emotional Response.' "[92]

Three aspects of Tolchin's article capture the crux of social workers' class identity during the decade. First, negotiations were complicated by what Tolchin highlighted in a subhead as the social workers' "identity crisis." Tolchin, it will be recalled, had a close friend who was a social worker in the strike and was himself a shop steward at the *Times*. An unnamed "agency man" had described social workers to Tolchin: " 'They're involved in an identity crisis. . . . They're caught up in a conflict between their identification as union members and their professional responsibilities to their clients.' " Tolchin's second observation, however, illuminates a critical difference between these social workers' identity of interests with agency supervisors and directors and the perspective of those of a generation earlier: "Unlike most labor disputes, the strike involves labor and management personnel who are ordinarily professional colleagues." The similarity of backgrounds and use of social work jargon by both labor and management in social work were not new, but their importance to a common middle-class identity of interest between caseworkers and managers had increased and undermined the ability of caseworkers to broaden the social base of their labor movement. Both sides attended the same schools, "received the same professional training, belong to the same professional organizations and share the same generally liberal political outlook." Indeed, most agency supervisors and directors had been union members themselves earlier in their social work careers. They even spoke the same language, what one labor negotiator bemoaned as "endless 'psychoanalyzing.' "[93]

A third element in Tolchin's account illustrates the ways in which the psychologizing of politics was gendered and reflected long-standing tendencies to debunk one's opponents by complaining that they exhibited attributes traditionally seen as feminine. Mary Gottsfeld, president of the union, objected that the JBG did not "react to our proposals, they give us their emotional responses."

As both a radical and a woman, Gottsfeld's dismissal of management as "emotional," rather than "rational," was ironic. But as New Left protest grew in the 1960s, the analysis of it in personal psychological terms had become a centerpiece of conservative social criticism that, in a familiar cultural trope, infantilized radicals or demeaned them as feminine and therefore weak. For instance, the University of Chicago's prominent child psychologist, Bruno Bettelheim, testified before Congress that radical protesters had been spoiled because their parents had followed the advice of Dr. Spock's permissive childrearing books. Spock, of course, was also a leader of the ban-the-bomb and antiwar movements of the 1950s and 1960s. In another widely iterated argument, social philosopher Lewis Feuer explained radical protest as a generational revolt of sons against fathers. Liberals, too, embraced the psychologizing reductionism of their opponents' positions by attributing to them traits conventionally viewed as "unprofessional" and feminine. AFSCME leaders, for example, privately viewed SSEU militants as "hysterical" and "irresponsible." Indeed, Gottsfeld's complaint about the JBG's "emotionalism" demonstrates that by the mid-1960s even some social work trade unionists had come to share with liberal and conservative social critics as well as their bosses a psychologizing lingo that described conflicts in personal rather than social terms.[94]

The labor struggles that rocked social service in New York City between 1964 and 1968 mixed locally and nationally in explosive urban politics and also gave new vitality to the racial script of middle-class identity. As disproportionate numbers of African American soldiers fought and died in Vietnam, black leaders questioned the nation's commitment to the war on poverty at home. Rallying under the banner of black power, a separatist and militant protest movement emerged, no longer content to wait for "whitey" to act on blacks' behalf. Not unlike a generation of labor organizers, civil rights protesters, and white student radicals, African Americans took to the streets in 1957 to voice their complaints. Harlem was one of many centers of black urban life to erupt in riots in 1964 and 1967; in fact, in 1967 racial violence broke out throughout the New York City metropolitan area.[95]

Two aspects of the black power movement galvanized the new politics of protest and identity in New York City: black separatism and black militancy. Constantly surrounded by armed, somber bodyguards, charismatic leaders such as Malcolm X in the Black Muslims and Eldridge Cleaver in the Black Panthers personified the "in your face" militancy of the movements. These groups refused to "turn the other cheek." In contrast to the nonviolence preached by Martin Luther King Jr., they advocated resistance to the enemies they saw around them and embellished their appeals with rhetorical flourishes. Among their "enemies" they counted the police, who they felt enforced an unjust and inequitable social order, and shopkeepers who profited at the expense of the black community.

Many of these shopkeepers were immigrant Jewish peddlers-cum-merchants who had established their businesses a generation or two earlier in what had been Jewish neighborhoods at the time. Disregarding the fact that many of them had been socialists, Jews averred that they had carved out a comfortable niche for themselves and their children in American society by dint of hard work—individual effort—not group power.[96]

Although Jews were rarely the majority of merchants in America's black communities, the persistent undercurrent of anti-Semitism in American culture and the interface between Jews and blacks in schools and welfare, two major institutions of life in the ghetto, made their stories inseparable. African Americans not only shopped in stores owned by Jews but often depended on them as social workers to certify their eligibility for welfare. Just as the nineteenth-century poor had characterized the Society for the Prevention of Cruelty to Children as "the cruelty," welfare recipients remained deeply suspicious of investigators, whom they saw as disapproving, prying snobs who required deference.[97] Blacks also confronted Jews in public schools, a conflict that came to a head in 1968 in Ocean Hill–Brownsville. As noted above, although a group of left-wing Jewish teachers supported the black community in this strike, the teachers' union did not. Led by their outspoken Jewish union president, Albert Shanker, the 1968 teachers' union strike further polarized relations between Jews and blacks.[98]

New York City's social workers were implicated in this conflict. When people complained of welfare costs, they meant AFDC, and by 1967 this single program dispensed almost twice as much money as the other relief programs for the aged, disabled, and blind. The majority of AFDC recipients nationally, 51.3 percent, continued to be white; the percentage of black AFDC families had only grown by 3 points since 1961, despite six years of intense civil rights activity. Two shifts, however, promoted the perception of welfare as black: the "explosion" in the numbers of new welfare cases occurred entirely in metropolitan areas, and as noted earlier, blacks increasingly dominated the rolls in the highly visible major metropolises of New York City, Chicago, and Los Angeles.[99]

At the same time that the mass media and politicians racialized welfare as black, policymakers problematized it in what historian Rickie Solinger has perceptively identified as racialized scripts on sexuality and the family. But it was a story with class differences, too. Conservative critics condemned sex outside marriage as "promiscuous," but a racialized class script focused blame on poor black women. The press lauded white, middle-class women who supposedly cast off the shackles of Victorianism in the sexual revolution; in contrast, it portrayed black and Hispanic single mothers as a population bomb triggered by pathological behavior.[100]

The findings of Harvard political scientist Daniel Patrick Moynihan in *The*

Negro Family: The Case for National Action (1965) became the text for such views. Ignoring the history of black family life under slavery and its reconstitution during Reconstruction, Moynihan attributed the high incidence of black single motherhood to a cultural pathology rooted in the legacy of slavery. Moynihan's book exonerated occupational discrimination and institutionalized white racism, and it focused social policy on "moral" values of work and direct aid. After his 1968 election, President Nixon appointed Moynihan to his cabinet to develop a new family policy for welfare. In fact, by that time the federal Department of Health, Education, and Welfare already contained the cornerstones of the racialized policy that would shape welfare to the present: welfare families could not be trusted with money but instead would receive food stamps and surplus commodities and would be directed into work relief programs.[101] Most important, their narrative of success implicated Jews in the new welfare policy as a counternarrative to black "failure." According to Jewish social historians such as Nathan Glazer, the high educational achievement and economic success of Jews correlated with their low divorce rates and presented a counternarrative to the black social profile. Recall, for example, Earl Morse's 1959 analysis of Jewish success on behalf of the FJF's Jewish Education Committee. Increasingly conservative social critics and some neoconservative Jews threw this Jewish success narrative in the face of blacks, placing the blame for their "failure" on their culture.[102]

As Jews, FJP social workers played an easily identifiable part in this story. FJP agencies felt the heightened racialization of the city because many agencies provided services in what had become African American and Hispanic communities. But Jewish social workers and agencies did not speak with one voice about these changes. For instance, FJP workers inhabited the same general social and political world as that of welfare workers, and many Jewish radicals and left-wing liberals continued to identify with and support the NWRO and struggles against racism. Others, however, did not.[103] Jews in the New Left also divided, especially on issues that involved Israel. Many young Jewish New Leftists identified with the Black Panthers and other black militants, which led to a debate among the Jewish left on whether to support or oppose Zionism. For some, Israel was an imperialist state that should not be supported by any progressive Marxist movement. Others argued that black nationalist support for Third World liberation movements should extend to ethnic nationalisms represented by Israel. Although such concerns were not discussed in social work literature, there is no reason to presume that the disagreement did not extend to radical Jewish social workers or that it did not sour black-Jewish solidarity.[104]

The debate over a new welfare policy mandating nonsectarian aid illustrates the deep division among agencies. To make sure that all institutions using public funds and serving the public were integrated, and "not just for 'residual cases,'" in March 1967, Commissioner Ginsberg, himself Jewish, implemented a new policy whereby welfare would henceforth not refer Jewish children only to sectarian Jewish agencies. Three FJP casework agencies that dealt with children—Louise Wise Services, the JBG, and the JCCA—divided on the policy. At one pole was the JCCA. It took the lead in openly disagreeing with the commissioner, issuing a public position paper (which it also sent to the FJP) on behalf of a committee of sixteen voluntary Catholic, Jewish, and Protestant agencies. The committee proposed that its agencies would fill any vacancies with nonsectarian children, in exchange for which it asked that public reimbursement rates be raised. Committed to the principle of sectarianism, the JCCA had just allotted twenty-two beds at its Pleasantville facility for non-Jewish children and opposed accepting any more.[105]

Justine Wise Polier and Florence Kreech, the president and executive director of Louise Wise Services, respectively, were furious that the JCCA had publicly voiced its opposition to Ginsberg and implicated the FJP. They countered with a withering critique of agencies such as the JCCA, challenging the moral legitimacy of the subsidy that made it possible for them to operate. Quotas at private voluntary agencies, they pointed out, had long been the basis of discrimination. Tax monies should not subsidize agencies that have "monopolistic control" of services simply because they provide aid but should insist that they provide needed services without regard to a prospective client's religious or racial background.[106]

JBG executives described their situation as "in the middle." Their facilities at Hawthorne were somewhat integrated, but they believed that to be more properly integrated they would have to accept another twenty to twenty-five black and Hispanic children. Whether Jewish children would be displaced and whether the agency's program would suffer remained open questions for the JBG, although the notion that the rehabilitation of delinquent children could suffer by admitting black children suggests the racial undercurrents in the discussion.[107]

By 1969, the FJP itself had to develop a general policy or risk losing its growing federal aid. The key, according to FJP president Samuel J. Silberman, was the "tipping point," the point at which the balance of clients in a Jewish agency shifts to non-Jews and the agency decides to halt services. What was the proper thing for a Jewish agency to do?[108]

As commentators on government policy, agencies gave widespread support for a just urban policy. That was easy. Establishing agency policy was trickier. In a lengthy discussion of urban problems following the assassinations of King and Robert Kennedy, for instance, the FJP's Executive Committee endorsed the recommendations of the Kerner Commission concerning urban violence and the Chicago police riot of 1968. FJP trustees regularly advocated support of public antipoverty programs. Speaking on behalf of the Committee on Religious Affairs, however, Gustave Levy told the trustees he opposed any support of an agency whose clientele was not prominently Jewish. The committee's report insisted that every needy Jew be served before any aid went to non-Jews. Such views, however, profoundly divided the trustees. New York Family Court judge Justine Wise Polier of the Louise Wise Services passionately opposed Levy's position, as did the chairman of the Committee on Communal Planning, Benjamin J. Buttenwieser. Buttenwieser commented that Levy's position would return the FJP agencies "to the ghetto from which their ancestors fought to escape."[109]

In May 1969, the FJP adopted a policy designed to bridge the deep divisions within the Jewish community. "Ethnic groups" would be encouraged to "develop their own institutions and services," and agency boards would be urged to add "representatives of the larger community [non-Jews]." The document made no mention of the issue of whether an agency was obligated to remain in a non-Jewish community. Leaving the matter unstated, the FJP implicitly acknowledged the extent to which ethnoreligious identity had returned to social work. Jewish social work was by Jews and for Jews, and the principle of agency autonomy left any agency free to leave a community in which the number of non-Jews had reached the "tipping point."[110]

With a certain irony, the growing Orthodox presence in the FJP and the quickened desire by some in the organization to reassert a Jewish identity in Jewish social service brought the struggle for status and social worker identity full circle. Between 1900 and 1930, social workers had struggled to liberate their emerging profession from the stigma of association with religious workers. The racialization of the city and welfare services, however, turned the sources of status on their head. Religious identification, especially with white, middle-class groups who had "succeeded," made some social workers begin to seek a separate space, a private place apart from the hostile, degrading world of welfare work. Some like Sam Liebner took the Hawthorne strike as an opportunity to leave casework for a new full-time career in education. Although he continued to supervise clinical practice at a neighborhood residence center run by the JBG on a part-time basis, Liebner became a professor of social work after the 1962 Hawthorne strike. By the end of the 1964 strike, the agency had lost a sizable core of its professional staff.[111]

The flight to a separate professional space, however, had definite gendered and racial patterns. Although social work radicalism of the 1960s, like the proletarianism of the 1930s, remained generally inattentive to issues of gender, the SSEU, the union that had helped organize the NWRO, had given voice to the caseworkers and other women who had felt excluded by the male supervisory staff that led Local 371 Thus, it is important to recognize that gendered prejudices continued to shape attitudes and policies at all times, whether toward clients as "welfare queens" or caseworkers as "emotional" bleeding hearts. Jewish and black women disproportionately supplied the frontline troops in these social service wars, but men, including important non-Jewish politicians, weighed in heavily on both sides. The subtle and uneasy coexistence of paternalism and feminism could be seen in the FJP contract covering 1969–71. The terms continued to ignore wage discrepancies between men and women but provided transportation for women who worked late, a policy that suggested the ways in which narratives of danger in the city and traditions of paternalism could transform what may have been a nascent feminist impulse.[112]

The emergence of the women's movement in the late 1960s intensified some white female social workers' sense of workplace inequities and undoubtedly hastened their movement out of casework in the following decades, a subject I pick up in the epilogue. Race and gender sensibilities structured social workers' alternatives. The general pattern for men was to either become executives or leave the field, whereas white women moved into supervisory positions or became therapists. Black and Hispanic women found an entirely new occupational category in social service open to them, albeit one with diminished status—the welfare aide. A smaller but significant core of African American social workers, male and female, found opportunity and social status within the increasingly racialized walls of the welfare bureaucracy, where they supervised both aides and clients from their communities. But by the end of the decade, two major developments in the reorganization of social work—the rise of the therapist and the creation of the welfare aide—would transform both the meaning of the occupation and middle-class identity for the rest of the century as they were understood by those in the field and those viewing it from outside. These two occupational categories, which illustrate that race and gender also provided several different understandings of what it meant to be middle class, shape the epilogue to this story.

Work and the Politics of the Middle Class

(A song sung by the vaudeville team of Democrat
and Republican)

Verse (Republican):
The liberal press will always try to say
Our policies make all the fat cats fatter.
Coincidence, no more, is what that is.
It's middle-class concerns that really matter.

Chorus (together):
Of classes, the middle's the best we've seen:
They're decent, hard-working. They're sparkling clean.
We're raising the middle from its morass.
There's nobody here but us middle class.

Verse (Democrat):
Conservatives will always try to say
All poor minorities have got our marker.
But middle class is what we really are—
The lighter middle class. Or tan. No darker.

Chorus (together):
Of classes, the middle's the best we've seen:
Not richer nor poorer but in between.
We're all middle now, every lad and lass.
There's nobody here but us middle class.
—Calvin Trillin, "Nobody Here but Us Middle Class,"
  The Nation, January 9/16, 1995

This study ends where it began: with a transformation of work that stimulated social workers to construct an identity as middle class in order to gain job security, status, and respectability. The very different notions of what it meant to be middle class that social workers held at the beginning and the end of the century profoundly affected their ability to respond to these transformations of their work. Defining themselves in the first half of the century as middle class against others above and below them—philanthropists, elite volunteers, and relief recipients—social workers organized professionally and in trade unions to maintain some control over their work. In contrast, the broad consumerist and heightened racialized meaning of "middle class" in the last quarter of the twentieth century obscured transformations in work; for social workers, this development disabled them more than it empowered them. Social workers rushed to join the would-be universal white "middle-class" bandwagon, but the diminution of a class "other" meant that, when confronted with economic anxieties that accompanied "downsizing" and the globalization of work, they could blame only racial others—blacks, Mexicans, Haitians, and so forth—or themselves.

Two major developments in the occupational structure of social service reshaped the distinct identities of different social workers—black, white, and brown, male and female—in post-1970 America. The first involved the use of the M.S.W. degree by many white social workers to redefine themselves as psychotherapists. The second occurred when bureaucrats replaced many case investigators in welfare with black and Hispanic women who had the job title of welfare service aide. This epilogue sketches the post-1970 history of social workers in the FJP and the DSS (later the Human Resources Administration) in order to illustrate how the politics of class and work in the late twentieth-century United States played out in key local situations. During these years, relief recipients and welfare workers continued to complain about excessive caseloads, red tape, and inadequate allowances. Across the political spectrum, many charged that welfare created dependency. The problem, they argued, was inadequate spending on job training and employment, not excessive coddling of the poor. In contrast, political conservatives in New York City and the nation castigated the social worker as a "bleeding-heart liberal" (by 1990, conservatives derided the word "liberal" itself as "the L word") and indicted welfare as a symbol of inflated government profligacy that bred dependence and crime. These politicians attacked the welfare state as not merely expensive but also socially and morally wrong. Indeed, by the 1990s, Democrats and Republicans alike chanted an antiwelfare litany, with differing vehemence, and neoconservatives cloaked fundamentalist gospel in social science garb when they asserted that welfare was the cause of poverty, not its relief; for these critics, welfare dependence created a pathological crime-prone "culture of poverty."

The new conservative agenda, launched by President Richard Nixon in 1968 and championed by Speaker of the House Newt Gingrich in 1995, began to revise Great Society programs, recasting the mission of social service to the poor as cultural and personal, not social. In retrospect, Nixon's Family Assistance Plan seems benign when compared to the Republicans' 1995 Contract with America. In the more recent assault on welfare, politicians brought a new militancy and punitive tone to old efforts to transform welfare into workfare, largely ignoring economists' analyses of economic restructuring and worklessness and racial discrimination in hiring.[1] Various state welfare proposals introduced in the mid-1990s limited material aid to a few years, penalized welfare mothers who had additional children, and required work in sub-minimum-wage jobs. Finally, in 1996 new federal legislation replaced AFDC with Temporary Aid to Needy Families and required states to place all able-bodied recipients in workfare programs within two years. Subsequent amendments have required minimum wages (usually without benefits), while at the same time municipal and state governments have insisted that as "recipients" of workfare these people cannot unionize. Meanwhile social workers were expected to instill a new work ethos in clients by placing them in jobs that many social workers and clients believed to be either unacceptable or unlikely to lead to permanent jobs. In the global economy, in which manufacturers reduced wage costs through the use of robotics or moved to nonunion low-wage areas, the service jobs that remained behind were unattractive. They paid poorly, often little more than welfare stipends, and usually lacked benefits, especially access to health care.

Uncomfortable with the notion of enforcing what they saw as a punitive welfare policy, many white social workers became private therapists. Other factors drove them out of welfare work, however; social work had become increasingly stigmatized for whites as an area of "nonwhite" employment. The taint of racism permeating the restructuring of social work may have helped push white women out of public assistance work, while their own sad experience with the discriminatory glass ceiling on social mobility in social service attracted them to therapy. Therapy not only provided higher status and income for those who could attract clients' fees (or copayments from insurance companies) but offered women independence from male psychiatrists and agency administrators as well as the opportunity to organize their family and work lives out of their own homes. The choice of therapy was not so new for white men; like administrative work in social service, it continued to be an alternative to a marginal career in a field already stigmatized as feminine.

The Welfare Service Aide

The dramatic rise in welfare rolls after 1965 forced public social service departments to reconsider how their already overextended staff could provide adequate service and what that might mean for both social workers and clients. Some people in public assistance had begun to worry that combining the functions of providing financial aid and offering counseling in one worker could lead to intrusive social control of clients. They urged that the two roles be separated. By late in the decade, new computer technologies made it possible to envision replacing welfare caseworkers with clerical workers who would perform a more limited function. Clerical workers would also be cheaper than caseworkers. In New York City, Mayor John Lindsay effected this functional division in social service by separating public relief from counseling, streamlining operations in his renamed Department of Social Services. By doing so, he also lowered the welfare budget. In his history of the SSEU, Mark H. Maier nicely summarized the transition: "Beginning in 1968, welfare aid was increasingly administered by clerical workers using computers rather than by social welfare workers, who previously managed a specified case load out of manila folders."[2] Nearly a decade later, apparently agreeing that the M.S.W. was not essential for welfare work, the federal government helped construct this group as a new and less well paid alternative "profession"—the human service worker. Some liberals also saw the creation of the human service worker as a way to break what they considered the NASW's stranglehold on "professional" jobs. They envisioned this as a new job opportunity for black and Hispanic workers, who, like many of their predecessors, often had little formal social work training and only a bachelor's degree. By 1981, the federal Department of Health, Education, and Welfare had changed its name to Health and Human Services.[3]

The responses of social workers to these changes were ambivalent, but probably no other occupation in the United States made a greater effort to confront racism in its ranks and in society. In New York City during 1969, to give their profession a more radical and less white public face on issues of race and war, the newly formed Association of Black Social Workers (ABSW) joined white radical social workers in seizing control of the annual meeting of the NASW. Around the same time, the National Federation of Settlements held a "technicolor caucus" of black, brown, red, and tan workers who insisted on representation and placement in executive positions. Indeed, professional associations tried to handle the racial crisis in different ways and did so with varying degrees of success. The point is not that they addressed the issue with unanimity or without resistance but that social workers within each group mounted serious movements for racial empowerment.[4]

The NASW's response reflected the ambivalence of many well-established social workers: the professional association pressed to oppose dilution of social work "standards" and to protect jobs, while it simultaneously strove to prevent agencies from using a divided labor force to undermine social workers' gains to date. Some in the NASW recognized that these job categories provided opportunities for minorities, and efforts to give them some professional standing seem to have represented a version of affirmative action. Agencies also had an interest in ensuring that these workers saw themselves as professionals: not only might the status help compensate for the appallingly low wage, but notions of professional objectivity would distance them from the clients they so resembled. This distance, they hoped would discourage absenteeism and strikes as professionally "irresponsible." So although the NASW and the Council on Social Work Education (CSWE) successfully pressed twenty-two states to license or regulate social workers' titles by 1978, under pressure from black social workers, the NASW admitted graduates with bachelor's degrees in social work in 1970. By 1983, the NASW had accorded graduates of new community college human services programs the preprofessional status of social service technician.[5]

The job title of service worker contradicted the effort to construct human service workers as professional social workers, however, and the Census Bureau was not prepared to accommodate either this ambiguity or affirmative action in its categories. In 1970 the U.S. Census revised its categorization of social work for the first time since 1930, and its new categorization framed the post-1970 history of social worker middle-class identity, much as it reflected social workers' crisis over being lumped with religious workers and fortune-tellers in the opening decades of the century. The occupational classification system for the 1970 census divided the 1960 census category of social and welfare workers into separate professional and service codes. The former included welfare caseworkers, interviewers, and investigators as well as the generic social worker; the service code consisted of welfare service aides. Those in the two codes still shared the same general workplace, but they spoke largely separate languages and came to invest their language and experiences with very different meanings. Between 1910 and 1930, social workers were vociferous about their right to professional status in the census. In contrast, they were silent about the service category in the 1970 census, suggesting either its irrelevance to their sense of professional status or their tacit acceptance of the Census Bureau's decision to deprofessionalize the welfare service aide. Difference from other social service workers had become an important source of caseworker status and identity.

The changing portrait of the typical welfare service aide reflected the segmentation of social service work and multiple middle-class identities by race, class, and gender. At first, there were few aides—there appear to have been almost fifteen to thirty times more social workers—but their distinct profile placed them in a social service ghetto. For instance, although women continued to make up about two-thirds of social workers through the 1990 census, from the beginning, a substantial majority of the welfare aides were women. More than three-quarters of the 14,569 welfare aides enumerated nationally in 1970 were women; by 1980, nearly all aides were women! At that time, women constituted

93.5 percent of the welfare service aides employed in the New York City metropolitan area (see appendix, table A.6).[6] Equally important, although 60.6 percent of the aides nationally were white, for the first time, whites were a minority in the social service census category for the New York City region. In the New York City–New Jersey metropolitan area, four of five aides were either black or Hispanic. At a time when policy analysts blamed poverty on the pathological behavior of the female-headed black family, the particularly low number of black male aides reemphasizes the pervasive discrimination against black men in the labor market, even for work that was in effect segregated.[7]

African American social worker Inabel Burns Lindsay attributed the meager presence of black men in social work to the low wages.[8] On average, however, black male aides made 50 percent more than their female counterparts, although neither earned more than a subsistence income (see appendix, table A.7). Hispanic social service workers fared even worse: annual earnings of a Hispanic female social worker were below those of a black male aide. Moreover, men needed more education to compete for jobs: nearly twice as many male aides had completed high school as female aides (73.3 and 38.8 percent, respectively).[9] Unfortunately, their higher pay also made men less attractive employees. Still, black men had good reasons to take such jobs: they had few job alternatives in the city, and although work as a welfare aide paid substantially less than casework, it beat unemployment. It was also public employment, and as such it offered reasonable job stability with medical benefits—no small matter.

Data comparing the family income of social service workers to that of other professionals in 1970 reveals how race and gender prejudice could undercut the aspirations of any woman who had to feed a family on an income from social work. Earnings below the poverty line for black and Hispanic female aides made income less an issue of aspirations than an issue of survival. Cuts in welfare devastated the poor, but as Frances Fox Piven and Richard A. Cloward have pointed out, they also hurt women of color who depended on social service jobs.[10] Although the metaphor may not do justice to the genuine sympathy that motivated many social service workers, welfare had become a free market plantation. Increasingly, black and Hispanic women clerical workers who were barely getting by themselves paternalistically oversaw subsistence relief to contain and motivate a female underclass from the "hood."

The Therapist

To the general public, the Census Bureau's distinction between welfare aides as service workers and social workers as professionals was moot. In highly publicized cases of child abuse by parents who were welfare recipients, media criticisms of the Child Welfare Administration usually did not distinguish between a protection service worker with a bachelor's degree and a caseworker with an M.S.W. To professionals coming out of graduate schools of social work, the difference was great. But politicians and representations in popular culture continued to lump service workers together with social workers, generally scorning all caseworkers, relief investigators, and aides who dispensed material support as either hard-hearted bureaucrats or "bleeding hearts."[11] The NASW's broad umbrella further obscured the distinctions. The organization sheltered aides, human service workers, therapists, counselors, investigators, and caseworkers as one, although it then divided them into an elaborate internal hierarchy containing six tiers of "competence."[12]

Although the NASW's inclusive policy may have helped human service workers feel a part of the profession, it did not mask the multiple ways in which caseworkers felt increasingly alienated from social work. Complaints of routinization and low pay had been long-standing; the increasing focus on eligibility in the 1950s and calls for efficiency and accountability had already compromised workers' autonomy. As caseloads escalated in the 1960s, counseling and therapy had to take a backseat to relief administration. At the same time, rising levels of drug use, juvenile delinquency, and violent crime in the city increased the number of challenging and demanding cases workers confronted on a daily basis.[13] Inevitably administrators and social workers were overwhelmed. The titles of three books published in 1980 highlight a persistent theme in social work literature—burnout: *Professional Burnout in the Human Service Organization*; *Staff Burnout: Job Stress in Human Services*; and *Burn-out: Stages of Disillusionment in the Helping Professions*.[14]

Dissatisfied, those who had M.S.W. degrees began to consider other possibilities. The conjunction of the black power and women's liberation movements in the late 1960s with the increased demands of casework probably propelled white female social workers, in particular, toward alternative careers as therapists or psychotherapists. The civil rights movement and the war on poverty had empowered black men and women to take up work not only as welfare service aides but also as social workers. Between 1960 and 1970, the ratio of black social workers more than doubled in New York City, rising to over one in four (26 percent). Nearly 5 percent of social workers were now Hispanic, but that percentage would triple in the next decade.[15] By 1980, more than two in five social workers in the New York City metropolitan area were "nonwhites," and by 1990, whites were barely a majority (see appendix, table A.8). Although it seems likely that a disproportionate number of "nonwhites" worked in the lower professional ranks with only a bachelor's degree and as aides, the black power movement and similar esprit among Hispanic workers helped give these men and women pride in their achievement. Given the dreary history of racial bias in employment, they had every reason to be proud. But the racialization of welfare and the city as black and the "de-classification" of some jobs lowered the status of the work, especially in the view of those with higher qualifications and other opportunities. Black pride and a history of welfare rights struggles also gave clients a greater sense of welfare as an entitlement, not a stigma. Some grew more assertive in their demands, pressing noncompliant social workers to provide benefits. The workplace had become more fractious and, especially for white workers, riven by racial antagonism. In this context, the move to therapy involved an element of white flight from social work.

Gender was an important component of the post-1970 development of the social worker as therapist, and its significance in that development also had considerably earlier roots. In an agency such as the JBG, with a strong tradition in psychiatric social work, white male social workers had often worked second jobs part-time as therapists since the 1940s. In 1951 Herschel Alt blamed the high turnover at both the Hawthorne–Cedar Knolls School and the Madeleine Borg Clinic of the Jewish Child Guidance Institute on the fact that married men were leaving for better-paying jobs as psychotherapists in private practice or in groups. Four years later, Alt proposed that the JBG consider allowing workers to see clients in private practice as a way of keeping married men in the agency, although he feared that private commitments would divert their energy from agency work. And by 1961, Alt's fears had been realized. Older caseworkers and psychologists no longer depended "primarily" on the JBG for their livelihood. Following the lead of staff psychiatrists over the past twenty years, a minority now earned at least as much or more in private practice on Saturdays and evenings as they did at the agency. The "problem," the Executive Committee reported, is the "divided attention of staff."[16]

By 1964, the countervailing tendencies of social protest and professional development had helped institutionalize the therapist in social work. Being temporarily without a source of income during the JBG strike, for instance, stimulated some female social workers to contemplate a new career as therapists. Thus, Hawthorne management noted with concern that some striking caseworkers were working in nonprofessional jobs such as babysitting and stenography—notably, jobs that suggested they were women—and were now talking about starting private practices.[17] That same year, the NASW granted formal recognition to therapy as a bona fide area of social work and adopted minimal standards for its practice.[18]

By the end of the year, FJP family agencies complained that private therapy had created a "serious shortage of trained workers." Seeking to counter the attractiveness of therapeutic work conditions—particularly higher wages and status and greater autonomy—a family casework agency executive, Robert Janover, proposed three changes. Besides suggesting a "possible" salary adjustment, Janover recommended "a revision of titles" so that senior workers would have the same status as supervisors and administrators. Finally, he recommended "payments on a case basis," a system that would replicate private practice but as worker-controlled piecework.[19]

Janover's suggestions revealed that at least one manager believed that the language and organization of work could meet social worker ambitions for middle-class status, but the modest changes that the BG implemented did little to stem the flood of social workers into private practice. As in the effort to professionalize human service workers, title changes were easier and cheaper to implement than meaningful changes in caseload or salary. In that regard, social service work was not unlike other industries. Caseworkers moved fluidly through three ranks into senior casework, much as bank workers, for instance, passed through assistant and associate manager ranks into vice presidencies. Wage increases came with the new social work titles, although on the whole, like the incomes of most industrial and middle-income white-collar workers, social workers' real incomes stagnated and they were hard-pressed to keep up with inflation.[20]

White women with the M.S.W. saw psychotherapy as an increasingly attractive alternative to casework, and not surprisingly, by the last two decades of the century, the racial and ethnic profile of the typical therapist contrasted with that of the welfare service aide and the social worker. (Compare appendix, tables A.6 and A.7, with table A.9.) By the mid-1980s, directors of community programs complained that it was difficult to find trained workers to do group work; all social workers continued to study group modalities, but many graduate schools of social work no longer trained workers in such a specialization. The New York University School of Social Work, for example, made clinical practice its exclusive focus. Its professors insisted that they had not forsaken their social mission; such work, they noted, still often took place in institutional settings such as community mental health programs. And some of it did. Although the 25,000 social work clinicians nearly equaled the number of psychiatrists in 1975, a large number undoubtedly worked in institutional settings. As the *New York Times* reported, "[S]ocial workers provide the bulk of therapy in institutions." In repeated interviews, however, 1980s graduates dismissed community work as neither interesting nor remunerative: like many of their professors, most students fully intended to take up private practice.[21]

By the 1980s, legal and economic incentives also encouraged women with the M.S.W. to move into therapy. Increased public acceptance of therapy and its commodification as a "middle-class" consumer good created a demand for social worker–therapists (especially since their fees appeared to be a bargain compared to those of psychiatrists); a fee structure that promised to double the salary of a social worker provided a personal attraction. After legitimizing private work in 1964, the NASW set out to persuade state legislatures to pass laws requiring insurance companies to reimburse social workers for psychotherapy. By 1985, fourteen states had passed such laws, including New York in 1984. The estimated 60,000 clinical social workers nationwide now outnumbered psychiatrists two to one. Many more supplemented agency work with part-time private practice but defined themselves by their full-time jobs. Still, with the availability of third-party insurance payments, the social work clinicians' preferred self-identification became that of therapist or psychotherapist.[22]

Social workers have disagreed even more than historians on the extent to which this race into therapy has jeopardized the historic mission of social work to advance the interests of "the needy." For historians and many social workers on the left, individualized, privatized treatment of fee-paying clients/consumers represents the ultimate commodification of therapy and the development of the "therapeutic self." Most recently, two professors of social work, Harry Specht and Mark E. Courtney, have analyzed the implications of this development in *Unfaithful Angels: How Social Work Has Abandoned Its Mission.* Therapy, they argue, advances a medical model of individual pathology and has turned its back on the poor.[23]

Not surprisingly, social workers who did therapy were ambivalent about this analysis. For instance, undoubtedly speaking for many in the professional establishment, Werner W. Boehm, the chair of the NASW committee that developed the profession's standards for private practice, criticized Specht and Courtney for underplaying the NASW's recognition that "private practice must move in a socially constructive direction."[24] And if one did not think of "the needy" simply as "the poor," social work therapists did provide a social service. Offering equivalent services at often two-thirds or half the fees charged by psychologists or psychiatrists, social workers made therapy available to a much broader range of people. Fees varied according to seniority and clientele, but in the mid-1990s, managed care typically allowed a New York City therapist with an M.S.W. about $65 per session; comparable rates for a psychologist with a Ph.D. and a psychiatrist were $75–$100 and $175–$200, respectively. At the same time, as the *New York Times* reported in 1985, "[A]ll but the most adamant of psychotherapists will acknowledge that the competence of a given therapist depends more on his training, experience and innate ability than on his academic credentials or licenses."[25]

Not only was this vision of the social worker as "discount therapist" profoundly different from the historic mission on behalf of the poor associated with Progressive Era, New Deal, and Great Society reformers, but it also did not address the old criticism that therapy emphasized individual adjustment rather than social change. Left-wing critics had raised this issue in regard to psychiatric social work since the 1920s. Psychotherapists, especially those with a left-wing perspective, responded by advancing "social" therapy, which in the post-1970 era came to be called "empowerment" or "consciousness raising." In this regard, radical therapists saw a client's investment in social activism as an alternative to stagnation and despair. Nonetheless, the private setting of this treatment—which, of course, was a relatively new development in social work in the second half of the century—and the relative affluence of the clientele kept the focus of treatment on the individual and his or her "needs" in the consumer society.[26]

It is important to note, however, that these people used the M.S.W. degree in order to become therapists, not social workers, and identified themselves as the former. Moreover, some within the therapeutic community agreed with the radical critique of much therapy and, styling themselves as "radical therapists," sought to separate themselves from mainstream therapists. Seeking a progressive alternative to private social work practice, such clinicians championed community mental health work in poor neighborhoods or advanced an "egalitarian" rather than "hierarchical" model of treatment in which client and therapist worked together.[27]

Still, there seems little doubt that as therapists social workers have distanced themselves from the historic roots of their craft. Left-wing social workers' calls for "empowerment" fall mostly on deaf ears, as social work programs increasingly train clinicians to be discount therapists to the "less affluent." This is not a view social workers would necessarily acknowledge, however. One therapist told me she felt she still upheld social work's commitment to the poor: she lowered the fees for some clients and did not charge other indigent clients. Ironically, in this scenario, the mission of social work returned to a different set of roots: the voluntarist pro bono labor of privileged women.[28]

Trade Union Responses

Let us briefly return to the history of the New York City social worker, in which the extensive trade union movement in the post-1958 era offers a good example of the profession's response to the reorganization of social work. Although many people with M.S.W. degrees increasingly refashioned themselves as therapists, welfare and private agencies continued to be staffed by people who defined themselves as social workers. The response of most social workers and their trade unions to the profession's historic concern with the "social problem"—whether cast as poverty or as class—was muted if not displaced after 1970 by an identity politics organized around distinct racial, ethnic, and gender interests.[29]

In New York City's HRA, the SSEU maintained its radical positions even after its merger with Local 371, District Council 37. But as Maier has concluded, the SSEU was "no longer the trend setter it once was." The merger agreement gave the local considerable independence: it was allowed to hire and fire its own organizers and control its own strike funds. As important to the local, at a time when George Meany and the AFL-CIO bureaucracy generally were falling in line behind government policy, the pact specifically permitted the local to maintain independent positions opposing the Vietnam War and the Office of Collective Bargaining. A militant cadre of leaders associated with left-wing sects such as the Maoist Progressive Labor Party and the Trotskyist Socialist Workers Party even persisted in defending clients' rights as part of a "worker alliance."[30] The key development, however, was the increasing isolation and containment of the rank-and-file dissidents under the District Council 37 umbrella.

To be sure, in the conservative context of national AFL-CIO policy, New York City's District Council 37 was one of the most progressive labor voices. The radical labor community had always been particularly strong in New York City, and hospital workers, communication workers, and District Council 65 of the distributive workers continued that tradition through the 1970s. The unions' liberalism on some national social issues should not be confused with the generally more conservative political style of their entrenched leaders. During the fiscal crisis that beset many American cities during the high inflation of the late 1970s, many leaders cemented their authority further. As managers pressed for cutbacks, give-backs, and downsizing, leaders became increasingly corporatist and consumerist, accepting tripartite collective bargaining as a way to minimize job losses and poor wage contracts during hard times. In the bargain, they sustained their personal power bases and, in the case of some neoconservative labor leaders such as Albert Shanker, the Jewish head of the teachers' union, shifted the focus from the failure of political economy to race. From his bully pulpit on the AFL-CIO national council, Shanker focused attention on affirmative action as reverse racial discrimination.

Using the authority vested in their power over New York City's municipal unions in the late 1960s, these labor leaders kept a tight rein on rank-and-file dissent. Four municipal unions struck in the late 1970s and 1980—sanitation and teachers in 1975, hospital workers in 1976, and transit workers in 1980—but only hospital workers did so with the support of their leadership. In fact, although Stanley Hill, an African American who was a onetime SSEU leader and had opposed the merger with Local 371, had become executive director of District Council 37 by 1986, the change in leaders had little impact on social welfare work or social policy.[31]

Although sketchy, the evidence suggests that work in welfare offices, never good, deteriorated further under the Reagan and Bush administrations. New demands on welfare services met increased government pressure to reduce costs. Privatization and the decline of the federal program to build public housing increased homelessness, while under the banner of "downsizing," many workers found themselves in lower-paid, nonunion jobs without medical benefits. Welfare was not immune to the give-back mood either, as New York City welfare workers found vacation benefits cut from four to two weeks.[32]

In this defensive environment, the 1987 recollections of a white Jewish woman social worker who worked in welfare suggest the extent to which racial strife came to characterize the work experience. Although District Council 37 leadership remained above the fray, locked in a defensive struggle to hold the line against cutbacks, according to Ruth Abramson, the work culture was divisive. Formerly, she remembered somewhat romantically, social workers had worked as a team, as "crusaders all fighting the same war." She recalled that 50 percent of the social workers were Jewish when she started in the late 1960s. Others were Italian or of Anglo-Saxon descent, and there was one Ukrainian and one black woman. By 1987, a racial "war" had come to divide the welfare workplace. Supervisors like Abramson were mostly white women; trainees were black and Hispanic women. And the "hostility" was palpable. As Abramson put it, how could a white supervisor tell a black worker how to deal with a black family? According to Abramson, "intolerance, disillusion and selfishness" now wracked the "team." When black staff, for example, took over the lounge to watch soap operas at lunch time older white staff felt that their space had been invaded and usurped. As a result, concluded Abramson, welfare workers today blame the problems of low morale and a bad physical plant on one another rather than on the administration.[33]

The struggle over leisure and work space reflected cultural differences among these women and helps explain the muddle over what it meant to be middle class and the social and political meanings of sameness and difference. The same words and ideas had different meanings to different people. If we return to where we began in the prologue, we will recall that polls at this time found widespread self-identification as middle class by people earning vastly different incomes. But, although social workers could urge policymakers to accord provisional professional status to welfare service aides, the abysmal service wage caused these jobs to be "de-classified" just when they became black and Hispanic enclaves. To many social workers, these were not the jobs, wages, or decorum of the middle-class professional, so they moved into therapy and left the welfare service aides behind.

"Middle class" also had multiple and racialized meanings in the black and Hispanic communities. Thus, black and Hispanic social workers had always constituted a vanguard black and Hispanic middle class since the 1920s, although it was separated from the white middle class by race In the post-1970 era, however, these social workers had to distinguish themselves from clients and then from welfare service aides by class. Subjects of racism, they could easily find themselves agents of classism. Perhaps black social workers' relationships to their clients were less guilt ridden than those of white social workers, but whatever the reason, supervisors like Abramson felt that they were usually less tolerant and more demanding of clients.[34]

The difference was more than one of perception, however, as women service workers and women social workers apparently often found themselves in different material circumstances (see appendix, table A.7). Reflecting the large number of black single mothers, the income of the average service worker household was not appreciably above an aide's earnings, suggesting that service workers usually lived in single-income households. Social workers had greater resources: they were usually married and lived in double-income families or were single women unburdened by families. Women social workers who headed families had nearly twice the household income of aides, whereas the wages of social worker wives usually constituted a second income. These women could easily define themselves by either their husbands' job or their household income.

One such woman is depicted in *A Loving Wife*, a novel by Violet Weingarten in which the main character, Molly Gilbert, is a Jewish social worker employed by an FJP casework agency in 1967.[35] Weingarten's novel contrasts with articles and short stories written by social workers for social workers in journals such as *Survey* and with plays and movies that portrayed representations of social workers to a broad public audience. *A Loving Wife* is part of a woman's fiction emerging in the 1950s and 1960s that incorporated the pleasures of travel, romance, and fantasy with the worlds of work and marriage. In this regard, Weingarten's novel explores an upgraded version of the 1920s professional woman's dilemma about reconciling tensions between work, marriage, consumption, and feminine identity.[36]

A Loving Wife amplifies this continuing dilemma by drawing on the author's local political knowledge. Molly's agency, Oak Hollow, resembles Hawthorne–Cedar Knolls; Weingarten describes it as a residential treatment center for emotionally disturbed children in a suburb of New York City, where, when the story opens, the cottage parents have gone out on strike. Indeed, the author had reason to know the conditions well: her husband headed the public relations firm the FJP employed during the 1964 strike! The author's sympathies with the downtrodden and with social workers in her books were genuine, however. A New York City journalist much of her life, she recounted in her autobiography, *Intimations of Mortality* (1978), her support for left-wing liberal political causes. Still, although *A Loving Wife* probably exaggerates the affluence of social workers, it does suggest the ways in which their life-style differed from that of welfare aides, who typically earned little more than the amount clients received from welfare. Molly, for example, explains that she started work right after getting her degree, stopping "*very* briefly" during childrearing until her housekeeper "knew enough" to care for her son. Molly had "deceived herself" into thinking the money she earned was unimportant, but the truth was that "[t]hey couldn't possibly have lived the way they did without her salary." The Gilberts upper-income life-style articulated the logic of both work and marriage for double-income families. Molly's husband was a research scientist, but "they had become accustomed to private schools and country weekends" at their summer home at "a Long Island resort."[37]

Weingarten depicts her fictional social worker as both a left-wing liberal on social issues and a materialistic grande dame. This reflects the mixture of industrial unionism and economism in the FJP's union. The FJP's social workers did not experience the job fragmentation that divided welfare workers. Although Local 1707, CSAE, no longer addressed client services, it continued to sustain a vestige of class advocacy. The union was an industrial organization representing clerical workers, maintenance workers, child care workers, and social workers. The homogeneity of the work force may help explain its ability to win contract settlements and mount labor protest. In the smaller private agencies, such as at the FJP, a shared ethnic tradition and collective ethos between clerical workers and professional staff was more likely to instill a sense of community. In the decade following the 1965 strike, Local 1707 signed biannual contracts with the FJP that won its members general cost-of-living increases and modest improvements in their pension and health benefits. Each contract also lowered their hourly work week, a bitter issue in the last strike. By 1976, workers' hours had been reduced to 36.25 hours a week, except during July and August, when they worked 35 hours.[38]

In the mid-1970s, the FJP staff went back out on strike on two occasions, but those would be the last strikes to date. After the UJA and the FJP's fund-raising efforts were consolidated, Local 1707 struck in November 1975 to win the staffs a unified contract at the higher UJA workers' standard. A month later, although management insisted on separate UJA and FJP contracts, workers won the same terms. The union held a second month-long strike in May 1977 over narrower wage issues. As usual, management attacked Local 1707 strikers for being "unprofessional, greedy and unrealistic." The settlement, however, showed that although FJP social workers might no longer be striking on behalf of their clients, they did fight alongside other white- and blue-collar staff, even though they accepted the internal wage hierarchy: maintenance, clerical, and child care workers all received annual increases of about $350; social workers won a $550 increase.[39]

As Local 1707 advanced its members' material interests, the new racial coding of social service and the entwined black and Jewish failure and success narratives continued to swirl about them. Old issues of agency autonomy and the suburbanization of services continued to complicate workers' ability to control their workplace. After the 1977 strike, the merger of the JFS and the JBG into the Jewish

Board of Family and Children's Services created a rationalized mega–family casework agency that left workers worried about job cutbacks.[40] But although Jewish social workers often could do little about FJP policy, they could not remain immune from the actions of the FJP and the larger Jewish community. A more complete picture of their unions' and professional association's responses emerges from the way social workers in each institution came to understand their own role and their relationship to the "other." Since these understandings were filtered through the lens of late-twentieth-century identity politics, we must now turn to that subject.

The Politics of Identity

People locate themselves in relation to others through their choice of language and categories, and nowhere is this more apparent than in late-twentieth-century U.S. political discourse about the language of class—most particularly the middle class—and the categories of work, worklessness, and welfare. Before 1930, "middle class" paid social workers emphasized their difference from both unpaid volunteers and poor immigrants. With the rise of the New Deal welfare state, radicalized social workers often dwelt on their conflicts with employers while debating among themselves the compatibility of professionalism and trade unionism. As we have seen, this debate was especially pronounced in New York City, where the trade union movement in social work was concentrated. But a sense of difference between public and private sector social workers also emerged throughout the country at this time, although it remained subordinate to social workers' general commitment to attain and defend their status as professional workers. The Great Depression made social workers keenly aware of the extent to which their own fragile economic situation paralleled that of their clients. The social worker's social identity was fractured between home and work, but class was a central component.

The postwar racialization of the city heightened the awareness of whiteness as a core element in middle-class identity. Then the total number of social workers more than doubled in the 1960s and nearly tripled in New York City as welfare personnel tried to keep up with the burgeoning demand for services. The explosion of the welfare rolls and the growth in the size of the government work force responsible for handling it obscured an equally important story: the racialization and engendering of welfare work.

Work on the feminization of poverty has highlighted the dominance of single black and Hispanic mothers and their children on post-1970s welfare rolls. Historically, women have also made up most of the work force. Less well known, however, is that the administration of relief has increasingly become a black and Hispanic enclave. The 115,799 social workers enumerated nationally in 1960 had grown to 218,281 in 1970 (see appendix, table A.1) and black social workers, and especially black women social workers, had become a substantial bloc within the field. Although the percentage of blacks remained about 3 percent from 1910 until 1940, it almost doubled in each decade since then, so that by 1970, more than 16.8 percent of female social workers were black. A decade later, one in three social workers in the New York City area was black and nearly one in two was either black or Hispanic.

Social Work and Globalization

The rise of a politics of identity took place against the backdrop of a fundamental reorganization of work in the United States after 1970 that paralleled the "declassification" of some welfare work, the rise of the therapist, and the racial and gendered divisions of these developments. This transformation was, however, only the most recent of three major reorganizations of work in the United States, each of which coincided with a reorganization of social work.

Social work's origins at the beginning of the Industrial Revolution in the mid-nineteenth century were in an era that social historians have associated with class formation, most especially with what E. P. Thompson called the "making of the working class." In recent years, historians in England and the United States have elaborated on middle-class formation during this era. As described by Leonore Davidoff and Catherine Hall for England and Mary P. Ryan for the United States, a propertied middle class arose in opposition to elites above and the disruptive ethos of workers below.[41] Charity work, however, emerged out of an elite and bourgeois milieu that shared concerns about the poor. Clergy, financiers, and the emerging merchant elite sat on boards of directors of philanthropic societies, while their wives ministered to the poor as "Ladies Bountiful," variously seeking to "uplift" the "unfortunate" and discipline them in the rhythms of industrial life.

By the turn of the century, the bureaucratic structures and service industries required of monopoly capitalism had produced C. Wright Mills's "new middle class" of white-collar workers. As social scientists sought to make social work scientific, industrial and community leaders recruited social workers to assimilate the strange ways of the immigrant worker to Americanism, some through industrial social work, some through the settlement house, and some through mental hygiene. In each case, social workers located themselves as middle-class paid professionals between others: above them, unpaid board directors, volunteers, and "ladies" they saw as playing at helping and managers and public officials who they felt identified with privilege and, below them, an immigrant working class they saw as in need of help. In either case, through World War II, otherness helped organize social workers' responses to social change.

In contrast, the nonclass content of the meanings of "middle class" since 1970 left workers unprepared to understand a third and equally fundamental shift in work and economic organization in America associated with deindustrialization: the globalization of capitalism and restructuring. With the decline of heavy industry and the manufacturing base in the old industrial cities of the Northeast and Midwest, urban economies increasingly have split into a low-paid service sector and a high-paid, high-tech sector involved in professional work. The "de-classification" of welfare work and the rise of the therapist in social work reflect this larger transformation of work in America.[42]

Although restructuring has occurred before, the impact of recent restructuring on managerial, professional, and technical workers, who traditionally have been seen as the backbone of the middle class, has been fundamentally different. Horizontal and vertical organization of industry in the late nineteenth century, Taylorism, automation, and the sad story of "runaway" textile mills, shoe factories, and garment shops have forced workers to endure speedups, unemployment, and wage reductions for a long time. In the past, however, as technology displaced workers, it often created abundant new jobs. Thus, the reorganization of work early in the century helped create the white-collar sector. In contrast, the late-twentieth-century transformation has sought to "downsize," a euphemism for sustaining productivity with a smaller work force. To workers, it has meant transporting jobs overseas to cheaper labor markets or firing part of the staff while speeding up the remaining workers. As significant, global restructuring is the first of these major transformations to affect the traditional security of managerial and white-collar jobs, a labor sector that had thought that its more privileged, "salaried," professional work was insulated from such traumas.

As white-collar workers who service the welfare state, social service workers have found themselves trapped at the center of a rhetorical crossroads of "middle-class" tax cuts and downsizing. The global reorganization of work put pressure on middle managers, supervisors, and professionals in the public sector to dismantle the welfare state. At the same time, antiurban federal and state policies (enacted by legislators representing suburban populations who dominate most state lower houses and have a de facto veto over urban policies) as well as heavier city tax loads also increased pressure on financially strapped municipalities to reduce the public work force. Thus, the "middle class" tax cut offered by politicians of both parties promised to save money for the same people it proposed to fire.[43]

Seeing "middle class" as a way of speaking about race, gender, or immorality —anything but class as a social category with an economic component—masks these contradictions, although it is unclear whether this discrepancy is ironic, tragic, or simply hypocritical. For instance, the gap between rich and poor in

American cities has widened since the mid-1970s. The New York City situation is among the worst, but the general trends it represents are not atypical. The difference between rich and poor has historically been great in New York City, but by the early 1990s, the fifth of the population in Manhattan with the highest incomes made thirty-two times as much as the bottom fifth. In an extraordinary commentary, the New York Times noted in 1994 that among the nation's counties, the gap between rich and poor in Manhattan was "surpassed only by a group of 70 households near a former leper colony in Hawaii."[44]

Identity Politics as Otherness

The irony of the formation of a ubiquitous middle-class identity in the late twentieth century is that it occurred just when multiculturalism, postmodernism, and identity politics celebrated the instability of identity and its fragmentation and multiplicities. The wide fascination in the humanities and social sciences with identity formation and deformation reflects this moment. Rooting the study of "middle-class" identity in a concrete historical circumstance of place makes it possible to see identity politics as a contest for authority and power, as the ability to "authorize" one's voice.[45] But several conceptual points must also be emphasized: it is important to acknowledge difference and otherness but to realize that some others are always "more" other. That is, blackness makes one a racial other in the United States in ways that, for example, "Italianness" or being a Baptist does not. Otherness also has different meanings at different historical times, so that "Italianness" may have been "more" other in the first half of the century than in the last.

Historically, the seeming disjuncture between an emergent universal middle class and a fragmented identity politics of difference lay in their distinct arenas and in their interdependence. In the first case, by late in the century, "middle class" had come to mean the denial of economic class. It also gave enhanced significance to political meanings of citizenship and respectability, of participation in the dream machine of consumption, which the middle class had long embraced. The politics of difference—originating in the black power and women's liberation movements of the late 1960s but becoming fragmented into ethnic power and gender difference by the 1980s—still had the power to shake dominant groups to the core. No group likes to have its voice ignored or debunked, especially when the "other" voice challenges core moral values, social standing, and political power. But stripped of class meaning, identity and difference translated the politics of identity into consumer strategies, such as ghetto "economic zones," "targets of opportunity," and fragmented advertising markets. In this context, all sides ascribed the language and status of the middle class to their own work and identity and disagreed about their appropriateness to others. The new language of class enabled the meaning of sameness and difference to coexist as pluralism or multiculturalism rather than as conflict.

Ironically, identity politics of the post-1970 era had its roots in an identity that, although it was not new to social workers, had lost much of its resonance: the identity of the radical. In the 1960s, radicals encouraged "liberation movements" among people they felt were discriminated against by privileged elites. By mid-decade, many radicals believed the "war at home" could not be separated from the war in Vietnam. Borrowing the language and categories of struggles in Third World countries, blacks and then women began to describe their own struggles as "liberation movements" of "Third World" peoples in the United States (or, using a metaphor of disenfranchisement, second-class citizens). Before long, interest groups defined by almost every type of social characteristic had emerged to press for equality. Groups promoting the rights of women, children, and retired persons (e.g., the Gray Panthers and the American Association of Retired Persons) demonstrated in support of specific welfare benefits, much as veterans groups and ethnic communities had done for some time. Some groups merged specific subsets of identities they saw as particularly aggrieved (i.e., women of color), but identity politics usually focused on ethno-national, racial, and gender identities.

Post-1970 identity politics fundamentally changed social workers' sense of themselves and what mattered to them. Previously, social worker politics usually split over ideological differences regarding professionalism versus trade unionism, functionalism versus diagnostic treatment, or advocacy versus neutrality. Jewish, female, and black social workers were often painfully aware of other differences, but although each group sometimes organized to advance its particular interest, these groups were not oppositional. Common policy objectives concerning professionalism, client services, and their own recompense united them as a class. Difference mattered, but their eyes were on the common prize.[46]

In contrast, racial and ethnic identity politics accompanied the deep divisions in the organization of work by occupational status (between service aides, caseworkers, and therapists) that characterized social work in the late twentieth century. As Ruth Abramson's description of her workplace suggests, blacks, who came to dominate the service category and made up nearly half of the caseworkers, and older whites who felt displaced increasingly saw each other as expressions of different worlds. To be sure, separate associations of Puerto Rican and black social workers and consciousness-raising groups of women social workers helped mobilize each group to fight distinct patterns of discrimination. The new lines of organization, however, also shifted social workers' axis of vision. The shift might have been small, but its impact was large. As a group, social workers remained among the most liberal in American society, but they became less focused on the broad structural changes in the industry and the ideological opponents of social service than on the occupational, cultural, and racial differences between each other.

Jews and Blacks

The political and social crisis within the FJP and the New York City Jewish community over what constituted appropriate Jewish social service was integral to the reconstitution of middle-class identity. Although EJP social workers were remarkably quiet about this crisis in extant professional accounts, in other roles, many Jews began to speak as if black protest threatened nothing less than the survival of the Jewish people.[47]

National political developments mirrored the growing antagonism between blacks and Jews that, as we have seen, came to a head in a paradigmatic struggle in New York City during the last years of the 1960s. As a symbolic rejection of the Great Society, Richard Nixon's election in 1968 was a watershed in the history of reform in America. The transition also pitted the Jewish success narrative against a black failure story to help justify what conservatives promoted as a less "indulgent" welfare policy. Resurrecting the language and categories of nineteenth-century attacks on the "undeserving poor," neoconservatives unleashed a rhetorical assault on the poor that by the 1990s would evolve into an effort to overturn sixty years of welfare entitlement programs. Nixon's appeals to Middle America and the silent majority recast the "disadvantaged" poor on welfare as "privileged" and idle malcontents coddled by what the new vice president, Spiro Agnew, called "effete" northeastern intellectuals. Although liberal critics would see the conservative welfare measures as punitive and harsh, Agnew's imagery represented them as simply an affirmation of "manly" American virtues from the heartland.

Approximately twenty-five years later, blurring their twin identities as historians and neoconservative proponents, House Speaker Newt Gingrich (with a doctorate in American history) and distinguished British historian Gertrude Himmelfarb buttressed a gathering attack on welfare with a historical sleight of hand, lauding the Victorian orphanage as an alternative to AFDC and foster care. In this conservative discourse, the American "middle" that had been "forgotten" by Great Society bureaucrats was mainstream, masculine, and nonclass. "Others" were placed outside (or "under") the discourse on what it meant to be American. Some "others" were radical and, like most urban welfare clients, feminine and/or black; still "others" were the black, Hispanic, and Jewish women who were thought to coddle them.

Although their awareness was unspoken, many Americans would have recognized Agnew's "effete intellectuals" as a reference to a putative Democratic liberal academic and media establishment they envisioned, ironically, as disproportionately Jewish. Some evidence was construed to support such contentions, but its meanings were generally more complicated than they were represented to be. German Jewish men did run many Hollywood film production houses in the 1930s. Jews were also active in education, especially in cities such as New York, where they were disproportionately represented on the faculties of the City University of New York (CUNY) and in the teachers' union. The production and reception of ideas cannot, however, be deduced so easily from such "facts." Not only did the movie studio system decline in subsequent decades, but the films it produced seem to have purveyed the American dream.[48] Similarly, presence in institutions did not automatically translate into political dominance of them, especially for a unitary position. Many Jewish teachers were secular; many were civil rights activists. Indeed, identity, whether Jewish or not, is not simple to interpret since people draw on many different identities and any single descriptor has multiple meanings. Still, as the discourse on blacks and Jews in the Ocean Hill–Brownsville dispute made clear, Jews were implicated in the welfare story from all sides: although conservative attitudes fueled by anti-Semitism cast liberal Jewish policymakers as the welfare problem, Jews could join with conservatives in celebrating Jewish social success as the solution to it. This contradiction and the fear of being associated with the liberal Jews may help explain why, just as black social workers had reason to want to distinguish themselves from black clients, Jewish neoconservative intellectuals at New York City's *Commentary* magazine raised their voices so high in support of both workfare and Jewish achievement.[49]

A March 1969 report on the "goals and purposes" of the FJP's Committee on Communal Planning must be seen against this backdrop. Recounting the demographic shifts in the Jewish community, it acknowledged that sectarian groups had "new responsibilities" to address "new problems" arising in New York City "from the substantial growth of Negro and Puerto Rican populations." Recommending that the FJP provide services to "non-Jewish clientele," the report focused on two abiding principles. First, reflecting the new conservative mood, it emphasized the centrality of voluntarism—what President George Bush would herald as "a thousand points of light"—to "the American way of life." The state should not intercede, and the FJP "should make a contribution to . . . non-Jewish clientele." Second, the report distinguished between nonsectarian service and sectarian service also open to non-Jews. FJP agencies should remain Jewish, providing services based on the fundamental Judaic commandment—the concept of *Tzedakah*. Although it carries implications for social justice, the concept signifies "righteousness in its broad sense and providing 'acts of loving kindness' with personal involvement rather than merely the giving of alms as acts of charity." Less grandiloquently, the report insisted that a "characteristic Jewish milieu" be respected.[50]

The ecumenical tone of the committee's report was challenged less than a year later by the JDL. The JDL had demanded that the FJP issue a policy statement on the "primacy and priority of Jewish problems," that it commit 25 percent of its budget to Jewish education and $12,500 for a Jewish police force, and that it democratize its decision-making processes and programs. Complaining that the FJP had not responded satisfactorily to any of these demands, Rabbi Meir Kahane's JDL militants picketed the February 1970 trustees' meeting.[51]

JDL protest raised a series of issues that troubled trustees: finances, vigilantism, autonomy, and what constituted Jewishness. The demand for a Jewish police force involved a minuscule sum of money but threatened to put the FJP at the center of a racial, religious war. One trustee suggested that it would amount to no more than a "self-styled constabulary." The amount the FJP would need to meet JDL education demands was quite another matter: it would require a 467 percent increase in the present allocation, from $1.5 to $7 million. This demand, however, raised an equally serious question for trustees about Jewish identity: at a time when, as the committee report had noted, the older Jewish community had become increasingly secular, what was a Jewish education?

This narrow debate over educational funding had broad implications for how the FJP would distribute Jewish aid and who spoke for the Jews. In a city such as New York where Jews had long been a vital liberal constituency in support of social programs, this controversy had immediate consequences for social welfare. Countless articles in the *New York Times* described growing "hostility" between a "resurgent" American Orthodox settlement and the older non-Orthodox Jewish community. The division among the Orthodox over some issues of polity into Hasidim, "strict" traditionalists, and "modern" Orthodoxy involved differences that were lost on most secular and reform Jews. JDL militants simply represented the most vocal and visible Orthodox group.[52]

The FJP rejected the JDL's initial demands, but the militants' continuing protest reflected the broader conservative success in shifting the political discourse to the right. In past decades, Jewish radicals and left-wing social worker trade unions had kept the FJP busy defending its left flank. After 1970, the JDL and conservative Jewry turned the FJP's concern on its head. For instance, after 100 JDL militants led a sit-in of FJP offices on April 8, 1970, the one family voice that usually supported dissenters now became their leading opponent. Of course, this was not left-wing but right-wing dissent, so trustee Lawrence Buttenwieser, Benjamin's son, pressed the FJP to get an injunction against the protesters. Then, when the Committee on Communal Planning proposed creating a committee on college youth funded with $75,000, he complained that this "sop to Jewish militants" would do little to meet the needs of Jewish youth on campuses. The proposal was tabled.[53] Still, the JDL's continuing harassment of FJP fund-raising events and its lawsuit against the organization for supposedly misallocating $1 million in funds donated by its supporters kept the FJP's focus on its right wing.

By 1973–74, two issues came together to narrow and propel the FJP's Jewish narrative into nothing less than a conservative defense of the history and survival of the Jewish people: the Yom Kippur War in October 1973 and *Wilder v. Sugarman* in September 1974, which charged FJP agencies with racial discrimination. To Jews, the former threatened the existence of Israel, and the Jewish victory reaffirmed the triumph of the Israeli David over the Arab (and Moslem) Goliath. Because the Jewish community's outpouring of contributions to the UJA's Israel aid fund threatened the FJP fund drive, FJP and UJA fund-raising efforts were combined in the future.

The *Sugarman* case, which symbolized the increasingly strained relations between Jews and blacks in New York City and nationwide, became, in some ways, a domestic cause célèbre akin to the defense of Israel. In *Sugarman*, the plaintiffs challenged the constitutionality of the provision of New York State aid to sectarian child care agencies. Specifically alleging that the JBG, the JCCA, and Louise Wise Services discriminated against black Protestant children, the plaintiffs asked that public funds be withdrawn from these agencies.[54] To Jews, the case threatened the integrity of their institutions; to blacks, it addressed the prejudicial treatment of their children by both Jews and the state. Like the conflict between Jews and blacks, the case remains unresolved (as of 1998), with FJP agencies continuing to insist that they have never discriminated and the city and black groups holding out for an admission of guilt, even if unintentional.[55]

Radicals and Feminists

Radical social workers did not disappear after 1970, but fewer were willing to embrace publicly a radical identity. As their trade union's social vision gave way to bread-and-butter issues and many social workers recast themselves as therapists, many radicals transformed themselves into liberals, an identity that conservatives increasingly stigmatized as profligacy; in public political debates, mainstream media considered radicals beyond the ken. Still, some self-declared radicals had an active presence in social work. Seeing themselves in the tradition of the Rank-and-File Movement of the 1930s and inspired by *Social Work Today*, a self-defined "group of radical social workers in New York City," many of whom were associated with the Hunter College School of Social Work, began to publish *Catalyst: A Socialist Journal of the Social Services* in 1978. In 1990 Haworth Press agreed to publish the journal, and the editorial collective renamed it the *Journal of Progressive Human Services*. Many of these same people organized the Bertha Capen Reynolds Society. At annual meetings, the society strategized about political action and sought to resurrect the occupation's radical past. The society's base of approximately 1,000 members was on the East Coast, overwhelmingly white, and largely in the academy. Nonetheless, it sought a more beneficent welfare policy and changes in the profession as a whole.[56] The fact that the group was named after the radical political activist and former associate director of the Smith College School of Social Work who was shunned by the AASW during the McCarthy era proclaimed its political engagement. As a pioneer psychiatric social worker and a social activist, Reynolds had impeccable professional and political credentials. To members, her illustrious career also refuted the alleged contradiction between individual therapy and social action. Radical leaders also looked to Reynolds's example to help them construct a feminist tradition in social work. Gisela Konopka, a German-Polish Jewish émigré with a revolutionary socialist background who was a professor of social work at the University of Minnesota from 1947 to 1973, echoed the New York City group's call to action. Lauding new community mental health projects, she insisted that social work needed "something as revolutionary as social group work" and that therapy should be combined with "social action."[57]

A few black and Hispanic social workers joined the Reynolds Society, but many more enrolled in a nationalist alternative that appealed to the larger African American community: the ABSW and its national organization, the National Association of Black Social Workers (NABSW). The ABSW formed on June 1, 1967, in Harlem, and the NABSW organized in San Francisco the following May. By the mid-1990s, the NABSW had enrolled approximately 3,000 members in 104 chapters across the country. Although both organizations arose as part of the radical ferment of the late 1960s, by 1990 they had shed much of their left-wing radicalism in favor of an Afrocentric orientation. Their Afrocentrism combined radical community organizing and political militancy with traditions of African American patriarchy, nationalism, and black essentialism, although at a time when black intellectuals such as Henry Louis Gates Jr. and Stuart Hall were emphasizing the culturally constructed nature of race. In its history from 1968 to 1996, the NABSW had a succession of six male presidents. Similarly, although women appeared to make up the bulk of local membership, virtually every local chapter elected a male president. In contrast, the vice presidency was a dead-end female slot.[58]

Although the organization's executive structure was hierarchical and patriarchal, its organizing and membership principles were inclusive and democratic. Seeing themselves as black social activists and interpreting social work as an intervention into their own communities, members welcomed African American students and community leaders into their organization. One in five members, for instance was an undergraduate or graduate student. Equally important, they acknowledged the problem of black welfare mothers and generally seemed to accept the discourse on black males as an endangered species.[59] Casting their lot with the African American community, black radical social workers expressed a racial solidarity with the black poor that denied the separateness of a black "underclass."

Not everyone was entirely comfortable with the NABSW's nationalist orientation. Ann Tanneyhill, for instance, longtime director of vocational guidance for the Urban League, rejected black separatism as an organizing principle but recognized that the "so-called middle class" could not obscure the common prejudice that distinguished the plight of all black people in America. When she came to New York City in 1930, Tanneyhill moved to Harlem because "there was no place else [for a black person] to live." In 1978 it was still her political and cultural community: "I think many people have risen from a lower group . . . and [have] . . . a better economic position and make more money, and they are in this so-called middle class. Some of them forget where they come from, and others will never forget. . . . I haven't deserted Harlem."[60]

It was also not uncommon for a generational divide to separate black social workers who had come of age before 1960 from their younger counterparts in the NABSW and the Reynolds Society. Typically, the black militancy of the 1960s and rising rates of illegitimacy and premarital sex troubled old-timers. Beulah S. Hester, head of the Robert Gould Shaw Settlement House in Boston from 1933 to 1964, explained in 1978 that others called her "old-fashioned and all that" but that she "can't get used to the change." From her perspective, race had not limited her: "Now, why should I go around all puffed up about white folks? They treated me all right. I can't bear the whole Negro race on my shoulders. I have enough to bear. When I go to them [white people] and ask for something, they always respond." In a related response, Frankie V. Adams, a social work educator at the Atlanta University School of Social Work from 1931 to 1964 who specialized in community organization, also rejected black separatism. She refused to allow a group of black social workers (one presumes from the NABSW) to set up a scholarship for blacks in her name. Explaining that being "Negro and female . . . has not affected her purpose or role in life," she supported mixed gender and racial organization.[61]

Available oral histories suggest that the older generation of black women leaders were especially unsympathetic to feminism. None of the women with careers in social work who were interviewed for the Schlesinger Library's Black Women's Oral History Project, for example, had a positive word to say about the women's movement. For Adams, it was a "dead subject." As essentially a "white middle-class" movement, it seemed irrelevant to Inabel Burns Lindsay. Since Tanneyhill never felt threatened by men, she found it "hard . . . to think of myself as a black female." She said she had "no interest" in feminism. And Hester explained her hostility to the women's movement as consistent with her earlier opposition to suffrage. She had associated suffrage with temperance, which she also opposed. She disagreed with the Equal Rights Amendment, which she saw as distorting women's feminine nature. As she explained, "It seems to me there are a lot of things a woman can do, and it seems there are things they should leave for men. . . . I can't see a woman putting on machine courses, or going on an engine and working on that."[62]

Even among the newer recruits to social work—black and white—the impact of second-wave feminism on women social workers was uneven, limited, and paradoxical. Feminists' greatest successes may have been on behalf of women clients rather than women social workers. Violence against women was not new, but police, politicians, and doctors had usually dismissed it as either female fantasy, male prerogative, or the result of female initiative. Women activists both inside and outside social service raised the awareness of violence against women and helped bring about its reconceptualization as male aggression that required state protection and aid for abused women and children. Heightened public awareness of the problem led to the development of shelters for battered women and children and rape crisis centers on college campuses and in the community as a direct outgrowth of feminist agitation.[63]

Some feminist (and usually white) social workers did see gender as a useful category for analysis in social work. Coincident with the rise of the women's movement in the late 1960s, articles in professional social work journals by both men and women began to evaluate sex discrimination in social work, the impact of feminism on social policy and treatment, and gender relations in casework as a historical and contemporary problem.[64] Since the mid-nineteenth century, as a matter of moral propriety, male and female staff members usually handled "personal" matters of male and female clients, respectively, and tailored diagnosis and treatment to distinctly gendered (and class) scripts.[65] Contemporary studies also came to understand gendered social work careers and practices as rooted in essentialist notions of femininity and masculinity. Just as vocational guidance books early in the century recommended social work as appropriate to women's nurturing "instinct," more recent studies found men to be more careerist, more committed to institutions of social work (rather than its practice in casework), and slightly more likely than women to place their own needs before those of clients.[66]

What feminist research failed to find, however, may have been as important as what it did find: feminism did not change fundamental patterns of gender discrimination in the workplace. As a 1974 review of the social work literature concluded, although social work analysts considered race, class, and ethnicity in their studies, "sex has not been integrated consistently into the profession's thinking."[67] The history of FJP contracts provides a good example. Gender seems to have appeared as a contractual issue in only two limited cases. The first involved paternalistic protective provisions for women employees who worked late. The second concerned the use of gender-neutral contract language: at the union's insistence, all references to "female" were deleted from the 1977 contract, and all references to "male" were changed to read "he/she" or "his/hers."[68]

The disparity between the rhetoric of equality and the workplace reality of inequality was not lost on female social workers. Men consistently received promotions faster and more often than women; overall, male workers in every classification received higher pay than women, although women usually had higher educational qualifications. As we saw in chapter 7, women like Martha K. Selig continued to find themselves deferring to men and giving them credit for their ideas.[69] Similarly, when interviewed, women debunked contractual gains as superficial. Ruth Abramson, for instance, commenting on the neutered contract language, laughed and contrasted it with the rapid rise into managerial ranks of the men with whom she had gone to social work school. A 1979 study conducted during the term of the first female president of the FJP, Billie Tishman, detailed the hostile environment in which women worked: 62 percent of female employees reported that they had experienced sex discrimination at the agency. Of these, 30 percent complained of "personal denigration," and 41 percent felt that discrimination was most apparent in wages and benefits.[70]

Women social workers' heightened consciousness of sex discrimination and entrenched patterns of male privilege and dominance created a feminist paradox. Dissatisfaction with agency work helps explain the movement of many women into psychotherapy, but the change could be simultaneously feminist and antifeminist. Clinical social work in private practice freed female social workers from the domination of male executives and psychiatrists and allowed them to have a flexible work routine compatible with family obligations. Self-employment afforded these clinicians the status of free professionals associated with C. Wright Mills's old middle class. The ultimate irony of social workers' feminist consciousness, however, was that although therapy freed women from the control of male supervisors, it also moved them back into the home, where they could continue to perform the duties of the double day as wife, mother, and professional. The model of the social worker as therapist was a kind of domestic feminine professionalism that was remarkably congruent with the model of the professional woman first articulated in the 1920s.

The fate of Molly Gilbert, Violet Weingarten's social work heroine in *A Loving Wife*, illustrates the continuing tensions in the professional woman identity for women social workers in the late twentieth century. Molly suffers from burnout, both in her work and in her personal life. Her marriage has grown stale, and she is having an affair with a trustee at Oak Hollow, the residential treatment center where she works. Work at the center "had become a miniature welfare state," and Molly despairs that it seems to make no difference: "We can give them all the services in the book, but it's a farce. You can't casework people out of poverty. It's like pasting paper over a rotten wall. The roaches and rats still come through. Sometimes I think we actually make things worse."[71]

Depicted as a liberal with a sincere dedication to the poor, Molly is a committed and humane social worker who derives more satisfaction from her work than from her domestic life. The success in her career, Molly explains, compensates for her feelings of inadequacy as a wife, mother, and homemaker: "At the Center, she knew who she was—a successful human being . . . [with] tangible proof of her worth—evaluations, promotions, consultations, gratitude, tenure and a paycheck. Whereas at home, life was a maze of questions—Was she really a good mother? Would the Bartons and Freedmans be good together, or should she make it cocktails and supper and invite three or four other couples as buffers?"[72]

Through all of her travails and self-doubt, Molly sustains a close personal relationship with Barbara Jean, a delinquent adolescent girl from the Lower East Side whom Molly has placed in one of the cottage houses at Oak Hollow. Molly sympathizes with Barbara Jean, but there is no mistaking the differences between the two. Molly's obsession with consumerism and status contrast with Barbara Jean's more mundane concerns with daily survival. Like many black single mothers on welfare, Barbara Jean and her single mother worry about daily survival with too many kids and too little money. Molly's social life and options are in stark contrast. Breaking off her affair and putting her marriage on hold, Molly can afford to take a few weeks off and fly to Italy to "find herself."

In Italy, Molly determines that her problem lies in her lack of self-confidence and her dependence on men. Reflecting on the ironies of the historical moment —that she is an "emancipated career woman"—Molly tells an Italian friend that she has been dependent on men all her life: "I've never been without a man to run interference for me—first my father, then Mike. I've never had to take care of baggage, or make a reservation, or tip anyone, except a waiter or doorman calling me a taxi. I've never even had to choose a restaurant except to have lunch near the office."[73]

Molly's dependence undoubtedly exaggerated that of most social workers, even though her solution resonated with the tensions in their careers as women. She despaired of the life and prospects of a single woman: "What has a woman alone to do in Manhattan?" One answer was to return to her job, something she did well. Back at work, "[s]he was safe, at last. Her office had been waiting for her all the time, four-cornered, rectangular, silent, hollow." The other answer was to rededicate herself to the obligations of the double day and return to the "safety" of her marriage as a loving wife. Molly's choices did not eliminate the tensions in the identity of the professional woman, but she resolved them in a separate bourgeois feminine space, one that set her off from both male supervisors and psychiatrists and the poverty of the single black mother in the ghetto.[74]

Conclusion

This historical narrative should make historians, journalists, and political pundits wary of using the term "middle class" without being historically specific. Post-1970 developments in social worker identity reveal not only the instability and multiplicity of middle-class identities but also the degree to which new political, ideological, and material conditions shape them.

In the post-1970 era, race and gender fragmented both social service work and social workers' middle-class identity. Welfare service aides were increasingly black and Hispanic women in a nonprofessional census category. In black and Hispanic communities, these modest semiskilled clerical jobs provided regular work and were preferred alternatives to servile work or unemployment. In minority communities, these jobs for women would be "middle income" and "middle class." The census, however, as we saw in chapter 1, constructed categories as much as it reflected them. NASW professionals, like their AASW predecessors, sought to distinguish their work as having professional status. Thus, although the identity of the welfare service aide may have been middle class for women of color, for whom the position was one of the best jobs available, for white social work "professionals" (and the smaller number of black caseworkers) who had fought since the 1910s for census recognition, it was "other." The census reflected this "white" view of professional labor. Social workers' rhetoric sought to confirm the reality as the social work establishment understood it: they were respectable and middle class, not workers "in service" to others but "caring" professionals acting "for" them. To whites (and many black caseworkers and administrators), the black middle class was not made up of welfare service aides; rather, it consisted of black men and women who had long worked as caseworkers and those who more recently had gained supervisory posts helping "administer" poverty within the welfare bureaucracy.

Gender also shaped work identities. Despite the restructuring and reorganizing of social work, media representations continued to imagine the social worker as a welfare worker, a harassed and aloof bureaucrat laboring in stripped-down proletarian conditions. Unable to change these perceptions, social workers increasingly sought other more congenial identities. The new jobs divided along lines essentialized as appropriately masculine and feminine. Male social workers, for example, had long cast themselves as managers, supervisors, and executives-in-training and often left the business if they did not move into such positions. White women now increasingly chose an alternate identity as therapists.

Meanwhile, for white women who continued to do casework, "professional work" remained riddled by the tensions in the model of the professional woman, much as it had since the 1920s. Second-wave feminism had raised women's consciousness of their discrimination and established legal pressures to

mitigate it, but feminism had also intensified male fears and reactions. A verita-
ble media industry, for instance, emerged around the genre of the career woman
as emasculating or a "spider woman." The genre had earlier roots in films such
as *Mildred Pierce* (1946) and *All about Eve* (1950), which could be read as postwar
Hollywood efforts to get Rosie the Riveter out of the factory. After 1980, comple-
menting the feminist backlash of the Reagan-Bush era, a series of films and
popular plays that dominated the public imagination—such as *Disclosure,
Oleanna, The Last Seduction,* and *Fatal Attraction*—portrayed career women as
predators who use violence and sexuality rather than business acumen to get
their way.[75]

The politics of social work also came to reflect the politics of what it meant to
be middle class in America. "Middle class" lost any vestiges of its class meaning.
Instead, serving to deny class, the category described "style"—not just standard
of living but the incorporation of "traditional" values that were antiurban,
antifeminist, and "white" around an idealized Middle American "modern" family.[76] Instead of traditional left-wing radicalism, in post-1968 New York City,
race, gender, and ethnicity replaced class as core elements of identity for Jewish,
black, and Hispanic social workers. Each term had a multitude of contested
meanings, however, as the difference between secular and religious Jews showed.
Blackness and whiteness both had constructed meanings that changed over
time, and one's subjective sense of race could also differ from how one was seen
by others. The one constant was the bias against blackness. From Daniel Patrick
Moynihan to Charles Murray, conservative policymakers advanced black culture
as pathological, rooted in genetic inferiority, and steeped in a culture of poverty.[77] Liberals attributed the exclusion of most blacks from the postwar American consumer cornucopia to systematic prejudice in jobs, housing, and education. The neoconservative analysis instead offered a version of social Darwinism
in modern dress: welfare was a retrogressive program that coddled the lazy and
encouraged dependence. According to the hotly contested and generally discredited eugenicist strain of this argument, blacks were the "unfit" consigned to
remain "under."[78]

The self-perception of race among Hispanics was also telling. Puerto Rican
social workers, for example, had developed their own organization to address
their demands as early as 1964, but the "Hispanic" census category covered
peoples from many countries in the Caribbean and South and Central America.
In nearly all of these countries, caste systems exist in which lighter-skinned
people usually have disproportionate political and economic power. These elites
often see themselves as white. In American cities, however, European descen-
dants may see all Hispanics as other than white and "black Hispanics" as simply
"more" other. Thus the U.S. government has historically given Cuban exiles and
light-skinned French-speaking Haitians preferential treatment over dark-

skinned poor Haitian people who speak Creole. Of course, U.S. anticommunism has complicated this scenario, but responses to the federal census by Hispanic social service workers suggest that they are not unaware of the power of whiteness in America. When 5,376 Hispanic welfare service aides nationally were asked in 1990 to describe their race, only 261 (4.8 percent) chose "black"; almost half (48.1 percent) opted for "white." Given additional choices of Asian, Aleut, Native American, Eskimo, and Pacific Islander, the clear second preference (44.5 percent) was "other race"—anything but black.[79]

Neither racism nor poverty in America has been limited to blacks,[80] but the dominant popular ideology has placed the failure narrative explaining middle-class exclusion on their backs. More recently, the consumer revolution has excluded Hispanics on the East Coast and Mexicans on the West Coast, but because Puerto Ricans and Hispanics generally also can be other than black, the welfare mark of Cain has labeled African Americans specially as beneath or "under" class. By the 1990s, the experience of Asians and some South Americans had replaced that of Jews as the counternarrative of success.[81]

Most people who go into social work continue to be distinguished by their concern for social justice. The profession retains its public image of being dedicated to helping the poor, even as more people use the M.S.W. degree to define themselves as therapists. Bureaucratic details also remain impediments to good service. Using their intimate knowledge of social service bureaucracy, however, social workers find ways to circumvent logjams to provide for clients as best they can. In response, critics complain of caseworker leniency and corruption. To caseworkers such as Leigh Benin, however, who juggled allocation categories to meet client needs in the late 1960s, such resourcefulness kept a beleaguered and underfunded social service functioning.

The transformation of social work between 1968 and the 1990s nonetheless did dilute the social work mission to the poor. In the twenty years after 1968, a study of social worker attitudes toward poverty and social action found that their analysis of poverty had become more structural and less personal, whereas the methods they endorsed had become consensual and less radical. According to the study, what had been a "dissenting profession" was now a "consenting profession."[82]

As the 104th Congress seeks to "reform" welfare as a central plank in the Republicans' Contract with America, the shift by social workers to more consensual politics has worrisome implications for the poor. The dominant political discourse of the day scapegoats welfare clients as black, female, and immoral. Simultaneously, the imposition of workfare and service limitations effectively translates into declining services and "downsized" staffs. To critics of such "reforms," the changes augur a new era of increased homelessness, unemployment, and poverty. Social workers have been a traditional base of organized resistance to such conditions. The nonclass content of middle-class identity, however threatens to complicate, if not undermine, social workers' opposition to this crisis. It remains to be seen, then, whether social workers will overcome this conservative shift to reactivate their mission to the poor or whether, as part of the middle class without a class, they will cast their die with the "taxpayer revolt" as consumers for whom the underclass is a world apart.

The conclusion to this story cannot yet be written since "downsizing" in the mid-1990s threatens to reverse the material bases of social worker identity as middle class. The rush into managed health care undermines the possibility of doing psychotherapy for many social workers as increased limitations on the authorization of therapy diminish their market. Proposed welfare cuts also augur reductions in public service job opportunities. The prospect of under-employment and unemployment among social service workers, however, places them on terrain that has long been familiar to industrial workers and, in-creasingly, many other professional and managerial workers. Ironically, how-ever, in the 1996 presidential campaign, as many politicians continued to appeal to a universal middle class, it was the neoconservative candidate, Pat Buchanan, who appreciated and began to give public voice to the increasing vulnerability of many Americans as "workers." Buchanan's attack was as much a nativist appeal to anti-immigrant prejudices as a populist critique of the privileged rich, but the latter nonetheless implicitly reinfused the language of class with class meanings.

The conservative assault on welfare and the new vulnerability of therapists with an M.S.W. to managed health care cutbacks may demoralize some but mobilize others. Hints of the latter can be seen in the recent infusion of a new radicalism into the NASW, the professional association that traditionally has rejected political action. The New York City chapter's selection in 1990 of Robert S. Schacter, a charter member of the Bertha Capen Reynolds Society, as its executive director reflected the chapter's new direction. As self-styled "radical conservatives" mounted their Contract with America in the fall of 1993, the New York City NASW chapter took the unprecedented step of forming a Social Action Committee. A week after the conservative landslide in November 1994, the chapter then joined a coalition of New York City social welfare agencies in forming a human chain around Mayor Rudolph W. Giuliani's City Hall offices in protest against threatened social service cutbacks. Evidence of such new directions was not confined to New York City. The Washington, D.C., NASW office, for instance, agreed to house the Women's Committee of 100, a political action lobby organized by leading feminist social service activists to defeat con-servative efforts to dismantle welfare. One leader of the committee was Frances Fox Piven, the longtime radical social work educator and activist.[83]

Whether these developments in the NASW herald the return of the "consenting profession" to its dissenting roots remains to be seen. The legacy of race and the ideology of the middle class as an open and generic social category constitute powerful counterforces, however, to any major shift in the language of class in America. Although white America continues to use race to separate an "underclass" from the rest of society, evidence of a professional black "middle class" confirms conservatives' belief that America remains a land of opportunity for those who can exercise their will and abilities. Such critics would point, for example, to the higher median income of black households than that of white households in the borough of Queens by the mid-1990s. Indeed, containing neighborhoods with pastoral names such as Forest Hills, Ridgewood, and Astoria, Queens has long been a symbol of New York City's "middle class." Building on such developments, titles of books by neoconservative writers such as Dinesh D'Souza announce "the end of racism."[84]

The evidence of an affluent black community, however, obscures as much about the language and meaning of class as it illuminates. To D'Souza and others, it refutes the argument that racial difference is a source of discrimination. But the different histories of black and white women and men in social work suggest otherwise. The history of social work demonstrates that the "middle class" is a racialized category with distinct meanings for white and black people. The experience of any black person trying to hail a taxicab at night, for instance, when many drivers view all blacks as potential criminals, illustrates the limitations of class distinctions for blacks. As African American literary critic Henry Louis Gates Jr. has argued, "[t]he enormous class disparities within the 'black community'" cannot be smoothed over. Building a genuine "community" requires "something we don't yet have: a way of speaking about black poverty without falsifying the reality of black advancement; a way of speaking about black advancement that doesn't distort the enduring realities of black poverty."[85] In Gates's challenge lies the present and future of the idea of the middle class as either a fulfillment of or an impediment to social justice.

appendix

Table A.1. Social Workers by Gender and Workplace in the United States and New York City, 1910–1970

	United States			New York City	
	Total	% Female	Public Sector (%)	Total	% Female
1910	15,970	55.7		1,741	69.2
1920	41,078	55.6		4,605	77.7
1930	31,341	79.0	20,307 (65.0)	3,573[a]	80.8
1940	75,197	54.3	46,088 (65.0)	9,860	62.9
1950	74,240	69.0	49,440 (64.3)	8,375	—
1960	115,799	57.0	74,111 (64.0)	11,933	—
1970	218,281	62.9	173,937 (79.7)	11,607	65.3

Sources: U.S. Department of Commerce, Bureau of the Census, *Census of Population, 1910–1970* (Washington, D.C.: Government Printing Office, 1973); BLS, *Social Workers in 1950: A Report on the Study of Salaries and Working Conditions in Social Work—Spring 1950* (New York: AASW, 1952) and *Salaries and Working Conditions of Social Welfare Manpower in 1960* (New York: National Social Welfare Assembly, [1961]).

Note: The figures are for religious and charity workers in 1910; religious, charity, and welfare workers in 1920; and social and welfare workers in 1930; and they include recreation but not group workers in 1960 and 1970.

[a]New York City also had 2,451 religious workers in 1930.

Table A.2. Religious and Charity Workers in the United States, 1910

Worker	Female	Male	Total (%)
White, native-born parents	4,753	3,855	8,608 (53.9)
Foreign/mixed parents	1,882	1,189	3,071 (19.2)
Foreign-born	1,916	1,813	3,729 (23.4)
African Americans	332	169	501 (3.1)
Others	6	55	61 (0.4)
Total	8,889 (55.7%)	7,081 (44.3%)	15,970

Source: U.S. Department of Commerce, Bureau of the Census, *Thirteenth Census of the United States: Population, 1910*, vol. 4, *Occupational Statistics* (Washington, D.C.: Government Printing Office, 1914), 93, table 1, 428, table 6.

Table A.3. Religious and Charity Workers in New York City, 1910

Worker	Female	Male	Total (%)[a]
White, native-born parents	480	179	659 (37.9)
Foreign/mixed parents	383	130	513 (29.5)
Foreign-born	320	220	540 (31.0)
African Americans	20	8	28 (1.1)
Others	1	0	1 (0.1)
Total New York City	1,204 (69.2%)	537 (30.8%)	1,741
Total New York State	1,640 (62.6%)	980 (37.4%)	2,620
Total United States	8,889 (55.7%)	7,081 (44.3%)	15,970

Source: U.S. Department of Commerce, Bureau of the Census, *Thirteenth Census of the United States: Population, 1910*, vol. 4, *Occupational Statistics* (Washington, D.C.: Government Printing Office, 1914), 93, table 1, 497, table 7, 573, table 8.
[a]Percentages do not add up to 100% because of averaging.

Table A.4. JBG Budget Sources, 1944–1956

Source	1944–45	1945–50	1955–56
FJP	74.2% ($452,498)	61.5%	48.2% ($809,847)
Public funds[a]	17.7 ($107,941)	—	27.1[b] ($455,329)
Private funds	4.6 ($28,052)	15.6	21.0 ($352,838)
Contributions and grants[c]	3.5 ($21,344)	—	3.7 ($62,167)
Total	$609,835		$1,680,181

Source: Minutes, Board of Trustees, Apr. 20, 1955, JBG, box 1235, JBGA.
[a]Non-FJP dollar amounts are based on FJP funds and are approximations.
[b]This figure, actually for 1954–55, is described as the "high" public share for the period.
[c]It is not clear how this category differs from public and private funds.

Table A.5. African American Social Workers in the United States and New York City, 1910–1960

Year	United States Total (%)	% Public Sector	% Private Sector	New York City Total (%)
1910[a]	501 (3.1)			28 (1.6)
1920[a]	1,231 (3.0)			96 (2.1)
1930	949 (3.2)			78 (2.2)
1940	2,720 (3.6)	72.1	27.9	—
1950	5,500 (7.2)	73.9[b]	24.3[b]	611 (7.3)
1960[c]	11,643 (12.2)	84.2	15.5	—

Source: Based on occupational data in the decennial U.S. censuses for population, 1910–60, by the U.S. Department of Commerce, Bureau of the Census (Washington, D.C.: Government Printing Office).
[a]The census category includes religious workers.
[b]The total does not equal 100% because of 60 self-employed and 30 unpaid family workers.
[c]This is the census total for "Nonwhite," of which 1,149 (1.2%) are "Other" than "Negro."

Table A.6. Social Workers and Welfare Service Aides in the New York City
Metropolitan Area, 1980

	Total (%)	White (%)	Black (%)	Hispanic (%)
Social workers				
Males	11,612 (36.3)	6,660 (36.4)	3,502 (34.5)	1,450 (43.8)
Females	20,131 (63.6)	11,621 (63.6)	6,652 (65.5)	1,858 (56.2)
Total	31,743	18,281 (57.5)	10,154 (31.9)	3,308 (10.4)
Welfare service aides				
Males	615 (6.5)	212 (11.0)	313 (5.0)	171 (9.3)
Females	9,551 (93.5)	1,721 (89.0)	5,931 (95.0)	1,672 (0.7)
Total	10,166	1,933 (19.0)	7,233 (61.4)	2,843 (18.1)

Source: U.S. Department of Commerce, Bureau of the Census, *Census of Population, 1980*, vol. 1, *Characteristics of the Population* (Washington, D.C.: Government Printing Office, 1983), pt. 34, 466–70.

Note: Totals do not reflect nonwhite "others" such as Asians.

Table A.7. Median Annual Earnings and Total Family Income by Gender and Race in the United States, 1969

Median Annual Earnings	Male	Female
Social workers		
All	$ 8,414	$6,475
Black	8,397	6,089
Hispanic origin	7,164	5,245
Welfare aides		
All	5,487	3,192
Black	5,336	3,541
Hispanic origin	4,235	3,245

Total Family Income	Male Headed	Female Headed
Social and recreation workers		
All	12,173	8,340
Black	13,000	6,956
Health service workers		
All	—	5,325
Black	—	4,956
Dentists	24,855	
Lawyers	23,037	
Engineers	15,788	
Accountants	14,220	

Source: U.S. Department of Commerce, Bureau of the Census, *Census of Population, 1970,* vol. 1, *Occupational Characteristics* (Washington, D.C.: Government Printing Office, 1973), tables 1, 17–18, 28.

Table A.8. Social Workers by Gender, Hispanic Origin, and Race in the New York City Metropolitan Area, 1990

Race	Male	Female	Total (%)[a]
Hispanic origin	2,724	6,363	9,087 (12.3)
White[b]	11,835	26,431	38,266 (52.0)
Black[b]	7,648	16,886	24,534 (33.3)
Asian or Pacific Islander[b]	443	880	1,323 (1.8)
Other[b]	136	245	381 (0.5)
Total	22,786	50,805	73,591

Source: U.S. Department of Commerce, Bureau of the Census, *1990 Census of Population and Housing*, Equal Employment Opportunity file, Region 300: social workers (occupational code 174), tape file 3C, United States Summary: Urbanized Areas and Their Components (Washington, D.C.: CD-Rom, Data User Services Division, 1993).
[a]Percentages do not add up to 100% because of averaging.
[b]Excluding those of Hispanic origin.

Table A.9. Therapists by Gender, Hispanic Origin, and Race in the United States, 1990

Race	Male	Female	Total (%)
Hispanic origin	991	2,009	3,000 (4.2)
White[a]	15,420	44,407	59,827 (83.8)
Black[a]	2,805	4,122	6,928 (9.7)
Asian or Pacific Islander[a]	375	826	1,201 (1.7)
Other[a]	164	283	447 (0.6)
Total	19,755	51,647	71,402

Source: U.S. Department of Commerce, Bureau of the Census, *1990 Census of Population and Housing*, Equal Employment Opportunity file, Region 010: therapists (occupational code 105), tape file 3C, United States Summary: Urbanized Areas and Their Components (Washington, D.C.: CD-Rom, Data User Services Division, 1993).

Note: This table excludes occupational, speech, and physical therapists, groups that more often provided employment for people of Hispanic origin or blacks than did psychotherapy.
[a]Excluding those of Hispanic origin.

notes

Abbreviations

In addition to the abbreviations listed in the front matter the following abbreviations are used throughout the notes.

AASW/NASWP	American Association of Social Workers/National Association of Social Workers Papers, SWHA
BLS	U.S. Bureau of Labor Statistics
BWOHP	Black Women's Oral History Project, vol. 10, Schlesinger Library, Radcliffe College, Harvard University, Cambridge, Mass.
DC65R	District Council 65 Records, WLA
DLL	U.S. Department of Labor Library, Washington, D.C.
FJPA	Federation of Jewish Philanthropies of New York Archive, New York, N.Y.
FJPOH	Federation of Jewish Philanthropies of New York Oral History Project, New York, N.Y.
JBGA	Jewish Board of Guardians Archive, Jewish Board of Family and Children's Services Archive, New York, N.Y.
JFP	Jacob Fisher Papers, Social Welfare History Archive, University of Minnesota, Minneapolis, Minn.
JPASA	Jewish Protectory and Aid Society Archive, Jewish Board of Family and Children's Services Archive, New York, N.Y.
MACNY	Municipal Archive of the City of New York, New York, N.Y.
NASWOH	National Association of Social Workers Oral History Project, Columbia University Oral History Research Office Butler Library, New York, N.Y.
NWROP	National Welfare Rights Organization Papers, Moorland-Spingarn Research Center, Manuscripts Division, Howard University, Washington, D.C.
RHC	Raymond M. Hilliard Collection, Chicago Historical Society, Chicago, Ill.

SSEUC   Social Service Employees Union Collection, Congress of Industrial Organization Archive, DLL

SSEU371R   Social Service Employees Union, Local 371, Records, WLA

SWHA   Social Welfare History Archive, University of Minnesota, Minneapolis, Minn.

UOPWAC   United Office and Professional Workers of America Collection, Congress of Industrial Organization Archive, DLL

WLA   Robert F. Wagner Labor Archive, Tamiment Library, New York University, New York, N.Y.

YIVO   YIVO Institute for Jewish Research Archive, New York, N.Y.

Preface

1. This Wingspread Conference on Work and Mental Health paper was published as Daniel J. Walkowitz and Peter R. Eisenstadt, "The Psychology of Work: Work and Mental Health in Historical Perspective," *Radical History Review* 34 (Jan. 1986): 7–31.

2. Martin Oppenheimer, *White Collar Politics* (New York: Monthly Review Press, 1985), 136–37.

3. Christopher Lasch, "The Siege of the Family," *New York Review of Books*, Nov. 24, 1977, 15–18, quoted in ibid., 136. The concept of the creation of a "market" for professionals is from Magali Larsen, *The Rise of Professionalism* (Berkeley: University of California Press, 1977), 14.

4. Robert Zussman, *Mechanics of the Middle Class: Work and Politics among American Engineers* (Berkeley: University of California Press, 1985), 1–13.

5. Peter Stallybrass and Allon White, *The Politics and Poetics of Transgression* (Ithaca: Cornell University Press, 1986), 24–26, 191–202.

6. Joan W. Scott, "On Language, Gender, and Working-Class History," *International Labor and Working-Class History* 31 (Spring 1987): 5. See the exchange between Scott and her critics in the "scholarly controversy" in *International Labor and Working-Class History* 31 (Spring 1987): 1–45, organized around her essay, "On Language, Gender, and Working-Class History," and Joan W. Scott, "A Reply to Criticism," *International Labor and Working-Class History* 32 (Fall 1987): 39–45; John E. Toews, "Intellectual History after the Linguistic Turn," *American Historical Review* 92, no. 4 (Oct. 1987): 879–907; and Gareth Stedman Jones, *Languages of Class: Studies in English Working Class History, 1832–1982* (Cambridge: Cambridge University Press, 1983). For a critique of the linguistic turn, see Bryan Palmer, *Descent into Discourse: The Reification of Language and the Writing of Social History* (Philadelphia: Temple University Press, 1990), esp. 120–44.

7. David Halle, *America's Working Man: Work, Home, and Politics among Blue Collar Property Owners* (Chicago: University of Chicago Press, 1984). Halle finds a third form of identity organized around the nation.

8. Zussman, *Mechanics of the Middle Class*, 205–7.

9. "U.S. Says Middle Class Shrinking," *New York Times*, Feb. 22, 1992; "Most Agree on Break for Middle Class but Who's a Member Is Taxing in Itself," *Baltimore Sun*, Jan. 28, 1992; "Taxpayers' Idea of Wealth May Not Be the Same as Mondale's," *New York Times*, Sept. 12, 1984; "Trapped in the Impoverished Middle Class," *New York Times*, Nov. 17, 1991. The

Census Bureau defined high incomes as twice the median income, low incomes as half. See also "Another Kind of Middle-Class Squeeze," *New York Times*, May 18, 1997, in which New York's governor George E. Pataki labeled all households making less than $75,000, or 99 percent of New Yorkers, as middle class.

10. Zussman, *Mechanics of the Middle Class* 206–14 'Most Agree on Break for Middle Class."

11. Bill Clinton, quoted in Nancy Folbre, "The Center Cannot Hold," *In These Times*, July 26, 1993, 14.

12. Jason DeParle, "Welfare to Work: A Sequel," *New York Times Magazine*, Dec. 28, 1997; "Success and Frustration, as Welfare Rules Change," *New York Times*, Dec. 30, 1997; "Workfare Study Finds High Penalty Rate," *New York Times*, Jan. 10, 1998.

13. Stephen Thernstrom and Abigail Thernstrom, *America in Black and White: One Nation, Indivisible* (New York: Simon and Schuster, 1997)

14. Nancy Fraser and Linda Gordon, "A Genealogy of 'Dependency': Tracing a Keyword of the U.S. Welfare State," in Nancy Fraser, *Justice Interruptus: Critical Reflections on the "Postsocialist" Condition* (New York: Routledge, 1997), 121–49

Prologue

1. Stanley Aronowitz, *The Politics of Identity: Class, Culture, and Social Movements* (New York: Routledge, 1992), 38.

2. Barry Bluestone, "In Support of the Deindustrialization Thesis," in *Deindustrialization and Plant Closures*, ed. Paul D. Standohar and Holly E. Brown (Lexington, Mass.: D. C. Heath, 1987), 41–52. On the restructuring of the steel industry, see Gordon L. Clark, "Corporate Restructuring in the Steel Industry: Adjustment Strategies and Local Labor Relations," in *America's New Market Geography: Nation, Region, and Metropolis*, ed. George Sternlieb and James W. Hughes (New Brunswick: Rutgers University Press, 1988), 179–214.

3. *Men 2000* (London: Mintel, 1994), cited in "Men Face Age of Uncertainty" and "Housework 'Sloths' Rife," *The Independent* (London), Feb. 21, 1994, 3

4. The "old" middle class, in conformance with the Marxist category of independent, propertied entrepreneurs, consisted mostly of farmers with goodly numbers of shopkeepers and independent professionals—doctors, lawyers, ministers. But the migration of Americans to cities had substantially reduced the percentage of farmers by 1940 to the point that an equal number worked in offices, followed by large numbers in sales and in the professions. See C. Wright Mills, *White Collar: The American Middle Classes* (New York: Oxford University Press, 1951).

5. Mary P. Ryan, *Cradle of the Middle Class: The Family in Oneida County, New York, 1790–1865* (New York: Cambridge University Press, 1981), and Lori D. Ginzberg, *Women and the Work of Benevolence: Morality, Politics, and Class in the Nineteenth-Century United States* (New Haven: Yale University Press, 1990), correctly note the emerging domestic and class perspectives of this class, but the women they study do relatively little work.

6. For data on clerical workers in 1870 and 1990, see U.S. Department of Commerce, Bureau of the Census, *Sixteenth Census of the United States: Comparative Occupational Statistics for the United States, 1870–1940* (Washington, D.C.: Government Printing Office, 1943), 101, 112 and U.S. Department of Labor, Women's Bureau, *Women's Occupations*

through Seven Decades, bulletin no. 218 (Washington, D.C.: Government Printing Office, n.d.), 75, 78. For intermediate data, see Everett M. Kassalow, "White Collar Unionism in the United States," in *White-Collar Trade Unions: Contemporary Developments in the Industrialized Societies*, ed. Adolf Sturmthal (Urbana: University of Illinois Press, 1966), 306–9.

7. Jürgen Kocka, *White Collar Workers in America, 1890–1940: A Social-Political History in International Perspective*, trans. Maura Kealey (Beverly Hills, Calif.: Sage Publications, 1980), 13.

8. Kassalow, "White Collar Unionism," 306. On stagnation in steel as a precursor of deindustrialization, see Clark, "Corporate Restructuring in the Steel Industry."

9. Kassalow, "White Collar Unionism," 310. See also Michael B. Fabricant and Steve Burghardt, *The Welfare State Crisis and the Transformation of Social Service Work* (Armonk, N.Y.: M. E. Sharpe, 1992).

10. See "Social Work and the Welfare State" in the bibliographical essay.

11. Kocka, *White Collar Workers in America*, 12–13, places social workers in the lower middle class because of their meager salaries and modicum of delegated authority. They do require higher educational qualifications and have more job security than those in the working class.

12. Judith Stacey, *Brave New Families: Stories of Domestic Upheaval in Late Twentieth Century America* (New York: Basic Books, 1990), 34–35.

13. Geoffrey Crossick, "From Gentlemen to the Residuum: Languages of Social Description in Victorian Britain," in *Language, History, and Class*, ed. Penelope J. Corfield (London: Basil Blackwell, 1991), 152, 159, 175. Stuart M. Blumin also bemoans the use of the term "middle class" by historians. See Stuart M. Blumin, "The Hypothesis of Middle-Class Formation in Nineteenth-Century America: A Critique and Some Proposals," *American Historical Review* 90, no. 2 (Apr. 1985): 299–338.

14. Ryan, *Cradle of the Middle Class*, 14. See also "Theorizing Class and Work" in the bibliographical essay.

15. See, for example, Herbert J. Gans, *The Levittowners: Ways of Life and Politics in a New Suburban Community* (New York: Columbia University Press, 1967), and Jules Henry, *Culture against Man* (New York: Random House, 1963). For examples of the best recent work, see Elaine Tyler May, *Homeward Bound: American Families in the Cold War Era* (New York: Basic Books, 1988), and Wini Breines, *Young, White, and Miserable: Growing Up Female in the Fifties* (Boston: Beacon Press, 1992).

16. See David Halle, *America's Working Man: Work, Home, and Politics among Blue Collar Property Owners* (Chicago: University of Chicago Press, 1984); Robert Zussman, *Mechanics of the Middle Class: Work and Politics among American Engineers* (Berkeley: University of California Press, 1985); Stacey, *Brave New Families*; and Barbara Ehrenreich, *Fear of Falling: The Inner Life of the Middle Class* (New York: Harper Collins, 1990).

17. It seems unfair to single out authors for what has been a commonplace vagueness about the concept of class in America, but a few works suggest the variety of different usages that have dominated much of the best writing of U.S. history. For instance, for the emergence of a professional middle class, see Paul Starr, *The Social Transformation of American Medicine: The Rise of a Sovereign Profession and the Making of a Vast Industry* (New York: Basic Books, 1982); for class as stratification, see John Bodnar, *The Transplanted: A History of Immigrants in Urban America* (Bloomington: Indiana University Press, 1985), 120; for class as income and status, see Gary R. Mormino and George E. Pozzetta, *The Immigrant World of*

Ybor City: Italians and Their Latin Neighbors in Tampa, 1885–1985 (Urbana: University of Illinois Press, 1987), 304; and for the essentialized use of the term "middle class" in a book distinguished by its attention to the constructed categories of race and gender, see Gail Bederman, *Manliness and Civilization: A Cultural History of Gender and Race in the United States, 1880–1917* (Chicago: University of Chicago Press, 1995). In his deliberate decision to use the term "bourgeoisie" or "upper class," T. J. Jackson Lears in *No Place of Grace: Antimodernism and the Transformation of American Culture, 1880–1920* (New York: Pantheon Books, 1981), is a notable exception in his use of the term "middle class."

18. Loïc J. D. Wacquant, "Making Class: The Middle Class(es) in Social Theory and Social Structure," in *Bringing Class Back In: Contemporary and Historical Perspectives*, ed. Scott G. McNall, Rhonda F. Levine, and Rick Fantasia (Boulder: Westview Press, 1991), 57. See also Pierre Bourdieu, "What Makes a Class?: On the Theoretical and Practical Existence of Groups," *Berkeley Journal of Sociology* 32 (Fall 1987): 1–18.

19. "'In between' spaces" is from Homi K. Bhabha, *The Location of Culture* (London: Routledge, 1994), 1–2. For a more detailed discussion, see below in this chapter.

20. Kocka, "Introduction," in *White Collar Workers in America*, also makes this point.

21. Zussman, *Mechanics of the Middle Class*, 1–13.

22. Warren I. Susman, *Culture as History: The Transformation of American Society in the Twentieth Century* (New York: Pantheon, 1984), xx–xxiii

23. Ryan, *Cradle of the Middle Class*; Stuart M. Blumin, *The Emergence of the Middle Class: Social Experience in the American City, 1760–1900* (Cambridge: Cambridge University Press, 1989); Richard Wightman Fox and T. J. Jackson Lears, eds., *The Culture of Consumption: Critical Essays in American History, 1880–1980* (New York: Pantheon, 1983); Susan Porter Benson, *Counter Cultures: Saleswomen, Managers, and Customers in American Department Stores, 1890–1940* (Urbana: University of Illinois Press, 1955).

24. Halle, *America's Working Man*; Zussman, *Mechanics of the Middle Class*.

25. Nancy Folbre, in "The Center Cannot Hold," *In These Times*, July 26, 1993, 17, notes, for instance, that women are almost three times more likely than men to be hired in many new assembly and service sector jobs. But when men lose their jobs, as nearly 100,000 "downsized" steelworkers in Pittsburgh did during the 1980s, such women's jobs, which pay less than those in the steel mills and often involve a loss of benefits, diminish the family wage. One study estimates, for instance, that it takes 163 electronic assembly jobs for women to provide wage parity with 100 steel workers. These women may appreciate the opportunity to work in jobs previously closed to them, but such jobs as breadwinners can take their toll on families in stress and the disruption of traditional gender roles. See, for example, Ruth Sidel, *Women and Children Last: The Plight of Poor Women in Affluent America* (New York: Penguin, 1986); Mimi Abramovitz, *Regulating the Lives of Women: Social Welfare Policy from Colonial Times to the Present* (Boston: South End Press, 1988), chap. 11; and Michael B. Katz, *The Undeserving Poor: From the War on Poverty to the War on Welfare* (New York: Pantheon, 1989), 66–78.

26. Linda Gordon, "What Does Welfare Regulate?," paper presented at the Conference on Gender and the Origin of the Welfare State, Harvard Center for European Studies, Cambridge, Mass., Apr. 16, 1988, and *Pitied but Not Entitled: Single Mothers and the History of Welfare, 1890–1935* (New York: Free Press, 1994); Abramovitz, *Regulating the Lives of Women*.

27. Rush Limbaugh, quoted in Folbre, "The Center Cannot Hold," 17.

28. For the most part, previous histories of social work have focused on professionalization and placed social workers within the sociological literature of medicine and the confines of medical history. Relatively little attention has been given to the work of these people, although a few doctoral theses have focused more narrowly on the social worker as trade unionist. For instance, Mark McColloch, *White Collar Workers in Transition: The Boom Years, 1940–1970* (Westport, Conn.: Greenwood Press, 1983), 74–77, 88–91, 102–3, 126–31, provides a useful outline of unionization in social work.

29. Ryan, *Cradle of the Middle Class*; Thorstein Veblen, *The Theory of the Leisure Class* (1899; reprint, New York: Penguin, 1979).

30. Kathy Peiss, *Cheap Amusements: Working Women and Leisure in Turn-of-the-Century New York* (Philadelphia: Temple University Press, 1986), 185; Joanne J. Meyerowitz, *Women Adrift: Independent Wage Earners in Chicago, 1880–1930* (Chicago: University of Chicago Press, 1988).

31. Leslie B. Alexander, "Organizing the Professional Social Worker: Union Development in Voluntary Social Work, 1930–1950" (Ph.D. diss., Bryn Mawr College, 1976), 198–99; John H. Ehrenreich, *The Altruistic Imagination: A History of Social Work and Social Policy in the United States* (Ithaca: Cornell University Press, 1985), 141–43.

32. Ava Baron, "An 'Other' Side of Gender Antagonism at Work: Men, Boys, and the Remasculinization of Printers' Work, 1830–1920," in *Work Engendered: Toward a New History of American Labor*, ed. Ava Baron (Ithaca: Cornell University Press, 1991), 47–69; Ileen A. DeVault, " 'Give the Boys a Trade': Gender and Job Choice in the 1890s," in Baron, *Work Engendered*, 211.

33. Peiss, *Cheap Amusements*; Meyerowitz, *Women Adrift*.

34. Ruth Wanger, *What Girls Can Do* (New York: H. Holt, 1926), 4. See also E. W. Weaver, *Profitable Vocations for Girls* (New York: A. S. Barnes, 1915).

35. WEIU, Department of Research, *Home and School Visiting as a Vocation for Women* (Boston: WEIU, 1911), *Organizing Charity as a Vocation for Women* (Boston: WEIU, 1912), *Settlement Work as a Vocation for Women* (Boston: WEIU, 1912), *Social Service for Children as a Vocation for Women* (Boston: WEIU, 1912), and *Studies in Economic Relations of Women*, vol. 1, pt. 2 (Boston: WEIU, 1914); Elizabeth Kemper Adams, *Women Professional Workers: A Study Made for the Women's Educational and Industrial Union* (Chautauqua, N.Y.: Chautauqua Press, 1921). On evangelical language used to legitimize women's work, see Ann Douglas, *The Feminization of American Culture* (New York: Knopf, 1977).

36. Vida D. Scudder, "Foreword," in WEIU, *Studies in Economic Relations*, 76–77. It seems unlikely that most female volunteers had nettlesome "business contacts," but the movement to paid labor for women seemed nonetheless logical.

37. WEIU, Department of Research, "Opportunities for Women in Social Service," in *Studies in Economic Relations of Women*, vol. 1, pt. 2 (Boston: WEIU, 1914), 77.

38. See Henry Louis Gates Jr., "Introduction: Writing 'Race' and the Difference It Makes" and "Talkin' That Talk," in *"Race," Writing, and Difference*, ed. Henry Louis Gates Jr. (Chicago: University of Chicago Press, 1985), 1–20, 402–9. The Baptist comment comes from *Western Recorder* (Louisville, Ky.), Jan. 30, 1896.

39. I am indebted to Douglas Rabinow for this discussion.

40. Linda Gordon, "Black and White Visions of Welfare: Women's Activism, 1890–1945," *Journal of American History* 78, no. 2 (Sept. 1991): 559–90.

41. On blacks and social service, see Evelyn Brooks Higgenbotham, *Righteous Discontent:*

The Women's Movement in the Black Baptist Church, 1880–1920 (Cambridge: Harvard University Press, 1989); Kevin K. Gaines, Uplifting the Race: Black Leadership, Politics, and Culture in the Twentieth Century (Chapel Hill: University of North Carolina Press, 1996); and Stephanie J. Shaw, What a Woman Ought to Be and to Do: Black Professional Women Workers during the Jim Crow Era (Chicago: University of Chicago Press, 1996). Race work among black social workers is discussed throughout this book, but their actions in the 1930s can be found in chapter 4.

42. Historians have emphasized that this period witnessed the proliferation of such seemingly diverse phenomena as consumer culture, advertising, scientific management, and leisure. See, for example, T. J. Jackson Lears, "From Salvation to Self-Realization: Advertising and the Therapeutic Roots of the Consumer Culture," in Fox and Lears, Culture of Consumption, 1–38; Benson, Counter Cultures; Stuart Ewen, Captains of Consciousness: Advertising and the Social Roots of the Consumer Culture (New York: McGraw-Hill, 1976); Harry Braverman, Labor and Monopoly Capital: The Degradation of Work in the Twentieth Century (New York: Monthly Review Press, 1974); Peiss, Cheap Amusements; Paula Fass, The Damned and the Beautiful: American Youth in the 1920s (New York: Oxford University Press, 1977); and Robert W. Snyder, The Voice of the City: Vaudeville and Popular Culture in New York (New York: Oxford University Press, 1989).

43. Michael B. Katz, In the Shadow of the Poorhouse: A Social History of Welfare in America (New York: Basic Books, 1986).

44. "Child-Protection System Falls Victim to a Paper Maneuver," New York Times, Jan. 2, 1989.

45. See U.S. Department of Commerce, Bureau of the Census, 1990 Census of Population and Housing, Equal Employment Opportunity file, United States and NY-NJ-CT Consolidated Metropolitan Statistical Area, social workers (occupational code 174) and welfare service workers (occupational code 465), tape file 3C, United States Summary: Urbanized Areas and Their Components (Washington, D.C.: CD-Rom, Data User Services Division, 1993). See also New York Times, Sept. 5, 1994.

46. Bhabha, Location of Culture, 1–2.

Chapter One

1. The New York School of Philanthropy would later become the prestigious New York School of Social Work and then the Columbia School of Social Work. See "Mary Ellen Richmond," Notable American Women, 1607–1950 (Cambridge: Harvard University Press, 1971), 152–54, and James Edward Hagerty, The Training of Social Workers (New York: McGraw-Hill, 1931), 23–27, 40–43.

2. Hagerty, Training of Social Workers, 23, 42–43.

3. The Oxford English Dictionary, 2d ed., vol. 15 (Oxford: Clarendon Press, 1989), 912.

4. Denise Riley, "Am I That Name?": Feminism and the Category of "Women" in History (Minneapolis: University of Minnesota Press, 1988), 50; International Encyclopedia of the Social Sciences, ed. David L. Sills (New York: Macmillan, 1968–79), 14:495. The gendered meaning of social work is the subject of chapter 3.

5. See, for example, Alba M. Edwards, in U.S. Department of Commerce, Bureau of the Census, Sixteenth Census of the United States: Comparative Occupational Statistics for the United

States, 1870–1940 (Washington, D.C.: Government Printing Office, 1943). See also Margo Anderson, *American Census: A Social History* (New Haven: Yale University Press, 1988).

6. U.S. Department of Commerce, Bureau of the Census, *Thirteenth Census of the United States: Population, 1910*, vol. 4, *Occupation Statistics* (Washington, D.C.: Government Printing Office, 1914), 93, table 1, 497, table 7, 573, table 8.

7. U.S. Department of Commerce, Bureau of the Census, *Fourteenth Census of the United States Taken for the Year 1920: Population*, vol. 3 (Washington, D.C.: Government Printing Office, 1922), 42, table 4, and *Fifteenth Census of the United States for 1930: Population*, vol. 4 (Washington, D.C.: Government Printing Office, 1933), 1100.

8. Roy Lubove, *The Professional Altruist: The Emergence of Social Work as a Career* (Cambridge: Harvard University Press, 1965), 49–62; Clarke A. Chambers, *Seedtime of Reform: American Social Service and Social Action, 1918–1933* (Minneapolis: University of Minnesota Press, 1963), 92. See also Abraham Flexner, "Is Social Work a Profession?," in *Proceedings of the National Conference of Charities and Correction, 1915* (Chicago, 1915), 576–90, and John H. Ehrenreich, *The Altruistic Imagination: A History of Social Work and Social Policy in the United States* (Ithaca: Cornell University Press, 1985), 57–58.

9. Report quoted in Mary Van Kleeck, "The Social Workers," *Survey*, Jan. 1, 1916, 386–89.

10. Esther Lucile Brown, *Social Work as a Profession* (New York: Russell Sage Foundation, 1935), 142–43.

11. Bureau of the Census, *Fifteenth Census: Population*, 1100. The Census Bureau's schedules for 1920 changed little by 1930. Both "keepers" and "workers" appeared as "semiprofessional pursuits," although the latter had been broadened to include "welfare workers."

12. Michael B. Katz, *In the Shadow of the Poorhouse: A Social History of Welfare in America* (New York: Basic Books, 1986), 13–21; David J. Rothman, *The Discovery of the Asylum: Social Order and Disorder in the New Republic* (Boston: Little, Brown, 1971); Gerald N. Grob, *Mental Institutions in America: Social Policy to 1875* (New York: Free Press, 1973).

13. Katz, *In the Shadow of the Poorhouse*, 107.

14. Ibid., 26–28.

15. Suzanne Lebsock, *The Free Women of Petersburg: Status and Culture in a Southern Town, 1784–1860* (New York: Norton, 1984), 196–236; Carroll Smith-Rosenberg, *Religion and the Rise of the American City: The New York City Mission Movement, 1812 to 1870* (Ithaca: Cornell University Press, 1971); Mary P. Ryan, *Cradle of the Middle Class: The Family in Oneida County, New York, 1790–1865* (New York: Cambridge University Press, 1981); Lori D. Ginzberg, *Women and the Work of Benevolence: Morality, Politics, and Class in the Nineteenth-Century United States* (New Haven: Yale University Press, 1990); Anne Boylan, "Women in Groups: An Analysis of Women's Benevolent Organizations in New York and Boston, 1797–1840," *Journal of American History* 71, no. 3 (Dec. 1984): 497–523; Nancy Hewitt, *Women's Activism and Social Change: Rochester, New York, 1822–1872* (Ithaca: Cornell University Press, 1984).

16. Ginzberg, *Women and the Work of Benevolence*, 1.

17. Christine Stansell, *City of Women: Sex and Class in New York, 1789–1860* (New York: Knopf, 1986), 67–69; Ginzberg, *Women and the Work of Benevolence*, 40–44.

18. Ginzberg, *Women and the Work of Benevolence*, 40; Katz, *In the Shadow of the Poorhouse*, 64.

19. Ginzberg, *Women and the Work of Benevolence*, 5, 135, 209; Katz, *In the Shadow of the Poorhouse*, 66.

20. Eric Foner, *Reconstruction: America's Unfinished Revolution, 1863–1877* (New York: Harper and Row, 1988), 489, quoted in Ginzberg, *Women and the Work of Benevolence*, 207–8.

21. Ginzberg, *Women and the Work of Benevolence*, 198

22. Katz, *In the Shadow of the Poorhouse*, chap. 3.

23. Marvin E. Gettleman, "The Whig Interpretation of Social Welfare History," *Smith College Studies in Social Work* 44, no. 3 (June 1974): 149–57, "Philanthropy as Social Control in Late Nineteenth-Century America: Some Hypotheses and Data on the Rise of Social Work," *Societas: A Journal of Social History* 5, no. 1 (Winter 1975): 49–59, and "John H. Findley and the Academic Origins of American Social Work," *Studies in History and Society* 2, nos. 1 and 2 (Fall 1969 and Spring 1970): 13–23; Katz, *In the Shadow of the Poorhouse*, 66–84; Ginzberg, *Women and the Work of Benevolence*, 48–49.

24. This view is shared by David M. Austin in "Historical Perspectives on Contemporary Social Work," *Urban and Social Change Review* 18, no. 2 (Summer 1985): 16–18.

25. Allen F. Davis, *Spearheads for Reform: The Social Settlements and the Progressive Movement, 1890–1914* (New York: Oxford University Press, 1967); Clarke A. Chambers, "Women in the Creation of the Profession of Social Work," *Social Service Review* 59 (Mar. 1986): 1–33.

26. WEIU, Department of Research, "Opportunities for Women in Social Service," in *Studies in Economic Relations of Women*, vol. 1, pt. 2 (Boston: WEIU, 1914), 102–3. Medical social work was represented by 210 workers, but 127 of these were district or visiting nurses, a field that had not yet distinguished itself from social work; 142 charity agents represented the older tradition of relief. Precursors of family caseworkers made up the rest: "97 women in children's societies, 76 matrons, and 70 visitors . . . , 10 probation officers, 8 investigators, 9 visitors to girls on parole, 6 directors of girls' clubs, and 1 attendance officer."

27. Vida D. Scudder, "Foreword," in WEIU, *Studies in Economic Relations of Women*, 76–77.

28. WEIU, "Opportunities for Women in Social Service," 77.

29. Davis, *Spearheads for Reform*, 33–37. Mary Simkhovitch, for instance, the founder of Greenwich House, attributed her social awareness to the influence of her minister, Henry Sylvester Nash, author of *Genesis of the Social Conscience*, and an edifying Thanksgiving visit to a Boston tenement with her Sunday school class. Although in retrospect she suspected that the scene was staged it had the intended effect: she was appalled to discover that some people were without food and clothing. See Mary Kingsbury Simkhovitch, *Neighborhood: My Story of Greenwich House* (New York: Norton, 1938), 17.

30. Judith Ann Trolander, *Professionalism and Social Change: From the Settlement House Movement to Neighborhood Centers, 1886 to the Present* (New York: Columbia University Press, 1987), 11–13; Davis, *Spearheads for Reform*, 33–37. Lillian Wald's relationship with her friend Mary Brewster is one such intimate friendship. Blanche Cook has speculated about the lesbian relationships among such reforming friends. See Blanche Cook, "Female Support Networks and Political Activism: Lillian Wald, Crystal Eastman, Emma Goldman," *Chrysalis* 3 (1977): 43–61, and Carroll Smith-Rosenberg, "The Female World of Love and Ritual: Relations between Women in Nineteenth-Century America," *Signs: Journal of Women in Culture and Society* 1 (1975): 1–30. For these settlement workers as "New Women," see Ellen Jacobs, "The 'New Woman' as Social Expert: Gender Consciousness in Social Investigation in Britain, 1880–1920," paper presented at the Berkshire Conference on the History of Women, Wellesley, Mass., June 1987.

31. Bureau of the Census, *Thirteenth Census: Population, Occupation Statistics*, 93, table 1, 428–29, table 6, 573, table 8.

32. Simkhovitch, *Neighborhood*, 252–55. For the historiography on settlements, see "Social Work and the Welfare State" in the bibliographical essay.

33. Albert Kennedy, Kathryn Farra, et al., *Social Settlements in New York City: Their Activities, Policies, and Administration* (New York: Columbia University Press, 1935), 498.

34. Linda Gordon, *Pitied but Not Entitled: Single Mothers and the History of Welfare, 1890–1935* (New York: Free Press, 1994); Kathryn Kish Sklar, *Florence Kelley and the Nation's Work: The Rise of Women's Political Culture, 1830–1900* (New Haven: Yale University Press, 1995).

35. Lillian Wald was called the "Angel of Henry Street," and similar images dominate the social worker novels of the era. See Beryl William Epstein, *Lillian Wald, Angel of Henry Street* (New York: J. Messner, 1948); Lucy Furman, *Mothering on Perilous* (New York: Macmillan, 1913); Henry Sydnor Harrison, *V. V.'s Eyes* (New York: Constable, 1913); and Mary Stanbery Watts, *Rise of Jennie Cushing* (New York: Macmillan, 1914). Arlien Johnson, a settlement worker at New York City's Hudson Guild in the early 1920s, remembers how Jane Addams's career shaped the public image of social work. See Arlien Johnson oral history, conducted by Vida S. Grayson, 1977–81, NASWOH.

36. Kathryn Kish Sklar, "Hull House in the 1890s: A Community of Women Reformers," *Signs: Journal of Women in Culture and Society* 10 (Summer 1985): 658, quoted in Maureen Weiner Greenwald, "Women and Class in Pittsburgh, 1850–1920," in *City on the Point*, ed. Samuel P. Hays (Pittsburgh: University of Pittsburgh Press, 1989), 58.

37. Simkhovitch, *Neighborhood*, 151.

38. Gordon, *Pitied but Not Entitled*, 56.

39. Davis, *Spearheads for Reform*, 21–22. Subsequent work by Lubove (*Professional Altruist*), Sklar (*Florence Kelley*), and others has supported the view that the settlements helped create a generation of women reformers.

40. Katz, *In the Shadow of the Poorhouse*, 162. See also Davis, *Spearheads for Reform*, 194–217.

41. Greenwald, "Women and Class in Pittsburgh," 33–67.

42. See, for example, the study of six Indianapolis and Gary, Indiana, settlements in Ruth Hutchinson Crocker, *Social Work and Social Order: The Settlement Movement in Two Industrial Cities, 1889–1930* (Urbana: University of Illinois Press, 1992); Mina Carson, *Settlement Folk: Social Thought and the American Settlement Movement, 1885–1930* (Chicago: University of Chicago Press, 1990); Rivka Lissak, *Pluralism and Progressives: Hull House and the New Immigrants* (Chicago: University of Chicago Press, 1989); Elizabeth Ewen, *Immigrant Women in the Land of Dollars: Life and Culture on the Lower East Side, 1890–1925* (New York: Monthly Review Press, 1985); and Elizabeth Lasch-Quinn, *Black Neighbors: Race and the Limits of Reform in the American Settlement House Movement, 1890–1945* (Chapel Hill: University of North Carolina Press, 1993).

43. Greenwich House History Workshop, Public History Program, Department of History, New York University, New York, N.Y., Apr. 1987. See also Elizabeth Ewen, *Immigrant Women*.

44. Undoubtedly learning from the bitter 1892 Homestead strike, U.S. Steel may have had the largest and earliest program in industrial social work. Crocker, *Social Work and Social Order*, describes the corporation's activity in Gary, Indiana. David Montgomery, *The Fall of the House of Labor: The Workplace, the State, and American Labor Activism, 1865–1925* (New

York: Cambridge University Press, 1987), 237, describes the Sociological Department of the Colorado Fuel and Iron Company as the "pioneering" corporate welfare program.

45. Stephen Meyer III, *The Five Dollar Day: Labor Management and Social Control in the Ford Motor Company, 1908–1921* (Albany, N.Y.: State University of New York Press, 1981), esp. 123–47.

46. George Brown, quoted in Olivier Zunz, *Making America Corporate, 1870–1920* (Chicago: University of Chicago Press, 1990), 134–38. Brown's views are not unlike those described in Meyer, *Five Dollar Day*, chap. 6.

47. Zunz, *Making America Corporate*, 93–94.

48. Angel Kwolek-Folland, "Gender, Self, and Work in the Life Insurance Industry, 1880–1930," in *Work Engendered: Toward a New History of American Labor*, ed. Ava Baron (Ithaca: Cornell University Press, 1991), 173–74.

49. Clifford W. Beers, *A Mind That Found Itself: An Autobiography* (1908; reprint, Garden City, N.Y.: Doubleday, 1953). See also Norman Dain, *Clifford W. Beers: Advocate for the Insane* (Pittsburgh: University of Pittsburgh Press, 1980).

50. Richard C. Cabot, *Social Work: Essays on the Meeting-Ground of Doctor and Social Worker* (Boston: Houghton Mifflin, 1919), xvi.

51. Ibid., 15, 142.

52. Ida M. Cannon, *Social Work in Hospitals: A Contribution to Progressive Medicine* (New York: Survey Associates, 1913), 148.

53. Cabot, *Social Work*, ix–x.

54. A sample of articles from 1918 gives a sense of the preoccupation with war disorders: John Collier, "The Management of War Neurosis and Allied Disorders in the Army," *Mental Hygiene* 2, no. 1 (1918): 1–18; F. H. Sexton, "Vocational Rehabilitation of Soldiers Suffering from Nervous Diseases," *Mental Hygiene* 2, no. 2 (1918): 265–76; and David Spence Hill, "Valid Uses of Psychology in the Rehabilitation of War Victims," *Mental Hygiene* 2, no. 4 (1918): 611–28.

55. Pearce Bailey, "Efficiency and Inefficiency: A Problem in Medicine," *Mental Hygiene* 1, no. 2 (1917): 196–210.

56. E. E. Southard, "The Movement for a Mental Hygiene of Industry," *Mental Hygiene* 4, no. 1 (1920): 43–64; "The Modern Specialist in Unrest: A Place for the Psychiatrist in Industry," *Mental Hygiene* 4, no. 3 (1920): 550–63; and "Trade Unionism and Temperament," *Mental Hygiene* 4, no. 2 (1920): 281–300. See also Mary C. Jarrett, "The Mental Health of Industry," *Mental Hygiene* 4, no. 4 (1920): 867–84, and Margaret J. Powers, "The Industrial Cost of the Psychopathic Employee," *Mental Hygiene* 4, no. 4 (1920): 932–39. The interest in industrial psychiatry, it should be noted, is coincident with the beginnings of the mental hygiene movement and much labor unrest. See, for example, Mary C. Jowett, "The Psychopathic Employee: A Problem of Industry," *Medicine and Surgery* 1 (Sept. 1917): 727–41, and E. E. Southard and K. C. Solomon, "Occupation Neuroses," in *Diseases of Occupations and Vocational Hygiene*, ed. George M. Kober and William C. Hansom (Philadelphia: Blakiston, 1916). John H. Ehrenreich provides an excellent discussion of mental hygiene in *The Altruistic Imagination*, 55–72.

57. Announcement for the Smith College School of Social Work, quoted in the reminiscence of Esther Cook, in *First Reunion, July 31–August 2, 1953* (Northampton, Mass.: Alumnae, Smith College School of Social Work, 1953), 17–18.

58. Ibid., 18–20.

59. Quoted in Lubove, *Professional Altruist*, 189.

60. Clarke A. Chambers, *Paul U. Kellogg and the* Survey: *Voices for Social Welfare and Social Justice* (Minneapolis: University of Minnesota Press, 1971).

61. John Haynes Holmes, "'Some Great Cause' and the Social Worker," *Survey*, July 8, 1911, 558–61; Thomas D. Eliot to the Editor, "A Social Workers' Party," *Survey*, June 10, 1911, 417–18.

62. "M." to the Editor, "Social Workishness," *Survey*, May 26, 1917, 199–200.

63. Edith S. Reider, "'Publicans and Sinners,'" *Survey*, Nov. 11, 1916, 138–40.

64. Ibid., 139. Of course, most of Reider's families were not "self-supporting."

65. *Survey*, Feb. 28, 1914, 661.

66. *Intolerance* was a 116-minute feature film directed by D. W. Griffith in 1926.

67. Frances C. L. Robbins, "Dressing the Part," *Survey*, Jan. 10, 1914, 415–16.

68. On the image of the "Lady Bountiful," see Kathleen D. McCarthy, *Noblesse Oblige, Charity, and Cultural Philanthropy in Chicago, 1849–1929* (Chicago: University of Chicago Press, 1982).

69. Sidney A. Teller to the Editor, "Is Social Work Essential?," *Survey*, Sept. 7, 1918, 646; Janet Hall to the Editor, "Essential Social Work," *Survey*, Oct. 19, 1918, 77.

70. *Salaried Positions for Men in Social Work*, booklet issued by the Department for Social Work of the Intercollegiate Bureau of Occupations and the Student Department of the International Committee of the YMCA, described in *Survey*, Mar. 28, 1914, 798; Katherine Bement Davis, cited in "Trained Social Workers Take Charge of New York City," *Survey*, Jan. 10, 1914, 430–33.

71. Gilbert Osofsky, *Harlem: The Making of a Ghetto* (New York: Harper and Row, 1963); U.S. Department of Commerce, Bureau of the Census, *Abstract of the Twelfth Census of the United States, 1900* (Washington, D.C.: Government Printing Office, 1902), 32, table 35, 101, table 80, and *Fourteenth Census: Population*, 676, table 1, 710, table 13; David Brody, *Steelworkers in America: The Nonunion Era* (Cambridge: Harvard University Press, 1960).

72. Bureau of the Census, *Fourteenth Census: Occupations*, 1160, table 2; Mary White Ovington, *Half a Man: The Status of the Negro in New York* (New York: Longmans, Green, 1911); Susan Brown, "Social Workers and Their Changing Attitudes towards Negroes during the Formative Years of the Profession" (M.S.W. thesis, Hunter College School of Social Work, 1968), chap. 5; Crocker, *Social Work and Social Order*, 3.

73. Crocker, *Social Work and Social Order*, 3–7, 68–93, 183–210; Lasch-Quinn, *Black Neighbors*.

74. "Negro Welfare Workers in Pittsburgh," *Survey*, Aug. 3, 1918, 513.

75. Ibid.

76. "Reform" was the byword, and feminist and settlement house historians have correctly noted that women social work leaders developed path-breaking social policy in health, safety, housing, sanitation, and so forth. But even in these nonindustrial settings, social workers' efforts to understand and, on occasion, to advocate the interests and positions of the working classes were often vitiated by assumptions that all class interests were ultimately consonant.

77. Elizabeth Kemper Adams, *Women Professional Workers: A Study Made for the Women's Educational and Industrial Union* (Chautauqua, N.Y.: Chautauqua Press, 1921). Adams discusses the debate over social work's professional status, noting that Vida Scudder referred to

it as a "transient profession" made necessary by present societal problems, and Cabot, *Social Work*, 157–62, referred to psychiatric social workers in Boston as "emerging professionals."

Chapter Two

1. Richard C. Cabot, *Social Work: Essays on the Meeting-Ground of Doctor and Social Worker* (Boston: Houghton Mifflin, 1919); *Notable American Women, 1607–1950*, vol. 3 (Cambridge: Harvard University Press, 1971), 152–54; Mary E. Richmond, *Friendly Visiting among the Poor: A Handbook for Charity Workers* (New York: Macmillan, 1899), and *Social Diagnosis* (New York: Russell Sage Foundation 1917).

2. See John H. Ehrenreich, *The Altruistic Imagination: A History of Social Work and Social Policy in the United States* (Ithaca: Cornell University Press, 1985), 64–70. I think Ehrenreich overstates the speed with which psychiatric social work took over the field.

3. Thomas W. Laquer, "Bodies, Details, and the Humanitarian Narrative," in *The New Cultural History*, ed. Lynn Hunt (Berkeley: University of California Press, 1989), 176–204. In practice, the distinction between casework and psychiatry was never so neat, as the medical model tended to emerge in all individual treatment.

4. Theodora L. Wilson, "Social Work from the Perspective of Fifty Years: A Personal History," *Smith College Studies in Social Work* 42, no. 2 (Feb. 1972): 102–3.

5. "Excerpts from Minutes and Reports, Tracing Purposes of Job Analysis Series," n.d., folder 43, AASW/NASWP. See also Louise Odencrantz, *The Social Worker in Family, Medical, and Psychiatric Social Work* (New York: Harper, 1929).

6. Odencrantz, *Social Worker*, 43–45.

7. James Edward Hagerty, *The Training of Social Workers* (New York: McGraw-Hill, 1931), 52–53, 194, cited in Stephanie J. Shaw, *What a Woman Ought to Be and to Do: Black Professional Women Workers during the Jim Crow Era* (Chicago: University of Chicago Press, 1996), 142.

8. Mary Palevsky, in *Proceedings*, Annual Session (1927), 178, NCJSS, YIVO. The classic statement on status and wealth is Thorstein Veblen, *The Theory of the Leisure Class* (1899; reprint, New York: Penguin, 1979).

9. See Harold Silver, "Social Work as I Found It," in *Proceedings*, Annual Session (1929), 198–206, NCJSS, YIVO. On routine in white-collar work, see Susan Porter Benson, *Counter Cultures: Saleswomen, Managers, and Customers in American Department Stores, 1890–1940* (Urbana: University of Illinois Press, 1986), and Sharon Hartman Strom, *Beyond the Typewriter: Gender, Class, and the Origins of Modern American Office Work, 1900–1930* (Urbana: University of Illinois Press, 1992).

10. Annual reports, 1921–29, box 1240, JBGA. See especially the 1923 report.

11. Strom, *Beyond the Typewriter*.

12. Annual reports, 1923, 1925, 1928, box 1240; 1930–31, box 1235, JBGA.

13. Before agreeing to undertake this study for the Rockefeller Foundation, Robert Lynd himself had been a minister. Secularization for the Lynds was the new materialism, the new dominance of business over social relations. See Robert S. Lynd and Helen Merrell Lynd, *Middletown: A Study in Modern American Culture* (1929; reprint, New York: Harcourt Brace Jovanovich, 1957), 496–502. See also Richard Wightman Fox, "Epitaph for Middletown," in

The Culture of Consumption: Critical Essays in American History, 1880–1980, ed. Richard Wightman Fox and T. J. Jackson Lears (New York: Pantheon, 1983), 101–42.

14. Lynd and Lynd, *Middletown*, 462–63.

15. Ibid., 465.

16. Ibid., 464–65.

17. Ibid., 22–23, 511, table 1.

18. Ibid., 466, n. 10.

19. See, for example, Michael B. Katz, *In the Shadow of the Poorhouse: A Social History of Welfare in America* (New York: Basic Books, 1986). The Salvation Army was a classic example of a proselytizing group. Such behavior was less overt in organizations such as the COS and the Children's Aid Society, but Catholics and Jews certainly felt it was justified by the need to maintain their own agencies for orphans and the indigent.

20. Warren I. Susman, *Culture as History: The Transformation of American Society in the Twentieth Century* (New York: Pantheon, 1984), 191–92.

21. For a discussion of the Jew and immigrant as alien, see David Feldman, *Englishmen and Jews: Social Relations and Political Culture, 1840–1914* (New Haven: Yale University Press, 1994).

22. E. Franklin Frazier, quoted in Tony Platt and Susan Chandler, "Constant Struggle: E. Franklin Frazier and Black Social Work in the 1920s," *Social Work* 33, no. 4 (July–Aug. 1988): 295.

23. Adam Clayton Powell, "The Church in Social Work," *Opportunity* 1, no. 1 (Jan. 1923): 15.

24. Shaw, *What a Woman Ought to Be*, 136–37, 170–79.

25. See Anzia Yezierska, *How I Found America: Collected Stories of Anzia Yezierska* (New York: Persea Books, 1991). The best example is probably her short story, "The Free Vacation House," 43–49, but biting critiques of the charities and of later social science also appear in "A Bed for the Night," 210–18; "The Lord Giveth," 233–44; "One Thousand Pages of Research," 279–84; and "A Window Full of Sky," 285–90. On the social distance of German Jewish women charity volunteers from eastern European relief recipients between 1890 and 1930, see Selma Berrol, "Class or Ethnicity: The Americanized German Jewish Woman and Her Middle Class Sisters in 1895," *Jewish Social Studies* 47 (Winter 1985): 21–32, and Charlotte Baum, Paula Hyman, and Sonya Michel, *The Jewish Woman in America* (New York: Dial Press, 1976), chaps. 2, 4, 6.

26. There was also considerable male backlash to women in all European societies. See Margaret Randolph Higgonet et al., eds., *Behind the Lines: Gender and the Two World Wars* (New Haven: Yale University Press, 1987).

27. See William M. Tuttle Jr., *Race Riot: Chicago in the Red Summer of 1919* (1970; reprint, New York: Atheneum, 1984), 3–31; Gilbert Osofsky, *Harlem: The Making of a Ghetto* (New York: Harper and Row, 1963), 17–23, 35–46. Dorothy Ross notes the ways in which the suppression of dissent in the 1920s affected social science, arguing that control was a central concern of the late Progressive Era that bloomed in the 1920s. See Dorothy Ross, *The Origins of American Social Science* (New York: Cambridge University Press, 1991), 311, 325–26. The impact of the repressive climate on black social work is seen in Atlanta, where E. Franklin Frazier was forced to resign as director of the Atlanta University School of Social Work in 1927. See Platt and Chandler, "Constant Struggle," 293–97.

28. The New York City Welfare Council still awaits its own historian. I presume that the size

of the city's welfare demands and the history of its strong ethnic financial support made ethnic and religious organizations unwilling to cede fiscal authority to a broader citywide agency.

29. U.S. Department of Commerce, Bureau of the Census, *Abstract of the Twelfth Census of the United States, 1900* (Washington, D.C.: Government Printing Office, 1902), 32, table 35, 101, table 80; Arthur A. Goren, *New York's Jews and the Quest for Community: The Kehillah Experiment, 1908–1922* (New York: Columbia University Press, 1970), 13–17. For data on crowded conditions on the Lower East Side at the end of the century, see David C. Hammack, *Power and Society: Greater New York at the Turn of the Century* (New York: Columbia University Press, 1987), 89–100. Crime and prostitution were threats to the status some had achieved and all sought, a point reiterated in a recent article by Seth Korelitz, "'A Magnificent Piece of Work': The Americanization of the National Council of Jewish Women," *American Jewish History* 83, no. 3 (1995): 200.

30. Theodore A. Bingham, quoted in "Foreign Criminals in New York," *North American Review*, Sept. 1908, cited in Goren, *New York's Jews*, 25.

31. Poverty often made prostitution a "best bad" choice for the poor, whereas the white slave trade narrative provided the affluent with a more compelling melodrama than poverty (and the low wages German Jewish factory owners paid). See Baum, Hyman, and Michel, *Jewish Woman in America*, 170–75.

32. "Reply of the Amsterdam Chamber of the West India Company to Peter Stuyvesant," quoted in Beth Wenger, "Ethnic Community in Economic Crisis: New York Jews and the Great Depression" (Ph.D. diss., Yale University, 1992), 173–74.

33. Goren, *New York's Jews*, 7–13.

34. Hyman Bogen, *The Luckiest Orphans: A History of the Hebrew Orphan Asylum of New York* (Urbana: University of Illinois Press, 1992), 1–12. Sephardic Jews first came to New York in the sixteenth century as Marianos, Jews from Spain via Dutch Brazil who outwardly practiced Christianity to avoid persecution.

35. For the case of London and an extended discussion of the problem of Jewish identity as it vied with the Jewish immigrant's adoption of an English national identity and an identity as working class, see Feldman, *Englishmen and Jews*.

36. U.S. Department of Commerce, Bureau of the Census, *Thirteenth Census of the United States: Population, 1910*, vol. 2 (Washington, D.C.: Government Printing Office, 1910), 573, table 8.

37. Daniel Soyer, *Jewish Immigrant Associations and American Identity in New York, 1880–1939* (Cambridge: Harvard University Press, 1997); Shelly Tenenbaum, *A Credit to Their Community: Jewish Loan Societies in the United States, 1880–1945* (Detroit: Wayne State University Press, 1993); Goren, *New York's Jews*, 47–48.

38. Bogen, *The Luckiest Orphans*, 68–72; annual report, 1916, UHC box 1240, JBGA. For a fuller picture of Jewish loan practices at the time, see Tenenbaum, *Credit to Their Community*. See also Beth S. Wenger, "Jewish Women and Voluntarism: Beyond the Myth of Enablers," *American Jewish History* 79, no. 1 (1989): 16–36, and Baum, Hyman, and Michel, *Jewish Woman in America*, 32–34.

39. Annual reports, 1902–16, box 1240, JPASA.

40. Annual reports, 1909, 1915, "By-Laws," Mar. 1915, box 1240, JPASA.

41. Anzia Yezierska, *Children of Loneliness: Stories of Immigrant Life in America* (New York: Funk and Wagnalls, 1923). One of these stories is discussed in chapter 3.

42. Goren, *New York's Jews*, 75–76.

43. Annual reports, 1912, 1913, 1915, box 1240, JPASA.

44. Minutes, Board of Trustees, Apr. 27, 1917, box 1085, FJPA.

45. Annual report, 1921, box 1240, JBGA.

46. Ibid.

47. Minutes, Board of Directors, May 9, 1921, box 1921, FJPA.

48. Cyrus Adler, *Jacob H. Schiff: His Life and Letters* (Garden City, N.Y.: Doubleday, 1928), 389, 391–92; Beryl William Epstein, *Lillian Wald, Angel of Henry Street* (New York: J. Messner, 1948).

49. Morris D. Waldman, quoted in Goren, *New York's Jews*, 16.

50. Baum, Hyman, and Michel, *Jewish Woman in America*, 29. Other recent studies emphasize work in the public realm itself as evidence of an enlarged woman's role. See Wenger, "Jewish Women and Voluntarism," and Korelitz, " 'A Magnificent Piece of Work,' " 177–203.

51. Roy Lubove, *The Professional Altruist: The Emergence of Social Work as a Career* (Cambridge: Harvard University Press, 1965); John H. Ehrenreich, *Altruistic Imagination*; Clarke A. Chambers, *Seedtime of Reform: American Social Service and Social Action, 1918–1933* (Minneapolis: University of Minnesota Press, 1963); James Leiby, *A History of Social Welfare and Social Work in the United States* (New York: Columbia University Press, 1978).

52. Annual reports, 1918, 1919, box 1240, JPASA.

53. Ruth J. Abram, ed., *Send Us a Lady Physician: Women Doctors in America, 1835–1920* (New York: Norton, 1985).

54. Annual reports, 1925, 1928, 1929, box 1240, JBGA.

55. Annual report, 1921, box 1240, JBGA. For medical views on the hypersexuality of girls, see Elizabeth Lunbeck, *The Psychiatric Persuasion: Knowledge, Gender, and Power in Modern America* (Princeton: Princeton University Press, 1994).

56. Annual report, 1924, box 1240, JBGA.

57. Annual reports, 1923, 1929, box 1240, JBGA.

58. Annual reports, 1921, 1923, 1929, box 1240, JBGA.

59. Louis M. Cahn, "The Lay Person and Professional Worker in Social Service," in *Proceedings*, Annual Session (1926), 2–9, NCJSS, YIVO.

60. On the ability of these women to afford domestic help, see Berrol, "Class or Ethnicity," 26–28.

61. Mrs. Abraham N. Davis, "Function of the Volunteer and Some Practical Applications in Family Case Work," in *Proceedings*, Annual Session (1929), 103–5, NCJSS, YIVO, divides volunteers into three types: board or committee members, clerical aides, and semiprofessionals with some training who work more than half time but are not paid. She sees the burden of making the volunteer valuable as resting on the paid professional.

62. Annual reports, 1924, 1928, box 1240, JBGA.

63. Annual reports, 1918, 1919, box 1240, JPASA.

64. Miscellaneous papers, 1937, Records, Clippings, 1927–50, NCJSS, YIVO.

65. Rabbi Abba Hillel Silver, in *Proceedings*, Annual Session (1926), 31, NCJSS, YIVO.

66. Judge Jacob M. Moses, in *Proceedings*, Annual Session (1923), 207–18, NCJSS, YIVO.

67. Ibid., 214–15, 233–34.

68. Ibid.

69. Ibid., 233–41. Agencies from St. Louis and Portland also noted that they had small Jewish labor movements.

70. William M. Leiserson, in *Proceedings*, Annual Session (1928), 162–65, Transfile 19/66a, NCJCS, YIVO.

71. Steve Fraser, "Dress Rehearsal for the New Deal: Shop-Floor Insurgents, Political Elites, and Industrial Democracy in the Amalgamated Clothing Workers," in *Working-Class America: Labor, Community, and American Society*, ed. Michael H. Frisch and Daniel J. Walkowitz (Urbana: University of Illinois Press, 1983), 212.

72. Sidney Hillman, in *Proceedings*, Annual Session (1928), 138–49, Transfile 19/66A, NCJCS, YIVO.

73. Solomon Lowenstein, in ibid., 162–65.

74. Bruno Lasker, in *Proceedings*, Annual Session (1928), 242, NCJSS, YIVO.

75. William Hodson, "Social Workers and Politics," *Survey*, Nov. 15, 1929, 199.

76. Staff of the Family Service Society, Columbus, Ohio, to Frank H. Howe, Oct. 2, 1923, Grievance Procedure Committee, folder 33, AASW/NASWP.

77. Petition from staff to Board of Managers, Family Service Society, Columbus, Ohio, Feb. 21, 1924, Grievance Procedure Committee, folder 33, AASW/NASWP.

78. "Report on the Break in Working Relations of the Community Fund and Family Service Society of Columbus, Ohio, and on Efforts at Securing a New Working Agreement," ca. May 1926, Grievance Procedure Committee, folder 33, AASW/NASWP.

79. Ibid.

80. Ibid.; J. H. Frantz to Frank H. Howe, Sept. 8, 1925, Grievance Procedure Committee, folder 33, AASW/NASWP; Columbus, Ohio, Family Service Society staff petition, Oct. 5, 1925, Grievance Procedure Committee, folder 33, AASW/NASWP.

81. Walter M. West to Philip Klein, Oct. 7, 1925, Grievance Procedure Committee, folder 33, AASW/NASWP.

82. Ibid.

83. Lucille K. Corbett et al. to Howard R. Knight, Nov. 6, 1925, Grievance Procedure Committee, folder 33, AASW/NASWP; Philip Klein and William Hodson, "Memorandum of Suggestions and Questions from the American Association of Social Workers in Regard to the Controversy That Has Arisen in Columbus between the Family Service Society and the Community Fund," n.d., Grievance Procedure Committee, folder 31, AASW/NASWP, reprinted in *Compass*, Dec. 1925, 1–2.

84. "Report on the Break"; "Report of the Sub-Committee of the American Association of Social Workers on the Break in the Working Relations between the Community Fund and the Family Service Society of Columbus, Ohio," ca. Dec. 1926, Grievance Procedure Committee, folder 33, AASW/NASWP. There are hints that the "personality" conflict may, in fact, have been about gender, but a confidential letter from the FSS president to Klein singled out the head of the fund as "not in the habit of cooperating." See Howard R. Knight to Philip Klein, Dec. 3, 1925, Grievance Procedure Committee, folder 33, AASW/NASWP.

85. Knight to Klein, Dec. 3, 1925; "Report of the Sub-Committee."

86. Grievants first had to appeal to local chapter committees, then if they were dissatisfied with the result, they could appeal to the national committee. See Grievance Procedure Committee, 1926–39, folder 31, AASW/NASWP.

Chapter Three

1. Hazel Newton, "Miss Case-Worker Goes Scientific," *Survey*, Jan. 15, 1930, 464–65. Newton had worked previously with Boston Italian immigrant families.

2. The gendered character of science is discussed in Margaret Rossiter, *Women Scientists in America: Struggles and Strategies to 1940* (Baltimore: Johns Hopkins University Press, 1982). Further tensions for women implicit in the professional model are analyzed in Nancy F. Cott, *The Grounding of Modern Feminism* (New Haven: Yale University Press, 1987); Joyce Antler, "The Educated Woman and Professionalization: The Struggle for a New Feminine Identity, 1890–1920" (Ph.D. diss., State University of New York at Stony Brook, 1977); Penina Migdal Glazer and Miriam Slater, *Unequal Colleagues: The Entrance of Women into the Professions* (New Brunswick: Rutgers University Press, 1987); Regina G. Kunzel, "The Professionalization of Benevolence: Evangelicals and Social Workers in the Florence Crittenton Homes, 1915 to 1945," *Journal of Social History* 22, no. 1 (Fall 1988): 21–43; Dee Garrison, *Apostles of Culture: The Public Librarian and American Society, 1876–1920* (New York: Free Press, 1976); and Clarke A. Chambers, "Women in the Creation of the Profession of Social Work," *Social Service Review* 59 (Mar. 1986): 1–33.

3. See prologue, n. 42.

4. Arthur Dunham oral history, conducted by Vida S. Greyson, 1977–81, NASWOH.

5. Harriet M. Bartlett oral history, conducted by Vida S. Greyson, 1977–81, NASWOH; Helen Harris Perlman oral history, conducted by Vida S. Greyson, 1977–81, NASWOH.

6. Beth S. Wenger, "Jewish Women and Voluntarism: Beyond the Myth of Enablers," *American Jewish History* 79, no. 1 (1989): 30.

7. See the masthead of the *Compass*, the monthly publication of the AASW (1921–48).

8. Reflecting the new emphasis on specialization and professionalization, both medical (hospital) and psychiatric social workers as well as visiting teachers organized their own associations between 1918 and 1926. The Milford Conference report suggested a common basis for organization and professional development. See AASW, *Social Case Work, Generic and Specific—An Outline: A Report of the Milford Conference*, Studies in the Practice of Social Work, no. 2 (New York: AASW, 1931). Barbara Melosh notes that the American Nursing Association had "low membership" too, suggesting that the AASW's enrollment of 15–20 percent of all social workers was in line with that of other feminized professions. See Barbara Melosh, *The Physician's Hand: Nurses and Nursing in the Twentieth Century* (Philadelphia: Temple University Press, 1982), 98.

9. On women in social work, see the citations in Chambers, "Women in the Creation of the Profession of Social Work." On women more generally, see Christine Stansell, *City of Women: Sex and Class in New York, 1789–1860* (New York: Knopf, 1986); Ava Baron, "Woman's 'Place' in Capitalist Production: A Study of Class Relations in the Nineteenth Century Printing Industry" (Ph.D. diss., New York University, 1981); Alice Kessler-Harris, *Out to Work: A History of Wage-Earning Women in the United States* (New York: Oxford University Press, 1982); Patricia A. Cooper, *Always a Cigarmaker: Men, Women, and Work Culture in American Cigar Factories, 1900–1919* (Urbana: University of Illinois Press, 1987); Ruth Milkman, *Gender at Work: The Dynamics of Job Segregation by Sex during World War II* (Urbana: University of Illinois Press, 1986); and Leslie Woodcock Tentler, *Wage-Earning Women: Industrial Work and Family Life in the United States, 1900–1930* (New York: Oxford University Press, 1979).

10. Arlien Johnson oral history, conducted by Vida S. Greyson, 1977–81, NASWOH.

11. I am indebted to Chambers, "Women in the Creation of the Profession of Social Work," 19, for this discussion. See also Susan Ware, *Partner and I: Molly Dewson, Feminism, and New Deal Politics* (New Haven: Yale University Press, 1987).

12. Theodora L. Wilson, "Social Work from the Perspective of Fifty Years: A Personal History," *Smith College Studies in Social Work* 42, no. 2 (Feb. 1972): 100.

13. Barbara J. Balliet, "'What Shall We Do with Our Daughters?': Middle-Class Women's Ideas about Work, 1840–1920" (Ph.D. diss., New York University, 1988). Balliet's women, from 1900 to 1920, were not daughters of immigrants; by the 1920s, they were more likely to be. Unlike the previous generation of women who filled the ranks of settlement house workers, most of these women would see spinsterhood as an impoverished and isolated existence. See, for example, Anzia Yezierska, *Bread Givers: A Novel* (1925; reprint, New York: Persea Books, 1975); Meredith Tax, *Rivington Street* (New York: Morrow, 1982), and *Union Square* (New York: Morrow, 1988); and Elizabeth Ewen, *Immigrant Women in the Land of Dollars: Life and Culture on the Lower East Side, 1890–1925* (New York: Monthly Review Press, 1985). On the demands of the double day, see Stephanie J. Shaw, *What a Woman Ought to Be and to Do: Black Professional Women Workers during the Jim Crow Era* (Chicago: University of Chicago Press, 1996), chap. 4.

14. The seventeen essays by professional women in *The Nation* are reprinted in Elaine Showalter, ed., *These Modern Women: Autobiographical Essays from the Twenties* (Old Westbury, N.Y.: Feminist Press, 1978). See also Joyce Antler, *Lucy Sprague Mitchell: The Making of a Modern Woman* (New Haven: Yale University Press, 1987; Estelle B. Freedman, "'The New Woman': Changing Views of Women in the 1920s," *Journal of American History* 61, no. 2 (1974): 372–93; Cott, *Modern Feminism*, 183; Robert W. Smuts, *Women and Work in America* (New York: Columbia University Press, 1959), 142–43; and Barbara M. Solomon, *In the Company of Educated Women* (New Haven: Yale University Press, 1985), 182–83, which cites a Radcliffe Alumnae Association survey in 1928 in which 50 percent of the 2,000 respondents hoped it was possible to combine marriage and work. A 1926 survey of women professionals conducted by the Bureau of Vocational Information concluded that they were an "advance guard" of working wives. See Virginia MacMakin Collier, *Marriage and Careers: A Study of One Hundred Women Who Are Mothers, Homemakers, and Professional Workers* (New York: Channel Bookshop, 1926). Two studies for the Russell Sage Foundation —Louise Odencrantz, *The Social Worker in Family, Medical, and Psychiatric Social Work* (New York: Harper, 1929), 87, and Margaretta A. Williamson, *The Social Worker in Child Care and Protection* (New York: Harper, 1931), 389—cite marriage as a reason for turnover and as a desirable situation for child care workers. Data for 1950 is found in BLS, *Social Workers in 1950: A Report on the Study of Salaries and Working Conditions in Social Work—Spring 1950* (New York: AASW, 1952), 42.

15. Andrew R. Heinze, *Adapting to Abundance: Jewish Immigrants, Mass Consumption, and the Search for American Identity* (New York: Columbia University Press, 1990).

16. James Walker Papers, DPW, 1926, folder 3, MACNY. Data on the ethnicity of social workers does not exist, but oral histories of caseworkers and staff reports from the FJP also suggest the entry of a new generation of social workers by the late 1920s. FJP leaders were German Jews whose wives had worked for the UHC; the new caseworkers were of eastern European background. See, for example, Martha K. Selig oral history, conducted by Judy E. Tenney, Feb. 9, 22, 1982, FJPOH. See also Cott, *Modern Feminism*, 217–19.

17. Louis M. Cahn, "The Lay Person and Professional Worker in Social Service," in *Proceedings*, Annual Session (1926), 2–9, NCJSS, YIVO. Women's nurturing roles are emphasized in most Progressive Era literature. See, for example, WEIU, Department of Research, *Home and School Visiting as a Vocation for Women* (Boston: WEIU, 1911), *Organizing Charity as a Vocation for Women* (Boston: WEIU, 1912), *Settlement Work as a Vocation for Women* (Boston: WEIU, 1912), *Social Service for Children as a Vocation for Women* (Boston: WEIU, 1912), and *Studies in Economic Relations of Women*, vol. 1, pt. 2 (Boston: WEIU, 1914); and Elizabeth Kemper Adams, *Women Professional Workers: A Study Made for the Women's Educational and Industrial Union* (Chautauqua, N.Y.: Chautauqua Press, 1921).

18. See Richard C. Cabot, *Social Work: Essays on the Meeting-Ground of Doctor and Social Worker* (Boston: Houghton Mifflin, 1919), and Mary C. Jarrett, "Psychiatric Social Work," *Mental Hygiene* 2, no. 2 (1918): 283–90.

19. Winifred D. Wandersee, *Women's Work and Family Values, 1920–1940* (Cambridge: Harvard University Press, 1981), 57; Jessica B. Peixotto, "Campus Standards of Living," *Survey Midmonthly*, Apr. 15, 1929, 119.

20. Florence Jacobs Edmonds oral history, 1980, BWOHP.

21. Shaw, *What a Woman Ought to Be*, chap. 4.

22. Odencrantz, *Social Worker*, 55, notes that 67 percent of 268 family caseworkers reported they had attended some college. Odencrantz's survey found that "a large majority" had some college education. According to Solomon, *Educated Women*, the percentage of all women who had attended college increased from 7.6 to 10.5 percent over the decade.

23. Annual reports, 1923, 1925, box 1240, JBGA. See also Nathan G. Hale Jr., *Freud and the Americans: The Beginnings of Psychoanalysis in the United States, 1876–1917* (New York: Oxford University Press, 1971) and *The Rise and Crisis of Psychoanalysis in America* (New York: Oxford University Press, 1995).

24. See annual report, 1925, box 1240, JBGA. The first good aggregate national data from which one can extrapolate occupational mobility in social work is from the 1940s. By the end of the decade, only about a fifth of the social workers were male, and most of them were either new workers in their twenties or married men over forty. See BLS, *Social Workers in 1950*.

25. Susan Porter Benson, "The 1920s through the Looking Glass of Gender: A Response to David Montgomery," *International Labor and Working Class History* 32 (Fall 1987): 31–38. Benson most forcefully has urged labor historians to integrate the history of twentieth-century labor with that of consumption. See also Kathy Peiss, *Cheap Amusements: Working Women and Leisure in Turn-of-the-Century New York* (Philadelphia: Temple University Press, 1986). John F. Kasson, *Amusing the Millions: Coney Island at the Turn of the Century* (New York: Hill and Wang, 1978), also demonstrates the appeal of amusement parks for the middle and working classes of the city.

26. The work culture is described in Susan Porter Benson, *Counter Cultures: Saleswomen, Managers, and Customers in American Department Stores, 1890–1940* (Urbana: University of Illinois Press, 1986), and Melosh, *Physician's Hand*. For a good recent survey of the standard-of-living literature, see Daniel Horowitz, *The Morality of Spending: Attitudes toward the Consumer Society in America, 1875–1940* (Baltimore: Johns Hopkins University Press, 1985), and Wandersee, *Women's Work*.

27. Most available information is about teachers and social workers. The most systematic survey of social workers' backgrounds is from the generation who began work in the

settlements, as described in Allen F. Davis, *Spearheads for Reform: The Social Settlements and the Progressive Movement, 1890–1914* (New York: Oxford University Press, 1967), 33–37.

28. John Mitchell, president of the United Mine Workers, identified the new consumer standard early in the century as the American "ideal": a "comfortable house of a least six rooms . . . , a bathroom, good sanitary plumbing, a parlor, dining-room, pictures, books, and furniture with which to make the home bright, comfortable and attractive for [the worker and] his family." See John Mitchell, *Organized Labor* (Philadelphia, 1903), 116, quoted in Ron Rothbart, "Work, Family, and Protest: Immigrant Labor in the Steel, Meat-packing, and Anthracite Industries, 1880–1920" (Ph.D. diss., University of California at Berkeley, 1988). Professional standards during the 1920s are described in Jessica B. Peixotto, *Getting and Spending at the Professional Standard of Living: A Study in the Costs of Living an Academic Life* (New York: Macmillan, 1927), and "Campus Standards of Living," 117–19. See also Wandersee, *Women's Work*, 1–13.

29. Elizabeth Healy, "Get Your Man," *Survey*, May 15, 1930, 202–5, 207.

30. Ralph G. Hurlin, "Social Worker Salaries," *Survey*, Feb. 15, 1926, 557–58. Ralph G. Hurlin, "Differences between Jewish and Non-Jewish Family Case-Work Agencies," in *Proceedings*, Annual Session (1930), 125–34, NCJSS, YIVO, finds salaries to be slightly higher in the Jewish agencies. A 1929 survey by the Philadelphia Federation of Jewish Philanthropies of twenty-nine agencies in various cities finds them lower. See Pauline Gollub, "Stabilizing Factors in the Profession of Social Work," in *Proceedings* Annual Session (1932), 195–97, NCJSS, YIVO. Poor conditions are described in E. Trotzkey, "The Recruiting and Training of Child Care Workers," in *Proceedings*, Annual Session (1924), 198–223, NCJSS, YIVO, and Odencrantz, *Social Worker*. Social workers and executives pressed to keep caseworker salaries commensurate with those of teachers. See, for example, minutes, Executive Board, Mar. 22, 1926, Mar. 19, 1928, box 1086, FJPA. Solomon Lowenstein, president of the FJP, attributed the slightly higher wages of teachers to their agitation. See Solomon Lowenstein, in *Proceedings*, Annual Session (1928), Transfile 19/66A, NCJCS, YIVO.

31. Jürgen Kocka, *White Collar Workers in America, 1890–1940: A Social-Political History in International Perspective*, trans. Maura Kealey (Beverly Hills, Calif.: Sage Publications, 1980), 168–69; Trotzkey, "Recruiting and Training of Child Care Workers"; Hurlin, "Social Worker Salaries"; Esther Lucile Brown, *Social Work as a Profession* (New York: Russell Sage Foundation, 1935), 167–80.

32. Shaw, *What a Woman Ought to Be*, 149.

33. Peixotto, "Campus Standards of Living," 119.

34. Brown, *Social Work as a Profession*, 168. For professional standards during the 1920s, see Peixotto, *Getting and Spending*, 252–59, and "Campus Standards of Living"; and Wandersee, *Women's Work*. A report of the Baltimore study appeared in Paul T. Beisser, "The Worthy Poor Social Worker," *Survey*, Aug. 15, 1928, 518. After the war, living costs rose dramatically, but they leveled off in 1923 until they began their depression-related decline in 1929. See National Industrial Conference Board, *The Cost of Living in the United States, 1914–1930* (New York: National Industrial Conference Board, 1931).

35. See T. J. Jackson Lears, *No Place of Grace: Antimodernism and the Transformation of American Culture, 1880–1920* (New York: Pantheon Books, 1981), and the essays in Richard Wightman Fox and T. J. Jackson Lears, eds., *The Culture of Consumption: Critical Essays in American History, 1880–1930* (New York: Pantheon, 1983).

36. There is a substantial body of recent writing on gender in popular representation.

Some of the literature is summarized by Lynn Hunt in her introduction to *The New Cultural History*, ed. Lynn Hunt (Berkeley: University of California Press, 1989). See also Joan Wallach Scott, *Gender and the Politics of History* (New York: Columbia University Press, 1988). Melosh, *Physician's Hand*, 59–63, imaginatively uses nurse fiction to talk about work and identity in that field.

37. The sixth edition of the *Fiction Catalogue* (New York: H. W. Wilson, 1950), which covers books published in American literature in the 1940s, for example, cites 111 American novels about teachers and 38 about nurses; only 21 focus on social workers. The seventh edition in 1961 covers the 1950s and contains similar ratios: teachers, nurses, and social workers figure in 88, 19, and 5 novels, respectively. Most of the social worker novels depict women aiding immigrant communities. There is no comparable list of books in which social workers play a secondary role, although Anzia Yezierska stories often fit into that category.

38. See Robert W. Snyder, *The Voice of the City: Vaudeville and Popular Culture in New York* (New York: Oxford University Press, 1989); Molly Haskell, *From Reverence to Rape: The Treatment of Women in the Movies* (New York: Holt, Rinehart, and Winston, 1974), chap. 2; Robert Sklar, *Movie-Made America: A Cultural History of American Movies* (New York: Vintage, 1975); Lary May, *Screening Out the Past: The Birth of Mass Culture and the Motion Picture Industry* (New York: Oxford University Press, 1980); Kasson, *Amusing the Millions*; Lewis A. Erenberg, *Steppin' Out: New York Nightlife and the Transformation of American Culture, 1890–1930* (Westport, Conn.: Greenwood Press, 1981); and Peiss, *Cheap Amusements*.

39. Samples can be found in Odencrantz, *Social Worker*, 136–43.

40. Louise Levitas Henrikson, *Anzia Yezierska: A Writer's Life* (New Brunswick: Rutgers University Press, 1988), 98, 157–84; Anzia Yezierska, *How I Found America: Collected Stories of Anzia Yezierska* (New York: Persea Books, 1991), and *Hungry Hearts* (Boston: Houghton Mifflin, 1920).

41. Anzia Yezierska, "The Lord Giveth," in *Children of Loneliness: Stories of Immigrant Life in America* (New York: Funk and Wagnalls, 1923), 125–41.

42. *Fiction Catalogue*, 7th ed. (1961), 220. Thanks to Barbara Melosh for her observations on Sinclair Lewis's confused and hostile portrait of gender in *Ann Vickers* (New York: Grosset and Dunlap, 1933).

43. Vickers does find some "earnest" workers, but the institutions they serve are hopelessly burdened by bureaucracy, are overrun with scoundrels, and "smelled of the sour smell of charity." Lewis, *Ann Vickers*, 236–37.

44. Ibid., 237.

45. Ibid., chaps. 23–29.

46. "We Get into the Movies—and Out," *Compass* 8, no. 7 (Apr. 1927): 1–3.

47. Ibid.; "What the Public Wants," *Compass* 11, no. 9 (May 1930): 6.

48. Adams, *Women Professional Workers*, 157–59; William Hodson, "Is Social Work Professional?: A Re-examination of the Question," in *Proceedings*, Annual Session (1925), 629–36, NCJSS, YIVO.

49. Cott, *Modern Feminism*, 237.

50. Traditionally, one of the major objectives of professionalism has been to control entry into a field. The large numbers of untrained relief workers who entered social work with the rise of state and federal New Deal programs after 1933 were a logical target of the stricter

entrance requirements. Although these new rules did block AASW membership for many of these public employees, the AASW had developed the new regulations prior to this era.

51. Lewis Miriam, "Report on Salary Schedules of Social Agencies," Nov. 15, 1932, Job Analysis Committee, Salary Data, 1931–34, folder 44, AASW/NASWP.

52. Many other letters, poems, and essays in *Survey* reflect the tensions over consumption, status, and work seen in these portraits, but none with quite the same dramatic flair and poignancy. Gertrude Springer's "Miss Bailey" essays, which appeared in *Survey* three years later, offer an interesting comparison with the stories recounted here. Written in the heart of the depression, the essays are not self-reflective. "Miss Bailey" variously gives practical advice to untrained relief workers laboring within the new federal and state bureaucracies and justifies relief workers owning their own cars as perhaps their only escape from relentless poverty. See, for example, Gertrude Springer, "When a Client Has a Car," *Survey*, Mar. 1933, 103–4.

53. Walker Papers, DPW, 1926, folder 3, MACNY.

54. The NASW's selection of Arthur Dunham as one of the eight social work leaders to be interviewed for its oral history of the profession is indicative of his prominence in the field. See Dunham oral history.

55. Esther S. Dunham, "Scatter-Brained Sally," *Survey*, July 15, 1930, 362–63.

56. Healy, "Get Your Man," 202–3, 207.

57. Karl de Schweinitz was a distinguished social work historian who is best known for his study of the origins of the English Poor Law: *England's Road to Social Security, from the Statute of Laborers in 1349 to the Beveridge Report of 1942* (Philadelphia: University of Pennsylvania Press, 1943).

58. Dorothea de Schweinitz, "Where Is He?," *Survey*, Sept. 15, 1930, 522–23.

59. *American Jewess*, quoted in Selma Berrol, "Class or Ethnicity: The Americanized German Jewish Woman and Her Middle Class Sisters in 1895," *Jewish Social Studies* 47 (Winter 1985): 27. See also Charlotte Baum, Paula Hyman, and Sonya Michel, *The Jewish Woman in America* (New York: Dial Press, 1976), 33–34.

60. Inabel Burns Lindsay oral history, 1977, EWOHP. Lindsay does not tell us the year she was married. She was born in 1900 and intimates that she was married the year before the St. Louis race riot in 1919.

61. See Sonia Ginsberg, "Experiences in Protective Organization for Social Workers in New York City," in *Proceedings*, Annual Session (1933), 116–19, NCJSS, YIVO, and John Earl Haynes, "The 'Rank and File Movement' in Private Social Work," *Labor History* 16, no. 1 (Winter 1975): 78–98. See also JFP and the autobiographical account by Jacob Fisher, who was editor of the Rank-and-File's journal, *Social Work Today* (1934–42): *The Response of Social Work to the Depression* (Boston: G. K. Hall, 1980). As many as 400 social workers and affiliated clerical workers may have been active in Workers Councils in New York City alone by the late 1920s, most of whom were Jewish workers employed in Jewish agencies.

62. Miss Levy and the chairman, in *Proceedings*, Annual Session (1923), 195–97, NCJSS, YIVO.

63. Moses W. Beckelman, "Protective Aspects of the Program of the American Association of Social Workers," in *Proceedings*, Annual Session (1933), 113–16, NCJSS, YIVO; Jacob Fisher, "Feasibility of a National Protective Organization for Social Workers," in *Proceedings*, Annual Session (1923), 119–23, NCJSS, YIVO.

64. The importance of these groups extends beyond their number, which was no more

than several hundred. They established an alternative typology that would emerge full-blown in the 1930s as a trade union tradition in social work. By 1926, there were two or three Workers' Councils in New York City Jewish social service. One was at the JBG, and the others seem to have been at the other large Jewish casework agencies providing child and family care.

65. Classic social welfare histories of this era (see "Social Work and the Welfare State" in the bibliographical essay) make no mention of the Workers' Councils. John H. Ehrenreich, *The Altruistic Imagination: A History of Social Work and Social Policy in the United States* (Ithaca: Cornell University Press, 1985), 110, gives them one sentence. Fisher, in *Response of Social Work*, recounts his leadership of the left-wing movement in the 1930s, minimizing the role of the Workers' Councils. They were not radical, but they did provide a network and an organizational base for the discussion groups that preceded the unions. See also Leslie Leighninger, *Social Work: Search for Identity* (New York: Greenwood Press, 1987), chaps. 2–5; Leslie B. Alexander, "Organizing the Professional Social Worker: Union Development in Voluntary Social Work, 1930–1950" (Ph.D. diss., Bryn Mawr College, 1976); Haynes, "'Rank and File Movement'"; and John C. Goldner, "Resolution of Major Crisis Situations in the New York City Department of Welfare, 1934–1949" (M.S.W. thesis, New York School of Social Work, 1949), Columbia University Library of Social Work, New York, N.Y.

66. Pearl Ortenberg and Frieda Fine, "Experiences in Participation," in *Proceedings*, Annual Session (1932), 201, NCJSS, YIVO. Ortenberg and Fine write that the Workers' Council "gained new life" in 1929 when a new JBG executive director opposed to the organization imposed a new "standard of work."

67. Beckelman, "Protective Aspects," 113; Ortenberg and Fine, "Experiences in Participation," 199–202; minutes, Executive Committee, Apr. 23, 1926, Apr. 18, 1929, JBGA; minutes, Central Council, May 24, 1930, JBGA.

68. Sonia Ginsberg, "Experiences in Protective Organization," 116–19.

69. Trade union interest among social workers could be seen at the 1928 NCJSS annual meeting, at which Sidney Hillman and a socialist economist from Antioch College, William M. Leiserson, discussed the relationship between social workers, social work, and trade unionism at a plenary luncheon. See *Proceedings*, Annual Session (1928), NCJSS, YIVO.

70. Cott, *Modern Feminism*; Van Gosse, "'To Organize in Every Neighborhood, in Every Home': The Gender Politics of the American Communists between the Wars," *Radical History Review* 50 (Spring 1991): 109–41.

71. Selig oral history; Elizabeth K. Radinsky oral history, conducted by Hannah K. Broder, Nov. 4, 1982, FJPOH; Francis Beatman oral history, conducted by Sally Pearce, Jan. 22, 1982, FJPOH; Sanford Solender oral history, conducted by Nikki Tanner, June–Aug. 1982, FJPOH.

72. For example, see chapter 7, where Martha K. Selig, a caseworker and supervisor at the JCCA in the 1930s, remembers how she manipulated situations to counter gender bias on the job.

Chapter Four

1. U.S. Department of Commerce, Bureau of the Census, *Sixteenth Census of the United States, 1940: Population, The Labor Force (Sample Statistics), Employment and Personal Characteristics* (Washington, D.C.: Government Printing Office, 1943).

2. U.S. Department of Commerce, Bureau of the Census, *Abstract of the Fifteenth Census, 1930* (Washington, D.C.: Government Printing Office, 1932), 357–59, and *Sixteenth Census of the United States: Comparative Occupational Statistics for the United States, 1870–1940* (Washington, D.C.: Government Printing Office, 1943), 78. The census enumeration for 1940 included 2,880 nonwhite social workers.

3. Susan Ware, "Women and the New Deal," in *Fifty Years Later: The New Deal Evaluated*, ed. Harvard Sitkoff (New York: Knopf, 1985), 113–32.

4. David M. Schneider and Albert Deutsch, *The History of Public Welfare in New York State, 1867–1940* (Chicago: University of Chicago Press, 1941), 332.

5. Jacob Fisher, "Feasibility of a National Protective Organization for Social Workers," in *Proceedings*, Annual Session (1933), 119–24, NCJSS, YIVO.

6. Edgar B. Shaw to Frank B. Taylor, June 28, 1933, James Walker Papers, Letters, box 635, MACNY.

7. Frank J. Taylor to Jay T. Fox, June 29, 1933, Walker Papers, Letters, box 635, MACNY.

8. Irwin Rosen, "The Economic Position of Jewish Youth," *Jewish Social Service Quarterly* 13, no. 1 (1936): 61–78, NCJSS, YIVO.

9. Lester B. Granger, "Harlem Comes of Age," *Social Work Today* 4 (May 1937): 9. Rick Spano reminded me of this reference. See Rick Spano, *The Rank and File Movement in Social Work* (Washington, D.C.: University Press of America, 1982), 234.

10. Leah Weiss (pseudonym) oral history, conducted by the author and Adina Back, Feb. 6, 1987, in author's possession. See also Sophie Grossman (pseudonym) oral history, conducted by the author and Adina Back, Feb. 5, 1987, in author's possession, and Marsha Treitman (pseudonym) oral history, conducted by the author, July 15, 1991, in author's possession. It is important to note that almost every social worker at agencies like the JBG joined the left-wing union in the 1930s.

11. Alan McKenzie and Henry Doliner, *The Negro Worker in the ERB* (New York: Association of Workers in Public Relief Agencies, AFSCME, 1937). Spano, *Rank and File Movement*, 235.

12. Frankwood E. Williams, "Understanding the Rank-and-Filers," *Survey Midmonthly*, May 15, 1935, 131–33; June 15, 1935, 170–72.

13. Mary E. Richmond, *Social Diagnosis* (New York: Russell Sage Foundation, 1917).

14. Williams, "Understanding the Rank-and-Filers," May 15, 1935, 132–33.

15. Leslie B. Alexander, "Organizing the Professional Social Worker: Union Development in Voluntary Social Work, 1930–1950" (Ph.D. diss., Bryn Mawr College, 1976), chap. 4. Although the largest local was in New York City, union locals existed in more than sixteen cities nationwide. The New York City local was spread over eighty-five agencies, but more than half were Jewish.

16. Ibid.

17. Lilian Brandt, *An Impressionistic View of the Winter of 1930–1931 in New York City: A Report Made to the Executive Committee of the Welfare Council's Coordinating Committee on Unemployment in the Course of the Research Bureau's Study of Social Welfare during the Business Depression* (New York: Welfare Council of New York, 1932), v, 22–23, 80.

18. Ibid., 60, 70.

19. Spano, *Rank and File Movement*, 67. Spano's book is a wonderful introduction to the Rank-and-File Movement and confirms many of my own readings of the movement. See also the history of the movement written by one of its leaders and the editor of *Social Work*

Today, Jacob Fisher, *The Response of Social Work to the Depression* (Boston: G. K. Hall, 1980); minutes, First National Convention of Rank-and-File Groups, Feb. 23, 1935, box 1, folder 3, JFP; and Jacob Fisher, "Rank and File Challenge: The First National Convention of Rank and File Groups in Social Work," *Social Work Today* 2 (Apr. 1935): 5–9.

20. Joseph H. Levy, "New Forms of Organization among Social Workers," *Social Work Today* 2 (Oct. 1934): 10–12, 30; Spano, *Rank and File Movement*, esp. 67–68.

21. Minutes and "Participating Groups," First National Convention of the Rank-and-File Groups, Feb. 22–24, 1935, box 1, folder 3, JFP; "Directory of Rank and File Organizations," *Social Work Today* 2 (Feb. 1935).

22. Social Worker Discussion Group, Chicago, 1933, "A Social Service Workers' Union," 1, cited in Spano, *Rank and File Movement*, 58.

23. "Social Welfare: Program Adopted by Rank and File Groups at Pittsburgh Convention," *Social Work Today* 2 (Apr. 1935): 6, reprinted from "Platform Adopted by Convention" and "Rank and File Speak," Feb. 22, 1935, box 1, folder 3, JFP.

24. "Report of the Labor Committee," in minutes, Board of Trustees, Mar. 8, Dec. 13, 1937, box 1088, FJPA.

25. Treitman and Grossman oral histories.

26. Nathan Glazer, *The Social Basis of American Communism* (New York: Harcourt, Brace, and World, 1961), has identified the UOPWA and the union of New York City's welfare employees, the SCMWA, led by Abe Flaxer, as among the U.S. unions in which communists were most prominent.

27. Fisher, *Response of Social Work*.

28. Spano, *Rank and File Movement*.

29. These people wrote for and served on the editorial board of *Social Work Today*. Further evidence of the movement's widespread support comes from the list of people who contributed money to *Social Work Today*. After 1937, when the magazine separated itself from the National Coordinating Committee of the Rank-and-File Movement, its list of financial supporters ("Cooperators") grew from 152 to 702 in 1941. The list included members of prominent German Jewish business families such as Mrs. Benjamin J. Buttenwieser, Sam A. Lewisohn, and Edward M. M. Warburg, as well as established social work leaders such as Mary K. Simkhovitch from Greenwich House and New York City councilman Stanley M. Isaacs. See "A Note of Appreciation," *Social Work Today* 5 (Jan. 1938): 17.

30. Indiana legislators voted to provide aid to the blind as early as 1830, and by 1930, nineteen more states did so. Mothers' aid laws dated to 1911, when Missouri and Illinois passed enabling legislation, and although mothers' pensions would be won and lost in the antifeminist backlash of the 1920s, legislation to aid children was passed in nearly every state in the Union by 1934. Finally, old-age assistance, which would be enshrined in the Social Security Act of 1935, had precedents in Montana provisions dating from 1925, some form of which had been enacted by California, New York, and Massachusetts legislators by 1930. See Clarke A. Chambers, *Seedtime of Reform: American Social Service and Social Activism, 1918– 1933* (Minneapolis: University of Minnesota Press, 1963), chap. 5, and Russell H. Kurtz, ed., *The Public Assistance Worker: His Responsibility to the Applicant, the Community, and Himself* (New York: Russell Sage Foundation, 1938), 13–14. For women reformers' contributions to the making of welfare law, see Seth Koven and Sonya Michel, "Womanly Duties: Maternalistic Politics and the Origins of Welfare States in France, Germany, Great Britain, and the United States," *American Historical Review* 95 (Oct. 1990): 1076–1108, and Kathryn Kish

Sklar, "The Historical Foundations of Women's Power in the Creation of the American Welfare State, 1830–1930," in *Mothers of a New World: Maternalist Politics and the Origins of Welfare States*, ed. Seth Koven and Sonya Michel (New York: Routledge, 1993): 43–93.

31. Aid to veterans and the homeless provided two of the more pertinent precedents for the subsequent history of public welfare. See Patrick J. Kelly, *Creating a National Home: Building the Veteran's Welfare State, 1860–1900* (Cambridge: Harvard University Press, 1997). By 1934, twenty-four states had passed laws providing relief to veterans. Kurtz, *Public Assistance Worker*, 14.

32. Linda Gordon, *Pitied but Not Entitled: Single Mothers and the History of Welfare, 1890–1935* (New York: Free Press, 1994), chap. 3; Clarke A. Chambers, personal communication with the author, Mar. 1995.

33. William B. Herlands, *Administration of Relief in New York City: Report to Honorable F. H. La Guardia* (New York: William B. Herlands, Commissioner of Investigation, 1940), 111.

34. Schneider and Deutsch, *History of Public Welfare*, 295–96.

35. Franklin D. Roosevelt, quoted in ibid., 297.

36. Herlands, *Administration of Relief*, ix; Kurtz, *Public Assistance Worker*, 16; Schneider and Deutsch, *History of Public Welfare*, 308.

37. Schneider and Deutsch, *History of Public Welfare*, 332.

38. Herlands, *Administration of Relief*, 309–10, 334–36.

39. New York State, TERA, Division of Research and Statistics, *Social Service Personnel in Local Public Relief Administration* (Albany: TERA, 1935), 22.

40. See Steve Fraser, "The 'Labor Question,'" in *The Rise and Fall of the New Deal Order, 1930–1980*, ed. Steve Fraser and Gary Gerstle (Princeton: Princeton University Press, 1989), 55–84, and Lizabeth Cohen, *Making a New Deal: Industrial Workers in Chicago, 1919–1939* (New York: Cambridge University Press, 1990), 213–360.

41. New York State, TERA, *Social Service Personnel*, 4.

42. Schneider and Deutsch, *History of Public Welfare*, 332.

43. Abe Flaxer, "Keeping One's Head above the Water," unpublished ms. (1989), pt. 2, 20–21, WLA.

44. On the central role of New York's social work leaders in the development of federal programs, see William H. Bremer, *Depression Winters: New York's Social Workers and the New Deal* (Philadelphia: Temple University Press, 1984). For a sense of the shifting terrain on New Deal scholarship, see Fraser and Gerstle, *Rise and Fall*.

45. American Public Welfare Association, *A Public Welfare Job Study: An Analysis of Selected Positions in Public Social Work* (Chicago: American Public Welfare Association, 1938), 32, 40.

46. Herlands, *Administration of Relief*, 112–13. "A Fellow Citizen" to Fiorello H. La Guardia, Oct. 23, 1935, Fiorello H. La Guardia Papers, DPW, Departmental Correspondence Received and Sent, box 43, folder 5, MACNY, urges La Guardia to "cut the arbitrary powers of the CASE WORKERS" and give "seasoned E.R.B. Workers" the "promotions they deserve."

47. Schneider and Deutsch, *History of Public Welfare*, 305.

48. Ibid., 299–332; Herlands, *Administration of Relief*, x.

49. Memo, Kenneth Drayton, Deputy Commissioner of Accounts, to Charlotte E. Carr, Executive Director, ERB, "Preliminary General Recommendations Based on Survey of Caseload," ca. July 1936, 7–8, 17, La Guardia Papers, DPW Departmental Correspondence Received and Sent, box 60, 1936, folder 1, MACNY.

50. Herbert A. O'Brien to the Editor, *New York Times*, ca. Oct. 23, 1939, La Guardia Papers, DW, Departmental Correspondence Received and Sent, box 131, folder 5, MACNY.

51. Ibid.

52. Memo, "Rank and File Veterans" to DPW, ca. early spring 1934, La Guardia Papers, DPW, Departmental Correspondence Received and Sent, box 20, folder 7, MACNY; "A Fellow Citizen" to Fiorello H. La Guardia, Oct. 23, 1935, La Guardia Papers, DPW, Departmental Correspondence Received and Sent, box 43, folder 5, MACNY.

53. Herman Figueroa to Fiorello H. La Guardia, May 18, 1935, La Guardia Papers, DPW, box 43, folder 2, MACNY.

54. Edward G. Rybicki to John P. O'Brien, Apr. 11, 1933, John P. O'Brien Papers, DPW, Letters Received, box 635, MACNY. Salary reductions reported for forty cities including New York ranged from 6 percent for the large number of investigators who made under $2,000 a year to 33.3 percent for top administrators who earned between $15,000 and $40,000.

55. The fullest accounts are Flaxer, "Keeping One's Head above the Water," esp. pt. 2; Jewel Bellush and Bernard Bellush, *Union Power and New York: Victor Gotbaum and District Council 37* (New York: Praeger, 1984), 4–7; and Richard Henry Mendes, "The Professional Union: A Study of the Social Service Employees Union of the New York City Department of Social Services" (Ph.D. diss., Columbia University, 1974). See also Spano, *Rank and File Movement*, esp. chaps. 4, 5; Alexander, "Organizing the Professional Social Worker"; and Mark McColloch, *White Collar Workers in Transition: The Boom Years, 1940–1970* (Westport, Conn.: Greenwood Press, 1983).

56. Jacob Fisher, "The Rank and File Movement, 1930–1936," *Social Work Today* 3 (Feb. 1936): 5–6; Flaxer, "Keeping One's Head above the Water," pt. 2; Spano, *Rank and File Movement*, chap. 4; Alexander, "Organizing the Professional Social Worker," 67.

57. Alexander, "Organizing the Professional Social Worker," 143; Flaxer, "Keeping One's Head above the Water," pt. 2; "Collective Bargaining in New York," *Social Work Today* 3 (Oct. 1935): 5; Bellush and Bellush, *Union Power and New York*, 4–7.

58. Bellush and Bellush, *Union Power and New York*, 1.

59. Speech (probably by Mayor La Guardia or Commissioner Hodson), ca. early 1935, La Guardia Papers, DPW, Departmental Correspondence Received and Sent, box 42, folder 2, MACNY.

60. Levy, "New Forms of Organization."

61. George Hauser, "When Clients Took Control," *Social Work Today* 2 (June 1934): 7–9; Eduard C. Lindeman, "The Future of the Professional," *Social Work Today* 2 (June 1934): 14–15.

62. As early as 1935, public agency social workers in Chicago, Cincinnati, Minneapolis, Newark, Cleveland, Pittsburgh, and Philadelphia organized, followed shortly thereafter by public agency social workers in Denver, Baltimore, Detroit, Los Angeles, Milwaukee, Oakland, St. Louis, St. Paul, and Washington, D.C. Countywide groups also formed in Ohio and Pennsylvania, and a statewide group organized in Michigan. See Alexander, "Organizing the Professional Social Worker," 67. Notably missing from this list are cities in the Deep South such as Atlanta and Birmingham. See chapter 5 for a discussion of Rank-and-File groups that developed in private agencies in most of these cities.

63. "Report of the Special Committee Appointed by the New York Chapter of the American Association of Social Workers to Investigate the Discharge of Miss Sidonia Dawson

from the Home Relief Bureau," n.d., Grievance Procedure Committee, Sidonia Dawson Case, 1934–35, folder 35, AASW/NASWP. See also Jerome Springer, "Cracking Down on Protest: The Dawson Case," *Social Work Today* 2 (Nov. 1934): 9–12, and an exchange of letters in *The Nation* between the president of the HRB employees' association, B. L. R. Riback, and the director of the HRB, William Hodson: B. L. R. Riback to the Editor, "Miss Dawson Is Fired," and William Hodson to the Editor, *The Nation*, Oct. 31, 1934, 508. Riback was himself fired the next year in a remarkably similar case. See George Hedin, "The Riback Firing," *Social Work Today* 2 (Feb. 1935): 16–17.

64. Alexander, "Organizing the Professional Social Worker," 10ff.

65. "Report of the Special Committee."

66. Ibid.

67. Ibid.

68. Executive Committee, New York City chapter of the AASW, "New York Chapter Reports on the Sidonia Dawson Case," Dec. 10, 1934, Grievance Procedure Committee, Sidonia Dawson Case, 1934–35, folder 35, AASW/NASWP.

69. Blanche Ferguson to Walter West, June 30, 1933, Grievance Procedure Committee, Denver, Colorado, Case, 1933–34, folder 34, AASW/NASWP.

70. Ibid.

71. Blanche Ferguson to Walter West, Oct. 9, 1933, and "Women Demand Local Labor Get Preference," clipping from *Denver Post*, June 21, 1933, Grievance Procedure Committee, Denver, Colorado, Case, 1933–34, folder 34, AASW/NASWP.

72. Adeline Jesse to Walter West, Oct. 14, 1933, and Celeste Post to Walter West, Mar. 8, 1934, Grievance Procedure Committee, Denver, Colorado, Case, 1933–34, folder 34, AASW/NASWP.

73. "Women Demand Local Labor Get Preference."

74. Although the Civil Service Commission specifically targeted appointments such as Post's, she was in fact exempted. See Celeste Post to Walter West, July 9, Oct. 4, 1933, Grievance Procedure Committee, Denver, Colorado, Case, 1933–34, folder 34, AASW/NASWP.

75. "Rector Ignores State Board in Appointing Relief Official," clipping from *Denver Post*, Mar. 8, 1934, Grievance Procedure Committee, Denver, Colorado, Case, 1933–34, folder 34, AASW/NASWP.

Chapter Five

1. Michael B. Katz makes two points that are central to the notion of a semiwelfare state: government programs are limited, and the public and private sectors are never completely distinct. Private agencies had always drawn on public funds and would increasingly do so. See Michael B. Katz, *In the Shadow of the Poorhouse: A Social History of Welfare in America* (New York: Basic Books 1986).

2. Marsha Treitman (pseudonym) oral history, conducted by the author, July 15, 1991, in author's possession.

3. Clarke A. Chambers, *Seedtime of Reform: American Social Service and Social Activism, 1918–1933* (Minneapolis: University of Minnesota Press, 1963), chap. 5.

4. Regina G. Kunzel, *Fallen Women, Problem Girls: Unmarried Mothers and the Professionalization of Social Work, 1890–1945* (New Haven: Yale University Press, 1993), 148; Leslie B.

Alexander, "Social Work's Freudian Deluge: Myth or Reality?," *Social Service Review* 46 (Dec. 1972): 517–18. Kunzel's fine book focuses on social workers in evangelical institutions.

5. George Z. Medalie, "Annual Report of the President," 1932, 8–9, box 1240, JBGA.

6. "Proposed Plan of Organization of the Jewish Board of Guardians," [1934], box 1240, JBGA.

7. Minutes, Executive Committee, Sept. 21, 1932, box 1240, JBGA.

8. Sophie Grossman (pseudonym) oral history, conducted by the author and Adina Back, Feb. 5, 1987, in author's possession.

9. Virginia P. Robinson, ed., *Jessie Taft, Therapist and Social Work Educator: A Professional Biography* (Philadelphia: University of Pennsylvania Press, 1962), 128; Jessie Taft, "Time as a Medium of the Helping Process," paper presented at the National Conference of Jewish Social Welfare, Cleveland, Ohio, June 1949, reprinted in Robinson, *Jessie Taft*, 312. Gordon Hamilton details her defense of the diagnostic position in *Theory and Practice of Social Case Work*, rev. ed. (New York: Columbia University Press, 1951). See also Rick Spano, *The Rank and File Movement in Social Work* (Washington, D.C.: University Press of America, 1982), 186–203.

10. John H. Ehrenreich, *The Altruistic Imagination: A History of Social Work and Social Policy in the United States* (Ithaca: Cornell University Press, 1985), 126. See also Robinson, *Jessie Taft*, 124–25, 155–57, 224, 270, 308, and Taft, "Time as a Medium of the Helping Process."

11. Spano, *Rank and File Movement*, 186–203.

12. Robinson, *Jessie Taft*, 309, quoted in Clarke A. Chambers, "Women in the Creation of the Profession of Social Work," *Social Service Review* 59 (Mar. 1986): 17.

13. Chambers, "Women in the Creation of the Profession of Social Work," 17; Robinson, *Jessie Taft*, 143.

14. Robinson, *Jessie Taft*, 269.

15. In the preface to *Theory and Practice of Social Case Work*, Hamilton, a leading exponent of the diagnostic school, notes that functionalism "had not [yet] become a definitive school of thought." In addition, Jessie Taft first published her famous description of functionalism, "The Relation of Function to Process in Social Case Work," in 1937, and the University of Pennsylvania School of Social Work only made her analysis a formal part of its curriculum in 1943. The paper was published as the introduction to *Journal of Social Work Process* 1, no. 1 (Nov. 1937). See also Robinson, *Jessie Taft*, 196–200.

16. Helen Perlman, quoted in Kunzel, *Fallen Women, Problem Girls*, 148; Alexander, "Social Work's Freudian Deluge," 517–18.

17. Theodora L. Wilson, "Social Work from the Perspective of Fifty Years: A Personal History," *Smith College Studies in Social Work* 42, no. 2 (Feb. 1972): 107–8; Jacob Fisher, *The Response of Social Work to the Depression* (Boston: G. K. Hall, 1980). Wilson actually slightly altered Muste's wording, which was "gone psychiatric in a world which has gone economic." Thanks to Clarke A. Chambers for identifying Muste for me.

18. Historians elsewhere have told the story of social worker unionization in the private sector and the primary role of the Jewish agency workers. See, for example, Leslie B. Alexander, "Organizing the Professional Social Worker: Union Development in Voluntary Social Work, 1930–1950" (Ph.D. diss., Bryn Mawr College, 1976); Spano, *Rank and File Movement*; and John Earl Haynes, "The 'Rank and File Movement' in Private Social Work," *Labor History* 16, no. 1 (Winter 1975): 78–98.

19. Helen Harris Perlman oral history, conducted by Vida S. Grayson, Aug. 11–14, 1978, NASWOH.

20. Federation trustees to all affiliated society presidents, Jan. 14, 1930, in minutes, Board of Trustees, Nov. 10, 1930, box 1036; June 25, Dec. 14, 1931, box 1036; and May 8, 1933, box 1087, FJPA.

21. Minutes, Board of Trustees, Dec. 11, 1933, box 1087, FJPA.

22. Minutes, Supervisors' Meeting, Feb. 20, Mar. 6, 1934, box 1243, JBGA.

23. Ibid.; minutes, Executive Committee, Mar. 21, 1934, box 1240, JBGA.

24. I. Gandel to Solomon Lowenstein, in minutes, Board of Trustees, Jan. 11, 1932, box 1036, FJPA.

25. Minutes, Board of Trustees, May 8, 1933, box 1087, FJPA.

26. Ibid., Mar. 11, 1935.

27. Minutes, Executive Committee, Dec. 20, 1933, box 1240, JBGA.

28. Minutes, Executive Committee, Mar. 21, May 23, 1934, box 1243, JBGA.

29. Ibid., Jan. 9, 1935.

30. Jennie Berman to Solomon Lowenstein, Feb. 26, 1935, and Solomon Lowenstein to Jennie Berman, Feb. 28 1935, in minutes, Board of Trustees, Mar. 11, 1935, box 1087, FJPA; minutes, Executive Committee, Feb. 27, 1935, box 1243, JBGA.

31. Minutes, Board of Trustees, Mar. 11, 1935, box 1087, FJPA. It is important to recognize that the business community, like labor, was not monolithic. It divided on policy and strategy. For this point in relation to business in the New Deal, see Thomas Ferguson, "Industrial Conflict and the Coming of the New Deal: The Triumph of Multinational Liberalism in America," in *The Rise and Fall of the New Deal Order, 1930–1980*, ed. Steve Fraser and Gary Gerstle (Princeton: Princeton University Press, 1989), 3–31.

32. Minutes, Board of Trustees, Mar. 11, 1935, box 1087, FJPA.

33. Ibid., Jan. 15, 1934.

34. "The A.F.W. Takes to Action," *Bulletin* 1, no. 4 (Mar. 1934), file 10, 1934–35, JFP. See also "Charities Lock Out Labor," *Jewish Frontier* 2, no. 9 (July 1935): 8–13.

35. Robert Miller, "Locked Out," *Social Work Today* 2 (July 1935): 11; "Reviewing the Lebanon Situation," *Bulletin* 4, no. 1 (Dec. 1935): 2, no. 6 (Apr. 1935), file 10, 1934–35, JFP.

36. Miller, "Locked Out," 10–12; "Staffs at 91 Hospitals Called Out on Two Hour Strike Today," *World-Telegram* May 14, 1935, 1.

37. Ibid.; minutes, Board of Trustees, Executive Session, Oct. 14, 1935, box 1087, FJPA.

38. Miller, "Locked Out."

39. "The Victory at Beth Moses," *Social Work Today* 3 (Oct. 1935): 6.

40. "Reviewing the Lebanon Situation."

41. Ibid. The support from the League of Women Shoppers may have reflected sisterhood since social service was also predominantly female. The locked-out workers, however, overwhelmingly seem to have been male. Fifteen of the eighteen who signed a letter of thanks to supporters had male first names.

42. "Reviewing the Lebanon Situation."

43. Minutes, Board of Trustees, Executive Session, Oct. 14, 1935, box 1087, FJPA.

44. George Z. Medalie, quoted in "Report of Committee on Personnel Practices," in minutes, Board of Trustees, Mar. 8, 1937, box 1088, FJPA.

45. The other locals were Pittsburgh, Local 38; Philadelphia, Local 21; and Chicago, Local 39. The SSEU had a brief prior life as an AFL affiliate but was quick to forsake the craft-

oriented AFL for the new CIO. See the weekly newsletter of Local 19, UOPWA, CIO (New York), *Social Service Employees Union Newsletter*, Sept. 16, Dec. 16, 1937, in SSEUC.

46. Piehl joined the JBG in 1935 and by the summer of 1937 had become chair of the agency's chapter of the SSEU. See minutes, Staff Conferences, Jan. 15, 1935, box 1243, JBGA; minutes, Personnel Committee, June 11, Sept. 24, 1937, box 1243, JBGA; and minutes, Board of Trustees, Oct. 11, 1937, box 1088, FJPA.

47. *Social Service Employees Union Newsletter*, Aug. 16, Oct. 25, 1937, in SSEUC.

48. Ibid., Aug. 23, 1937.

49. Stanley Isaacs, speech at Oct. 22, 1937, rally, quoted in ibid., Oct. 25, 1937.

50. "Report of Committee on Personnel Practices," in minutes, Board of Trustees, Mar. 6, 1937, box 1088, FJPA.

51. Jacob Fisher, quoted in minutes, Board of Trustees, Oct. 11, 1937, box 1088, FJPA.

52. Minutes, Board of Trustees, Dec. 13, 1937, box 1088, FJPA.

53. *Social Service Employees Union Newsletter*, Oct. 25, Nov. 23, 1937, in SSEUC.

54. Ibid., Nov. 9, 1937.

55. Minutes, Board of Trustees, Dec. 13, 1937, box 1088, FJPA.

56. Jacob Proskauer, quoted in ibid., Mar. 6, 1937; minutes, Board of Trustees, Apr. 29, 1935, box 1087, FJPA.

57. Minutes, Board of Trustees, Dec. 13, 1937, box 1088, FJPA.

58. Ibid., Jan. 10, 1938; *Social Service Employees Union Newsletter*, July 6, 1938, in SSEUC.

59. "Relation of the Jewish Social Worker to the Jewish Community," report of the New York Committee of the Case-Workers' Section of the NCJSS, Clara Rabinowitz, Chair, in *Proceedings*, Annual Session (1934), 82–86, NCJSS, YIVO.

60. Clarke A. Chambers, *Paul U. Kellogg and the Survey: Voices for Social Welfare and Social Justice* (Minneapolis: University of Minnesota Press, 1971), 143–46.

61. See, for example, Gertrude Springer, "The Children Can't Wait," "Too Old to Change," and "Kith and Kin," in "Miss Bailey Says," *Survey Midmonthly*, May 15, 1935–Jan. 15, 1936.

62. Gertrude Springer, "Miss Bailey Says: 'Maybe When We Get Our Growth . . . ,'" *Survey Midmonthly*, May 15, 1938, 169.

63. Ibid., 169–70.

64. Ibid., 170.

65. Ibid., 170–71.

66. Elizabeth Faue, "Public Soldiers, Solidarity Warriors: Labor, Sex, and Solidarity on the American Left, 1929–1945," paper presented at the annual meeting of the Organization of American Historians, St. Louis, Mo., Apr. 8, 1989.

67. Minutes, Executive Committee, Nov. 10, 1937, box 1243, and Mar. 8, 1933, box 1240, JBGA.

68. *Social Service Employees Union Newsletter*, Apr. 13, 1939, in SSEUC.

69. Louis Gordon, *The White Collar Workers Organize* (New York: Local 19, UOPWA, 1938), 18, in UOPWAC.

70. See Spano, *Rank and File Movement*, 243–62.

71. Elizabeth Lunbeck, "'A New Generation of Women': Progressive Psychiatrists and the Hypersexual Female," *Feminist Studies* 13 (Fall 1987): 513–44; Kunzel, *Fallen Women, Problem Girls*.

72. Minutes, Staff Meetings, Supervisors' Seminars, Oct. 4, 1934–May 15, 1935, box 1243, JBGA.

73. Treitman oral history. Census data on age cohorts of social workers by sex throughout the century documents the relative disappearance of older male caseworkers and the dominance of older men within administrative ranks.

74. Barbara Abel, "The Clean Up," *Survey Midmonthly*. Sept. 15. 1938, 274–77.

75. "People and Things," *Survey Midmonthly*, Aug. 15, 1939, 256.

76. Edith Abbott, quoted in National Coordinating Committee of Social Service Employee Groups, "Statement on the Negro Issue at the National Conference of Social Work," Jan. 1936, box 1, folder 6, JFP.

77. Alan McKenzie, "Negro in Social Work," speech given at the Rank-and-File Convention, Feb. 22, 1936, box 1, folder 5, JFP.

78. William B. Herlands, *Administration of Relief in New York City: Report to Honorable F. H. La Guardia* (New York: William B. Herlands, Commissioner of Investigation, 1940). These firings are discussed in chapter 4 See also telegram, Metropolitan Guild to Fiorello H. La Guardia, Mar. 3, 1938, Fiorello H. La Guardia Papers, DW, Correspondence Received and Sent, box 109, folder 1, MACNY. The telegram claims that a civil service exam would result in the disproportionate dismissal of "Negro members of the staff," especially in Harlem. In 1939, responding to social worker pressure, Commissioner Hodson appointed 600 provisional investigators, more than 200 of whom were African Americans. See William Hodson to Fiorello H. La Guardia, May 15, 1939, La Guardia Papers, DW, box 131, folder 2, MACNY.

79. Inabel Burns Lindsay oral history, conducted by Vida S. Grayson, 1977–81, NASWOH; Inabel Burns Lindsay oral history, 1977, BWOHP. Lindsay gives several accounts of prejudice she encountered in St. Louis in her oral history with the BWOHP.

80. Frankie V. Adams oral history, 1977, BWOHP.

81. On southern racism in social work, see Spano, *Rank and File Movement*. African Americans did make significant inroads into social work outside New York City, however, even if their history was a complicated one of uplift, benevolence, and social control. Although her study closes in the 1920s, see Ruth Hutchinson Crocker, *Social Work and Social Order: The Settlement Movement in Two Industrial Cities, 1889–1930* (Urbana: University of Illinois Press, 1992). Andor Skotnes, "The Black Freedom Movement and the Workers' Movement, Baltimore, Maryland, 1930–1939" (Ph.D. diss., Rutgers University, 1990), chap. 6, notes that black reformers were able to compel Baltimore's emergency relief program to hire eighteen black investigators in 1934.

82. See the case of Beulah Whitby in Stephanie J. Shaw, *What a Woman Ought to Be and to Do: Black Professional Women Workers during the Jim Crow Era* (Chicago: University of Chicago Press, 1996), 191–96.

83. Dorothy I. Haight oral history, 1974, BWOHP.

84. Beth Wenger, *New York Jews and the Great Depression: Uncertain Promises* (New Haven: Yale University Press, 1996); Suzanne Rachel Wasserman, "The Good Old Days of Poverty: The Battle over the Fate of New York City's Lower East Side during the Depression" (Ph.D. diss., New York University, 1990), esp. chap. 6.

85. Perlman oral history.

86. Beth Wenger, "Ethnic Community in Economic Crisis: New York Jews and the Great Depression" (Ph.D. diss, Yale University, 1992), 213–14.

87. Hasia R. Diner, *In the Almost Promised Land: American Jews and Blacks, 1915–1935* (Westport, Conn.: Greenwood Press, 1977), 35, 191, 237.

88. Ibid., 111.

89. Virginia P. Robinson, "Is Unionization Compatible with Social Work?," *Compass* 18, no. 8 (May 1937): 5–9. The paper was presented in March 1937 at a forum sponsored by the Coordinating Committee of Social Service Employees of Philadelphia.

90. Ibid.

91. *Social Service Employees Union Newsletter*, Apr. 12, 1939, in SSEUC.

92. Jacob Fisher, "Professional Goals and the Trade Union," speech given at a conference at Pennsylvania State University, Feb. 18, 1939, box 1, folder 8, JFP.

93. Ibid.

Chapter Six

1. This point has been made by several others, although they tend to set the development in the 1940s, which is earlier than I think is warranted. See, for example, Regina G. Kunzel, *Fallen Women, Problem Girls: Unmarried Mothers and the Professionalization of Social Work, 1890–1945* (New Haven: Yale University Press, 1993), chap. 6, and Ira Katznelson, "Was the Great Society a Lost Opportunity?," in *The Rise and Fall of the New Deal Order, 1930–1980,* ed. Steve Fraser and Gary Gerstle (Princeton: Princeton University Press, 1989), 212–42. Two later important transitional moments were in the 1950s, when the city and welfare were marked as black in the popular imagination, and between 1968 and 1972, when the term "middle class" became a way to avoid talking explicitly about class and to speak instead about race (and secondarily gender).

2. *Office and Professional News* 6 (July–Aug. 1941).

3. Stanley Wenocur and Michael Reisch, *From Charity to Enterprise: The Development of American Social Work in a Market Economy* (Urbana: University of Illinois Press, 1989), 202–4; Leslie B. Alexander, "Organizing the Professional Social Worker: Union Development in Voluntary Social Work, 1930–1950" (Ph.D. diss., Bryn Mawr College, 1976). Wenocur and Reisch are especially good at framing the history of the social work profession as a business within the changing structure of the economy.

4. This program is described in Bertha Capen Reynolds, *Social Work and Social Living: Explorations in Philosophy and Practice* (New York: Citadel Press, 1951), 54–57.

5. Ibid., 5–9, 52–61, 86–88.

6. Wenocur and Reisch, *From Charity to Enterprise*, 199–202; *Social Work Today* 7 (Jan. 1940): 5–6.

7. Rick Spano, *The Rank and File Movement in Social Work* (Washington, D.C.: University Press of America, 1982), 174; Wenocur and Reisch, *From Charity to Enterprise*, 202–7.

8. "The Impact of War on Public Welfare," *Public Welfare News* 10, no. 1 (Jan. 1942): 1, and "Introduction of the New Worker to the Agency," *Public Welfare News* 10, no. 7 (July 1942): 2–3, 8, DLL.

9. Minutes, Executive Committee, Jan. 14, Dec. 7, 1942, Nov. 10, 1943, box 1243, JBGA. The war also affected treatment: fear of air raids prevented some children from keeping appointments; in treatment, children expressed heightened anxieties associated with the war, such as the possibility of losing their parents.

10. The best treatment of Jewish "suburbanization" and social mobility to the outer boroughs from the 1920s to the war is Deborah Dash Moore, *At Home in America: Second Generation New York Jews* (New York: Columbia University Press, 1981), chap. 2. See also

minutes, Board of Trustees, June 10, 1940, box 1089; Apr. 12, May 10, June 14, 1943, Nov. 13, 1944, box 1090; and Dec. 8, 1947, box 1091, FJPA.

11. Minutes, Board of Trustees, Dec. 8, 1947, box 1091, FJPA.

12. Ibid., Feb. 19, 1940, box 1089.

13. "Distribution Committee Report," in minutes, Board of Trustees, June 28, 1948, box 1092, FJPA.

14. Minutes, Board of Trustees, Oct. 18, 1943, box 1090, FJPA.

15. Ibid., Feb. 7, 1944.

16. The JSSA did sign a contract in 1940. See Mark McColloch, *White Collar Workers in Transition: The Boom Years, 1940–1970* (Westport, Conn.: Greenwood Press, 1983), 45. Jacob Fisher, *The Response of Social Work to the Depression* (Boston: G. K. Hall, 1980), and Alexander, "Organizing the Professional Social Worker," both acknowledge the congeniality of many union members to party positions but consider the relationship irrelevant to their union activities. John Earl Haynes, "The 'Rank and File Movement' in Private Social Work," *Labor History* 16, no. 1 (Winter 1975): 78–98, disagrees.

17. See Sanford Solender oral history, conducted by Nikki Tanner, June–Aug. 1982, FJPOH; Marjorie S. Dammann oral history, conducted by Sally Pearce and Laura Strauss, Nov. 1, 1982, Mar. 3, 1983, FJPOH; Martha K. Selig oral history, conducted by Judy E. Tenney, Feb. 9, 22, 1982, FJPOH; and Jerome M. Goldsmith oral history, conducted by Hannah N. Broder, Dec. 23, 1982, Apr. 18, 1983, FJPOH.

18. The FJP did employ its own staff and bargain with it. See minutes, Executive Committee, Dec. 19, 1945, Jan. 16, Mar. 20, Apr. 17, Dec. 18, 1946, box 1244, JBGA.

19. Ibid., Dec. 6, 1950 minutes, Board of Trustees, Sept. 12, Oct. 10, 1949, box 1092, FJPA.

20. Jewel Bellush and Bernard Bellush, *Union Power and New York: Victor Gotbaum and District Council 37* (New York: Praeger, 1984), 2.

21. Ibid., 3. For a good review of the problems of white-collar unions, see Martin Oppenheimer, *White Collar Politics* (New York: Monthly Review Press, 1985), 165–67.

22. American Business Consultants, "Objective Study of United Office and Professional Workers of America, CIO," *Counterattack: The Newsletter of Facts on Communism*, Special Report no. 1, July 1947, in UOPWAC; UOPWA, CIO, "Report of Executive Board Committee Appointed by President Murray to Investigate Charges against the United Office and Professional Workers of America," 1950, in UOPWAC; UOPWA, CIO, "Statement by United Office and Public Workers of America, CIO, to CIO," miscellaneous publication no. 18, Dec. 19, 1949, in UOPWAC.

23. Nelson Lichtenstein, "From Corporatism to Collective Bargaining: Organized Labor and the Eclipse of Social Democracy in the Postwar Era," in Fraser and Gerstle, *Rise and Fall of the New Deal Order*, 122.

24. Ibid., 122–52; Katznelson, "Was the Great Society a Lost Opportunity?"; Bellush and Bellush, *Union Power and New York*, 6–14.

25. Confidential Files, Grievance Committee, 1946–55, folders 264–314, AASW/NASWP.

26. McColloch, *White Collar Workers*, 52–53, 74–77; William O'Dwyer Papers, Subject file, Strikes and Labor Troubles, 1945–48, MACNY.

27. McColloch, *White Collar Workers*, 17.

28. Minutes, Executive Committee, Mar. 20, Apr. 17, 1945, box 1244, JBGA; *Welfare*, Apr. 1946, in SSEUC. Winning a contract after more than a decade of agitation was not without symbolic significance, although according to Local 19 leader Bernard R. Segal, the union

and its lawyers felt the Code of Personnel Practices that had been agreed to in a signed cover letter had the legal status of a contract all along. See Bernard R. Segal oral history, conducted by the author and Dorothy Fennell, July 14, 1992, in author's possession.

29. Minutes, Board of Trustees, June 26, 1946, Apr. 11, 1949, box 1090, FJPA.

30. "Social Worker's Salary Doesn't Allow Him to Live 'At a Professional Level,'" *Welfare*, Dec. 1945, 4, in SSEUC.

31. Joseph H. Levy, in *Proceedings*, Sixth Convention, Feb. 18–22, 1946, UOPWA, in UOPWAC. Levy's speech was preceded by the reading of a letter to the convention from Albert Einstein that urged the organization of salaried intellectual workers, whom he described as no different from people paid daily, monthly, or annual fees.

32. "Can Social Workers Defend Hardships Forced on Workers by Inadequate Salaries?," *Welfare*, Oct. 1945, in SSEUC.

33. Ibid.

34. Hawthorne–Cedar Knolls annual report, 1948–49, in minutes, Executive Committee, 1949, box 1244, JBGA.

35. Minutes, Executive Committee, Dec. 12, 1948, box 1244, JBGA.

36. "Case Worker's Dilemma," *Staff: The Magazine of the Social Service Employee* (UOPWA, Social Service Division), 1, no. 2 (Feb. 1947): 7, in UOPWAC.

37. "Manual of Procedures," 1942, box 1243, file 31, JBGA.

38. Minutes, Board of Trustees, Oct. 10, 1949, box 1092, FJPA; minutes, Administrative Committee, Dec. 6, 1943, Feb. 9, 1944, Dec. 19, 1945, box 1244, JBGA; minutes, Executive Committee, June 19, 1946, box 1244, JBGA.

39. *Manual of Social Service Policies in Public Assistance* (New York: Department of Welfare, 1945), and "Additional Pages for the *Manual*," Feb. 13, 1946, O'Dwyer Papers, DW, Departmental Letters, box 18, MACNY.

40. Edward E. Rhatigan to William O'Dwyer, Jan. 31, 1946, O'Dwyer Papers, DW, Departmental Letters, box 18, MACNY.

41. See Welfare (miscellaneous), Dec. 21, 1939, and Department of Welfare Orders, July–Dec. 1945, Fiorello H. La Guardia Papers, DW, Departmental Letters, box 849, Subject files, pt. 4 (W), MACNY. See also "Report of the Mayor's Executive Committee . . . ," Oct. 24, 1947, and memo, Mr. Condello to Deputy Mayor, "Summary of the State Hearing on City Welfare," Dec. 1947, O'Dwyer Papers, DW, Departmental Letters, box 33, MACNY.

42. "Officials Worried by Influx of Migrant Puerto Ricans," *New York Times*, Aug. 3, 1947.

43. C. Wright Mills to Hon. Jesús T. Piñero, Governor of Puerto Rico, "Puerto Rican Migration Study," Columbia University, Bureau of Applied Social Research, June 15, 1948, unpublished manuscript, Center for Puerto Rican Studies, Hunter College, City University of New York, New York, N.Y. Nelida Perez graciously forwarded this document to me.

44. Marsha Treitman (pseudonym) oral history, conducted by the author, July 15, 1991, in author's possession.

45. Mills, "Puerto Rican Migration Study," 4. Of the other Puerto Ricans, 5 percent said they were black, 15 percent said they were mulatto, and 17 percent "were in the mixed group known in Puerto Rico as 'grife' or 'indio.'"

46. U.S. racial prejudice against people of "color" has been a compelling practical reason for some to elect to describe themselves as "white." Other evidence is somewhat impres-

sionistic, but, for example, as a graduate student decades ago, I read references to Italians as "not quite white" in the Baptist press at the turn of the century.

47. No firm data exists on union membership in the immediate postwar years, but ex-commissioner Rhatigan asserted in December 1947 that 99 percent of the DW staff members were unionized. No more than 500 seem to have ever joined the conservative alternative to the UPW, the CSF. Since the DW employed 5,761 people at the end of 1947, UPW membership may have ranged from 5,000 to 2,100 just before the UPW disbanded in 1950. See Rhatigan to O'Dwyer, Jan. 31, 1946, and Edward E. Rhatigan testimony, New York State Hearing on City Welfare Department, Ninth and Tenth Sessions, Dec. 2, 1947, O'Dwyer Papers, DW, Departmental Letters, box 33, MACNY.

48. Nelson Lichtenstein, *Labor's War at Home: The CIO in World War II* (Cambridge: Cambridge University Press, 1982), esp. chaps. 7, 8.

49. See *Public Record*, May–Dec. 1947, esp. "Local 1 Offers 10 Point Plan on Welfare," *Public Record*, Jan. 1948, 7, in UOPWAC. See also McColloch, *White Collar Workers*, 74–75.

50. Press release, Feb. 26, 1947, O'Dwyer Papers, DW, Departmental Letters, box 32, MACNY.

51. Edward E. Rhatigan press release, May 28, 1947, and Report to the Mayor, Oct. 24, 1947, O'Dwyer Papers, DW, Departmental Letters, box 33, MACNY.

52. "Woman in Mink with $60,000 Lived on Relief in a Hotel, Inquiry by State Discloses," *New York Times*, Oct. 30, Nov. 1, 1947.

53. Fielding justified relief to the "woman in mink," for instance, as falling under AFDC guidelines: she was a single mother with a four-month-old child who had gotten her money in a divorce settlement seven years ago. See *New York Times*, Nov. 1, 1947.

54. I am unaware of a good comparative history of how Puerto Ricans have been treated by welfare in New York City and Puerto Rico. It is a subject with much promise.

55. McColloch, *White Collar Workers*, 52–53, 74–77; O'Dwyer Papers, Subject file, Strikes and Labor Troubles, 1945–48, MACNY; Edward E. Rhatigan to William O'Dwyer, Apr. 18, Mar. 12, 1946, O'Dwyer Papers, DW, Departmental Letters, box 18, MACNY; Alexander, "Organizing the Professional Social Worker," 3–5, 204–5.

56. Condello, "Summary of the State Hearing on City Welfare"; Rhatigan testimony, New York State Hearing on City Welfare Department.

57. Raymond M. Hilliard press release, Nov. 3 1948, O'Dwyer Papers, DW, Departmental Letters, box 45, MACNY.

58. Jerome Beatty, "The Most Hated Man in Town," *American Magazine*, Sept. 1, 1950, 24–25, 116–20.

59. *New York Times*, May 22, 1948. Gunnar Myrdal had documented black exclusion from U.S. economic expansion as early as 1944 in his landmark study, *An American Dilemma: The Negro Problem and Modern Democracy* (New York: Harper and Brothers, 1944).

60. *New York Times*, June 4, 1948

61. Ibid.

62. Raymond M. Hilliard to Ben Davidson, Liberal Party head, July 21, 1948, O'Dwyer Papers, DW, Departmental Letters, box 45, MACNY.

63. Beatty, "Most Hated Man in Town," 25.

64. The "retraining" of the New York City welfare workers is described in chapter 7.

65. Hilliard cited the federal Hatch Act and argued that federal aid implicated municipal employees. See Beatty, "Most Hated Man in Town," 119, and "Summary of Welfare Newspaper Coverage," Aug. 31, 1948, O'Dwyer Papers, DW, Departmental Letters, box 45, MACNY.

66. Shirley Kleid et al. to William O'Dwyer, June 1, 1950; "Expulsion of United Public Workers," Mar. 9, 1950; and Raymond M. Hilliard to Staff, Mar. 30, 1950, O'Dwyer–Vincent R. Impellitteri Papers, DW, Departmental File, box 1111 (old no.), MACNY.

67. *New York Times*, Aug. 21, 1948; Beatty, "Most Hated Man in Town," 119; McColloch, *White Collar Workers*, 76.

68. *Super-Ego Newsletter*, 1, no. 1 (ca. 1950), Sheltering Arms Children's Services, box 132, file 19, DC65R. The newsletter was a publication of the student chapter of the SSEU at the New York School of Social Work.

69. Kleid et al. to O'Dwyer, June 1, 1950.

70. Minutes, Board of Trustees, Feb. 2, Dec. 12, 1949, box 1092, FJPA.

71. *New York Times*, Jan. 14, 1947.

72. Ibid., Mar. 31, 1947; Helen Mangold, "Dangerous Dismissal," *Staff* 1, no. 2 (Feb. 1947): 6, in UOPWAC.

73. *New York Times*, Mar. 31, Aug. 11, 1947, Jan. 23, 1948.

74. Summary of staff meeting, Mar. 17, 1950, WJCS, box 142, file 22, DC65R.

75. Anonymous letter, Mar. 20, 1950, WJCS, box 142, file 22, DC65R.

76. Draft Code, Oct. 23, 1950, and Luchansky et al. to Board Members, Dec. 1, 4, 1950, WJCS, box 142, file 22, DC65R.

77. WJCS to Board of Directors, Dec. 1, 4, 1950, Feb. 21, 1951, WJCS, box 142, file 22, DC65R; minutes, Board of Trustees, Nov. 13, 1950, box 1093, FJPA.

78. Minutes, Board of Trustees, May 14, 1951, box 1093, FJPA.

79. Memo, Mrs. Walter Mendelsohn to staff, Sept. 24, 1951, in minutes, Executive Committee, box 1244, JBGA.

80. Minutes, Mar. 29, 1951, WJCS, box 12, folder 14, DC65R.

81. To improve its organizing base, during the past year the UOPWA and its Local 19 had been absorbed into District Council 65, a CIO local of the distributive workers' union, which had also organized department store workers. Ibid., Mar. 19, 1951.

82. *New York Times*, June 16, 1948.

83. McColloch, *White Collar Workers*.

84. See John C. Burnham, "The Influence of Psychoanalysis upon American Culture," in *American Psychoanalysis: Origins and Developments*, ed. Jacques M. Quen and Eric T. Carlson (New York: Brunner/Mazel, 1978), 52–72; Kunzel, *Fallen Women, Problem Girls*, 148; Nathan G. Hale Jr., *Freud and the Americans: The Beginnings of Psychoanalysis in the United States, 1876–1917* (New York: Oxford University Press, 1971) and *The Rise and Crisis of Psychoanalysis in America* (New York: Oxford University Press, 1995); and Walter Bromberg, *From Shaman to Psychotherapist: A History of the Treatment of Mental Illness* (Chicago: Henry Regnery, 1975), chaps. 12–14.

85. Burnham, "Influence of Psychoanalysis," 54.

86. Gerald N. Grob, *From Asylum to Community: Mental Health Policy in Modern America* (Princeton: Princeton University Press, 1991), 10–12.

87. Ibid., 11–17; Burnham, "Influence of Psychoanalysis," 58–62; Don Martindale and Edith Martindale, *Mental Disability in America since World War II* (New York: Philosophical

Library, 1985); George Rosen, *Madness in Society: Chapters in the Historical Sociology of Mental Illness* (London: Routledge and Kegan Paul, 1968), 313; U.S. National Research Council, *Psychology for the Fighting Man: What You Should Know about Yourself and Others* (Washington, D.C.: Infantry Journal, 1943).

88. I am indebted for all of these popular references to Burnham, "Influence of Psychoanalysis," 58–62.

89. Kunzel, *Fallen Women, Problem Girls*, 152; Rebecca Jo Plant, "The Menace of Momism: The Popularization of Psychiatry and the Anti-Woman Backlash in the Post World War II Era," seminar paper, Johns Hopkins University, Department of History, spring 1991.

90. Minutes, Executive Committee, Oct. 17, 1945, Dec. 18, 1946, box 1244, JBGA. On divorce, see Elaine Tyler May, *Great Expectations: Marriage and Divorce in Post-Victorian America* (Chicago: University of Chicago Press, 1980).

91. Minutes, Executive Committee, Oct. 6, Nov. 3, 1943 box 1244, JBGA.

92. Ann Douglas, *Terrible Honesty: Mongrel Manhattan in the 1920s* (New York: Farrar, Straus, and Giroux, 1995).

93. Jack Yeaman Bryan, "Vote of Confidence for Social Work," *Survey Midmonthly*, Nov. 15, 1945, 287–89.

94. *Survey* did not ask where the remaining 75 percent would turn for help. The presumption of the article is that although some may have been willing to go to a psychiatrist, most would have rejected therapy altogether and relied on friends, kin, or perhaps a cleric for support.

95. Male and female social workers had slightly different profiles; it was always more difficult to recruit men into the business. See CSWE, *Undergraduate Programs in Social Work: Guidelines to Curriculum, Content, Field Instruction, and Organization* (New York: CSWE, 1971), and *Student Selection: The Role of School and Agency* (New York: CSWE, 1958); Bernard Ross and Philip Lichtenberg, *Education in Schools of Social Work, 1950–1960* (New York: CSWE, 1963); and Arnulf M. Pins, *An Overview of Undergraduate Education in Social Welfare: Past Issues, Current Developments, and Future Potentials* (New York: CSWE, 1968).

96. These social worker views are quoted in Kunzel, *Fallen Women, Problem Girls*, 146.

97. The JBG instituted fees in 1946. Fees, it is worth noting, held particular appeal for the Rankean functionalists who increasingly dominated New York City's Jewish casework agencies. They believed paying fees helped clients assume responsibility. See minutes, Executive Committee, Dec. 18, 1946, Feb. 19, 1947, box 1244, JBGA.

98. Rose Bernstein, quoted in Kunzel, *Fallen Women, Problem Girls*, 147.

99. See the discussion of battered women and children in Linda Gordon, *Heroes of Their Own Lives: The Politics and History of Family Violence, Boston, 1880–1960* (New York: Viking, 1988).

100. Katznelson, quoted in Fraser and Gerstle, "Introduction," in *Rise and Fall of the New Deal Order*, lxix.

101. Minutes, Executive Committee, Jan. 5, 1949, box 1244, JBGA; minutes, Board of Trustees, June 13, 1949, box 1092, FJPA.

102. Dorothy I. Haight oral history, 1974, BWOHP.

103. Fraser and Gerstle, "Introduction," in *Rise and Fall of the New Deal Order*, xix. The authors are referring to the argument made in Katznelson, "Was the Great Society a Lost Opportunity?"

1. Thomas C. Holt, quoted in Earl Lewis, "Invoking Concepts, Problematizing Identities: The Life of Charles N. Hunter and the Implications for the Study of Gender and Labor," *Labor History* 34, nos. 2–3 (Spring–Summer 1993): 296. See also John Kenneth Galbraith, *The Affluent Society* (Boston: Houghton Mifflin, 1960), and William H. Whyte, *The Organization Man* (New York: Simon and Schuster, 1956). On the family during this era, see Elaine Tyler May, *Homeward Bound: American Families in the Cold War Era* (New York: Basic Books, 1988).

2. Michael Frisch was especially helpful with this formulation. May, *Homeward Bound*, describes the revitalization of the middle-class family in the context of the 1950s Cold War mentality. The disparity and tensions between the stereotyped white, middle-class housewife in 1950s sitcoms and the work realities of many women are traced in essays in Joanne Meyerowitz, ed., *Not June Cleaver: Women and Gender in Postwar America, 1945–1960* (Philadelphia: Temple University Press, 1994). In "Introduction: Women and Gender in Postwar America, 1945–1960," in ibid., 1–16, Meyerowitz argues that this tension helps explain the welcome Betty Friedan's *Feminine Mystique* (1963) received from many women.

3. The nation's population increased 18 percent between 1950 and 1960, and the number of social welfare workers rose 42 percent to 105,350. Two out of three of these employees worked in the public sector, where more than half served in public assistance programs. The big gain, however, was in child welfare, which now accounted for 21 percent of all jobs (up from 17 percent). The role of social worker as therapist was still in its infancy.

4. BLS, *Salaries and Working Conditions of Social Welfare Manpower in 1960* (New York: National Social Welfare Assembly, [1961]), 1–14, and *Social Workers in 1950: A Report on the Study of Salaries and Working Conditions in Social Work—Spring 1950* (New York: AASW, 1952).

5. Daniel J. Walkowitz, "New York: A Tale of Two Cities," in *Snowbelt Cities: Metropolitan Politics in the Northeast and Midwest since World War II* (Bloomington: Indiana University Press, 1990), 192.

6. U.S. Department of Commerce, Bureau of the Census, *Sixteenth Census of the United States, 1940: Population, The Labor Force (Sample Statistics), Employment and Personal Characteristics* (Washington, D.C.: Government Printing Office, 1943); BLS, *Social Workers in 1950*, 6.

7. Agency requirements that employees own automobiles were considered "a relatively insignificant factor" in auto ownership. See "1950 Study—Analysis and Interpretation, 1951," 49–75, Suppl. 2, Personnel Series, box 48, AASW/NASWP. National data on automobile ownership is in BLS, *Social Workers in 1950*, 73, table D-53.

8. Lucy's comedy draws on the slightly transgressive nature of her marriage to a Cuban, who is depicted as a white exotic in a white world. Thanks to Dorothy Ross for this observation.

9. David Marc, "Comic Visions of the City: New York and the Television Sitcom," *Radical History Review* 42 (Fall 1988): 48–63. See also George Lipsitz, *Time Passages: Collective Memory and American Popular Culture* (Minneapolis: University of Minnesota Press, 1994), 266–67.

10. David Halle, *America's Working Man: Work, Home, and Politics among Blue Collar Property Owners* (Chicago: University of Chicago Press, 1984).

11. See Leon Fink and Brian Greenberg, *Upheaval in the Quiet Zone: A History of Hospital Workers' Union 1199* (Urbana: University of Illinois Press, 1989), 17–19; Joshua B. Freeman, *In Transit: The Transit Workers' Union in New York City, 1933–1966* (New York: Oxford University Press, 1989), 267–317; and Marjorie Murphy, *Blackboard Unions: The AFT and the NEA, 1900–1980* (Ithaca: Cornell University Press, 1990), 184–95.

12. Thomas Dewey, quoted in *New York Times*, Nov. 11, 1952.

13. Galbraith, *Affluent Society*; Wini Breines, *Young, White, and Miserable: Growing Up Female in the Fifties* (Boston: Beacon Press, 1992), 3. Galbraith's book was actually critical of the maldistribution of wealth, but its title shaped how people thought of the book.

14. James B. Gilbert, *A Cycle of Outrage: America's Reaction to the Juvenile Delinquent in the 1950s* (New York: Oxford University Press, 1986), 7.

15. BLS, *Salaries and Working Conditions*; Walkowitz, "Tale of Two Cities."

16. See the documentary film *The Life and Time of Rosie the Riveter* (Direct Cinema, 1980), produced and directed by Connie Field, and on "Momism," see Philip Wylie, *Generation of Vipers* (New York: Rinehart, 1942).

17. See "The National Pastime: Inning Six," in the documentary series *Baseball* by Ken Burns (PBS, 1994).

18. Howard P. Chudacoff, *The Evolution of American Urban Society*, 2d ed. (Englewood Cliffs, N.J.: Prentice-Hall, 1981), 264–66; Herbert J. Gans, *The Levittowners: Ways of Life and Politics in a New Suburban Community* (New York: Pantheon Books, 1967).

19. Evelyn Brooks Higginbotham, "African-American Women's History and the Metalanguage of Race," *Signs* 17 (Winter 1992): 251–74, cited in Lewis, "Invoking Concepts, Problematizing Identities," 292–308.

20. *The Blackboard Jungle* (Warner Brothers, 1955), feature film directed by Richard Brooks, based on the novel by Evan Hunter, *The Blackboard Jungle* (London: Constable, 1955).

21. American Legion, quoted in Gilbert, *Cycle of Outrage*, 184–85. It is interesting to note that the opening scene, which depicts boys dancing together (at a boys school), did not provoke any homophobic commentary. On the incorporation of African American music into vernacular (white) working-class culture via rock 'n' roll, see Lipsitz, *Time Passages*, 13.

22. *West Side Story* (United Artists, 1961), feature film directed by Robert Wise and Jerome Robbins, based on the play *West Side Story* (1957), directed by Jerome Robbins, lyrics by Stephen Sondheim, music by Leonard Bernstein, and book by Arthur Laurents.

23. Minutes, Board of Trustees, May 14, 1951, box 1093, JPA.

24. One of the two organizers for Local 19, District Council 65, was Norma Aronson, and 17 of the 29 people attending the August 1951 Executive Board meeting were women, but only 11 of 29 shop stewards were women. See minutes of Local 19, Executive Board, Aug. 1, 1951, Industry Minutes, Social Service, box 1G, file 75, DC65R. District Council 65 and Local 19 fought "Jim Crowed [*sic*] work loads, sought to integrate Stuyvesant Town where many social workers lived, and pressed for maternity benefits." See "Report on Women—Headquarters and Membership Meeting—April 17, 1951," Area Minutes, box 13, file 1, DC65R; minutes, Oct. 14, 1949, Local 19, Sheltering Arms, box 132, file 19, DC65R; and Area Minutes, Gramercy Area, Jan. 16, 1951, box 13, file 1, folder 5, DC65R.

25. "History," Finder's Guide, SSEU371R. See also Mark H. Maier, *City Unions: Managing Discontent in New York City* (New Brunswick: Rutgers University Press, 1987), and Richard Henry Mendes, "The Professional Union: A Study of the Social Service Employees Union of the New York City Department of Social Services" (Ph.D. diss., Columbia University, 1974).

26. Committee for a More Militant and Representative Union in Welfare, Elections, [1959], box 2, file 54, SSEU371R.

27. It is estimated that almost four-fifths of the trained social workers in New York City remained unorganized during even the most active union era. I suspect that a disproportionate number of the unorganized worked in private agencies, especially those funded by the Catholic church. Leslie B. Alexander, "Organizing the Professional Social Worker: Union Development in Voluntary Social Work, 1930–1950" (Ph.D. diss., Bryn Mawr College, 1976), 144, estimates the national UOPWA membership in 1940 at 3,200.

28. Jewel Bellush and Bernard Bellush, *Union Power and New York: Victor Gotbaum and District Council 37* (New York: Praeger, 1984), 112; Mendes, "Professional Union," 23–29; Mark McColloch, *White Collar Workers in Transition: The Boom Years, 1940–1970* (Westport, Conn.: Greenwood Press, 1983), 63–112.

29. The president of the CSAE was Sam Friedman, an old socialist. See Sam Liebner (pseudonym) oral history, conducted by the author and Adina Back, Feb. 3, 1987, in author's possession. Leah Weiss notes that the new union was accused by the old union "of being Trots." See Leah Weiss (pseudonym) oral history, conducted by the author and Adina Back, Feb. 6, 1987, in author's possession. Bernie Segal refers to the new CSAE leaders as "red-baiters." See Bernard R. Segal oral history, conducted by the author and Dorothy Fennell, July 14, 1992, in author's possession.

30. Clarke A. Chambers, "Foreword," in Jacob Fisher, *The Response of Social Work to the Depression* (Boston: G. K. Hall, 1980), xiv. See also Abe Flaxer, "Keeping One's Head above Water," unpublished manuscript (1989), WLA, and Segal oral history.

31. Raymond M. Hilliard, "We Threw the Commies Out," *Saturday Evening Post*, July 1951; Dorothy Doan to Sally Iselin, June 29, 1951, and "Summary of . . . ," *Trends and Developments Exposing the Communist Conspiracy* 4, no. 7 (July 1951): 27, in Personal Papers, 1951 files, RHC.

32. Edward E. Rhatigan testimony, New York State Hearing on City Welfare Department, Ninth and Tenth Sessions, Dec. 2, 1947, William O'Dwyer Papers, DW, Departmental Letters, box 33, MACNY.

33. With the Senate's Kefauver Committee ready to summon O'Dwyer to testify, O'Dwyer moved to Mexico City as U.S. ambassador. See Walkowitz, "Tale of Two Cities," 198. The Welfare Council selected Hilliard despite opposition from New York City's AASW chapter and the FJP's decision to reject council membership. See *New York Times*, Jan. 31, Mar. 29, 1951, and Marsha Treitman (pseudonym) oral history, conducted by the author, July 15, 1991, in author's possession.

34. Henry L. McCarthy oral history, conducted by Cullum Davis, 1981, Columbia University Oral History Research Office, Butler Library, New York, N.Y.

35. *New York Times*, Mar. 20, 1951, Nov. 11, 1952.

36. Report of the NCSWE, quoted in *New York Times*, Dec. 7, 1951.

37. The DW's Negro History Week began in 1943 and featured speakers such as Thurgood Marshall, Roy Wilkins, and psychologist Kenneth Clark. See Lindsay H. White to Raymond M. Hilliard, July 12, 1951; Raymond M. Hilliard to Arthur B. Spingarn, July 23, 1951; Raymond M. Hilliard to Lindsay H. White, July 23, 1951; James K. Brown to Raymond M. Hilliard, Aug. 16, 1951; and Raymond M. Hilliard to James K. Brown, Aug. 31, 1951, Personal Papers, 1951 files, RHC.

38. *Welfarer* 4, no. 9 (Sept. 1952): 6–7, in Vincent R. Impellitteri Papers, DW, Departmental Correspondence, box 22, MACNY.

39. Clarke A. Chambers, quoted in Walter I. Trattner, *From Poor Law to Welfare State: A History of Social Welfare in America*, 4th ed. (New York: Free Press, 1989), 280.

40. *Welfarer* 4, no. 9 (Sep. 1952): 6–7.

41. Ibid.

42. "Report on Eligibility Case Review and Statement on Administrative Study in the New York City Department of Welfare," Jan. 18, 1952, Impellitteri Papers, DW, Departmental Correspondence, box 22, MACNY.

43. Caseload statistics, Dec. 29, 1953, Impellitteri Papers, DW, Departmental Correspondence, box 34, MACNY; press release on case reduction, Dec. 20, 1948, O'Dwyer Papers, DW, Departmental Correspondence, box 44, MACNY; press release on case reduction, Aug. 18, 1950, O'Dwyer-Impellitteri Papers, DW, Departmental Correspondence, box 1111, MACNY; McCarthy oral history.

44. Working conditions and salaries were worse for the three-quarters of women social workers who were single or widowed. Even black caseworkers as a group averaged $20 a year more than women as a group. See BLS, *Social Workers in 1950*.

45. *New York Times*, Dec. 10, 1942; Minutes, Board of Trustees, Oct. 1953, box 1235, JBGA.

46. *Proceedings*, Annual Sessions (1930–60), NCJSS, YIVO.

47. The title of the JBG's 1958 report summed up its turnover problem: "The Case of the Vanishing American Social Worker . . . ," 1958, Social Work Recruitment, 1956–62, box 1243, JBGA. See also minutes, Board of Trustees, Apr. 20, 1955, box 1235, JBGA, and "Social Work Recruitment, 1956–62," Board of Trustees, box 1243, JBGA. On CSAE contracts with the FJP in 1952 and 1953, see minutes, Board of Trustees, Nov. 2, 1952, box 1094, JBGA, and minutes, Board of Trustees, Oct. 19, 1953, box 1095, FJPA.

48. Public assistance workers, who constituted 40 percent of all social workers (another 27 percent worked in the public sector but in child welfare and other programs), earned considerably less than schoolteachers. Workers in private agencies fared better, but because Jewish caseworker agencies employed many of the best-educated psychiatric social workers, they had to deal with people with high expectations about receiving top dollar. See U.S. Department of Commerce, Bureau of the Census, *Historical Statistics of the United States*, series D (Washington, D.C.: Government Printing Office, 1953), 97, and BLS, *Social Workers in 1950*.

49. Minutes, Board of Trustees, June 14, 1954, box 1095, FJPA; "Report of the Distribution Committee for the 1958–59 Budget Year," Board of Trustees, June 13, 1958, box 1097, FJPA; "Distribution Committee Report," Board of Trustees, Apr. 20, 1959, box 1098, FJPA; Herschel Alt to the Trustees, "Volume of Service to the Clients," Board of Trustees, Sept. 21, 1959, box 139, JBGA; Herschel Alt to David L. Benetar, "Amount of Client Service Given by Caseworkers," Board of Trustees, Apr. 27, 1960, box 139, JBGA.

50. Minutes, Executive Committee, Nov. 7, 1951, box 1094, JBGA.

51. Social workers did not administer drugs, of course, but referred patients to doctors for pharmacological intervention. The use of Thorazine and reserpine is noted in ibid., Apr. 20, 1955, box 1235.

52. Regina G. Kunzel, *Fallen Women, Problem Girls: Unmarried Mothers and the Professionalization of Social Work, 1890–1945* (New Haven: Yale University Press, 1993), chap. 6.

53. Career and Salary Plan Classification Appeal of Stephan Ross, General Grievances, 1958–62, box 2, folder 32, SSEU371R.

54. Marc, "Comic Visions of the City," 56–57

55. For oral histories consulted, see the bibliographical essay. Women in the agencies may never, of course, have seen the Nellie cartoons in the *Welfarer*.

56. Helen Harris Perlman and Arlien Johnson oral histories, 1977–81, NASWOH. See also Beulah S. Hester oral history, 1978, BWOHP, and Gertrude Wilson oral history, 1977–81, NASWOH.

57. Verne Weed, quoted in Yvonne T. Cullen, "An Alternative Tradition in Social Work: Bertha Reynolds, 1885–1978," *Catalyst* 15 (1983): 55–73. Cullen also refers to Bertha Reynolds, *McCarthyism versus Social Work* (New York: National Council of the Arts, Sciences, and Professions, 1954), 11.

58. Because some of the women remain sensitive about old political issues, I have agreed to preserve their anonymity. Weiss is such a woman. Women interviewed as part of the FJPOH are identified by their real names. For the most part, the FJPOH did not inquire about union ties or political work.

59. Martha K. Selig oral history, conducted by Judy E. Tenney, Feb. 9, 1982, FJPOH. Selig, who had moved on to become an administrator herself and a dear friend of Hexter's, did not address this in her interview.

60. Weiss oral history.

61. Ibid.

62. Laura Lewis, *Enter In* (New York: Pilot, 1959). Treitman spoke about this again in a telephone interview with the author, Mar. 22, 1992. Her memory of her decision to publish the book under a pseudonym remained vague, but she proffered that "to have a [Jewish] identity would work against the appeal of the book."

63. Treitman spoke with me in her modest apartment on immodest Central Park West, to which she and her social work sister had moved in the late 1950s by pooling their resources. Such a fashionable address ensured that neither she nor her clients would presume to share a class identity. As neither a communist nor a union leader, Treitman quietly managed to remove herself from the fray and avoid any agency recriminations against her. See Treitman oral history.

64. I owe a considerable debt to Clarke A. Chambers for this discussion.

65. John H. Ehrenreich, *The Altruistic Imagination: A History of Social Work and Social Policy in the United States* (Ithaca: Cornell University Press, 1985), 136–38.

66. Weiss and Liebner oral histories.

67. Mendes, "Professional Union," 29. Much the same point is made in Bellush and Bellush, *Union Power and New York*, 112.

68. Deborah Dash Moore, *At Home in America: Second Generation New York Jews* (New York: Columbia University Press, 1991), and *To the Golden Cities: Pursuing the American Jewish Dream in Miami and Los Angeles* (New York: Free Press, 1994); Suzanne Rachel Wasserman, "The Good Old Days of Poverty: The Battle over the Fate of New York City's Lower East Side during the Depression" (Ph.D. diss., New York University, 1990).

69. Nelson Lichtenstein, "No Labor Party in the United States? What Difference Did It Make?," Beasley Society Lecture, University College, London, Eng., May 4, 1994.

70. Allison Davies, "Ability and Survival," *Survey*, Feb. 1951, 60–63.

71. Michael B. Katz, *The Undeserving Poor: From the War on Poverty to the War on Welfare* (New York: Pantheon, 1989), 16–35.

72. Treitman oral history. This is a complicated piece of evidence to read because it reflects her 1991 attitudes about and memories of views she held over thirty years ago. Since

1959, racial conflict between the Jewish and black communities also sharpened, and Treitman's comment in 1991 may have revealed as much about that shift as it suggests about an underlying weakness in her 1959 interracialism.

73. "Domestic Relations Court of the City of New York vs. Department of Welfare," Oct. 30, 1951, Impellitteri Papers, DW, Departmental Correspondence, box 11, MACNY.

74. Ibid.

75. See Michael B. Katz, *In the Shadow of the Poorhouse: A Social History of Welfare in America* (New York: Basic Books, 1986), chap. 9.

76. "Domestic Relations Court."

77. McCarthy oral history.

78. W. Allen to Francis J. Petrocelli, July 12, 1959, General Grievances, 1958–64, box 2, file 32, SSEU371R.

79. The city comptroller insisted that the city bore no responsibility and refused to legitimize Schaeffer's claim to a work-related injury; he denied Schaeffer's request for $30 in damages. See Controller of the City of New York to Francis J. Petrocelli, Feb. 13, 1959, General Grievances, 1958–64, box 2, file 32, SSEU371R.

80. See, for example, the account of the conflicts between Birmingham's black social workers and their clients during the New Deal in Robin D. G. Kelley, *Hammer and Hoe: Alabama Communists during the Great Depression* (Chapel Hill: University of North Carolina Press, 1990).

81. Renee Newman, "Transposed Parts: Race, Culture, and Identity at the Music School Settlement for Colored People," seminar paper, New York University, fall 1993.

82. James H. Hubert, "Social Work in New York City," *Opportunity: A Journal of Negro Life* 4, no. 3 (Mar. 1926): 102–3; *Opportunity* 5, no. 6 (June 1927): 159.

83. *Opportunity* 5, no. 6 (June 1927): 159.

84. L. Hollingsworth Wood, "The New York Colored Mission: Good Samaritan," *Opportunity* 5, no. 3 (Mar. 1927): 82–83.

85. Walkowitz, "Tale of Two Cities."

86. See "James R. Dumpson," in *Who's Who among Black Americans*, 4th ed. (Lake Forest, Ill.: Education Communications, 1985), 239.

87. Treitman oral history. On the comments about discrimination in Harlem, see chapter 4.

88. See "Report of the Committee on Puerto Ricans in New York City," Welfare Council of New York City, Jan. 1948, and C. Wright Mills to Hon. Jesús Piñero, Governor of Puerto Rico, "Puerto Rican Migration Study," Columbia University, Bureau of Applied Social Research, June 15, 1948, unpublished manuscript, Center for Puerto Rican Studies, Hunter College, City University of New York, New York, N.Y.; General Grievances, 1958–64, box 2, folder 32, SSEU371R.

89. Dorothy I. Haight oral history, 1974, BWOHP.

90. Ann Tanneyhill oral history, 1978, BWOHP.

91. Benjamin E. Youngdahl (1949) and Savilla Millis Simons (1956), in *Proceedings*, Annual Session (1956), NCSW, cited in Frank J. Bruno, *Trends in Social Work, 1874–1956: A History Based on the Proceedings of the National Conference on Social Welfare* (New York: Columbia University Press, 1957), 389–93. The limitations of social work on questions of race are discussed in Stanley Wenocur and Michael Reisch, *From Charity to Enterprise: The Development of American Social Work in a Market Economy* (Urbana: University of Illinois Press, 1989), 256–59. I am indebted to Clarke A. Chambers for this paragraph.

92. Kunzel, *Fallen Women, Problem Girls*, 165; Frances Fox Piven and Richard A. Cloward, *Regulating the Poor: The Functions of Public Welfare* (New York: Random House, 1971).

93. Kunzel, *Fallen Women, Problem Girls*, 164–65; Rickie Solinger, *Wake Up Little Susie: Single Pregnancy and Race before* Roe v. Wade (New York: Routledge, 1992), 205–31. The role of the Catholic church in welfare birth control policy needs to be studied. Commissioners Hilliard, McCarthy, and Dumpson were all Catholics who prohibited social investigators from discussing birth control with clients. Hilliard resigned from the Welfare Council after it agreed to admit Planned Parenthood to its membership. See "Statement by Raymond M. Hilliard on Leaving the Welfare Council of New York City," June 15, 1953, Personal Papers, 1953 files, RHC. On black sexuality, see Treitman oral history.

94. "Social Workers on the Race Issue," *Opportunity* 5, no. 5 (May 1927): 159. All sessions in Memphis were integrated, and when hotels refused to serve African Americans, the conference moved its meals to the Elks Building and the Catholic Club. The hotel also barred blacks from the president's reception, so the president and about twenty delegates appeared at a separate reception for the African American delegation. See *Opportunity* 6, no. 6 (June 1928): 162.

95. Case of Mrs. J. and baby Marilyn (anonymous), Mar. 23, 1959, Rietta May (Hines) Herbert Papers, Schomburg Center for Research in Black Culture, New York, N.Y.

96. Deposition of Anthony Quiñones, Nov. 1958, Grievances, 1952–59, box 2, folder 32, SSEU371R.

97. Mimi Abramovitz, *Regulating the Lives of Women: Social Welfare Policy from Colonial Times to the Present* (Boston: South End Press, 1991), 21, 313–80; Barbara Ehrenreich, *Fear of Falling: The Inner Life of the Middle Class* (New York: Harper Collins, 1989), esp. 108.

98. BLS, *Salaries and Working Conditions*, 10.

99. BLS, *Social Workers in 1950*.

100. Bureau of the Census, *Historical Statistics*, 97; BLS, *Social Workers in 1950*.

101. BLS, *Social Workers in 1950*.

102. Treitman, Weiss, and Selig oral histories; Herbert Papers, Schomburg Center for Research in Black Culture, New York, N.Y. See also minutes, Board of Trustees, Dec. 8, 1952, box 1094, FJPA.

103. Weiss oral history.

104. Selig oral history.

105. Robin D. G. Kelley suggested this pattern of black male identity to me. See, for example, the discussion of work on black social workers in Philadelphia in Vincent P. Franklin, *The Education of Black Philadelphia: The Social and Educational History of a Minority Community, 1900–1950* (Philadelphia: University of Pennsylvania Press, 1979), and Carl H. Nightengale, *On the Edge: A History of Poor Black Children and Their American Dreams* (New York: Basic Books, 1993).

106. See the essays in Ava Baron, ed., *Work Engendered: Toward a New History of American Labor* (Ithaca: Cornell University Press, 1991).

107. Treitman oral history.

108. Liebner oral history.

109. BLS, *Social Workers in 1950*. Social workers with an M.S.W. concentrated in child and family service agencies like those in the FJP under study here. Only 25 public assistance workers in the entire country (out of over 30,000) had an M.S.W. See James Leiby, *A History*

of Social Welfare and Social Work in the United States (New York: Columbia University Press, 1978), 279.

110. This is discussed more fully in chapter 8. See Leigh Benin oral history, conducted by the author and Adina Back, Jan. 28, 1987, in author's possession, and William Schleicher, personal communication with the author, Nov. 9, 1995.

111. "Alcoholism," *Better Times*, Dec. 5, 12, 1952, reprinted in *Welfarer* 4, no. 12 (Dec. 1952), in Impellitteri Papers, DW, Departmental Correspondence, box 22, MACNY.

112. Minutes, Board of Trustees, 1955–56, box 1235, JBGA.

113. Grievance Committee, folders 264–71, 275–77, 279–86, 285–314, AASW/NASWP. See also Wenocur and Reisch, *From Charity to Enterprise*, 242–43.

114. For example, see "Report and Recommendations of the Subcommittee to Study Types of Legal Regulation of Social Work Practice in New York State,' 1957, NASW, New York City Chapter, Suppl. 2, Personnel Series, box 47, National Social Welfare Assembly, SWHA.

115. Minutes, Executive Committee, Oct. 20, 1959, box 139, JBGA.

116. U.S. Department of Commerce, Bureau of the Census, *Census of Population, 1950*, vol. 4, pt. 1, *Subject Reports, Occupational Characteristics* (Washington, D.C.: Government Printing Office, 1952), 129, table 13, and *Census of Population, 1960*, vol. 1, *Subject Reports, Occupational Characteristics* (Washington, D.C.: Government Printing Office, 1961), table 21.

Chapter Eight

1. "Minorities" (identified as blacks, Hispanics, and women) struggled with Italian- and Irish-dominated unions over discriminatory hiring practices in the construction industry and uniformed trades (sanitation, police, fire).

2. Felicia Kornbluh, "A Right to Welfare?: Poor Women, Professionals, and Poverty Programs, 1935–1975" (Ph.D. diss., Princeton University, forthcoming), notes that this demand was central to the NWRO's quest for a guaranteed adequate income in 1966–67.

3. Minutes, Board of Trustees, Jan. 11, 1960, box 1098, FJPA.

4. I was one such person. Living in New Jersey I attended a summer camp run by the FJP in the early 1950s and later took advantage of its vocational testing program.

5. Willens did not try to answer these questions but merely suggested that non-Jews be added to boards to reflect the agencies' present constituency. See minutes, Board of Trustees, Nov. 18, 1957, box 1096, FJPA.

6. Ibid., Mar. 20, 1959, box 1098.

7. Ibid.

8. Ibid.

9. *New York Times*, Nov. 13, 1963.

10. Ibid.

11. Minutes, Executive Committee, Nov. 14, 1963, box 138, JBGA.

12. Frances Fox Piven and Richard A. Cloward, *Regulating the Poor: The Functions of Public Welfare* (New York: Random House, 1971), 183–92.

13. Ibid. Welfare rolls grew elsewhere irrespective of increases in benefit levels. Increased benefits might help explain the quadrupled rolls in New York City, except that rolls also quadrupled in Los Angeles, where there was no comparable increase in benefits.

14. Ibid., 138, 329, n. 32.

15. See Bret N. Eynon, "Democracy, Community, and the Reconstruction of Political Life: The Civil Rights Influence on New Left Political Culture, Ann Arbor, 1958–68" (Ph.D. diss., New York University, 1993); Kornbluh, "A Right to Welfare?"; and Saul Alinsky, *Reveille for Radicals* (New York: Vintage, 1969), and *Rules for Radicals: A Practical Primer for Realistic Radicals* (New York: Random House, 1971).

16. Piven and Cloward, *Regulating the Poor*, 329.

17. Blacks' conflict with Asians, which would constitute a second counternarrative of the African American experience, became equally important in the late 1980s.

18. Murray Polner, review of Hillel Levine, *The Death of an American Jewish Community: A Tragedy of Good Intentions* (New York: Free Press, 1992), in *The Nation*, Mar. 2, 1992, 276–79.

19. See Suzanne Rachel Wasserman, "The Good Old Days of Poverty: The Battle over the Fate of New York City's Lower East Side during the Depression" (Ph.D. diss., New York University, 1990). The growth of Orthodox Judaism needs study. It may be attributed to high birth rates among the Orthodox, in-migration (from both Israel and Russia), and New Age spiritualism among Jewish cultural radicals in the 1960s that made secular Jews especially receptive to Lubavitcher outreach programs. At the same time, as intermarriage among less-religious Jews rose to nearly 50 percent, the celebration of the search for one's "roots" (and identity politics) may have increased the appeal of the Orthodox tradition.

20. Ibid.

21. The story of the largely Jewish teachers' union conflict with the black community of Ocean Hill–Brownsville in 1968 has been told often, most recently in Marjorie Murphy, *Blackboard Unions: The AFT and the NEA, 1900–1980* (Ithaca: Cornell University Press, 1990). On segregated New York City schools, see Adina Back, "Up South in New York: The 1950s School Desegregation Struggles" (Ph.D. diss., New York University, 1997).

22. Jeffrey S. Gurok, *The Men and Women of Yeshiva: Higher Education, Orthodoxy, and American Judaism* (New York: Columbia University Press, 1988), 217–18. Seeking to counter this trend within their own community, approximately sixty Yeshiva University students formed the Yeshiva University Neighborhood Youth Corp to "mend fences" in the Washington Heights neighborhood.

23. See Paul Berman, ed., *Blacks and Jews: Alliances and Arguments* (New York: Delacorte Press, 1994).

24. Kevin Phillips, *The Emerging Republican Majority* (New Rochelle, N.Y.: Arlington Press, 1969); James Albert Michener, *America vs. America: The Revolution in Middle-Class Values* (New York: New American Library, 1969); Lowell D. Streiker and Gerald S. Strober, *Religion and the New Majority: Billy Graham, Middle America, and the Politics of the 70s* (New York: Association Press, 1972). Robert Coldwell Wood, *The Necessary Majority: Middle America and the Urban Crisis* (New York: Columbia University Press, 1972), critiques this neoconservative explanation.

25. Phillips, *Emerging Republican Majority*, 119.

26. Cynthia Ozick, "Literary Blacks and Jews," in Berman, *Blacks and Jews*, 46–47.

27. Ibid. See also Norman Podhoretz, "My Negro Problem—and Ours (1963), with Post-script (1993)," and Ellen Willis, "The Myth of the Powerful Jew (1979), with Prologue (1994)," in Berman, *Blacks and Jews*, 76–96, 183–203.

28. The fascinating history of this and subsequent strikes in this decade has been told well

in Richard Henry Mendes, "The Professional Union: A Study of the Social Service Employees Union of the New York City Department of Social Services" (Ph.D. diss., Columbia University, 1974), and Mark H. Maier, *City Unions: Managing Discontent in New York City* (New Brunswick: Rutgers University Press, 1987), 57–76. See also Jewel Bellush and Bernard Bellush, *Union Power and New York: Victor Gotbaum and District Council 37* (New York: Praeger, 1984), 111–39. Unfortunately, the detailed FJP history of this era will have to be told another time.

29. Maier, *City Unions*, 59. Diana became assistant for labor relations to Mayor Wagner, Russo became commissioner of labor relations and Petrocelli became executive officer in the DW. Some sense of Petrocelli's cordial working relationship with Dumpson can be gleaned from union records. See Summary of Meeting with Dumpson, Nov. 24, 1959, box 2, file 13, SSEU371R.

30. Committee for a More Militant and Representative Union in Welfare to Members, n.d., and Frank Petroceli to Fellow Member, May 2, 1959, box 2, file 54, SSEU371R. The two slates differed in important ways. In addition to its moderate, conciliatory mode, Local 371 was dominated by supervisory and clerical personnel of Italian and Irish descent. The Podell slate was all male; was seemingly all Jewish; was made up primarily, if not exclusively, of caseworkers; and emphasized an adversarial position with the commissioner.

31. Election results, May 18, 1959, box 2, file 54, SSEU371R. Running for vice president, Podell lost to Nicholas Buccinna, 518 to 405.

32. Ibid.; "1963 Local 371 Election, Committee for Union Democracy," n.d., box 2, file 56, SSEU371R.

33. In the DW, 6,370 people in 17 job titles were eligible to join the union. See Bellush and Bellush, *Union Power and New York*, 112, and Maier, *City Unions*, 59–60.

34. Maier, *City Unions*, 60.

35. Ibid., 61–62; Mendes, "Professional Union," 47–60.

36. Bellush and Bellush, *Union Power and New York*, 115; *New York Times*, May 31, 1962; Leigh Benin, "Radicals in the 'Real' World: The Social Service Employees Union and the Limits of the New Radicalism of the 1960s," seminar paper, New York University, 1988.

37. See Martha K. Selig oral history, conducted by Judy E. Tenney Feb. 9, 22, 1982, FJPOH; Marsha Treitman (pseudonym) oral history, conducted by the author, July 15, 1991, in author's possession. Gender relations during third-wave feminism are discussed further in the epilogue.

38. "New working class" theory developed after the publication of Serge Mallet, *Nouvelle classe ouvrière* (Paris: Editions du Seuil, 1963), and Andre Gorz, *Stratégie ouvrière et neo-capitalisme* (Paris: Editions du Seuil, 1964). Gorz's book was published in English three years later as *Strategy for Labor: A Radical Proposal* (Boston: Beacon, 1967). See also Serge Mallet, ed., *Essays on the New Working Class* (St. Louis: Telos Press, 1975).

39. Maier, *City Unions*, 62 accepts the view of Mendes, "Professional Union," that SSEU members came from "two distinct backgrounds": an older one rooted in the depression and a newer one made up of migrants to the city. This analysis ignores younger New Left activists like Mage who also came from the city and gives little attention to the New Left or the intervening history of the 1950s. Benin, "Radicals in the 'Real' World," develops the place of "new working class" theory in social work.

40. SSEU, "Introducing the Social Service Employees Union" (1963), quoted in Benin, "Radicals in the 'Real' World," 9.

41. Bellush and Bellush, *Union Power and New York*, 116; Benin, "Radicals in the 'Real' World."

42. Piven and Cloward, *Regulating the Poor*, 183–98, 290–330; Gregory K. Raynor, "The Ford Foundation's War on Poverty: Private Philanthropy and Race Relations in New York City, 1948–1968," in *Studying Philanthropic Foundations: New Scholarship, New Possibilities* (Bloomington: Indiana University Press, forthcoming), chap. 9.

43. Felicia Kornbluh kindly shared her conversations with Piven and Cloward with me: Felicia Kornbluh to the author, Jan. 12, 1996. Piven and Cloward strategized in *The Nation* (1966) that in order to gain political support for decent welfare provisions, it would be necessary to create a "crisis" in service.

44. Piven and Cloward, *Regulating the Poor*, 147–61; Rickie Solinger, *Wake Up Little Susie: Single Pregnancy and Race before* Roe v. Wade (New York: Routledge, 1992), 152–53. See also Michael B. Katz, *The Undeserving Poor: From the War on Poverty to the War on Welfare* (New York: Pantheon, 1989).

45. William Schleicher, personal communication with the author, Nov. 9, 1995.

46. Leigh Benin oral history, conducted by the author and Adina Back, Jan. 28, 1987, in author's possession.

47. Ibid.

48. After the purge of the UPW, the city established a career and salary plan for the DW in 1954 that placed questions of caseloads and working conditions outside the scope of labor relations.

49. "Primary Loyalty," Nov. 17, 1966, box 2010, SSEU-NY file, NWROP. Thanks to Felicia Kornbluh for this document.

50. "To All Welfare Client Groups in New York City," May 27, 1966, box 2010, SSEU-NY file, NWROP.

51. Benin, "Radicals in the 'Real' World"; Maier, *City Unions*, 64–67.

52. Maier, *City Unions*, 65–66.

53. SSEU, "Second Bargaining Contract between the City of New York and the Social Service Employees Union," June 7, 1965, quoted in Benin, "Radicals in the 'Real' World," 16–17.

54. Maier, *City Unions*, 67, 81–82. The SSEU agreed to mediation only after the city agreed to allow the union to contest Condon-Wadlin's legality.

55. Ibid., 56, 67–68, 71; Benin, "Radicals in the 'Real' World," 18.

56. Maier, *City Unions*, 78–82.

57. Ibid., 69. In the face of considerable public pressure, the city released the funds two years later, but with the understanding that it would not acknowledge the union's authority in such matters again.

58. "New Welfare Title May Eliminate Caseworkers," *Civil Service Leader*, Dec. 20, 1966, 1, 16, reprinted as a one-page flier by the SSEU. Felicia Kornbluh kindly supplied this document.

59. Benin, "Radicals in the 'Real' World," 22; Bellush and Bellush, *Union Power and New York*; Maier, *City Unions*, 70–71.

60. These strikes are detailed nicely in Maier, *City Unions*, chap. 5; Bellush and Bellush, *Union Power and New York*, 130–36; Mendes, "Professional Union"; and Benin, "Radicals in the 'Real' World," 24–36.

61. *New York Times*, June 20, 24, 1967, cited in Maier, *City Unions*, 71.

62. Maier, *City Union*, 70–71; Benin, "Radicals in the 'Real' World," 27.

63. Benin, "Radicals in the 'Real' World," 37; Judith Mage, in *Civil Service Leader*, Nov. 14, 1967, cited in Benin, "Radicals in the 'Real' World," 37.

64. Benin oral history.

65. Gilbert Y. Steiner, *State of Welfare* (Washington, D.C.: Brookings Institute, 1971), 300.

66. Maier, *City Union*, 73.

67. Ibid., 72; Bellush and Bellush, *Union Power and New York*, 132. Lindsay established the Office of Collective Bargaining in 1968 in an effort to rationalize the city's labor relations.

68. The two sides always reached accord, although usually not without the threat of strikes and cliff-hanger settlements. See Sam Liebner (pseudonym) oral history, conducted by the author and Adina Back, Feb. 3, 1987, in author's possession. See also minutes, Board of Trustees, Nov. 9, 1959, box 1098, FJPA, and "Union, 1961," Oct. 25, Nov. 20, 1961, box 47, JBGA.

69. Sam Liebner remembered these years as the "golden age" at Hawthorne–Cedar Knolls, when people from all over the world visited the facilities to see the latest in psychiatric social work care and treatment. Liebner oral history.

70. Ibid.

71. Herschel Alt to the public, Feb. 28, 1962, and Negotiations Staff Petition, Feb. 8, 1962, "Union, 1962," box 47, JBGA.

72. "Union, 1961–62," Feb. 22, 28, 1962, box 47, JBGA; *New York Times*, Feb. 17, 18, 21, 22, 27, 1962; Liebner oral history; Albert Benghiat, quoted in *White Plains Reporter-Dispatch*, Feb. 17, 1962, in "Union, 1961–62," box 47, JBGA. Pleasantville cottage parents opposed the strike by Hawthorne–Cedar Knolls cottage parents, but when Herschel Alt, the JBG's executive director, and Jerome Goldsmith, the school's executive director, refused to engage the issues raised by the staff, strike support spread.

73. *Process*, no. 35 (Feb. 1962/Aug. 1963), in "Union, 1962–63," box 47, JBGA. Also, Liebner left Hawthorne after the strike. As a cottage supervisor, he felt his friendship with social workers had undermined his ability to work with administrators. He also had misgivings about a strike at a facility such as Hawthorne. See Liebner oral history.

74. *New York Times*, Feb. 22, 27, 1962.

75. "Union, 1962," Apr. 4, June 7, 1962, box 47, JBGA.

76. Ibid., Sept. 19, 1962.

77. Minutes, Board of Trustees, May 13, 1963, box 1100, FJPA.

78. *New York Times*, Feb. 21, Mar. 3, 1964.

79. Liebner oral history.

80. *New York Times*, Feb. 22, 27, 1964; "Union, 1964," Mar. 2, 1964, box 47, JBGA.

81. *New York Times*, Mar. 3, 1964; memo, D. J. Merwin to Executive Committee, Mar. 30, 1964, "Union, 1964," box 47, JBGA; Martin Tolchin, telephone conversation with the author, Dec. 1994.

82. Merwin to Executive Committee, Mar. 30, 1964. Merwin crossed out several passages to obscure the intervention of the trustees with the *New York Times* editors.

83. D. J. Merwin to Herschel Alt, Feb. 28, 1964, "1964 Strike," box 47, JBGA.

84. An acrimonious struggle for the top leadership post in the international union exacerbated the dispute. Jerry Wurf, the executive director of AFSCME's District Council 37 in New York City, had lost a close election for AFSCME president to Arnold Zander two years before. With a new election pending, both sides sought every opportunity to demon-

strate that they could do more for the striking workers. See *New York Herald Tribune*, Mar. 15, 1964. See also Personnel Committee, Mar. 15, 1964, box 197, FJPA, and *New York Times*, Feb. 21, Mar. 3, 1964.

85. "Union, 1964," Mar. 12, Apr. 24, 1964, box 47, JBGA.

86. *New York Times*, Mar. 9, 11, 12, July 9, 1964.

87. "Review of Last Meeting of Personnel Committee," Apr. 8, 1964, box 47, JBGA.

88. Minutes, Board of Trustees, Nov. 22, 1965, box 1101, FJPA.

89. FJP trustees congratulated themselves that the cost of the settlement ($95,000) would be offset by savings of $150,000 during the strike. See minutes, Board of Trustees, Nov. 18, 1963, box 1100, and Nov. 22, 1965, box 1101, FJPA.

90. "Union, 1963," Apr. 30, 1963, box 47, JBGA. See also Barbara Ehrenreich and John H. Ehrenreich, "The Professional-Managerial Class," in *Between Labor and Capital: The Professional Managerial Class*, ed. Pat Walker (Boston: South End Press, 1979), 5–45.

91. "Union, 1964," Feb. 21, 1964, box 47, JBGA.

92. Martin Tolchin, "Psyches Conflict in Strike Parley," *New York Times*, Mar. 9, 1964.

93. Ibid.

94. Ibid. Bruno Bettelheim, author of *Social Change and Prejudice* (New York: Free Press, 1964), lambasted radical protesters in testimony before Congress in the mid-1960s. See also Lewis Samuel Feuer, *The Conflict of Generations: The Character and Significance of Student Movements* (New York: Basic Books, 1969), and Maier, *City Unions*.

95. Otto Kerner et al., *The National Advisory Commission on Civil Disorders* (New York: Dutton, 1968), 35–41, 56–84, 112–16.

96. Jerald E. Podair, " 'White' Values, 'Black' Values: The Ocean Hill–Brownsville Controversy and New York City Culture, 1965–1975," *Radical History Review* 59 (Spring 1994): 36–59.

97. Benin oral history. Benin sympathetically describes the hostility he felt from clients and the stilted way they acted in his presence, fearful of losing support if the investigator disliked them.

98. See Murphy, *Blackboard Unions*, and Back, "Up South in New York."

99. Steiner, *State of Welfare*, 26–42.

100. Solinger, *Wake Up Little Susie*, 205–31.

101. U.S. Department of Labor, Office of Policy Planning and Research, *The Negro Family: The Case for National Action* (Washington, D.C.: Government Printing Office, 1965); Steiner, *State of Welfare*, 26. On Moynihan, see Michael B. Katz, "The Urban 'Underclass' as a Metaphor of Social Transformation," in *The "Underclass" Debate: Views from History*, ed. Michael B. Katz (Princeton: Princeton University Press, 1993), 12–13, and *Undeserving Poor*, 44–52.

102. Nathan Glazer and Daniel Patrick Moynihan, *Beyond the Melting Pot: The Negroes, Puerto Ricans, Jews, Italians, and Irish of New York City* (New York: M.I.T. Press, 1963).

103. See Piven and Cloward, *Regulating the Poor*, and Steiner, *State of Welfare*, 295–305.

104. See Balfour Brickner, "Jewish Youth, Israel, and the Third World," *Reconstructionist*, Mar. 27, 1970, 7–13; Robert G. Weisbord and Arthur Stein, "Black Nationalism and the Arab-Israelite Conflict," *Patterns of Prejudice* 3 (Nov.–Dec. 1969): 1–9; and Arthur Liebman, *Jews and the Left* (New York: John Wiley and Sons, 1979), 564–68. Thanks to Robin D. G. Kelley for these citations.

105. Minutes, Executive Committee, Mar. 8, 31, 1967, box 138, JBGA.

106. Ibid., Apr. 24, 1967.

107. Ibid., May 10, 1967.

108. Minutes, Board of Trustees, Jan. 13, 1969, box 1102, FJPA.

109. Ibid., Mar. 10, Apr. 14, 1969.

110. Ibid., May 12, 1969.

111. Liebner oral history.

112. Minutes, Board of Trustees, Oct. 21, 1968, box 1102, FJPA.

Epilogue

1. See Walter I. Trattner, *From Poor Law to Welfare State: A History of Social Welfare in America*, 4th ed. (New York Free Press, 1989), chap. 5; Barry Bluestone and Bennett Harrison, *The Deindustrialization of America: Plant Closings, Community Abandonment, and the Dismantling of Basic Industries* (New York: Basic Books, 1982); Juliet B. Schor, *The Overworked American: The Unexpected Decline of Leisure* (New York: Basic Books, 1991); and Michael B. Fabricant and Steve Burghardt, *The Welfare State Crisis and the Transformation of Social Service Work* (Armonk, N.Y.: M. E. Sharpe, 1992).

2. Mark H. Maier, *City Unions: Managing Discontent in New York City* (New Brunswick: Rutgers University Press, 1987), 72.

3. For an excellent summary of the early human services field, see Betty Reid Mandell, "Blurring Definitions of Social Services: Human Services v. Social Work," *Catalyst: A Socialist Journal of the Social Services* 4, no. 3 (1983): 5–21. See also Stanley Wenocur and Michael Reisch, *From Charity to Enterprise: The Development of American Social Work in a Market Economy* (Urbana: University of Illinois Press, 1989), 266.

4. Clarke A. Chambers, personal communication with the author, Mar. 1995; Trattner, *From Poor Law to Welfare State*, 311. In contrast to social workers, men in the New York City uniformed services (police, fire, sanitation) and construction industry were cool, if not hostile, to African American and Hispanic workers (and women) entering their preserves.

5. Mandell, "Blurring Definitions." Mandell also notes that the new careers movement, as part of the war on poverty in the mid-1960s, sought to create jobs for poor people. See also Arthur Pearl and Frank Reissman, *New Careers for the Poor* (New York: Free Press, 1965).

6. See U.S. Department of Commerce, Bureau of the Census, *1990 Census of Population and Housing*, Equal Employment Opportunity file, United States, welfare service workers (occupational code 465), tape file 3C, United States Summary: Urbanized Areas and Their Components (Washington, D.C.: CD-Rom, Data User Services Division, 1993). See also *New York Times*, Sept. 5, 1994. Nationally, 83.7 percent of the welfare service aides were female.

7. Ibid., Region 300: NY-NJ-Ct CMSA, finds that white aides had become a minority of 49.9 percent, even with the inclusion of the Long Island, New Jersey, and Connecticut suburban areas.

8. Inabel Burns Lindsay oral history, conducted by Vida S. Grayson, 1977–81, NASWOH.

9. U.S. Department of Commerce, Bureau of the Census *Census of Population, 1970*, vol. 1, *Occupational Characteristics* (Washington, D.C.: Government Printing Office, 1973), 59–86, table 5. Two-thirds of the social workers enumerated in 1970 had completed college, compared to only 7.2 percent of the aides. Not surprisingly, almost all (93.6 percent) caseworkers had high school diplomas.

10. Frances Fox Piven and Richard A. Cloward, *The New Class War: Reagan's Attack on the Welfare State and Its Consequences* (New York: Pantheon, 1982).

11. The negative image of social workers is reflected in the continuing lack of novels in which they are featured. For the post-1965 era, see Charlotte Armstrong, "The Turret Room," in *The Charlotte Armstrong Reader* (New York: Coward, McCann, 1970), 325–474, and Violet Weingarten, *A Loving Wife* (New York: Knopf, 1969). Negative film and theatrical representations include *Brother from Another Planet* (Cinecom International Films, 1984; directed by John Sayles, produced by Peggy Rajski and Maggie Renzi) and the revival of the play *Annie*. Conservative talk radio programs also debunk social workers.

12. Mandell, "Blurring Definitions," 15.

13. On crime, one piece of data illustrates the changing incidence of violent crime since 1960: the number of homicides recorded in New York City rose from 390 in 1960 to 2,250 in 1990. See *New York Times*, Jan. 1, 1995.

14. See, for example, Gary Cherniss, *Professional Burnout in Human Service Organization* (New York: Praeger, 1980) and *Staff Burnout: Job Stress in the Human Services* (Beverly Hills: Sage Publications, 1980); Jerry Edelwick, *Burn-out: Stages of Disillusionment in the Helping Professions* (New York: Human Sciences Press, 1980); Kristine Siefert, Jayaratha Srinika, and Wayne A. Chessil, "Job Satisfaction, Burnout, and Turnover in Health Care Social Workers," *Health and Social Work* 16 (Aug. 1991): 193–202; and Joan Arches, "Social Structure, Burnout, and Job Satisfaction," *Social Work* 36 (May 1991): 202–6.

15. Bureau of the Census, *Census of Population, 1970*, vol. 1, *Characteristics of the Population*, pt. 34, chap. D, *Detailed Population Characteristics*, 420, 466–70, table 219, 856–57, table 226.

16. Minutes, Executive Committee, Oct. 3, 1951, box 139, JBGA; minutes, Board of Trustees, Oct. 19, 1955, box 1235, JBGA; minutes, Executive Committee, Oct. 18, 1961, box 139, JBGA.

17. Memo, Donald J. Merwin to Herschel Alt, Mar. 6, 1964, "Union, 1964," box 47, JBGA.

18. Harry Specht and Mark E. Courtney, *Unfaithful Angels: How Social Work Has Abandoned Its Mission* (New York: Free Press, 1994), chap. 5.

19. Minutes, Board of Trustees, Dec. 14, 1964, box 1100, FJPA.

20. See Schor, *Overworked American*.

21. *BCR Reports* (Bertha Capen Reynolds Society) 2, nos. 3 and 4 (Winter 1990): 5; Shirley Sealy, "Social-Work Field Gains Size, Status," *New York University Magazine* 1, no. 2 (Winter 1986): 75–76; Daniel Coleman, "Social Workers Take Leading Role in Therapy," *New York Times*, Apr. 30, 1985; Karen Brothers and Sue Daley, "Practice Interests and Client Group Preferences of New York University M.S.W. Students," Dec. 1996, unpublished paper in author's possession.

22. Coleman, "Social Workers Take Leading Role in Therapy."

23. Specht and Courtney, *Unfaithful Angels*. See also John H. Ehrenreich, *The Altruistic Imagination: A History of Social Work and Social Policy in the United States* (Ithaca: Cornell University Press, 1985), chap. 8; Wenocur and Reisch, *From Charity to Enterprise*, 268–69; Regina G. Kunzel, *Fallen Women, Problem Girls: Unmarried Mothers and the Professionalization of Social Work, 1890–1945* (New Haven: Yale University Press, 1993), 148–52; and Richard Wightman Fox and T. J. Jackson Lears, eds., *The Culture of Consumption: Critical Essays in American History, 1880–1980* (New York: Pantheon, 1983).

24. Werner W. Boehm, review of Specht and Courtney, *Unfaithful Angels*, *Social Welfare History Group Newsletter*, no. 86 (Aug. 1994): n.p.

25. *New York Times*, Apr. 30, 1985. I am familiar with New York City fees from discussion with various therapists and clients and from personal experience. Managed care rates as of mid-1997 were provided by Professor Sam Rosenberg, a licensed social worker and educator, from a review of Manhattan fees authorized by the Health Insurance Plan (HIP) of Greater New York, the Oxford Health Plan, and U.S. Healthcare.

26. See Barbara Levy Solomon, "Rethinking Empowerment," *Journal of Progressive Human Services* 1, no. 1 (1990): 27–39.

27. See *Issues in Radical Therapy*, 1973–82. Published principally by psychologists, this journal spoke to all radical therapists. The description of radical therapy as egalitarian is by Brandeis University professor of social work David G. Gil in "Clinical Practice and Politics of Human Liberation," *Catalyst* 1, no. 2 (1978): 68.

28. Evelyn Blake (pseudonym), personal communication with the author, Jan. 1995.

29. For example, see Karen Stallard, Barbara Ehrenreich, and Holly Sklar, *Poverty in the American Dream: Women and Children First* (New York: Institute for New Communications, 1983), and Annette Fuentes and Barbara Ehrenreich, *Women in the Global Factory* (Boston: Institute for Communication, 1983). Earlier versions of both books appeared in *Ms.*, July 1982, Jan. 1981, respectively.

30. Maier, *City Unions*, 75–76; Leigh Benin oral history, conducted by the author and Adina Back, Jan. 28, 1987, in author's possession.

31. Maier, *City Unions*, 171, 174.

32. Ruth Abramson (pseudonym) oral history, conducted by the author and Adina Back, Mar. 7, 1987, in author's possession.

33. Ibid.

34. Ibid.

35. Weingarten wrote for the *Brooklyn Eagle* from 1935 into the 1950s. *A Loving Wife* was the second of her four novels. She also wrote four nonfiction books, the last of which is an autobiographical account of her losing battle with cancer, *Intimations of Mortality* (New York: Knopf, 1978). She was deeply committed to social welfare and also wrote film scripts for nonprofit health and welfare agencies. Calling both Sutton Place South in Manhattan and the Westchester suburb of Mt. Kisco, New York, home, Weingarten lived the life of affluence she described. Her husband, Victor, was president of the Institute of Public Affairs. Her obituary appears in the *New York Times*, July 18, 1976.

36. See Joanne Meyerowitz, ed., *Not June Cleaver: Women and Gender in Postwar America, 1945–1960* (Philadelphia: Temple University Press, 1994).

37. Weingarten, *A Loving Wife*, 55.

38. *JTA Daily News Bulletin*, Dec. 12, 1975, in minutes, Executive Office, box 2433, 1975 file, FJPA.

39. Frederick P. Rose to Boards of Directors, Federation-UJA agencies, [Nov. 1975], and Adie Cooper to Sanford Solender, June 13, 1977, Executive Office, box 2433, 1975 and 1977 files, FJPA; minutes, Board of Trustees, Oct. 27, Nov. 10, 1975, box 1106, 1975 file, FJPA; miscellaneous papers, Apr.–June 1977, box 1233, Community Services, Strike file, FJPA.

40. Minutes, Board of Trustees, Apr. 11, 1970, box 1103; Oct. 8, 1973, box 1104, FJPA; "Reject the Offer!," leaflet, ca. May 1977, box 1233, Community Services, Strike file, FJPA. The JCCA was expected to join this umbrella unit but finally resisted the merger for complicated reasons that may have had as much to do with concerns about autonomy as with policy differences with the other agencies reflected in the dispute over integrated services.

41. Leonore Davidoff and Catherine Hall, *Family Fortunes: Men and Women of the English Middle Class, 1780–1850* (Chicago: University of Chicago Press, 1990); Mary P. Ryan, *Cradle of the Middle Class: The Family in Oneida County, New York, 1790–1865* (New York: Cambridge University Press, 1981). See also E. P. Thompson, *The Making of the English Working Class* (New York: Vintage Books, 1963).

42. John Hull Mollenkopf and Manuel Castells, eds., *Dual City: Restructuring New York* (New York: Russell Sage Foundation, 1991); Daniel J. Walkowitz, "New York: A Tale of Two Cities," in *Snowbelt Cities: Metropolitan Politics in the Northeast and Midwest since World War II* (Bloomington: Indiana University Press, 1990), 189–208.

43. On globalization, see Saskia Sassen, *The Global City: New York, London, Tokyo* (Princeton: Princeton University Press, 1991), and *The Mobility of Labor and Capital: A Study in International Investment and Labor Flow* (Cambridge: Cambridge University Press, 1987); and Fuentes and Barbara Ehrenreich, *Women in the Global Factory*. The impact on professional managerial workers is detailed in Barbara Ehrenreich, *Fear of Falling: The Inner Life of the Middle Class* (New York: Pantheon, 1989).

44. Sam Roberts, "Gap between Rich and Poor in New York City Grows Wider," *New York Times*, Dec. 25, 1994.

45. Michael Keith and Steve Pile, "Introduction Part One: The Politics of Place" and "Introduction Part Two: The Place of Politics," in *Place and the Politics of Identity*, ed. Michael Keith and Steve Pile (London: Routledge, 1993), 1–40. See also David Harvey, "Class Relations, Social Justice, and the Politics of Difference," in Keith and Pile, *Place and the Politics of Identity*, 41–66.

46. Danny L. Jorgensen, "The Social Construction of Professional Knowledge: Social Work Ideology, 1956–1973," *Journal of Sociology and Social Welfare* 6, no. 4 (1979): 434–63, finds that agency workers and workers with an M.S.W. tend to support and define professionalism as "clinicalism rather than social reform."

47. See Paul Berman's splendid anthology of documents on black-Jewish relations since the mid-1960s: *Blacks and Jews: Alliances and Arguments* (New York: Delacorte Press, 1994).

48. See Neal Gabler, *An Empire of Their Own: How the Jews Invented Hollywood* (New York: Crown, 1988), and David Desser and Lester D. Friedman, *American Jewish Filmmakers: Traditions and Trends* (Urbana: University of Illinois Press, 1993). Between 1990 and 1993, the head of the City College of New York, CUNY, African American Studies Department, Leonard Jeffries, popularized the view of Jewish domination as part of a cabal against blacks. For an assessment of the earlier history of Jews in the academy, see Susanne Klingenstein, *Jews in the American Academy, 1900–1940: The Dynamics of Intellectual Assimilation* (New Haven: Yale University Press, 1991).

49. See, in particular, Norman Podhoretz, "My Negro Problem—and Ours (1963), with Postscript (1993)," and Clayborne Carson, "The Politics of Relations between African-Americans and Jews," in Berman, *Blacks and Jews*, 76–96, 131–43. *Commentary* was funded by the American Jewish Committee, and although the committee did not necessarily agree with its views, it was easy for outsiders to blur the distinction.

50. Committee on Communal Planning, "Goals and Purposes of the Federation of Jewish Philanthropies of New York," Mar. 31, 1969, Board of Trustees, box 1102, 1969 file, FJPA.

51. Minutes, Board of Trustees, Mar. 9, 1970, box 1102, FJPA.

52. A front-page feature article in the *New York Times*, Mar. 29, 1984, describes the Orthodox resurgence and the varieties of its expression.

53. Minutes, Board of Trustees, Apr. 11, June 8, 1970, box 1103, FJPA. I am particularly in-debted to Gail Katz for sharing her experience in the Brooklyn Orthodox community with me.

54. Ibid., Oct. 8, 1973, box 1104; Sept. 9, Dec 9, 1974, box 1105.

55. Strained relations between blacks and Jews can be seen in the numerous references under "Jews" in the annual index to the *New York Times* after 1970. By 1984, Reverend Jesse Jackson's well-publicized reference to "Hymietown" and Reverend Louis Farrakhan's de-scription of Judaism as a "gutter religion" had led the American Jewish Committee to describe the strains as an "open rift." See *New York Times*, May 4, 1984. The New York American Civil Liberties Union actively continues to press the *Sugarman* case on behalf of the plaintiffs.

56. Marti Bombyk and Mimi Abramovitz, founding editors of *Catalyst*, confirmed this profile of the Reynolds Society in telephone conversations with the author, Apr. 1996.

57. See "Introduction: Transitions," *Journal of Progressive Human Service* 1, no. 1 (1990): 1–2; John H. Ehrenreich, *Altruistic Imagination*, 13, 72, 118–19, 203; Reynolds Society call to annual meetings, in author's possession; and Gisela Konopka oral history, conducted by Vida S. Grayson, 1979, NASWOH.

58. See NABSW, program, Twenty-seventh Annual Conference, Apr. 12–16, 1995, New York, N.Y., and *News* (ABSW, New York City chapter) 1, no. 12 (Summer/Fall 1995). Dean Lucretia Phillips of the New York University School of Social Work kindly supplied these materials. The NABSW office provided the estimate of its membership in April 1996.

59. NABSW, program, Twenty-seventh Annual Conference, Apr. 12–16, 1995, New York, N.Y.; *News* (ABSW New York City chapter) 1, no. 12 (Summer/Fall 1995).

60. Ann Tanneyhill oral history, 1978, BWOHP.

61. Beulah S. Hester oral history, 1978, BWOHP; Frankie V. Adams oral history, 1977, BWOHP.

62. Adams, Lindsay, Tanneyhill, and Hester oral histories.

63. Linda Gordon publicizes the sorry history of violence against women in her classic book, *Heroes of Their Own Lives: The Politics and History of Family Violence, Boston, 1880–1960* (New York: Viking, 1988).

64. See, for example, George Brages and John A. Michael, "The Sex Distribution in Social Work: Causes and Consequences," *Social Casework* 50, no. 10 (Dec. 1969): 595–601; Mary C. Schwartz, "The Importance of the Sex of Workers and Clients," *Social Service Review* 19 (Mar. 1974): 177–85; Jamie Wood Wetzel, "Interaction of Feminism and Social Work in America," *Social Casework* 57, no. 4 (Apr. 1976): 227–36; Wynne S. Kerr, "Exploring Differ-ences among Women in Social Work," *Social Service Review* 60 (Dec. 1986): 555–67; and Carolyn Morell, "Cause *Is* Function: Toward a Feminist Model of Integration for Social Work," *Social Service Review* 61 (Dec. 1987): 610–22. One professor of social work has written a feminist history of social work: Mimi Abramovitz, *Regulating the Lives of Women: Social Welfare Policy from Colonial Times to the Present* (Boston: South End Press, 1988).

65. Daniel J. Walkowitz and Peter R. Eisenstadt, "The Psychology of Work: Work and Mental Health in Historical Perspective," *Radical History Review* 34 (Jan. 1986): 7–31.

66. Brages and Michael, "Sex Distribution in Social Work."

67. Schwartz, "Importance of the Sex of Workers and Clients," 183–84.

68. Minutes, Executive Committee, Board of Trustees, Oct. 10, 1968, box 2222, FJPA; minutes, Board of Trustees, Oct. 18, 1971, box 1103, FJPA; Executive Office Records, June 17, 1977, box 2433, FJPA.

69. Martha K. Selig oral history, conducted by Judy E. Tenney, Feb. 9, 22, 1982, FJPOH.

70. Abramson oral history; "Report of the Task Force on Federation Personnel of the Council of Jewish Federations," rev. draft, Historical, box 1422, 1979 file, FJPA. By the 1970s, approximately one-third of the over 100 trustees were women. Their elite social profile does not appear to have differed from that of the men. Moreover, committee assignments continued to reflect gender stereotypes: men dominated most committees, except for those dealing with women and the family. See committee assignments in minutes, Board of Trustees, Oct. 12, 1976, box 1106, FJPA.

71. Weingarten, *A Loving Wife*, 31.

72. Ibid., 158–59.

73. Ibid., 231.

74. Ibid., 168, 188.

75. See *New York Times*, Dec. 11, 1994.

76. See Judith Stacey, *Brave New Families: Stories of Domestic Upheaval in Late Twentieth Century America* (New York: Basic Books, 1990).

77. Michael B. Katz, ed., *The "Underclass" Debate: Views from History* (Princeton: Princeton University Press, 1993).

78. The most explicit eugenicist position of the neoconservative analysis is given in Richard Herrnstein and Charles Murray, *The Bell Curve: Intelligence and Class Structure in American Life* (New York: Free Press, 1994).

79. Hispanics' sense of themselves as either black or white can be seen by comparing census tables where "Hispanic" is an option with those where it is not. See, for example, Bureau of the Census, *1990 Census of Population and Housing*, Equal Employment Opportunity file, United States, welfare service workers (occupational code 465). In contrast to the national profile, New York City Hispanics were three times more likely to identify themselves as black. The explanation for these decisions must remain tentative, although they may reflect the presence of a particular Caribbean group in New York City or a more positive association with black identity in the radicalized urban setting. It would be helpful to see photos of the respondents.

80. One only has to recall the genocide of Native Americans, the internment of Japanese Americans during World War II, and the passage of Proposition 387 in California, which deprived undocumented Mexican immigrants of social services without trial.

81. Conflicts between Korean grocery dealers in Queens and Brooklyn are one example; the social mobility of migrants from Brazil, Argentina, and the Caribbean is another. See Paule Marshall's novel of Bahamians in Brooklyn, *Brown Girl, Brownstones* (1959; reprint, Old Westbury, N.Y.: Feminist Press, 1981).

82. Linda Cherrey Reeser and Irwin Epstein, "Social Workers' Attitudes toward Poverty and Social Action," *Social Service Review* 61 (Dec. 1987): 610–22.

83. Robert S. Schacter, telephone interview with the author, Apr. 25, 1996; Marti Bombyk, telephone interview with the author, Apr. 22, 1996.

84. Dinesh D'Souza, *The End of Racism: Principles for a Multiracial Society* (New York: Free Press, 1995).

85. Henry Louis Gates Jr., "The Gap between Black Leaders and Their Constituents," *Chronicle of Higher Education*, Apr. 5, 1996, B7, quoted in Henry Louis Gates Jr. and Cornell West, *The Future of Race* (New York: Knopf, 1996).

bibliographical essay

Theorizing Class and Work

This book is based on sources from various institutional archives and articles in a wide range of professional and popular journals and magazines that reflect the history of social welfare in the United States. My broader concerns with the problem of middle-class identity, however, build on important earlier work, some of which is discussed in the prologue. From among the vast body of theoretical work on class, C. Wright Mills, *White Collar: The American Middle Classes* (New York: Oxford University Press, 1951), is still a good starting point. Barbara Ehrenreich and John H. Ehrenreich developed the idea of the professional-managerial class in "The Professional-Managerial Class," in *Between Labor and Capital: The Professional Managerial Class*, ed. Pat Walker (Boston: South End Press, 1979), 5–45, and Barbara Ehrenreich extended this analysis in her book, *Fear of Falling: The Inner Life of the Middle Class* (New York: Harper Collins, 1990). Loïc J. D. Wacquant's theorizing of the relationship between class as a discursive site and class as a set of concrete material conditions is most helpful: "Making Class: The Middle Class(es) in Social Theory and Social Structure," in *Bringing Class Back In: Contemporary and Historical Perspectives*, ed. Scott G. McNall, Rhonda F. Levine, and Rick Fantasia (Boulder: Westview Press, 1991), 39–64. Wacquant's article is also a solid introduction for readers who wish to engage the wider theoretical literature on class.

A whole generation of labor historians have been challenged by the debate between Joan W. Scott, Gareth Stedman Jones, and others that first appeared prominently as a "scholarly controversy" in *International Labor and Working-Class History* 31 (Spring 1987): 1–45, organized around Scott's essay, "On Language, Gender, and Working-Class History," 1–13. However, it was *The Politics and Poetics of Transgression* (Ithaca: Cornell University Press, 1986), by literary critics Peter Stallybrass and Allon White, that most stimulated my rethinking about how to combine postmodern concerns with subjectivity and social history in writing about the meaning of class in twentieth-century America. I recommend it heartily to all historians, even though it is not about America, the twentieth century, or class per se.

I have also drawn on a growing literature on the history of the middle class. With some important exceptions, the best of this work has been on the first half of the nineteenth century: Paul E. Johnson, *Shopkeeper's Millennium: Society and Revivals in Rochester, New*

York, 1815–1837 (New York: Hill and Wang, 1978); Mary P. Ryan, *Cradle of the Middle Class: The Family in Oneida County, New York, 1790–1865* (New York: Cambridge University Press, 1981); and Leonore Davidoff and Catherine Hall, *Family Fortunes: Men and Women of the English Middle Class, 1780–1850* (Chicago: University of Chicago Press, 1990). Geoffrey Crossick's article on the "lower middle class" in Victorian England is especially attuned to the language of class: "From Gentlemen to the Residuum: Languages of Social Description in Victorian Britain," in *Language, History, and Class*, ed. Penelope J. Corfield (London: Basil Blackwell, 1991), 150–75.

Most historical studies of the American middle class end before 1920 and therefore only anticipate the dominance of white-collar work in the twentieth-century United States. Stuart M. Blumin has provided an ambitious comprehensive summary of much of this literature in *The Emergence of the Middle Class: Social Experience in the American City, 1760–1900* (Cambridge: Cambridge University Press, 1989). Blumin's contribution, however, reflects the limitations of the secondary work on which he draws (including my own): subjectivity takes a backseat to empirical categories that distinguish middle-class behavior— residential location, limitation of family size, socialization for "achievement" and "respectability," delayed marriage, and so forth. Blumin acknowledges, however, that this middle-class work world existed before the emergence of the twin problems of "feminization" and "proletarianization" that would play such a major role in twentieth-century white-collar labor. For a more gendered treatment, see Lori D. Ginzberg, *Women and the Work of Benevolence: Morality, Politics, and Class in the Nineteenth-Century United States* (New Haven: Yale University Press, 1990).

Cindy Sondik Aron, *Ladies and Gentlemen of the Civil Service: Middle-Class Workers in Victorian America* (New York: Oxford University Press, 1987), and Olivier Zunz, *Making America Corporate, 1870–1920* (Chicago: University of Chicago Press, 1990), suggest the strengths and weaknesses of the literature on the middle-class identity of early white-collar workers. Aron's study describes a generation of women clerks who worked for the federal government as early as the last half of the nineteenth century as part of a burgeoning middle class. Aron, however, only begins to examine these women's subjectivity or the meanings they give to class. Instead, class remains an assumed category. We learn that most of these women were recruited from the middle class; the fathers of 65 percent of the women were professionals, small businessmen, or the like, and 94 percent of the women were able to remain in school until age sixteen.

Zunz brings the story of middle-class re-formation into the twentieth century. In his study, however, the middle class is primarily represented by middle-management men in the emerging corporate bureaucracies of Dupont, Ford, and Metropolitan Life; Zunz devotes only one chapter to Met Life's female clerks. Criticizing the view that feminization involves proletarianization, Zunz rejects the idea that these workers might have had different identities at home and at work, as suggested in Susan Porter Benson's study of department store clerks, *Counter Cultures: Saleswomen, Managers, and Customers in American Department Stores, 1890–1940* (Urbana: University of Illinois Press, 1986). Unlike Aron's clerks, Zunz's generation of white-collar workers become a study of bourgeoisification: they come out of working-class or petite bourgeois occupations to become the backbone of the new corporate order. White, native-born, and usually male, Zunz's middle class re-forms itself against an immigrant "other," so that Zunz projects its post-1920 history in terms that forecast the stereotype of the homogeneous middle class as a combination of H. L. Mencken's Boobus Americanus and William H. Whyte's organization man. Zunz concludes that it was as the middle class that middle management "identified with corporations" to create a "simplified cultural system" in a "homogeneous society."

My understanding of the middle class in the twentieth century has been enriched most by the work of two historical sociologists. For the complicated languages of class deployed by chemical and engineering workers and their families later in the century as they navigated home and workplace, see David Halle, *America's Working Man: Work, Home, and Politics among Blue Collar Property Owners* (Chicago: University of Chicago Press, 1984), and Robert Zussman, *Mechanics of the Middle Class: Work and Politics among American Engineers* (Berkeley: University of California Press, 1985).

Finally, for an overview of the transformation of work in America, see David Gordon, Michael Reich, and Richard Edwards, *Segmented Work, Divided Workers: The Historical Transformation of Work in the United States* (Cambridge: Cambridge University Press, 1982). More specifically, Harry Braverman, *Labor and Monopoly Capital: The Degradation of Work in the Twentieth Century* (New York: Monthly Review Press, 1974), is a primer on the transformations of work and industry at the turn of the century. Labor and managerial developments are detailed respectively, in David Montgomery, *The Fall of the House of Labor: The Workplace, the State, and American Labor Activism, 1865–1925* (New York: Cambridge University Press, 1987), and Alfred D. Chandler, *The Visible Hand: The Managerial Revolution in American Business* (Cambridge: Harvard University Press, 1977). For the transformation of work from the 1960s to the 1990s, see Barry Bluestone and Bennett Harrison, *The Deindustrialization of America: Plant Closings, Community Abandonment, and the Dismantling of Basic Industries* (New York: Basic Books, 1982), and Daniel J. Walkowitz, "'Normal Life': The Crisis of Identity among Donetsk's Miners," in Lewis H. Siegelbaum and Daniel J. Walkowitz, *Workers of the Donbass Speak: Survival and Identity in the New Ukraine, 1989–1992* (Albany: State University of New York Press, 1995), 159–84.

Social Work and the Welfare State

The especially rich history of social work and social welfare policy provides a solid base for scholars. See Clarke A. Chambers, *Seedtime of Reform: American Social Service and Social Action, 1918–1933* (Minneapolis: University of Minnesota Press, 1963); Allen F. Davis, *Spearheads for Reform: The Social Settlements and the Progressive Movement, 1890–1914* (New York: Oxford University Press, 1967); Judith Trolander, *Settlement Houses and the Great Depression* (Detroit: Wayne State University Press, 1975); James Leiby, *A History of Social Welfare and Social Work in the United States* (New York: Columbia University Press, 1978); John H. Ehrenreich, *The Altruistic Imagination: A History of Social Work and Social Policy in the United States* (Ithaca: Cornell University Press, 1985); Michael B. Katz, *In the Shadow of the Poorhouse: A Social History of Welfare in America* (New York: Basic Books, 1986); Leslie Leighninger, *Social Work: Search for Identity* (New York: Greenwood Press, 1987); Walter I. Trattner, *From Poor Law to Welfare State: A History of Social Welfare in America*, 4th ed. (New York: Free Press, 1989); Stanley Wenocur and Michael Reisch, *From Charity to Enterprise: The Development of American Social Work in a Market Economy* (Urbana: University of Illinois Press, 1989); Mina Carson, *Settlement Folk: Social Thought and the American Settlement Movement, 1885–1930* (Chicago: University of Chicago Press, 1990); and Ruth

Hutchinson Crocker, *Social Work and Social Order: The Settlement Movement in Two Industrial Cities, 1889–1930* (Urbana: University of Illinois Press, 1992). Finally, the classic insider's history of welfare and the national welfare rights movement in the post–World War II era remains Frances Fox Piven and Richard A. Cloward, *Regulating the Poor: The Functions of Public Welfare* (New York: Random House, 1971).

In one of the richest areas of contemporary historiography, feminist historians have documented the gendered character of social workers' diagnosis of behavior and of welfare policy. See Linda Gordon, *Heroes of Their Own Lives: The Politics and History of Family Violence, Boston, 1880–1960* (New York: Viking, 1988) and *Pitied but Not Entitled: Single Mothers and the History of Welfare, 1890–1935* (New York: Free Press, 1994); Mimi Abramovitz, *Regulating the Lives of Women: Social Welfare Policy from Colonial Times to the Present* (Boston: South End Press, 1988); and Regina G. Kunzel, *Fallen Women, Problem Girls: Unmarried Mothers and the Professionalization of Social Work, 1890–1945* (New Haven: Yale University Press, 1993). See also Clarke A. Chambers's path-breaking essay, "Women in the Creation of the Profession of Social Work," *Social Service Review* 59 (March 1986): 1–33.

Welfare state formation plays an important, although indirect, role in the construction of middle-class identity, and once again, feminist historians have been most influential in examining this process. See Stephen Skowronek, *Building a New American State: The Expansion of National Administrative Capacities, 1877–1920* (Cambridge: Cambridge University Press, 1982); Gwendolyn Mink, *Old Labor and New Immigrants in American Political Development: Union, Party, and State, 1875–1980* (Princeton: Princeton University Press, 1986); Theda Skocpol, Margaret Weir, and Ann Shola Orloff, eds., *The Politics of Social Policy in the United States* (Princeton: Princeton University Press, 1988); Steve Fraser and Gary Gerstle, eds., *The Rise and Fall of the New Deal Order, 1930–1980* (Princeton: Princeton University Press, 1989); Linda Gordon, ed., *Women, the State, and Welfare* (Madison: University of Wisconsin Press, 1990); Theda Skocpol, *Protecting Soldiers and Mothers: The Political Origins of Social Policy in the United States* (Cambridge: Harvard University Press, 1992); Seth Koven and Sonya Michel, eds., *Mothers of a New World: Maternalist Politics and the Origins of Welfare States* (New York: Routledge, 1993); and William Julius Wilson, *When Work Disappears: The World of the New Urban Poor* (New York: Knopf, 1997). The tendency to understate the perspective of social workers and to focus on the indictment of clients can be seen in important work by Linda Gordon (*Heroes of Their Own Lives*), Kunzel (*Fallen Women, Problem Girls*), and Rickie Solinger (*Wake Up Little Susie: Single Pregnancy and Race before* Roe v. Wade [New York: Routledge, 1992]). Finally, Lynne Haney, in the recent essay "Homeboys, Babies, Men in Suits: The State and the Reproduction of Male Dominance," *American Sociological Review* 61 (October 1996): 759–78, demonstrates that clients play various state agents against one another, illuminating how the state operates on several layers and does not always speak with one voice.

Labor in Social Work

The history of white-collar workers and their unions in America is traced through the twentieth century in two books: Jürgen Kocka, *White Collar Workers in America, 1890–1940: A Social-Political History in International Perspective*, trans. Maura Kealey (Beverly Hills, Calif.: Sage Publications, 1980), and Mark McColloch, *White Collar Workers in Transition:*

The Boom Years, 1940–1970 (Westport. Conn.: Greenwood Press, 1983). The unionization of social workers in the 1930s is recounted in Rick Spano, The Rank and File Movement in Social Work (Washington, D.C.: University Press of America, 1982), and Leslie B. Alexander, "Organizing the Professional Social Worker: Union Development in Voluntary Social Work, 1930–1950" (Ph.D. diss., Bryn Mawr College, 1976). Jacob Fisher, the editor of Social Work Today and a Rank-and-File leader in the 1930s, has written an informative account of those years: The Response of Social Work to the Depression (Boston: G. K. Hall, 1980). See also John Earl Haynes, "The 'Rank and File Movement' in Private Social Work," Labor History 16, no. 1 (Winter 1975): 78–98.

The best postwar histories of social work unionization are John C. Goldner, "Resolution of Major Crisis Situations in the New York City Department of Welfare, 1939–1949" (M.S.W. thesis, New York School of Social Work, Columbia University, 1949); Richard Henry Mendes, "The Professional Union: A Study of the Social Service Employees Union of the New York City Department of Social Services" (Ph.D diss., Columbia University, 1974); and Leigh Benin, "Radicals in the 'Real' World: The Social Service Employees Union and the Limits of the New Radicalism of the 1960s," seminar paper, New York University, 1988. In addition, see Al Nash, "Local 1707, CSAE: Facets of a Union in the Non-Profit Field," Labor History 20, no. 2 (Spring 1979): 256–77. Finally, Mark H. Maier, City Unions: Managing Discontent in New York City (New Brunswick: Rutgers University Press, 1987), does an excellent job of placing the postwar history of New York City's municipal unions in the context of city politics, whereas Jewel Bellush and Bernard Bellush, Union Power and New York: Victor Gotbaum and District Council 37 (New York: Praeger, 1984), offers an insider's view of Victor Gotbaum and District Council 37 of the AFSCME, AFL-CIO.

Professionalization

Among the vast literature on professionalism, I have found Magali Sarfatti Larson, The Rise of Professionalism (Berkeley: University of California Press, 1977), most useful. The most influential works have been Thomas L. Haskell, The Emergence of Professional Social Science (Urbana: University of Illinois Press, 1972); Eliot Friedson, The Professions and Their Prospects (Beverly Hills, Calif.: Sage Publications, 1973); Burton J. Bledstein, The Culture of Professionalism: The Middle Class and the Development of Higher Education in America (New York: Norton, 1976); Martin Oppenheimer, White Collar Politics (New York: Monthly Review Press, 1985); and Dorothy Ross, The Origins of American Social Science (New York: Cambridge University Press, 1991). For more traditional sociological literature, see William J. Goode, "Community within a Community: The Professions," American Sociological Review 22 (April 1957): 194–200; Amitai Etzioni, ed., The Semi-Professions and Their Organization: Teachers, Nurses, Social Workers (New York: Free Press, 1969); Elliot Friedson, "Theory of Professions: State of the Art," in The Sociology of the Professions: Lawyers, Doctors, and Others, ed. R. Dingwall and P. Lewis (New York: St. Martin's Press, 1983), 19–37; and Sydney A. Halpern, American Pediatrics: The Social Dynamics of Professionalism, 1880–1980 (Berkeley: University of California Press, 1988).

Many histories of social work focus on the occupation's concern with professionalism. For instance, Roy Lubove, The Professional Altruist: The Emergence of Social Work as a Career (Cambridge: Harvard University Press 1965), illuminates the beginnings of the profession but concludes in the 1920s; Leiby, *History of Social Welfare*, chronicles the history of welfare policy and social institutions; and most recently, John H. Ehrenreich, *The Altruistic Imagination*, links the development of professional ideology in social work with social policy.

Recent work by feminist and African Americanist historians has revealed the constructed character of professionalism and its multiplicity of meanings. On gender and professionalism, three historians have most influenced me: Barbara Melosh, *The Physician's Hand: Nurses and Nursing in the Twentieth Century* (Philadelphia: Temple University Press, 1982); Nancy F. Cott, *The Grounding of Modern Feminism* (New Haven: Yale University Press, 1987); and Kunzel, *Fallen Women, Problem Girls*. On race, class, and professionalism, see Evelyn Brooks Higgenbotham, *Righteous Discontent: The Women's Movement in the Black Baptist Church, 1880–1920* (Cambridge: Harvard University Press, 1989); Stephanie J. Shaw, *What a Woman Ought to Be and to Do: Black Professional Women Workers during the Jim Crow Era* (Chicago: University of Chicago Press, 1996); and Kevin K. Gaines, *Uplifting the Race: Black Leadership, Politics, and Culture in the Twentieth Century* (Chapel Hill: University of North Carolina Press, 1996) and "Rethinking Race and Class in African-American Struggles for Equality, 1885–1941," *American Historical Review* 102, no. 2 (April 1997): 378–87.

Jewish History

For the years during which Jews immigrated to the United States, good starting places include Arthur A. Goren, *New York's Jews and the Quest for Community: The Kehillah Experiment, 1908–1922* (New York: Columbia University Press, 1970); Charlotte Baum, Paula Hyman, and Sonya Michel, *The Jewish Woman in America* (New York: Dial Press, 1976); Hyman Bogen, *The Luckiest Orphans: A History of the Hebrew Orphan Asylum of New York* (Urbana: University of Illinois Press, 1992); Daniel Soyer, *Jewish Immigrant Associations and American Identity in New York, 1880–1939* (Cambridge: Harvard University Press, 1997); Shelly Tenenbaum, *A Credit to Their Community: Jewish Loan Societies in the United States, 1880–1945* (Detroit: Wayne State University Press, 1993); and Beth Wenger, *New York Jews and the Great Depression: Uncertain Promises* (New Haven: Yale University Press, 1996). On Jews and consumerism in the 1920s, see Andrew R. Heinze, *Adapting to Abundance: Jewish Immigrants, Mass Consumption, and the Search for American Identity* (New York: Columbia University Press, 1990), and Deborah Dash Moore, *At Home in America: Second Generation New York Jews* (New York: Columbia University Press, 1981). On how Jews on New York City's Lower East Side endured the depression and began to romanticize their experience, see Suzanne Rachel Wasserman, "The Good Old Days of Poverty: The Battle over the Fate of New York City's Lower East Side during the Depression" (Ph.D. diss., New York University, 1990).

The postwar cultural history of Jews in Deborah Dash Moore, *To the Golden Cities: Pursuing the American Jewish Dream in Miami and Los Angeles* (New York: Free Press, 1994), is limited to Sunbelt settlements but does speak to Jewish suburbanization. The experience of Jews in New York City is enmeshed in social histories ostensibly about broader subjects, such as the Ocean Hill–Brownsville school dispute or the history of the teachers' union. See, for example, Diane Ravitch, *The Great School Wars, New York City, 1805–1973: A History of the Public Schools as Battleground of Social Change* (New York: Basic Books, 1974); Marjorie Murphy, *Blackboard Unions: The AFT and the NEA, 1900–1980* (Ithaca: Cornell University

Press, 1990); and Adina Back, "Up South in New York: The 1950s School Desegregation Struggles" (Ph.D. diss. New York University, 1997). The study of the relationship between Jews and blacks has become a small cottage industry in the 1990s that is nicely anthologized in Paul Berman, ed., *Blacks and Jews: Alliances and Arguments* (New York: Delacorte Press, 1994).

Primary Materials

The self-representations and attitudes of social workers at the center of this book were gleaned from articles in a wide range of journals and magazines that have national distribution. Many of these sources are professional publications, including publications of specific interest groups, especially Jewish, black, and radical social worker organizations. Prominent among these are *Social Work Today*, the magazine of the Rank-and-File Movement in the 1930s; the *Survey*, a widely read national social reform magazine; the *Compass*, the official journal of the AASW; and the *Jewish Social Service Quarterly*, the journal of the professional association of Jewish social workers. Other important sources of general attitudes and national developments come from popular culture, especially novels, short stories, and representations in film, photographs, and drawings.

The New York City case draws on the Municipal Archive of the City of New York for records of the DW. Both the Federation of Jewish Philanthropies of New York Archive and the Jewish Board of Family and Children's Services Archive house the records of Jewish family casework agency workers (including the JBG). Diagnosis and therapy were relatively tangential to my concern with social workers' subjectivity and middle-class identity, so I did not rely on case records as much as personnel and administrative records. In this regard, JBG papers and DW records did include a few casework-related materials, although general case records remain closed or have been destroyed. Records of the various social worker labor unions are in the Robert F. Wagner Labor Archive, Tamiment Library, New York University. The Columbia School of Social Work (formerly the New York School of Social Work) and the Bobst Library of New York University provided records of each institution's school of social work, as well as publications of the Russell Sage Foundation. Finally, the *New York Times* has provided regular and extensive coverage of New York's (and often national) welfare and philanthropy efforts and struggles from the onset of the New Deal to the present.

Archival Sources

Center for Puerto Rican Studies, Hunter College, City University of New York, New York, N.Y.
 Miscellaneous papers
Chicago Historical Society, Chicago, Ill.
 Raymond M. Hilliard Collection
Columbia University School of Social Work Library, New York, N.Y.
 New York School of Social Work: *Bulletin*, 1930–56; *The New York School of Social Work: A Graduate Directory, 1898–1956* (1956); *New York School of Social Work: A Graduate Census* (1956); M.S W. theses; miscellaneous records
Federation of Jewish Philanthropies of New York Archive, New York, N.Y.

Board of Trustees minutes; Executive Committee minutes; budgets; public relations material; historical material; Personnel Committee records; correspondence; strike records

Jewish Board of Family and Children's Services Archive, New York, N.Y.

Jewish Board of Guardians Archive: manuals of proceedings; Executive Committee minutes; Board of Directors minutes; Administrative Committee minutes; Evaluation Committee reports on staff work; annual reports; federation materials; staff records; union matters; volunteer records; Herschel Alt Papers

Jewish Family Services: administrative materials; manuals; personnel reports; union contracts

Jewish Family Welfare Society: miscellaneous records

Jewish Protectory and Aid Society Archive: miscellaneous records

Jewish Social Service Association: annual reports; miscellaneous records

Rena Schulman Papers

United Hebrew Charities of the City of New York: annual reports

Moorland-Spingarn Research Center, Manuscripts Division, Howard University, Washington, D.C.

National Welfare Rights Organization Papers

Municipal Archive of the City of New York, New York, N.Y.

Department of Public Welfare (Department of Welfare after 1937): letters received

Mayors' Papers, Department of Public Welfare (Department of Welfare, Department of Social Services, and Human Resources Administration) (James Walker, John P. O'Brien, Fiorello H. La Guardia, William O'Dwyer, Vincent R. Impellitteri, Robert F. Wagner, John Lindsay)

Robert F. Wagner Labor Archive, Tamiment Library, New York University, New York, N.Y.

District Council 65 Records

Social Service Employees Union, Local 371, Records

UOPWA, SSEU, District Council 65, Local 19: UOPWA records, proceedings, annual conventions

Schomburg Center for Research in Black Culture, New York Public Library, New York, N.Y.

Rietta May (Hines) Herbert Papers

Smith College School of Social Work, Northampton, Mass.

Bulletin, 1930–31, 1935–36; First Reunion, July 31–August 2, 1953 (Northampton, Mass.: Alumnae, Smith College School of Social Work, 1953)

Social Welfare History Archive, University of Minnesota, Minneapolis, Minn.

American Association of Social Workers/National Association of Social Workers Papers: pamphlets; personnel practices material; letters; labor relations records; practitioners movement materials; Columbus, Ohio, case, 1926–33; grievances

Jacob Fisher Papers

Paul Underwood Kellogg Papers

National Social Welfare Assembly: Personnel Committee records; labor relations materials

U.S. Department of Labor Library, Washington, D.C.

Congress of Industrial Organization Archive: Social Service Employees Union Collection; United Office and Professional Workers of America Collection; Official Reports on the Expulsion of Communist-Dominated Organizations from the CIO, Washington, D.C., 1954

YIVO Institute for Jewish Research Archive, New York, N.Y.

National Conference of Jewish Communal Service: miscellaneous records
National Conference of Jewish Social Service: conference proceedings; clippings;
National Conference of Jewish Social Workers records

Periodicals and Newspapers

Bulletin of the Association of Neighborhood Workers, 1916–18
Catalyst: A Socialist Journal of Social Service, 1978–90; *Journal of Progressive Human Services*, 1990–
Charities and the Commons, 1890–1911; *Survey*, 1911–52
Compass, 1921–47; *Social Work*, 1947–
Health and Social Work, 1976–
Issues in Radical Therapy, 1973–82
Jewish Frontier, 1934–39
Jewish Social Service Quarterly, 1924–56; *Journal of Jewish Communal Service*, 1956–
Ledger, Bookkeepers', Stenographers', and Accountants' Union, Local 12646, New York, N.Y., 1934–38
Mental Hygiene, 1917–21
New York Times, 1915–
Proceedings, National Conference of Charities and Correction, 1874–1917, National Conference of Social Work, 1917–33
Public Welfare News, American Public Welfare Association, Chicago, Ill., 1932–42
Radical Therapist, 1970–72
Social Casework, 1950–39
Social Service Review, 1927–
Social Work Today, 1934–42
Social Work Yearbook, 1929–60
Staff, SSEU, UOPWA, CIO, Local 19, 1947
U.O.P.W.A. News, 1934–35
Welfare, SSEU, UOPWA, CIO, Local 19, also named *Social Service Employees Union Newsletter, Newsletter, News*, 1937–48

General Works

American Public Welfare Association, *A Public Welfare Job Study: An Analysis of Selected Positions in Public Social Work* (Chicago: American Public Welfare Association, 1938).
Esther Lucile Brown, *Social Work as a Profession* (New York: Russell Sage Foundation, 1935).
Joseph Chapin Brown, *Public Relief, 1929–1939* (New York: Holt, 1940).
William B. Herlands, *Administration of Relief in New York City: Report to Honorable F. H. La Guardia* (New York: William B. Herlands, Commissioner of Investigation, 1940).
Russell H. Kurtz, ed., *The Public Assistance Worker: His Responsibility to the Applicant, the Community, and Himself* (New York: Russell Sage Foundation, 1938).
New York State, TERA, Division of Research and Statistics, *Social Service Personnel in Local Public Relief Administration* (Albany: TERA 1935).
Louise Odencrantz, *The Social Worker in Family, Medical, and Psychiatric Social Work* (New York: Harper, 1929).

U.S. Bureau of Labor Statistics, *Salaries and Working Conditions of Social Welfare Manpower in 1960* (New York: National Social Welfare Assembly, [1961]).

U.S. Bureau of Labor Statistics, *Social Workers in 1950: A Report on the Study of Salaries and Working Conditions in Social Work—Spring 1950* (New York: AASW, 1952).

U.S. Department of Commerce, Bureau of the Census, *Census of Population, 1900–1990* (Washington, D.C.: Government Printing Office, 1902–93).

WEIU, Department of Research, *Home and School Visiting as a Vocation for Women* (Boston: WEIU, 1911).

WEIU, Department of Research, *Organizing Charity as a Vocation for Women* (Boston: WEIU, 1912).

WEIU, Department of Research, *Settlement Work as a Vocation for Women* (Boston: WEIU, 1912).

WEIU, Department of Research, *Social Service for Children as a Vocation for Women* (Boston: WEIU, 1912).

WEIU, Department of Research, *Studies in Economic Relations of Women*, vol. 1, pt. 2 (Boston: WEIU, 1914).

Margaretta A. Williamson, *The Social Worker in Child Care and Protection* (New York: Harper, 1931).

Novels and Short Stories

Erskine Caldwell, *Tragic Ground* (New York: Duell, Sloan, and Pearce, 1944).

Sinclair Lewis, *Ann Vickers* (New York: Grosset and Dunlap, 1933).

Violet Weingarten, *A Loving Wife* (New York: Knopf, 1969).

Anzia Yezierska, *The Open Cage: An Anzia Yezierska Collection*, ed. Alice Kessler-Harris (New York: Persea Books, 1979), and *Children of Loneliness: Stories of Immigrant Life in America* (New York: Funk and Wagnalls, 1923).

Autobiographies

Harriet Bartlett, *50 Years of Social Work in the Medical Setting: Past Significances/Future Outlook* (New York: NASW, 1957).

Abe Flaxer, "Keeping One's Head above the Water," unpublished manuscript (1989), Robert F. Wagner Labor Archive, Tamiment Library, New York University, New York, N.Y.

Oral Histories

Black Women's Oral History Project, vol. 10, Schlesinger Library, Radcliffe College, Harvard University, Cambridge, Mass.
    Frankie V. Adams
    Florence Jacobs Edmonds
    Dorothy I. Haight
    Beulah S. Hester
    Inabel Burns Lindsay
    Ann Tanneyhill
Columbia University Oral History Research Office, Butler Library, New York, N.Y. (CUOHRO)
    Henry L. McCarthy

Federation of Jewish Philanthropies of New York Oral History Project, New York, N.Y.

Francis Beatman

Graenum Berger

Marjorie S. Dammann

Jerome M. Goldsmith

Maurice B. Hexter

Elizabeth K. Radinsky

Martha K. Selig

John Slawson

Robert I. Smith

Sanford Solender

Peggy Tishman

National Association of Social Workers Oral History Project, CUOHRO

Harriet M. Bartlett

Arthur Dunham

Arlien Johnson

Gisela Konopka

Inabel Burns Lindsay

Helen Harris Perlman

Gladys Ryland

Gertrude Wilson

Oral histories conducted by the author (in author's possession)

Marsha Treitman (pseudonym)

Oral histories conducted by the author and Adina Back (in author's possession)

Ruth Abramson (pseudonym)

Leigh Benin

Sophie Grossman (pseudonym)

Sam Liebner (pseudonym)

Leah Weiss (pseudonym)

Oral histories conducted by the author and Dorothy Fennell (in author's possession)

Bernard R. Segal

Personal Communications

Mimi Abramovitz

Evelyn Blake (pseudonym)

Marti Bombyk

Clarke A. Chambers

Sam Rosenberg

Robert S. Schacter

William Schleicher

index

status, 29, 30, 68, 80, 103; and social workers' image, 80, 103; and social workers' grievances, 83–85, 137–38, 184, 250; male executives' domination in, 89, 108, 166; membership requirements of, 90, 104, 110, 123, 162, 350–51 (n. 50); size of, 90, 162; local chapters of, 100, 139

American Federation of Labor (AFL), 77, 134

American Federation of Labor–Congress of Industrial Organizations (AFL-CIO), 219–20, 300

American Federation of State, County, and Municipal Employees (AFSCME), 250, 283; in 1930s, 134, 184. *See also* District Council 37, AFSCME; Welfare Employees Local 371, District Council 37, AFSCME

American Public Welfare Association, 129

"American Standard of Living," 95–97

Ann Vickers (Lewis), 102–3, 201

Anticommunism, 196–99; use of, against left-wing unions, 177–78, 183–85, 190–92, 193–95, 198–99, 215, 219, 220. *See also* McCarthyism

Antipoverty workers, 274

Anti-Semitism, 260, 284

Antman, Joseph, 197–98

Arab-Israeli wars, 260, 263, 312

Aron, Cindy Sondik, 5, 7

Aronson, Norma, 184, 221

Asians, 242, 320

Association of Black Social Workers (ABSW), 292, 313–14

Association of Brooklyn Federation Workers, 155

Association of Colored Social Workers, 241

Association of Federation Workers (AFW), 108–9, 122, 124–25, 151, 152–53, 157

Association of Professional Schools, 90

Association of Workers in Public Relief Agencies (AWPRA), 133

Atlanta University School of Social Work, 66, 207, 213, 241

Automation, 254, 275. *See also* Welfare service aides

Autonomy: professionalism as an attempt to achieve, 59; decreased, 61, 177, 186–87, 229

AWPRA. *See* Association of Workers in Public Relief Agencies

Baldwin, Roger, 125

Baltimore, 27, 57, 78, 125, 161

Baron, Ava, 13

Bartlett, Harriet M., 88–89

Bauer, Frederick E., 93

Beatman, Francis, 109

Beers, Clifford W., 44

Bellush, Bernard, 266

Bellush, Jewel, 266

Benghiat, Albert, 277

Benghiat, Rose, 277

Benin, Leigh, 268–69, 274, 320

Benson, Susan Porter, 95

Berkman, Miriam, 166

Berman, Jennie, 152

Bernstein, Rose, 206

Bertha Capen Reynolds Society, 312–13, 321

Beth Moses Hospital, 155

Bettelheim, Bruno, 283

Bhabha, Homi K., 23

Bingham, Theodore A., 68–69

Black, Bertram, 202

The Blackboard Jungle, 218–19, 240

Black churches, 15, 63, 66

Black power movement, 283–84, 295

Blacks. *See* African Americans

Black separatism, 313–14

Bledstein, Burton J., 5

Blumin, Stuart M., 5

Boehm, Werner W., 298

Boston, 78, 123, 125, 161

Boston Psychopathic Hospital, 45, 46

Boston School of Social Work, 46

Bourdieu, Pierre, 6

Braverman, Harry, 5

Breines, Wini, 216

Brill, A. A., 46

Brown, George, 42

Buchanan, Pat, 321

Burnham, John C., 200, 201

Community and Social Agency Employees (CSAE), 198, 199, 221, 229, 250, 275–82, 303

Condon-Wadlin Act, 177, 183, 270, 271, 280

Congress of Industrial Organizations (CIO), 121, 183–84, 196, 199

Congress of Racial Equality (CORE), 268, 270, 277

Consumerism, 216, 236; and middle-class identity, 8, 16, 213–14, 236, 249, 281; and female social workers, 8, 95–100, 185–86

Cook, Esther, 46

CORE. *See* Congress of Racial Equality

Cortez, Jessica, 20

COS. *See* Charity Organization Society

Cott, Nancy, 103

Council on Social Work Education (CSWE), 90, 293

Courtney, Mark E., 298

Craft unionism, 253

Crocker, Ruth Hutchinson, 52

Crossick, Geoffrey, 4–5

CSAE. *See* Community and Social Agency Employees

CSF. *See* Civil Service Forum

CSWE. *See* Council on Social Work Education

"Culture of containment," 211

"Culture of poverty," xvi, 237. *See also* "Underclass"

Davidoff, Leonore, 5, 305

Davis, Allen F., 36, 37, 38

Davis, Katherine Bement, 51

Dawson, Sidonia, 136–38

Deardorff, Neva R., 89, 90

Denver, 78, 135, 138–40, 161

Department of Child Welfare (New York City), 178, 188

Department of Health, Education, and Welfare, 285

Department of Public Welfare of the City of New York (DPW), 93, 115–16, 128, 131–32, 143, 172; racial/ethnic hiring patterns in, 93, 172; merger of, into DW, 130

Department of Social Services of the City of New York (DSS), 275, 292

Department of Welfare of the City of New York (DW), 21–22, 128, 178, 238–40; size of workforce in, 22, 128; focus of, on policing eligibility, 22, 130–32, 222, 223, 227, 238–40; working conditions in, 128–29, 187–88, 227; creation of, 130; political pressures on, 131, 189–96; merger of Department of Child Welfare with, 178; political purges in, 190–92, 193–96, 219–20; unions in, 221; policy changes in, 221–27; renaming of, 274–75. *See also* Social Service Employees Union; United Public Workers; Welfare Employees Local 371, District Council 37, AFSCME

Depression of 1930s, 121–22, 143

De Schweinitz, Dorothea, 106–7

Detroit, 122, 125

DeVault, Ileen A., 13

Dewey, Thomas, 215, 223

Dexter, Elizabeth, 144, 150

Diana, Raymond, 265

Dies Committee, 184

Diner, Hasia R., 173–74

Dinwiddie, Emily, 39

District Council 37, AFSCME, 37, 265, 267, 270, 271, 274, 300, 301. *See also* Welfare Employees Local 371, District Council 37, AFSCME

Double day, women's, 15, 74, 206, 212, 231, 246, 316

DPW. *See* Department of Public Welfare of the City of New York

Dreyfuss, Milton L., 155

Drug therapy, 229

D'Souza, Dinesh, 322

DSS. *See* Department of Social Services of the City of New York

Dublin, Louis Israel, 43

Dumpson, James R., 242, 258, 265, 266, 275, 278

Dunham, Arthur, 88, 105

Dunham, Esther, 104–5

DW. *See* Department of Welfare of the City of New York

Edmonds, Florence Jacobs, 94

Edwards, Alba M., 28–29

Ehrenreich, John H., 145

Eligibility: focus on restricting, 22, 31, 130–32, 222, 223, 227, 238–40

Elsey, Florence, 137

Ely, Richard T., 57

ERB. *See* New York City Emergency Relief Bureau

Family and child casework, 35, 94, 97, 187, 216, 246–47, 296–97

Family Service Association of America, 243

Family Service Society (FSS) (Columbus, Ohio), 81–84

Farmer, James, 270

Faue, Elizabeth, 163

Federal Employment Relief Administration, 129–30

Federation of Jewish Philanthropies of New York (FJP), 21–22, 149, 172–73, 285–87; founding of, 70–71, 72; agencies' nominal autonomy from, 73, 80, 149–50, 152–53, 160, 229; and unions, 124, 148–60, 182, 185, 187, 196–99, 219, 221, 276, 303; and radicalism, 159–60, 184, 196–99, 219; changing clientele of, 180–81, 213, 254–57; and strikes, 227–28, 275, 280–81; and gender issues, 247, 315–16; and issues of Jewish identity, 254–56, 286–87, 310–12. *See also* Jewish private agencies

Female social workers, 12–15; differences of, from volunteers, 10, 13–14, 74, 75–76, 94, 104; percentage of, among all social workers, 12, 29, 115, 212, 323; and middle-class identity, 13–15, 135–86, 245–48; double day of, 15, 74, 206, 231, 246, 316; growing numbers of, 29, 67; discrimination against, in promotions, 88–89, 94–95, 167, 206, 231, 246, 316; and professional woman identity, 91, 103–7, 109, 110, 118, 139, 316; discrimination against, in wages, 95, 97, 166, 206, 246, 294; representations of, 102–3, 230; discrimination against, 107, 115, 185–86, 206, 247,

315–17; in unions, 163–66, 219, 220, 287; unions and discrimination against, 166, 219, 281, 315; as working mothers, 216; movement of, into private therapy, 291, 297–99, 301, 316, 318

Femininity, 12–13, 118, 167, 170

Feminism, 314–15, 318–19; and psychiatric social work, 146, 316

Ferguson, Blanche, 138, 139

Feuer, Lewis, 283

Fielding, Benjamin, 190

Fisher, Jacob, 116, 125, 147, 157, 158, 175–76, 221

Fitch, John A., 89

FJP. *See* Federation of Jewish Philanthropies of New York

Flaxer, Abe, 125, 129, 133–34, 184, 221

Flexner, Abraham, 29, 48, 54

Folbre, Nancy, 9

Foner, Eric, 33

Foot, Marsha, 20

Ford Motor Company, 41–42

Frankel, Lee K., 43

Frazier, E. Franklin, 66

Freud, Anna, 202

Freudian therapy, 46, 94, 166–67, 234

Friedman, H. G., 152

Friedman, Sam, 275

FSS. *See* Family Service Society

Functional (Rankian) therapy, 145–47, 166, 174, 234

Galbraith, John Kenneth, 216

Gary, Indiana, 52

Gates, Henry Louis, Jr., 15, 313, 322

German Jews, 68, 71, 78

Gilbert, James B., 216

Gingrich, Newt, 291, 309

Ginsberg, Mitchell, 272, 286

Ginzberg, Lori D., 5, 32

Giuliani, Rudolph W., 321

Glasberg, Benjamin, 140

Glazer, Nathan, 285

Globalization, 2, 3, 306

Goding, Eleanor, 189

Goldstein, Paula Jacobs, 166

Gordon, Linda, 39, 206
Goren, Arthur A., 69
Gotbaum, Victor, 271, 273
Gottsfeld, Mary, 282–83
Government and Civic Employees Organizing Committee, CIO, 221
Graduate education, 46, 90. *See also* Schools of social work
Graduate School for Jewish Social Work, 76
Granger, Lester B., 118–19
Greenwich House, 39, 40
Griffith, D. W., 50
Grob, Gerald N., 200
Grossman, Sophie, 125, 144–45
Gurok, Jeffrey S., 262

Hagerty, James Edward, 61
Haight, Dorothy I., 172, 207, 242
Hall, Catherine, 5, 305
Hall, Janet, 51
Hall, Stuart, 313
Halle, David, xiv–xv, 9, 11, 18, 215, 253
Halpern, George E., 155
Hawthorne–Cedar Knolls School, 276–77, 296; clientele of, 258, 286; strikes at, 277, 278, 279–80, 282, 287, 302. *See also* Cedar Knolls School for Girls; Hawthorne School for Boys
Hawthorne School for Boys, 71–72, 180, 186, 207, 233, 235
Healy, Elizabeth, 97, 105–6
Heinze, Andrew R., 93
Herbert, Rietta May, 244–45, 246–47
Herbst, Frank, 185
Herlands, William B., 128
Herzfeld, Elsa, 39
Hester, Beulah S., 314–15
Hexter, Maurice B., 198, 219, 232, 247
Hill, Stanley, 300
Hilliard, Raymond M., 192, 193–96, 221–22, 223, 227, 238
Hillman, Sidney, 79
Himmelfarb, Gertrude, 222, 309
Hispanics, 212; racial classifications of, 15, 189; as public assistance clients, 17, 213,
216, 242, 249, 259, 286; as social workers, 17, 213, 294, 295, 301–2, 304–5, 319–20, 328. *See also* Puerto Ricans
Hitler-Stalin Pact, 179–80
Hochman, Julius, 158
Hodson, William, 80, 81, 83, 89, 129, 131
Holmes, John Haynes, 48–49
Holt, Thomas C., 211
Home Relief Bureau Employees Association, 133
Home Relief Bureau of New York (HRB), 116, 133, 204
Hook, Sidney, 197
Hoover administration, 127
Horney, Karen, 145
Hospitals: as branch of social work, 44–46, 47, 154; strikes in, 153–57
Howe, Frank H., 81
HRA. *See* Human Resources Administration
HRB. *See* Home Relief Bureau of New York
Human Resources Administration (New York City) (HRA), 20, 274, 290, 299
Hunt, Richard, 279–80
Hunter College School of Social Work, 312
Hurlin, Ralph G., 89
Hyman, Louise, 39

Identity: historical and contingent nature of, xiii–xiv, 9. *See also* Jewish identity; Male identity; Middle-class identity; Professional woman identity; Professional worker identity
Identity politics, 308
Immigrants, 68–69; as social workers, 37–38, 93; as clients, 40, 51
Impellitteri, Vincent R., 222
Indianapolis, 52
Industrial social work, 41–44, 47, 53, 54
Industrial unionism, 123, 124, 151, 153, 303; abandonment of, 265, 267, 281
Industrial Workers of the World, 77
Insurance companies, 298
Intercollegiate Bureau of Occupations, 29, 51